Virtues of Authenticity

Virtues of Authenticity

ESSAYS ON PLATO AND SOCRATES

Alexander Nehamas

PRINCETON UNIVERSITY PRESS

PRINCETON, NEW JERSEY

Copyright © 1999 by Princeton University Press
Published by Princeton University Press, 41 William Street,
Princeton, New Jersey 08540
In the United Kingdom: Princeton University Press, Chichester, West Sussex

Library of Congress Cataloging-in-Publication Data

Nehamas, Alexander, 1946–
Virtues of authenticity : essays on Plato and Socrates / Alexander
Nehamas.
p.   cm.
Includes bibliographical references and indexes.
ISBN 0-691-00177-4 (alk. paper). — ISBN 0-691-00178-2 (pbk. :
alk. paper)
1. Plato. 2. Socrates. I. Title.
B395.N44 1998
184—dc21   98-7109
                                                                          CIP

This book has been composed in Galliard

Princeton University Press books are printed on acid-free paper
and meet the guidelines for permanence and durability of the
Committee on Production Guidelines for Book Longevity of the
Council on Library Resources
http://pup.princeton.edu

Printed in the United States of America

1 3 5 7 9 10 8 6 4 2
1 3 5 7 9 10 8 6 4 2

In memory of Gregory Vlastos

———————————————

CONTENTS

III. *Plato: Questions of Beauty and the Arts*

IV. *Plato: Individual Works*

ACKNOWLEDGMENTS

THE ESSAYS collected here were written over roughly the past twenty-five years. They cover a number of issues raised by Plato's writing, and I would never have been able to compose them if it had not been for the help, criticism, and encouragement I received from all those named in various notes throughout this volume, and others besides. Some must also be named here.

Gregory Vlastos, to whom these essays are dedicated, stands behind many of the questions I have asked of Plato so far. My ideas on Socrates and on Plato's metaphysics, epistemology, and philosophy of language were sparked by his own brilliant work. My answers have not always been the same as his, but the questions, and, by and large, the framework within which I have tried to answer them, have been established by him and are common to us both. I would hope that our divergences, particularly in what he probably would have described as my more "literary" approach to Plato's treatment of Socrates and to the nature of the dialogues as a whole, are only instances of what Nietzsche had in mind when he wrote that one repays a teacher badly if one always remains only a pupil. I owe him an immense debt of gratitude.

Since 1971, I have had the good fortune to have always been a friend and, for most of that time as well, a colleague of John Cooper. We have discussed Greek philosophy on innumerable occasions, in public and in private. We have often disagreed, but I have learned more from his remarkable dialectical ability and his even more remarkable persistence in the pursuit of philosophical understanding than from anyone else. He has established for me the standards for the clear, textured, productive, and philosophical interpretation of all the texts and issues that concern us in common and many that do not. His own collected essays, which are to appear at about the same time as this volume, represent philosophical thinking of a level to which it is as easy to aspire as it is difficult to attain.

Paul Guyer, whose own interests lie far from the Greek authors, but who has a sense of the philosophical importance of the history of philosophy, has also been a friend and, on two distinct occasions, a colleague during this period. He has been the most generous and sympathetic of listeners, always able and willing to make the effort to translate the often abstruse discussions of classical scholars and to translate them into clear and philosophically significant terms. He has given me a rare gift—a sense that philosophy is unified, that we need not remain isolated each within our own little area, and that the effort to cross the limits of the many narrow subfields of which our discipline so unfortunately consists today is still worth making.

More intermittent, though equally intense and all-pervasive, has been my friendship with Myles Burnyeat, whom I first met when I was his teaching assistant in Princeton in 1970. Burnyeat has an uncanny ability to pick up a philosophical thread wherever he finds himself and whenever he had last dropped it. And so he has done with me, in various parts of the world and in the most unusual circumstances. His calming intellectual companionship, balancing sharpness of argument, deep erudition, and a soaring philosophical imagination, has been one of my chief joys; and it has shown me how difficult it is to distinguish between the personal and the intellectual—another reason for which I am grateful to him.

On two occasions, Paul Woodruff and I collaborated on translating Plato into English. Those occasions, as well as many others since we were graduate students together, have been among the most exciting intellectual events in my life. I am immensely in his debt for his interest in my work and for his allowing me to reprint the introductions to the *Symposium* and the *Phaedrus* in this volume.

I wish Plato was also thinking of intelligence and sensibility when he wrote κοινὰ τὰ τῶν φίλων, "friends have everything in common." For my sake, moreover, I wish he had been correct.

The essays of which this volume consists originally appeared as follows:

"Meno's Paradox and Socrates as a Teacher" first appeared in *Oxford Studies in Ancient Philosophy* 3, edited by Julia Annas (Oxford: Clarendon Press, 1985), 1–30.

"Socratic Intellectualism" first appeared in *Proceedings of the Boston Area Colloquium in Ancient Philosophy* 2, edited by John J. Cleary (Langham, Md.: University Press of America, 1987), 275–316. Reprinted by permission.

"What Did Socrates Teach and to Whom Did He Teach It?" first appeared in *Review of Metaphysics* 46 (1992): 279–306. Reprinted by permission.

"Voices of Silence: On Gregory Vlastos's Socrates" first appeared in *Arion,* 3d Series, 2 (1992): 157–86. Reprinted by permission.

"Eristic, Antilogic, Sophistic, Dialectic" first appeared in *History of Philosophy Quarterly* 7 (1990): 3–16. Reprinted by permission.

"On Parmenides' Three Ways of Inquiry" first appeared, along with a modern Greek translation, in *Deukalion* 33/34 (1981): 97–112. Reprinted by permission.

"Plato on the Imperfection of the Sensible World" first appeared in *American Philosophical Quarterly* 12 (1975): 105–17. Reprinted by permission.

"Confusing Universals and Particulars in Plato's Early Dialogues" first appeared in *Review of Metaphysics* 29 (1975): 287–306. Reprinted by permission.

"Self-Predication and Plato's Theory of Forms" first appeared in *American Philosophical Quarterly* 16 (1979): 93–103. Reprinted by permission.

"Participation and Predication in Plato's Later Thought" first appeared in *Review of Metaphysics* 36 (1982): 343–74. Reprinted by permission.

"*Epistēmē* and *Logos* in Plato's Later Thought" first appeared in *Archiv für Geschichte der Philosophie* 66 (1984): 11–36. Reprinted by permission.

"Plato on Imitation and Poetry in *Republic* X" first appeared in *Plato on Beauty, Wisdom and the Arts,* edited by J.M.E. Moravcsik and Philip Temko (Totowa, N.J.: Rowman and Littlefield, 1982), 47–78. Reprinted by permission.

"Plato and the Mass Media" first appeared in *The Monist* 71 (1988): 214–34. Copyright © 1988, *The Monist,* La Salle, Illinois 61301. Reprinted by permission.

"The *Symposium*" first appeared as the introduction to *Plato's "Symposium,"* translated by Alexander Nehamas and Paul Woodruff (Indianapolis: Hackett Publishing Company, 1989), xi–xxvi. Reprinted by permission.

"The *Republic*" first appeared as the introduction to *The Republic,* translated by A. D. Lindsay (London: Everyman's Library, 1992), vii–xxii. Reprinted by permission.

"The *Phaedrus*" first appeared as the introduction to *Plato's "Phaedrus,"* translated by Alexander Nehamas and Paul Woodruff (Indianapolis: Hackett Publishing Company, 1995), ix–xlvii. Reprinted by permission.

ABBREVIATIONS

The following abbreviations and references have been used in the text and notes.

Plato

Alc.	*Alcibiades*
Ap.	*Apology*
Chrm.	*Charmides*
Crat.	*Cratylus*
Cr.	*Crito*
Euthd.	*Euthydemus*
Eu.	*Euthyphro*
G.	*Gorgias*
Hi.Ma.	*Hippias Major*
Hi.Mi.	*Hippias Minor*
Ion	*Ion*
La.	*Laches*
Lg.	*Laws (Leges)*
Ly.	*Lysis*
Mx.	*Menexenus*
M.	*Meno*
Prm.	*Parmenides*
Phd.	*Phaedo*
Phdr.	*Phaedrus*
Phil.	*Philebus*
Pol.	*Politicus*
Prt.	*Protagoras*
Rep.	*Republic*
Sph.	*Sophist*
Smp.	*Symposium*
Tht.	*Theaetetus*
Thg.	*Theages*
Tim.	*Timaeus*

Aristotle

Cat.	*Categories*
EE	*Eudemian Ethics*
Met.	*Metaphysics*
EN	*Nicomachean Ethics*

Gen.Corr.	*On Generation and Corruption*
Phys.	*Physics*
Poet.	*Poetics*
An.Po.	*Posterior Analytics*
Rhet.	*Rhetoric*
Soph.El.	*Sophistical Refutations (Sophistici Elenchi)*
Top.	*Topics*

Xenophon

Ap.Soc.	*Apology of Socrates*
Mem.	*Memorabilia*
Smp.	*Symposium*

Additional References

DK	Diels, H., and W. Kranz, eds. *Die Fragmente der Vorsokratiker* (Berlin, 10th ed. 1960)
LSJ	Liddell, H. G., R. Scott, and H. S. Jones, eds. *A Greek-English Lexicon* (Oxford, rev. ed. 1968)

INTRODUCTION

How CAN WE go about trying to understand Plato, when so much—the whole history of Western philosophy—separates us from him? How well can we ever hope to understand him? And what can we possibly expect to learn from him today?[1]

It is tempting to answer these questions in a resigned, negative manner. We might think that there is no good method of approaching a thinker who wrote dramatic philosophical works from which he excluded himself as a character and who therefore never spoke in his own voice; no hope that, whatever approach we adopt, we will be able to understand at all well an author who lived—socially, intellectually, emotionally, and ideologically —in a world so different from ours; and no likelihood that, no matter how well we understand him, we can derive from him much that is significant for the questions that concern us today. Reading Plato, on this line of thought, is simply an exercise in the "history" of philosophy, where this disparaging term—contrasted with what passes as "systematic" philosophy—suggests that to determine what he said and thought, if it is at all possible, and however important it may be in its own right (and opinions differ even about that), is of no importance to the questions that confront both contemporary academic philosophy and the general public.

I

The essays collected in this volume, written roughly over the last twenty-five years, reject these skeptical answers. First, I believe—and I have written all these essays in that belief—that there are many fruitful ways of approaching Plato's complex, elusive, and in many respects foreign mode of writing. I emphasize the plural "many ways." Plato wrote a set of dialogues, canonized by now as literary works in their own right, in which (with two minor exceptions)[2] he does not himself participate as a character—not treatises in which, perhaps like Aristotle, he expressed in no uncertain (though not thereby always clear) terms what his own positions may have been. But these dialogues often contain arguments of great complexity and immense interest in their own right. They regularly present elaborate theories, sometimes expressed by Socrates, who is by far the most common main character in the dialogues, sometimes by others. Some dialogues are short, with an intense dramatic structure, depending on the interplay—dialectical and psychological—between their participants; others, which are often much longer, employ the secondary characters simply in order to agree with the direction of the hero's dialectic. And just as the dialogues are produced by many sorts of philosophical writing, so they must be understood by many sorts of philosophical reading.

Sometimes, it is proper to pay primary attention to the arguments by means of which Plato has a character (most often, as we have noted, Socrates, but also Parmenides in the dialogue named after him, or the Eleatic Stranger in the *Sophist* and the *Statesman*) present an elaborate theory in metaphysics, epistemology, or ethics. Whether or not Plato "really" believed the theory in question—and there is no reason to think that he did not unless strong considerations are offered to the contrary—a great part of the importance of the works that have come to us under Plato's name consists precisely in those views and in the reasons offered for them: the theory of Forms and our knowledge of them, the construction of the universe, the division and immortality of the human soul, the structure of the ideal city, the nature of pleasure, the place of poetry in the economy of life. These are the views that have defined Platonism—and therefore Plato— for us, and it is crucial to understand what considerations led to their formulation and the advantages they possess as well as the problems they raise. The essays on Plato's metaphysics, philosophy of language, and epistemology included in Part II of this volume exemplify that approach to Plato. They assume that the views presented in various dialogues and in the various arguments and considerations used to support them are to be understood as philosophical achievements in their own right. On the whole, they abstract from "the literary form" through which those views are presented.

On the whole, but not completely. In "*Epistēmē* and *Logos* in Plato's Later Thought," I address Plato's arguments in the *Theaetetus* to the effect that no definition of *epistēmē* (usually translated as "knowledge" but, I argue, closer to our notion of understanding) as a true belief that is accompanied by a *logos* (account or justification) is possible. But I also claim that the negative conclusion with which the dialogue ends does not represent Plato's actual view of the matter. The dialogue aims to show that no single formula can encompass what *epistēmē* is because Plato believes that to understand anything is to know its interrelations with everything else to which it is connected; and it is quite possible that everything is connected to everything else. To understand anything we may therefore have to understand everything. To understand what *epistēmē* is, therefore, we must understand everything to which it in turn is connected. But that is an empty idea unless we are given a number of such interrelated structures, each one of which constitutes at least a partial instance of *epistēmē* of a particular field. To give that empty idea content, therefore, Plato writes the *Sophist* and the *Statesman,* which he describes explicitly as the *Theaetetus'* dramatic sequels. In these works he defines the sophist and the statesman by means of the method of "collection and division," which places the activity of each within a vast network of other related activities, each of which is in turn related to still others in a spiraling structure that can only be encompassed by the synoptic understanding of everything that is supplied by philosophy. And that understanding cannot be represented within a dialogue; it can only be exhibited and finally grasped in the very practice of philosophy itself, to which these dialogues, by engaging in it, urge their readers to devote themselves.

It seems, then, that even when we are centrally concerned with Plato's arguments, our interpretation of his dialogues must still include attention to their literary form. But it is crucial to realize that the fact that the dialogues constitute a literary form does not force one particular line of interpretation upon us: the form is not used, in the same way, in order to convey the same message. This has sometimes been the view associated with Leo Strauss and a number of his followers, who often argue that the dramatic form of the dialogues, when these are carefully read, almost always produces a covert, "esoteric" thesis that undercuts the obvious message that a straightforward, "doctrinal," or "exoteric" reading would derive from each work. Allan Bloom, for example, made this approach popular in his interpretation of the *Republic*. Bloom interpreted Plato's call for a city governed by "philosopher-kings" who share their spouses and possess no private property to be the exact opposite of the work's real thesis, which is that "gentlemen," aristocratic young men represented by Glaucon and Adeimantus, Socrates' interlocutors, should actually govern the city in order to allow the philosophers to pursue their intellectual studies (which far from being beneficial to the city, as Plato seems to argue, are really inimical to it) undisturbed.[3]

My own view is that Plato wrote dialogues not for any specific, strategic reason (such as his desire to be understood, as Strauss claimed, only by an appropriate few), but simply because that was the genre one had to use if one were to write about Socrates at the end of the fifth century B.C. and the beginning of the fourth century B.C.: the Socratic dialogue was a genre as much as the choral lyric or the satyr drama is. That is not to say that Plato did not exploit the dialogue form for his own purposes; but it is to say that he was not faced with a number of choices between various ways of representing Socrates and that he decided, for some independent reason that we can identify and use as a general principle of interpretation, to choose to write dialogues as opposed, say, to treatises or epics. By refusing to attribute a single goal to Plato's literary practice, we can begin to search for, and to find, different effects in different works. At the same time, we can also, as I have said already, attribute to Plato himself at least some of the views his characters express in his works, as we do with any literary author when our attribution is based on a reasonable interpretation. We need not assume either that Plato always speaks for himself through his main characters or that he never does.

So, for example, Plato's discussion of Socrates' ethics and views of human action in his earlier works, included here in Part I, can be taken seriously as an effort on his part to exhibit the main features that characterized the thought, the practice and the life of his greatest teacher. But we must be careful about the term "teacher" in this context, since Socrates, as Plato depicts him in these works, consistently denied that he was a teacher of anything, especially of *aretē* (which is usually translated "virtue," but which, we shall see, must be given a broader interpretation). And not only is Socrates made to deny that role, but Plato does not once show him to have a long-lasting beneficial effect on anyone with whom he came into contact: that is part of the point of "What Did Socrates Teach and to Whom Did He Teach It?" Furthermore, as I argue in "Meno's Paradox and Socrates as a Teacher" and in "Socratic Intellectualism," certain assumptions that Plato attributes to Socrates make it plausible to think that the only way one can recognize a good person is to be convinced by that person's views regarding the good life. But, according to the same assumptions, if you are convinced that a view is correct, you necessarily act on it: Socrates believes that we always do what we think is best. To recognize a good person, therefore, is to be oneself good, since to recognize such a person is to accept their views of how to act, and to accept those views means that one inevitably acts on them.

Socrates, however, did not only go unrecognized as a good person by his contemporaries; he was actually executed like a common criminal. How, then, do we recognize him today as a paradigm of goodness, whatever our reservations about his views and theories may be? The answer is that he was recognized as such by the only character whom he never addresses in Plato's dialogues—namely, by Plato himself, who thus makes the supremely arrogant claim that he, alone among his contemporaries, was as good a human being as Socrates was. In that way, again, the doctrinal and the literary elements of Plato's writings are intertwined, and an adequate reading of the dialogues cannot be given without giving each an equal and independent status. It is of course true that most of Plato's works are dramatic. But they are dramas whose characters include arguments and ideas, which, like those of all characters, we must interpret and appreciate in their own right before we can understand and evaluate their contribution to the overall sense of the dialogues to which they belong.

Literary elements are in the foreground in the essays included in Part IV, which serve as introductions to the *Symposium*, the *Republic*, and the *Phaedrus*, especially in the case of the *Symposium* and the *Phaedrus*. In all of them, as in all of his earlier works, Plato praises Socrates and what he takes him to have stood for and, implicitly or explicitly, defends him against the misunderstanding of the Athenians. In fact, we can interpret Plato's whole philosophical project as a lifelong struggle to understand Socrates' strange personality, to account for the strength of his convictions and for his devotion to living well, and as an effort to make sure that he could construct a world, at least in imagination, in which Socrates and others like him would be consistently recognized as the best human beings there could be. But Plato's devotion to Socrates was neither blind nor unqualified. The ideal city of the *Republic* is designed to make sure that people like Socrates—whom Plato was the first to call "philosophers"— will appear regularly with every generation, not as "a divine accident" but as the result of careful and coordinated planning. As "kings," the philosophers will be the state's most powerful, most respected, and most admired citizens. Yet Plato does not refrain from criticizing many aspects of his hero's views and practices even as he constructs such a place. In the *Republic* itself, for example, we find an explicit attack against Socrates' practice of allowing young men to engage in dialectic before they were, according to Plato, mature enough to profit from it; and against their using dialectic simply for negative purposes that, perhaps not without reason, would enrage the rest of the city. That criticism, which, ironically, is not so different from the charge of "corrupting the young" that Socrates had faced in his actual trial, is part of the topic of the essay titled "Eristic, Antilogic, Sophistic, Dialectic," and it is explicitly doctrinal. But not all of Plato's criticisms of Socrates are made in such theoretical terms. For example, in the *Gorgias,* which I do not discuss here in its own right, Plato makes it perfectly clear through his dramatic practice (that is, through the inconclusive confrontation between Socrates' austere morality and Callicles' hedonism) that he knew that Socrates' view that it is wrong to live a life devoted to pursuing pleasure and satisfying whatever desires we happen to find ourselves to have could not be supported by the psychology he had developed so far.[4] We cannot, therefore, assume that Socrates is always speaking for Plato or that Plato endorses everything he makes his central character say in his works: sometimes he does, and sometimes he does not. We must interpret each particular case with an eye to its specific theoretical and dramatic details. No general position on the issue is possible.

II

There is, then, no single key to understanding Plato, no privileged method for unlocking the secrets of his dialogues. But even if we were to agree that we must read his works in many ways in order to interpret them at all, one might still think that Plato is so far from us, that he thought and wrote within such a different context, in such radically different terms from our own, that however flexibly we approach him, we can never hope to understand what he himself was about. That, of course, is a general problem connected with the interpretation of all authors who are far removed from their readers. I have no original thoughts on the subject, but I feel I should at least explain the reasons that allow me to think that the distance that separates us from Plato does not constitute an unbridgeable gap. Coming to terms with this issue will also lead me naturally to a discussion of the question of what, if anything, Plato has to say that is relevant to our philosophical and social concerns today.

The flexible methodological approach I presented above, combined with a particular attitude toward the substance of his philosophy, which I will sketch out below, allows us to hope that we can understand Plato fairly well. I emphasize the qualification "fairly." That is much more difficult to explain than it might seem at first. In order to explain what I mean by it, it might be best to begin by contrasting my view with the most optimistic position on our ability to understand Plato that has ever been expressed so far. That is the position taken by Immanuel Kant in the famous passage of the *Critique of Pure Reason*, where he discusses Plato's idea of "recollection" in particular and philosophy in general:

> I do not wish [Kant writes] to go into any literary investigation here, in order to make out the sense which the sublime philosopher combined with his word. I note only that when we compare the thoughts that an author expresses about a subject, in ordinary speech as in writings, it is not at all unusual to find that we understand him even better than he understood himself, since he may not have determined his concept sufficiently and hence sometimes spoke, or even thought, contrary to his own intention.[5]

That is not a view I can accept. I do not believe that we can say such things as "The question Plato really meant to ask was one that was different from the one he did in fact ask, and the answer he gave it was one that was different from the one he meant to give it." But we must note that to disagree with Kant is not to say that we are obliged always to agree with Plato, to believe that his statement of his problems is always correct and that his views of the matters he discusses are always right. Plato could well be wrong both about the way he conceived of a question and about the solution he gave it. We can therefore well disagree with him, at least on occasion, about both. What we cannot do is to think that, instead of the wrong question Plato asked and the wrong answer he gave it, he "really" meant to ask another, "better" question and to give it another, "better" answer. One of the problems with such an attitude is, of course, the anachronism it involves, since what count as better questions and answers in this context often concern subjects that could not have been conceived by an older author. Kant's own interpretation of Plato's ideal city as embodying the "necessary idea" of a constitution that guaranteed its citizens the greatest freedom consistent with the freedom of all others is a perfect case in point: freedom, as Kant came to understand it, which is so important to the political theory of the Enlightenment, plays no role in the conception of the *Republic's* ideal city.

Another, more serious problem with Kant's approach is that it involves the wrong terms of comparison. For Kant does not simply say that as Plato is read again and again with every new generation, he may come to be understood better than he has ever been understood before. There are moments when I believe that such an idea may be right, that as interpretations of Plato's work multiply, even when they are in conflict with one another, they result, collectively, in a more complete—certainly a more complex—picture of his thought than had been possible earlier. But even if all these interpretations collectively result in a better understanding of Plato, to understand Plato is not the same as to understand how Plato "understood himself." Plato's own self-understanding is a psychological category, a view that Plato may or may not have held of himself. And, as in all cases of interpretation, our object is not to grasp how authors understood what they produced once (or while) they produced it, but what exactly it is that they produced in the first place. Our goal is not to recapture or reconstruct the mental state of an author, but to offer a reasonable interpretation of a text.

But a text, obviously, constitutes someone's work. We generally cannot understand actions and their products, which is what works are, without understanding the agents who produced them. Is it not true then that to understand the work is also to understand the author whose work it is? And is understanding who produced the work not the same as understanding, as we often say, what the author meant by it? And is not that, in turn, to determine how an author—in this case, Plato—understood his work, and therefore himself? The answer to the first question is "Yes"; to the second, "Yes and No"; and to the third, "No."

In interpreting a text, whether of literature or philosophy, we necessarily attribute it to an author, whose work we construe it to be.[6] Our interpretation of the text is guided by everything else we know that author to have said and written—keeping always in mind that determining what that is will in turn depend on what we are taking the text we are actually interpreting to mean. The process, like all interpretation, is circular, beginning with provisional hypotheses about the nature of the texts and the author we are reading and concluding with further, sometimes less provisional hypotheses about them, hypotheses that will guide further attempts at interpretation, which will sometimes become parts of new interpretations and will sometimes be rejected once new hypotheses have been reached by their means. To understand a work is to place it within a context that includes everything else its author is responsible for, just as to understand what the movement of someone's arm in the distance is we need to understand whether our friend is waving good-bye or warning us about a danger coming from behind. The difference is only one of degree and complexity. To understand a text is to understand its author. That is why the answer to the first question above is "Yes."

In all these cases, we juxtapose our provisional understanding of a particular text with our provisional understanding of the author whose work it is, or, better, whose work we want that text to turn out to be—by which I mean that we try to interpret texts so that we can reasonably attribute them to their authors consistently with everything else we know about them, even though, sometimes, we may change our mind about that in that very process. The "author" here refers not to the actual historical person who composed the text, not, that is, to that author's self-understanding, but to the character who is manifested in the work that is a product of that author's activity. That character, in turn, is a plausible historical variant of the writer. That is, the author is a character the writer could have been, consistently with everything we know about biography, history, psychology, literature, philosophy, and much else besides (that is, everything). Note this "could." The author and the writer need not coincide: the writer need not have consciously accepted the interpretation of a text we find most convincing; more important, the writer might not accept that interpretation even if confronted with it. In the terminology I am using here, though each text is the product of its writer, the work that text is taken to constitute as a result of interpretation can be attributed to an author who is not identical with that writer. The writer is an individual. The author is a character consistent with everything we know about the writer but not necessarily a character the writer actually was. I say that authors must be historically plausible variants of writers in order to make sure that we avoid anachronism and, with it, unfettered arbitrariness in interpretation.

On this view of interpretation, our goal is to understand an author. And that is very different from trying to reconstruct how a particular writer understood himself. To interpret a text is to determine what its author meant by it, but not necessarily what its writer actually did mean (or thought he meant) by it. That is why the answer to our second question, whether understanding a text was not understanding what its author meant by it, was "Yes and No." And the same considerations show why the answer to the third question has to be a "No." To understand Plato, even if we construe that as understanding what Plato meant by his works, is not the same as understanding how Plato understood himself.

When, then, I said that we can hope to understand Plato "fairly" well, I did not mean that we could only recapture part of what he had in mind when he composed his dialogues. Rather, I meant that interpretation can never, in the nature of the case, be complete. Philosophical texts, no less than literary ones, are inexhaustible—not because they have many meanings, but because there is no such thing as the ultimate meaning of a text, a meaning that can be determined once and for all. As history proceeds, as new texts come into being, as new possibilities of understanding emerge, old texts get interpreted again and again. And though I believe that the process of interpretation is at least partly cumulative, that newer interpretations often incorporate elements of earlier ones and sometimes build upon them, I do not believe that, as long as history proceeds, that process can ever reach a final conclusion—except when our interest in a work is, for various reasons, exhausted. A text is to its many interpretations as the world is to the many theories we develop about it: each is inexhaustible, but not because the text has a plurality of meanings nor because the world turns out to be a plurality of universes.

III

Suppose, then, that the distance that separates us from Plato does not in itself prevent us from understanding him, as I have put it, fairly well, especially if we approach his enigmatic works in the pliant manner I have tried to characterize. Can we, in that case, hope to learn something from him that will be of more than "mere historical interest," something that, despite the radically different context within which it was originally conceived and expressed, can be relevant to the questions that philosophers, and the rest of the world, are asking today?

Before we do anything else, we must stop right here at the beginning and question the very notion of "mere historical interest," which is so often used today in order to distinguish the work of historians of philosophy from the work of those who think of themselves as "systematic" or plain philosophers, without qualification. I do not mean that there are no differences between historical work in philosophy and writing to which the history of the subject is, at least at first sight, irrelevant. Nor do I think that every bit of esoteric research concerning the views of a philosopher of the past on an issue that, for various reasons, is no longer discussed today, will somehow always affect the writings of philosophers who are working on problems set to them by their contemporaries. (Nor should we forget, on the other hand, that many of these very problems will, in turn, cease to be discussed in the future, and not always because they have been definitively solved.) But it will not do to claim—as it was once claimed, partly in jest— that as the history of physics is studied in departments of history or the history of science, the history of philosophy should be pursued in similar independent units in order to allow the actual business of philosophy, which is to solve actual problems and not to understand the views of dead people, to go forward.

A number of years ago, Thomas Kuhn distinguished the sciences from the arts partly on the ground of their different relations to their past:

> Though contemporaries address them with an altered sensibility, the past products of artistic activity are still vital parts of the artistic scene. Picasso's success has not relegated Rembrandt's paintings to the storage vaults of the art museums . . . [even though] neither the artist nor his audience would accept these same masterpieces as legitimate products of contemporary activity. In no area is the contrast between art and science clearer. Science textbooks are studded with the names and sometimes with portraits of old heroes, but only historians read old scientific works. . . . Unlike art, science destroys its past.[7]

What I want to suggest is that, in some respects at least, philosophy is more like art than the view that philosophy and its history constitute different disciplines presupposes. Some fields of philosophy—logic, perhaps philosophy of mind (now renamed "cognitive science"), aspects of the philosophy of language or the philosophy of science—may be closer to scientific projects. Others—including moral philosophy and psychology, the philosophy of art, parts of metaphysics and epistemology—exhibit some of the features Kuhn attributes to the arts: understanding, appreciating, and being able to make substantive contributions to them is inseparable from knowing their history. The books of the authors of the past are not made obsolete by the journal articles of our contemporaries.

In the United States, the study of Greek philosophy was accepted as a branch of analytical philosophy primarily through the work of Gregory Vlastos and of G.E.L. Owen, who was writing at the time in England, in the mid-1950s. Vlastos reclaimed Plato (who had been studied mostly by classicists in the period preceding Vlastos's first studies) for philosophers by emphasizing two aspects of his writing. First, Vlastos focused attention on Plato's arguments, which he claimed were the primary, and most rewarding, objects of the philosophical study of the dialogues. Plato's arguments, Vlastos showed, were complex, intriguing, sophisticated, often valid, and, what was very important at a time when symbolic logic was widely considered the essence of philosophy, amenable to formal analysis. The study of textual and literary issues, though Vlastos allowed it constituted a proper object for the discipline of Classics, was irrelevant to the philosophical (argumentative and doctrinal) content of the dialogues. Second, Vlastos argued to great effect that many of the questions Plato was asking in his works were identical to some of the questions that were exercising analytical philosophers at that time. Since the analysis of concepts, sentences, or propositions into perspicuous or canonical form required being able to define terms clearly and adequately, as well as knowing when such definitions were successful, it also required a clear and adequate account of the nature of definition itself. But the aim of many of Plato's dialogues is precisely to offer and test definitions of various terms, many of them regarding the virtues: the *Euthyphro,* for example, is an effort to define piety, courage is the topic of the *Laches,* and temperance that of the *Charmides,* while justice is the subject of the first book of the *Republic.* What is more, the dialogues do not simply offer definitions of particular notions; they discuss the very issue of the nature of good definitions, exhibiting the obvious errors people can make who have not considered the issue enough, and even offering, as in the *Meno,* a sweeping methodological discussion of the conditions under which definitions can hope to be successful. By exhibiting the strictly logical structure of Socrates' method for evaluating (and, in the end, always rejecting) definitions, Vlastos showed that Plato seemed to be involved in what could easily be recognized as a project that was essential to contemporary philosophy.[8] He was asking our own methodological questions.

In "The 'Third Man' Argument in the *Parmenides,*"[9] Vlastos turned to the substance of Plato's views. He took the theory of Forms, which had often seemed like a wild flight of fancy to many philosophers, and, so to speak, domesticated it. Vlastos interpreted the theory as a sophisticated effort to offer an account of the status and nature of universals, of objects like properties or meanings, that can exist, like the property of tallness or the meaning of the word "tall," in many places at the same time—in all the countless tall things and all the uses of the word "tall"—without losing their unity and integrity. The problem of universals was also a problem that was very much in the forefront of philosophical interest at the time, and Plato was therefore drawn in as a collaborator in a common and vital enterprise.[10]

Vlastos's effort was immensely successful both intellectually and institutionally, and the earliest essays in this volume, the essays on Plato's metaphysics and philosophy of language that are included in Part II, are—as, indeed, is everything else I have written on Plato—deeply indebted to his work. Readers of these early essays will notice their almost exclusive emphasis on Plato's arguments as well as a tendency to assume that Plato's questions were the questions that contemporary philosophers were concerned with. Following Vlastos, I believed that Plato developed the theory of Forms and his philosophy of language within the following general context. Plato knew, like all of us, that we use a single word, like "tall," to describe a vast number of things in the world: that operation, predication, is one of our most elementary linguistic activities. When we predicate, we say that all these things have something in common—in this case, tallness.

But what is that thing, tallness, which all large things have in common, and how can it be present in all of them at the same time? The theory of Forms provided an answer to that question. Tallness is a Form, an intelligible object that exists beyond the sensible world around us and in which sensible objects that happen to be tall "participate"—a concept that Plato did not find easy to explain. To say that something is tall, then, is to say that it participates in the Form of Tallness. "Socrates participates in Tallness" is, according to this interpretation, Plato's *analysis* of the sentence "Socrates is tall"; it shows that the "is" that connects subject and predicate in such a sentence expresses a relation between a particular object, Socrates, and the universal Tallness.

The problem with this theory, Vlastos argued in "The 'Third Man' Argument in the *Parmenides*," is that, for some inexplicable reason, Plato insisted that the Form of Tallness is itself tall, just as the Form of Equality is itself equal, the Form of Justice is itself just, and so on for all the Forms. The Forms are not only universals that are shared by many particulars, but are also paradigms of the properties for which they stand, perfect instances of what they denote. Tallness is not only tall, but it is the most perfect (perhaps the tallest?) tall thing in the world. But how can it then be a universal, a logical entity that is simply shared among many particulars?

Vlastos called the view that each Form itself possesses the property it stands for the "self-predication" assumption, and he found it impossible to explain why Plato had been tempted to hold it, since it amounts to the absurd belief that every property itself *has* the property it *is*. He suggested that certain peculiarities of Greek linguistic usage may have tempted Plato to believe it, but rejected this suggestion since, as he wrote, "other philosophers, using the same language made no such assumption." Instead, he concluded in what was clearly an admission that Plato's view was incomprehensible, that the "assumption has far deeper roots, notably religious ones, which I cannot explore in this paper" (Vlastos 181). This strange assumption, combined with certain other views Plato appeared to hold, created insuperable problems for the theory of Forms, and vitiated its ultimate usefulness as a theory of universals. Nevertheless, a wrong theory about a subject of great importance to philosophers is nothing to sneer at—how many correct theories about important subjects do we actually have, after all?

The more I thought about this topic, the more dissatisfied I became with this understanding of self-predication and with the view that the theory of Forms was a theory of universals. According to Vlastos, Plato understood perfectly well that to say that Socrates was tall was to say that Socrates was a tall thing, or a member of the class of tall things. That is, Plato understood what predication is. What he did not understand is what the tallness was that named the class of things to which Socrates belongs.

And when he tried to answer that question, Plato for some strange reason concluded that Tallness, too, was tall. That, in turn, was to say that Tallness is a tall thing, which is absurd on its face and, along with some other views that I discuss in Part II in "Self-Predication and Plato's Theory of Forms," prevented the theory from answering the questions it had been designed to resolve.

At that point, I noticed that Plato always introduced the idea of self-predication without ever suggesting that it needed any justification: to him, it seemed like a self-evident idea, not like the absurdity it appeared to be to us. That fact, along with my study of Parmenides, whose influence on Plato's early and middle works has been deeply underestimated, made me think that the general picture of the theory of Forms to which we had been accustomed needed to be reversed. What, that is, if Plato did *not* understand how it was possible for many things to be truly described by one word, or "name" (*onoma*)? What if he did *not* understand what predication was in the first place? What if he began from the assumption that each thing can be properly described or "named" (Greek used mostly this one word for most linguistic terms) only by a name that expresses its very nature, as "Prometheus" and "Epimetheus," for example, express the nature of the two Titans they name? If that were so, then Plato would not be asking what the object is that many things (say, the many tall things in the world) somehow share. Rather, on the assumption that the name "tall" is the proper name of Tallness, he would be asking how it is possible for that term to name all those other things as well. If Plato believed that a name has a natural affinity for what it names and applies to it because it reveals its nature, then the idea that Tallness is tall, that it is named by the name "tall," ceases to be a gratuitous assumption. By contrast, the problem now becomes how "tall" can also name all the various tall things in the world whose nature it does not and cannot express. For if it did, then since things that share their nature are the same, all tall things would turn out to be the same thing after all!

Given, then, that set of assumptions, as I argue in "Self-Predication and Plato's Theory of Forms," the theory of Forms turns out to be not a theory of universals but a first attempt to explain how predication, the application of a single term to many objects—what is *now* considered one of the most elementary operations of language—is possible. I also offer a brief account of the historical antecedents of such an approach in "On Parmenides' Three Ways of Inquiry," which is why it is included in this volume even though its connection with Plato is relatively indirect. One of the main differences between my view of the theory of Forms and the influential version made popular by Vlastos is that I do not believe that the statement "Socrates participates in Tallness" is an *analysis* of the statement "Socrates is tall." Instead, I believe that in his middle dialogues, from the

Phaedo and the *Symposium* through the first part of the *Parmenides,* where he himself discusses the problems his theory has created for him, Plato believed that "Socrates participates in Tallness" is a *replacement* for the statement "Socrates is tall." Only the Forms can be properly qualified by Being, only Tallness and nothing else really *is* tall; everything else merely participates in the Forms and, being excluded from the realm of Being, belongs to the inferior realm of Becoming. Only in his later works, in the second part of the *Parmenides* and in the *Sophist,* does Plato come to see that constituting the nature of a property is not the only way of being qualified by the property in question; and only then, as I claim in "Participation and Predication in Plato's Later Thought," does he offer the first theory of predication in Western thought—a simple and naive theory perhaps, but an indispensable step for the sophisticated views on which we pride ourselves today.

I realize that what I have just written is hardly comprehensible in its own right. But my reason for presenting these two alternative approaches to Plato's metaphysics and philosophy of language was not to explain the theories and argue for the merits of one over the other. My purpose was to show that sometimes the way to make Plato speak to us is not to assume that he is asking our questions, for we may then find his answers to them quite bad. By contrast, my view of the theory of Forms assumes that Plato's questions were very different from ours, but that the answers he provided to them were superb. The question how it can be that many things are described by a single term—how predication is possible—is hardly asked today. But the reason it is not is that Plato, working only with the notion of a name that could at best be the name of one and only one thing, gradually developed the concepts that eventually resulted in the distinctions between naming and describing, essence and accident, identity and multiplicity, that have allowed us to think (though not necessarily correctly) that predication no longer constitutes a philosophical problem.

This way of understanding Plato, which supplies him with good answers to old questions rather than with bad answers to new questions, may appear to remove him even farther from the contemporary philosophical scene. But that appearance is deceiving. For to see that Plato's views on predication are not weak competitors to today's theories but rather strong ancestors to them is to realize that even some of the most general and abstract problems of philosophy are historically situated and that their nature is not exhausted by the most recent manner in which they have been posed. Their nature, rather, consists in the whole history of solutions that have produced the questions we are asking today. A different understanding of the history of a problem can therefore generate a different understanding of the nature of the problem, and therefore of the very problem itself. Further, since, as I firmly believe that there is no single, distinctive method for pursuing philosophical questions, we are much more likely to learn more about how philosophy is done well by seeing novel and exciting answers to unexpected questions than problematic answers to questions with which we are already familiar. That is not, of course, a "substantive" contribution to philosophical understanding. But since substantive contributions can generally be made by people who are familiar with the best substantive contributions so far, it is indispensable nonetheless.

In most of the essays in this volume I aim not to take Plato's questions and his interests for granted, in order to avoid reading him in those terms that are readiest to hand and most familiar to us in our own thought and language.[11] Sometimes, as in the case of predication, the result is that his problems appear to be indeed more different from ours than we might have expected. At other times, however, the opposite is the case. That is true, for example, in connection with the essays on Plato's "philosophy of art" in Part III. The *Republic*, of course, is shocking for many reasons. One of the most famous among them is that it ends with a proscription of poetry (and, some wrongly believe, of painting as well) from the ideal city it envisages. Now, in the terms that are readiest to hand and most familiar to us, poetry and painting are paradigm instances of the fine arts as we understand them. Plato then appears to be an implacable enemy of art in general—a view that is strange and repulsive on its own, but which is also disturbing because it makes him blind to the fact that his own dialogues are themselves paradigm instances of the fine arts as we understand them. Countless efforts to discount Plato's attitude, to explain it away or even partially to justify it, have been made, and I discuss some of them in "Plato on Imitation and Poetry in *Republic* X." I believe that they all fail.

The reason is that they attribute to Plato the wrong questions. That is the argument of the essay "Plato and the Mass Media." If we pay close attention to the concerns Plato expresses, to the considerations to which he appeals in proscribing poetry and to the place and function of poetry, both epic and dramatic, in classical and postclassical Athens, a very different picture begins to emerge. The poetry Plato attacks, though it has by now become as paradigmatic of "great art" as his own dialogues, was, at the time he was writing, the popular entertainment of Athens. Both structurally—in the kinds of lurid, often immoral stories it told, in the fact that those stories were repeated with ingenious variations and appreciated on their account by people who were familiar with them in many versions, and in its inherently realistic status—and socially—in its appeal to the broadest possible audience, in its bearing a particular, most often democratic, ideology, and in the festival atmosphere within which it was produced—the dramatic poetry of Athens was much closer to the plays of the Elizabethan era, the novels of the eighteenth century, and the movies that defined the beginning of the twentieth century as well as the television that epitomizes its end. When Plato therefore argues that poetry conflates the authentic and the fake, that it is suited for representing only vulgar and violent subjects, and that it induces even the most intelligent members of its audience to live in ways they would have otherwise considered despicable, he is presenting the kernel of every attack by the intelligentsia against popular culture and entertainment since his time. And unless we can show that the parallel I have mentioned does not hold, we are faced with a serious dilemma. For either Plato was wrong about the horrible effects of Homer and Aeschylus and misunderstood the artistic value of their work (in that case many of those who scoff at popular entertainment for Plato's reasons are as wrong as he was, and also misunderstand its artistic potential), or we are right about the depraved nature of our popular entertainment, in which case we cannot dismiss Plato's proscription of Sophocles and Euripides as easily as we would like to. In both cases, Plato becomes a direct participant in a crucial contemporary debate—not primarily the debate on "the morality of art" as that is discussed in the professional journals but, rather, the overwhelmingly serious public dispute over the role of popular culture and entertainment in the general economy of life. And many of the same people who find Plato to be, at best, of "mere historical interest" are simply repeating his arguments and sharing his attitude without knowing what they are doing. Such ignorance is not neutral; it produces worse arguments, and sillier views. "Historical" importance and "systematic" importance cannot in this case be distinguished at all.

The essays on Socrates' ethics, moral psychology, personality, and life that constitute Part I of this volume represent, on the whole, the most recent work included here. They probably combine the various features of the general approach to reading Plato, which I have outlined so far, more than any others. The analysis of arguments occurs alongside serious attention to the dialogues' dramatic effect, and, I claim, that shows that, despite the overwhelming impression that Socrates devoted his life to the improvement of his contemporaries, his project was essentially more individualist than we have generally taken it to be. Socrates' primary concern was what he called "the care of the self" (*epimeleia heautou*), where that self was, above all, his own. He did urge his contemporaries to do the same, but even that involved an irreducible personal element. Socrates admitted, as we have seen, that he did not know what *aretē* was, but he also believed that only one good person can recognize another. If people, then, did care for themselves in the way he required, became good and convinced him that they had, then Socrates, in recognizing them, would know that he had accomplished his own goal and that he had attained *aretē* for himself. Socrates was therefore much less of a teacher of others than we have tended to believe. Improving others, though a worthwhile and valuable end in its own right as well, was not a central part of the care he devoted to his own self.

The problem of the exact nature of *aretē* requires a reinterpretation of the questions we find Plato posing in his dialogues. Most people agree that the Greek term is considerably broader than the English term "virtue," by which it is most often translated, and that *aretē* concerns much more than moral goodness—it applies, for example, to animals and to inanimate objects, all of which exhibit their own characteristic *aretē*. Yet, once the discussion of Plato's views begins, these qualifications tend to be forgotten: Socrates' desire to learn what *aretē* is, and whether it can be taught, is understood as a concern with what it is that makes people morally good and how, if at all, moral virtue can be transmitted. But those questions do not capture the extreme nature of the debate between Socrates and the other members of what George Kerferd has called "the Sophistic movement,"[12] who claimed they could teach their pupils, for a fee, how to acquire *aretē* and who identified what they taught with political power and economic success (cf., for example, *Protagoras* 318e–320c). Taking *aretē* as moral goodness, Benjamin Jowett, among others, wrote in connection with Meno's asking Socrates whether such a thing can be taught that "no one would either ask or answer such a question in modern times."[13] The issue appears, again, to be of mere historical interest.

Yet if, on grounds I try to provide in the essays on Socrates included here, we interpret *aretē* more broadly, as something more akin to "success" than to moral goodness, as what it is that is responsible for people having a good reputation among their peers, then the ancient debate acquires an immediate contemporary resonance. For the question now turns out to be what it is to be successful and how one can secure success for oneself. Success, much more than moral goodness, is what is often called an "essentially contested concept." And what we observe in the conflicts between Socrates and Plato, on the one hand, and Protagoras, Gorgias, or Evenus, on the other, is a deep disagreement about the very nature of the state that they are willing to name *aretē* in the first place. Where Protagoras promises to show his students how to secure economic well-being and political power, Socrates insists that *aretē* consists in possessing what we now call the moral virtues. Where the world identifies success with public acclaim, Socrates insists that "real" success consists in having a harmonious soul. The sophistic insistence that success can be taught is countered by the Socratic view that, even if it can, it constitutes at best a poor substitute for what makes a human being truly worthwhile. Today, the primarily oral mode of teaching of the sophists has been replaced with print and electronic versions. But many individuals make fortunes— fortunes equivalent to that which Protagoras is said to have amassed for himself—by showing people the "secrets" of various forms of success—in personal relationships, in business ventures, in acquiring power—while intellectuals in general and philosophers in particular pass those people by in silent disdain and contempt. Though we are convinced that such hucksters fail to teach what they advertise, and that, even if they do, they impart a debased conception of what constitutes a valuable human life, we refuse to face them and to articulate directly and in public an alternative conception of what such a life would consist in. But that is just what Socrates, and Plato following him, did: they refused to pass such people by, they attacked them squarely and plainly, they claimed that what they taught, if they taught it at all, was merely apparent success and not worth learning in the first place, and they presented a conception of real success, which makes human beings admirable for a good reason.

IV

The contrast between apparent and real success brings me now to a common thread that, in retrospect, I see running through the essays in this volume. These pieces were written at different times, in different contexts, for different audiences, and as a result of different preoccupations on my own part. But many, perhaps most of them, address in one way or another and from different points of view a single problem that I now see is absolutely central to Plato's philosophical project. That is the problem of establishing—in ethics, in metaphysics, and in the philosophy of art—the difference between what is authentic and what is fake, what is genuine and what is at best only an imitation.

Plato's preoccupation with that issue begins, I think, with Socrates. Socrates, who disputed whether what the teachers of *aretē* promised to impart to their students was a genuine human accomplishment, was himself in Plato's eyes the best exemplar so far of the authentic success that can guarantee the satisfaction of all our natural, and therefore justified, desires. And yet, as I have said a number of times already, Socrates not only went unrecognized by his contemporaries, but he was put to death as a criminal—condemned as the opposite of everything he had stood and lived for. Plato felt that the Athenians failed to recognize an authentically good, a truly successful, person and mistook him instead for a failure. The gap between the genuine, represented by Socrates, and the fake, represented by the jury's conception of what a good human being was, could not have been greater.

Why was that gap so great? And why was it so difficult to recognize? The reason, Plato gradually came to believe, was that the public at large, whose intellectual abilities were limited to begin with, had been encouraged by the political, rhetorical, and poetic discourse of the time to look for paradigms of genuine goodness in what was closest to hand, in the heroes of the archaic tradition, or the democratic politicians of the fifth century B.C., who were admired on grounds supplied simply by the traditions they themselves sustained—an aristocratic code in the first case, and a democratic one in the second. But Socrates, who was aware that traditions differ and that, for example, the idea that courage consists in standing your ground against your enemy held only for Greek hoplites but not for Scythian cavalry (see *Laches* 189e–190b), insisted that *aretē* transcends tradition and depends on standards that cannot vary from place to place or from time to time. Yet Socrates could not explain where those standards were derived from or how it was possible for people to learn what they are.

It was in order to answer ethical questions of this sort that Plato first developed the theory of Forms, though the fact that widely disparate forms of behavior, like the examples of courage we just mentioned, could all be described in certain circumstances as instances of *aretē* could not have been far from his mind either. The standards according to which genuinely good human behavior can be judged are provided by the Forms, which Plato came to believe exist beyond the sensible world and are accessible only through reason, whose power in most people he considered deficient. The theory of recollection, which he first presented in the *Meno* and the *Phaedo*, and which he supplemented by the immensely ambitious educational program of the *Republic*, supplied the epistemic means for those with the required rational abilities to come to know what those standards actually are. But the theory of Forms highlighted for Plato another dimension of approaching the problem of authenticity, which grew into a problem in its own right, far beyond its original connection with the character and worth of Socrates.

The theory of Forms, as I interpret it here, depends on the assumption that nothing is authentically what we say it is unless it is the very nature of that thing. Nothing is authentically beautiful unless it is the very nature of beauty; nothing is authentically large unless it is the very nature of largeness; nothing is authentically equal unless it is the very nature of equality. Plato, following Parmenides, who had convinced two generations of philosophers before him, understood the simple term "is," which connects subject and predicate in a sentence like "Equality is equal," as the complex notion "what it is to be." If we interpret "Equality is equal" in the most obvious way, as "Equality is an equal thing," the sentence turns out to be absurd: To what is Equality equal? Does it perhaps consist of two perfectly equal things? What could such things possibly be? But if we grant Plato his unusual understanding of "is" and interpret the sentence in a more unusual manner, "Equality is equal" now comes to express the reasonable view that Equality, whatever it turns out to be when we define it successfully, is what it is to be equal. It simply says, for example, that having identical measurements in some dimension is what to be equal is. Plato does not believe, as we saw Vlastos claim earlier, that a property *has* the property it *is,* but that only the very nature of equality can, on this under-standing of "being," be truly, genuinely, or authentically equal. That is not to say that equality is an equal thing, but, rather, to claim that to be an equal thing—which, as Plato never tires of pointing out, involves being equal to some things but unequal to others, equal from some points of view but unequal from others, equal according to some people but un-equal according to others—is an imperfect, inauthentic way of being equal. Once again, we see that Plato assumes that in the first place predication—the application of a general term to many objects that it characterizes only under particular circumstances—is the problematic no-tion, and that his notion of "participation" is the first systematic effort to offer an account of this universal, but not yet understood, operation of language.

Just, then, as authentically good people model their behavior on the standards supplied by the Forms while the rest of the world is satisfied with deceiving appearances of goodness, so the Forms themselves provide the authentic objects of which the changing, qualified objects of the sensible world around us are at best misleading imitations. And at this point, po-etry comes back into our general discussion. For one of Plato's main accu-sations against epic and dramatic poetry is that they depict characters like Agamemnon, Achilles, Medea, or Oedipus, whom he considers at least flawed if not totally odious, as if they were not simply objects but also models of imitation—as if they were, in fact, authentic paradigms of proper human behavior. Painting, too, he argues in the tenth book of the *Republic,* presents imitations of objects as if they were the real thing. But, even though painting can occasionally mislead simple people into the wrong ideas about life and the world, Plato does not believe that it has the disastrous ethical consequences of poetry. He is therefore satisfied to issue a warning against it, to alert us not to consider it as more than a trifle or a game (*paidia*) and to let it continue to function in his ideal city. Poetry, however, depicts depraved characters as virtuous and tempts even virtuous people into the depravity such characters exemplify. Its confusion of the authentic and the fake is not only an ontological error, but an ethical dan-ger. That is why it has no place within the ideal city or the good life.

For Plato, the inauthentic is the unethical. There is virtue in being au-thentic, and there is authenticity in all virtue. Nothing fake can be good, and nothing good can be fake. Only the genuine can be a proper model of imitation, and nothing short of the genuine can ever be perfect. These are strong views, and they have, on Plato's own grounds, very negative conse-quences for the life of most, perhaps all, people, since he believes that unalloyed authenticity is impossible while the soul is incarnate and a pris-oner, as he was tempted to put it, of the body. These are views with which, for the most part, I disagree very sharply. I am suspicious of Plato's deep distinction between the authentic and the sham and of his radical privileging of the former over the latter. I believe that a better life both for individuals and for society can be secured within a naturalistic framework that offers us only worldly hopes. I reject the idea that the real world is distinct from the world in which we live. I find much greater value in popular culture and entertainment than Plato and his modern followers—who, lacking Plato's courage and forthrightness, are contemptuous of the public at the same time that they champion its political interests—are willing to find in them.

Yet despite all these difficulties, and many others besides, Plato's early portrait of Socrates (sketched out in some of the following essays)[14] as someone who fashioned a life of his own, changing the world as he changed himself without trying to impose his views upon others, is a paradigmatic philosophical achievement, and my own life would be poorer without it. My disagreements with Plato are many. But like Alcibiades, one of Socrates' greatest admirers, I too first felt in Socrates' words what Alcibiades in the *Symposium* (218a) calls the bite "of philosophy, whose grip on young and eager souls is much more vicious than a viper's and makes them do the most amazing things." And like Nietzsche, one of Plato's greatest enemies, I too still revel in "the charm of the Platonic way thinking, which was a *noble* way of thinking, [and which] consisted precisely in *resistance* to obvious sense-evidence."[15] Plato's resistance to sense-evidence led him too far away from where I think we should remain. But in resisting the *obvious*, in refusing to take what the world around him was taking for granted, in constructing, through the picture of Socrates in his early works, an admirable mode of life that denied what most people at the time considered proper and right, in presenting as complete a picture of the world and of the place of human beings within it and in being able to accomplish all that through the most powerful combination of literary and dialectical skill imaginable, Plato remains, if I may use these terms here, the perfect model of a genuine philosopher, the authentic standard by which philosophy, including especially the philosophy of today, must measure itself.

NOTES

1. I am grateful to Myles Burnyeat for his comments on a draft of this essay.

2. *Apology* (*Ap.*) 38b6, where Socrates says that along with Crito and some other friends present at his trial, Plato will guarantee a fine of thirty minae, which Socrates proposes as a counterpenalty to Meletus' proposal that he be executed for his activities. See also *Phaedo* (*Phd.*) 59b10, where Phaedo says that Plato was absent on the day of Socrates' execution because he was ill.

3. Allan Bloom, *The Republic of Plato, Translated, with Notes and an Interpretive Essay* (New York: Basic Books, 1968). A controversial, but firm, criticism of this general approach to the interpretation of Plato has been offered by M. F. Burnyeat, "Sphinx Without a Secret," *New York Review of Books,* May 30, 1985: 30–36.

4. For a demonstration of this point, see John M. Cooper, "Socrates and Plato in Plato's *Gorgias,*" in John M. Cooper, *Emotion and Value: Essays on Ancient Moral Psychology and Ethical Theory* (Princeton: Princeton University Press, in press).

5. Immanuel Kant, *Critique of Pure Reason,* edited and translated by Paul D. Guyer and Allen Wood (New York: Cambridge University Press, 1998), A313–14; B370.

6. I have offered detailed arguments for the position summarized here in "The Postulated Author: Critical Monism as a Regulative Principle," *Critical Inquiry* 8 (1981): 131–49, and in "Writer, Text, Work, Author," in A. J. Cascardi, ed., *Literature and the Question of Philosophy* (Baltimore: Johns Hopkins University Press, 1987), 265–91. The general theory is put into practice in my *Nietzsche: Life as Literature* (Cambridge, Mass.: Harvard University Press, 1985).

7. Thomas S. Kuhn, "Comment on the Relations of Science and Art," in his *The Essential Tension: Selected Studies in Scientific Tradition and Change* (Chicago: University of Chicago Press), 340–51, 345.

8. Vlastos presented the first, and perhaps most influential, of his many discussions of this issue in his introduction to Martin Ostwald's revision of Jowett's translation of Plato's *Protagoras* (Indianapolis: Bobbs-Merrill, 1956).

9. "The 'Third Man' Argument in the *Parmenides,*" *Philosophical Review* 63 (1954): 319–49. Reprinted in his *Studies in Greek Philosophy,* vol. 2, edited by Daniel W. Graham (Princeton: Princeton University Press, 1995), 166–90, to which citations will be made below.

10. In another influential paper, "Reasons and Causes in the *Phaedo,*" *Philosophical Review* 78 (1969): 291–325, Vlastos argued that some of the epistemological aspects of the theory of Forms were continuous with the interest in the contrast between a priori and a posteriori knowledge that had exercised modern philosophers like Leibniz and Kant and, though he did not make an explicit issue of it, contemporary philosophers like Rudolf Carnap, under the guise of the distinction between analytic and synthetic statements.

11. See Arnold Isenberg, "Some Problems in Interpretation," in his *Aesthetics and the Theory of Criticism,* edited by William Callaghan et al. (Chicago: University of Chicago Press, 1973), 199–215, 215.

12. George Kerferd, *The Sophistic Movement* (Cambridge: Cambridge University Press, 1981).

13. B. Jowett, *The Dialogues of Plato,* 4th ed., edited by D. J. Allan and H. E. Dale (Oxford: Oxford University Press, 1953), 252. I discuss this view in detail in "Meno's Paradox and Socrates as a Teacher" as well as in "Socratic Intellectualism."

14. And developed in detail in *The Art of Living: Socratic Reflections from Plato to Foucault* (Berkeley: University of California Press, 1998).

15. Friedrich Nietzsche, *Beyond Good and Evil,* translated by Walter Kaufmann (New York: Random House, 1968), sec. 14.

PART I

Socrates: Questions of Goodness and Method

One

MENO'S PARADOX AND SOCRATES AS A TEACHER

MENO has always been considered one of the least gifted and cooperative characters in Plato's dialogues. Commentators have disdained him generally, but their greatest disdain is reserved for the argument he introduces to the effect that all learning is impossible, at *Meno* 80d5–9. Shorey, who had no patience for the view expressed in the paradox itself, referred to it disparagingly as "this eristic and lazy argument."[1] Taylor liked neither the argument nor Meno's reasons for bringing it up: "Meno," he wrote, "again tries to run off on an irrelevant issue. He brings up the sophistic puzzle."[2] Klein thought of the negative influence of the paradox on all desire to learn anything new and wrote that Meno himself "was conspicuously reluctant to make the effort Socrates requested of him. It seems that his behaviour throughout the conversation was in agreement with the consequence that flows from the argument he has just presented."[3] Bernard Phillips, who with many other writers takes the argument itself quite seriously, nevertheless insists that for Meno personally "it is merely a dodge."[4] Even Bluck, who is slightly more sympathetic to Meno than other writers are, cannot approve of him in this instance: "So far as Meno is concerned, this question may be regarded as a convenient dodge, an eristic trick; but for Plato, it had important philosophical implications."[5]

Plato himself certainly took Meno's paradox seriously, as we can see from the care with which he develops his own controversial and complicated solution to the problem (*Meno* 81a5–86c2) and from the intimate connection of that solution, the theory of recollection, to the theory of Forms when the latter eventually appears, as it does not in the *Meno*, in Plato's texts.[6] But does Plato take only the argument, and not Meno himself, seriously? Is Meno merely dodging the issue and trying to win a debating point from Socrates? Is his paradox simply a pretext for Plato to present his own, recently acquired, epistemological ideas?

This view is invested with considerable authority, but does not seem to me to be true. To see that it is not, we must first examine the general situation that prompts Meno to present his paradox as well as the precise wording of his statement. If we can show that Plato thinks that Meno himself has good reason to raise this difficulty then we shall be able to connect this passage with certain other issues, some of which were of considerable importance in Plato's philosophical thinking.

I

The question whether *arete* is teachable, inborn, or acquired in some other way, with which Meno so abruptly opens the dialogue (*M.* 71a1–4), was a commonplace of early Greek speculation. That it concerned not only Socrates but also, more generally, the sophistic movement is already indicated by the Gorgianic style of Meno's question.[7] More traditionally, the issue applied not only to *arete* but also to *sophia* (wisdom); this may appear surprising in view of the fact that Socrates finds it uncontroversial to claim that if *arete* is *episteme* (knowledge or understanding, often used interchangeably with *sophia*), then it is surely teachable (*M.* 87c5–6).[8] Already by the end of the fifth century, the author (unknown) of *Dissoi Logoi* (403–395 B.C.) can refer to the "neither true nor new argument that *sophie and areta* can neither be taught nor learned" (6.1).[9] In a famous passage of *Olympian* II.86–88, Pindar had already claimed that the wise (which in this case refers to the poet) is so by nature, the rest being to him like cacophonous crows in comparison.[10] Isocrates was to argue that *arete* and *dikaiosune* (justice) are not purely teachable, without, that is, the proper nature (*Contra Sophistas* 14–18, 21)[11]—a position with some affinities to Plato's view in the *Republic*. Finally, a similar position in regard to *andreia* (courage) is attributed to Socrates by Xenophon at *Memorabilia* III.9.

But though this question was commonplace, there was little, if any, agreement as to the nature of what it concerned, the nature of *arete*. What concerns me is not the specific debate over the distinction between "quiet" or "cooperative" and competitive virtues. Mine is the much simpler point that *arete* has an immensely broader range of application than its conventional English translation "virtue," while the more recent "excellence" strikes me as too weak and vague. *Arete* not only applies to more human qualities than "virtue" does, but it also covers features that are in no way specifically human. This is, of course, perfectly clear from *Republic* 352d–354a, where Plato discusses explicitly the *arete* of instruments and, by implication, that of animals. But this usage is not found only in Plato. Already in Homer, horses are said to possess *arete* (*Iliad* XXIII.276, 374). Even inanimate objects can have their characteristic excellence: fertile soil (Thucydides I.2.4) and fine cotton (Herodotus III.106.2) are cases in point. If it were not for this, we might do well to construe *arete* as "success" or as the quality that constitutes or that accounts for it. If nothing else, this would show that the ancient debate is relevant to the many contemporary promises to ensure success, for an appropriate fee, in all sorts of fields and endeavors and that it prompts Socratic and Platonic responses from all those who look down upon the notion of success implicit in these promises and upon the endeavors themselves. We may thus be able to answer Jowett, who, construing *aretē* as virtue, claimed that "no one would either ask or answer such a question [as Meno's] in modern times."[12]

In order to account for the application of *aretē* to animals as well as to inanimate objects, it might be better to construe it as that quality or set of qualities, whatever that may be, that makes something *outstanding* in its group. We might even consider it as what accounts for an object's *justified notability*. Both suggestions concern not only intrinsic features of such objects but also, in one way or another, their reputation. And this is as it should be. For from the earliest times on, the notion of *aretē* was intrinsically social, sometimes almost equivalent to fame (*kleos*). That this was so even in late periods is shown by Hypereides, who in his *Epitaphios* wrote that those who die for their city "leave *aretē* behind them" (41). Also, an epigraph commemorating the Athenians who fell at Potidaea states that "having placed their lives onto the scale, they received *aretē* in return."[13]

The question, therefore, whether *aretē* can be taught is the question whether one can be taught what it takes to have a justifiably high reputation among one's peers.[14] But this, of course, leaves the prior question unanswered; the term is not noncontroversially connected with any particular set of human qualities. We still do not know the proper domain within which one is supposed to be outstanding or, even more importantly, in what being outstanding itself consists.

This last reasonable doubt, expressed in appropriate Socratic vocabulary, suggests that Socrates' own response to Meno's opening question makes rather good sense. In the persona of an imaginary Athenian, Socrates tells Meno not only that he does not know whether it can be taught but also that he does not know "in any way at all (*to parapan*) what *aretē* itself is" (71a5–7).[15] Now as long as we think of *aretē* as virtue we have enough intuitions about what that is to think that Socrates' reply must be prompted by metaphysical or epistemological considerations. He, too, we suppose, has a pretty good idea of what virtue is, but insists that he does not in order to make a purely philosophical point about the priority of definition. Yet, though not without important metaphysical implications, Socrates' response to Meno's precipitate question is quite independently reasonable. Meno asks without preamble a commonplace question that nonetheless depends on many disputable presuppositions. Socrates' reaction is, simply, to try to slow Meno and the discussion down.[16]

In light of this, I follow Bluck (209) in taking *to parapan* at 71a6 closely with *oude*. Socrates is disclaiming all knowledge of the nature of *aretē*, and he does exactly the same at 71b4: *ouk eidōs peri aretēs to parapan*. I also take it that his very next point—that one cannot know whether Meno is beautiful, rich, or noble, if one does not in any way (*to parapan*) know who Meno is—is strictly parallel. Socrates is not appealing to a distinction between knowledge by acquaintance and knowledge by description as Bluck (32–33, 213–14) among others, has claimed, nor is he introducing, at least implicitly, a technical distinction between knowledge and belief and claiming that though one can have all sorts of beliefs about the object of one's inquiry, these beliefs cannot become knowledge unless they are supplemented by knowledge of the definition of the nature of the object in question.[17] His point is simple and intuitive: if he has *no* idea who Meno is, how can he answer any questions about him? That this is so is shown by the fact that Meno immediately accepts Socrates' general view, as he should not on either of the two interpretations above. What he cannot believe is that Socrates is quite as ignorant as he claims to be about the nature of *aretē*.

Nevertheless, and in characteristic fashion, Socrates insists on his ignorance and asks Meno, who claims to know, to tell him what *aretē* is. Meno makes three efforts (71e ff., 73c ff., 76b ff.). But in each case he can only produce many *aretai* instead of the one that Socrates wants in answer to his question. Meno is originally unwilling to agree that *aretē* is one (73a1–5). He then agrees to go along with Socrates without necessarily accepting his view (*eiper hen ge ti zēteis kata pantōn*, 73d1). He finally appears to accept Socrates' arguments to that effect (79a7–e4). Willing as he is to cooperate with Socrates, Meno is led from thinking that he knew what *aretē* is to being unable to say anything satisfactory about his topic, each time unexpectedly, and in a different way, being shown to make the very same error.

It is only after the failure of his third effort that Meno begins to lose his patience. Even so, he very politely concedes that Socrates seems correct in what he says (cf. 79d5, e4) and rather ingenuously confesses that he cannot answer the question. Through his famous comparison of Socrates to the torpedo fish, he claims that though he had earlier spoken at length and well about *aretē* his contact with Socrates seems to have robbed him of all ability to do so now (79c7–80b3).

It is very important to notice the exact expression Meno uses at this point:

nun de oud' hoti estin to parapan echō eipein (80b4)

He admits that he is unable to say even in the most general terms what *aretē* is, that he is totally lost and confused. And by the repetition of the crucial term *to parapan*, through which Socrates had earlier disavowed all ability to lead the discussion, Plato now places Meno, even if against his will, in the very same position that Socrates had eagerly taken up at the opening of the dialogue.

Socrates refuses to return Meno's compliment and offers a simile in his turn (80c3–6). If he has reduced Meno to perplexity, he says, it is only because he is himself perplexed.

καὶ νῦν περὶ ἀρετῆς ὅ ἐστιν ἐγὼ μὲν οὐκ οἶδα, σὺ μέντοι ἴσως πρότερον μὲν ἤδησθα πρὶν ἐμοῦ ἅψασθαι, νῦν μέντοι ὅμοιος εἶ οὐκ εἰδότι. (80d1–3)

This passage is important. We should notice, for one thing, the irony of the final phrase, in which Socrates, despite his earlier disclaimer, does after all offer a simile for Meno; though, of course, to say as he does that Meno is "similar to someone who does not know" is literally true.[18] We should also notice that in saying that Meno may have known earlier what *aretē* is, Socrates suggests, equally ironically, that something that is known can actually be forgotten. In one sense this is quite true, and it forms the central point of the theory of recollection. But once something comes to be known, once (in Plato's terms) it is recollected, then it becomes more difficult to forget it or to be persuaded to change one's mind about it. This, after all, is how Socrates distinguishes *doxa* from *epistēmē* at 97d6–98d5. True beliefs, he claims, like Daedalus' statues, are always escaping from the soul. But when they are bound down by an "account of the explanation," which, "as we earlier agreed, is recollection" (98a3–5), they are transformed into *epistēmē* and become permanent. There is a serious question here about the sorts of things that, once learned, become permanent. Does Plato believe, for example, that if you know the road to Larissa (97a9–11) you cannot ever forget it? Or would he more plausibly be willing to allow gradations of permanence that would prevent geometrical or ethical truths from being forgotten but that would allow lower-level truths to escape the soul either through forgetfulness or through contrary argument? We shall return to this question toward the end of this essay.

Our present passage, 80d1–3, is finally important because it completes the stage setting for the raising of Meno's paradox. Since Meno has now admitted that he is totally lost with respect to *aretē* and since Socrates has repeated his earlier complete inability to say anything about it, neither of them can even know where to begin the investigation. It is only at this point and faced with yet a further exhortation by Socrates to say what *aretē* is (80d3–4) that the much-maligned Meno raises the not unreasonable question of how, if this is indeed their situation, they can possibly go on with the inquiry. In stating the paradox Meno once again repeats Socrates' word *to parapan*: "In what way," he asks, "can you search for something when you are altogether ignorant of what it is?" (80d5–6). Plato has gone to great lengths in order to emphasize Socrates' ignorance and to strip Meno of all claims to knowledge. Given this situation, and far from being a contentious move, Meno's raising of the paradox of inquiry is natural and well motivated.

II

Plato takes Meno's paradox, that you cannot look for what you do not know and do not need to look for what you know, very seriously in its own right.[19] In addition, he provides Meno with good reason to raise it. He uses the paradox not only in order to discuss serious epistemological issues, but also to resolve a number of dialectical difficulties to which Socrates' practice had given rise.

Of course, Meno's paradox could easily be put to contentious use, as it was, in two related versions, in the *Euthydemus*. At 275d3–4, Euthydemus asks Cleinias whether those who learn are the wise or the ignorant; at 276d7–8, he asks him whether one learns things one already knows or things one does not. In each case Cleinias is made to contradict himself. Having claimed that it is the wise who learn, he is forced to admit that it has to be the ignorant instead (276b4–5), and immediately following he is made to concede that in fact those who learn are, after all, the wise (276c6–7). Having claimed that one learns what one does not know, he is forced to agree that what one learns one actually knows (277a8–b4) and, at that point, Dionysiodorus enters the argument and argues that one learns only what one does not know (277c6–7).

Socrates replies on Cleinias' behalf that such paradoxes depend merely on verbal trickery. They equivocate between two senses of *manthanein* ("to learn"), one involving the acquisition at some time of knowledge that was not at all possessed previously and the other involving the exercising of knowledge that has already been acquired in the past (277e3–278b2). In this he is followed to the letter by Aristotle, who, in *Sophistici Elenchi* 4 (*Soph. El.* 165b30–34), classifies this as a paradox due to verbal homonymy.

When such paradoxes, therefore, are offered contentiously, Plato is perfectly capable of giving them a short and easy reply. His reply in the *Euthydemus* depends crucially and unselfconsciously on the notion of the absolute acquisition of knowledge. But, in the *Meno*, Plato finds this reply deeply problematic. At the very least, he does not think that the paradox to which he can also supply a merely verbal solution has merely verbal force. What, then, accounts for this difference in attitude?

We have already said that Meno uses the term *to parapan* in stating his paradox. Some commentators have taken it that Meno simply overstates his case, and that Plato solves the problem by pointing this out. Their case depends primarily on the fact that Socrates omits this qualification in his restatement of Meno's problem (*M.* 80e1–5). Thomas, for example, writes:

> This immediately destroys the thrust of the original puzzle for, lacking "parapan," the crucial premise reads "if a man does not have some knowledge"

rather than "if a man has no knowledge whatsoever." The reformulated dilemma is consistent with the possession of some knowledge. . . . Plato is not making much of an effort to meet the eristics in their . . . own terms. How could he, since to do so would be to concede them victory? Why should he, when the dilemma proscribes the possible? One is not obliged to take seriously intellectual chicanery that prohibits us from doing what we already do.[20]

But to assume that this is chicanery and that we can perfectly well do what the paradox denies, being a begging of the question, is itself a prime case of chicanery. Despite the similar views of Moravcsik[21] and Scolnicov,[22] it does not seem to me that Socrates refutes Meno by changing the terms of the argument. He may try to show that we do all possess some knowledge already, but he cannot begin from that fact. In this respect, at least, White is correct in writing that there is no substantive difference between Meno's and Socrates' statement of the paradox: "What Socrates does is simply to make clear that Meno's puzzle can be cast in the form of a dilemma" (290 n. 4). The function of *to parapan* is important and ineliminable.

Discussions of this passage often claim that Plato is only concerned with one among the many species of learning. Gregory Vlastos, for example, writes that:

Manthanein . . . is being used in this context in the restricted sense of learning to have propositional knowledge. The acquisition of inarticulate skills, though well within the scope of the word in ordinary usage, is tacitly excluded.[23]

Moravcsik also believes that the paradox concerns only "learning taking the form of inquiry" (53). Plato, he continues, is not concerned with the learning of nonintellectual skills, with learning by being told, or with learning by imitation (54).

This is in a way correct, since the *Meno* does discuss only learning by inquiry.[24] But we must avoid the implication, which perhaps these writers themselves do not want, that Plato acknowledges many ways of learning but discusses only one in this context. Instead, Plato seems to hold the view that any learning and *epistēmē* worth the name must be achieved through inquiry and that therefore all learning, not just one particular form of it, must, in Moravcsik's words, "be given direction by the learner himself" (54). Plato is not simply excluding the learning or inarticulate skills from his discussion. Rather, he seems at least implicitly to be denying that inarticulate skills are acquired through learning and that they are therefore, strictly speaking, objects of *epistēmē*. Similarly, he appears to deny that being told or imitating can, in themselves, constitute learning and produce understanding.

But if learning can proceed only through inquiry and if neither Socrates nor Meno knows how to go on, then their impasse is very serious indeed. Where can the elenchus even begin? In addition, Gorgias, who had been earlier mentioned as a possible teacher of *aretē* and who might have helped the discussion, has already been disqualified. Since Meno accepts his views, it was agreed that to include him in the discussion would have been superfluous (*M.* 71c5–d5). And in any case, his account of what *aretē* is (71e1–72a5; cf. Aristotle, *Politics* I.13.1260a20–28) did not survive Socrates' arguments.

III

It would seem, then, that for the discussion to proceed, Socrates and Meno are in need of another teacher who might guide them out of their impasse. Such teachers are mentioned later on in the *Meno*. Why does Plato not bring them into the discussion now? Is it simply because he is not interested in the case of learning by being told by another, or is the matter, as I shall now try to suggest, considerably more complicated?

Three classes of possible teachers of *aretē* are brought up in the *Meno*: sophists, notably successful citizens, and, in a rather cursory way, poets (89e–96b). The sophists are disqualified because they cannot agree among themselves whether *aretē* can or cannot be taught (95b–c); also because, unlike the case of any other subject, those who claim to teach what *aretē* is are not acknowledged as proper teachers of their subject by others and are even claimed to lack that which they profess to teach (96a6–b1; cf. 91c1–92c5). Good and noble citizens, men like Pericles, Themistocles, Aristeides, and Thucydides, are disqualified because not one of them has been capable of teaching his own sons what *aretē* is (93b–94e); also because they, no less than the sophists, cannot agree on whether this is a teachable topic (95a–b, 96b1–3).[25] Finally, the poets, through a quick examination of Theognis, are summarily dismissed because they cannot even produce internally coherent views on the subject (95c–96a).

These arguments against particular sorts of teachers of *aretē* are common, indeed commonplace.[26] In addition to them, however, Plato offers a more subtle and much more far-ranging argument against any self-professed teachers of success. The argument is implicit in a not very widely discussed passage of the *Protagoras* (*Prt.* 313a1–314c2). In this passage, Socrates is warning Hippocrates against going to the sophist for instruction without first thinking the matter through very carefully. In addition, however, his warning involves an important paradox with some serious implications for our own discussion.

Socrates, we said, warns Hippocrates not to rush into Protagoras' company. He describes the sophist as "a merchant or peddler of the goods by which the soul is nourished" (313c4–5). The soul, he continues, is nourished by what it learns (*mathēmata*, 313c7). He then offers an analogy between sophists, so construed, and those who sell any sort of food for the body (*ponēron ē chrēston*) but praise everything they sell indiscriminately (313d1–3). The buyers of such food also lack the necessary knowledge, unless they happen to be experts on such issues, gymnasts or physicians (313d3–5). The same is at least possible in the case of the peddlers of mental nourishment: some of them, too, may well be "ignorant of whether what they sell is harmful or beneficial to the soul" (*chrēston ē ponēron pros tēn psuchēn*, 313d8–31). And the analogy holds further true of their clients, unless one among them happens to be "a physician with regard to the soul" (*peri tēn psuchēn iatrikos*, 313e1–2). Now if, Socrates continues, "you happen to be an expert regarding which of those things are beneficial or harmful, then it is safe for you to buy learning from Protagoras or from anyone else" (313e2–5). But if not, the danger is great, much greater indeed in this case than in the case of physical nourishment. Physical food can be taken away from the peddlers in a separate vessel and examined by an expert before it is consumed (314a3–b1). But this is not possible with food for thought:

> You cannot carry learning away in a jar. Once you have paid for it you must receive it directly into the soul and having learned it you must leave already harmed or benefited. (*Prt.* 314b1–4)

The discussion is at least cautionary, but it makes an additional point. Buying, or more generally receiving, learning presents some special difficulties of its own. When buying food one can always ask a third party, an acknowledged expert, for advice before the fact and act accordingly. But when buying learning the expert cannot be consulted, so to speak, after the initial transaction. One must determine in advance of all contact whether listening to the sophist or to any other professor of *aretē* is likely to help or harm one's soul. But at least part of the additional problem in regard to learning is that in this case there are no acknowledged experts. And therefore the same difficulty that applied to the sophists will also apply to such putative experts: how is one to tell whether their advice is itself harmful or beneficial?

The predicament gets worse. The dangers involved in approaching the sophist, concerning as they do what is most dear and precious to us, the soul, are immense. The implication, though it is not explicitly drawn in the text, is that one should not approach such a professor unless one is certain that one knows that what is offered will be beneficial. Now to benefit or harm the soul, is, obviously, to make it better or worse (cf.

318a6–9, d7–e5). And a discussion in the *Laches* adds a special urgency to this connection.

In the *Laches*, Lysimachus and Milesias ask Socrates, Laches, and Nicias whether they should train their sons in armed combat. The two generals having disagreed on this issue, Socrates questions whether any one of them there is an expert (*technikos, La.* 185a1) on the issue at hand. In typical fashion, he immediately generalizes that issue to apply not only to fighting but to the large question whether the boys will or will not become good (*agathoi,* 185a6). This in turn he construes as the problem of how to make the boys' souls as good as possible (186a5–6). But to know how to accomplish this, he continues, they must know what it is that makes the soul better when it is present in it. And to know this, of course, is to know what *aretē* is (189d–190a).

In order to know whether a course of learning, therefore, will harm or benefit the soul, the expert (*iatrikos, epaiōn*) of the *Protagoras* must, like the expert (*technikos*) of the *Laches,* know what *aretē* is. But if the expert knows this, why bother to go to the sophist at all, why not learn instead from one who has already been determined to know? But the point is that there are no such acknowledged experts. Therefore, learners can only be certain that their soul will not be harmed by the sophist (or by the expert) if they themselves can tell whether such advice or instruction will be beneficial or harmful. But to know this, we have just shown, is to know oneself what *aretē* is. Therefore, unless one already knows what *aretē* is, and thus precisely what sophists claim to teach, one should never approach any professors of *aretē*. The sophists, and all who claim to teach what *aretē* is, are quite useless!

IV

None of the problems discussed here, of course, could ever be problems for Socrates, since he never claimed to teach what *aretē* is. It is true that in *Alcibiades I* Socrates makes some startlingly extravagant claims about his importance to Alcibiades and his political ambitions (*Alc.* 105d ff.). But his point there, I should think, is to satirize the wooing practices of Athenian men.[27] In general, Socrates steadfastly refuses the teacher's role or function in Plato's early dialogues.[28]

These problems, therefore, could not have seriously disturbed Socrates. But they did become very serious indeed for Plato, who gradually, in the very process of portraying him as refusing that role, came to see Socrates not only as "the best, the wisest, and the most just" man of his generation (*Phaedo* 118a16–17) but also as the ablest, thus far, teacher of *aretē*. For Socrates' sons, like the sons of Pericles, Aristeides, and Themistocles, did little to distinguish themselves in their city. His friends and companions, like the friends and companions of Protagoras and Gorgias, remained mediocre, like Crito, or became vicious, like Charmides, Critias, or especially Alcibiades. Though perhaps ironically motivated, his views on whether *aretē* can be taught did not remain stable. And he certainly was not universally acknowledged as an expert on *aretē*. On the contrary, his life no less than his reputation suffered worse in the hands of the Athenians than the lives and reputations of many who, in Plato's eyes, had no claim to *aretē* whatsoever compared to him.

How, we should finally ask, could Socrates be exempt from the paradox that the teacher of *aretē* is useless? How could Plato, the disciple who may have thought he learned something from him, believe that Socrates could be approached even if one did not already know what was good and what was bad?

The answer to this question goes to the heart of Socrates' personality as well as of his method. It is that Socrates, unlike all other teachers of *aretē* does not constitute a danger to his students precisely because he refuses to tell anyone what *aretē* is, especially since he denies having that knowledge in the first place. Whatever claim Socrates has to the teaching of *aretē* lies exactly in his disclaiming any such ability. The contrast around which the *Protagoras* and many other early Platonic dialogues revolve is a contrast between a method that depends on telling one's students what *aretē* is, on transmitting information to them, and one that does not.

But if Socrates' refusal or inability to offer positive views makes it safe to approach him, it generates another problem: how does the elenctic method result in any learning? How do two people who are ignorant of the answer to a given question discover that answer, and how do they realize that they have discovered it? If the elenchus presents a serious methodological question, this is it. And this is the very question that Meno raises in the paradox with which we have been concerned.

Plato tries to answer this question in the *Meno* through the examination of the slave and the theory of recollection, though his views on these issues never remain unchanged. In claiming that Meno's paradox is well motivated and that it goes to the heart of Socratic dialectic, I find myself in agreement with Irwin, who writes that "the examination of the slave is a scale-model of a Socratic elenchos, with a commentary to explain and justify the procedure" (139). However, I cannot agree with Irwin on the question of the resolution of the paradox. He thinks that the paradox depends on the view that if I know nothing about an object, I cannot identify it as the subject of my enquiry and I cannot therefore inquire into it at all (138–39).[29] According to Irwin, Socrates rejects this view and claims that though the slave does not know, he has true beliefs about the questions discussed. . . . To inquire into x we need only enough true beliefs about x to fix the reference of the term "x" so that when the inquiry is over, we can still see we refer to the same thing. (Irwin, 139)

To support his view, Irwin relies crucially on *Meno* 85c6–7, where Socrates asks whether one who does not know does not still possess true beliefs about the things he does not know (316 n. 14). But, for one thing, the position of the passage announces it more as an intermediate step of the argument rather than as a conclusion to it.[30] More importantly, the question of identification does not seem to me so crucial to Plato's resolution of the paradox. It is quite true that Plato writes that before the inquiry begins the slave has true beliefs concerning the geometrical problem discussed. But these beliefs were in no way available to him as such at the time. They were mixed together with all sorts of false beliefs, some of which were both elicited and eliminated by Socrates during his questioning. These true beliefs are recovered by the slave at the end of his examination by Socrates; they could not therefore play the identificatory role Irwin asks of them and that requires them to be there consciously at its very beginning. Further, the knowledge that the slave is said to be eventually able to recover is also said to be in him, just as those true beliefs are possessed in a particular manner, different from that in which knowledge is possessed and that therefore would enable them to have the different function Irwin's account assigns to them.

For true belief to secure the stable identification of the object of inquiry, it is necessary for it and for knowledge to be independent of each other. But this does not seem to be the case. Plato writes that the slave who now has only belief will acquire knowledge through repeated questioning (85c9–d1). This statement is not by itself very explicit, but it becomes a bit more clear when we connect it to the later discussion of "the reasoning out of the explanation" at 97e–98a. Once this is achieved, Plato writes, true beliefs "become *epistēmai*." That is, these beliefs do not simply fix the object of which knowledge is to be acquired or, in Plato's terms, recovered; rather once acquired (recovered) themselves they become that knowledge when they have been properly organized and systematized.[31]

But before we offer some tentative remarks about Plato's resolution of the paradox we must raise one further, rather complicated problem. What exactly does recollection cover for Plato? Does it apply to the whole process of learning or only to part of it? Or, not to beg any questions about learning, which part of the slave's examination actually involves him in recollection?

The manner in which Socrates introduces the theory of recollection and his rather general statements at 81d2–3, d4–5, and 82a1–2 suggest that recollection applies to all the different stages that may be, however loosely, associated with the process of learning. Accordingly, we expect that everything that takes place during the slave's examination constitutes an instance of recollection. Socrates strengthens this expectation when he prefaces his examination by urging Meno to see whether the slave will be recollecting or learning from him (82b6–7), and by saying at the end of its first stage that he is only asking questions of the slave and not telling him anything (82e4–6).

But does not Socrates teach or tell the slave all sorts of things during their discussion? How else can we construe the questions of 82c7–8 and d1–2 or the leading (that is, misleading) question of 82d8–e2 that prompts the slave to offer one of his many wrong solutions to the geometrical problem? In addition, we must not forget the passages 83c8–d1 and d4–5, where Socrates does not even bother to ask a question but himself draws the inference, marked in each case by *ara,* for the slave.

Bluck, who was exercised by this problem, answered that Socrates does not teach the slave "in the sophistic way, by merely presenting him with propositions that he must accept." He gradually "leads" the slave to the correct solution and at that point the slave is "able to 'see' that what was said was true. The argument is simply that such 'seeing' or comprehension would not be possible if the slave had not had previous acquaintance with the truth" (12).

But is it so clear that there was such a thing as "the" sophistic way of teaching? And if there were, is Bluck's description of it accurate? Some sophists, Hippias and sometimes Protagoras (*Pr.* 320c2–4), may have taught in this manner. But Euthydemus and Dionysiodorus used a questioning method that, at least superficially, did not differ so drastically from the elenchus.[32] Bluck's appeal to "seeing," in addition, seems to me rather empty. The point is not simply that, especially in the *Meno,* the text gives little warrant to the identification of the slave's understanding with "his feeling of inner conviction" (12). More importantly, it is not clear that, even if such a feeling exists, the slave has it only when he "sees" the right answer and not also when he gives the wrong one. On the contrary, Socrates' comment at *Meno* 82e5–6 to the effect that the slave now thinks he knows the solution suggests that subjectively there is no difference between merely thinking one has knowledge and actually having it. If there were, and assuming that everyone knows at least one thing, learning should proceed on its own until this feeling of inner conviction is acquired.

In the course of questioning the slave, Socrates produces in him, or elicits from him, a number of false geometric beliefs. In the present case, he continues to clear them out and to replace them by true ones instead. But what if he had not? What if, in particular, their conversation concerned *aretē,* of which Socrates is himself ignorant, and thus the very soul of the slave? Would Socrates not be capable of causing at least as much harm to the slave as the sophists have earlier been said to cause their students unless these already know the answers to their questions?

It is at this point that we should take Socrates very seriously, if rather liberally, when he insists that he does not teach anyone anything. He does not mean that he will ask no obvious or leading questions, or that he will not make statements or even sometimes long speeches.[33] He does mean that he requires his interlocutor to assent only to what he thinks is true, nothing more and nothing less. This is what Vlastos has called the "say what you believe" requirement of the elenchus.[34] Socrates' practice is in stark contrast to the method of Euthydemus, despite their apparent similarity. For Euthydemus insists that Socrates answer his questions in ways with which he is deeply dissatisfied, dropping a number of essential qualifications, in order to prove to him that (again in a way superficially and perhaps deliberately reminiscent of the *Meno*) he has always known everything, even before he or the whole universe came into being, provided Euthydemus "wants it that way" (*Euthd.* 295e–296d).

If knowledge consisted in a feeling of inner conviction, Socrates would have been quite dangerous to his interlocutors. For since knowledge and belief, true or false, do not differ subjectively, there might in fact be no way of telling, from the inside, whether a particular answer reached to a problem is true or false. But, of course, Socrates never ends his questioning when he has simply elicited a statement. The major burden of the elenchus is to *test* such statements and Socrates assumes that no false statement can survive these tests. Whether he is engaged in the more negative elenchus of the earlier dialogues or in the more positive investigation of the *Gorgias*,[35] Socrates consistently makes his interlocutors answer for their beliefs. What determines whether a belief is true or false has nothing to do with how the respondent feels and everything to do with that belief's dialectical impregnability.

The elenchus, therefore, depends solely on a dialectical test for truth: a belief is true if it cannot be overthrown by sound, noncontentious argument. To which, of course, one might be tempted to reply: but how can we know that a belief will not be overthrown? Socrates, I think, had no clear answer to this question. Plato may have tried to devise one: we can know this to be the case when we master the whole interconnected set of truths to which our particular belief refers. We have *epistēmē* when we have learned the axiomatic structure of the system in question and can prove any one of its elements.[36]

But even though Socrates' leading questions may be harmless to the slave, his claim that the whole examination involves recollection is misleading for the readers of the *Meno*. The slave only produces a false belief in the first stretch of the argument (82b9–83e3). Are we to infer that coming to have (or recovering) false beliefs is a case of recollection?[37]

By opening the second stretch of the examination by asking Meno to watch how the slave will now properly engage in orderly recollection (82e11–12), Socrates again suggests that the slave will be actually recollecting in what follows. What occurs here, of course, is that the slave is made to realize that he does not know the answer to Socrates' question (82e14–84a2). Are we to infer that recollection applies to the realization that one's beliefs about a topic are false?

Part of the answer to this question depends on the interpretation of Socrates' next question, which occurs in his summary of this second stretch of argument:

Ἐννοεῖς αὖ, ὦ Μένων, οὗ ἐστιν ἤδη βαδίζων ὅδε τοῦ ἀναμιμνήσκεσθαι; (84a3–4)

Thompson construes this as asking "what point on the track of reminiscence he has now reached," and believes that recollection has already begun.[38] On the other hand, we could take the question to concern "what point on the track *to* reminiscence he has now reached," in which case Socrates would be saying that the path to recollection is now open, not that recollection has already begun. In that case, we may take his earlier remarks about the slave's recollecting to apply not specifically to the first part of the discussion but, more generally and programmatically, to the whole examination. Recollection may be more restricted than is sometimes supposed.

This impression is reinforced by Socrates' summary of the last section of his questioning. He and Meno agree that the slave has only replied with beliefs that were his own (85b8–9) and that he has true beliefs about what he does not yet know (85c2–7). Socrates now claims that if "someone asks him the same question many times and in many ways" he will finally have as much knowledge about these topics as anyone else (85c9–d1).[39] From this it is clear that the slave still does not have *epistēmē* of the subject and Socrates drives the point home by locating the slave's knowledge in the future in his very next question (*epistēsetai*, 85d3–4). He then goes on to say that it is just this recovery of knowledge that is still all in the *future* for the slave, that is recollection (85d6–7). Recollection thus seems limited to a very small part of the process of learning.

Despite the tension it creates with the general statement at 81d4–5, such a restricted interpretation of recollection fits well with Socrates' later distinction between *doxa* and *epistēmē*: the former, he says, "is worth little until it is tied down by reasoning about the explanation" (98a3–4). And it is *this* (*touto*, 98a4), he continues, that, "as we agreed earlier, is recollection" (98a4–5). But the *aitias logismos,* as far as I can see, corresponds to nothing in the first stages of the slave's interrogation. The only process to which it can be connected is the repeated questioning that will eventually lead to the recovery of *epistēmē* (85c–d) and which we were just now, on independent grounds, considering as a candidate for recollection.

Suppose now that we restrict recollection in this way. Since we are explicitly told that the slave does not yet have any *epistēmē* does it not follow that he has not engaged in recollection in the dialogue? And if this is so, what is the point of his long examination? What has Plato succeeded in demonstrating by its means?

It is quite possible that recollection, strictly speaking, is not shown to occur anywhere in the *Meno.* Nevertheless, I think that the last stage of the slave's questioning, in which Socrates elicits the correct solution to the problem from him, is deeply representative of the process. It represents it, that is, because it is a part of it. The slave, Socrates says, will come to have knowledge "if one asks him the very same questions [or: questions about the very same things] many times and in many ways" (85c10–11). What brings about the *aitias logismos* and transforms *doxai* into *epistēmē* is not a new operation, additional to the eliciting of true *doxa,* but rather the eliciting of enough true *doxa* about the subject to make having them *constitute* the *aitias logismos.* The very same true beliefs the slave now has, Socrates claims at 86a7–8, "having been aroused by questioning, become knowledge" (*epistēmai*).

Plato does not explain how this transformation is to occur, and it is very difficult to know what is involved in the transition. Certainly, simply having many *doxai* about geometry cannot be itself sufficient for *epistēmē.* One must also acquire the ability to organize them systematically, to become able to move from one of them to another properly and on one's own, to know how they are supported by one another. This is one of the reasons Plato emphasizes the role of questioning in the recovery of knowledge. Having the answers to as many questions as one pleases does not constitute *epistēmē* unless one is also capable of answering ever new questions as well as of formulating questions of one's own. The *aitias logismos* and recollection, strictly speaking, consist in this ability, which transcends merely having answers to different questions but which is acquired (or revealed) only in the course of learning them.[40]

Implicitly, true beliefs are in one in just the way that knowledge is supposed to be; explicitly, they enter the process of learning and recollection midway. It is therefore unlikely that Meno's paradox is resolved by appealing to them in order to secure, from the very beginning of the inquiry, reference to the object that the inquiry concerns. Plato seems to deny the claim, on which the paradox depends, that "one cannot search for what one does not know for one does not even know what to search for"

(80e5), on slightly different grounds. One does know what one does not know because questioning and the inability to answer continued questions determine that knowledge is lacking. Conversely, the continued ability to answer such questions suggests that knowledge has been reached and that "you have happened upon" what you did not know (80d8). On the other hand, he also denies the claim that "one cannot search for what one knows—for one knows, and one who knows does not need to search" (80e3–5). For one need not know what one knows since knowledge may be, and usually is, forgotten and is brought out only by questioning. Knowledge is reached when what one knew that one does not know is matched with what one did not know that one knows. The role of questioning in bringing this matching about is crucial: Plato's resolution of Meno's paradox is dialectical rather than logical.

V

The dialectical resolution of Meno's paradox, even when supported by the nondialectical explanation offered through the theory of recollection,[41] does not by itself account for Socrates' continued insistence that he is not, in this or in any other case, engaged in teaching. We have seen that part of this account is that had Socrates been willing to offer positive views on the nature of *aretē*, he should not have been approached any more than the sophists should. But in the *Meno* the question does not concern *aretē*, and Socrates is quite aware of the correct answer. Why does Plato insist that the slave must come to it on his own? Why is he so eager to point out that even when Socrates is transmitting information to the slave (which he has him do on a number of occasions) the slave is still only recovering knowledge from within himself?

Plato appears to believe that even in matters that do not concern the soul's welfare as directly as *aretē* does, *epistēmē* cannot and must not be reached through the transmission of information. But knowledge depends essentially on the transmission of information and is itself transmissible. What is crucial to knowledge is that the information in which it consists has been acquired in the proper way, no less and no more. As Bernard Williams has written, in regard to knowledge in general,

> not only is it not necessary that the knower be able to support or ground his belief by reference to other propositions, but it is not necessary that he be in any special state in regard to this belief at all, at least at the level of what he can consciously rehearse. What is necessary . . . is that one or more of a class of conditions should obtain . . . conditions which can best be summarized by the formula that, given the truth of p, it is no accident that A believes that p rather than not p.[42]

Though this formulation, as Williams himself admits, needs much further refinement, it seems to me quite true. However, Williams's conditions are remarkably weaker than Plato's and even explicitly exclude what Plato considers most crucial to *epistēmē:* the ability to "support or ground (a) belief," to give an account, a *logos* of the object of *epistēmē.*[43]

We might want to say that Plato insists upon an unduly restrictive notion of knowledge; but we would do better, I think, to say that when he is discussing *epistēmē* he is not producing unreasonable conditions on knowledge, but, rather, quite reasonable conditions on what it is to understand something. For unlike knowledge, understanding involves, in rough and ready terms, the ability to *explain* what one understands. By contrast, many items of knowledge, for example, particular facts, are not even the sorts of things to which explanation is applicable in this context.[44]

In the case of mathematical knowledge, at least so far as nonelementary propositions are concerned, Williams accepts "the Platonic view," that such knowledge involves *aitias logismos,* which he glosses as "a chain of proof." But he goes on to claim that whether or not having such proof makes true beliefs more permanent, as Plato believes, is irrelevant to the main point

> that the access to mathematical truth must necessarily be through proof, and
> that therefore the notion of non-accidental true belief in mathematics essen-
> tially involves the notion of mathematical proof (the points which the Pla-
> tonic model of *recollection* precisely serves to obscure). (9)

But Plato's emphasis on the permanence of *epistēmē* is anything but irrelevant. For one thing, the permanence of one's understanding of a topic is in itself a measure of the degree to which one understands it. At some earlier time, I was capable of dealing with quadratic equations; my present total inability to do so strongly argues that I never understood that subject very well. For understanding the nature of quadratic equations is not an isolated act concerning an isolated object; it involves, at least in principle, the understanding of a vast number of mathematical propositions and operations, perhaps of all of algebra. And the more of a field one understands, the more systematically one's abilities with respect to it are organized, the less likely it is that the relevant beliefs will be forgotten: the more likely it is that they will be, in Plato's word, permanent (*monimoi,* 96a6). It is very easy, it is in fact inevitable, to forget whether it rained here three years ago today or to be persuaded that my recollection is wrong. It is also easy to forget how to get from one part of one's country to another. It is easy to forget how to determine the circumference of the circle, if you were only taught it once at school. But it seems more difficult to say that one has forgotten geometry, and almost totally absurd to claim to have forgotten what *aretē* is.[45] The broader and more encompassing the field to which a proposition belongs, the more permanent beliefs concerning that field, once mastered, are likely to be. The more worthy, therefore, that field is, in Plato's eyes, as an object of *epistēmē*.

Plato's model of recollection, though it may obscure Williams's points about knowledge, is crucial in emphasizing the necessity of working out a proof or of reaching any sort of understanding through and for oneself. Knowledge of fact, we have said, is transmissible, and the

> mechanism by which knowledge is transmitted is *belief.* More precisely . . . it is sufficient and necessary for the transmission of your knowledge that *p* to me that I *believe you* when, speaking (or writing) from knowledge, you tell me that *p*.[46]

But, as Augustine also saw and argued in *De Magistro* (40), understanding cannot be handed down in this manner. In an important discussion of this dialogue that connects it to Plato's concerns, Burnyeat describes its main thesis, "that no man can teach another knowledge (*scientia*)," as

> the claim that no man can teach another to understand something. The argument will not be that information cannot be transmitted from one person to another, but that the appreciation or understanding of any such information is something that each person must work out for himself. . . . The conveying of information is not enough for teaching in the sense of bringing the learner to know something.[47]

Burnyeat wants to connect Augustine's view that learning comes about through "first-hand learning, by the intellect or by my own sense-perception" with a number of cases discussed by Plato. He mentions in particular Plato's insistence that the slave in the *Meno* can learn mathematics only through reasoning and with his claim that only someone who has actually gone on the road to Larissa knows the way there (*M.* 97a–b). He also brings in the view of the *Theaetetus* (*Tht.* 201b–c) that only an eyewitness to a crime can have knowledge about it (Burnyeat 16). My own view is that Plato considers the examples of the traveler and of the eyewitness not as instances of *epistēmē* but as indispensable analogies by which to explain his view of it. Their function is to highlight the crucial condition that *epistēmē* must be acquired firsthand; and in so far as they satisfy this condition, they may be, catachrestically, considered as cases of *epistēmē*. But in a stricter sense,[48] *epistēmē* applies only to cases that in addition to firsthand acquisition also involve systematization, proof, explanation, or account: this is the *aitias logismos* of the *Meno* and the *logos* of the *Theaetetus* (202d5). Neither the case of the traveler nor that of the eyewitness seems to me capable of satisfying this additional constraint.

What, then, is the difference between *epistēmē* and *orthē doxa*? According to Burnyeat, the case of the eyewitness shows that if he tells me I may come to know much of what he knows himself (though not, of course, on his grounds); still, there will "typically" be other things I will not know because eyewitnesses "nearly always" know more than they tell. What marks the difference between us is the eyewitness's synoptic grasp of something of which I at best know some isolated elements. And Burnyeat concludes that

> the important difference between knowledge and understanding is this, that knowledge can be piecemeal, can grasp related truths one by one, but understanding always involves seeing the connections and relations between the items known. (17)

The conclusion itself is quite correct, but I doubt that the case of the eyewitness testifies in its favor. First, I am not sure that it would be correct to say that the eyewitness does have understanding of what occurs. More importantly, the manner in which Burnyeat constructs his case (through the qualifications "typically" and "nearly always") suggests that he may think that eyewitnesses can on occasion tell all they see. But the difference between the eyewitness and me (if we attribute understanding to the eyewitness) cannot be, as this construal implies, merely one of degree. For if it depends simply on the amount of the information transmitted, then teaching may be after all, at least in principle, a matter of degree: what we would need would simply be a *very good* eyewitness. I think that the problem is caused by taking this case to constitute for Plato an actual instance of *epistēmē*. If, as I suggest, we take it only as a partial illustration of what *epistēmē* involves, then we will not feel it necessary to locate the difference between *epistēmē* and *orthē doxa* through it.

Instead, we can turn to the case of the slave and of mathematical knowledge. For here, the difference between belief (or even knowledge) and understanding is more clearly qualitative. Here, the connections and relations between the objects of knowledge, which were not easy to discern in the previous case, are much more central. For it is these relations and connections that produce understanding, and this limits understanding to fields that, unlike empirical low-level matters, involve them crucially. And it is precisely the mastering of these connections and relations that cannot be transmitted (cf. *Republic* 518b6–7) because these connections are methods and rules for proceeding in a properly justified manner, from one item of knowledge to another. And even if such rules and methods can be formulated, and in that sense transmitted, what cannot be transmitted in the same manner is the ability to follow the methods and to apply the rules.[49] And if we can formulate methods and rules for following the previous set, we will again face the question of how these new rules and methods are to be correctly applied. The notion of recollection provides Plato both with an account of the inward, firsthand nature of all *epistēmē* and with a way of ending this regress: its power lies in its double contribution to Plato's philosophical purposes.[50]

In relation to *aretē* the connections we have been discussing are what allows one to do the right thing on all occasions and not only sometimes or capriciously. Unless it is in order to fool someone, the geometrician will not consciously produce a fallacious proof of a theorem. And unless it is in order to harm someone, the *agathos* will not willingly do the wrong thing. But part of being *agathos,* of course, is never to want to harm anyone, as Socrates consistently argued in Plato's dialogues. The *agathos,* therefore, will never do the wrong thing.

Socrates, in Plato's eyes, never did the wrong thing and thus seemed to him to be the best man of his generation. But Socrates steadfastly refused the role of teacher: he claimed not to know how to make people good, and not even to understand at all what *aretē* itself consisted in. For practical and ethical reasons, Socrates had never wanted to tell his students (for students he certainly wanted, and had no less than any of the distinguished sophists) anything about the subject that they wanted to learn from him. For epistemological reasons, Plato came not to want Socrates to have believed that he was capable of doing so. Meno's paradox brought together Socrates' immediate concern with not harming his friends (a rather old-fashioned conception of *aretē* in its own right) with Plato's theoretical interest in the nature of understanding. The theory of recollection, whatever its ultimate shortcomings, succeeded in accounting systematically for both, even if in the process some of the mystery of Socrates gave way to the mysticism of Plato.[51]

NOTES

1. Paul Shorey, *What Plato Said* (Chicago, 1983), 157.

2. A. E. Taylor, *Plato: The Man and His Work* (London, 1937), 137.

3. Jacob Klein, *A Commentary on Plato's Meno* (Chapel Hill, 1965), 92.

4. Bernard Phillips, "The Significance of Meno's Paradox," in *Plato's Meno: Text and Criticism,* ed. Alexander Sesonske and Noel Fleming (Belmont, 1965), 78.

5. R. S. Bluck, *Plato's Meno* (Cambridge, 1964), 8. Bluck's mixed view of Meno can be found on pp. 125–26.

6. The contrary views of Cherniss and Guthrie have been recently discussed by Michael Morgan, "Belief, Knowledge and Learning in Plato's Middle Dialogues" *Canadian Journal of Philosophy,* suppl. vol. 9 (1983): 63–100, with full references.

7. Cf. also G. B. Kerferd, *The Sophistic Movement* (Cambridge, 1981), 131–38.

8. Cf. *Protagoras* (*Prt.*) 361a5–b3 and contrast *Euthydemus* (*Euthd.*) 282c1–8.

9. On the date of the *Dissoi Logoi,* cf. T. M. Robinson, *Contrasting Arguments: An Edition of the Dissoi Logoi* (New York, 1979), 34–41.

10. Cf. *Nemean* III.41.

11. Cf. *Antidosis* 186–92, 274–75. For further references, cf. Klein, above n. 3, 39 n. 18.

12. B. Jowett, *The Dialogues of Plato,* 4th ed., ed. D. J. Allan and H. F. Dale (Oxford, 1953), 252.

13. W. Peek, *Griechische Versinschriften,* vol. i (Berlin, 1955), 20.11.

14. The question of the public aspects of *aretē,* though very complicated, has not been widely discussed. My suspicion, though highly speculative and in need of extensive support before it can be taken seriously, is that Plato was centrally concerned with it. Part of his purpose in the *Republic,* I would want (and have) to argue, is to ensure that *aretē* will always have a proper audience, and that those who possess it will necessarily be recognized as such by everyone in their social group.

15. There is considerable irony in putting this reply in the mouth of an imaginary Athenian, since Anytus is later shown not to have any doubts about the fact that any good Athenian citizen can make another better (92e ff.).

16. The abrupt opening of the *Meno* concerns both Bluck (above n. 5, 199) and Klein (above n. 3, 38). The discussion above may offer an adequate dramatic justification for it.

17. This view has become popular recently. It is supported for example, by Terence Irwin, *Plato's Moral Theory* (Oxford, 1977), 40–41, 63; by Gerasimos Xenophon Santas, *Socrates* (London, Boston, and Henley, 1979), 118–22; 311 n. 26; and by Paul Woodruff, *Plato: Hippias Major* (Indianapolis, 1982), 138, 141. The issue is much too complicated to be discussed here, and it will occupy me in this book's essay "Socratic Intellectualism." A careful examination of the passages cited in this connection (*Laches* 190b8–c2; *Protagoras* 361c3–6; *Charmides* 157e7–159a3; *Meno* 100b4–6; *Lysis* 223b4–8; *Hippias Major* 286c8–d2, 304d4–e3; *Republic* 345b3–c3) has convinced me that Socrates does not, and need not, appeal to the distinction between knowledge and belief in order to justify his views on the priority of definition. The present case is, I think, even more straightforward.

18. Cp. 80d3 with *homoiotatos . . . narkēi,* and cf. Bluck, above n. 5, 271.

19. Cf. Nicholas White, "Inquiry," *Review of Metaphysics* XXVIII (1974), 289 with n. 1.

20. John E. Thomas, *Musings on the Meno* (The Hague, 1980), 123, 128–29.

21. J.M.E. Moravcsik, "Learning as Recollection," in *Plato: Metaphysics and Epistemology,* ed. Gregory Vlastos (Garden City, N.Y., 1971), 57.

22. Samuel Scolnicov, "Three Aspects of Plato's Philosophy of Learning and Instruction," *Paideia* V (1976), 52.

23. Gregory Vlastos, "*Anamnesis* in the *Meno,*" *Dialogue* IV (1965), 143 n. 1.

24. Cf. White, above n. 19, and Irwin, above n. 17, 315 n. 13.

25. Similar arguments can be found at *Protagoras* 319e–320b, *Alcibiades I* 118c–119a.

26. Cf. *Dissoi Logoi* 6.3, 4.

27. On which see Kenneth Dover, *Greek Homosexuality* (Cambridge, Mass., 1978), 81–100. In the course of the dialogue Socrates insists that he is not telling Alcibiades anything as their discussion proceeds (112d ff.), and he readily admits that he, no less than Alcibiades, is in need of an education (124b1–c2). In a final

ironic reversal, moreover, the dialogue ends with Alcibiades assuming the teacher's role and assigning to Socrates the student's position (135d–e).

28. Socrates often describes himself as a willing disciple of someone who claims to know something about *aretē;* cf., e.g., *Euthyphro* 5a3–b7.

29. White (above n. 19) offers a related account, more concerned with identifying the object inquired into throughout the inquiry, on 294–97.

30. Cf. Michael Morgan, "How Does Plato Solve the Paradox of Inquiry in the *Meno*?," in *Essays in Ancient Greek Philosophy: Plato,* ed. J. Anton and A. Preus (Albany, 1989), 169–82.

31. I have discussed some of the issues involved in this transition in the essay "*Epistēmē* and *Logos* in Plato's Later Thought" in this book.

32. For some material on sophistic teaching methods, cf. Kerferd, above n. 7, 59–67.

33. For example, despite his insistence on short questions and answers at *Gorgias* 448e–449a, 49b4–c7, Socrates makes many longer speeches than Gorgias in the course of their conversation (451a3–c9, 452a1–a4, 455a8–e5, 457c3–458c8).

34. Gregory Vlastos, "The Socratic Elenchus," in *Oxford Studies in Ancient Philosophy,* vol. i (Oxford, 1983), 27–58, with full references.

35. Vlastos's evidence, in "The Socratic Elenchus," for his construal of the elenchus as a method for reaching positive ethical conclusions mainly comes, as he himself admits, from the *Gorgias.*

36. This view is supported in "*Epistēmē* and *Logos* in Plato's Later Thought" (above n. 31).

37. Theodor Ebert, *Meinung und Wissen in der Philosophie Platons* (Berlin, 1974), 83–104, and "Plato's Theory of Recollection Reconsidered: An Interpretation of *Meno* 80a–86c," *Man and World* VI (1973), 163–81, thinks that it is because he thinks that Plato believes that learning is only analogous to recollection, and not an instance of it. But, I think, Plato's view is much stronger than that, and it would be very strange of him to consider that both the recovery of knowledge and the recovery of false beliefs are equally cases of recollection.

38. E. S. Thompson, *Plato's Meno* (London, 1901), 137.

39. Plato radically qualifies this extremely optimistic view, of course, in the *Republic.* The myth of Er and the theory of recollection as presented in the *Phaedrus* provide a rationale for his more cautious claims about the ability of people to reach *epistēmē.*

40. Restricting recollection in this way may help account for Socrates' argument of 96d ff. that though *aretē* is beneficial it may still not be *epistēmē* but *orthē doxa* instead and thus not teachable. For recollection provides Socrates' alternative account of teaching and learning. If it applied to the recovery of a single true belief (or to a small number of them), then this recovery would definitely be a matter of teaching, and Socrates would have no grounds for arguing that *aretē* cannot be taught. But if recollection only follows the recovery, or mere possession, of true belief, he may have just such a reason: teaching produces orderly recollection.

41. On the question whether the paradox is resolved primarily by the examination or by the theory of recollection, I agree with Irwin (above n. 17, 139, and n.

13; *contra* White, above n. 19, 289, and *Plato on Knowledge and Reality* (Indianapolis, 1976), 40–41): the paradox is disarmed in the examination, and recollection explains how that is possible.

42. Bernard Williams, "Knowledge and Reasons," in *Problems in the Theory of Knowledge,* ed. G. H. von Wright (The Hague, 1972), 5.

43. I have presented a full case for that claim in "*Epistēmē* and *Logos* in Plato's Later Thought"; cf. also Jon Moline, *Plato's Theory of Understanding* (Madison, 1981), 32–51.

44. This is not to say that the fact, which I know, that it is raining cannot be explained. It is only to say that my knowledge of that (meteorological) explanation has no bearing on whether I know the fact in question. Most people know the latter, when it is the case, and ignore the former.

45. Cf. Hesiod, *Works and Days,* 293–94: 'He is the very best who understands everything having considered it himself and knows what is good later and to the end' (quoted by Moline, above n. 43, 19; the translation is different).

46. Michael Welbourne, "The Transmission of Knowledge," *Philosophical Quarterly* XXIX (1979): 3.

47. M. F. Burnyeat, "Augustine *De Magistro*" (unpublished manuscript, 1982), 9, 11.

48. This stricter sense, as I proceed to suggest, can be found in the *Meno* and in the *Theaetetus,* contrary to Burnyeat's suggestion, above n. 47, 16.

49. The problem is discussed, but not resolved, by Gilbert Ryle, "Teaching and Training," in *Plato's Meno,* ed. Malcolm Brown (Indianapolis, 1971), 243–46.

50. Recollection does not perpetuate the regress, for the requisite abilities have, according to Plato (*M.* 85e–86b), always been in the soul.

51. For comments on an earlier version of this essay, I am grateful to M. F. Burnyeat, Rosemary Desjardins, Steven Strange, and Gregory Vlastos. I must also thank Paul Kalligas, who discussed these issues exhaustively with me and who gave me extensive and helpful comments.

Two

SOCRATIC INTELLECTUALISM

> And yet not once did he profess to be a teacher of
> virtue; still, being so obviously virtuous himself, he
> made those who spent time with him hope that by
> acting like him they too would become virtuous.
> —Xenophon, *Memorabilia* I.ii.3

APART FROM the legal charges that Plato may or may not have refuted in
the *Apology*, a philosophical charge against Socrates still remains. It is,
appropriately, an ancient charge (*Ap.* 18b–c), first and most crudely made
in Aristophanes' *Clouds*. Plato may have also made it himself when, in the
Republic, he divided the human soul into different capacities, not all of
them rational, and offered a detailed program designed to educate and
bring them into harmony with one another. Plato's implicit criticism was,
characteristically, made explicit by Aristotle (*Eudemian Ethics* [*EE*]
I.7.1216b3–26; *Nichomachean Ethics* [*EN*] VI.13.1144b17–30). And
George Grote both expressed the consensus of the ages and set the stage
for modern attitudes toward Socrates when he attributed to him "the error . . . of dwelling exclusively on the intellectual conditions of human
conduct, and omitting to give proper attention to the emotional and
volitional."[1]

Socrates' intellectualism has proved to be a spur as well as a hurdle to
our understanding him. How could such a supremely intelligent man fail
to realize that intelligence is not enough for being good and, as it followed
for him, for being happy?[2] Given his own view that to commit injustice is
to harm oneself (*Ap.* 30c5–d5), how could it be that "he had no suspicion
of the extent to which his mental superiority had raised fear and hatred
against him in the hearts of men towards whom he was conscious of nothing but good will and good service,"[3] and that he therefore may have after
all, though perhaps inadvertently, harmed them himself?

How could someone learn to live the life of reason, virtue, and happiness Socrates praised? (And did Socrates himself live that way?) Does Socrates offer us a moral philosophy? Plato's early dialogues suggest that Socrates believed that to live the good life, we must first learn what virtue is.
To act virtuously, we must know the definition of virtue. But this may
present another serious problem. On an ethical level, it may seem that
knowledge of what is good is not sufficient to make us do it. On a logical

and metaphysical level, it may now appear, Socrates' belief in "the priority of definition" may make it impossible to acquire that knowledge in the first place. Socrates' refusal to look at concrete cases of action, and to learn about the virtues from them, it has been thought, is yet another instance of his "despotic" intellectualism.[4]

The problem, then, seems to be this. Socrates' ethical intellectualism makes him believe that once people acquire knowledge of virtue, they will be able to tell what the good thing to do is in all circumstances, and will in fact do it. They will therefore always act well and be happy. But the transition from knowledge to action seems highly doubtful. In addition, his definitional intellectualism, his view that knowledge of the definition of virtue is necessary in order to tell what the good thing to do is, seems to make the acquisition of the knowledge necessary for the good life impossible. The Socratic project of teaching people how to be good appears to fail at two crucial places: it considers a certain knowledge sufficient for right action when it is not, and it makes the acquisition of that knowledge impossible in the first place.

I

We will first turn to this latter problem, which, if it is real, undermines the whole Socratic project. Readers of Plato's early dialogues are universally agreed that Socrates believes that definition is prior to something.[5] But various and conflicting answers have been given to the question of precisely what it is that the definition is prior to. In what follows, I shall offer my own answer to that question. I will argue that little, if anything, is wrong with Socrates' view on this issue. And I will suggest that this problem is deeply connected with the question of moral education, with which our discussion began.

One way of interpreting the priority of definition is to take it as the view that if one does not know, say, the definition of piety, then one is never in a position to tell whether any individual person or action is or is not pious. If we add to this the idea that it is impossible to arrive at the definition of piety through an examination of specific examples of pious actions or pious people, it is easy to see that this principle is vicious. If you cannot recognize cases of piety without knowing what piety is, then how can you appeal to such cases in order to arrive at that knowledge? Wittgenstein criticized both Plato and Socrates for accepting this view,[6] and the criticism became broadly known as "the Socratic fallacy" when Peter Geach claimed to locate it in the *Euthyphro* and described it as the assumption

> (A) that if you know you are correctly predicating a given term 'T' you must know "what it is to be T," in the sense of being able to give a general criterion

of a thing's being T; (B) that it is no use to try and arrive at the meaning of 'T' by citing examples of things that are T.[7]

Now, at least in connection with the *Euthyphro,* it can be shown that Socrates does not endorse this unacceptable principle. He makes, instead, a much weaker claim. This is that if Euthyphro is convinced that his highly controversial legal action against his father (the shocking nature of which Plato clearly underscores: *Eu.* 4a11, b4–6, e4–9) is in fact pious, then he is bound to have an account of piety that justifies his confidence. Socrates need not depend on general principles in order to ask for a definition in this case. His request is a dialectically motivated and reasonable response to Euthyphro's startling claim that he feels as secure as he claims to be in prosecuting his own father on a murder charge.[8] But Geach's charge, as we shall soon see, can be refuted on more general grounds in any case.

A second way of construing the priority of definition concerns further features of the very object we are trying to define and not instances in which a virtue is or is not manifested. Terence Irwin, for example, writes that at *Meno* 71b1–8 "Socrates insists as usual that a definition of virtue is prior to any knowledge of what it is like."[9] This principle, too, can be stated so that learning is impossible. For if no features of a virtue can guide us in our effort to define it, how can we have even the faintest idea of what it is that we are trying to define in the first place?

We should take a good look at the *Meno.* For Socrates offers an example of what he means when he says that, not knowing what virtue is, he also does not know if it is teachable or, more generally, what sort of thing it is (ὁποῖόν τι). This is the famous case of Meno himself, and it repays close attention:

> Do you think that it is possible for someone who is altogether ignorant of who Meno is to know if he is noble, wealthy or high-born, or the opposite of these? (*M.* 71b4–7)[10]

The traditional reading of this passage depends on attributing to Plato, and agreeing with, the view that "knowing Meno is of course a matter of acquaintance."[11] The example is then taken to be an illustration of the Platonic theory that some sort of intellectual acquaintance with the Forms is necessary if we are to have any knowledge of them at all.[12]

Serious doubts about whether Plato ever held this theory have been consistently raised.[13] These may or may not be justified, though I personally believe they are. But we should concentrate on the specific example at hand before we examine such general claims. And in connection with this example it is crucial to notice that, given Bluck's interpretation, what Socrates says about Meno is obviously and strikingly wrong. Being acquainted with Meno is neither necessary for knowing whether he is rich (since we can know this without being acquainted with him) nor sufficient for such knowledge (since we can be acquainted with him and still have no idea of his wealth). If Socrates is trying to show that we need to be directly acquainted with an object before we can know what any of its features are, then he has chosen a very bad example indeed.[14]

What, then, is the point of the example, and what does it show about the priority of definition? Before I offer my own answer to these questions I would like to consider what has emerged as one of the most popular responses to Geach's charge against Plato. This response depends essentially on drawing a sharp distinction between knowledge and true belief. If Socrates observes this distinction, whether or not he draws it explicitly, then, as Irwin writes, he

> can insist that without knowledge of what virtue is we cannot have fully justified beliefs [i.e., knowledge] about virtue, and still allow us true beliefs to recognize examples of virtue. . . . He allows both his interlocutors and himself true beliefs without knowledge. (Irwin, *PMT,* 41)

According to this interpretation, the definition of virtue (or anything else) is prior to knowledge of its properties or instances. But we can have true beliefs about these before we know the definition. These beliefs, though not "fully justified," can guide us in our effort to reach the definition, and Geach's charge is defused.

This defense is also offered by Gerasimos Santas, who distinguishes two assumptions Socrates might have made.[15] The first is that "knowledge of the definition of, say, courage is a necessary condition for knowing that a given action is courageous." The second is the much stronger view that such knowledge "is a necessary condition for judging or believing that a given act is courageous." Socrates, Santas argues, may have possibly held the first view, but he "certainly does not hold" the second. And it is, of course, only the second that would give rise to "the Socratic fallacy." Santas attributes the first assumption to Socrates on the basis of the *Hippias Major* (286c) and the *Lysis* (223b). But he admits that these passages, which we shall examine soon and interpret quite differently, "are not in the least conclusive."

Santas's and Irwin's responses are without question formally correct: they extricate Socrates from Geach's difficulties. Are they what Plato's texts require? The point is not simply that Socrates does not himself draw the distinction between knowledge and belief on which this solution depends—a distinction that in fact belongs among the factors that characterize Plato's middle, post-Socratic thought and that is actually first encountered toward the very end of the *Meno* itself (*M.* 96c ff.).[16] This, though surely relevant, is not sufficient reason for rejecting this approach.[17]

The real question is whether we need this solution at all—whether Socrates' method creates a problem that calls for a solution in the first place. We would need this approach,[18] whatever distinctions Socrates did or did not explicitly draw, if we accepted the assumption, which Geach's opponents freely grant him, that Socrates "often . . . says or implies that we cannot know anything about, say, virtue until we know what virtue is."[19] This is the assumption that Socrates is making a general logical or epistemological point: for any property F that is true of any object a, we cannot have any knowledge regarding F and its application to a unless we already know the definition of a. The case of virtue is a special instance of this general principle. And indeed the passage to which Irwin appeals as evidence for this principle, "How could I know what sort of thing something is when I don't know what it is?" (ὃ δὲ μὴ οἶδα τί ἐστιν, πῶς ἂν ὁποῖόν γέ τι εἰδείην;, M. 71b3–4) appears general enough to support this unrestricted view.

And yet the distinction between knowledge and belief does not apply well to the case of *Meno*, which is immediately offered as an illustration of this general statement (71b4–8). For it is quite unclear that, in the technical philosophical sense of these terms, any sensible object, Meno included, could ever be either known or defined. It is, I think, much more plausible to believe that Plato is making a simpler and more intuitive point through his example.[20]

This point would be just that someone who does not in any way (τὸ παράπαν) know who Meno is will also not know whether he is noble, wealthy, or highborn. Plato selects the relevant features of Meno quite carefully; they do not constitute a haphazard list. In particular, καλός must not be taken as "beautiful"; this encourages the idea that you must see (be acquainted with) Meno before you can decide whether he is handsome or not. The word is equally connected with the idea of nobility. All the features Plato mentions here belong to Meno as a function of his social position. To know whether they are true of him, it is necessary to know "who Meno is" in the everyday sense, absolutely basic to Greek views of who people are, of knowing his geographical, familial, and social origins. If Meno does have an "essence," this is an intuitively obvious one: it is his provenance. And knowing this is indeed necessary in order to know (in any sense you like) whether nobility, wealth, and a distinguished birth, all of which are a function of his provenance and to that extent "essential" to him, do or do not belong to him.[21]

Socrates' example, I would therefore like to suggest, is not profoundly philosophical. Meno is perfectly willing to accept it as it concerns himself and he seems equally willing to accept the principle Socrates' conditional is intended to illustrate. What he does refuse to believe is that Socrates is in fact ignorant of the nature of virtue (71b9–c2). But what exactly is the principle that Socrates illustrates by his claim that if he did not know who Meno was he also would not know whether he was noble, rich, or high-born? How broad and unrestricted is that principle?

The sentence "How could I know what sort of thing something is when I don't know what it is?" (*M.* 71b3–4), taken by itself, is quite general. It may seem to apply to all the features of virtue and, indeed, of everything else: it sounds like an unrestricted philosophical principle. Yet it is made in a very specific context. And this context, together with the force of the example through which Socrates illustrates the principle, places severe limits on the range of features of virtue about which he claims to be igno-rant as long as he is also ignorant of its definition.

The *Meno* is essentially concerned with the question whether or not virtue can be taught, and this is the issue explicitly under discussion here. We could now say that whether or not virtue is teachable is as disputable a question as the question of what constitutes its essence. Alternatively, we could say that it is a feature that, whether or not it is strictly speaking essential, belongs to virtue directly on account of what the essence of vir-tue is.[22]

Perhaps, then, Socrates' claim is more restricted than Geach thought and not subject to the difficulties from which Irwin, Santas, and Woodruff, who all accept Geach's assumption, try to protect it. In light of what we have seen so far, we may attribute to Socrates the modest claim that there are some features of virtue (those which are as disputable as its definition or essentially connected with it) about which he can have no knowledge, or any other cognitive attitude, without first knowing what virtue itself is. The unrestricted appearance of the principle of *Meno* 71b3–4 is not by itself sufficient to attribute to Plato the unrestricted view we have been discussing.[23] The view he holds cannot be determined by general consid-eration. We must take a close look at Plato's actual practice.

The following three passages are always cited in support of the view that Socrates accepts the unrestricted principle:

> For if we did not in any way (τὸ παράπαν) know what virtue is, how could we possibly advise anyone about how best to acquire it? (*Laches* 190b8–c2)[24]

> Now . . . I would like to have all this well explained and to also discuss what virtue is and again consider whether it is or is not teachable. (*Protagoras* 361c2–6)[25]

> We shall have clear knowledge about it when, before we try to determine how it comes to be present to people, we first try to discover what virtue itself is. (*Meno* 100b4–6)[26]

It is a remarkable, though not sufficiently remarked, fact that these three passages all concern the very same question. This is just the question dis-

cussed at the opening of the *Meno*—namely, How is virtue acquired?—
and of which the problem whether it can be taught is a special case. Plato
does not seem concerned with arbitrary features of virtue, and he seems
even less concerned with features of arbitrary objects. Socrates is raising a
very special problem: the fact that, as he believes, it is necessary to know
what virtue is before we can tell how it is acquired. His view, in my opinion, is very reasonable. But whether or not it is reasonable, it is simply not
general enough to provoke Geach's attack or to require the broad defense
we have been discussing so far.[27]

Two passages in the *Hippias Major*, however, appear to commit Socrates
to the stronger view that one simply cannot recognize any case of the fine
or nobility without knowing its definition:

> Just now someone got me badly stuck when I was finding fault with part of
> some speeches for being foul, and praising other parts as fine. He questioned
> me this way, really insultingly: "Socrates, how do *you* know what sort of
> things (ὁποῖα) are fine and foul? Look, would you be able to say what the fine
> is?" (*Hi.Ma.* 286c5–d2)

> He asks if I'm not ashamed that I dare discuss fine activities when I've been so
> plainly refuted about the fine, and it's clear I don't even know at all what that
> is itself! "Look," he'll say, "how will you know whose speech—or any other
> action—is finely presented or not, when you are ignorant of the fine? And
> when you're in a state like that, do you think it's any better for you to live
> than die?" (*Hi.Ma.* 304d5–e3; trans. Woodruff)

But in both cases Socrates claims that he had been discoursing on the
subject and was then caught out. The emphasis is not on the recognition
of individual instances of the fine. On the contrary, it seems to me, the
questioner seems to ask whether Socrates can tell in general what is and is
not fine without knowing what the fine is. Alternatively, the questioner
suggests that Socrates cannot defend his praise and faultfinding (ἐπαι-
νοῦντα . . . ψέγοντα) and cannot justify his discoursing (διαλέγεσθαι) on
the subject without knowing the definition.[28] Either of those interpretations, which are compatible with each other, implies that the issue Socrates
raises does not concern the mere recognition of individual cases of the
fine.[29] The issue is not even one directly for Socrates himself, in any case.
For his questioner, Socrates says (*Hi.Ma.* 304c1–d3), attacks him at specific moments. Those are the moments when Socrates, instead of simply
manifesting his ignorance and confusion (ἀπορία) to the wise, tries to act
like them. That is, those are moments when Socrates professes to speak
about the fine. But, then, as the dialogues clearly indicate, Socrates never
tries to do this. It is only Hippias and others like him who speak about the
fine and the other virtues in general terms, implying that they know what

these are but betraying their ignorance when pressed. Socrates uses his imaginary interlocutor to put questions to Hippias, not to himself. And it is just Hippias' ignorance of his ignorance that, Socrates says through that interlocutor, makes his life not preferable to death.

Socrates does not accept a view open to Geach's charge in the *Lysis,* either. At 212a4–6, Socrates claims that he is so far from possessing (the virtue of) friendship that he does not even know how one person comes to be a friend of another. The question of acquisition is still paramount.[30] And at 223b4–8, Socrates says that he and his interlocutors have appeared "ridiculous" since they consider themselves as friends of one another "but have not yet been able to discover what a friend is." This, too, is not a strong statement. It implies at most that if some people are, or take themselves to be, friends, then they are more likely than others to know what friendship is—or at least that they should be able to learn what it is once they apply themselves to that task. This is, incidentally, all that is implied in connection with temperance at *Charmides* 158c7–159a3, a passage in which Socrates explicitly mentions belief (δόξα)—but without distinguishing it from knowledge (ἐπιστήμη). But to return to the *Lysis,* Socrates and his friends appear ridiculous for they have not yet (οὔπω) said what friendship is. Socrates may in fact be wrong in his optimistic conviction, though being a friend probably is at least a necessary condition for knowing what friendship is. But right or wrong, his view does not amount to the strong principle that we cannot know whether a relationship between two people is an instance of friendship without knowing what friendship is.

The final passage always cited in this connection is the end of *Republic* I (354b–c). Here Socrates says that instead of pursuing the definition of justice, he wandered away into asking whether it is evil and ignorance or wisdom and virtue and whether justice is more beneficial than injustice, so that now he is totally confused.

> [For] if I do not know what justice is, I shall hardly know whether it is a virtue or not and whether whoever possesses it is or is not happy. (354c1–3)

One may be unwilling to appeal to this passage on the grounds that it represents Plato's, and not Socrates', views.[31] But even if we do, we shall see that the claim Socrates makes here is characteristically narrow. The features of justice with which Socrates is concerned have all, at least in this context, been highly disputed by Thrasymachus (significantly, they included the possibility that justice is wisdom (σοφία) and thus introduced the issue of its teachability).[32] In order to decide whether such features, once they have been denied in connection to justice by Thrasymachus, are actually true of it, we may well have to know first what the definition or essence of justice is.

Socrates' insistence on the priority of definition is therefore very narrowly circumscribed. First, it seems to concern primarily the virtues and not every thing or every term, as Geach supposed. Second, it seems to apply only to specific issues, and not to all the features of virtue, as Geach's opponents actually conceded to him. Socrates seems to believe that we need to know the definition of a virtue in order to decide whether certain disputable features (either traditionally disputed, like teachability, or disputed on particular occasions, like its benefits in the case of Thrasymachus) are or are not true of it.[33] We also need to know it in order to decide whether particularly disputable courses of action do or do not fall under it. And we need to know it in order to discourse generally about it; that is, in order to present ourselves, as Hippias does, in the guise of experts in its regard. None of this amounts to a fallacy, and none of it requires a broad methodological response.

In fact, Socrates often claims to have a number of views about some of the features of virtue as well as about some of its instances. He claims, for example, that noble (καλά) things are beneficial (ὠφέλιμα) and good (ἀγαθά) and that courage is noble (*La.* 192c5–6; *Hi.Ma.* 296cd, 297c; *M.* 77b6–7). Actually, as we now know, he relies heavily on these and other such views in practicing the elenchus; without them many of his arguments against proposed definitions could never proceed. We might of course want to say that he only has true belief and not knowledge about them. But since we are no longer bothered by Geach's charge, why should we? Why not say instead that Socrates claims to know a number of non-controversial features of the virtues?[34] Socrates can also believe that he is able to distinguish some virtuous actions from others that are vicious. He can still claim, consistently with the above and reasonably in any case, that he is unable to answer controversial questions about the virtues themselves or about their instances without knowing their definitions, and he can very well expect anyone who offers answers to such questions to be able to offer, and to defend, the appropriate account.

In short, Socrates' insistence on the priority of definition occurs within a carefully delineated context, not only in the *Meno,* but also in many other Platonic dialogues. It is indeed necessary to know what virtue is in order to know whether it has features that are as much in dispute as the nature of virtue itself and that are therefore parts of that nature. But knowledge of the definition is not prior to knowledge of all features or instances of virtue. On the contrary, as the practice of the dialogues shows, the search for definition depends on presupposing such knowledge. This is knowledge that no one in the dialogues disputes.

No one, that is, except Thrasymachus. Even Callicles is willing to concede that real, as opposed to conventional, justice is a virtue (*Gorgias* 488b8–489c7). But Thrasymachus boldly refuses to agree that justice is a virtue at *Republic* I.348c ff.—a position that eventually prompts Socrates' peculiar statement at the end of Book I. In fact, and not unexpectedly, Socrates' response to Thrasymachus, after he has made sure that Thrasymachus means what he says, is that it is very hard to know how to reply to such a view (348e5–6). He goes on to argue in a roundabout way for the conclusion that, whether justice is or is not a virtue, it is still more beneficial than injustice. For it is just by denying this view that Thrasymachus was led to his counterintuitive position in the first place. But as the end of *Republic* I suggests, Socrates is not totally pleased with his efforts.

To return to where we started, Plato's example involving the knowledge of Meno, like all his views on the priority of definition, is straightforward and uncontroversial. It says that if I have no idea who Meno is, I can also have no idea of the features that depend on who he is. The example transfers to virtue in that it shows that if I do not know what virtue is I cannot know whether or not it can be taught—a feature that I characterized as disputable in the same way as the definition of virtue is disputable and which is directly connected with virtue's nature.

My conclusion, then, is that Socrates' belief in the priority of definition is much less radical than we have often tended to suppose. It depends neither on a general theory of meaning nor on an epistemological view about the grounding of belief in knowledge. It does not even depend on a general theory of definition. Aristotle (*Metaphysics* M.4.1078b23–25), who also limits Socrates' interest to the virtues,[35] suggests that Socrates was motivated to look for definitions because definition is prior to syllogistic argument. He may well have been right about the latter point, but that was not, I think, Socrates' reason for his search, though it was perfectly consistent with it. Though Plato's Socratic dialogues contain crucial logical, semantical, epistemological, and metaphysical ideas, and though such ideas are among the greatest and most lasting contributions to our philosophical heritage, these dialogues are not, as such, logical, semantical, epistemological, or metaphysical treatises. Socrates did not consider definition in general as an end in itself. Nor did he think that it was the necessary beginning of all knowledge whatever. To that extent, at least, the first charge of intellectualism against him fails. But he certainly did consider definition essential, and he pursued it relentlessly as a means for answering a question he did in fact see as an end in itself, the only one he really cared about, the question of the nature and the content of the good life, of *eudaimonia*.

II

Did Socrates succeed in answering his question? Could he, with the means he put at his disposal? We have seen that he did not believe that knowledge of virtue is necessary for recognizing every case of virtuous action or even for acting virtuously on occasion. But acting virtuously on occasion is not the same as being virtuous, as Aristotle also clearly pointed out in the *Nicomachean Ethics* (*EN* II.3.1105a26–b12); this does seem to involve knowledge as well as constancy and stability of motivation. But if knowledge of the nature of virtue is at least necessary as well as sufficient for the good life, and yet Socrates never acquired that knowledge, was his life a failure? And if Socrates was wrong, and knowledge of virtue must be supplemented by good upbringing and by the independent training of character in order to secure virtue and happiness, was his teaching a mistake? In either case, his moral intellectualism appears to condemn him: either a failed person, or a failed teacher, or perhaps both. Is this the Socrates we have to live with?

These are immensely complicated questions. They presuppose answers to other equally complicated questions and give rise to still further questions, which we cannot hope to answer at once, or perhaps ever. What follows, then, is, in more than one sense of that term, only the slightest beginning. The question on which I will concentrate concerns Socrates as a teacher of *aretē*. This is the word I have translated as "virtue" so far, but which, it is well known, covers a much broader range than its morally oriented conventional English equivalent. Generally speaking, I take *aretē* to concern the capacity for achieving a justifiably high reputation among one's peers, and the achieved reputation as well, as success in a very broad sense.[36] Our question then becomes whether this was something of which Socrates was a successful teacher.

The answer to this question emerges, in my opinion, quite clearly in Plato's earlier dialogues. Within the world of these dialogues Socrates is not depicted as a good teacher of *aretē*, especially by his own standards. The most crucial reason seems to be that Socrates is convinced that in order to be a teacher of anything, one must first know the subject oneself. This is, of course, the point with which the *Meno* (the first half of which is thoroughly Socratic) begins; it is also made explicitly at *Alcibiades I*.111a11–12. Even to be an adviser on how something is to be acquired, even to point out its proper teachers, Socrates claims, one must know what the subject in question is (in the context from which this point is taken, *La.* 190b7–c2, the subject is *aretē* itself). Yet Socrates is the first to admit, and steadfastly to insist, that he does not know what *aretē* or any of its parts (justice, temperance, and the other virtues) is.[37] His view that *aretē* is knowledge of good and evil, if he in fact holds it (*Chrm.* 135a3–8, *La.* 199c4–e9), is, in my opinion, not sufficient to count as a definition because without an explicit account of what constitutes good and evil such knowledge cannot possibly be a guide to, much less a guarantor of, goodness and *eudaimonia*. Knowledge of good and evil cannot in itself constitute a definition of virtue unless one can say independently what these are (*La.* 190c6; cf. Xenophon, *Memorabilia* IV.vi.1).

But there are other reasons as well for Socrates' failure as a teacher. In his earlier dialogues, Plato raises a number of problems for those who profess, or are claimed by others to be able, to teach what *aretē* is. One such argument is that the great Athenian statesmen (the most successful people of their time) were not even able to accomplish the least one would expect of such teachers; that is, to make their own children good (*Prt.* 319d7–320b3, *M.* 92e1–94e2: cf. *Alc.* I.118c–119e).[38] In the *Gorgias,* more radically and perhaps more as Plato's own spokesman, Socrates is made to deny that the great statesmen even possessed *aretē* themselves since, he argues, they seem to have left the citizens actually worse than they found them when they came to power. Pericles, for example, is disqualified by a strangely poignant argument: how could he be considered to have tended his people well if toward the end of his rule he was brought to trial for theft and almost sentenced to death? (*G.* 515e10–516a3; 515c4–517a6 is all relevant to this issue.)

In addition, the sophists are disqualified as teachers of *aretē* for at least two reasons. First, through the complicated general arguments of which the *Protagoras,* the *Euthydemus,* the *Hippias Major,* and the *Gorgias* consist.[39] Secondly, because, as the *Meno* claims, they cannot even agree with one another about whether *aretē* can or cannot be taught, a point that also applies to the notables discussed in the previous paragraph (*M.* 95b9–c8; cf. *Alc.* I.111b3–4).[40] Finally, the *Meno* dismisses the poets as teachers of *aretē* because, as a quick examination of Theognis is supposed to show, their views on *aretē* are not even internally consistent (*M.* 95c9–96a5), and the *Ion* denies that they possess any knowledge of their subject matter.

But the most serious argument against the professors of *aretē* occurs, as I have argued in detail elsewhere,[41] in the opening pages of the *Protagoras* (313a1–314c2). Socrates here warns Hippocrates, who is passionately eager to become Protagoras' student, of the grave dangers involved in approaching the sophist or anyone else who professes to teach what *aretē* is, especially though not necessarily for a fee. Unlike food for the body, the appropriateness of which we can check with an expert before we consume it, learning, which is food for the soul, has to be carried away directly within the soul itself. There is no time, as it were, between obtaining it and consuming it, to consult an expert about its possible harms and benefits. In addition, there seem to be no acknowledged experts in the field in any case. We must therefore ourselves know beforehand whether what the professor or *aretē* offers is or is not good for the soul. And to know this is to know how a soul is made better or worse. But to know this, as is argued explicitly in the *Laches* (189d4–190c6), is just to know in what the soul's goodness consists. And that is nothing other than *aretē*. We should therefore approach professors of *aretē* in order to learn from them without fear only if we already know what they profess to teach. Teachers of *aretē* are simply useless.

There may seem to be two problems with this account. First, it could be argued that Socrates was capable of determining whether Protagoras, say, or Hippias was a proper teacher of *aretē* without being such an expert himself. This is true. But all it shows is that you do not need to be an expert in order to disqualify such a professor. But what about determining that someone does know, and can teach, what *aretē* is? This generates the second apparent problem for my view. For, one might argue, if experts on *aretē* existed, they could approach its professors first, and if they determined that their teachings were worthwhile, they could encourage us to approach them. But, first, no such experts on *aretē* seem to exist. Secondly, and more importantly, it would follow by our previous argument that if they existed they themselves would be at least as good teachers of *aretē* as the professors they examined. In that case, we could bypass the teachers altogether and attach ourselves to the experts. But how, in that case, would we be able to recognize the experts? Would not our earlier problem apply to them as well? In a community with no clear criteria for distinguishing experts from charlatans, it is not easy to see how an expert can be recognized by someone who does not already possess knowledge of the subject in question.

The notion of an expert raises very difficult problems for the interpretation of Plato. "The expert in a particular craft," Terence Irwin writes, "offers authoritative advice, supported by a rational account; and Socrates argues that we should seek someone equally authoritative in morals" (Irwin, *PMT,* 71). I think it is true that Socrates often wishes that virtue were like a craft, of which there could be recognizable experts. I am not so sure, however, that Socrates took the "craft analogy" as seriously as Irwin claims. His attitude, in my opinion, is more equivocal.

Irwin considers that it is essential to a craft that it have a clear, rational, teachable method (*PMT,* 34), that the method can be explained to nonexperts (*PMT,* 23), and that disputes within a craft can always be decided by reference to the quality of its end products (*PMT,* 24). Now it is clear, of course, that the crafts are teachable. But it is not so clear that their method is "rational" if by that we mean that their procedure can be explained to outsiders. Perhaps a craftsman can explain why he acts in a particular way at a particular time. But the stronger claim, which Irwin claims to find at *Apology* 22d3–4 (*PMT,* 73), seems to me neither true nor in the text. All that Socrates says in the *Apology* is that, relative to their work, the craftsmen "knew things I didn't and were to that extent wiser than I was." He implies that the craftsmen know what they are doing, but not that they can explain what they are doing to others. And if even this weak implication is missing, so is the much stronger implication that the practice of a craft can be taught on the basis solely of rational and intellectual factors. Socrates, himself a statuary and a statuary's son (*Diogenes Laertius* V.I.18), knew perfectly well that in ancient Athens the crafts were most often transmitted along with their "secrets within the family from generation to generation."[42] The overwhelming evidence is that fathers trained their sons and even that "training probably began at an earlier age than in modern times."[43] Habituation no less than "rational method" is essential for the practice if not also for the appreciation of a craft. And disputes, we should recall, were not so easily settled: the famous case of the constant competitiveness between Zeuxis and Parrhasius is only one of many, and the invective heaped by the author of *On Ancient Medicine* on conceptions of medicine differing from his own, another.[44]

Still, there is no question about the fact that Socrates often brings the crafts into his discussion of *aretē* and that he sometimes claims that an expert on the subject, "if there is an expert," would be of great help to us in learning to be good (*Crito* 47c8–48c10). But, implicit in all of Plato's early dialogues and particularly important in the passage of the *Protagoras* we have already discussed, there is a very serious problem concerning the expert of *aretē*. This is a problem we have already mentioned; how are we to recognize an expert even if one actually does exist? The issue, in my opinion, is very serious, and it has deep implications for Socrates' views on moral character and on the nature of the ability to live well.

In *Socrates and the State,* Richard Kraut argues that, contrary to what most people have thought, Socrates was not an absolute opponent of Athenian democracy. Kraut agrees that Socrates believed that "if there ever are moral experts, then they alone should have political power; they should give commands to the other citizens, and these commands should be obeyed" (233). But since Socrates also believed that no moral expert (himself included) existed, he was willing to accept the rule of the many as the best available alternative.

Kraut's view of the moral expert is not too far removed from that of Irwin, though it is more authoritarian. It gives, in fact, relatively little weight to the role of argument and persuasion in Socrates' view of the nature of the expert of *aretē* and of the process of recognizing him. Kraut seems to argue that once moral experts are somehow recognized, then Socrates is perfectly willing to give them the power to issue commands to the rest of the citizens. These commands will then be obeyed to a great extent just because they are the commands of these acknowledged experts.

This voluntaristic approach to moral expertise, however, immediately seems to conflict with the central Socratic idea that "the unexamined life is not worth living for a human being" (*Ap.* 38a5–6). Kraut is aware of the conflict, but he thinks it is only apparent. The idea of examination, he argues, applies only to understanding and not to obeying the expert's commands:

> If you acquire your beliefs from someone you recognize as a moral expert, then you can be fairly sure that nothing you believe is false. But that still leaves a good deal of work for you to do. Just accepting what someone says doesn't give you much understanding of what he says. (Kraut, *SS*, 241)

But can we plausibly attribute to Socrates, in the context of the conduct of life, this sort of distinction between accepting someone's view and understanding it? The elenchus depends essentially on the idea that you must neither offer nor receive a view as your own unless it is truly a view of your own—unless, that is, you are sure you accept it.[45] But to be sure that you accept a view you must first understand it, or at least think that you do. For to accept a view as your own is to believe that it does not conflict with other views of your own. To accept a view you must first, both logically and temporally, understand it.

In fairness to Kraut, we should point out that he applies the distinction between accepting and understanding a view to the conduct of life only on the assumption that moral experts exist. This is to assume that the conduct of life does bear some deep similarities to the practice of the crafts. In the crafts, both outsiders and apprentices accept the master's word just because it is issued by the master. Perhaps a particular master could explain a particular view then and there, but does not; perhaps we could only understand it after we had become fairly proficient in the craft ourselves. And in either case, provided an expert has been determined to exist, the distinction between accepting and understanding a view can be clearly drawn.

Yet the problem with moral experts does not concern only their existence but also, as we have seen, their recognition. Even if disagreements in the crafts are more common than Irwin suggests, we can still accept his view that we have a reasonably good idea about which craftsmen are better than others, and we also know that learning a craft takes time and practice. But even if we agree that moral experts do exist, it still would not be clear that we could recognize them independently of the fact that their arguments in favor of these views, their reasons for living as they did, were *convincing*. And because of this problem the distinction between understanding and obeying appears, once again, to collapse. Kraut believes that moral experts must not only give commands: they must also try to "get others to understand" their reasons for issuing them (Kraut, *SS*, 248). But moral experts, so far as I can tell, are simply those people who can convincingly explain why we should act in one way rather than in another.

Consider, for example, the argument in the *Euthyphro* where Socrates refuses to accept as a definition of the pious its specification as being what all the gods love. His reason is that this is not consistent with the fact that the gods love the pious because it is pious, since it construes as the pious whatever it is that the gods happen to love (*Eu.* 9e1–11b1). The clear implication is that the gods (moral experts, if anyone is a moral expert) love the pious for a reason, and that this reason explains not only why the pious is pious but also why (as Euthyphro believes) they command us to do it. But this reason, and not the gods' love, is then what constitutes piety itself. This extreme objectivism bypasses the experts altogether. The only factor in the situation that matters is their reason for wanting us to act in some ways and not in others. And this reason can be convincing, and therefore worthy of obedience, only if we understand what it is and find it rationally acceptable.[46]

Kraut's view, in my opinion, leans toward voluntarism more than Socrates would be willing to allow. At least, Kraut's view is voluntarist for the intermediate stages of moral development, within which, in general, he distinguishes four. Kraut believes that Socrates has reached a point in his moral development at which he can discern a moral expert without being one himself. In support of his view, he cites, for example, *Euthyphro* 6e3–6, which says that if I know what piety is then I can use it as a standard to decide whether anything is or is not pious. Kraut writes:

> It would be natural for Socrates to assume that anyone who possesses such a standard ought to be in a position of authority. For why should decisions be made by majority rule, when someone already knows what the outcome of such decisions should be? (*SS*, Kraut, 233)

The situation, however, is in my view considerably more complicated and equivocal. Socrates is here asking Euthyphro, with obvious emphasis on the word, to *teach* (διδάσκειν) him what the standard of piety, which he claims to know, is (*Eu.* 6e3; cf. 5a3–4, c4–5, 15e5–7). He wants to learn what that standard is so that *he,* Socrates, can discriminate correctly between pious and impious courses of action. He never says or implies that if Euthyphro knows the definition of piety then, as Kraut's view suggests, Euthyphro should make decisions on Socrates' behalf. Ironically, presupposing that Euthyphro is an expert, Socrates presents himself, equally ironically, as his student. But the point he makes is not itself ironical.

This is the point that one attaches oneself to experts in order to gain understanding from them, and that only the acquisition of understanding can convince us that our putative expert was also an expert in fact—which is exactly what Euthyphro is not. Socrates can reach understanding only through an examination, an elenchus, of Euthyphro. His elenchus fails to yield a definition and thus succeeds in leading him to understanding as little as it succeeds in undermining Euthyphro's claim to possessing it— that is, not at all.[47] But if his elenchus had actually led to a definition of piety that was, so far as anyone could tell, immune to dialectical attack, then Socrates, in grasping that definition (no easy task itself), would have become himself an expert on piety. Perhaps a city, as Kraut correctly notes, cannot function without commands accepted just because they are issued by those with authority. But what I am arguing is that Plato's Socrates simply does not seem concerned with the general problem of the nature of political community. The farthest he goes in that direction essentially involves his own relationship to the state insofar as that relationship is relevant to his living well. This, of course, is the problem of the *Crito*.

What seems to follow from this is not that moral experts, if they exist, should issue commands to the rest of us, as Kraut thinks.[48] What follows is that such experts would devote all their efforts to imparting their understanding to the rest of us, thus making us experts too, and securing their recognition. This, in my opinion, is one of the most crucial, interesting, and paradoxical consequences of Socrates' view on moral education: only one good human being can recognize another.

In general, I think that the whole notion of obedience and submission, which becomes central to the educational schemes of both Plato and Aristotle, is deeply unimportant to Socrates. In particular, I do not think it plays a serious role in the passage on which Kraut depends crucially for his view. This is the famous sentence of the *Apology* (29b6–7):

> To do an injustice and disobey a superior, whether divine or human: that, I know, is bad and shameful.

Kraut writes:

> Socrates talks about obedience to god and to man in the same breath: the absolute submission owed to an immortal is also owed to a human superior. (*SS*, 234)[49]

Two points are important here. First, we should take issue with Kraut's idea of "the absolute submission owed to an immortal." To be sure, Socrates never disobeyed his *daimonion*, which was, I think, as much of a mystery to him as it is to us. But just a few pages earlier in the same speech, he tells the jurors that when he received Apollo's oracle that he was the wisest of the Athenians, he was very puzzled. He claims to have known that the god could not have lied, but, nevertheless, he decided he had to put the oracle to the test (ἐλέγξων, 21c1) in order to be able to say, "This man here is wiser than I am, though you claimed I was the one" (*Ap.* 21c2–3). It is only after his many conversations with the politicians, the poets, and the artisans (20c–23a) that Socrates came to see that the god might have been right to proclaim him wise on the grounds that he, at least, was aware of his ignorance (23a5–14). There is no question that Socrates feels he owed the god "absolute submission"; on the contrary, he *tests* the oracle's wisdom as rigorously as he tests the wisdom of those by means of whom he tests the oracle itself.

But does not Socrates claim throughout the *Apology* that the god has "ordered" him to practice philosophy and that to stop doing so would be to "disobey" the oracle (28d6–91a1, 30a5, 33c4–7, 37e5–38a)? This is true, but it is crucial to remember that Socrates interprets the oracle as an "order" to do philosophy only after, as we just put it, he tests it in order to determine whether or not it is true. And, I think, it is Socrates' conviction that the god was right, when he said that he was the wisest of the Athenians, that provides the grounds for Socrates' practicing the elenchus. The god, after all, never issued a direct command to Socrates. Socrates' effort to prove the oracle wrong turned out to be the practice of philosophy—and, for all that the elenchus can show, Socrates may still run into someone who knows something "good and noble"(21d4), and thus show the oracle to be wrong after all. But, in the meantime, he has been convinced that this is the "best" post for him to have (28d7, 10; 30a7–b2). And at *Apology* 38a1–8 he claims explicitly, after again alluding to the god's command, that the elenchus, which is the daily concern with *aretē,* is "the greatest human good." There is, in my opinion, not a trace of voluntarism in Socrates' "obedience" to the god; on the contrary, he only does, as he always has done, what he thinks is, on independent grounds, the best thing.

This brings us to a second point in connection with *Apology* 29b6–7. The word Kraut translates here as "disobey" is ἀπειϑεῖν, and it is, of course, clear that "obey" and "disobey" are common enough senses of the verbs πείϑεσϑαι and ἀπειϑεῖν.[50] For example, the most plausible translation of πείσομαι at 29d3, just a few lines below, may be "obey."[51] But the etymological connection between πείϑω and its cognates and the notion of persuasion is never, I think, far from the surface in the uses of these terms. In any case, immediately after 29b6–7, there occurs an important passage. Socrates here considers the possibility that the court might refuse to believe Anytus (ἀπιστήσαντες)[52] and set him free. He goes on to imagine that, not having been *convinced* (οὐ πεισόμεϑα) by Anytus' call for the death penalty, they will spare him on condition that he no longer engage in philosophy—something which, he says, he would refuse to do. It is clear, I think, that the Greek word here must be translated as I have given it, and not as "obey": the court is referring to Anytus' arguments and to their effects upon it. There can be no question of the court obeying one of the parties involved in the dispute.

What this suggests is that Socrates envisages that the same relationship holds between himself and whoever is better than he is, god or human, between Anytus and the jury, and perhaps between himself and the jury as well. The central idea is that at 29b6–7 Socrates is saying that it would be bad and shameful to fail to be convinced or persuaded by either a human or a divine moral expert. The question of submission, I think, is not raised. Socrates characteristically claims that the expert is just whoever has the knowledge necessary to convince us that a course of action is right or wrong. His terminology may suggest that a convincing argument may be recognized but not followed. But this, in my opinion, is a rhetorical maneuver intended to introduce the terms κακόν and αἰσχρόν. Given his view that knowledge is sufficient for virtue, Socrates cannot believe that we can act against our conviction that a certain action is or is not to be performed.[53]

Experts, then, cannot be recognized unless you are convinced by their arguments. But what does such conviction involve? It involves accepting the conclusions of these arguments as well as the methods by which the arguments reach their directions for how to act. And what, in turn, is this? Is it not a way of saying that one has become, at least to that extent, a moral expert, a virtuous agent, oneself? Is it not to say that only one virtuous person can recognize another?

But if this is the case, and if a moral expert must possess knowledge of the definition of virtue (which is more than knowledge of a few formulae concerning it),[54] how can one become a moral agent? How can one learn to be good? The elenchus could succeed in showing that someone did in fact know what virtue is only if the questioner arrived at that knowledge himself during the questioning. Socrates' repeated willingness to continue his discussions indefinitely suggests just this: the elenchus can succeed positively only if both parties reach the relevant understanding together.[55] The recognition of a moral expert, that is, a virtuous agent, through the elenchus can ultimately only be mutual. It always involves one of the participants becoming noncoercively convinced of the views, and therefore of the ways, of the other.[56]

The elenchus, then, works only through persuasion. But this seems to compound against Socrates the charges of moral intellectualism with which we began. Socrates seems to believe that only knowledge is relevant to right action. He also appears to hold that such knowledge can only be reached by means of the elenchus, by means, that is, of strictly intellectual argument. Our character and the other affective features of our personality are irrelevant to such argument. This may now be put together with the view, plausibly attributed to Socrates, that knowledge is not only sufficient but also necessary for virtue (*Ap.* 29d2–30a1).[57] What appears to follow is that knowledge and virtue go hand in hand, that Socrates does not have the relevant knowledge, and that he assumes he can determine what virtue is and can therefore act well by paying attention only to our intellect. But this is a doomed project. If virtue is only a matter of learning, strictly speaking, then it never has been learned. And neither can it ever be learned.

The ancient charges against Socrates as a moral educator have been recently revived.[58] Plato and Aristotle seem to have accused him of caring only for the intellect and not also for the character, habits, and dispositions of his students. Aristophanes may have claimed against him that, because of this intellectualism, Socrates would engage in conversation with anyone, whatever his moral character, and that his teaching could therefore easily lead to immorality. In addition, though Socrates criticized the traditional moral education of Athens, he lacked a positive moral program of his own. These charges, it has been argued, can all be truly made of Socrates as he is depicted in Plato's early dialogues.[59]

Yet even if we suppose that Socrates did literally think that *aretē* was a craft, we need not further believe that the crafts are purely intellectual activities, or that Socrates thought that they were. If *aretē* was a craft, then Socrates must have known that, like any craft, it could be learned only through an early beginning and after long training. Such training does not only impart knowledge; it also trains one's habits and dispositions. *Aretē*, moreover, could be a superordinate craft. It could involve not only knowledge of how to produce specific, independently given ends but also knowledge of which ends are good, which ends, that is, ought to be produced. If this is so, then the mere analogy between *aretē* and the crafts is not sufficient to convict Socrates of blind intellectualism.[60]

Socrates, we must now insist, did not make it his practice to engage in discussion indiscriminately. Plato is careful to show how he questioned only those who claimed to have knowledge of *aretē* and that he took pains to examine the moral qualities of the younger men he proposed to spend time with (*Charmides* 154e1). His *daimonion,* we are told, often prevented him from associating with particular individuals (*Theages* 129e ff.; cf. *Theaetetus* 151c).[61]

What cannot be denied is that, with the possible but unclear exception of the hedonism for which he may have argued in the *Protagoras,*[62] Socrates did not offer a program of positive moral education. But that he should have provided such a program is a view that presupposes that Socrates was in fact a moral educator. This presupposition, crudely made by Aristophanes, eventually becomes the assumption that Socrates was concerned to offer a general theory of virtue and happiness as well as a method for acquiring them. This assumption, in turn, is that he was, and that he should have been, a philosopher in the mode of Plato when he wrote the *Republic* or of Aristotle when he wrote his various *Ethics*. The view, however, that it is essential for philosophers to offer general instructions for how to live the good life is deeply debatable. I want to resist it. In his early dialogues Plato makes Socrates explicitly insist, again and again, that he has no such instructions to offer and that he lacks the knowledge of what virtue is. I think that we should take his disavowals of knowledge very seriously indeed. And since Socrates is also made to insist that it is necessary to know what virtue is in order to teach people how to live well, I think that we must take his disavowal of the role of teacher or moral educator seriously as well (*Ap.* 19d8–e2, 23a 3–5; *La.* 200e1–201a1). If anything, Socrates often declares that he wants to become the pupil of whoever it might be who might have the knowledge in question (*Eu.* 5a3–67; *La.* 201a1–b5).

But is not Socrates' disavowal of knowledge and of his role as a teacher ironical? No, it is not, as Gregory Vlastos has conclusively shown.[63] Vlastos, however, believes that this creates a paradox, since he is convinced that Socrates claims, with equal seriousness, to possess the knowledge in question. Yet the vast majority of the passages in which Socrates unambiguously claims to have knowledge come from the *Gorgias* and *Republic* I, which mark the early stages of Plato's middle period. The early dialogues are much more equivocal on this issue. Vlastos himself writes that "the only place in Plato's earliest dialogues where Socrates avows flatly, without resort to indirection of any sort, that he knows a moral truth" is *Apology* 29b6–7, which he translates as follows: "but that to do injustice and disobey my superior, god or man, this I know to be evil and base."[64]

We have already discussed this passage, and the possibility of translating ἀπειθεῖν as "not being convinced by" may now suggest that this is not after all such a substantive moral principle. How deeply inconsistent is Socrates when he claims, on the one hand, that he is "wise in nothing great or small" (*Ap.* 21b4–5) and that he "knows nothing noble and good" (*Ap.* 21d4) and, on the other, that he knows that injustice (whatever it turns out to be) is wrong? Surely the idea that injustice is wrong is quite conventional and noncontroversial; it is Callicles who produces a novel and debatable view when he argues that it is not. Socrates' view is simply that, as he also argues in the *Crito* (47d7–48a11), if you are convinced by argument that a course of action is unjust, you must not pursue it.

To think that Socrates' view that you should not do what you take to be injust is inconsistent with his claim to lack moral knowledge depends, I think, on a crucial presupposition. This is the idea that Socrates believes that you cannot recognize any action as unjust without knowing what justice is. Since, then, he clearly does not know this latter, he also, it would seem, cannot know the former. But the first part of this essay has been aimed at showing that Socrates does not believe that knowledge of virtue is necessary for knowledge that some particular action is virtuous, or for knowing that justice is a virtue, and injustice wrong. What Socrates would consider as knowledge of something "noble and good" is knowledge of the definition of justice, which would provide a standard for evaluating every action. This is knowledge that, indeed, he lacks. But this lack does not involve him in paradox.

Socrates, then, disavows the role of moral teacher in all seriousness, and we must believe him when he says so. He spent a large part of his life looking for such a teacher, in the hope (perhaps ironic) that if he found one then he, too, would *ipso facto* become virtuous and happy. He failed not only in finding such a teacher but also, at least as he is depicted in Plato's early dialogues, in being one himself. This, of course, was not a problem for him directly, since he would have been the first to acknowledge that the problems he raised for those who professed to teach what *aretē* is were problems for him as well: his sons never achieved excellence, he is not shown to have had a single distinguished disciple, and he never made up his own mind unconditionally about whether *aretē* could or could not be taught.[65] In the *Gorgias,* as we have remarked already, Socrates claims that Pericles failed to make the Athenians good since they eventually prosecuted him and almost sentenced him to death (*G.* 515e10–516a3). But does this argument not apply even more directly to Socrates himself, who, "toward the end of his life" (*G.* 516a1 with *Ap.* 38c5–7), was not nearly but actually and horribly executed by his own countrymen?

Was Socrates then a complete failure?[66] Failed as a teacher, since he is not shown to have made anyone else good, and failed as a student, since he never discovered what the virtues are, we might say that he should attract our attention only for some specific innovations in moral thought that he may have introduced or for the uniqueness of his character.[67] But in saying this, and in making his character the object of our concern, we have given ourselves a whole new dimension against which to measure his moral and philosophical stature.

In Plato's early dialogues, Socrates finds no teachers and no students worthy of him. The key words here are "worthy of him." For despite his failure, Plato's Socrates is still depicted as the best of men:

> No man ever breathed greater assurance that his feet were planted firmly on the path of right. He never voices a doubt of the moral rightness of any of his acts or decision, never betrays a sense of sin. He goes to his death confident that "no evil thing can happen to a good man" (*Ap.* 41d)—that "good man" is himself.[68]

Vlastos's description of Socrates' sense of himself is just right. Now this is the sense of himself Socrates is depicted to have in the Platonic dialogues, and it is reflected and encapsulated in the closing words of the *Phaedo:* He was the best, the wisest, and the most just man of his generation (*Phd.* 118a16–17). This description, therefore, necessarily gets Plato's view of Socrates and of Socrates' sense of himself just right as well. And here, I think, we may find the beginnings of a solution to our problem.

Being convinced that virtue was either identical with or very closely related to knowledge, Socrates spent a great part of his life trying to acquire that knowledge. Though he seemed to have failed in his quest, he still lived the life of someone who appeared to possess the virtues and who also, therefore, must in some way or another (if his view was at all correct) have possessed the knowledge in question.

More importantly, this shows that Socrates was after all recognized as a virtuous man and, despite his own disclaimers, as having come the closest to being the very moral expert for whom he had always been looking in others. That is, Socrates did in the end have a student who recognized him as virtuous. If the argument of this essay is at all correct, this recognition depended on the student becoming convinced of at least many of his teacher's views. And if the recognition of a virtuous agent is, as I have argued, a mutual affair, that student must have claimed to be at least as expert in matters of morality as his own teacher. This student is, of course, just the one whom we never see depicted in the dialogues and who constantly describes the failure of others to see Socrates for what he was, or for what he at least took him to be. His absence as a character in the dialogues allows him never to have to make his claim to expertise explicit, but his presence as their author compels him to issue it whenever they are read.

What Plato saw in Socrates has by now become for most of us Socrates himself. But what did he see? He saw a man who placed the pursuit of a knowledge or wisdom he thought he lacked at the very center of his life and who, in pursuing that wisdom, succeeded in living a virtuous life and, to that extent, in exhibiting the very knowledge he claimed not to have.

Socrates offered to teach no one, since he believed he had nothing to teach. He did not even claim to provide an example for others, as Xenophon at least occasionally realized. For in the passage that serves as epigraph to this essay, Xenophon writes only that Socrates' mode of life made others hope that if they lived as he did they would become like him, not that he ever set himself up as their model (but contrast *Memorabilia* I.ii.8, 18, 48). In one of the most famous passages of the *Nicomachean Ethics* (II.2.1103b26–29), Aristotle claims that the goal of moral inquiry is not simply knowledge, but possession, of *aretē*. Yet it was just the pursuit of knowledge that led Socrates to do, habitually, the right thing. The charge of intellectualism is defused when we take Socrates at his word and do not consider him as someone who offered a method for becoming good.

Nevertheless, Socrates was virtuous, and yet he had no explanation of that fact. And neither did Plato until he began to consider that the elenchus could be taken positively as well as negatively, that it could be a method for acquiring knowledge as well as a means for removing ignorance.[69] What he had to explain was how one could learn from Socrates even if Socrates had nothing to teach. And he connected this with the view that the knowledge Socrates was looking for is already within us, capable of being recollected perhaps by all (as he may have thought at *Meno*

85c10–12) or perhaps only by some (as he came to think in the *Republic*).[70] Plato, who *was* a moral educator if anyone ever was, took it as his task to make sure that Socrates' influence on him, or what he took that influence to be, would no longer be a matter of chance and accident. He also wanted to make sure that moral *aretē* would never again result in the disgraceful treatment Socrates received from his compatriots. On the contrary, he tried to describe a state in which moral *aretē* would necessarily bring along the public honor and recognition more traditional conceptions of *aretē* had always involved. Knowledge, virtue, and reputation were no longer to diverge from one another. To that end, Plato began to articulate the structure of the knowledge necessary for virtue so that it could be acquired systematically. He turned his attention to the project of identifying, as early as possible, those who were capable of acquiring that knowledge and, with it, *aretē* and genuine *eudaimonia* as well.

It is true that Plato's project, like Aristotle's, involves paying much greater attention to character than Socrates ever did. But Plato had to do so, because his views were addressed directly to all. Even when Socrates admits that he had a mission in Athens, his essentially individualist bent is unmistakable: the greatest benefit he has conferred on his city, he says, has been his effort to convince everyone that one must "cultivate oneself" (ἑαυτοῦ ἐπιμελεῖσθαι) before anything else (*Ap.* 38c3–7). Perhaps such "cultivation" consists only in intellectual activity, but, in his case at least, such intellectual activity led to *aretē*. Plato, by contrast, wants to improve everyone's lot directly, and he assigns every citizen a clear position in his new system. He wants to teach everyone, and he needs docile or at least willing and cooperative students. He gives rules for saving everybody's soul.[71] But behind these rules there lurks the solitary pursuer of knowledge for its own sake, or, what may come to the same thing, for *his* own sake, who may not have worried about character because he already had the right habits and desires. It is in fact remarkable to what extent the life of Socrates, combining the search for knowledge with moral virtue, remains the ideal to which both Plato's and Aristotle's philosophies, not to mention many later, moral philosophies, aspire. Socrates may have never learned nor taught how to save another's soul. Is this a criticism? Or might it be the key to understanding how he may just possibly have saved his own?[72]

NOTES

1. George Grote, *Plato and the Other Companions of Sokrates* (London, 1875), vol. I, 399.

2. A recent discussion of the complexities of the relationship between virtue and happiness in Socrates' thought, rejecting the view that the two are identical but

also correctly insisting that virtue is not simply instrumental to happiness, can be found in Gregory Vlastos, "Happiness and Virtue in Socrates' Moral Theory," *Proceedings of the Cambridge Philological Society* 210 (N.S. 30, 1984), 181–213.

3. George Bernard Shaw, Preface to *Saint Joan* (Harmondsworth, 1957), 8.

4. The word is taken over from Nietzsche's *Birth of Tragedy*, sec. 15, and used, in a different context, by Gregory Vlastos, "The Paradox of Socrates," in his *Socrates: A Collection of Critical Essays* (Garden City, N.Y., 1971), 17; hereafter referred to as PS.

5. The principle of the priority of definition also seems accepted in the late *Theaetetus* (146c ff.). Plato's reversion to the Socratic form in this work is significant; cf. the essay "*Epistēmē* and *Logos* in Plato's Later Thought" in this book.

6. Ludwig Wittgenstein, *The Blue and Brown Books* (New York, 1964), 20; cf. John McDowell, *Plato: "Theaetetus"* (Oxford, 1973), 115.

7. P. T. Geach, "Plato's *Euthyphro*: An Analysis and Commentary," *The Monist* 50 (1966): 369–82. The quotation comes from page 371. Geach's view has been anticipated by W. D. Ross, *Plato's Theory of Ideas* (Oxford, 1951), 16, as well as by Richard Robinson, *Plato's Earlier Dialectic*, 2d ed. (Oxford, 1953), 51–53.

8. I have given a detailed argument for this view in the essay "Confusing Universals and Particulars in Plato's Early Dialogues." A slightly different defense of Socrates had been offered by Gerasimos Santas, "The Socratic Fallacy," *Journal of the History of Philosophy* 10 (1972): 127–41 (Santas later modified his view; I discuss it below). M. F. Burnyeat argued that Santas's view of Socrates' reliance on examples as data from which definitions could be reached is wrong on the grounds that Socrates considers examples to be as disputable as definitions. Socrates, Burnyeat writes, wants to know what piety is "in order to be able to tell what is an instance of the concept and what is not," in "Examples in Epistemology: Socrates, Theaetetus and G. E. Moore," *Philosophy* 52 (1977): 381–98, 386. But the statement to which Burnyeat refers to support his view, *Euthyphro* 6e5–6, need not be read as claiming that a definition is necessary in order to tell whether *anything* is or is not pious. More weakly, and more plausibly, it can be taken to assert that if we have the definition we shall be able to tell in every case whether we do or do not have an instance of piety. Burnyeat's own view, though not central to his concern in this article and though more dialectical than theirs, is related to those of Irwin, of Woodruff, and of Santas's later *Socrates*, which I discuss below.

9. Terence Irwin, *Plato's Moral Theory: The Early and Middle Dialogues* (Oxford, 1977), 133, referred to as *PMT* below. These two versions of the thesis of the priority of definition are not always clearly distinguished. I tried to do so in a note that appeared in the *Proceedings of the Second International Symposium of Philosophy*, held in Athens in 1984. The distinction is now drawn by Gregory Vlastos in "Socrates' Disavowal of Knowledge" (hereafter referred to as SDK), *Philosophical Quarterly* (1985): 1–31; cf. 26 and n. 65.

10. I have stressed the importance of the qualification "altogether" (τὸ παράπαν) in this passage, as well as in the closely connected text of 71a6–7, 63, 80b4, d4–5 in "Meno's Paradox and Socrates as a Teacher."

11. R. S. Bluck, *Plato's Meno* (Cambridge, 1961), 213.

12. Bluck, *Plato's Meno*, 214.

13. For example, by M. F. Burnyeat, "The Simple and the Complex in the *Theaetetus*," unpublished manuscript, 1970, and Gail J. Fine, "Knowledge and *Logos* in the *Theaetetus*," *Philosophical Review* 88 (1979): 366–97.

14. Consider also the following point. If Socrates' example is supposed to illustrate a technical philosophical position concerning the necessity of direct acquaintance with intelligible objects, as Bluck maintains, it becomes difficult to explain why Meno is so willing to accept it (cf. οὐκ ἔμοιγε, 71b9). Even if Meno accepts the example itself as an accurate account of everyday situations (which, as we have just shown, it is not), he should still need much better reason in order to agree that it applies to the case of the controversial abstract objects that Socrates is allegedly introducing along with his controversial epistemology. Meno is not generally easy to convince, and he is one of Socrates' less malleable interlocutors. He is often unwilling to accept Socrates' philosophical views without argument (cf. *M.* 73a4–5, on the unity of virtue). His easy and casually offered assent in the present instance should make us pause before we agree that Socrates is making such a controversial point—especially if, as Bluck believes, this is the first time the idea is broached in Plato's dialogues.

15. Gerasimos Xenophon Santas, *Socrates: Philosophy in Plato's Early Dialogues* (London, 1979), 311 n. 26.

16. The distinction between knowledge and true belief can also be found at *Gorgias* (*G.*) 454d. The *Gorgias* seems to be contemporary with the *Meno:* it plays for Socrates' moral philosophy the role the *Meno* plays for his methodology. Both dialogues signal Plato's departure from, or perhaps generalization of, Socrates' approach to inquiry. The methodological orientation of the *Meno* naturally gives the distinction between knowledge and true belief a more prominent role.

17. As Irwin (*PMT,* 294 n. 4) remarks, even if the distinction is not explicitly drawn in Plato's early dialogues, Socrates may still be consistently observing it in practice.

18. Also accepted by Paul Woodruff, *Plato: "Hippias Major"* (Indianapolis, 1982), 140–41.

19. Irwin, *PMT,* 40; cf. 294 n. 4.

20. Cf. notes 4 and 72.

21. Anna Greco and Steven Strange helped me to see the import of Socrates' example in this way.

22. If virtue is (essentially) knowledge and knowledge is (essentially) teachable (*M.* 86c5–6, *Prt.* 361b1–3; cf. *EN* VI.3.1139b25–26), then its teachability is straightforwardly one of its essential features. But we could relax the connection between virtue and knowledge and still maintain that the latter is essential to the former. Such a view, harking back to, but also differing from, that of Aristotle has been accepted, in general terms, by Thomas Nagel, *The View from Nowhere* (New York, 1986), 48.

23. This, of course, is the import of my argument concerning the example of Meno. In addition, Plato often offers views that seem to be perfectly general but which, the context shows, he understands in restrictive ways. This is particularly true of his specifications of the domain of the Forms, which I discuss in "Predication and Forms of Opposites in the *Phaedo*," *Review of Metaphysics* 26 (1973): 461–91.

24. Cited as such evidence by Irwin, *PMT,* 40, 294 n. 4.

25. Cited by Irwin, *PMT,* 294 n. 4; by Richard Kraut, *Socrates and the State* (Princeton, 1984), 303 n. 82 (hereafter referred to as *SS*); and by C.C.W. Taylor, *Plato: "Protagoras"* (Oxford, 1976), 212: "The thesis that it is impossible to any subject x and predicate F, to answer the question 'Is x F?' until one can answer the question 'What is x?' is familiar Socratic doctrine." The generality of this passage is correctly denied by Vlastos, SDK, 26 n. 65, who, however, believes (as does Kraut, *SS,* 278–79) that *M.* 71b, like *Rep.* 354b–c, is unrestricted. We have already discussed the passage of the *Meno* above, and we will soon examine that of the *Republic.*

26. Cited by Irwin, *PMT,* 294 n. 4, and by Woodruff, *Plato: "Hippias Major,"* 140.

27. Some relevant remarks, though they are inspired by different passages and lead in a different direction, can be found in Santas, *Socrates,* 123–24.

28. This is also Santas's view of the first of these two passages (Santas, *Socrates,* 119).

29. This is Woodruff's view (*Plato: "Hippias Major,"* 140), as well as Irwin's (*PMT,* 294 n. 4). For another objection to their effort to defend Socrates by attributing to him a distinction between knowledge and true belief, cf. Vlastos, SDK, 22–26. Vlastos himself believes that the *Hippias Major* is a postelenctic dialogue, and that it commits Plato (though not Socrates) to the unrestricted principle he also accepts at *Meno* 71b3–4. For the reasons given above, I do not agree that Plato accepts this unrestricted principle in the *Meno.* I do agree with Vlastos's general resolution of the issue of "the Socratic fallacy"; he claims that it simply is not committed in the early Socratic dialogues. But I am not convinced by the distinction between "philosophical" or "certain" and "elenctic" knowledge, which Vlastos wants to attribute to Socrates. I also think that Vlastos's discussion of the *Hippias* passage is subject to an independent problem. Vlastos attributes to Socrates the view that a life lived in ignorance of the definition of virtue is not worth living. But this view is much too strong, even for the author of the *Republic* (with whom, for Vlastos, the author of the *Hippias Major* is more nearly contemporary). Most people, according to Plato, are ignorant of the definition of the virtues, yet the life they lead in the *Republic* is not only preferable to death, but as good a life as a human being can live—and Plato gives no indication that this is not, in more absolute terms, a good life.

30. *Contra* Irwin, *PMT,* 294 n. 4, who writes that this passage "suggests that we cannot be friends unless we know how one person becomes friend to another." The point, I would argue, is similar to that made at the opening of the *Meno.* Similarly, Irwin's view that *Lysis* 223b4–8 (discussed presently) "suggests that we cannot be friends unless . . . we know what a friend is" does not have to be accepted.

31. For a late date for *Republic* I, see Irwin, *PMT,* 178–79, 183–84, 292 n. 3. He still cites it as evidence for the view that "I must know what x is to know anything about x" (294 n. 4). Vlastos, who prefers an early date for *Republic* I, claims that the closing passage of the book has been "tacked on" to the main text (Vlastos, SDK, 26 n. 65) because it contains the claim that Socrates does not know

whether justice is a virtue. But this claim, he argues, contradicts the conclusion, previously agreed upon (*Rep.* 351a5–6), that injustice is ignorance, hence its corollary that justice is knowledge and therefore that it is a virtue (350b5). But Socrates has engaged in a number of dialectical moves that Thrasymachus has conceded only with great reluctance (cf. *Rep.* 350c–d). There would therefore be, in my opinion, nothing wrong with Socrates being willing to reopen the whole question from the very beginning. This, of course, is exactly what the *Republic* proceeds to do. The "contradiction" signifies not that the end of Book I has been added to a text with which Plato remains in agreement but that Plato is not satisfied with the arguments he has given so far. Later dates for the *Hippias Major* and the *Lysis* have also been proposed by Vlastos, "The Socratic Elenchus," *Oxford Studies in Ancient Philosophy* 1(1983): 25–88, esp. 57–58.

32. Though, as we have seen (n. 22 above), knowledge and teachings are closely connected both for Plato and for Aristotle, the *Dissoi Logoi* (VI.1) could raise the question whether wisdom (σοφίη) as well as *aretē* is teachable.

33. Richard Kraut has objected that this account makes knowledge depend on what is and is not actually disputed. I know a proposition, he claims, "if everyone agrees with me. But if someone disagrees, that makes my claim controversial, and I no longer know it." I respond that Socrates is primarily concerned with features of virtue that have been in fact traditionally disputed. He gives no indication that he is willing to take seriously any doubt raised by anyone on any grounds. If someone, like Thrasymachus, wants to dispute a feature that has not in fact been in dispute, then the burden of making the claim at least *prima facie* plausible is his. If the case is strong, and if the disputed feature turns out to depend on the essence of virtue, then it may in fact follow that to answer the challenge we must offer an account of what virtue is.

34. None of the transitions alluded to in the texts above is supported by argument, which strongly suggests that they all have intuitive appeal. A similar move is made at *G.* 468d–569b; cf. Vlastos, "Happiness and Virtue in Socrates' Moral Theory," 203 n. 14.

35. Contrast Kraut, *SS,* 247 n. 7.

36. I have provided some evidence for this account, which, with suitable substitutions for "peers," applies to animals and even to inanimate objects (*Iliad* XXIII.267, 374; *Thucydides* I.2.4: *Herodotus* III.106.2) in this book's essay "Meno's Paradox and Socrates as a Teacher." Amélie Rorty points out that reputation in this context depends on having lived a good life, and that it is the capacity for this latter that is of essence to *aretē* (Amélie O. Rorty, "The Limits to Socratic Intellectualism: Did Socrates Teach Aretē?" *Proceedings of the Boston Area Colloquium in Ancient Philosophy,* vol. II, ed. John J. Cleary [Lanham, MD., 1987], 317–30). I think that the notion of success does bring in the idea of the good life, without the more strictly moral connotations introduced by the term "good." The question "Does success ensure happiness?" is as plausible in English as the parallel question about *aretē* and *eudaimonia* was in Greek.

37. I am inclined to take Socrates' profession of ignorance with regard to the "What is x?" question quite seriously, at least when the subject in question is *aretē* (*Eu.* 5a3–c5, 6d9–36, 11b11–5, d2–e5, 14b8–c5, 15c11–a4; *Chrm.* 165b5–c1,

166c77–d6, 175c2–176b4; *La.* 185c4–186c5, 199e11–12, 200e2–201b5; *Prt.* 361c3–6; *Hi. Ma.* 286c3–e4, 304d4–e3; *Ly.* 212a4–7, 223b4–8; *M.* 71a5–7, 80c8–d1, 100b4–6; *G.* 506a3–5, 509a4–6; *Rep.* I, 337d3–4, 354c1–3; cf. Aristotle, *Soph.El.* 186b6–8). Many of these passages, some of which we have already discussed, are cited by Kraut, *SS*, 247 n. 7. The moral Kraut draws from them, however, is that "Socrates cannot answer his 'What is x?' question even when x is not a virtue." I don't think I accept this. First, because of the general reasons offered in the first part of this essay. Second, because the implication in these passages that more than virtue is at issue is not at all easy to find. Third, because Socrates sometimes suggests that he does in fact have answers for his "What is x?" question when *aretē* is not the subject: *La.* 192a1–b4, *Eu.* 765–d5, *M.* 72a6–c5, 75b8–76a7. It is, of course, a further question whether the definitions given or implied in these passages are ultimately acceptable; cf. Irwin, *PMT,* 44–46.

For reasons stated earlier, I do not accept Irwin's view that Socrates lacks knowledge, but possesses true beliefs about the virtues. In any case, I don't think Irwin and I would disagree on the particular case of the answer to the "What is x?" question: we would agree that Socrates lacks it. For if he possessed it, then on Irwin's view, Socrates' true beliefs about *aretē* would thereby become knowledge—which, as Irwin correctly insists, Socrates lacks.

Gregory Vlastos's position, in SDK, is more difficult to come to terms with. His distinction between deductive, philosophical, or certain knowledge and knowledge arrived at through the elenchus, and always subject to revision, accounts for more of Plato's texts than Irwin's. For Socrates, as Vlastos points out, claims to have knowledge more often than we suppose. On the other hand, Vlastos's distinction (already prefigured, though not developed in *PS,* 9–12) is not easy to accept. Vlastos's claim that Socrates contrasts elenctic knowledge with a higher sort of philosophical knowledge is problematic: we need more evidence than we are given in order to agree that such a stronger conception of knowledge already existed and could provide a sensible term for the contrast. Vlastos interestingly appeals to Parmenides' presentation of his position through "hierophantic trappings," which suggest to him a commitment to certainty (17). Still, in *DK* B7, Parmenides characterizes his view, and asks that it be rationally evaluated, as a *poludēris elenchos;* the occurrence of this term raises serious questions about the status of Parmenides' argument and, in fact, about the sense of the word itself. Another factor that needs to be carefully considered is whether, as Vlastos assumes, different methods for reaching knowledge (the tentative elenchus as opposed to a more systematic deductive approach, assuming the concept had application before Plato) necessarily produce different kinds of knowledge.

38. The argument of the *Meno* is particularly ironical. Recall that in answering Meno's opening question regarding the acquisition of *aretē,* Socrates replies that, in possible contrast to Thessaly, Athens is suffering from an apparent drought of wisdom. *Any* Athenian to whom Meno might put his question, Socrates continues, would reply that he is ignorant not only of whether or not virtue can be taught but also of its very nature (*M.* 71a1–7). Yet when Anytus, who is of course one of the Athenians on behalf of whom Socrates had earlier spoken, enters the discussion he confidently asserts that any good (καλὸς κἀγαθός) citizen would know how to

make Meno, or anyone else, a better person. This, of course, would qualify any Athenian as a teacher of *aretē* and therefore as knowing what its nature is (*M.* 92e3–6). Socrates is the only one, it seems, who lacks the knowledge in question.

39. Useful remarks on Plato's attitude toward the sophists as teachers of *aretē* can be found in C. J. Rowe, "Plato on the Sophists as Teachers of Virtue," *History of Political Thought* 4 (1983): 409–27. My only reservation about this interesting article is that it tends to assimilate too quickly the attitude toward the sophists expressed in Plato's early works with the much more complicated, metaphysically loaded account offered in the late *Sophist*.

40. According to Xenophon, *Memorabilia* I.i.13 f., Socrates was also suspicious of natural philosophers because they were in such violent disagreement with one another about the most fundamental issues that concerned them.

41. Cf. the essay "Meno's Paradox and Socrates as a Teacher."

42. Alison Burford, *Craftsmen in Greek and Roman Society* (Ithaca, 1972), 82.

43. Burford, *Craftsmen in Greek and Roman Society,* 89. Burford also writes: "Craftsmen . . . had to undergo long and thorough training. Constant application was required of a man if he was to become fully acquainted with his craft. Once he had learnt it, he must continue to exercise his skill, otherwise it would decay and die on him" (69). Pliny, for example, writes that Apelles drew every day in order to maintain his ability in top form (*Natural History* [*NH*] 35, 84). Such statements invite both contrast and comparison with Aristotle's view that *aretē* is almost impossible to lose since it is by nature such as to be constantly manifested in action (*EN* III.5.1114b30–1115a4; IV.10.1152a28–33). One could well ask whether Apelles had to force himself to draw or whether, like the virtuous agent who finds pleasure in right action, he preferred it to other activities. Cf. also Maurice Pope, *The Ancient Greeks: How They Lived and Worked* (Newton, Mass., 1976), 73.

44. *On Ancient Medicine* I.13–19, and cf. the commentary of A. J. Festugiere, in *Hippocrate: L'Ancienne médecine* (Paris, 1948; repr. 1979). On the dispute between Zeuxis and Parrhasius, cf. Pliny, *NH* 35, 61; on the competition between Apelles and Protogenes, *NH* 35, 79; a related story occurs in *NH* 36, 61. Richard Kraut has objected that I hold the implausible view that "no craft need be rationally explainable to any outsider." The fact is that I do not hold that view. Of course crafts can be taught and learned. But this, as I argue, requires time, training, and habituation. All I argue is that a craft cannot be learned simply by intellectual methods. In addition, I do not want to deny that particular actions within a craft can be explained to outsiders. Pheidias could well explain why a specific part of the statue of Pallas Athena needed to be made of ivory (though not, perhaps, why he had requested as much as he had). This would not be very different from what, for example, Socrates himself does in the *Crito* when he argues, to his satisfaction, that he should not attempt to escape from prison.

45. I take this to be a legitimate extension of the requirement on the elenchus that Gregory Vlastos has termed the "say what you believe" condition; cf. his "The Socratic Elenchus," 35.

46. Cf. S. Marc Cohen, "Socrates on the Definition of Piety: *Euthyphro 10A–11B*," in Vlastos, *Socrates,* 158–75, esp. 175: "If a moral concept M is such that there is an authority whose judgement whether or not something falls under M is

decisive and is rationally grounded, then 'M' cannot be defined in terms of that authority's judgement." Cohen's view is stronger than what we need to believe in order to disagree with Kraut. Even if a virtue is not to be defined as what a moral expert commands, our recognition of someone as an expert depends on his being able to *persuade* us that his judgment is rational. On Socrates' antivoluntarism, cf. Santas, *Socrates,* 56. A discussion of voluntarism and objectivism, tracing the debate back to the *Euthyphro,* can be found in William Mann, "Modality, Morality, and God," unpublished manuscript, 1986.

47. For his own reasons, to which we shall allude below, Socrates never stops pretending to believe that Euthyphro knows what piety is; cf. *Eu.* 15d5–e2.

48. Kraut (*SS,* 233) also appeals to *Laches* 184e8–9 as evidence for his views. But Socrates' example of an expert here is a teacher of gymnastics, whom there may be good reason to obey even if the motivation for his commands is not obvious. In any case, this linguistic point I am about to make, if acceptable, provides further evidence against him.

49. Cf. Richard Kraut, "Plato's *Apology* and *Crito:* Two Recent Studies." *Ethics* 91 (1981): 651–64, esp. 659.

50. Cf. LSJ, s.v. ἀπειθέω; s.v. πείθω, I.2.

51. Cf. Kraut, "Plato's *Apology* and *Crito,*" 658–59, where he is disputing the translation of the verb as "be persuaded by" by A. D. Woozley, *Law and Obedience: The Argument of Plato's Crito* (London, 1979), 44–46.

52. Cf. LSJ, s.v. ἀπιστεύω, I.2.

53. This last is the important point. Even if we insist on translating ἀπειθεῖν as "to disobey," Socrates is not making a substantive point. Once you have recognized that someone is better than you are, you have become convinced by that person's views. And, on Socratic grounds, it is impossible to fail to act on those views.

Notice also the statement at *Apology* 28d6–29a1, where Socrates speaks of obeying his commanders, human and divine. What he says is that you must pursue any course of action that you chose "having considered it the best" or which was ordered by your commander. The first alternative clearly introduces the idea of judging the rightness of an action for oneself. The latter, I think, depends on Socrates' obeying his commanders in a particular case having already agreed, on rational grounds, to obey them in general, as Richard Kraut himself demonstrates in *Socrates and the State.*

54. Kraut, *SS,* 279–85, shows the complexity of the knowledge involved in knowing the definition of the virtues.

55. Cf., for example, *Eu.* 15e3–4, *Chrm.* 176a6 ff., *La.* 210b6–c5, *Ly.* 223a1–b3, *Prt.* 361e5–6.

56. This, though I am not sure, may be the point of *Apology* 26a1–4. Socrates here claims that if Meletus thought that Socrates was harming the young involuntarily, he should "have taken him aside, taught, and put sense in him"; for, he continues, "it is clear that once I have learned (what is good), I shall stop doing what I have only been doing involuntarily."

57. Cf. Irwin, *PMT,* 90. I am not sure that *Lysis* 212a1–7, 223b4–8, which Irwin cites in this connection, actually support this view, as our earlier discussion may indicate. *Laches* 193d11–e6 is, in my opinion, a more likely candidate.

58. In general terms, among others, by M. F. Burnyeat, "Aristotle on Learning to be Good," in Amélie Rorty, ed., *Essays on Aristotle's Ethics* (Berkeley, 1980), 69–92. More specifically, by Martha C. Nussbaum, "Aristophanes and Socrates on Learning Practical Wisdom," *Yale Classical Studies* 26 (1980): 43–97.

59. Cf. Nussbaum, "Aristophanes and Socrates," 79–88. Kraut, *SS,* 218–28, gives some persuasive arguments that Socrates was much less opposed to traditional moral education than is often supposed.

60. Cf. the discussion of M. J. O'Brien, *The Socratic Paradoxes and the Greek Mind* (Chapel Hill, 1967), ch. 2.

61. This was also, of course, Xenophon's view of Socrates: *Mem.* I.ii.2, vi.5 ff.; vi.13f.; *Ap.* 16. W.K.C. Guthrie, *A History of Greek Philosophy,* vol. III.1 (Cambridge, 1971), 39, writes that this is only Xenophon's, and not Plato's view; but contrast vol. III.2, 83. A careful examination of the evidence and an account of those passages in both Plato and Xenophon which suggest that Socrates was open to all is offered by David L. Blank, "Socratics versus Sophists on Payment for Teaching," *California Studies in Classical Philology* (1985): 1–49, which also includes all the relevant testimonia. Blank argues that Socrates was not open to all. His own view, that Socrates chose his associates on the basis of an erotic attraction, though suggestive, is not developed in detail.

62. This has become an issue of serious dispute since Taylor, *Plato: "Protagoras,"* 166–70; Irwin, *PMT,* ch. 4; and J.C.B. Gosling and C.C.W. Taylor, *The Greeks on Pleasure* (Oxford, 1982), chs. 2, 3, attributed the hedonism discussed here to Socrates himself. *Contra* Donald Zeyl, "Socrates and Hedonism—*Protagoras* 351b–348d," *Phronesis* 25 (1980): 250–69.

63. Vlastos, SDK, 2–5.

64. Vlastos, SDK, 6–7.

65. The relevant texts and some comments are given in the essay "Meno's Paradox and Socrates as a Teacher" in this book.

66. An interestingly equivocal answer to this question is offered by Vlastos, *PS,* 15–21. His view, I think, depends on taking Socrates to be a positive moral teacher.

67. Vlastos, *PS,* 18–19.

68. Vlastos, *PS,* 7.

69. Here I rely on Vlastos, "The Socratic Elenchus," and on his "Afterthoughts on the Socratic Elenchus," *Oxford Studies in Ancient Philosophy* 1(1983): 71–74. I particularly have in mind his statement that his main evidence for construing the elenchus positively comes from the *Gorgias* (Vlastos, 74 n. 8).

70. Cf. the essay "Meno's Paradox and Socrates as a Teacher" in this book; and Vlastos, "The Socratic Elenchus," 55–57.

71. I use the term "rules" in a loose sense, in light of Gisela Striker's "On the Greek Origins of the Concept of Natural Law," *Proceedings of the Boston Area Colloquium in Ancient Philosophy,* vol. II, ed. John J. Cleary (Lanham, Md., 1987), 79–94.

72. For comments on earlier versions of this paper, I am grateful to Richard Kraut, Amélie Rorty, Steven Strange, and Gregory Vlastos.

Three

WHAT DID SOCRATES TEACH AND TO WHOM DID HE TEACH IT?

I

A LARGE NUMBER OF PEOPLE, ancient and modern alike, have always found in Socrates what seemed to them a suspicious, if not actually repugnant, aspect. This aspect, to put the point first in crude terms, is his devotion to philosophy, which presupposes an apparently unshakable faith in reason, in the power of understanding to secure goodness, and in the power of goodness to provide us with happiness.

But philosophy, Plato has Callicles say in the *Gorgias,* emasculates even those who may possess great talents: it makes them avoid public life, where serious matters are decided and real reputations are established; instead, philosophers "live out their lives skulking in some corner whispering with three or four boys, never saying anything grand, great or important."[1] Seen from the outside, this is not a totally inaccurate description of the picture that Socrates' life, as Plato depicts it in his dialogues, may have presented to many of his contemporaries.

For Nietzsche, whose repugnance for Socrates was indissolubly mixed with admiration, Socrates' trust in reason was one of his most despicable features. Socrates, Nietzsche sneered early on in his writings, "is the prototype of the theoretical optimist who, with his faith that the nature of things can be fathomed, ascribes to knowledge and insight the power of a panacea, while understanding error as the evil par excellence."[2] The sneer only becomes more pronounced in the later works:

> One chooses dialectic only when one has no other means. One knows that one arouses mistrust with it, that it is not very persuasive. Nothing is easier to erase than a dialectical effect: the experience of every meeting at which there are speeches proves this. It can only be *self-defense* for those who no longer have other weapons.[3]

Nietzsche's remark about dialectic's inability to convince is worth thinking about further, and we shall return to it. For the moment, I am concerned to specify exactly what in Socrates has provoked such criticism, both traditional and contemporary.[4] As a first approximation, we may say that this is the element in his philosophy and in his personality that has come to be known as his intellectualism.

Intellectualism involves a number of features. First, it seems to identify virtue with knowledge and therefore appears to consider the affective side of our nature irrelevant to our virtue, to what counts as a good human life. Just for this reason, intellectualists pay no heed to the necessity of social-ization and habituation, to the importance of the careful, long-term atten-tion to our noncognitive side that, it seems plausible to claim, is at least as necessary for becoming good as is the knowledge of the nature of goodness.[5]

Second, intellectualism as we find it in Socrates seems to be a view that considers virtue not only necessary but also sufficient for the good life and for happiness: being good, in some way, is the essence of being happy—nothing else matters. To quote one criticism of Socrates on this issue, it may seem that, unconcerned with anything but virtue, especially with the things that luck or chance might give us or take away without any respon-sibility on our part, Socrates "can't lose" in the game of life,

> because he does not care so deeply for the things that are subject to risk that their loss would be a serious loss to him. *There* is his strangeness, awe-inspiring and alarming. And it leaves the question: Is this a good way for a human being to live?[6]

The third feature of intellectualism is the following. Since Socrates be-lieved that only knowledge and argument,[7] not the whole nature of one's personality, can lead us to virtue, and since reason seems to be the most universal human capacity, he made it his business to address his questions to everyone indiscriminately. Not caring whether those he engaged in dis-cussion, particularly the young among them, had the character appropriate for philosophy, he encouraged the wrong people—like Critias, Charmides, and Alcibiades—to engage in philosophy to the detriment both of the youths and of philosophy. Gregory Vlastos, who does not find fault with Socrates on this issue, promotes this conception of Socrates' indiscrimi-nate approach to his audience when he describes him as a "street-philosopher," a "missionary to the unwashed":[8] "not only does he allow question-breeding argument about good and evil to all and sundry, he positively thrusts it upon them."[9]

Socrates, then, wrongly equates knowledge with virtue, inhumanly identifies virtue with happiness, and imprudently encourages everyone, whatever their moral fiber, to become well versed in the sort of argument that can as easily destroy as establish moral value.[10] These are serious charges, not obviously compatible with his canonical status as moral exemplar.

It is deeply ironic that one of the earliest versions of these charges was made by none other than Plato himself.[11] The criticism appears at *Repub-lic* 539b–d. The charge is that argument (*logos*) should not be taught to very young men, who are likely to indulge in it only for the pleasure of contradicting others. Their constant refutation of other people's views, whatever they happen to be, results in their "believing nothing of what they earlier believed," thus being bereft of new ideals with which to replace their former values. It produces an agnosticism or even cynicism that may, under some circumstances, be correctly described as "corruption."[12] This gives them a bad name, and harms the very cause of philosophy. Older men, by contrast, who deal with dialectic conversation (*dialegesthai*) seriously, for the sake of finding the truth and not just for contradiction, will become themselves more measured (*metriōteroi*, 539c8, in contrast to the impetuous, puppylike young at 539b4–6), and will bring honor to philosophy. Plato finally sums up all these points concerning age and connects them with one's character:

> Indeed, all that we said before this was said for the sake of caution, that those whom one allows to partake in reasoned discourse [*hoi logoi*] should by nature be orderly and steady [*tas phuseis kosmioi kai stasimoi*] not as now when anyone engages in it, even if he is quite unfit. (539d3–6)[13]

With the exception of the charge that Socrates discoursed about natural phenomena and the gods, and with the addition of the view that philosophy, when properly practiced, does lead to the greatest goods, Plato's criticism is not so distant, after all, from the picture of Socrates that Aristophanes presented in the *Clouds* some forty to fifty years before the composition of the *Republic*.

To this charge that Socrates was a serious failure as a teacher, we can add another, more personal accusation. If virtue is knowledge, if it is necessary to know the good in order to do it, then is it not after all the case that Socrates, who consistently admits that he does not know what virtue is, also failed as an individual? How can he claim, or how can anyone else claim on his behalf, that he had led a virtuous and happy life? His shortcomings seem to keep proliferating.

II

In order to defuse the seriousness of the first set of charges against Socrates, I tried on a number of earlier occasions to construct an interpretation of his character as we find it in Plato's early works, according to which Socrates, no matter how intellectualist he is, is totally unconcerned with the moral improvement of others. I argued that Plato's Socrates believes sincerely, not at all ironically, that he had nothing of his own, no positive ethical views, to impart to the world. If Socrates was not a teacher; if he did not have, even in its most rudimentary form, the sort of program for moral education that Plato and Aristotle developed after him; if all he was concerned about was the salvation of his own and not of any other soul, then, I thought, the charge of intellectualism, as amplified in the passage from the *Republic,* would lose much of its point.[14]

I still believe that this hypothesis is true. I am, however, less confident about the truth of its antecedent, the point about Socrates' teaching and positive views. I now believe that I ran together a number of different ideas, and that separating them from one another will be a good thing both for me personally (one can always safely be that much of an intellectualist) and for the discussion of the problem generally, since the differences between these ideas are not always clearly marked when they are discussed in the secondary literature.

One point that needs to be stated clearly and distinguished from others concerns the question whether Socrates was or was not a teacher. I still believe that he was not—that he was not, that is, a teacher of *aretē;* I will argue for the claim in what follows. But I do not want to claim that Socrates was not *perceived* as a teacher—he certainly was, by Plato as well as by Xenophon (for their different reasons), and also by a number of other Athenians, both friends and enemies. I believe, however, that Socrates, at least as he is depicted in Plato's early dialogues, did not see himself as such a teacher, and that—whatever Plato's actual intentions may have been— his moral stature derives directly from his refusal to accept that role. In other words, we must not distinguish only between what Socrates took himself to be and what others thought of him, but also between the way he is represented in Plato's dialogues and whatever we believe Plato's own attitude toward his representation to have been.

What is it, then, to be a teacher of *aretē,* an ethical teacher who can show others how to live a good and successful life? One can try to do this in at least two ways. One may in fact know (or claim to know) what the good and successful life is, and one may be able (or claim to be able) to transmit that knowledge to others. Or one can set oneself up as an example, perhaps as the only example, of what it is to lead a good and successful life. I am quite sure that Socrates was not a teacher in the first sense. With the exception of some passages in Plato's *Apology,* which I will discuss a little later, I also believe we have no evidence for thinking that Plato's Socrates set his life up as a model of what the good life is, even if Plato may have seen and presented him as the best human being of his time.

In contrast to Plato's version, Xenophon definitely portrays Socrates as someone constantly involved in giving explicit advice to his companions. The trouble with this representation of Socrates, however, is that Xenophon's refrain, "So saying and doing such things himself, he made his companions more pious and prudent,"[15] consistently closes conversations that it is hard to imagine as having had *any* effect, especially one that was serious and lasting, on anyone. In any case, Xenophon's most general statement about Socrates' teaching (at *Memorabilia* I.2.3) is profoundly equivocal: at best, it attributes to him the status of moral exemplar and not that of systematic teacher.[16]

In trying to avoid portraying Socrates as any sort of teacher, I argued at one point that unless Socrates renounced *all* claims to any positive views whatever regarding virtue, he would have had to present himself as having the knowledge professed by the teachers of *aretē* with whom he did not want to be identified—precisely those people from whom Plato took such pains to distinguish him, the people we call sophists today. Accordingly, I tried to interpret what seemed to be one of his most substantive claims in a way that would make it turn out to be a very weak, almost trivial, claim indeed.[17] This is the famous passage of the *Apology:* "To do injustice and to disobey a superior, whether divine or human: that I know to be bad and shameful" (29b6–7).

My argument was that the Greek word for "disobey," *apeithein,* should be translated, as it certainly can be, as "to fail to be persuaded by"; and the Greek word for "superior," *beltiōn,* translated as "a better person." And since, because of Socrates' very intellectualism, one cannot recognize a better person independently of being persuaded of that person's moral views, I argued that all that the statement comes down to is the common-place that injustice is wrong. I now think that this was an overstatement, especially since a few lines before making the statement quoted above, Socrates refers to his military commanders at Potidaea, Amphipolis, and Delium as his superiors, though he does not use the word *beltiōn* to describe them; and there is no reason to think that he would have thought of them as better human beings than he.[18]

The word *beltiōn,* then, should be interpreted as "superior" in a broad sense. In the *Apology,* Plato has Socrates make the sensible point that in some particular cases there are people who are superior to oneself. For example, in time of war, generals are the relevant experts who know what is good and bad in military affairs, and one should perform the tasks that they assign. In other cases, we assign ourselves tasks that we consider the best in the circumstances (*hēgēsamenos beltiston einai,* 28d6). In both types of cases—including of course the most important type, the case of the god's command to Socrates to practice philosophy, which is what is really at issue here—someone, either oneself or an acknowledged expert, has set one a task. Socrates claims that he knows that it is bad and shameful to refuse to perform this task, especially if one is motivated by a fear of death (*Ap.* 28d9, 28e6) or of anything else (29e1) greater than the fear of what is shameful (*Ap.* 28d9–10; cf. *Crito* 48d3–5).

Socrates' claim is not trivial. The idea that injustice is shameful, however, is not in fact terribly controversial: Polus readily concedes it,[19] and it takes a person of views as extreme as those Callicles holds to defend it.

Moreover, though the thesis that it is wrong to consider death worse than disgrace can be debated at length, it is still a proposition that, in general, is not especially easy to reject. Accordingly, I would like to suggest that Socrates relies on substantive though not particularly controversial premises in his argument that he will not abandon philosophy.

It seems to me that we can attribute such ideas to him, because having some moral views about the world is not sufficient to qualify one as a teacher of *aretē*, as I earlier thought. What Socrates considers necessary for being able to claim that role is a very specific kind of knowledge, not simply the conviction that some moral positions, which may in fact be very important to him, have so far survived all dialectical attacks. To be a teacher, you need not only this conviction, which is compatible with the possibility of your ideas turning out to be false upon their next examination,[20] but also a certainty that the views you are claiming to teach are true. So, at least, Socrates seems to have believed: in *Gorgias* (506a) he claims for himself the role of seeker and nothing more precisely because he lacks that certainty (cf. 509a). In addition, you must be in a position to explain the truth of these ideas: if not to all and sundry, at least to those who, like apprentices to a master craftsman, gradually become habituated into a craft.[21] This is just the sort of knowledge that, all scholars agree, Socrates lacks, and, moreover, believes he lacks.

Socrates does, however, sometimes depend on more controversial ideas in his discussions. Most famous among these ideas is his claim in the *Crito* that "one should never return an injustice nor harm another human being, no matter what one suffers at their hands" (49c10–11). Still, we must ask how substantive a commitment on his part this view constitutes; and is it a proposition that he can be said to teach to others? In order to answer these questions, we must first note that Socrates introduces his principle in terms that show that he himself considers it terribly controversial and subject to irresoluble disagreement:

> For I know that this seems and will seem so to few people. Now, between those who think so and those who don't, there is no common counsel— necessarily they have nothing but contempt for one another when they observe what those of the other group decide. (*Cr.* 49d2–5)

We do not know how Socrates reaches his conclusion about returning injustice, a view "which still now seems to him as it has always seemed" (*Cr.* 49c1). There is a strong implication, however, that it is an idea the maintaining of which has never caused him to lose a dialectical bout, an elenchus (49b3–c6). Now, in view of how controversial Socrates takes the view to be, of the fallibility of the method by which he has been brought to believe it, and of his constant pressure on Crito to consider for himself whether he does or does not accept it (49d5–e2), it is difficult to believe that this is the sort of idea of which Socrates can claim (or be claimed, by Plato) to be a teacher. Though everything here is morally robust, it is dialectically light and tentative. Socrates makes it perfectly clear to Crito that he is willing to take up the argument for this position from the beginning, if that is what Crito wants. He seems to lack just the sort of confidence that would allow him to present himself as a teacher of this view to anyone else.

Ironically, today we often refer to "Socratic teaching" as a method that is tentative in that it depends essentially on questions, though we always presume that teachers—usually law professors but sometimes Socrates himself—secretly know the truth and are not at all tentative in their conviction regarding it. In fact, no mode of teaching is more dogmatic than what goes by the name of "the Socratic method" today. In this we are completely untrue to the Socrates who appears in Plato's early dialogues, for reasons I will mention later on. Socrates is light and tentative all the way down. Though he insists on following his own dialectical method, he is constantly expressing the willingness to reexamine his views and to review his arguments. He does not believe that such tentativeness is compatible with teaching.

There is a remarkable difference between the way Socrates presents his "rejection of retaliation" in the *Crito* and his attitude toward the same principle in the *Gorgias*. In the latter, we find him saying to Polus, "I and you and [all] other people think that committing injustice is worse than being treated unjustly and that avoiding punishment is worse than being punished (*G.* 474b3–5; cf. 475e2–6). Though he still presents the idea as controversial, Socrates now claims that everybody in fact already believes it: the sharp line he draws in the *Crito* between those who do and those who do not accept the rejection of retaliation is gone. It is true that in strictly logical terms his views in the two dialogues are mutually compatible. It is possible, after all, for people who share the same beliefs but are not in fact aware of this fact to have only contempt for one another on the basis of what they *think* the others believe, and not to be able to "deliberate" (*bouleuesthai*) together. But the idea that underneath our apparent disagreements there exists a fundamentally similar approach to the world, and that dialectical discussion may actually be capable of revealing it, seems to me totally absent from the *Crito*. I believe that this constitutes a very significant difference between the two dialogues.

The difference is significant because it suggests that it was only between the time when he wrote the *Crito* and the date when he composed the *Gorgias,* and not throughout his early period, as Gregory Vlastos has so forcefully argued, that Plato came to the view that everyone possesses a stock of true moral beliefs that entail the negation of any false moral belief they may also hold.[22] Furthermore, it is of course not only perfectly consistent with this idea, but evidence in its support, that only in the *Gorgias* does Plato have Socrates, for the first time, commit himself to the truth of the results of elenctic investigation (*G.* 486e5–6; cf. 478e8, 487e6–7). If everyone does indeed possess a sufficient stock of true beliefs "within," then the results of the elenchus are not simply dialectically but also epistemically secure. The very idea of our having beliefs "within," however, which is introduced without explanation in the *Gorgias,* is a later Platonic innovation and not a Socratic thesis. It receives its first explanation through the theory of recollection presented in the *Gorgias*'s companion piece, the *Meno,* which Vlastos acknowledges as a work belonging to the beginnings of Plato's Postsocratic middle period.[23]

If the results of the elenchus, which are reached on the basis of views asserted by an interlocutor, are to be true, then they must be reached on the basis of beliefs that are not only sincerely held but that are also themselves true. But how do we acquire such beliefs? The answer to this question is one of the great intellectual contributions of the *Meno,* in which, from some true mathematical beliefs of a slave, Socrates derives a further, much less obvious, view. Moreover, the theory of recollection is introduced right here precisely in order to explain how those true beliefs can be in the slave's (or in anyone else's) soul in the first place. The question the *Gorgias* raises implicitly, then, is answered explicitly in the *Meno.* The two dialogues go hand in hand. Both begin as traditional Socratic dialogues. At the point where Socratic dialogues reach an impasse, however, both these works literally explode into the presentation of extremely radical substantive theses: the *Gorgias* produces new ideas in ethics and politics; and the *Meno* inaugurates a new attitude toward dialectical method, metaphysics, and epistemology. Both works constitute Plato's first attempts to explain what underwrites Socrates' practice of the elenchus and his ethical views. Both, of course, need serious expansion and revision. This is exactly what they receive in what we now call Plato's middle dialogues, to which they provide a tight and intelligible transition.

It is important to note that despite his positive claims for the truth of the results of the elenchus in the *Gorgias* (cf. *G.* 508e6–509a3), Socrates, as Vlastos has also shown, adds an explicit disclaimer regarding his knowledge of these matters: "But as for me, my position [*logos*] is always the same: I do not know how these things are" (509a4–6). In other words, the elenchus, as practiced by Socrates, even if it reaches a conclusion that Socrates regards as true, does not constitute teaching, and Socrates can still claim that he does not have knowledge concerning the conclusion in question. Truth, as we have seen, is a necessary but not a sufficient condition for knowledge that can be taught; the ability to explain the views in question is also needed.[24] This distinction is captured by the contrast between knowledge, which is accompanied by the ability to offer an explanation, and true belief, which is not. This contrast, in turn, which is centrally important to the *Meno* (*M*. 85b–86a, 97a–98b) and to all of Plato's subsequent works, is first introduced in the *Gorgias* (*G*. 454d–e)—a further indication that these two dialogues are to be read as companion pieces, summing up and extending Socratic ethics and dialectic.

The question we now need to ask, then, is what the knowledge is that Socrates lacks and that therefore prevents him from being a teacher of the good life. Vlastos has argued that though Socrates possesses a sort of dialectical, fallible knowledge reached by means of the elenchus, and is willing to avow possessing it, he is also aware that he lacks a kind of knowledge that is philosophical, deductive, and certain.[25] It is just the possession of this second sort of knowledge that Socrates disavows, and that might have made him a teacher if he had only had it.

A problem with this interpretation, however, is that such a notion of "philosophical" knowledge is systematically articulated only in the middle and later writings of Plato and in the texts of Aristotle.[26] There is very little evidence for thinking that this notion constituted an idea disseminated widely enough—of, for that matter, articulated sufficiently—by Socrates' time (or even by the time of Plato's early works) to provide a sensible term of contrast with Socrates' elenctic method of dialectic. Unless such a concept was current at the time, Socrates could not reasonably deny possessing it; and evidence that it was current is very weak indeed. Vlastos provides only two passages from Democritus, and appeals to Parmenides' strong claims for his view of the world.[27] But the passages of Democritus do not seen to me to be enough to show that a systematic conception of philosophical knowledge that entailed certainty was available, and the Eleatics' reliance on deductive proof was used almost exclusively for the refutation of commonsense views rather than for the establishment of positive conclusions.

General considerations of this sort, however, are unlikely to resolve the problem. Let us, instead, look at our texts. In *Apology* 20d6–e2 Socrates claims to possess only what he calls "human wisdom," in contrast to what some other people to whom he claims to have just referred may profess. Who are these people, and what knowledge do they believe they have? According to Vlastos, they are the natural philosophers (referred to at *Ap*. 19a–20d) and the sophists (19d–20c). On his view, therefore, Socrates disavows the "philosophical" knowledge he must be attributing to the natural philosophers, and uses a single term "to refer to two radically different cognitive achievements, one of which [he] dares claim to have while disclaiming the other."[28]

The situation, however, is considerably more complicated than this suggests. First, Socrates, in repeating the "ancient" accusation that he claims is behind Meletus' writ, considers that it describes him both as a natural philosopher and as a teacher of rhetoric, since it is supposed to refer both to his investigations of natural phenomena and to his teaching of how to "make the weaker argument stronger" (*Ap.* 19b4–c1). Accordingly, when he denies having an interest in these topics, he cannot be thinking simply of natural philosophy: he must be thinking of rhetoric as well. But it is quite unlikely that Socrates would have attributed "philosophical" or certain knowledge to the rhetoricians if his notion of this knowledge was supposed to be derived from natural philosophy.

Second, Socrates remains explicitly agnostic about what it is, if anything, that natural philosophers and rhetoricians know: "I do not speak of this sort of knowledge in order to put it down—if indeed someone is wise concerning such matters . . . , but, really, Athenians, I take no part whatsoever in such affairs" (*Ap.* 19c5–8). Since he considers that natural philosophy and rhetoric are totally beyond his concerns, and since he expresses serious reservations about what is known in their regard, it is very difficult to believe that Socrates contrasts his own knowledge with the knowledge those people may have claimed for themselves. Moreover, it is equally implausible to believe that he considers the knowledge of the natural philosophers and the rhetoricians—if indeed they have any knowledge in the first place—to be superior to his own.

Of course, Socrates may well be being ironical in attributing wisdom and knowledge to the philosophers and to the rhetoricians. His real view may be that knowledge is god's prerogative (23a). In that case, however, we cannot appeal to the deductive features of the knowledge the philosophers allegedly possess in order to establish a notion of knowledge with which Socrates can be contrasting his own: either Socrates seriously accepts the philosophical concept of knowledge that he claims to lack, or he doubts it exists, in which case he cannot be contrasting *his* kind of knowledge with it.

For these reasons, it seems to me much more likely to suppose that the people of whom Socrates says he was just speaking (*Ap.* 20d9–e1) and with whom he contrasts himself are just the sophists who are concerned with rhetoric, grammar, or virtue: Gorgias, Prodicus, Hippias, and Evenus. Two reasons make this supposition plausible. First, these are in fact the people about whom Socrates has been speaking for the past whole Stephanus page (19d–20d); the natural philosophers have been left far behind. Second, since Socrates does discuss virtue incessantly and uses dialectical approaches not dissimilar to theirs,[29] it might seem obvious to the people of Athens that he is part of their group. It is therefore important to him to distinguish his position from theirs as clearly as possible. He claims that if, like them and like Evenus in particular, he himself possesses the knowledge (*epistēmē*) of *aretē* and the craft (*technē*) of teaching it, then he would indeed be "puffed up with vanity and pride" (20c1–2).

If so, then the domain with which Socrates is concerned is exclusively ethical, and the knowledge he claims to lack is the knowledge that the sophists—not the natural philosophers—claim to possess. More accurately put, he says he lacks the knowledge he believes these people must lay claim to if they can be teachers of anything. His concern, as David Reeve writes, is to try "to explain how his wisdom differs from that of Gorgias and the other sophists and how, despite the fact that he knows nothing of the things they claim to know (*Ap.* 20c1–3), his wisdom got confused with theirs (20c4–24b2)."[30] But the sophists' wisdom cannot have been the philosophical, deductive knowledge that may have been in the process of being articulated by Parmenides, Anaxagoras, and Democritus. If anything, the sophists represented, to a great extent, a repudiation of traditional natural philosophy.

The knowledge the sophists claim for themselves does not have anything to do with certainty and deduction. Rather, what they claim to have is what we might call technical or expert knowledge of *aretē*, knowledge that they can articulate and transmit to others with a reasonable assurance of success.[31] Perhaps it is not even the case that all of them make that strong a claim. Protagoras, for example, may be unwilling to identify his teaching too closely with what occurs in other *technai*.[32] Socrates is convinced, however, that if some people can teach virtue (or any other subject), then they must possess what he would consider technical knowledge, and he interprets their claim in this manner. This is a knowledge he disavows, while he is willing to claim for himself what we might call common, nontechnical, or nonexpert knowledge of *aretē*: he was convinced about some of its features, perhaps features that were quite controversial, by means of the fallible method provided by the elenchus. In addition, he was able to do with the greatest consistency the right thing on all occasions; this, I believe, must have been the greatest problem Plato faced regarding his "teacher": How could Socrates always do what is right without the knowledge he himself seemed to consider necessary for doing it? But Socrates' knowledge can neither explain why the truths it captures are true ("I do not know how it is [*hopōs echei*] that these things are so," he says at *Gorgias* 509a5), nor can it be transmitted from one person to another, as the artisans can transmit their knowledge in virtue of being able to explain the reasons for proceeding as they do in their work. The contrast is not between dialectical and apodeictic knowledge; it is, rather, between dialectic and craft—between pure persuasion by means of argument on the one hand, and an authority that can justify itself by its tried and true accomplishments on the other.

III

The most common approach to Socrates' disclaiming of the role of teacher is to consider it ironical. One of the most sophisticated expressions of this approach is found in Gregory Vlastos's concept of "complex irony." In complex irony, a word is used in two senses, denied in one while it is being asserted in the other. Many of Socrates' most paradoxical positions, including his attitude toward his teaching, turn out to be instances of this trope:

> In the conventional sense, where to "teach" is simply to transfer knowledge from a teacher's to a learner's mind, Socrates means what he says. But in the sense which *he* would give to "teaching"—engaging would-be learners in elenctic argument to make them aware of their own ignorance and enable them to discover for themselves *the truth the teacher had held back*—in that sense of "teaching" Socrates would want to say that he *is* a teacher, the only true teacher: his dialogue with his fellows is meant to have, and does have, the effect of evoking and assisting their efforts at moral self-improvement.[33]

This Socrates is, in the ancient sense of the term, a dogmatist: he knows the truth as certainly as anyone ever did. His ironic insistence that he neither knows nor teaches it, once interpreted in this manner, disappears into a protreptic device. This is the heart of Vlastos's controversial new interpretation of Socrates. But should we allow Socratic irony to transform itself so readily into an educational ploy? Is this irony at all?

I believe that it is not and that we should, instead, leave Socrates' irony intact, for a number of reasons. One is that this interpretation of Socratic irony seems tailor-made for the *Gorgias* (521d, 515a), a dialogue in which Plato's Socrates does reveal a newly found dogmatic streak. As I have already argued, however, the *Gorgias* should be seen as a text in which Plato goes beyond his previous understanding of Socrates. In fact, the *Gorgias* is the earliest in a long series of efforts to come to terms with Socrates' irony, to disarm it, and to claim Socrates as the first in a venerable tradition of moral teachers. In other words, I believe that the evidence of the *Gorgias,* like that of the *Meno,* is evidence for Plato's own controversial interpretation of what he had up to that point presented as Socratic philosophy.

Another reason for not reading Socrates' disavowal of teaching as a complex irony is the perhaps unfortunate fact that is it is far from clear that Socrates' dialogue with his fellows, as depicted in Plato's early works, "does have" the beneficial effect Vlastos so confidently attributes to it. Protagoras, Gorgias, Polus, Callicles, Hippias, Euthydemus, and Dionysiodorus remain unmoved. So do Euthyphro, Ion, and Meno. "Moral improvement" simply misdescribes the direction toward which Critias' and Charmides' lives tend. The *Laches* and the *Lysis* end with a promise to continue the efforts begun in these works, but they still leave the question of Socrates' long-term effects completely unresolved. As to his influence on Alcibiades, we have, apart from the testimony of history, the confession Plato himself attributes to Alcibiades in the *Symposium:* "I know perfectly well that I can't prove him wrong when he tells me what I should do; yet, the moment I leave his side, I go back to my old ways: I cave in to my desire to please the crowd" (*Smp.* 216b).

As a description of Socrates' efforts and effects as they are depicted in Plato's early dialogues, Nietzsche's point that dialectic "arouses mistrust," "that it is not very persuasive," "that nothing is easier to erase than a dialectical effect,"[34] seems to me to be exactly right. Though we know, through the existence of the various Socratic *logoi,* that some people at least were converted by him and tried to continue what they each took his mission to be, the fact remains that Socrates' direct, immediate effect on his contemporaries' morality was minimal.

It is true that both his enemies and his friends considered Socrates a teacher, but that is no reason to refuse to take his own disavowal of that role at face value. There is little ground for supposing that Socrates' contemporaries and near-contemporaries—the authors of the Socratic *logoi* that contained such incredibly different pictures of him—must have understood him better than we do. Kierkegaard was right: "Even if I were to imagine myself his contemporary," he writes, "he would still always be difficult to comprehend."[35]

Taking Socrates' attitude toward his teaching as ironical robs him of much of his strangeness. Taking it as sincere supplies him, paradoxically, with a much more profound ironical mask—a mask that is very difficult, perhaps impossible, to remove. For here we have someone who, precisely in disavowing ethical knowledge and the ability to supply it to others, succeeded in living as moral (if not necessarily as perfectly human) a life as anyone ever did who belonged to a tradition he himself had initiated. And he does not let us know how.

This—we must be very clear—is a profound instance of irony. For irony cannot simply be defined (as Vlastos, following the tradition begun by Quintilian, defines it) as saying one thing and meaning the opposite. The idea that ironists are always in clear possession of a truth they are holding back is itself part of the trope, part of what irony represents itself as, but not necessarily a part it communicates. To believe this idea is in many cases to miss the irony, to fail to notice that ironists can be ironical toward themselves as well. Often, irony consists simply in letting your audience know that something is taking place inside you that they are not allowed to see—but it also leaves open the question whether you are seeing it yourself. Irony often communicates that we are not seeing the whole picture, but it does not imply that the speaker is; in fact, it does not always imply that there is a whole picture to be seen in the first place.[36]

Irony, as I have been saying, provides a mask. It does not show what, if anything, is masked. It suggests depth, but it does not guarantee it. Furthermore, I believe, the Socrates of Plato's early dialogues has no depth, no underlying story distinct from what we are given in the texts. Intimations that his practice is underwritten by a set of views and theories different from those he expresses appear only in the *Gorgias* and in the *Meno;* and the first effort to display his depth explicitly is made when Plato composes Alcibiades' speech in the *Symposium*. These works are the beginning of Plato's attempt to endow Socrates with a depth that can explain his paradoxical life.

In our many discussions of Socratic irony we often forget that Socrates is after all Plato's literary creature and that the issue of Platonic irony, of the irony of the author, is at least as important as the irony of his character. Plato's irony, I believe, is more disturbing than Socrates': it is deep, dark, and disdainful. It expresses deep contempt, especially since Plato never engages in it directly in his own person, but only through the effect of his works.

Consider, for example, the way the *Euthyphro* manipulates its readers. By and large, even if we do not agree with all of Socrates' arguments, we finish the dialogue convinced that whether Euthyphro knows it or not, he has lost the day. We are put in the position of taking Socrates' side, of believing that he is absolutely right in thinking that Euthyphro does not know what piety is while yet he is determined to proceed with his astounding suit against his own father. Euthyphro's last words—"Some other time, Socrates; for, right now, I am in a hurry to get somewhere, and it's time for me to leave" (*Eu.* 15e3–4)—with which he avoids a discussion that he had taken such pains to initiate, show that he has missed Socrates' point completely: the argument must go on if he is to go on with his suit. Having taken Socrates' side, however, we ourselves close the book. Just like Euthyphro himself, we turn to our previous engagements instead of doing what agreement with Socrates entails: devoting ourselves, just like him, to the search for the good life—and this not simply in a metaphorical sense. What Socrates and Plato ask their respective audiences to do is neither uncontroversial nor easy. But agreeing that it is the right thing to do and not doing it, knowing the better but choosing the worse, places us, as Plato's readers and Socrates' admirers, in a very peculiar situation indeed.[37] To believe that Socrates' effect, either on his own interlocutors or on the readers of the dialogues, is generally beneficial is to be taken in by Platonic irony and to show ourselves to be missing the point in our very claim to see it. It is nothing other than displaying our ignorance of our ignorance.

Another reason for taking Socrates at face value when he denies being a teacher is the contrast between *Apology* 33a–b and *Gorgias* 456c–461b.[38] In the latter passage, Gorgias, having claimed to be a teacher of rhetoric, disclaims any responsibility for the use to which his students might put the knowledge he gives them. Socrates then argues that since Gorgias has claimed that the nature of justice is part of what his course on rhetoric reveals, his students should never be unjust. Gorgias accepts this conclusion, but the contradiction is left unresolved. The implication is that either rhetoric does not concern justice (for then the orator would never be unjust), or that Gorgias does not after all teach his students what he professes. In the *Apology*, however, Socrates claims for himself just the position he refuses to allow Gorgias to occupy. In very strong terms he says that since he never was the teacher of anyone, he cannot be held in any way responsible for the character and behavior of those who made it *their* business to listen to his discussions. I think that if there ever was a sense, any sense, in which Socrates did think of himself as a teacher of *aretē*, he would never have disavowed this central responsibility.

Who were the people who wanted to listen while he was discussing and minding his own business (*ta emautou prattontos*)? To whom did Socrates turn in order both to interpret and, once interpreted, to obey, the Delphic oracle? What did he tell them?

In Plato's Socratic dialogues, Socrates addresses a very small class of people (Crito, his closest friend, constitutes a very special case). This class includes acknowledged experts (Protagoras, Hippias, Gorgias and his companions, Euthydemus and Dionysiodorus, Ion, Laches, and Nicias), self-professed experts (Euthyphro, perhaps Critias [*Charmides* 162b–c], Meno, and Anytus), or handsome young men (Charmides, Lysis, Menexenus, and Alcibiades). Very often it is not Socrates who initiates the conversation, but it is his interlocutors who invite him into their discussion; consider, for example, how long it takes him to engage in the discussion of the *Laches,* or the pressure Hippocrates exerts on him, in the opening pages of the *Protagoras,* to introduce him to the sophist.

These are, however, all special people. How can their exclusive presence in their dialogues fit with Socrates' repeated claims in the *Apology* that he addresses absolutely every one he meets? (*Ap.* 29d6, 31b3–4; cf. 36c4–5). One possible answer to this question would be that these dialogues depict Socrates at the early stage of his elenctic career, before the incidents described in the *Apology* occur. They represent the set of disputations that provoked Chairephon to send to Delphi for the oracle, the time before Socrates took it upon himself to do the god's work in Athens and approach every ordinary person there. But the response fails. In the *Apology* Socrates says explicitly that he approached the experts after he received the oracle; and the examination of Euthyphro occurs just before his trial, well after the oracle was received.[39]

Let us now look at the passages of the *Apology* a little more closely. How strongly do they testify to Socrates' "universalism," to his being the popular figure of the "street philosopher" he is regularly taken to be? I am not sure we can answer this question unequivocally; but I do believe that the *Apology* presents a more complex picture of Socrates' activities than we often suppose.

Consider, first, Socrates' response to the oracle. Puzzled by its declaration, he approaches the three classes of people who had a reputation for wisdom: politicians, poets, and craftsmen. Moreover, Socrates describes his examination of the "wise," which was part of his effort at the elenchus of the oracle, as an activity "in accordance with the god's wish" (*kata ton theon,* 22a4)—an expression that suggests that his very attempt to interpret, perhaps even to refute, the oracle, was also part of his divine mission. That is, Socrates' mission does not begin *only* after he has determined the meaning of the oracle and has established the worth of his "human wisdom."

He comes to this interpretation after he has examined these people.[40] That is, he finally understands that the message of the oracle was that human wisdom is of little value and that he was chosen as an example of someone, perhaps the only person, aware of this. He then describes what he did next, characterizing it three times as divinely ordained: *kata ton theon* (23b5), *tōi theōi boēthōn* (23b7), *dia tēn tou theou latreian* (23c1). What is crucial here is the fact that Socrates consistently identifies his divine mission as a search for someone wise and a demonstration that no one with that reputation really deserves it. He does not depict his task as an effort to teach anyone the truth about virtue. In addition, he claims that the rich young men who have the leisure to "follow him around" do so purely on their own initiative (*automatoi,* 23c2–3). He does not offer himself as their teacher.

Plato is writing carefully here, and we should read him in the same way. He is equally careful later, when, beginning again with Socrates' effect on the young, he makes him expand on the content of the divine command:

> They enjoy listening to the examination of those who think they are wise but actually are not, for this is not without its pleasure. Just this, I claim, has been set to me as my task by the god both through oracles and dreams and in every way in which any other divine arrangement ever set a human being to doing something. (*Ap.* 33c2–7)

This famous passage, which asserts in the strongest terms that Socrates is obeying a divine command, tells us that he was ordered not to approach "all and sundry," but to examine those who believe they are wise, but in fact are not, and to expose their arrogance. The scope of Socrates' mission once again appears considerably more narrow than we often take it to be.

What of his long speech to the jury in the hypothetical case that they might allow him to live if he did not do philosophy? (*Ap.* 29d2–30c1). Does not Socrates clearly say here that he will still say *to anyone he happens upon* that what really matters is not wealth, fame, or honor, but the care of the soul? To answer this question correctly we must recall that this speech is addressed directly to the jury, which, by hypothesis, might allow Socrates to live if he were to abandon philosophy and—what comes to the same for him—the pursuit of virtue. What he tells *these members of the jury* is that he will not stop philosophizing. On the contrary, he will miss no opportunity of addressing them—that is, the very people who think, after all, that a life not lived in search of virtue is still worth living—on that very subject. For their hypothetical decision to let him live without philosophy would amount precisely to such an evaluation of life. So, even in this case, Socrates' audience is not unlimited. He begins his hypothetical speech by addressing it to an unnamed Athenian citizen (29d7–8), but he is speaking to the jurors, to whom he has been referring consistently as "Athenians," and who have expressed an explicit and controversial view on the value of life.[41] If any one of them (*ean tis humōn*), he continues, replies that he does care for what is worth caring for, Socrates will attach himself to him and will examine him in detail, showing him up as a hypocrite, if that is what he is.

What Socrates promises he will do to the members of the jury is in fact the point of the elenchus, as practiced on those who claim to be wise. Socrates now focuses on this point and says that he will engage in discussion of it "whomever I happen upon, young or old, citizen or foreigner, though preferably a citizen" (*Ap.* 30a2–4). Given the context, however, which concerns the practice of the elenchus on those who think they are wise, "whomever I happen upon" need not refer to everyone indiscriminately, but only to those for whom Socrates considers the elenchus appropriate, wherever they are from. That is, Socrates need not be saying, "I will walk about town and I will practice the elenchus on everyone I meet." Instead he may be saying, "Having determined that someone needs to be subjected to the elenchus, I will do so, whoever he is, young or old, citizen or foreigner."

A final point needs to be addressed now. When Socrates announces what he will say to the people he approaches, he does not rest content with the specifications of the elenchus he has given so far. He offers a much more general statement about the fundamentally greater importance of the care of the soul over concern with other goods (*Ap.* 30a–b). This is true. But we are not obligated to take his words to specify the surface content of his interaction with these people. His statement, rather, describes the covert point of the elenchus, which is in fact to show that the care of the soul is the most important activity in life, and which is established by the demonstration that people who believe they are wise actually are not.[42]

This speculation, about which I am far from certain, contains two parts. The first is that Socrates does not say that he addresses everyone he meets—though those he addresses are often to be found in public, in the streets. The second is that his "protreptic" description of what he will tell those he encounters is not an exact description of his words, but an explanation of the elenchus's point. Nothing prevents him, however, from thinking that by addressing elenctically the particular people who invite his intervention he is also improving not only their own personal fortune but the lot of the city as a whole.

If this is right, then Socrates can in all seriousness disclaim the role of teacher, though not on the grounds that he holds absolutely no positive views of his own. If he can disclaim that role, then the charge of intellectualism cannot show that his project is fundamentally flawed. Why should he not concentrate on the intellectual aspects of his interlocutors if those interlocutors claim on their own accord to know the nature of virtue and of the good life and, knowing it, to live it?

IV

Socrates may well have believed that the unexamined life is not worth living, and that his life, to the extent that it was examined, was the best a human being could have. But he came to this belief because he realized that it was the god's command (*Ap.* 37e–38a). How did he come to this realization? What enabled him to heed the god's desire to care for his own soul? What enabled the god to communicate that message to Socrates in the first place? The problem is one both for Socrates and for the god. As Vlastos writes,

> How could the god make the Athenians care for their soul? He could send them signs to that effect, dreams and oracles galore. But unless they brought the right beliefs to the interpretation of those signs, they would not be able to read them correctly. And they could not have come by those right beliefs unless they had already engaged in the quest for moral truth. So the god is stuck. . . . He must depend on someone who does have the right beliefs and can read signs correctly to assist the god.[43]

The god is in a quandary, indeed, in a quandary worse than this. As C.C.W. Taylor put the problem,

> There is one good product which [the gods] can't produce without human assistance, namely, good human souls. For a good human soul is a self-directed soul.[44]

Unless one wants to be good, the gods are powerless to help. But how can one want to be good if one is ignorant of what goodness is and, worse, ignorant of that very ignorance? In the case of Socrates, the god, if we may put the point as a near oxymoron, was lucky. *There was no reason* why Socrates was correctly motivated to inquire into virtue so as to be able to interpret the god's command correctly.[45]

In addition, the problem for which Socrates provides a solution on behalf of the god is at least as much of a problem for Socrates himself: how is *he* to make himself understood to his fellows? The situation, for the god and for Socrates, is strictly parallel: only one good agent can recognize another. What Socrates does, during the whole of his life, is look for a good agent: he is convinced that if he recognizes one, he will thereby show himself to be good as well, and will be recognized as good by that other good human being. Far from having anything to teach, Socrates is engaged in a search in the most literal sense of the term.[46]

It could well be, however, that someone, having somehow recognized Socrates as a good man, wanted Socrates' motivation, character, and activity to be not simply a matter of luck, of a "divine accident,"[47] but rather to be the product of a *technē*. One may have wanted to make sure that there will always be people like him in society and that they will always be honored for what they are; that *aretē* in the sense of having a good soul and *aretē* in the sense of having a great reputation will never again diverge as they did so tragically in Socrates' case. One will then turn to education in a most profound and systematic way: education, if we know what we want, will produce good people and the ability, in those who are not so good, to recognize them. This turn, which did occur, was profound and systematic enough to convince most of us that philosophy necessarily involves showing others what the good life is. This is a view that, though inspired by Socrates, was not, I believe, his own. It is also a view that radically separates the ability to lead a good life from the ability to recognize one who does.

If one, in addition, has just learned, and has become rapt with, a method of learning that itself does not depend on luck and good will, but only on ability and persistence—a method that offers no choice, but imposes the obligation to accept its conclusions once you begin to follow it—then that one will devise a system for the direct education of the souls of one and all. That one's name, as it happens, is Plato. His method will be in its higher reaches mathematical, and his attention will focus on the affective side of his pupils. For it will now be necessary to start when they are young and to get them to *want* to have the right beliefs. It will also be necessary to ensure that those with talent will in fact develop the systematic ability to do the right thing that Socrates possessed without ever knowing how he had learned it.

It is deeply ironical that Socrates' paradoxical ignorance gave rise to Plato's systematic effort to articulate the notion that the life of knowledge and, in particular, of philosophy, is the best life for all human beings. It also gave rise to Plato's conviction that philosophers can tell the rest of the people how they can live best. These two ideas go together. As long as we identify the life of philosophy as the best life, it seems reasonable to expect philosophers also to know how others should live. It seems to me, however, that the first of these two ideas is now lost. Far from constituting the best mode of life, philosophy is often not even seen as such a thing at all: it no longer represents, in Aristotle's words, a *prohairesis tou biou*—a choice of life—but has itself become a *technē*. In that case, however, the second idea, that philosophers are particularly qualified to understand the nature of the good life and to show it to others, also must lose some of its hold on our imagination. Socrates' suspicions about a *technē* that can teach us how to live well—suspicions we share while reading Plato's early dialogues— must remain with us after we close our books.

Separated from Plato's own systematic educational interests, Socrates constitutes a peculiar figure, concerned primarily if not exclusively with the improvement of his own soul. He therefore prompts us to reexamine our assumption that philosophy must be essentially directed toward public affairs. Perhaps his own private goals are enough; perhaps one can change the world, as Nietzsche would have said, only through changing oneself. Those who find such narrower goals unacceptable and want to reclaim a public voice for philosophy must then try hard to find the proper modulation for that voice. In fact, they must go back to the Plato of the *Republic:* his grand claims for the value of philosophy can be made only on the basis of a conception of the discipline that is itself as grand as his own. Is Platonism, even understood in the broadest terms, a possible choice today? Or should we return to Socrates' superficially more modest approach, knowing, however, that once we engage in the care of the self we will never know when we can stop, that the limits of the self are also the limits of the world?[48]

NOTES

1. *Gorgias* 485d3–e2. Unless otherwise noted, translations from the Greek are my own.

2. Friedrich Nietzsche, *The Birth of Tragedy,* trans. Walter Kaufmann, in *Basic Writings of Nietzsche* (New York, 1966), sec. 15.

3. Friedrich Nietzsche, *The Twilight of the Idols,* trans. Walter Kaufmann, in *The Viking Portable Nietzsche* (New York, 1968), 476.

4. For examples of the latter, see, among others, Myles F. Burnyeat, "Aristotle on Learning to be Good," in *Essays on Aristotle's Ethics,* ed. Amélie O. Rorty (Berkeley, 1980), 60–92; and Martha C. Nussbaum, "Aristophanes and Socrates on Learning Practical Wisdom," *Yale Classical Studies* 26 (1980): 43–97.

5. An extensive discussion of habituation in the formation of character and in the attainment of the good life, as Aristotle conceives them, can be found in Nancy Sherman, *The Fabric of Character* (Oxford, 1989), esp. ch. 5.

6. Martha C. Nussbaum, "The Chill of Virtue," a review of Gregory Vlastos, *Socrates: Ironist and Moral Philosopher,* in *The New Republic,* September 16 and 23, 1991: 40.

7. In what follows, I shall mainly use "argument" as a translation of the Greek *logos* when the latter refers to Socratic conversation and dialectic. This is sometimes too narrow, since Socrates' discussions often are informal and do not always involve logical demonstration. But I still think that "argument," broadly construed as dialectical give and take, is the best we can do. An alternative would be "discussion" (a suggestion made to me by Paul Woodruff), but I find this term too general; and it fails to suggest the sharpness that characterizes the edges of Socrates' particular method of conversation. Occasionally, however, context will demand the use of this broader term.

8. Gregory Vlastos, *Socrates: Ironist and Moral Philosopher* (Cambridge, 1991), 253.

9. Ibid., 110.

10. Cf., however, Xenophon, *Memorabilia* IV.4.11.

11. That in his middle and late works Plato is willing to criticize Socrates, often through the persona of Socrates himself, is one indication that in his earlier works he *does* try to represent Socrates as he genuinely sees him to be, whether or not we can trust his representation to be accurate.

12. The irony is compounded by the fact that Gregory Vlastos, in his discussion of this passage of the *Republic,* writes that if young men were to come to philosophy unprepared, "they would be sure to be corrupted"; Vlastos, *Socrates: Ironist and Moral Philosopher,* 110. Though he does not explicitly endorse Plato's criticism, Vlastos uses the very term Socrates' own accusers used in their indictment, despite the fact that Plato himself (very carefully, in my opinion) consistently avoids the word *diaphtheirein* ("to corrupt") throughout the criticism of Socrates' approach at hand.

13. This translation is taken from G.M.A. Grube, *Plato's Republic* (Indianapolis, 1974).

14. Cf. my essays in this book: "Meno's Paradox and Socrates as a Teacher," "Socratic Intellectualism," and "Eristic, Antilogic, Sophistic, Dialectic."

15. Xenophon, *Memorabilia* IV.3.8; cf. IV.3.25.

16. Vlastos argues that I take Xenophon's statement as evidence "that Socrates not only did not *promise* to teach virtue, but *did not teach it,* and did not even *try* to teach it, which Xenophon does not say and certainly does not mean; cf. *Mem.* IV.7.1"; Vlastos, *Socrates: Ironist and Moral Philosopher,* 241 n. 26. This reply, however, conflates the two senses of teaching, by communication of doctrine on the one hand and by setting a moral example on the other, which I have argued we must keep distinct. My point in "Socratic Intellectualism" (see note 14 above) was that Xenophon, in the statement we are discussing here, does not attribute to Socrates any version of the former approach. It is true that at many other points in the *Memorabilia* Xenophon lavishly attributes to Socrates the desire (and, ineffec-

tively, the ability) to teach. But Xenophon's not always consistent evidence does not affect the interpretation of this text, which appears so early and so prominently in his account. For another criticism of my view, see Donald Morrison, "Xenophon's Socrates as Teacher," in *The Socratic Movement,* ed. Paul A. Vander Waerdt (Ithaca, 1992).

17. See my essay "Socratic Intellectualism" in this book.

18. See *Apology* 28d10–29a1. The point is well argued in C.D.C. Reeve, *Socrates in the* Apology (Indianapolis, 1989), 109–11. See also Thomas C. Brickhouse and Nicholas D. Smith, *Socrates on Trial* (Princeton, 1989), 141–42.

19. *Gorgias* 474c.

20. The fact that a particular thesis "has always proved true [that is, has survived the elenchus] in the past offers absolutely no certainty that it always will in the future: it may have been vindicated in a thousand elenchi in the past and prove false in the very next one after that"; Vlastos, *Socrates: Ironist and Moral Philosopher,* 114.

21. On the idea that technical or "expert" knowledge involves the ability to explain that which one knows, see Reeve, *Socrates in the* Apology, 37–45.

22. See Vlastos, *Socrates: Ironist and Moral Philosopher,* 113–15. Vlastos presents and defends his view more extensively in "The Socratic Elenchus," *Oxford Studies in Ancient Philosophy* 1 (1983): 27–58, esp. 52–53, and 74, with n. 8.

23. See Vlastos, *Socrates: Ironist and Moral Philosopher,* 47, with n. 8; 117–26.

24. See Reeve, *Socrates in the* Apology, 52.

25. Gregory Vlastos, "Socrates' Disavowal of Knowledge," *Philosophical Quarterly* 35 (1981): 1–35.

26. Vlastos's evidence from these authors is collected in "Socrates' Disavowal of Knowledge," 13–16.

27. Democritus, B117 and B9 Diels-Kranz; cited in "Socrates' Disavowal of Knowledge," 17.

28. Vlastos, "Socrates' Disavowal of Knowledge," 27, with n. 68; cf. Vlastos, *Socrates: Ironist and Moral Philosopher,* 238–39.

29. The argument for the methodological similarities between Socrates and the "sophists" can be found in the essay "Eristic, Antilogic, Sophistic, Dialectic" in this book.

30. Reeve, *Socrates in the* Apology, 10–11. I am particularly indebted to Reeve's clear analysis of the "ancient" accusation against Socrates and of his manner of responding to it.

31. On "expert" knowledge, see Paul Woodruff, *Plato:* Hippias Major (Indianapolis, 1982), 79–112; and Reeve, *Socrates in the* Apology, 37–53.

32. On this hypothesis, see Paul Woodruff, "Socrates' Debt to Protagoras" (unpublished manuscript, 1992). He writes that in the *Protagoras,* "Protagoras uses the analogy of virtue to *technē* delicately, recognizing—and showing—that it does not hold in every respect; and he draws encouragement from it for the teaching of virtue (as flutists can teach music to their sons to varying degrees, depending on their natural talents). Socrates, on the other hand, drives the analogy hard in order to undermine it and so to cast suspicion on claims that Sophists teach virtue" (12). The issue is complex and needs further discussion, in which, unfortunately, I can-

not engage on this occasion. Woodruff's own position is well presented in "Plato's Early Theory of Knowledge," in *Epistemology*, ed. Stephen Everson (Cambridge, 1990), 60–84.

33. Vlastos, *Socrates: Ironist and Moral Philosopher*, 32; the second set of italics is mine. Other Socratic statements that Vlastos interprets as complex ironies are Socrates' disavowal of knowledge and his disavowal of being engaged in politics; see ch. 1, and pp. 236–42.

34. See note 3 above.

35. Søren Kierkegaard, *The Concept of Irony (With Continual Reference to Socrates)*, ed. and trans. Howard V. Hong and Edna H. Hong (Princeton, 1989), 12.

36. This can be seen even through one of Vlastos's simplest examples of irony, the response of Mae West to an invitation to dinner at the Ford White House: "It's an awful long way to go for just one meal"; Vlastos, *Socrates: Ironist and Moral Philosopher*, 21–22. Vlastos acknowledges that there is a "riddling" element in this statement. The case, however, is more complex—not perhaps as irony itself, but as an instance to be explained by the traditional interpretation of irony. What we learn from Mae West is that she is not going to dinner with the President. But I can think of no function that takes us from her uttered words to their "opposite," whatever that might be.

37. Diogenes Laertius claims that Socrates actually diverted Euthyphro from his course of action as a result of their conversation on piety (*Lives of the Philosophers*, II.5.29).

38. Cf., however, Xenophon, *Memorabilia* I.2.19, I.2.23, I.2.27. For the distinction between the two stages of Socrates' elenctic enterprise, though not for this use of it, see Reeve, *Socrates in the* Apology, 45.

39. David Blank, in "Socratics vs. Sophists on Payment for Teaching," *California Studies in Classical Philology* 48 (1985): 1–49, has argued that the evidence of the *Apology* should be discounted. It is a work, he writes, "with a strong apologetic tendency [and] the only Platonic work containing such a statement. Any elitism on Socrates' part might have lent support to the charge, unspoken at his trial, that he had been involved in the preparation of young men for the oligarchy of the Thirty. . . . Plato's *Apology* is . . . concerned to bring out Socrates' civic-mindedness" (20). There is something to this idea, but taken by itself it does not remove a sense of deep uneasiness about Plato's practice.

40. Note, incidentally, Socrates' subtle suggestion that there *are* some people in Athens who, without having that reputation, do know something about the good; *Apology* 22a4. It is an interesting question whom he had in mind.

41. On the possible significance of Socrates' addressing the jury only as "Athenians" and not as "judges" (*dikastai*), see Brickhouse and Smith, *Socrates on Trial*, 210–11, with references.

42. This, I believe, is also the point Socrates makes at *Apology* 36c.

43. Vlastos, *Socrates: Ironist and Moral Philosopher*, 173.

44. C.C.W. Taylor, "The End of the *Euthyphro*," *Phronesis* 27 (1982): 113.

45. Vlastos's solution to this problem (see *Socrates: Ironist and Moral Philosopher*, 173–74) is that Socrates had the "right beliefs" that enabled him to understand the god's good wish. This does not, however, answer the question, because

we must now determine how Socrates came to have those true beliefs. Vlastos seems to suggest that Socrates may have come to them as a result of his "street-philosophizing," but this does not explain why Socrates engaged in such "street-philosophizing" in the first place.

46. A more complete version of this case is made in this book's essay "Meno's Paradox and Socrates as a Teacher."

47. Cf. *Republic* 492a.

48. The earliest version of this paper was written when Gregory Vlastos invited me to speak at one of his National Endowment for the Humanities Summer Seminars for College Teachers in Berkeley, July 1989. I am grateful to the participants in that seminar for a lively and productive discussion. Vlastos and I disagreed about the essay, in a friendly though spirited manner, until his death. A later version was presented at the Leonard Conference held at the University of Nevada at Reno, October 1991, where it received a number of very valuable criticisms. Roslyn Weiss corrected a number of my errors. I am also indebted to Paul Woodruff for his written comments on that version.

Four

VOICES OF SILENCE:
ON GREGORY VLASTOS'S SOCRATES

> What Socrates himself prized so highly, namely,
> standing still and contemplating—in other words,
> silence—this is his whole life in terms of world history.
> He has left nothing by which a later age can judge
> him; indeed, even if I were to imagine myself his
> contemporary, he would still always be difficult to
> comprehend. In other words, he belonged to that
> breed of persons with whom the outer as such is not
> the stopping point. The outer continually pointed to
> something other and opposite.
> —Søren Kierkegaard, *The Concept of Irony*

KIERKEGAARD, whose picture of Socrates is an extended effort to fill in the outline he draws in this passage,[1] is not often mentioned in Gregory Vlastos's *Socrates: Ironist and Moral Philosopher*.[2] Nevertheless, the portrait Vlastos paints in this work seems at times to have been composed specifically in order to dispute Kierkegaard's picture—particularly his contrast between the public face Socrates' contemporaries saw and the opposite inner life he kept to himself. Vlastos's Socrates, no less than Kierkegaard's, is also "difficult to comprehend"; but the difficulties he presents can be overcome, and the public and the private, the inner and the outer, finally merge. In no uncertain terms, Vlastos's book invites us to come to know Socrates as he really was.

It is far from clear that Kierkegaard's view that Socrates' interior was so directly opposite to his exterior can be correct. In my view, we know too little about Socrates to be in a position to have even that much of a conception of his "interiority." But this should not cause us to overlook the crucial importance of that feature of Socrates to which Kierkegaard refers as his *silence*. Vlastos in fact builds his interpretation upon it, even though he does not think of it in Kierkegaard's terms.

Socrates' silence takes three forms, ranging from the more literal to the more metaphorical and, perhaps, from the less central to the more essential.

I

The first and most literal sort of silence is described on two occasions in Plato's *Symposium*. On one of them, Aristodemus, who is accompanying Socrates to Agathon's celebration, realizes that he has reached Agathon's house alone: on the way there, Socrates had wandered off. A slave, dispatched to find him, returns to report that Socrates has "gone off to the neighbor's porch. He's standing there and won't come in even though I called him several times." And Aristodemus explains, "It's one of his habits: every now and then he just goes off like that and stands motionless, wherever he happens to be," speechless and unresponsive (*Smp.* 174e–175b). On the other occasion, Alcibiades describes how, as the sun rose on a day during the siege of Potidaea, Socrates "started thinking about some problem or other; he just stood outside, trying to figure it out. He couldn't resolve it, but he wouldn't give up. He simply stood there, glued to the same spot. . . . He only left next morning, when the sun came out, and he made his prayers to the new day" (*Smp.* 220c–d).

We shall never know what occupied Socrates during his habitual and often long periods of silence. They must have even baffled Plato himself, since he never tries to explain them: they are for him simply part of what Socrates was. But they also contrast starkly with Socrates' passionate, one might even say obsessive, devotion to talk, to conversation, to argument, and to his own understanding of his mission in life: "I do nothing but go about persuading you, young and old, to have your first and greatest concern not for your body or for your money, but for your soul, that it should be as excellent as possible" (*Apology* 30a–b). Socrates' silences may have been either interruptions or essential elements of his communicative endeavor: we shall never know.

But if Socrates' mission was what Plato says it is, then "silence," contrary to Kierkegaard, may appear to be a very inappropriate term for describing his "whole life," devoted as that was to dialogue and discussion, to the effort to "give an account" (*logon didonai*). For to give such an account was precisely to refrain from remaining silent over the things that matter most, over the quality of one's whole life (*Laches* 187e–188b).

This silence, then, cannot be what Kierkegaard had in mind. At best, in its existence as well as in its inexplicability, it can function as an emblem for two other forms of silence—one characteristic of Socrates' actual life as it is represented in all our sources and the other a feature of the most important and influential representation of his character. Socrates was silent because he never wrote anything himself; and he is silent because he is so unwilling, in Plato's dialogues, to present views of his own. These forms of silence lead us directly into the most central questions raised by any interpretation of Socrates' life, views, and influence. They provide, in addition, the background against which Vlastos's study was composed and in relation to which it must be read. *Socrates: Ironist and Moral Philosopher* does not take these forms of silence for granted: it confronts them directly and tries to listen through them. The first thing to understand about this major and—despite its pervasively conciliatory tone—extremely controversial and revisionary book is that it is an extended effort to break these forms of silence, to hear the voice that still, Vlastos believes, is speaking to us through them.

II

Nietzsche once described Socrates as "the one who doesn't write." This authorial silence leads directly into "the Socratic problem," the annoyingly recalcitrant question of who the historical personage known as "Socrates" really was. W.K.C. Guthrie, in his account of Greek philosophy from Thales to Aristotle, puts the matter succinctly and well: "There is, and shall always be, a 'Socratic problem.' This is inevitable, since he wrote nothing."[3]

The problem is this. Socrates himself has left us no writing of his own, no self-representation. We only have his images, as drawn by others. We have no direct access to the thoughts and actions of one of our most central moral exemplars. The character who is credited with the distinction between reflection and original is known to us only as a set of reflections of an original perhaps forever lost. One of the single most important characters in our moral and intellectual tradition—crucial not only for the content of his thought, for the force of his personality, or for the shape of his life, but most of all for their interrelation, for the manner in which each supports the others and adds further dimensions to them—has survived only through the words of a few people who knew him.

In many other cases, this might not have been a problem. But despite his immense emphasis on the vital importance of thought and reason, Socrates was not simply a theoretical philosopher—so those who knew him have convinced us. More than any other figure in our secular intellectual history he seems to have lived and died as he thought: holding that thought and action are continuous, he actually drew no line between what he believed and what he did. The question, therefore, who he really was, whether what we know of him in any way corresponds to historical reality, seems absolutely crucial. If Socrates was in reality radically different from his representations, then it is not clear that he deserves his status. In such a case, some of our most cherished conceptions of the nature of a good human life may turn out to be simply fictions. Can a "merely" literary figure, which is what he would in that case be, provide us with a paradigm of how actually to live? If it cannot, what of the various conceptions of the good life that have in fact been articulated under his influence? If it can, what exactly is the place of imaginative literature within the moral life?

Socrates' legacy is defined for us mainly by the texts of four ancient authors. Aristophanes lampooned Socrates incidentally in the *Frogs* and centrally in the *Clouds,* in which he is the central figure. Xenophon wrote a number of works, the *Memorabilia,* the *Symposium,* the *Oeconomicus,* and the *Apology of Socrates,* which aimed at vindicating Socrates against a number of accusations that had been made against him during his life and after his death. Aristotle refers to Socrates' philosophical views on a number of occasions in his treatises. But by far the most important sources for our understanding of Socrates are the dialogues of Plato, in which his philosophical views and his enigmatic personality are given the most detailed, the most intimately interconnected, and therefore the most vivid presentations.

Plato was certainly not the only one among his friends and companions to write dialogues in which Socrates was the central character. A whole genre of "Socratic *logoi,*" as Aristotle testifies (*Poetics* 1447b11), had sprung around him. But with the exception of some fragments from the dialogues of Aeschines of Sphettus, and a few sentences of Antisthenes and Phaedo of Elis, nothing remains of the works of authors like Aristippus, Cebes, and many others.[4] It is, of course, not likely that having more texts about Socrates would make it easier to answer the question of his historical substance. Our four existing sources are often in deep disagreement. We know from various reports that the other Socratics, each one of whom traced the origins of his views to Socrates himself, attributed to him the most various, often directly contradictory positions. And it is therefore quite likely that the more information we had about him, the less we would understand him.

Not that we understand him so well as it is. Consider, as one among many examples, what Aristophanes, Plato, and Xenophon (the three of our original source-authors who knew Socrates personally) tell us about his attitude toward *physiologia,* or natural philosophy.

In the *Clouds,* Aristophanes depicts Socrates as the head of a school, the *phrontistērion,* where astronomy and meteorology, geometry, geology and geography, and, in particular, natural history are studied intensively: the first thing we learn about Socrates is his "brilliant" calculation of how many flea-feet's worth a flea is capable of jumping (143 ff.).[5] Aristophanes' intent was, of course, comic. But if we were to go by his testimony alone, we would have to conclude that Socrates must have been seriously involved in the investigation of the phenomena of nature.

Xenophon, by contrast, writes not only that Socrates was uninterested in such investigations but that he actually believed that those who were concerned with them were "fools" (*Memorabilia* i.1.11). Still, Xenophon also claims that Socrates did encourage his companions to learn, to the extent that they were practically useful, all the subjects a well-educated man should know, including geometry and astronomy. And though, Xenophon continues, Socrates considered the theoretical study of these subjects "useless," he himself was both experienced in higher mathematics and had attended lectures concerning them (*Mem.* iv.7.1–5).

Now when Plato, in his *Apology*, makes Socrates address the common view that he was, in one way or another, well versed in natural science and philosophy, he makes him say that "of such things I know nothing, great or small. Not that I would speak disparagingly of such science, if anyone is really wise regarding it. . . . But the fact is, Athenians, that I have no share in it" (19c). Contrary to the characterizations of both Aristophanes and Xenophon, Plato's Socrates is totally uninvolved in natural science, both theoretically and practically, though he is not, as Xenophon claims, disrespectful of its achievements—if achievements in fact they are.

Even casual attention to our sources will show in how many ways the sketches of Socrates presented by those who knew him best are difficult, if not impossible, to combine into a coherent portrait. Once this is realized, then it becomes necessary to establish some principles by means of which we can be satisfied that some of the reports that have reached us do in fact describe Socrates as he actually was. What these principles can be and how dependable the conclusions are that can be derived from them regarding Socrates constitute the core of "the Socratic problem."

It is commonly thought that the Socratic problem was first posed in the nineteenth century by Friedrich Schleiermacher, who believed that both Xenophon and Plato were reporting on the historical Socrates and hoped that the discrepancies between them could be eliminated, or at least minimized, by always keeping the following question in mind: What *could* Socrates have been above and beyond the testimony of Xenophon without contradicting those traits of character and the rules of life that Xenophon attributes to him without qualification, and what *must* he have been like so as to give Plato the right and the grounds for presenting him as he does in his dialogues?[6] Schleiermacher's influence on the study of Plato is immense. But in fact the problem had already been posed by a number of Enlightenment scholars, who toward the end of the eighteenth century had attempted to establish a number of facts about Socrates' actual life and thought, particularly concerning the events surrounding his trial and execution by the Athenian courts in 399 B.C.[7]

This is not the place for a history of the Socratic problem. My purpose is simply to locate the approach of *Socrates: Ironist and Moral Philosopher* within the context of more recent approaches to the views and character of the historical Socrates, since one of Vlastos's central aims in his book is to face that question squarely and give it a controversial answer.

Which of our four sources are we to choose as authentic, to the detriment or even the exclusion of the rest? Guthrie, again, puts the matter well:

A. Diès speaks entertainingly of how few scholars have . . . had the courage to mount the quadriga and drive all four horses. Most have preferred to disqualify all but one whom, rather than guide, they allow to run as he pleases. Plato was the first to enjoy this privilege, then Xenophon, then Aristotle; one or two backed Aristophanes, then round came the wheel to Plato again in this century with the British scholars Burnet and Taylor.[8]

Taylor's reliance on Plato was, at least in principle, moderate: " 'Socrates' in Plato," he wrote, "is neither . . . the historical Socrates nor . . . the historical Plato, but the hero of the Platonic drama. The hero's character is largely modelled on that of the actual Socrates, his opinions are often those of the historical Plato, but he is still distinct from them both."[9] In practice, however, Taylor sided[10] with Burnet, who was given to rather extravagant claims: Burnet believed, for example, that the cosmology and philosophy attributed to Socrates in Plato's *Phaedo,* including the full-blown theory of Forms, must have been Socrates' actual views:

I cannot, indeed [Burnet admits] feel sure that all the incidents of the narrative are strictly historical. . . . But the religious and philosophical teaching of the *Phaedo* is on a very different footing. Whatever Plato may or may not have done in other dialogues . . . I cannot bring myself to believe that he falsified the story of his master's last hours on earth by using him as a mere mouthpiece for novel doctrines of his own.[11]

In reaction to such an extreme view, many scholars have chosen to follow a different approach altogether. They argue, instead, that the name "Socrates" refers to a purely literary, fictional character who appears in a number of ancient texts and who does not exist outside them. No one disputes, of course, that a historical person of that name existed and that some facts about him, like the dates of his birth and death or the names of his parents, can be known. But everything we learn about him as a character and as a philosopher must be considered strictly as a literary invention that cannot intersect with history. This view has been argued by, among others, Dupréel,[12] Gigon,[13] and Chroust, who believes not only that our sources are not faithful to the historical Socrates but also that they were never intended to be:

This whole literary tradition never really intended to concern itself with historical reporting of fact. We must surmise, therefore, that this tradition was aimed primarily at creating a legend or fiction. Hence we may also claim that the literary Socrates is essentially a legendary Socrates. He is above all a legend or the product of a legend, created by a host of myth-makers.[14]

The view that Socrates should be treated as a literary character, without extensive concern for his historicity, has been dominant in recent discussions. Such an approach is justified if we are only interested in the theoretical views Plato attributes to his creature. But many scholars are also interested in the mutual influence of Socrates' theoretical and practical views, in his status as a moral exemplar. This, in turn, forces us to ask whether our conception of this human being answers to anything in reality, whether the life he is represented as having lived is in fact worth living and, more important, whether it can actually be lived. If we are supposed, in some ways, to be like him, we must know if Socrates *himself* could have been as our sources represent him. At the very least, the question must be raised, if only to be put aside.

Gregory Vlastos follows a sophisticated middle course between straightforward historicism and absolute fictionalism. By and large discarding the verse of Aristophanes, he practices a sort of "triangulation" on our three other source-authors. He believes that by means of such a procedure we may be able to determine a number of features of Socrates, both personal and philosophical, that correspond to the historical substance of the man who inspired them.

On such an approach, Socrates' silence as an author, his leaving no personal written record of himself, need not prevent us from hearing, at least sometimes, the sound of his own voice. It emerges when the voices of Plato, Xenophon, and Aristotle sound, so to speak, in harmony with one another.

Vlastos follows Burnet and Taylor in taking Plato as our main source for a reconstruction of the views of the historical Socrates. But in stark contrast to their view that the character depicted in the dialogues is one and the same throughout, he draws a sharp distinction between the Socrates whom we meet in Plato's earlier works and the character of the same name who is the central speaker of most (though not all) of the works of Plato's middle and later periods. Relying mostly on philosophical but also on stylistic criteria, Vlastos considers that the following dialogues constitute Plato's earlier output, which he divides, in turn, into two groups. To the first belong the "elenctic" dialogues, in which Socrates is depicted mostly as a practitioner of the dialectical method that came to be known as the elenchus and which reach mostly negative results: these are the *Apology,* the *Charmides,* the *Crito,* the *Euthyphro,* the *Gorgias,* the *Hippias Minor,* the *Ion,* the *Laches,* the *Protagoras,* and *Republic* I. The second consists of "transitional" dialogues, in which the elenchus is abandoned but in which the full metaphysics, epistemology, cosmology, and moral and political philosophy characteristic of Plato's great middle works are not yet to be found: to this group belong the *Euthydemus,* the *Hippias Major,* the *Lysis,* the *Menexenus,* and the *Meno.*

Vlastos relies on these dialogues, especially those of the first group, and in particular on the *Apology* and the *Gorgias* (of the five hundred or so references to the elenctic dialogues in his index, over three hundred are to

these two texts alone), in order to extract views that can be attributed to
the historical Socrates.

But Vlastos's extraordinary reliance on the *Gorgias* raises some very serious questions. The dialogue, as Vlastos had earlier conceded,[15] attributes
a number of views to Socrates that cannot be found in the other early
dialogues. These concessions are not noted in the present book. Further,
the *Gorgias* has generally been considered among the last of Plato's early
dialogues (including those of Vlastos's second group). On textual and
philosophical grounds, W. H. Thompson places it close to the *Republic;*[16]
E. R. Dodds, after the *Euthydemus* and close to the *Meno;*[17] and Terence
Irwin finds it to be in a number of respects different from the early works
and similar to the middle ones.[18] In many ways, I would argue, the
Gorgias and the *Meno* are structurally and philosophically companion
pieces, efforts on Plato's part to explain, by appealing to ideas that are
wholly his own, the practice of his teacher rather than attempts simply to
present him at work. Vlastos's crucial reliance on the *Gorgias,* therefore,
for the historical Socrates' views seems to me to present a serious obstacle
to his reconstruction.[19]

According to this reconstruction, in his early works Plato shared Socrates' own philosophical convictions and tried to produce as coherent a system of Socratic philosophy as he could. "In doing this," Vlastos writes,

> Plato is producing, not reproducing, Socratic philosophizing. Employing a
> literary medium which allows Socrates to speak for himself, Plato makes him
> say whatever *he*—Plato—thinks *at the time of writing* would be the most
> reasonable thing for Socrates to be saying just then in expounding and de-
> fending his own philosophy. (50)

In the dialogues of Plato's middle and later periods, however, Socrates
becomes a mouthpiece for views that are purely Plato's own. Some of
these views Plato reached by further reflection on Socratic ideas; to the
most important ones, according to Vlastos, he probably came after learning of the achievements of the mathematicians of his time, as a result of
meeting Archytas of Tarentum during one of his visits to Sicily. The second
chapter of Vlastos's book contains a detailed contrast between the Socrates
of Plato's early dialogues and the character of the same name who appears
in Plato's later works. In very general terms, the former (who corresponds,
according to Vlastos, to the historical figure) is purely a moral philosopher
who refuses to speculate about ontology, epistemology, cosmology, political philosophy, or philosophy of art. He is a moral philosopher, moreover,
of a peculiar sort. The Socrates of the middle works tirelessly expounds
one controversial theory after another in all fields of philosophical inquiry.
But the Socrates of the early dialogues, apart from staying away from such
theorizing, also denies any knowledge of importance concerning the only

subject he ever investigates—the question of how we are to live: his "dis-avowal of knowledge" is one of his most salient characteristics. He is, al-most without qualification, a philosopher of search and questions, not of answers. And his search is rigorously circumscribed: he does not stray from its pursuit, and does not believe that answering any of the other questions that occupy Plato in his later works could ever be of any help to him.

Another crucial difference between the early and the middle Socrates, to which Plato's discovery of mathematics is directly relevant, is that the early Socrates relies exclusively on a dialectical method, the elenchus, which can never guarantee certainty. The elenchus is essentially adversarial: it allows you to refute your opponent; it gives you positive reason to accept a view only to the extent that you have never been refuted while maintaining it. But it provides no assurance whatever that, when you engage in it next, you will be able to emerge victorious from your dialectical encounter: there is no logical reason to believe that a view on which you may have based your whole life will not be demolished, together with your life, the very next time you enter an argument. By contrast, mathematical knowl-edge, on which Plato eventually comes to model all knowledge worth the name, is completely immune to this kind of uncertainty: once attained, a proof is forever unassailable.

Why, though, should we believe that the protagonist of Plato's early dialogues is an accurate representation of a historical figure? Why, as Vlastos himself puts it, should we accept

> the claim that through a "Socrates" in Plato we can come to know the Socra-tes of history—the Socrates who made history, taught Plato and others, changed their thinking and their lives, and through them changed the course of Western thought[?] (45)

His answer is this. The Socrates of the early dialogues, who according to Vlastos corresponds to the figure of history, is distinguished from the Soc-rates of the later works who expressed views held only by Plato, by exhibit-ing a different approach on ten important issues. Vlastos concentrates on four among them. We have already mentioned two: the early Socrates is interested exclusively in moral issues: he looks for knowledge only through the elenchus and habitually disavows having any; by contrast, the middle Socrates' philosophical concerns are universal, and he believes that he pos-sesses a demonstrative and indubitable method for acquiring the knowl-edge he earlier lacked. Add to these contrasts the following two: first, the fact that the metaphysical theory of the "separate" Forms, perhaps the single view for which Plato is best known, is totally absent from his early works; second, that the early Socrates believes that the human soul is per-fectly unified and that, since all its desires aim at the good, *akrasia*—doing the worse while knowing that something else is better—is impossible, whereas the Platonic Socrates holds that the soul is divided into three parts and that *akrasia* is not only possible but inevitable if the right part—reason—is not strong enough to "rule" the others.

Even if these contrasts are substantiated, as they are, the conclusion that the earlier Socrates mirrors the historical man does not follow: it could still be the case that all the views Socrates is made to express in Plato's dialogues were always Plato's own and that the change in the views Socrates holds simply reflects Plato's changed and broadened philosophical interests. It is at this point, however, that the "triangulation" of which I spoke earlier enters the picture. By means of a careful study of Xenophon's and Aristotle's reports about Socrates, Vlastos comes to the conclusion that on almost every issue concerning these four features both authors attribute to the character *they* call "Socrates" the same views we find attributed to him in Plato's early dialogues. But if, the argument proceeds, two authors who differ from Plato in so many ways can agree with him on these features of Socrates, then, on these points at least, we can be sure that Plato is describing the ideas of a person who existed above and beyond his own works. This, then, is how Vlastos summarizes his findings on the Socratic problem:

> Asking our two main witnesses, Aristotle and Xenophon, to speak to the hypothesis that on four salient points . . . on which [the early] Socrates differs from [the later one], the former speaks for Socrates in Plato, the latter only for Plato, we find Aristotle confirming the hypothesis on all four counts, Xenophon confirming on three out of four,[20] disagreeing with Aristotle on only one of the four, and on this disagreeing with himself. The hypothesis has been confirmed. (106)

My main difficulty with this conclusion can be put simply: Vlastos's hypothesis can be confirmed only if Aristotle and Xenophon had independent access to those views of Socrates that they attribute to him in agreement with Plato—and if, in fact, they agree with Plato as extensively as Vlastos believes they do. If their source for attributing those views to him were Plato's dialogues themselves, which I believe to be the case with most of the important passages in Aristotle and some in Xenophon as well, and if they agree with Plato less than Vlastos believes, which I believe to be the case with Xenophon, then they cannot help much in bringing us closer to the historical character.

Consider the case of Aristotle. First, Vlastos argues that Aristotle distinguishes between the historical Socrates and Plato's character on the basis of his "substantial, though not invariable observance of . . . the so-called 'Fitzgerald's canon,' *Sōkratēs* for the historical figure, *ho Sōkratēs* [the name preceded by the definite article] . . . for the Platonic figure" (97 n. 67). Second, he claims that the views Aristotle attributes to the historical

Socrates, identified by means of his observance of the canon, are just the views Plato attributes to the Socrates of his early dialogues. Finally, he states that Aristotle must have found support for his distinction in the many Socratic dialogues composed by Socrates' other disciples as well as through various people who had known Socrates and whom "Aristotle would have ample opportunity to interrogate" (97).

Every step of this argument raises serious questions. To begin with, as Vlastos admits, Aristotle's observance of Fitzgerald's canon is not invariable. For example, in *Rhetoric* II.23.1398b29–32, Aristotle refers to what can only be the historical Socrates by means of the definite article, which is supposed to be reserved only for his fictional counterpart. By contrast, in *Rhetoric* III.14.1415b30–32, and III.18.1419a8–12, he refers to the fictional character without the definite article.[21] In *Nicomachean Ethics* III.2.1116b3–5, in the course of a discussion of courage, we find the expression *ho Sōkratēs* in a context where, according to Deman, everything, including the tense of the main verb, suggests that the historical Socrates must be the subject.[22] Finally, it seems to me significant that the famous passage of the *Nicomachean Ethics* (VII.2.1145b21 ff.) in which Aristotle discusses the issue of *akrasia* contains only uses of *Sōkratēs* without the article. For Aristotle's allusion to Plato's *Protagoras* 352c is so obvious that even Vlastos admits that this constitutes a "very striking" case of "the fact that many of Aristotle's testimonia about Socrates seem derived directly from Plato's earlier dialogues" (97 n. 69). But if Aristotle can use the expression supposed to designate the historical Socrates even when he is signaling his dependence on Plato's texts, then we cannot rely securely on the view that his usage is a good guide to the distinction it was supposed to mark.

Let us, however, grant that Aristotle's usage is consistent enough and that his texts support a clear distinction between Socrates as a mouthpiece for Platonic views on the one hand and another Socrates on the other. Who is this other Socrates?

Before we try to answer this question, we should make a preliminary remark. It is true, as Vlastos claims, that "in over a third of the 42 testimonia about Socrates included in Deman . . . there is no indication of a Platonic source" (97 n. 69). Still, most of the seventeen Aristotelian texts that Deman classifies as discussing "the great Socratic positions," including his exclusively ethical interests, his concern with definition,[23] his view that knowledge is virtue, and his claim that *akrasia* is impossible, have clear Platonic sources, all among the earlier dialogues. This suggests that Aristotle's reliance on Plato for what he considered as Socrates' main contributions to philosophical thought was quite extensive.[24]

More would follow if, indeed, we knew that historical accuracy was central to Aristotle's concerns and that he actually compared Plato's version with others and found it adequate. But the scholarly approach Vlastos envisions Aristotle to have followed seems both uncharacteristic and anachronistic to me. Still, suppose that Aristotle had in fact checked with other sources. What would he have been likely to find? Clearly, not much on which Aeschines, Antisthenes, Aristippus, "and the rest" (97), who differed so radically from one another in their interpretations of Socrates, would have been in agreement. Their versions of Socrates would have been much more likely to provide further incompatible versions of Socrates than to supply him with clear independent evidence to allow him to accept Plato's (or anyone else's) account as accurate. As Kierkegaard saw, trying to get closer in time to Socrates is not a particularly good way of coming closer to understanding him: the man was a mystery from the very beginning.

Though Vlastos is in general critical and dismissive of Xenophon's testimony regarding Socrates' philosophical positions, he is willing to rely on him as an independent check on Plato's reports of his teacher's actual views. But, in my opinion, Xenophon is not helpful in allowing the genuine Socrates' voice to sound.

Quickly and perhaps dogmatically expressed, the problem is this. It involves two issues. First, the question whether Xenophon's intention was to portray Socrates in a historically accurate way. To Guthrie's view that at least in the *Memorabilia* Xenophon's "earnest desire to reproduce accurately the substance of what he has learned is, in accordance with his purpose, beyond doubt" (345), we must oppose, among many others, the statement of Momigliano that in this work "Xenophon created or perfected a biographical form—the report of conversations preceded by a general introduction to the character of the main speaker—but in actual fact used this form for what amounted as fiction."[25] That is, very serious questions persist about the overall intention of the *Memorabilia*—not to mention Xenophon's *Apology of Socrates*, of which even Guthrie admits that "it is of little or no independent value, and may be set aside in favor of a serious consideration of Plato's writings on the same subject" (20),[26] or his *Symposium*, whose complex relationship to Plato's work of the same title has been the subject of serious discussion.[27]

Perhaps, then, Xenophon's general intention was not to present an accurate picture of the historical Socrates but, rather, an apologetically motivated portrait that was, at best, loosely anchored in reality. Even so, however, it could be argued that on some important issues his portrait does capture Socrates as he actually was. That this is so, and that on those issues Xenophon by and large supports Plato's picture and bolsters its claims to historicity, is Vlastos's claim. But this raises the second issue that confronts his use of Xenophon.

For example, Vlastos claims that at *Memorabilia* iii.9.5, Xenophon attributes to Socrates "part of" his doctrine of the impossibility of incontinence, or *akrasia*. Xenophon does indeed write here that Socrates believed that virtue is wisdom and that those who know what is good will always pursue it and nothing else. Vlastos also tries to interpret a passage at *Memorabilia* iv.5.6, where Xenophon seems to attribute to Socrates a view to the effect that *akrasia* is after all possible so that Xenophon, instead of simply contradicting himself, only misses Socrates' point that no one, temperate or intemperate, can be incontinent (99–101). But even if we accept Vlastos's reading of this passage, the fact remains that Xenophon (on the assumption that Plato gets Socrates' view correctly) is still too confused to be reliable. Plato's *Protagoras* (352a–359a) contains a complex argument for the conclusion that every case of knowing the better and doing the worse is simply a matter of ignorance (of what is truly better and worse) and that in fact there is no such phenomenon as *akrasia*. Yet Xenophon, just before the first of the two passages we are discussing (*Mem.* iii.9.4), attributes to Socrates the view that those who do not know what is good and what is bad are only ignorant *but also incontinent*. Whatever else is the case, then, he attributes a solid existence to the phenomenon Plato's Socrates believed never occurred.

One more example will have to do. "On Socrates' turning away from speculation of the nature of the whole universe," Vlastos writes, "Xenophon is, if anything, even more explicit and emphatic than are Plato and Aristotle" (102). But even though it is correct to say that Xenophon's Socrates considered abstract cosmological speculation as "folly" (*Mem.* i.1.11, with Plato, *Ap.* 19b–d), Xenophon, as we have already seen, attributes to his Socrates, in contrast to Plato's, both a knowledge of and an interest in a number of aspects of geometry, astronomy, and arithmetic (*Mem.* iv.7).

In short, in the case of neither of these crucial features of the Socrates of Plato's early dialogues does Xenophon's testimony give clear and unequivocal support to Plato's interpretation. Add to this the fact that Socrates' most intriguing feature, his disavowal of knowledge, appears only once—and then indirectly—in Xenophon (*Mem.* iv.4.9), while the bulk of his work consists of examples of his rather heavy-handed homespun wisdom, and Xenophon's credentials as an independent source of verification of Plato's picture seem to be at best negligible.

III

We have seen that the silence that consists in Socrates' having written nothing himself has not prevented Vlastos from determining at least part of what he considers to be his genuine voice. This, he believes, is the voice sounding in Plato's early dialogues, to the extent that echoes of it rebound

from the writings of Xenophon and Aristotle. The view, as I have suggested, faces serious difficulties. But suppose that, along with Vlastos and
other scholars, we accept it and rely on Plato for understanding what Socrates was really like.

Once we do this, we are confronted with Socrates' third form of silence,
the most haunting and complex silence we are to encounter.

Xenophon's Socrates, for example, is constantly dispensing advice,
simple wisdom, and explicit guidelines for the behavior of his friends and
companions—and is precisely for that reason, Vlastos correctly argues,
incomparably less interesting than his Platonic counterpart. Far from remaining silent, Xenophon's Socrates is often overwhelmingly voluble—
that is one of the reasons for Kierkegaard's contempt.[28] With Xenophon,
Socrates is all on the surface: both his intentions and his motives are obvious. By contrast, even though the Socrates of Plato's early dialogues
does hold explicit and complex views,[29] as a character he remains deeply
mysterious.

Not that Plato's Socrates is silent in every sense of the term. On the
contrary, he is untiringly engaged in torrential discussions. Though he
often disavows any inclination or ability for long speeches, he is often portrayed delivering them with considerable relish: having tried to abandon
his confrontation with Protagoras on the grounds that, unlike the sophist,
he is only competent in short questions and answers (*Prt.* 334c–338e), he
proceeds to deliver an analysis of Simonides' poem (339d–347a), which is
almost exactly as long as Protagoras' "Great Speech" earlier on in the
dialogue (320c–327d). But though his life, as Plato depicts it, consists of
relentless communication, his talk ultimately communicates very little
about himself.

Gregory Vlastos would never have accepted this claim of mine. Both his
method of investigation, most clearly exhibited in his discussion of Socratic irony, and the substance of his study, which offers a profound personal and philosophical interpretation of Socrates' life and thought, are
based on the following principle regarding Plato's representation of his
teacher:

> Since the depicted character was, above any philosopher of the West, a man
> who lived his philosophy, the writer, deeply conscious of that fact, has reason
> to tell us much about the man's life, including his inner life, allowing us a
> fuller, more intimate, view of the man than is given us of any character, real or
> fictional, in the whole of ancient Greek literature. (51)

In radical disagreement with Kierkegaard, for whom Socrates' exterior in-
timates an inner life that is fundamentally and directly opposed to it,
Vlastos finds in Plato's portrayal of Socrates no dark or incomplete
patches. Though we cannot learn "everything" about Socrates from Plato,

what we learn, so to speak, goes all the way down: it supplies and illuminates a depth that is harmonious with, and accounts for, the surface of its subject: we can succeed where Alcibiades failed.

To see the issue involved here, consider the case of another character, Sophocles' Antigone, who, like Socrates, chooses to die rather than to betray the principles she considers most important in her life. Antigone and Socrates have been treated over the years by different authors in importantly different ways. Critical disagreements about Antigone exist, and various interpreters offer conflicting interpretations of her motivation and actions. But the truly important versions of her character—those of Hegel, for example, and Anouilh—are not *competitors* to Sophocles' vision. Receiving from him the limits, the outline of what she did, they offer alternative combinations of reasons and desires that could have led her to act as she did and, in the process, redescribe the texture and perhaps the substance of her actions. For Hegel, Antigone displays an absolute allegiance to what was only a partial conception of duty and morality; for Anouilh, she is moved by a spirit of resistance to the politically treasonous conformism of Creon.

In saying that these versions are not competitors to Sophocles', that different productions of both Sophocles' and Anouilh's dramas can stand side by side, I do not mean that we cannot decide whether one version is not more convincing or more valuable than another. But however convincing or valuable we find any particular version, our preference does not entail that those we rank lower are inadequate or wrong. Even different critical interpretations of Sophocles' own character, if they are global and convincing enough to underwrite a production of the play, can be placed side by side. Antigone keeps being reinterpreted by critics and dramatists. The proliferation of alternative interpretations of her actions, despite the depth of Sophocles' original characterization, is not only possible but desirable. New versions of Antigone add to their predecessors; they do not displace them. And they add to Antigone herself.

Not so with our versions of Socrates. For Antisthenes, Socrates was the inspiration for Cynicism; for Aristippus, the first Hedonist; for Plato, the figure the present book, among so many others, is trying to decipher. Even his contemporaries, that is, were radically, passionately divided about the nature of his views, the substance of his actions, and the structure of his motives. The situation remained the same in later antiquity. In the eyes of the Academics, he was the first skeptic; for the Stoics, he was as free of disturbing passion as any man who had ever lived; and even the Peripatetics, if Cicero is to be believed (*De Officiis* I.2.5), claimed a connection with him. In modern times, Montaigne saw him as the paradigm of the human being who knew and lived within his natural limits; Kierkegaard approached him as the sophist who uses sophistry to lead people to the truth; Nietzsche, irreconcilably divided, excoriated him for his faith in reason and his admiration of moral virtue and at the same time envied and admired "this most brilliant of all self-outwitters" for the depth of his paradoxical self-understanding.[30] But can these approaches to Socrates survive together? Need none predominate at the others' expense?

There is a fundamental difference between the proliferation of images of Socrates and of renderings of Antigone. Each of the many versions of Socrates makes a strong claim, not made by most of those of Antigone, to being true. If we accept Nietzsche's view of Socrates (and it is a view, we must emphasize, which refers back to roughly the same texts of Plato that are also Vlastos's own concern), then we simply cannot accept Vlastos's interpretation, and conversely. If one is correct, the other is not. Or so it seems.

The most obvious response to this asymmetry is to argue that Antigone, who is simply a literary or fictional character, has no "real story" to which we are to be faithful. By contrast, Socrates was surely a historical character, even if we have no reliable account of what he had to say, and there must have been a real story about him that needs to be recaptured. This real story, which can be only one in number, accounts for the competition between the different accounts of his thought.[31]

But the situation is not so simple. Even if we agree that there must be a "real story" behind Socrates' various representations, we need not believe that this story would consist of his accepting one of the various approaches that his disciples and later interpreters were eager to attribute to him. Perhaps the most central element in Socrates' "real story" is precisely his ability to have given rise to so many diametrically opposed interpretations. Perhaps the most accurate retelling of his real story would be an account that explained, if at all possible, how a single man could have been understood so differently by so many of his closest associates.[32]

It would be better, I believe, to argue that the fundamental difference between Antigone and Socrates is that the latter, however literary a creation, is still a *philosopher*, the truth of whose views is essential to the nature of his character. Accordingly, one might say, it is an ineradicable part of the enterprise of understanding Socrates to determine whether the views attributed to him are or are not true—a concern that does not affect our understanding of the tragic nature of Antigone and her choice. What matters with her is, to a great extent, the intensity of her conviction that her position is right; but such a conviction is not sufficient in Socrates' case. Unless Socrates is not only passionately committed to his views but also correct, then his life, no less than his philosophy, loses a large part of its claim to our allegiance and admiration. Under some interpretation of the nature of the values that he accepts, in fact, it may even become (as it does, for example, on some versions of Nietzsche's reading) not a mode of life to follow but one to avoid.

Yet this explanation of the difference is only partially correct. The strength of Antigone's convictions is not quite enough to make her the character she is; others, after all, including Creon, could hold on to their beliefs with equal or even greater passion. Antigone goes to her death not for any chance view or value, but for a set of principles that we consider intrinsically important and worth dying for. To this extent, she and Socrates are not so different from one another. The serious difference between them emerges when we ask about Antigone's motivation for going to her death rather than betraying her values. All sorts of different motives, some of them quite incompatible with others, still permit her to remain, if not always an admirable person, at least a great literary character. So a production of Sophocles' tragedy that explained her behavior more in terms of a pathological attachment to her brother rather than in terms of her devotion to justice could stand next to a large number of other interpretations.

This is impossible in the case of Socrates. Precisely because he is a philosopher, he can be admirable only if he acts out of a belief that his principles are true: he can have no other motives. Any attempt to give an alternative account of his motivation (Nietzsche's effort, for example, to portray him as a decadent whose instincts were too strong for him to control without tyrannizing them) robs him of a large measure of his ethical stature. It is in that sense that Socrates must be correct as well as passionate if he is to play the exemplary role that is so often claimed for him.

If this interpretation is correct, however, then it points to a further truth that should make us pause before we conclude that we do, in fact, know who Socrates was, that our knowledge of his inner life is as intimate as the present book claims. As we have already said, the history of Socrates' influence is a history of the most intense and profound disagreement. With the exception of the Epicureans, every philosophical school in antiquity, whatever is orientation, saw in him either its actual founder or the type of person to whom its adherents were to aspire. Conflict over his views has not stopped at the question of their nature, but has extended even to the issue whether he did or did not hold any views at all in the first place.

If we keep in mind that most of these (and many other) disputes are ultimately provoked by Plato's early dialogues, then we may well come to wonder what Plato actually tells us about the "inner life" of his hero. And even if we refuse to accept Kierkegaard's view that Socrates' exterior points to an interior fundamentally opposed to it, we may still suspect that, however detailed Plato's picture actually is, it is nothing like the "full" and "intimate" picture Vlastos envisages—if these words describe an account that presents not only the texture of its subject but also an explanation of what makes that texture what it is.

I would like to suggest that the construction of an intimate picture in this sense is not at all Plato's creation but, perhaps ironically, the great achievement of Gregory Vlastos's book. For it is Vlastos who goes, so to speak, under the surface of the Platonic Socrates and provides strands that can hold his peculiar views and mode of life together. Vlastos has produced one of the most systematic interpretations of Socrates' views and personality ever to have been accomplished. In its sweep and generality, in its attention to the interactions between Socrates' thought, character, and life, this book rises above all recent scholarship. Its rivals, and equals, are the two great nineteenth-century works on Socrates, Grote's and Zeller's.[33] One might even say that its approach is so systematic and the positions it attributes to Socrates are so definite and clear that it may well raise the question of how this Socrates could have provoked so many diverse readings and reconstructions over the centuries.

IV

What is particularly striking about this study is that it belongs squarely to the "analytical" approach to the history of Greek philosophy. This is an approach that Gregory Vlastos himself pioneered in the United States in the mid-1950s. It pays particular attention to argument and addresses problems that can be put in direct contact with questions attracting contemporary attention. Although it attracted a whole generation of scholars, its considerable gains were obtained at a certain cost. Extensive attention to Plato's arguments obscures a view of the overall literary structure of his dialogues. More to our present point, it made it difficult to pay attention to Socrates as a whole, as a character and a personality no less than as a proponent of arguments and an advocate of theories. The discussion of various substantive views that could be found in the dialogues flourished in an unprecedented manner in the past half-century. But throughout this period, the personality of Socrates, which is one of the main reasons why Plato continues to fascinate, to attract, and, often, even to repel so many readers, was systematically ignored. The manner in which analytical philosophy addressed the dialogues appeared to leave no room for attention to this crucial issue.

But, as it turns out, the appearance was deceptive, and it took the originator of the approach to show how much more it could accomplish. Vlastos remains very close to the Platonic text and examines minutely the texture of Socrates' arguments. Nevertheless, he reconstructs much more than a set of theories that Socrates may have held. He also constructs a person, a complex and lively character with whom we can come to terms only as a whole.

Vlastos's main device for constructing that character is his version of Socrates' irony. This constitutes, in my opinion, the most provocative and controversial aspect of this work. Vlastos's interpretation of irony enables him to attribute to Socrates a complex attitude both toward his own theories and toward the manner in which he wants his disciples to come to accept them. Very briefly, the idea is the following.

Socrates is for Vlastos an ironist of a very peculiar kind. When he uses words ironically in a philosophical context, he always operates with two senses in mind, explicitly denying, for example, that he possesses knowledge, or that he is a teacher, or that he engages in politics, in one sense of these terms, but implicitly affirming the very same thesis in another. In contrast to "simple" irony, where what is said is simply the opposite of what is meant, Socrates' "complex" irony involves his not meaning what he says in the common, accepted sense of these words and hence his appearing profoundly paradoxical; Socrates does, however, mean what he says when his words are taken according to his own, innovative understanding. Most important, he absolutely refuses to explain to his interlocutors what the difference between those two senses is: this, like so much else in connection with his views, his teaching, his personality, and even his feelings (as Alcibiades inadvertently reveals in the *Symposium*), was something he wanted them to come to learn solely by themselves.

Vlastos can therefore attribute to Socrates a large number of substantive moral views despite the latter's consistent denials that he holds them. For the denials are ironical, and irony now turns out to be only a mask and a teacher's device:

> In the conventional sense, where to "teach" is simply to transfer knowledge from a teacher's to a learner's mind, Socrates means what he says. But in the sense *he* would give to "teaching"—engaging would-be learners in elenctic argument to make them aware of their own ignorance and enable them to discover for themselves *the truth the teacher had held back*—in that sense of "teaching" Socrates would want to say that he is a teacher, the only true teacher: his dialogue with his fellows is meant to have, and does have, the effect of evoking and assisting their efforts at moral self-improvement. (32)

The phrase I have italicized within this quotation constitutes the heart of the interpretation of Socrates to be found in this book. Not that there is not much else to that interpretation besides: Vlastos's rationalist interpretation of Socrates' religiosity—one of the most engaging and convincing elements in the work—his attribution to him of an absolute rejection of retaliation as a moral procedure, his interpretation of Socrates' eudaimonism as involving what Vlastos calls the "sovereignty" of virtue—all these are substantial theories, supported by careful argument, and bound to be discussed at length. But the most important and most controversial element in Vlastos's interpretation of Socrates is his governing assumption that there are truths that Socrates knows and that he knows that he knows.

This Socrates is, in the ancient sense of that term, a dogmatist: he knows the truth. His ironic denials that he possesses knowledge and that he teaches it, once interpreted as Vlastos proposes, disappear into protreptic devices designed to get others to see that truth for themselves.

Should we then allow Socratic irony to transform itself so quickly into an educational ploy? Does Socrates really abandon his silence, dividing his listeners into two groups, one (which includes all of his interlocutors in Plato's dialogues) consisting of those who "may indeed see but not perceive, and may indeed hear but not understand," and another (which, it fortunately turns out, includes most of us) consisting of those who both see and perceive, who both hear and understand, and for whom his silence is only an invitation to listen more carefully for his voice? Could the Socrates presented in this book have inspired the almost endlessly different efforts to come to terms with him and with his "strangeness"? Is, in fact, this strangeness something we should want to account for, to explain, perhaps even to explain away? Or should we rather try to leave it intact, considering any effort to come to terms with it, such as Vlastos's own, as just one more of its products, another one of its symptoms?

I believe we should try to leave Socratic irony intact, for many reasons. One is that Vlastos's main evidence for his interpretation of Socratic irony—an interpretation, note, that identifies it closely with what passes for the "Socratic method" in the practice of many of our law schools today—comes from the *Gorgias* (515a, 521d). But the *Gorgias,* as I have already argued, is much more plausibly read as a Platonic text and, along with the *Meno,* as one of the very earliest efforts—Plato's own—to come to terms with Socrates' silence, to disarm his irony, and to claim him as the first in a long tradition of moral teachers eager to transmit positive views to others.

Another reason is that I do not believe Plato's early dialogues show that Socrates "does have" the beneficial effect Vlastos attributes to him in the passage I quoted above. Protagoras, Gorgias, Polus, Callicles, Hippias, Thrasymachus, Euthydemus, and Dionysiodorus remain totally unmoved. So do Euthyphro and Meno. "Moral improvement" is not really an apt characterization of the trajectory of Critias' and Charmides' lives. The end of the *Laches,* as well as that of the *Lysis,* leaves the question of Socrates' long-term influence completely unresolved. And as for Alcibiades, neither history nor his own admission (*Symposium* 216b) can leave us with any illusions.

Both his friends and his enemies considered Socrates a teacher and believed he had knowledge that he would not divulge. But this is no reason to refuse to take his own disavowals at face value—unless we make the dubious assumption, denied by Kierkegaard, that his contemporaries must have known him better than we do. Taking his disavowals as complex ironies robs him of his strangeness and in fact eliminates his irony. Assuming, by contrast, that he was sincere supplies him with a much more profound ironical mask after all—a mask that it is difficult, if not impossible, to remove. For now he turns out to be someone who, precisely in disavowing ethical knowledge and the ability to provide it for others, succeeded in living as moral a life as anyone who belongs in the tradition he himself originated.

And he does not let us know how. This, in turn, is a profound instance of irony. For irony cannot simply be defined, as Vlastos, following the tradition originating in Quintilian, defines it, as saying one thing and meaning the opposite—a definition that ultimately applies to complex irony as well. Often, irony consists in letting your audience know that something is taking place inside you that they simply are not allowed to see. But it also, more radically, leaves open the question whether you are seeing it yourself: speakers are not always in the privileged position in relation to themselves that Quintilian attributes to them. Irony often communicates the fact that the audience is not getting the whole picture; but it does not necessarily imply that the speaker has that picture or that, indeed, there is a whole picture to be understood in the first place.[34]

Irony constructs a mask. It leaves open the question what, if anything, is masked. It is because of this that I am unwilling to accept Vlastos's view that Plato's earlier dialogues allow us to see into Socrates' depths. On the contrary, I believe that, in this sense, the Socrates we meet in these texts has no depth. That he does is an idea that emerges in the *Gorgias* and the *Meno* and finds its first extensive expression in Alcibiades' speech in the *Symposium,* even though Alcibiades' revelations leave his mystery untouched.[35]

Coming to terms with Socrates involves explaining why he has given rise to so many diametrically opposed interpretations even when he is studied only through Plato's texts. The conception of irony of which I have given the barest idea here can help in this endeavor. It is certainly not a conception Gregory Vlastos would have accepted, and it forms the basis of a profound disagreement between us. But I believe that, if I were able to support it as it should be supported, he would have been eager to discuss it with me. His passion for argument, for intense but friendly intellectual confrontation, was phenomenal. It is a passion evident throughout *Socrates: Ironist and Moral Philosopher,* which invites debate at every turn. Methodologically novel, the work combines a theoretical with a personal approach to Socrates, and takes a position both on the nature of the literary character depicted in Plato's dialogues and on the relation of that character to the historical figure who inspired it. Whether we agree with Vlastos's conclusions or not, we must admire the way in which the book combines the ancients' fascination with Socrates' virtue with the moderns' concern with his rationality. In pursuing these two traits and their interconnections, it succeeds in exhibiting them itself. And so it manifests the very features of the Socrates it has created and adds its own, marvelous voice to the echoes that answer Socrates' paradoxical silence.[36]

Notes

1. Søren Kierkegaard, *The Concept of Irony* (*With Continual References to Socrates*), ed. and trans. Howard V. Hong and Edna H. Hong (Princeton, 1989), 11–12.

2. Gregory Vlastos, *Socrates: Ironist and Moral Philosopher* (Ithaca, 1991).

3. W.K.C. Guthrie, *A History of Greek Philosophy*, vol. 3: *The Fifth-Century Enlightenment* (Cambridge, 1971), 326.

4. A complete edition of the writings of, and of the reports about, the "minor Socratics," with the exception of Aeschines, is available in Gabriele Giannantoni, *Socraticorum Reliquiae*, 2d ed. (Rome, 1990). For Aeschines, see Heinrich Dittmar, *Aischines von Sphettos: Studien zu Literaturgeschichte der Sokratiker* (Berlin, 1912).

5. A detailed account of Socrates' portrayal in the *Clouds* can be found in the introduction to K. J. Dover's edition, *Aristophanes' "Clouds"* (Oxford, 1968). Dover's presentation of the evidence is masterful, though his interpretation, to the effect that Aristophanes satirizes Socrates only as a representative of the interests of the time, as a "generic intellectual," is not totally convincing. This does not, however, imply that Aristophanes' play, correcting for the comic poet's exaggerations, ultimately offers direct and deserved criticisms of Socrates (this is the position of Martha Nussbaum, "Aristophanes and Socrates on Learning the Practical Wisdom," *Yale Classical Studies* 26 [1980]: 43–97). An excellent alternative interpretation can be found in John A. Palmer, "Aristophanes' Parody of Socrates," unpublished manuscript, Princeton University, 1991. Palmer argues, among other things, that the play establishes a series of parallels between Socrates and Aristophanes himself, and that Aristophanes' parody (in contrast to satire) of Socrates is also an attack on a public who failed to understand Socrates as it failed to appreciate, and award the prize to, Aristophanes' "most clever (*sōphōtatē*) comedy" (*Nu.* 522).

6. The principle is stated in F. Schleiermacher, *Über den Wert des Sokrates als Philosophen*, in his *Gesammelte Werke*, vol. III, 2 (Berlin, 1838), 297.

7. An interesting selection of such writings, along with a surprisingly extensive bibliography, can be found in Mario Montuori, *De Socrate Iuste Damnato: The Rise of the Socratic Problem in the Eighteenth Century* (Amsterdam, 1981).

8. Guthrie, 329. The reference is to Auguste Diès, *Autour de Platon* (Paris, 1927), 157–59.

9. A. E. Taylor, *The Mind of Plato* (Ann Arbor, 1960), 32.

10. See A. E. Taylor, *Plato: The Man and His Work* (Cleveland, 1956), 199–200.

11. John Burnet, *Plato's "Phaedo": edited with introduction and notes by John Burnet* (Oxford, 1911), xi–xii. Burnet's introduction to the dialogue still remains one of the great essays on Plato and Socrates.

12. E. Dupréel, *La légende socratique et les sources de Plato* (Brussels, 1922).

13. Olof Gigon, *Sokrates, sein Bild in Dichtung und Geschichte* (Bern, 1947).

14. Anton-Hermann Chroust, *Socrates, Man and Myth* (London, 1977), xii.

15. See his "Afterthoughts on the Socratic Elenchus," *Oxford Studies in Ancient Philosophy* 1 (1983): 71–74.

16. W. H. Thompson, *The "Gorgias" of Plato* (London, 1871), ix, xii–xx.

17. E. R. Dodds, *Plato: "Gorgias"* (Oxford, 1959), 18–30.

18. Terence Irwin, *Plato: "Gorgias"* (Oxford, 1979), 5–9.

19. An unorthodox position, reading the *Gorgias* as one of Plato's earliest philosophical dialogues, has been maintained in a series of articles by Charles Kahn. See, for example, "Did Plato Write Socratic Dialogues?" *Classical Quarterly* 31 (1981): 305–20, and "On the Relative Date of the *Gorgias* and the *Protagoras*," *Oxford Studies in Ancient Philosophy* 6 (1988): 69–102.

20. This qualification needs to be explained. On the issue of Socrates' profession of ignorance, Xenophon's testimony does not support the picture of Plato and Aristotle; in general, Xenophon is quite silent on this issue. But on one occasion (*Mem.* iv.4.9), he actually gives an indication that he, too, is aware of Socrates' refusal (or inability) to produce positive views of his own.

21. Aristotle is here referring indirectly to Plato's *Menexenus* 235d and *Apology* 27c–e. Thomas Deman, *Le témoignage d'Aristotle sur Socrate* (Paris, 1942), who generally tries to show that Aristotle's usage is consistent, suggests that Aristotle may be referring to the historical Socrates, "though through the discourse of Plato" (63). In the case of *Magna Moralia* I.1.1183b8–11, where Aristotle uses the article to refer to Socrates in what might seem a historical context despite his omission of it in a number of nearby texts, Deman writes that since Socrates had been named earlier in the text, the use of the article could well signify something like "the aforementioned (*le dit*) Socrates" (95). But the reference Deman has in mind seems to occur at 1182a15–23, which seems somewhat far for the sort of connection he needs to have been established.

22. See Deman, 102–3, for a statement of the situation and an effort to establish an alternative to the position of W. D. Ross, *Aristotle's Metaphysics* (Oxford, 1924), xl, that this is the fictional Socrates, without having to conclude that Aristotle's usage is inconsistent (Ross's whole discussion of this issue, xxxix–xli, is worth consulting).

23. Though Aristotle's claim that Socrates was concerned with the definition of "universal," which he did not (in contrast to Plato) "separate" from sensible objects, as a basis for engaging in syllogistic thought (cf. *Metaphysics* I.6.987b1–6, XIII.9.1086a37–b5, XIII.4.1078b17–32) seems to me to go beyond the Platonic evidence and to represent a clear instance of Aristotle's practice of reading his own interests into his predecessors' endeavors.

24. W. D. Ross, in his own effort to argue that Aristotle affords us evidence about Socrates that is independent of Plato, argues that Aristotle "could not have learned from the dialogues that Cratylus was Plato's first master; nothing in the *Cratylus* or elsewhere in Plato suggests it" ("The Problem of Socrates," in Andreas Patzer, ed., *Der historische Sokrates* [Darmstadt, 1987], 234). But, of course, that Aristotle had independent evidence about *Plato's* career—which is what this testimony concerns—is totally irrelevant to showing that his knowledge of Socrates

was not derived from Plato. Interestingly, Vlastos misquotes Ross's statement, which he quotes approvingly, and substitutes "Socrates" for "Plato" in the phrase concerning Cratylus, Plato's "first master" (97 n. 69).

25. Arnaldo Momigliano, *The Development of Greek Biography* (Cambridge, Mass., 1971), 54.

26. On Xenophon's *Apology of Socrates,* see also Paul Vander Waerdt, "Socratic Justice and Self-Sufficiency: The Story of the Delphic Oracle in Xenophon's *Apology of Socrates,*" unpublished manuscript, 1992.

27. On this issue, and for a negative assessment of Xenophon as a source for the views of the historical Socrates, see Heinrich Maier, *Sokrates, sein Werk und seine geschichtliche Stellung* (Tübingen, 1913), esp. 17–19.

28. "Xenophon portrays in Socrates not that beautiful, harmonious unity of natural determinant and freedom indicated in the term σωφροσύνη but a graceless composite of cynicism and bourgeois philistinism. . . . Instead of the good, we have the useful, instead of the beautiful the utilitarian, instead of the true the established, instead of the sympathetic the lucrative, instead of harmonious unity the pedestrian"; Kierkegaard, *The Concept of Irony,* 24–25.

29. For example, chapter 7 of Vlastos's book, "Socrates' Rejection of Retaliation," presents just such an articulate and carefully thought-out position on Socrates' part—though the question whether the position is Socrates' or Plato's own is still, in my opinion, open.

30. Friedrich Nietzsche, *The Twilight of the Idols,* in Walter Kaufmann, ed., *The Viking Portable Nietzsche* (New York, 1954), 479.

31. This point was put to me in eloquent terms by Charles Kahn, for whose comments on an earlier version of this essay I am very grateful.

32. See Donald Morrison, "On Professor Vlastos's Xenophon," *Ancient Philosophy* 7 (1987): 9–22, who urges that we should cease paying attention to

the *noumenon* Socrates—Socrates in himself, the way he actually, historically was—while retaining a vivid interest in the *phenomenon* Socrates—that is, Socrates as he is manifested through his influence on his followers, and more generally on the culture around him. Think of each of the Socratics as a facet through which Socrates may be viewed. The view through each facet is different. The views are of the same object, yet they are not reducible to any simple unity. (19)

33. See George Grote, *Plato and the Other Companions of Sokrates,* 3d ed. (London, 1875), and Eduard Zeller, *Sokrates und die Sokratiker,* in *Die Philosophie der Griechen,* 4th ed. (Berlin, 1889).

34. This feature of irony is obvious even in one of Vlastos's own examples of "simple" irony, the case of Mae West declining Gerald Ford's invitation to dinner at the White House because, she said, "It's an awful long way to go for just one meal" (21–22). Though Vlastos suggests that Mae West may be presenting us with a riddle here, he does not notice that it is very difficult to say exactly what "the opposite" of what she said actually is. In fact, I believe there is no such opposite, even if, behaviorally, the net result of her statement was that Mae West did not have dinner with the Fords. Even everyday cases of irony, that is, leave the issue of what the speaker "really meant" less determinate than rhetorical theory tempts us to suppose.

35. An issue left untouched in discussions of Socratic irony is that of the irony exhibited in *Plato's* own text—a deep and disdainful irony directed toward his readers. This is too large a subject even to broach here. I discuss some aspects of it in this book's essay "What Did Socrates Teach and to Whom Did He Teach It?" in which some of the material presented above can also be found, along with a number of other questions raised by Vlastos's *Socrates: Ironist and Moral Philosopher.*

36. Paul Kalligas read an earlier version of this essay. I am grateful for his detailed comments and his valuable suggestions.

Five

ERISTIC, ANTILOGIC, SOPHISTIC, DIALECTIC: PLATO'S DEMARCATION OF PHILOSOPHY FROM SOPHISTRY

WRITING in 345 B.C.—over fifty years after Socrates' death and over twenty after the composition of the *Republic*—the orator Aeschines could refer to Socrates as "the sophist" without giving any indication that he felt his description needed any justification.[1] And already in 370 B.C., Isocrates had grouped together a number of people in a way that, at least to us today, may appear absolutely unacceptable. Three classes of people, Isocrates writes in his *Helen,* find pleasure in offering plausible defenses of implausible theses: first, those who argue that falsehood and contradiction do not exist; second, those who occupy themselves with contentious disputations (ἔριδες) that benefit none and annoy all; finally—and this is where the shock comes—those who, presumably like Socrates and Plato, believe that all the virtues are one and connected with a single kind of knowledge.[2]

These texts indicate that in the eyes of the generation or two following him no less than in the mind of his contemporaries (as Aristophanes' *Clouds* demonstrates), Socrates remained closely connected with those who, at least in Plato's dialogues, are portrayed as his most bitter and dangerous opponents. And, at least for Isocrates, Plato himself was on the sophistic and eristic side of the distinction between philosophy and its early rivals.

It is perhaps tempting simply to dismiss this classification of Socrates as a sophist and an eristic as the result of a philistine misunderstanding, a superficial confusion between sophistry and genuine philosophy, for which Aristophanes' crude wit may have been ultimately responsible. But the cost of this easy dismissal, I believe, is both historical inaccuracy and philosophical shallowness. It is worth our while to consider our evidence once again. In particular, it is important to reexamine the way in which Plato tried to distinguish Socrates from the sophists, and dialectic from eristic.

In the course of such a reexamination it is important to keep in mind the fact that Plato and Aristotle are not the only authors to have been concerned with the nature of philosophy during the fourth century B.C. The reason for keeping this in mind is not that Plato, with whom I shall mainly be concerned in what follows, is unjustifiably partial or misleading. On the contrary, I propose to argue, Plato's own views are considerably more equivocal and complicated than we commonly suppose. But if we pay no attention to his rivals' different points of view, we lose the opportunity to develop what we might describe as a stereoscopic image of the issue and to construct a deeper and richer picture of the relationship between philosophy and sophistry.

The testimony of Isocrates, who fought long and hard to win the term "philosophy" for his own educational scheme and to deny it of the system of Plato, is particularly important. But Plato, though certainly the most significant, was not Isocrates' only rival. What is crucial for our own purposes is the company in which Isocrates places Plato, the group that, as a whole, he opposes to philosophy as he conceives it.

Isocrates contrasts himself with Protagoras and Gorgias, who were universally acknowledged as sophists: Protagoras, according to Plato, made much of his willingness to accept that characterization (*Prt.* 316c–317c). Isocrates classifies Gorgias and Protagoras together with Zeno and Melissus, whom Plato and Aristotle would have been willing to consider— though perhaps not without reservations—among their own predecessors, and hence as philosophers of a sort.[3] He describes Parmenides and Empedocles, whom Plato took extremely seriously, explicitly as sophists, and claims that they are at best useful as a propaedeutic to real philosophy.[4] Isocrates considers Parmenides and Empedocles as members of the camp of Alcmaeon, Ion, Melissus, and Gorgias because, he makes it very clear, he finds all their views on the natural universe equally unacceptable. He puts into one single category both "those who are skilled in contentious arguments" (οἱ ἐν τοῖς ἐριστικοῖς λόγοις δυναστεύοντες) and the teachers of geometry, astronomy, and other scientific subjects–a group that presumably included Theodorus and Eudoxus as well as Hippias. And he claims that, at the very best, these people and their subjects have a limited usefulness—if, that is, they function as preparation for philosophy.[5]

In this last, Isocrates sounds like a direct echo of Plato. But the similarity between their views is purely verbal. Philosophy for Isocrates has nothing to do with the abstract study of reality with which Plato identifies it in the *Phaedo*, the *Republic*, and thereafter. Isocrates thinks of a philosophy as ἡ τῶν λόγων παιδεία, the ability to speak well, which in turn reflects and is the product of the ability to think well and shrewdly about practical matters.[6] His picture is just the inverse of the picture Plato develops in the middle books of the *Republic* and to which, in this respect at least, he returns in the *Philebus* (55c–58b). Plato argues that the more a method of investigation depends on mathematics, the closer it comes to the truth. Isocrates dismisses mathematical precision as a waste of time. He urges his listeners toward an overwhelmingly practical direction, and considers the

mathematical and dialectical training advocated by Plato only a hindrance.
Isocrates urges us

> to search for the truth and to educate our associates in connection with the
> activities regarding the government of the city and to train them in relation to
> the experience of these things, keeping in mind that it is much better to have
> reasonable opinions about useful matters than precise knowledge about mat-
> ters of no use and to have a slight advantage in important matters rather than
> to excel greatly in matters of no importance and of no value to life.[7]

It is not my purpose here to argue that either Plato or Isocrates was correct
in his conception of the nature of philosophy, especially since I believe, on
independent grounds, that this is not a question that can ever be answered.
Indeed, I might say that this is precisely the point I am trying to make in
historical terms in this essay.

The reason why it is important to remind ourselves of Isocrates' views,
crude as they may appear, is that they make it clear that in the fourth
century B.C. terms like "philosophy," "dialectic," and "sophistry" do not
seem to have had a widely agreed-upon application. On the contrary, different authors seem to have fought with one another with the purpose of
appropriating the term "philosophy," each for his own practice and educational scheme. In the long run, of course, Plato (followed in this respect,
and despite their many differences, by Aristotle) emerged victorious. He
thereby established what philosophy is by contrasting it not only with sophistry but also with rhetoric, poetry, traditional religion, and the specialized sciences. This was a grandiose project, and on this occasion I can
only take a quick look at one of its smaller parts: the way in which Plato
proposed to distinguish Socrates from the sophists.

The most influential modern account of the distinction between Socrates and the sophists describes it as a difference in *method* of investigation
and argument. This account goes back to Henry Sidgwick and George
Grote.[8] A closer look, however, shows that when Grote and Sidgwick
wrote of "method" they had very different things in mind.

Sidgwick believed that Socrates was the inventor of the method of
question-and-answer that he is shown to practice in Plato's early dialogues, while the sophists developed the art of delivering long speeches,
often called ἐπιδείξεις, on given subjects. But not only is there no independent evidence that this method was in fact Socrates' invention: on the
contrary, the sophists are frequently portrayed as capable of practicing it in
Plato's dialogues. Gorgias, for example, claims that he can answer questions διὰ μακρῶν, which suggests that he could deliver an oration in answer to a specific question, as well as ἐν βραχυτέροις or διὰ βραχυλογίας,
which is much more in line with the Socratic elenchus (*G.* 449b–c). Socrates relies on Protagoras' reputation to be skilled both in μακρολογία

("speaking long") and in βραχυλογία ("speaking short") in order to insist that their discussion proceed by means of question-and-answer, the only method with which he claims to be comfortable.[9] Protagoras in fact claims that these two modes of speaking are species of dialectic, of conversation, and that though he is skilled in both, he is not willing always to follow the method his interlocutors prefer: if he did, he asks, how could he have won his dialectical bouts as consistently as he did (*Prt.* 335a)? Finally, and notoriously, Euthydemus and Dionysiodorus are clearly both practitioners and teachers of an art of question-and-answer, referred to by Socrates as ἐριστικὴ σοφία ("eristic wisdom").[10] The method of question-and-answer is not the exclusive province of Socrates.

In contrast to Sidgwick, when Grote wrote that the difference between Euthydemus and Dionysiodorus on the one hand and Socrates on the other "consists, first, in the pretensions—next in method,"[11] he meant that the two sophists were arrogant, professed to teach anyone what virtue is, and were ready to claim a fee for their services. But Socrates never asked for money, was uncertain whether virtue could be taught, and claimed to be able to help only willing pupils. He aimed to encourage and guide, and was indifferent to his effect on the rest of his audience, while the sophists aimed to humiliate the young Cleinias by any means that would win the approval and the applause of the bystanders.

I think that Grote's use of the term "method" in this context was particularly unfortunate. For, with the exception of the conscious use of fallacious argument, to which I shall return, none of the features mentioned in the previous paragraph are strictly speaking methodological features at all. In fact, Grote saw that the central difference between Socrates and the two sophists lies in their different moral interests, in their overall purpose:[12] Grote's view was a modern expression of Aristotle's statement that philosophy differs from sophistry "in that it chooses a different kind of life" (*Metaphysics* IV.2.1004b24–25). But the word "method" unfortunately took hold, and various authors have tried to distinguish Socrates from the sophists in general by means of appealing to differences in their respective methods.

A most sophisticated variant of such an effort appears in George Kerferd's *The Sophistic Movement*.[13] Kerferd approaches this issue by turning his attention to Plato's use of the related terms "eristic," "antilogic," and "dialectic," and by trying to determine Plato's conception of and attitude toward the activities associated with them. His view has been at least partly accepted by both Gregory Vlastos and Terence Irwin.[14]

To begin with, Kerferd writes, Plato considers dialectic to be, if not identical with philosophy, at least its proper method. Kerferd then argues that though eristic is not a method of argument, antilogic is such a method; moreover, if it is followed properly, antilogic constitutes the first stage of dialectic. These distinctions allow Kerferd to claim that Plato can draw a *neutral* distinction between philosophy and other argumentative practices, like sophistry, on the basis of their respective methods. Sophistry is eristic, and consists in the misguided practice of antilogic; dialectic, by contrast, begins with antilogic correctly practiced and proceeds to true philosophy. Kerferd writes:

> As Plato uses the term, eristic means "seeking victory in argument," and the art which cultivates and provides appropriate means for so doing. Concern for the truth is not a necessary part of the art—victory in argument can be secured without it, sometimes more easily so. It follows that eristic as such is not strictly speaking a *technique* of argument. It can use any one or more than one of a series of techniques in order to achieve its aim, which is success in debate or at least the appearance of such success. (62–63)

Though I am perfectly willing to agree that for Plato eristic does not constitute a method of argument, I must also make two additional remarks. First, it is far from obvious that Plato believes that to argue eristically is consciously to use fallacious arguments.[15] A treatise like Protagoras' *Technē Eristikōn* need not have contained instructions for the use of fallacious arguments, and we have no evidence that it did. Plato, moreover, does not portray Protagoras as likely to use such arguments. On the contrary, it is Protagoras who catches Socrates arguing fallaciously at *Protagoras* 350c ff. Second, if people like Euthydemus and Dionysiodorus did in fact exist and did use fallacious arguments intentionally, they would not, I think, be willing to grant the distinction between real and merely apparent victory that Kerferd draws above. The distinction between what is real and what is merely apparent is, precisely, an involved philosophical idea that, as Plato clearly shows in the *Sophist*, cannot be accepted without complicated and controversial argument.

This strikes me as an important point. One of the features that distinguishes Socrates from the sophists, as Gregory Vlastos has reminded us, is that though the Socratic elenchus is an adversarial procedure, its object is always the discovery of the truth. The elenchus, Vlastos writes,

> remains in principle a method of searching for truth, which eristic is not, but only a method (or set of methods—a whole bag of tricks) for winning arguments, regardless of whether or not you take what you are arguing for to be true. (31 n. 14)

Now I think that it is absolutely correct to say that Socrates always pursues the elenchus in order to discover the truth. But, we must ask, what criterion of truth does the elenchus afford? What else but the always fallible criterion supplied by dialectical victory, by the ability to defend your position against dialectical attack? As late as the middle books of the *Republic*,

Plato himself envisages a connection between victory in argument and knowledge of the truth:

> The man who cannot by reason distinguish the Form of the Good from all others, who does not, *as in a battle,* survive all refutations, eager to argue according to reality and not according to opinion, and who does not come through *all the tests* without faltering in reasoned discourse—such a man you will say does not know the Good itself, nor any kind of good. (*Rep.* 534c; trans. Grube, italics added)

Plato may have by then relegated dialectical invincibility to the status of what is at most a necessary condition for knowing the truth: awareness of the Forms and of their interrelations is also essential. But victory in argument, I think, had to be close to being both necessary and sufficient for the knowledge of the truth in the Socratic dialogues, from which both the Forms and their apprehension are markedly absent.

Now one could say, quite correctly, that a major difference between Socrates and sophists like Euthydemus and Dionysiodorus was that, unlike them, he was never willing to use arguments that he knew to be fallacious. Socrates would never ascribe to himself the desire or the ability "to fight in verbal battles and to refute anything that is said, regardless of whether it is true or false" (*Euthydemus* 272b). But to be able to appeal to this as a neutral, methodological distinction, we need a general theory of fallacious arguments, of the sophisms or eristic syllogisms that Aristotle, significantly, defined as "syllogisms which start from opinions that seem to be reputable, but are not really such, or again which merely seem to reason from opinions that are or seem to be reputable" (*Topics* I.100b23–25; cf. *Sophistici Elenchi* 11). The definition is significant because it shows that we have to appeal to the distinction between reality and appearance in order to support the distinction between real and apparent victory in argument and to claim, with Aristotle, that eristic syllogism should not really be called "syllogism, since it appears to deduce, but in fact does not" (*Top.* I.1.101a3–4). Without such a theory, I think, it is difficult to say why fallacious arguments should in general be avoided.

As I said above, however, I think that Kerferd is still quite correct in holding that Plato uses the term "eristic" as a term of abuse, not in order to refer to a method of argument but, instead, to various *misuses* of dialectic. What I do not accept is his view that antilogic, by contrast,

> when used in argument . . . constitutes a specific and fairly definite technique, namely that of proceeding from a given logos, say the position adopted by an opponent, to the establishment of a contrary or contradictory logos in such a way that the opponent must either accept both logoi, or at least abandon his first position. (63)

Kerferd claims to find this conception of antilogic expressed at *Lysis* 216a. But this passage does not serve him well. Socrates here has argued to the view that opposites are most friendly to one another. He now describes this as ἀλλόκοτον (wildly strange or weird) and claims that, on hearing it, "those most wise people, the antilogicians, will immediately and gleefully leap upon us" and argue that since enmity is the opposite of friendship, it follows by this argument that it is enemies who after all will be friends of one another. The passage definitely shows that there is a close connection of some sort between antilogic and contradiction. But the antilogicians' conclusion, which, it is imperative to notice, Socrates himself accepts, and on account of which he abandons the view that opposites are friendly to one another, is not reached, as Kerferd believes, by means of an independent specific method. On the contrary, it is reached by Socrates' habitual methods, whatever they are, and by Socrates himself.

In fact, Kerferd's description of antilogic applies very well to the Socratic elenchus itself. It is even echoed at the very beginning of the *Topics,* where Aristotle writes that the aim of his treatise on dialectic includes the determination of the means by which "we shall ourselves, when standing up to an argument, avoid saying anything contrary to it."[16] Antilogic seems to be not a method distinct from dialectic, but rather the use of dialectic for the purpose of generating (or avoiding) a contradiction. And how different is this from what Socrates actually succeeds in doing time after time in Plato's early dialogues, whatever his stated purpose may have been?

Consider now this famous passage of the *Republic:*

> When youths get their first taste of reasoned discourse they take it as a game and always use it to contradict. They imitate those who cross-examined them and themselves cross-examine others, rejoicing like puppies to drag along and tear to bits in argument whoever is near them. (539b2–7, trans. Grube)

Kerferd writes that this passage expresses Plato's "constant fear over the danger of [antilogic's] misuse, especially in the hands of those who are young" (64). But a careful reading of the text shows that what is misused is not antilogic; on the contrary, the objects of misuse (κατάχρησις) are arguments themselves (*logoi*); and their misuse consists in that they are employed simply for the purpose of establishing antilogies (εἰς ἀντι-λογίαν). Plato is not afraid that antilogic, a particular method of argument distinct from dialectic, is subject to misuse. Rather, he fears that argument, the very matter of dialectic, can be itself misused for merely contentious purposes. Antilogic is no more distinct a *method* of argument from dialectic than eristic is.

Because young men are apt to continue to engage in contentious cross-examination, Plato now writes, they themselves and the whole of philosophy are discredited in the eyes of other men. . . . An older man . . . would not want to take part in such folly; he will rather act like one who is willing to converse in order to discover the truth rather than one who is merely playing and contradicting for play. (539c2–8; Grube trans., slightly modified)

This passage shows clearly that the proper contrast is not between two different methods of argument, but between two purposes that argument can serve, one serious and the other not. The whole point of the present discussion in the *Republic* is that only those who are mature enough are to be exposed to dialectic. Even Kerferd's own writing inadvertently concedes this point, for, having claimed that the elenchus "is for Plato regularly a necessary part of the process of dialectic," he continues: "Plato is condemning the abuse of the elenchus when it is used for frivolous purposes, but by implication he is approving of it when used for the purposes of dialectic" (66). The contrast is purely one of purpose, not of method. One and the same method of argument can be used or misused according to what one proposes to make of it.

It is, unfortunately, true that we know very little about dialectic as Plato conceives it in his middle works. As Richard Robinson once wrote, throughout Plato's philosophical career dialectic seems to be "the ideal method, whatever it may be."[17] But one feature of dialectic of which we can be reasonably confident, according to Kerferd, is that dialectic "necessarily involves an approach to the Platonic Forms and it is this more than anything else which distinguishes it from antilogic" (65).

I think that Kerferd's statement is in a serious sense correct and that, perhaps ironically, its correctness generates a very serious problem that is not at all easy to resolve.

The problem is that if we incorporate the theory of Forms in our conception of dialectic we become incapable of distinguishing Socrates, who did not himself envisage the existence of the Forms as these are presented in Plato's middle dialogues, from his sophistic opponents. Socrates may well have claimed that his purpose in argument was always the discovery of the truth. But if, as I have argued, the test of truth in the elenchus is essentially dialectical, then the truth can be established only to the extent that you continue to win the argument—and it can therefore be tested only negatively: the fact that you have so far been victorious in your argument with me does not in any way guarantee that a new consideration undermining your position will not be found. Both Socrates and his opponents, therefore, necessarily aimed at victory. In this respect at least, Socrates cannot have differed in method from those sophists who practiced the method of question-and-answer and who did not intentionally use fallacious reasoning.

We might, however, say that Socrates' aim was not victory as such but rather the determination in each case of the victorious argument, independently of whether that was his own or his opponent's: "What kind of man am I?" he says to Gorgias. "One of those who would be pleased to be refuted if I say something untrue, and pleased to refute if someone else were to say something untrue, yet not at all less pleased to be refuted than to refute" (*G.* 458a; trans. Irwin, slightly modified). Socrates seeks victory for the correct argument, not for himself.

This point is connected with one of the most central features of the Socratic elenchus, Socrates' insistence that his interlocutors always answer him with views they truly believe. In Plato's *Euthydemus* (275d–e), the sophist Dionysiodorus assures Socrates that the young Cleinias will be refuted whatever he says—whether he believes what he says or not is irrelevant. But Socrates always makes sure that the answers he receives are views his interlocutors accept.

This requirement has been called the "say-what-you-believe" constraint by Vlastos.[18] It reflects, as Vlastos claims, the fact that Socrates aims to discover the truth and not merely to win the argument, his desire to test his interlocutors' seriousness, and his effort to change their very lives.

This "say-what-you-believe" requirement also reflects something else. This is the fact that Socrates engages in the elenchus because, as he says, he does not know what virtue and happiness are. He therefore makes it his practice to question those who actually have views about those issues in order, perhaps, to learn from them that which they claim to know—if in fact they do.[19] Given his profession of ignorance, Socrates needs to be answered truthfully. Though he may only succeed in refuting his interlocutors, Socrates' purpose is not to refute but to learn from his opponents, and he cannot learn from them unless they tell him what they believe.

Socrates' insistence on receiving answers his interlocutors truly accept reflects a crucial difference between him and the sophists. And that is his constant and consistent insistence that whatever else he knew he did not know what virtue was and that, in contrast to them, he was not a teacher of anything. He was not a teacher of virtue, as Protagoras claimed to be, of rhetoric, which was the province of Gorgias, of grammar, in which Prodicus specialized, or of any other *technē*—disclaiming, naturally, Hippias' polymathy. As he is made to say by Aeschines the Socratic in connection with Alcibiades, "If I thought that it was by some craft (*technē*) that I was able to benefit him, I would find myself guilty of great folly."[20]

This difference provides us with a neutral, nonpartisan way of distinguishing Socrates from his sophistic opponents. It is a difference more in purpose than in method, and we should be prepared to take it very seriously indeed. But we should also concede that it might easily have failed to impress—as it patently did not on the whole impress—those of his contemporaries who had been reduced to embarrassing and humiliating perplexity by him or by one of his followers.[21]

From our point of view, then, we can distinguish between Socrates and the sophists by means of his refusal to present himself as a teacher of others (leaving open, all the while, the question whether he actually did or did not succeed in teaching). The difference between Socrates and the people with whom he was often and not so unreasonably confused is ultimately a difference in purpose, in the sort of life he chose to follow.

Unfortunately, however, this approach cannot possibly distinguish philosophy, as Plato eventually comes to conceive it, from sophistry. For Plato became convinced that, in contrast to Socrates, he *did* know what virtue was and undertook to teach it to others: he came to the conclusion that virtue and happiness consist in the life of philosophy itself. But Plato's ambitious and controversial conception of the nature, function, and value of philosophy, articulated in detail in the *Republic,* creates a new problem for him. If philosophers aim to teach the true art of virtue (that is, philosophy itself), then their purpose appears to be at least superficially identical with the purpose of many of the sophists.[22]

Plato's magnificent solution to this problem was to press relentlessly the conceptual implications of the term "superficially" and of the whole family of distinctions it brings in its train. He defines dialectic as a method of argument that aims at the discovery of the real nature of things and is not guided by those merely verbal distinctions that at best indicate how the world appears to us (*Rep.* 454a–c, *Tht.* 164c–d). And, of course, he insists that the real nature of things is constituted by the Forms in which these things participate. The dialectician studies the Forms and therefore the theory of Forms, which Plato introduces in his middle works and which constitutes a deeply controversial metaphysical theory, also functions to underwrite the nature and practice of dialectic: the dialectician and the sophist now do something fundamentally different and in different ways; their methods are no longer the same, even though they may appear identical.

Terence Irwin, who thinks that this view of Plato's development "is far from the truth," argues that even in the *Republic* dialectic is nothing but "the familiar Socratic conversation."[23] But though the connections between dialectic and conversation are certainly not abandoned in the *Republic,* Plato explicitly writes that the dialectician tries, "without any help from the senses but by means of reason, to set out to find each true reality and does not give up before apprehending the Good itself with reason alone" (532a–b). The exclusion of the senses, the reliance on reason, and the very idea of the Good itself constitute critical innovations on Plato's middle period: nothing like them can be found in his Socratic dialogues. In fact, Plato actually argues that conversation of the sort in which Socrates engaged undermines traditional views of nobility, justice, and goodness in the mind of young men without giving them a notion of what these things really are. It therefore also undermines their character as well as the esteem in which philosophy is held by most people. And this, he concludes, was only to be expected. Young people should not be exposed to dialectic before they are mature enough to realize that the refutation of traditional values is to be made only in the name of the radically new but utterly objective values determined through the Forms (*Rep.* 537e–540c).

Plato's new conception of the relationship between philosophy and sophistry is reflected in the famous passage on "misology" in the *Phaedo* (89d–91c). Plato here argues that antilogical arguments, practiced ἄνευ τέχνης (without art) and opposing contrary but apparently equally supported views to one another, lead to the conclusion that the world itself, in line with the arguments that reflect it, lacks a stable nature. But arguing with *technē*, he continues, leads instead to the discovery of a "true and secure argument" (90c) and to the realization that the world is ultimately stable because it depends on and manifests the Forms—the real, unchanging natures of things. Once again, dialectic and the theory of Forms are closely connected to one another.

Misology, the hatred and distrust of arguments and things, is one result of such "untechnical" concern with argument. A related consequence, according to the *Republic* (492a–495b), is the perversion of the truly philosophic nature by traditional education. Plato calls such education "sophistry" in this passage. And the reason for this seems to be that he attributes to it an exclusive concern with "the many beautifuls" (τὰ πολλὰ καλά, 493e3), which are "no more beautiful than ugly" (479a6–7): they are thus the perfect subjects of antilogical argument in contrast to "the beautiful itself" (493e1–2), which is the only subject fit for the philosopher.

The main point is the following. Socrates did not differ from the sophists in method but in overall purpose, whereas Plato's sweeping moral vision identified his overall purpose with theirs. Plato therefore had to distance himself from the sophists, and from everyone else who claimed to teach people how to live their lives, in a new way. His resolution of this problem made essential use of a specific philosophical theory, the theory of Forms, which allowed him to claim that the sophists and all his various other opponents were trapped in the world of appearance. What they therefore taught (or appeared to teach) was only apparent wisdom and virtue.

Plato's metaphysical views thus allow him to agree that the sophist may well appear identical to the philosopher; but this, he could now insist, is a *mere* appearance, just like the sensible world, which merely appears to be, but is not, real. This is, of course, the central point for which Plato argues in the *Sophist*. In this dialogue, after a long metaphysical discussion aimed precisely at the articulation of the distinction between appearance and reality, the sophist is finally defined as μιμητὴς τοῦ σοφοῦ ("imitator of the wise") (*Sph.* 268c1), an idea echoed closely by Aristotle (*Soph. El.* 165b22–23; cf. *Met.* IV.1004b25 ff.).[24] Significantly, the *Sophist* describes the Socratic elenchus as merely as preparation for philosophy, purging the soul of false benefits that stand in the way of learning (*Sph.* 230d). And, most astonishingly, Plato goes on to characterize the elenchus as a species of sophistry, though one of "noble lineage" (230d, 231b). Even in Plato's own eyes, the elenctic method is not sufficient to distinguish clearly between Socratic and sophistic inquiry.

We must not, however, conclude that such a distinction cannot be drawn. On the contrary, a neutral distinction that begs no questions can be drawn on the grounds that Socrates, in contrast to the sophists, claimed not to be a teacher. This was not, however, a claim Plato was willing to make. Nor is it always effective in practice: the *effects* of the elenchus, as even Plato himself eventually came to believe, may be sometimes difficult to distinguish from the effects of sophistic teaching.

Sophistic influence can be securely avoided, Plato agues in the *Phaedo,* the *Republic,* and the *Sophist,* only by supplementing the elenchus with the study of the unchanging nature of the world, which demonstrates both how argument should ideally proceed and how life should properly be lived. But distinguishing philosophy from sophistry in this manner is no longer neutral. It presupposes accepting a specific and deeply controversial philosophical theory and, even more radically, a family of distinctions between appearance and reality that is itself equally partisan. The distinction between philosophy and sophistry is no longer neutral; it is drawn from within the point of view of philosophy itself.

It seems clear to me that denying the metaphysical distinction between appearance and reality does not by itself lead to sophistry construed as naked relativism and as the effort to win all arguments by any means. Of course, trivially, it leads to sophistry construed as a dialectical and perhaps even a moral practice that does not depend on this distinction. It is at least an open question, and one well worth pursuing, whether these two interpretations of sophistry are logically connected with one another. Socrates, as Plato himself depicts him in his early dialogues, was eager to argue with each sophist on particular questions. In his middle works, Plato seems to have wanted to show that such argument is out of place, because the sophists' place itself is outside philosophy.

But to agree too quickly with Plato on this issue may commit us to a restrictive and perhaps problematic conception of philosophy—at least insofar as Platonism is a view of limited appeal. If "sophistry" is a term of abuse, then "philosophy" is not a term that really describes anything. If, on the other hand, "philosophy" does describe a specific activity, then it is not clear what is wrong with being, along with the sophists, outside it. The most dialectical attitude, after all, may well be a view of philosophy that attributes to it neither a clear beginning nor a clear end.

The effort to set limits to philosophy is in fact as old as philosophy itself. This is shown by a passage from Aristotle's *Protrepticus*:

> If we are to engage in philosophy, we are to engage in philosophy; and if we are not to engage in philosophy, we are to engage in philosophy. In every case, therefore, we are to engage in philosophy. For if philosophy is possible, then we must in every way engage in it, since it exists. And if it is not possible, in this case too we ought to inquire how it is possible for philosophy not to be, and in inquiring we engage in philosophy: for inquiry is the cause of philosophy.[25]

The limits that Aristotle here refuses to accept may indeed sometimes prevent pretenders from masquerading as philosophers. But they may, at least as often, prevent philosophers from engaging with the opponents Socrates so eagerly sought and from asking the questions in which he delighted, for which he lived and died. Philosophy can include even the garrulous Isocrates: one can always count against him his garrulity, that is, his dialectical incompetence.[26]

Notes

1. *In Timarchum* 173. Very interestingly, Aeschines also describes Demosthenes as a sophist in the very same speech (125, 175). He describes him both as τὰς τῶν λόγων τέχνας κατεπαγγελόμενος τοὺς νέους διδάσκειν ("actively professing to teach young men the skills involved in speech and argument") (117) and as someone who περιήει τὴν πόλιν θηρεύων νέους πλουσίους ("wandered about town hunting for young men") (170). The latter description harks directly to Plato's *Sophist*, which was probably composed in the decade preceding the composition of Aeschines' speech, and testifies either to Plato's influence or to the preexisting popularity of this description; cf. *Sophist* 231d2–3, νέων καὶ πλουσίων ἔμμισθος θηρευτής ("a paid hunter of rich young men").

2. *Helen* (*Hel.*) 1. Though Isocrates does not mention Plato and Socrates by name, his allusion to them—a specific allusion, perhaps, to the *Protagoras*—is unmistakable.

3. *Hel.* 2–3. For Plato's and Aristotle's reservations, cf. *Phaedrus* 261d and *Physics* A.2–3, respectively.

4. *Antidosis* 268.

5. *Antid.* 261–66, *Panathenaicus* 26–29.

6. *Antid.* 253–55; *ad Nicoclem* 1.

7. *Hel.* 5. On "experience" (ἐμπειρία), contrast Plato's contemptuous and dismissive attitude at *G.* 462c.

8. Henry Sidgwick, "The Sophists," *Journal of Philology* 4 (1872): 288–307,

and 5 (1873): 66–68; George Grote, *Plato and the Other Companions of Sokrates* (London, 1875).

9. *Protagoras* 334c–335c. Socrates' identification of *brachulogia* with the elenctic method argues against Dodds's claim that *brachulogia* simply refers to "a laconic style"; cf. E. R. Dodds, *Plato "Gorgias"* (Oxford, 1959), n. *ad* 449c2.

10. *Euthydemus* 272d. A partial defense of Sidgwick's view is given by Norman Gulley, *The Philosophy of Socrates* (London: Macmillan, 1968), 28–31. The view that *brachulogia* and *makrologia* in fact refer simply to two different modes of engaging in question-and-answer and not to the contrast between question-and-answer on the one hand and oration on the other (as claimed, e.g., by George Kerferd, *The Sophistic Movement* [Cambridge, 1982], 32) is given support by Keith Knightenhelser, "Makrologia and Brachulogia," unpublished manuscript, 1986.

11. Grote, op. cit., vol. II, 198–99.

12. Grote, 202–3, 211.

13. London, 1981.

14. Gregory Vlastos, "The Socratic Elenchus," *Oxford Studies in Ancient Philosophy* 1 (1983): 27–58, 31 n. 14. T. H. Irwin, "Coercion and Objectivity in Plato's Dialectic," *Révue Internationale de Philosophie* 40 (1986): 49–74, 61 n. 18.

15. Such a relation is not envisaged, for example, in the brief (and admittedly incomplete) characterizations of eristic offered at *Meno* 75c–d and *Lysis* 216b–c. The latter is particularly interesting in this connection because though Socrates attributes to the antilogicians an argument of dubious worth, he is perfectly willing to abandon the conclusion he has reached as a result of its being vulnerable to that argument.

16. *Topics* A1.100a20–21; cf. 101a35.

17. *Plato's Earlier Dialectic* (Oxford, 1953), 70.

18. Vlastos, "The Socratic Elenchus," 35–38, with references and accounts of some notable exceptions. To the references supplied by Vlastos, one may add *Gorgias* 495a–b and *Laches* 193c.

19. Vlastos, "The Socratic Elenchus," 34, refers to *Apology* 29d and 30a to show that Socrates manifests "the aggressive outreach, the indiscriminate address to all and sundry, of the street evangelist." But, though Socrates does in these two apologetic passages suggest that he addresses everyone, his practice, as Plato depicts it in his other dialogues, belies his claim. His interlocutors are persons of note, renowned in one way or another (Protagoras, Gorgias, Hippias), people who claim to possess knowledge (Euthyphro, Polus), experts who can be reasonably expected to have it (Laches, Nicias), or attractive young men (Charmides, Lysis). In correspondence, Gregory Vlastos has objected that "the Platonic dialogues are not meant to develop a biographically informative account of when, with whom, and how Socrates spends his days. They are meant to develop Socratic views and arguments on key topics of philosophical interest. If so, we cannot take their personnel to indicate that Socrates' interlocutors are not [just anyone], but a select bunch." Two points need to be made in response. First, if the dialogues are not meant as accurate biographical information about Socrates, it is not obvious that the *Apology,* in contrast to them, can be considered truthful. Second, if the *Apology* is indeed truthful, then Socrates' eagerness to engage in philosophical discussion with

everybody is *itself* a "key topic of philosophical interest" and should therefore have been the subject of at least some of the dialogues.

20. Aeschines, *Alcibiades,* frag. 11.

21. I discuss Socrates and his connection to teaching in the essays "Meno's Paradox and Socrates as a Teacher" and "Socratic Intellectualism."

22. The qualification is inserted in view of *M.* 95c, where Gorgias is said not to be a teacher of virtue. But cf. W.K.C. Guthrie, *A History of Greek Philosophy,* vol. 3 (Cambridge, 1969), 271–72. Furthermore, since the *Phaedrus* (272a–b) seems to attribute to the philosopher the abilities of the true rhetorician, the overlap in purpose between philosophy and sophistry conceived as "the art of speech" is even more pronounced.

23. Irwin, "Coercion and Objectivity in Plato's Dialectic," 54.

24. For our purposes, a crucial question regarding the *Sophist* is whether Plato's effort to attribute to images and appearances a status of their own, different from reality but not equivalent to nothingness, is successful independently of his own specific metaphysical views. This is an immensely complex issue, and I plan to address it in a separate study.

25. W. D. Ross, *Aristotelis Fragmenta Selecta* (Oxford, 1955), 28.

26. Charles Kahn, Phillip Mitsis, and Steven Strange made valuable observations on earlier versions of this essay. I am particularly grateful to Gregory Vlastos for his detailed, extensive, and generous advice.

PART II

Plato: Questions of Metaphysics and Epistemology

Six

ON PARMENIDES' THREE WAYS OF INQUIRY

WE OFTEN take Parmenides to distinguish three "ways of inquiry" in his poem: the way of being, that of not-being, and the way that combines being and not-being; and to hold that of these only the first is to be followed.

This approach, originating in Reinhardt,[1] is now canonical.[2] G.E.L. Owen, for example, writes that Parmenides aims

> to rule out two wrong roads which, together with the remaining right road, make up an exhaustive set of possible answers to the question ἔστιν ἢ οὐκ ἔστιν; . . . The right path is an unqualified yes. The first wrong path is an equally unqualified no. . . . There is no suggestion that anyone ever takes the first wrong road. . . . It is the second, the blind alley described in . . . B6, that is followed by "mortals." . . . To take this well-trodden path . . . is to say, very naturally, that the question ἔστιν ἢ οὐκ ἔστιν; can be answered either yes or no.[3]

The text of B6.1–5 is as follows:

> χρὴ τὸ λέγειν τε νοεῖν τ' ἐὸν ἔμμεναι· ἔστι γὰρ εἶναι,
> μηδὲν δ' οὐκ ἔστιν· τὰ σ' ἐγὼ φράζεσθαι ἄνωγα.
> πρώτης γὰρ σ' ἀφ' ὁδοῦ ταύτης διζήσιος εἴργω
> αὐτὰρ ἔπειτ' ἀπὸ τῆς, ἣν δὴ βροτοὶ εἰδότες οὐδέν
> πλάττονται, δίκρανοι . . .

and can be translated as:

> What is for saying and for thinking must be;[4] for it can be,
> while nothing cannot; I ask you to consider this.
> For, first, I hold you back from this way of inquiry,
> and then again from that, on which mortals, knowing nothing,
> wander aimlessly, two headed . . .

Simplicius' manuscript, where this fragment is found, contains a lacuna after διζήσιος in line 3. Diels supplied εἴργω and took lines 4 ff. to follow directly afterward.[5] Thus, the goddess seems to proscribe two ways of inquiring into being. This text, however, exhibits certain peculiarities that suggest that this view faces serious difficulties. The purpose of this paper is to present these peculiarities, discuss the difficulties, and suggest, if cautiously, an alternative to the text and to the view it engenders.

I

Leonardo Tarán, for example, discusses the problem of the referent of ταύτης in line 3.[6] We know that the second way the goddess proscribes, "the way of mortals," combines being and not-being (B6.5–6). The first way, to which ταύτης seems to refer, must therefore be the way of "pure" not-being (cf. B2.5). But αὕτη usually refers backward, to an antecedent already stated. Yet where, in lines 1–2, can we find a reference to the way of not-being?

In answer, some scholars, for example Guthrie,[7] separate sharply between ἔστι γὰρ εἶναι in line 1 and μηδὲν δ᾽ οὐκ ἔστιν in line 2. They argue that the former states the way of being, while the latter, that of not-being. But, as Tarán replies,[8] "Nothing cannot be," far from being a statement of a wrong road, belongs essentially to the way of being, which was originally introduced in B2.3 by such a double construction:

ἡ μὲν ὅπως ἔστιν τε καὶ ὡς οὐκ ἔστι μὴ εἶναι.

If, then, ταύτης refers backward, it can only refer to the way of being. But why should that path be forbidden? To resolve this, Tarán postulates a longer lacuna after διζήσιος than Diels had done. And he speculates that in this missing text the goddess says that she is setting that way aside "for the present" in order to discuss other matters. That is, the way is not proscribed, but its discussion is temporarily postponed.

Tarán's positive view is rather confusing. At times he suggests that altogether there are three ways of inquiry (61). But his considered view seems to be that Parmenides envisages only two: "This fragment [B6] is not a third way" (72); "The *Doxa* is not a third way which combines Being and non-Being; there is no such third way" (208); "The *Doxa* itself is the way of not being" (230). Since, however, he refuses to identify the way of mortals in B6 with that of not-being, he never explains which way the mortals take. At one point he writes that this is not a way of inquiry at all: B6 "does not assert that Being and non-Being exist," but simply "criticizes as the extreme of folly a doctrine that cannot even distinguish between" them (72).

This serious unclarity aside, Stokes has raised a serious objection to Tarán's postulated lacuna. He argues that since line 4 contains neither a main verb nor a temporal qualification of its own, it must depend on εἴργω in line 3 and on whatever qualification εἴργω would have received in that lacuna. But this makes the asymmetry that Tarán intended to secure impossible: "Either the two abandonments are both temporary or they are both absolute."[9]

Stokes, who agrees with Tarán that two ways are proscribed in B6, but who believes that the proscription is permanent, needs to find a reference to another wrong way to which ταύτης can refer. His solution is to assume, with some evidence,[10] that the pronoun refers forward, to what follows it in the text.

The difficulty is that nothing in what follows ταύτης can be its antecedent; all we have is the second way, that of mortals. Stokes, therefore, is also forced to postulate a longer lacuna after διζήσιος, and conjectures that it contained a description of the way of "pure" not-being. This is possible, though, we shall see, not without difficulties. Its main drawback is that it tries to make sense of the text by assuming that just what is needed for that purpose is just what is missing from it.

A less extravagant view is offered by Mourelatos, who also agrees that two ways are proscribed in B6.[11] He accepts the view that ταύτης refers backward, to lines 1–2, but denies that it must therefore refer to the correct way of being. He claims that ταύτης need not "refer to a route *explicitly* mentioned" (my emphasis). His view thus is that B6.1–2 does after all contain a reference to a wrong way of inquiry.

Mourelatos argues first that B6.1–2 describes not only the positive way of being but also "the doctrine that sanctions it to the exclusion of the negative route." But this, he claims, is sufficient to secure an *implicit* reference to the way of not-being.

Mourelatos claims that his interpretation preserves the parallelism between B6.1–3 and B7.1–3,

> οὐ γὰρ μήποτε τοῦτο δαμῇ εἶναι μὴ ἐόντα·
> ἀλλὰ σὺ τῆσδ᾽ ἀφ᾽ ὁδοῦ διζήσιος εἶργε νόημα,
> μηδὲ σ᾽ ἔθος πολύπειρον ὁδὸν κατὰ τήνδε βιάσθω . . .

> For never shall this be proved,[12] that what is not is;
> but hold your thought back from this way of inquiry,
> nor let much-inured habit force you upon that way . . .

The fragments are supposed to be parallel in that both begin by recalling the doctrine that supports being and excludes not-being: B6, positively, by approving of the way of being; B7, negatively, by rejecting not-being. Both warn against two alternatives to being: B6, positively, through γάρ; B7, negatively, through ἀλλά. B6 distinguishes its alternatives positively, through αὐτὰρ ἔπειτα; B7, negatively, through μηδέ. The contrast ταύτης . . . τῆς of B6 is echoed by the contrast τῆσδε . . . τήνδε of B7.

Neither consideration is convincing. First, it is unclear how the goddess's expression of preference for the way of being at B6.1–2, however explicit, enables her to refer to one of its opposites simply by the pronoun "this," which surely needs more solid referential support. In this respect, the argument of Tarán and Stokes remains undislodged.

Secondly, the parallelism between B6.1–3 and B7.1–3 is questionable.

Though B6.1–2 contains the doctrine that supports being and excludes not-being (cf. B2.7–8), B7.1–2 does not. These lines simply assert the falseness of the way of not-being without in any way justifying that assertion.

Mourelatos claims that the contrasts ταύτης . . . τῆς and τῆσδε . . . τήνδε are "weak" because he thinks that the two wrong ways finally lapse into each other.[13] Now if there is any contrast in B7 at all, it is weak enough for Parmenides to use the very same pronoun in referring to these two ways. But in B6 he employs distinct grammatical forms, and marks a forceful contrast. Again, the parallelism fails.

But is there a contrast between two ways of inquiry at all in B7? Though it is usually thought so, I cannot find it there. Apart from the grammatical point just mentioned, this view has a curious consequence that seems not to have been noticed. If B7 contrasts two wrong ways, it implies that reason takes the first (not-being), while habit takes the second (both being and not-being). Yet why should Parmenides think this? This peculiar correlation, which is absent elsewhere in the poem, does not fit with the grammar of the text. For the contrast expressed by μηδέ seems to hold directly between reason and habit (εἶργε νόημα/μηδὲ σ᾽ ἔθος) rather than between ways of inquiry. The juxtaposition of reason and habit suggests that we are warned against two different ways of falling into a wrong path, rather than against two wrong paths. The pronouns τῆσδε and τήνδε have the same antecedent, and the goddess in effect says:

> but hold your thought back from this way of inquiry,
> nor let much-inured habit force you upon it . . .

We can thus account for the repetition τῆσδε . . . τήνδε in B7, as opposed to the contrast ταύτης . . . τῆς in B6, and also attribute a reasonable claim to the goddess. Accordingly, no parallelism between B6 and B7 remains.

Before we examine the consequences of this reading we must examine one more consideration against the view of Mourelatos and Stokes and, indeed, against any approach that finds an injunction *against* certain ways of inquiry in B6.

The presence of γάρ ("because") shows that B6.3 ff. offers support for the argument in lines 1–2. Mourelatos claims that B6.3 "reminds" us of the doctrine supporting being and excluding not-being and that γάρ "introduces the injunction of restraint." Stokes, who takes B6.1–2 to argue for the way of being, finds that "this argument is buttressed—whence the γάρ—by the exclusion of the two alternatives."[14] Both thus suppose that the exclusion of the wrong ways supports the claim that precedes it. But, contrary to their view, what precedes this directly is not an argument about being, but the phrase τὰ σ᾽ἐγὼ φράζεσθαι ἄνωγα, which is, therefore, what the phrase including the γάρ must support. But why should excluding the wrong ways facilitate considering the argument for the correct one? In reality, the order is precisely the converse, since that argument provides the grounds for excluding those ways. The logical connection should be that the argument be considered *in order to* exclude the wrong ways. But γάρ will not tolerate that sense. In fact, the presence of the γάρ suggests that as the youth considers the argument for the right way, he must also think about (without accepting) whatever wrong ways of inquiry there are in order to see the truth of the former and the deceptiveness of the latter. This is, after all, what is also suggested by B1.28–31, which tells the youth that he must learn the view of mortals along with the truth.

It begins to appear that our difficulties with B6 may be caused by the one assumption that we have not questioned so far: the idea that the goddess is *proscribing* certain ways of inquiry in this passage. We now turn to that assumption.

II

So far, we have taken it that in B6 the goddess tells the youth *not* to do something, not to follow either of two ways of inquiring into being. Yet she only seems to mention one wrong way. Faced with this problem, we have, broadly speaking, two alternatives. Since the way of being is mentioned, we can try to find a suitable sense in which this way, too, may be left aside. Or we can insist that, despite the appearance of the text, a second wrong way is being excluded.

The first alternative (which is Tarán's) is to suppose not that the way of being is abandoned, but that its discussion is postponed. The second (that of Stokes and Mourelatos) assumes that the goddess has the same attitude toward the two ways she discusses here; since she wants to abandon the way of mortals, she must also want to abandon the other way, and therefore a second wrong way is somehow to be found in the passage.

The difficulty of finding a reference to such a way suggests that perhaps no third way is to be found in Parmenides. This is in fact likely on general grounds.

First, the overall structure of the poem is dualistic with a vengeance. There are just two parts, the *Alētheia* and the *Doxa,* and we know that the former demonstrates the way of being. It is thus to that extent plausible that Parmenides considers only one alternative to that way, which he discusses in the *Doxa*.

This contrast between truth and appearance is reflected in the contrast between the goddess's road (B1.23, 27) and the people's well-trodden path (B1.27), and in that between the truth the goddess possesses (B1.29, B8.50–51) and the opinions among which mortals wander (B1.29, B8.51). Most importantly, however, the goddess states unequivocally that there are *only* (μοῦναι) two ways of inquiry (B2.2). By itself, this statement creates an intolerable inconsistency for those who find three ways in B6, and we cannot dismiss it as easily as the following comment suggests:

> Though Parmenides has in B2 suggested that there are only two "conceivable ways of inquiry" . . . it now appears [B6, B7] . . . that in addition to the true premiss there are actually two premisses that must be rejected.[15]

This view faces a further difficulty. Parmenides distinguishes between truth and appearance, the way of the goddess and the way of mortals. If he also distinguishes the way of being not only from the way of not-being but from the way of both being and not-being as well, how are we to relate the terms of these different contrasts to each other?

We can easily identify truth with the goddess's way and the way of being. Now B6 characterizes the way of mortals as the way both of being and not-being: is this also the way discussed in the *Doxa,* as Reinhardt, Owen, and Kirk and Raven claim? If it is, then the way of not-being, originally introduced in B2 as the only alternative to the way of being, is not discussed in the poem. In addition, we must now attribute to the goddess the following unreasonable procedure: she begins (B1.27 ff.) by contrasting her way with that of mortals (i.e., on this view, being and not-being); she now says (B2) that her way can only be contrasted with that of "pure" not-being; she mentions this way again at B6.3, only to drop it and, without explanation or warning, return to the combined way at B6.4.

If, on the other hand, we identify the *Doxa* with the way of not-being (so Burnet[16] and Tarán), little is said of the way of mortals. In particular, we will be unable to explain why it is not discussed in the detail promised at B1.27 ff. and B8.50–52.

Again, our problems spring from taking the goddess to proscribe certain ways of inquiry in B6, and this in turn depends on accepting Diels's supplying of εἴργω at B6.3.[17] What is the positive evidence for this problematic emendation?

Diels supplied εἴργω because of the verbal resemblance between B6.3 and B7.2. In itself, of course, this resemblance is not telling.[18] But two other reasons are also relevant.

First, it may seem that Simplicius attributed two forbidden ways to Parmenides:

> μεμψάμενος γὰρ τοῖς τὸ ὂν καὶ τὸ μὴ ὂν συμφέρουσιν ἐν τῷ νοητῷ,
> "οἷς τὸ πέλειν τε καὶ οὐκ εἶναι ταὐτὸν νενόμισται κοὐ ταὐτόν", καὶ
> ἀποστρέψας τῆς ὁδοῦ τῆς τὸ μὴ ὂν ζητούσης, "ἀλλὰ σὺ τῆσδ᾽ ἀφ᾽
> ὁδοῦ διζήσιος εἶργε νόημα", ἐπάγει. (78.2 ff.)

Tarán claims that this passage "proves" that Simplicius took Parmenides to distinguish two wrong ways. Stokes, more cautiously, writes that "Simplicius appears to hold that Parmenides refects two ways" (115). Nevertheless, the most natural reading of the passage need not attribute this idea to Simplicius:

> For, censuring those who combine in thought being with not being, "those to whom being and not being seem to be the same and not the same," and turning away from the path that seeks not being ("but hold your thought back from this way of inquiry") he concludes . . .

Parmenides, Simplicius writes, attacks those who combine being with not-being and turns away from the road that seeks not-being. In the absence of other evidence, the most natural supposition is to take that those who make this combination are on the road of not-being, and that only one wrong way is involved.

A second, more serious, reason in favor of εἴργω is given by the grammatical appearance of B6.3. It seems obvious that σ᾽ here is the elision of σέ; and since ἀπό commonly means "away from," we are faced with the sentence-frame

I ——— you away from this way of inquiry,

which seems tailor-made for a verb like εἴργω. In view of this, all other considerations become, quite rightly, secondary.

Yet σ᾽ need not necessarily be the elision of σέ. In epic verse, of which Parmenides' is an instance, it can also be the elision of σοί, the pronoun's dative. So, for example, *Iliad* I.170–71,

> . . . οὐδὲ σ᾽ ὀίω
> ἐνθάδ᾽ ἄτιμος ἐὼν ἄφενος καὶ πλοῦτον ἀφύξειν,
> . . . nor do I intend,
> staying here dishonorably to draw booty and riches for you,

contains just such an elision.[19] And so, probably, does *Iliad* XXI.122–23,[20] while Helmut Saake has recently adopted this reading for σ᾽ in lines 18–19 of Sappho's "Ode to Aphrodite."[21]

Since the elision of σοί is possible, the goddess may be saying:

I ——— *for you* from this way of inquiry,

and now a significantly different interpretation of this line becomes possible. For it now appears that a verb expressing opposition is no longer mandatory. In view of this, we might construe our incomplete line as follows:

πρώτης γὰρ σ(οι) ἀφ᾽ ὁδοῦ ταύτης διζήσιος ἄρξω.

The use of ἄρχειν, "to begin," with ἀπό is noticed in LSJ (s.v. ἄρχω, I.2). Smyth considers ἀπό parallel to ἐκ;[22] ἀπό often suggests a point of origin, and Parmenides uses it in just that sense at B8.51 to signify the beginning of the *Doxa*. In Homer it is sometimes used in parallel to ἐπί ("upon"), but always involving the notion of origin, as in the common expressions ἀφ᾽ ἵππων or ἀπὸ νεῶν μάχεσθαι. It may then be that in B6 the goddess says:

> For, first, I will begin for you from this way of inquiry,
> and then again from that on which mortals, knowing nothing,
> wander aimlessly, two headed.

That the discussion of either way can be a beginning echoes nicely B5:

> ξυνὸν δέ μοί ἐστιν
> ὁππόθεν ἄρξωμαι· τόθι γὰρ πάλιν ἵξομαι αὖθις.

> And it is the same to me
> whence I begin; for I shall again reach the same spot.

This "spot" is just the doctrine that what is not can neither be known nor said (B2.7–8) or, as in B6 itself, that all there is to say and think is what is. The youth is asked to consider this doctrine, and to do this he is to hear the true way of being and the false way of not-being, so he can realize how the doctrine supports the former and excludes the latter.[23]

The poem now acquires a remarkably clear structure. The goddess contrasts her road with the people's (B1.27), but tells the youth that he must learn everything (B1.28), not only "the heart of truth" but the opinions of mortals as well (B1.29–30). She gives a preliminary specification of these two ways of inquiry in B2.[24] She warns against the wrong way, supporting her warning with the central doctrine of B2.7–8. She asks the youth to keep that thesis in mind (B6.1–2) because (and now the function of the γάρ at B6.3 finally becomes clear) she will, as B1 promised, *take* him through these two ways—first through the way of being, in the *Alētheia*, and then through that of not-being, in the *Doxa*.

Fragment B6 does not therefore reject any way of inquiry. On the contrary, it says that the goddess will follow (demonstrate) two methods of inquiring into nature—which is just what she does.

The vehemence with which the way of mortals is denounced is due to the fact that the youth will have to travel along it and because habit may make him want to remain there. As Odysseus protected himself against the Sirens, the youth must not allow the apparent attractiveness, the intuitive appeal, of this road to deceive him. The wrong road is exposed (cf. B8.51–54, 60–61; perhaps B19) because the youth must take it yet not mistake it for the truth.

III

Our interpretation implies that the content of the *Doxa*, the way of mortals, the way of not-being, and the way that combines being and not-being are all the same. To defend this last, and most problematic, identification I will assume, controversially, that Parmenides' "being" is neither existential,[25] nor both existential and predicative,[26] but fundamentally predicative. My view owes much to Owen[27] and to Mourelatos;[28] I have discussed in detail on other occasions the sense of being to which I appeal below in connection with those of Plato's doctrines, notably his view of self-predication, which have an Eleatic origin.[29]

The assumption is that Parmenides understands "is" in the very strong sense of "is what it is to be." Thus if he talks, for example, of what is wood, he takes it that he is talking of what it is to be wood, the very nature of wood. And if so, then his denial of generation (B8.6–9) becomes more plausible. For to say that wood ever came to be is to say that what it is to be wood came out of something that itself was not what it is to be wood. And that, in turn, is to say not only that the nature of things is generable but that the very nature of one thing can be transformed into the very nature of another. But how could this be? To say that the nature of wood ever came to be is to say that something other than this nature came to be that nature. But "the nature of a thing" is the ultimate subject of predication. To say that it came to be out of something else is to postulate a further subject of predication. And this only generates the same problem. For whatever it was that changed proves to be not the nature of the thing in question (not, for example, what it is to be wood); and the thing that underlies the change, whatever it is, turns out to be the only unchangeable, and therefore real, thing. Lacking the Aristotelian doctrine of matter, which his own arguments caused to be developed, Parmenides could only conclude that whatever it is that things really are is itself unchanging. For if it changed in any way, it would no longer be what it is, and there would be no subject for us even to talk about. Concerned as he was with the very natures of things, Parmenides concluded, by generalizing from cases of this sort, that what is cannot not be. This means, for example, that what it is to be wood (if there is such a thing) cannot in any way, at any time, and from any point of view, not be wood. Nature is unchanging. Whenever we observe change, we are still within the realm of appearance. If wood does change into ash, then neither wood nor ash are real, but only appearances unrelated to the unchanging reality of things. The way of mortals is the commonsense view that things can change, and the philosophical, Milesian, view that everything in the world is somehow generated out of an undifferentiated principle. Parmenides' response is to argue that such change is only apparent. Real things, things that are *F* in the strong sense of being what it is to be *F*, cannot change. For to be what it is to be *F*, to be the nature of *F*, is to be *F* in every way and at all times. If such a thing changed in any way, it would cease being what it is, and thus what is (what it is to be) *F* would turn out not to be (what it is to be) *F*. But this is to say that what is is not, that being and not-being are the same. And this is the result of saying of any subject, which is assumed to be real, that it is subject to change.

But why did Parmenides, after ostensibly outlawing this way of mortals, proceed to describe it in such detail in the *Doxa*? If change is impossible, because it involves saying of its subject that it is not, why does he devote so much time to detailing its workings?

Through a careful analysis of B1.31–32, Owen has shown that no "approximate" truth is accorded to the *Doxa*.[30] Why is it then introduced at all? Owen answers that Parmenides' purpose was "wholly dialectical." To me, however, it seems peculiar that Parmenides would construct a (totally false) cosmology only so that "no mortal will ever give an account which presents fewer violations of the laws of Truth."[31] Parmenides seems to have constructed the *Doxa* with great care, and the suspicion lingers that he is competing with the φυσιολόγοι, that he is offering a theory of the world in which, in some sense, he believes. This suspicion is supported by Aristotle's testimony, which, though not unequivocal, often attributes the dualistic cosmology of the *Doxa* to Parmenides himself.[32] I now want to suggest that we can attribute such a cosmology to Parmenides and still respect Owen's sound arguments.

At B1.31–32 we read:

> ἀλλ' ἔμπης καὶ ταῦτα μαθήσεαι, ὡς τὰ δοκοῦντα
> χρῆν δοκίμως εἶναι, διὰ παντὸς πάντα περ ὄντα.

> Still, you will learn these things too, how what seems
> had to be real, being indeed the whole of things.

The mortals' error is described in the phrase ὡς . . . ὄντα. And this mistake is to confuse things as they appear with things as they are, to take what seems for what is. We can thus distinguish two aspects of the question of the truth of the *Doxa*. We can ask either if the *Doxa* contains a correct description of phenomena or if any such description, however correct of phenomena, can be an adequate account of reality. We can now explain why Parmenides cheerfully constructs the *Doxa* despite the devastating proofs of the *Alētheia*. Unlike common mortals, he knows that the *Doxa* can only tell us how the world appears to be, and that the way the world appears to be and the way it is are totally distinct. The deceptiveness of the *Doxa* does not consist in its relation to appearance, which it describes (in

Parmenides' view) quite correctly, but in its plausible claim that it is also a description of reality.

Parmenides then draws, perhaps for the first time in Western thought, the distinction between appearance and reality: not only does the world appear to be other than it is, but the world that appears is other than the world that is. Parmenides' challenge (ἔλεγχος) to cosmology was not to argue that physics was impossible; this would be difficult to reconcile with his own relentless pursuit of it. His refutation consisted in arguing that cosmology only touches appearance, and not the world of reality, whose true description is in the *Alētheia*. He writes the *Doxa* because its false-hood consists not in its being a *wrong* description of appearance but in its being only a description of *appearance* and in its apparent claim to describe reality.

In writing the *Doxa,* and in using negative predications, Parmenides is not trapped in the paradox of having to say what cannot be said.[33] "What cannot be said" is not how things seem to be, something to the saying of which Parmenides devoted considerable enthusiasm. Rather it is that how things appear to be (and hence, he would have inferred, are not) is how they are. Any aspect in respect of which a thing changes is part of that thing's appearance, and hence no part of what the thing is. To think that things really change would indeed be to think that what is not, is. This is what cannot be said and what Parmenides never tries to say.

Parmenides' absolute distinction between being and not-being, be-tween reality and appearance, is thus an ancestor of the distinction be-tween essence and accident. Instead of proclaiming wrongly, as we have often thought, the end of cosmology, he showed how, given its own as-sumptions, its field of application and its claim to truth were severely lim-ited. In so doing, he also showed that philosophy was necessary to put physics upon the secure path of science.

NOTES

1. Karl Reinhardt, *Parmenides und die Geschichte der Griechischen Philosophie* (Bonn, 1916; repr. Frankfurt, 1959), 18–32.

2. David J. Furley, "Notes on Parmenides," in E. M. Lee et al., *Exegesis and Argument: Studies in Greek Philosophy Presented to Gregory Vlastos* (Assen, 1973), 1–15; W.K.C. Guthrie, *A History of Greek Philosophy,* vol. 2 (Cambridge, 1965); G. S. Kirk and J. E. Raven, *The Presocratic Philosophers* (Cambridge, 1957); A.P.D. Mourelatos, *The Route of Parmenides* (New Haven, 1970); G.E.L. Owen, "Eleatic Questions," *Classical Quarterly,* N.S. 10 (1960): 85–102; Michael C. Stokes, *One and Many in Presocratic Philosophy* (Cambridge, Mass., 1971). Hereafter, I shall refer to these works by their author's name.

3. Owen, 90–91.

4. For this construction, see Furley, 11.

5. See Diels's comment in his apparatus to the Prussian Academy edition of Simplicius' commentary on Aristotle's *Physics* (Berlin, 1882), 117.

6. Leonardo Tarán, *Parmenides: A Text with Translation, Commentary, and Critical Essays* (Princeton, 1965), 59–72.

7. Guthrie, 22.

8. Cf. Stokes, 113.

9. Stokes, 113. Stokes and Tarán both reject the attempt of Rosamond Kent Sprague ("Parmenides: A Suggested Rearrangement of the Fragments in the Way of Truth," *Classical Philology* 50 [1955]: 124–26) to avoid this problem by changing the order of the fragments. Cf. Stokes, 113; Tarán, 60–61. Furley suggests (10) that ταύτης refers back to the specification of the wrong way of not-being in B2.5. But this is surely too far back for the reference to be understandable, especially since different subjects have intervened.

10. Stokes, 115 n. 27.

11. Mourelatos, 77 n. 7. All references to Mourelatos on this question concern this passage.

12. δάμνημι is not quite equivalent to "prove," but this does not concern us now. Cf. Mourelatos, 28 n. 27.

13. Mourelatos thinks that the two routes "amount to" each other, but insists that "the route of mortals cannot be identified with the negative route directly or *simpliciter*" (91 n. 47).

14. Stokes, 114.

15. Kirk and Raven, 271.

16. John Burnet, *Early Greek Philosophy*, 4th ed. (London, 1930), 183–84.

17. Diels's emendation has been accepted universally, with one exception noted below (nn. 18, 23). Cf. Tarán, 61; Stokes, 114; Furley, 10 n. 29.

18. Cf. Nestor-Luis Cordero, "Les deux chemins de Parménide dans les fragments 6 et 7," *Phronesis* 24 (1979): 11: "La ressemblance qui existe entre 6.3 . . . et 7.2 . . . est indeniable. Mais il s'agit d'une ressemblance exterieure, donc trompeuse." Cf. n. 23 below.

19. Cf. Pierre Chantraine, *Grammaire Homérique* (Paris, 1942), 86.

20. Cf. Walter Leaf and M. A. Bayfield, *The Iliad of Homer* (London, 1895), vol. 2, 506. Cf. also W. Leaf, *The Iliad* (2d ed. London, 1900), vol. 1, n. *ad* I.170; Georg Autenrieth, *A Homeric Dictionary* (Norman, Okla., 1969), s.v. σ᾽, and Herbert Weir Smyth, *Greek Grammar* (Cambridge, Mass., 1956), 23.

21. Helmut Saake, *Zur Kunst Sapphos* (Munich, 1971), 54–65. I thank Edwin Floyd for bringing this reference to my attention and for discussing this question with me.

22. Smyth, 371.

23. After this article was written, Nestor-Luis Cordero subjected fragments B6 and B7 to an exhaustive philological examination. His article, referred to above in note 18, is extremely valuable. Given his examination of the manuscripts of Simplicius, he prefers the reading of (elided) τε instead of (elided) σοί as I propose. He, like me, considers that a form of the verb ἄρχειν is necessary to complete the sense of B6.3. His own proposal is:

πρώτης γὰρ τ' ἀφ' ὁδοῦ ταύτης διζήσιος ἄρξει
For you shall first begin from this way of inquiry.

I find the closeness of our views extremely gratifying, especially since the sense we attribute to the text is virtually identical.

24. These lines do not contain the goddess's full description of the two ways of inquiry. The μῦθος (B2.1) that she wants the youth to carry back with him is the μῦθος of B8.1 and the κόσμος ἐπέων ἀπατηλῶν of B8.52. It is in B8 and the following parts of the poem that the ways are fully specified.

25. This is the view of Tarán, Burnet, and Owen ("Eleatic Questions"; he may have changed his mind by the time he wrote the paper referred to in note 27 below). Tarán (33–35) gives more references, and Mourelatos (269–78) offers an exhaustive classification of every possible alternative.

26. For example, Guido Calogero, *Studi sull' Eleatismo* (Rome, 1932), who claims that Parmenides does not distinguish existence from predication, and Kirk and Raven. Montgomery Furth, "Elements of Eleatic Ontology," in A.P.D. Mourelatos, ed., *The Presocratics* (Garden City, N.Y., 1974), 241–70, argues that Parmenides "fuses" but does not confuse existence and predication, and that his argument is plausible under either alternative. Furley ("Notes on Parmenides," 13–14), follows Furth's approach.

27. "Plato on Not-Being," in Gregory Vlastos, ed., *Plato I: Metaphysics and Epistemology* (Garden City, N.Y., 1971), 223–67.

28. Mourelatos, 47–93.

29. See this book's essays "Confusing Universals and Particulars in Plato's Early Dialogues" and especially "Self-Predication and Plato's Theory of Forms."

30. Owen, "Eleatic Questions," 84–89; cf. Mourelatos, 194–221.

31. Stokes, following Owen, 148; cf. A. A. Long, "The Principles of Parmenides' Cosmogony," *Phronesis* 8 (1963): 90–107.

32. Aristotle often treats Parmenides as denying physics altogether, e.g., in *Physics* A2.185a ff. Yet at *Physics* A5.188a19 ff., he attributes a cosmogony to him. At *Metaphysics* A3.984b3–4, he grudgingly attributes to him a dualistic cosmogony, while at A5.986b27 ff., he suggests that Parmenides, "forced to follow the observed facts," accepts such a theory. At *De Generatione et Corruptione* A3.318a6–7, he attributes such a dualistic view straightforwardly to Parmenides (cf. also 330b13–19, 335b15–16). Interestingly, H. H. Joachim (*Aristotle on Coming-to-Be and Passing-Away* [Oxford, 1922], 100) hastens to comment that Parmenides presents this theory as "prevalent, but erroneous," and follows Burnet in thinking that Aristotle attributes this view not to Parmenides himself but to the poem that Parmenides composed, referring to it by its author's name, much in the way a contemporary literary critic might proceed.

33. Furth, "Elements of Eleatic Ontology," 269–70.

Seven

PLATO ON THE IMPERFECTION
OF THE SENSIBLE WORLD

IT IS A COMMONPLACE, both among philosophers and among the more general public, that Plato believed that the sensible world is imperfect in comparison to the world of Forms. There is also a received tradition as to exactly how the world's imperfection manifests itself that has by now become a commonplace in its own right. I have no quarrel with the first of these two commonplaces: as stated, it is too vague to command close attention. It is only when it is interpreted in terms of the received tradition that it becomes informative enough to require consideration. And when it is so interpreted, it requires not only consideration but also careful examination. For these two commonplaces, taken together, create a radically mistaken picture of Plato's view of the sensible world, and of its relation to the Forms.

In what follows, I will first set out the received tradition by means of a number of quotations, for which I ask my readers' patience: it is important to realize just how broad that tradition is. I will then suggest a view of the relation between the sensible world and the Forms that conflicts with the received tradition, and I will finally examine the merits of the two approaches.

I

Plato often tells his readers that the Forms are, in some sense, superior to the sensible objects that participate in them. He speaks of the Forms as completely and purely real at *Republic* 477–79 (παντελῶς ὄν, εἰλικρινῶς ὄν); as perfectly and really real at *Republic* 597 (τελέως ὄν, ὄντως ὄν). He says that particulars fall short (ἐνδεῖ τι) of being such as the Form is in which they participate (*Phaedo* 74d); that particulars desire (ὀρέγεται) to be like Forms, but fall short (ἔχει ἐνδεεστέρως) of that end (*Phd.* 75a); that particulars are inferior (φαυλότερα) to Forms (*Phd.* 75b). He makes this point forcefully at *Symposium* 210e–212a, and he also exhibits this attitude at *Republic* 515d, *Phaedrus* 247c, *Philebus* 59d, and elsewhere.[1]

We are trying to understand what Plato had in mind when he compared sensible objects so unfavorably to the Forms. It is to this question that the received tradition has provided the answer with which I disagree.

Why are particulars imperfect in comparison to Forms? Because, writes A. E. Taylor in his *Plato,*

the pure logical concept (viz., the Form) is never fully embodied in any sensible example: two things, for instance, which at first blush appear equal, on close comparison will be found to be only approximately so; the visible diagram which we take to stand for a triangle . . . has never really the properties which we attribute to "the triangle" in our definition; the conduct we praise as just may, on close scrutiny, turn out to be only imperfectly just.[2]

In *Plato: The Man and his Work,* Taylor writes that

the so-called sticks and stones we do see are not exactly, but only approximately equal,[3]

and expands this as follows:

The same visual sensations which suggest the notion "straight" to me, for example, are the foundation of the judgment that no visible stick is perfectly straight. The form is thus never contained in, or presented by, the sensible experience that suggests it. Like the "limit" of an infinite series it is approximated but never reached.[4]

Burnet, commenting on *Euthyphro* 6e4, writes:

The identical "form" will not be fully embodied in any of the particulars, but it is the exemplar to which they more or less approximate.[5]

while he glosses *Phd.* 74a9 as follows:

The "forms" are *types* (παραδείγματα) to which particular sensible things approximate more or less closely.[6]

W. D. Ross follows suit on this issue:

. . . all sensible apparent equals both aspire to that which is equal and fall short of it;[7]

apparent equals are objects between which

we can detect no difference in size [while] exact instruments of measurement reveal inequalities where the eye does not detect them, and . . . in all probability we have never seen two physical objects that were exactly equal.[8]

Paul Shorey also suggests this attitude:

Experience can never give us the pure mathematical ideas which sensation and perception awaken in our minds. There are no perfect circles or equalities in nature. Yet we do conceive them, and we feel how far concrete circles and equalities fall short of the ideal toward which they strive. . . . We are reminded by the imperfect copies in the world of sense of something that we have seen or known in another state of existence.[9]

And, finally, Hugh Tredennick conjectures that

> Plato's reasoning may have been something like this. "Knowledge must be possible; Socrates was sure of it, and the world makes nonsense if it is not. But the things of this world cannot be truly known, because they are changeable and imperfect, and therefore not real; for *what is* is changeless. Now in geometry (for Plato was an expert mathematician) the properties which we know and can prove to be of circles and triangles and so on are not strictly true of this particular figure which I draw, because it too is imperfect and impermanent, They are true of the 'look' or Form of circle (or triangle), which exists somewhere in eternal perfection. Surely, it must be the same with everything else. The things of this world are all imperfect copies of Forms which exist eternally somewhere; which are the true and only objects of knowledge, but can only be apprehended by direct contemplation of the mind, freed as far as possible from the confusing imperfections of the physical world."[10]

These writings cover roughly fifty years of scholarship. They range from technical commentaries to popular introductions to Plato's work. They are written by scholars on either side of the unitarian/developmental dispute about Plato's thought. Yet they all exhibit a remarkable agreement on a number of issues, examples, and vocabulary; the points agreed upon constitute the received tradition on Plato's disparagement of the sensible world. They are the following:

1. Plato was inspired to formulate the theory of Forms by his attitude toward mathematics, especially toward geometry. Geometrical truths do not concern sensible equal things, squares, or circles. Such objects are only illustrations of the intelligible and unitary objects (equality, the square, the circle) about which the theorems of geometry are really formulated.[11]

2. Sensible objects only approximate the intelligible objects which they represent in geometrical contexts. They are imperfect in the sense that the definition of, say, "circle" never quite applies to any drawn circle; a drawn circle could always be closer to being the locus of points equidistant to a given point. Measurement can always be further refined, and each refinement will reveal, for example, that objects previously judged to be equal are not equal relative to the new procedure. It is in this sense that sensible equal objects are never "really" equal, and sensible circles are never "really" circular. Geometrical illustrations, no matter how carefully they have been constructed, are always "fuzzy."

3. Plato, either consciously or unconsciously, applied this sense of imperfection to objects belonging to ethical and aesthetic contexts.[12] Just as geometrical illustrations are always only approximately and never exactly equal, circular, or square, so beautiful people, just actions, and healthy animals are only approximately and never exactly beautiful, just, or healthy. That is, they could

always be more beautiful, more just, or healthier. It is in this sense that the Form of, say, beauty, which is perfectly (namely, exactly) beautiful, is like the limit of an infinite series.[13]

The first of these three theses is not crucial to my purpose. Already in 1912, Gillespie had cast doubts on Taylor's (and Burnet's) contention that the theory of Forms was a direct application of Pythagorean geometry by Plato.[14] Also, on this historical view, geometrical objects were thought to be unitary, and Plato was supposed to have duplicated this feature in postulating a single Form for each multiplicity of objects that interested him; but this obviously conflicts with Aristotle's statement that "mathematical objects . . . differ from sensible objects in being eternal and unchanging, and from Forms in being *many of each sort*, while each Form is itself solitary" (*Metaphysics* A6.987b16–19). Finally, this account does not explain certain crucial features of the theory of Forms, which we shall examine as we discuss in detail theses *(2)* and *(3);* for convenience, I shall refer to these two theses jointly as "the approximation view."

The approximation view interprets in a particular way the relation between geometrical illustrations and the "objects" these illustrate. And it attributes to Plato both that interpretation and also a radical generalization of it to other contexts: "Surely it must be the same with everything else."[15] Plato's fondness for generalization notwithstanding, I find this particular instance intolerable; and, I believe, Plato himself found it unthinkable: he never made it.

On the approximation view, earthly squares and circles are fuzzy squares and circles—their outlines could always as a matter of logical possibility approximate more closely their respective ideal, which is exactly square and circular. So with justice and beauty: their earthly manifestations could always benefit from improvement along specified lines. The sensible world is imperfect because it is only approximately whatever we say it is; the Forms are perfect because they are exactly whatever we say they are. Particulars are imperfect copies of the Forms in which they participate. They are copies in that they "strive to be like" the relevant Forms: they do possess the relevant properties. They are imperfect in that they "fall short of being like" the relevant Forms: they possess the relevant properties only to an extent or a degree. In other words, particulars resemble the Forms in which they participate (and this makes them copies). But the resemblance is defective in the very respect in which it holds (and this makes them imperfect). Helen is not really (perfectly, that is, exactly) beautiful, nor is Phaedo really tall, much like this page, which is not exactly rectangular, or like a portrait of Simmias, which, on this account, cannot match Simmias' complexion perfectly. "Perfection" is explicated as "exactness," and "imperfection" as "approximation."

On this view, a Form is never manifested in the sensible objects that participate in it. This is a crucial consequence, and the proponents of the approximation thesis accept it willingly.[16] The imperfection of the sensible world consists in the imperfection of those very properties the possession of which makes it a copy of the world of Forms. This is, as Mr. Crombie has put it, "a doctrine to the effect that Helen's beauty was . . . analogous to but not identical with true beauty . . . [and] would entail the consequence that forms are to be distinguished from [the common features of actual things. It is not the doctrine] that forms are imperfectly embodied by things, [but] the doctrine that forms are imperfectly embodied in the properties of things."[17]

II

Having given a brief characterization of the approximation view, I would like to stop for a moment and also give a brief characterization of an alternative view of the relation between sensible particulars and Forms. This is a view for which I have argued in detail elsewhere.[18] Here, I will simply restate the main points, and I hope that the subsequent discussion will make my approach slightly clearer and somewhat more plausible.

Plato, I believe, was to a great extent led to formulate the theory of Forms in the *Phaedo,* the *Symposium,* and the *Republic* out of a concern with definition springing from Socrates' unsuccessful attempts to define a number of a family of terms, attempts that Plato himself made in the early or Socratic dialogues. These terms, prominent among which are terms for the moral virtues (justice, virtue, courage, piety, temperance, beauty) and terms for properties involving measurement or comparison (largeness or tallness, equality, heat), created a peculiar problem. Although these terms did not seem to be ambiguous, not only they but also their contraries seemed to apply to the same objects without obvious contradiction. Thus the same person could (in different contexts) be truly described as both beautiful and ugly, tall and short, courageous and cowardly. Further, there seemed to be no plausible single candidate to account for the application of these terms to different objects; what seemed to account for courage in one situation could also explain cowardice in another, what explained beauty in one context could equally well account for ugliness in another. No sensible object could function as the *definiens* of terms like "beauty," "virtue," or "tallness"; for any such object, which should have explained the application of these terms and the exclusion of their contraries, also seemed to account for the application of their contraries and the exclusion of the original terms. Thus no sensible object seemed to be really or, if one prefers, essentially just, beautiful, or tall; that is, beautiful in itself, independently of whatever context in which it happened to be placed, present in all and only those objects that we might truly consider beautiful. Individual objects were beautiful only in relation to other objects, and they were also, without undergoing any change in themselves, ugly in relation to still other objects. Any definitional candidate for such terms did not isolate the instances of beauty or of justice, but it applied equally well to instances of ugliness or of injustice.[19]

Predicates like these are all incomplete; they are attributive or relational. And they are to be contrasted with predicates like "is a man," "is a finger," or "is a stick," which are complete, both grammatically and logically one-place. Objects are men, fingers, or wooden sticks in themselves, independently of any relation to other things. As long as Simmias is the same object, he will be a man, and conversely. Complete terms like these are connected with the identity of the objects to which they apply, and do not generate the paradoxes that incomplete terms seem to generate. Plato, in fact, contrasted these two classes of terms: explicitly at *Republic* 523–25 and *Alcibiades* I.111b11–c2, and implicitly, as I shall argue below, at *Phaedo* 74a9–c5.

My view is that, at least in the *Phaedo* and the middle books of the *Republic*, Plato envisaged Forms for these incomplete predicates only. In the *Phaedo* (100b–105c) Socrates distinguishes between sensible particulars, their properties or characters, and the Forms. These Forms, and all the Forms mentioned elsewhere in the *Phaedo* and in the middle books of the *Republic*, correspond to incomplete predicates. Plato is introducing a new class of objects that the soul, confused by the contradictory reports of the senses (*cf. Rep.* 524b–d), has to contemplate if it is to grasp what beauty, justice, or tallness are in themselves. Unlike sensible particulars, the Form and the characters of beauty are completely, essentially, beautiful. If a particular is beautiful, it will also be ugly in another context: that very same particular will be ugly, without undergoing any change. But the Form and the characters of beauty would cease to be what they are if they were ever qualified by ugliness. Socrates' language is significant: neither the Form nor the character of tallness that a tall particular object possesses, he says,

> will consent to being other than it is by remaining and accepting shortness. Whereas, remaining and accepting shortness, still being who I am, I become short without changing, it will not dare, being tall, to become short. (*Phd.* 102e2–6)

There is a clear parallel between Socrates' "being who he is" and tallness's "being tall." Socrates cannot cease to be a man and still be Socrates; and tallness cannot cease to be tall and still be what it is: for what it is is, in an essential way, *tall*.

By introducing this new class of intelligible objects Plato managed to resolve one of the problems of the early dialogues. We do "mean one thing" when we call many objects beautiful, just, or tall; the terms are not ambiguous: their meaning, and reference, is the Form of beauty, justice, and tallness, respectively. Sensible objects are both beautiful and ugly, just and unjust, tall and short, because they are not *really* beautiful, just, or tall; they only participate in beauty, justice, or tallness by possessing a relevant character. And it is only the Forms and the characters that really are beautiful, just, or tall: they are beautiful, just, or tall in themselves, without qualification, in every context, and they are present in all and only those cases where we can speak of beautiful, just, or tall sensible objects.

If this view is correct, then when Plato says that sensible objects are only imperfectly beautiful or just, he does not mean that they are approximately beautiful or just. Rather, he means that they are only accidentally beautiful or just, while the Form and its characters possess the relevant property in an essential manner. Notice also that on this approach, not only the Form but also the properties of particulars (the characters) exhibit this perfection. Thus the properties that particulars possess are perfect copies of the Forms in which these particulars participate. The imperfection of the sensible world does not consist in those very properties that it shares with the world of Forms. It consists, rather, in that sensible objects possess their perfect (i.e., exact) properties imperfectly (i.e., incompletely, temporarily, accidentally). Particulars are not imperfect copies of the Forms, as the approximation view would have it; they are imperfect: that is, copies of the Forms. For we shall see, in what follows, that to be a copy for Plato is the same as to "fall short" of, to be imperfect in comparison to, the model. The copies' imperfection does not reside in the properties that make them copies, but in the way these perfect properties are possessed. When we say that particulars are only imperfectly F in comparison to the Form of F-ness, the imperfection belongs to the "being" rather to the "F" in "being F."[20]

I am afraid that this all-too-sketchy account is all I can give here by way of exposition. Perhaps the examination of the approximation view, to which we must now return, will help to put my position in a clearer perspective.

III

The approximation view holds that, say, two particulars are equal to each other because each participates in equality with respect to the other, or that Helen is beautiful because she participates in beauty, and so on.[21] But also, on this view, no sensible object ever is equal, beautiful, and so on, because of the fact that such objects are only approximately whatever we say they are. Here, then, is a problem. On what grounds can we justify our saying that the particulars participate in equality and Helen in beauty? How can we avoid saying that our particulars really participate in inequality and Helen in ugliness? If, as Taylor says, the same visual sensations that suggest the notion "straight" also show that nothing in the world is perfectly straight (and one can wonder at this point on what grounds this "perfectly" was included), why does the notion of being straight ever get suggested in the first place? Why not deduce from these sensations that visible lines strive after perfect inequality? On such grounds as these, the postulation of the Forms is no more legitimate than is the postulation of material objects in order to explain the regularities of our perception, when *all* we are "acquainted with" in perception is supposed to be only our own sense-experience. Both postulations are equally illegitimate, and both show that more than is supposed is given to us in perception.[22]

I can think of only one way in which a defender of the approximation view could try to circumvent this criticism. That would be to claim that although no two sensible objects are perfectly equal, still sensible objects participate more or less in equality. If participation were a matter of degree, then it might be argued that every pair of objects participates in equality to some extent, that we consider equal those objects whose participation in equality is very great (that is, whose dimensions yield very close measurements), and that no objects are exactly equal, although that notion is reached by approximation. But I don't think that this suggestion can work at all. First, because there is not one shred of evidence that Plato thought of participation as an ordinal relation: particulars participate in the Forms in different respects or in different contexts, but never, so far as I can tell, in different degrees. Secondly, and perhaps more importantly, because this suggestion reverses the logical relations between "being F" and "participating in F." Plato introduces the relation of participation to explain the notion of, say, being equal. He says that sensible objects participate in equality because he feels that he cannot say that sensible objects are (really) equal; but his concern has nothing to do with the exactness of the instantiations of equality: it is with their accidental nature. He begins by observing that objects are equal, or just, or beautiful, but only in certain respects, or in relation to certain objects, and he introduces their participation in the Forms on account for this latter feature. And he also limits participation in the Form of F-ness only to those objects that we can, in certain respects or contexts, truly consider as F. By contrast, the suggestion we are examining takes Plato's technical term, interpreted as an ordinal relation, as basic, and constructs the notions of equality, beauty, or justice as special cases of that relation.

A number of issues are involved in this question, and we shall examine them as we proceed. For the moment, we must turn to Plato's own writings and see whether the approximation view can give a reasonable interpretation of Plato's expressed position on the imperfection of sensible objects. A key passage, which has furnished the received tradition with its favorite example, is *Phaedo* 72e–78b, where Socrates tries to prove the soul's immortality by appealing to the theory of recollection.

I cannot possibly give an exhaustive analysis of this notorious passage here.[23] My question concerns the adequacy of the approximation view in explaining Socrates' distinction between equal particulars and the equal itself and his statement that the former are "inferior" to the latter. On at least one problem I will be quite dogmatic: I will assume that Plato is only referring to the unitary[24] Form of equality by all three expressions that he uses in this passage, namely, "the equals themselves" (αὐτὰ τὰ ἴσα, 74c1), "equality" (ἰσότης, 74c1), and "the equal itself" (αὐτὸ τὸ ἴσον, 74c4–5); neither mathematical intermediaries[25] nor "things insofar as they are equal"[26] are involved in his argument.[27] I will not be quite as dogmatic, however, on the interpretation of the phrase "equal . . . to one . . . unequal to another" (τῷ μὲν . . . ἴσα . . . τῷ δ᾽ οὔ, 74b8–9), and I will not be at all dogmatic on the interpretation of the way in which particulars "fall short" of the Forms.

These last two points are quite distinct on the approximation view, whose reconstruction is as follows: Socrates first distinguishes equal particulars from the equal itself on the vague and incomplete grounds that "sticks and stones, sometimes, being the same, appear equal to one, unequal to another" (*Phd.* 74b8–9),[28] while on no occasion do "the equals themselves appear unequal to you (viz., Simmias), or equality, inequality" (74c1–2). He then goes on to say that equal particulars fall short of equality, in that they are only approximately and not exactly equal (74d4–7). Finally, he generalizes this to all particulars and properties at 74d9–75b8.

The points are distinct because on no interpretation of the first does it follow that equal things, in contrast to equality, are only approximately equal. Whether sticks and stones appear to one *person* equal, to another person unequal; whether they appear equal to one *thing*, unequal to another thing; or whether they appear *sometimes* equal and sometimes unequal: none of these alternatives implies that their relative or temporary equality is only approximate. On the contrary, it seems to me, roughly the same predicaments, if they are predicaments, would befall things that were exactly equal. If two things were perfectly equal in this sense, then from some perspective they must appear unequal to an observer, and they must appear (and be) unequal to some things that measure differently. As to the "sometimes" reading, we have two alternatives: we can either take it as "they sometimes appear equal, sometimes unequal, to each other," in which case we have two only unequal things appearing to be equal on some occasions, probably because of perspectival variation; or we can take it as "they sometimes appear equal to some things, sometimes unequal to other things." On either alternative, the case collapses to one of the two previous possibilities; and neither of these supports the approximation interpretation of imperfection.

So, Ross's claim that in distinguishing equal things from the equal itself, Plato "is thinking, perhaps, of the effect of perspective" cannot stand.[29] In fact, to appear equal, or square, from all angles, apart from being impossible, is also to my mind a mark of imperfection: an object that appears square from all angles cannot be a square, it must be an impossible-object construction; it would, by contrast, be a mark of the perfect square that at such-and-such a tilt, it would project exactly such-and-such a trapezoid![30]

This, then, is one shortcoming of the approximation view in interpreting Plato's argument. The distinction between particulars and Forms is quite independent of the inferiority of the former to the latter, although there should be some connection between them. Because of this, the imperfection of particulars is left undefended on this account: Socrates simply asks Simmias if this is not the case (*Phd.* 74d5-7), Simmias immediately agrees (74d8), and Socrates generalizes his conclusion. But why should Simmias agree to such an idea? Perhaps he might have found it plausible if it concerned only squares and circles (drawn circles being only approximately circular by geometrical standards); but it does not. He might have been tempted, although that would have been a very mild temptation, if it concerned only equality. But Socrates proceeds to generalize to "the larger, the smaller, and all such things"; his argument, he says, "is not more about the equal than it is about the beautiful itself, the good itself, the just, the pious, and, I mean, about everything to which we give our seal of 'that which is' in our discussions" (75c9-d3). This generalization, which Simmias also accepts without argument, certainly needs support. But before I show how Socrates does argue for it, and how the two points are connected, I must discuss another difficulty for the approximation view, which was first pointed out by Gosling.[31]

Suppose that the approximation view is correct and that particulars are deficient in the very respect in which they resemble the relevant Form. Now, in this argument, Plato is trying to prove that our knowledge of equality is an instance of recollection. To this end, he specifies four conditions that cases of recollection should satisfy. Two are given at *Phaedo* 73c6-d1:

> If someone saw, heard, or by another sense perceived something, and came to know not only that thing but also became aware of another, the knowledge of which is not the same but different, would we not be justified in saying that he remembered what he became aware of?

First, the perception of one thing must give rise to knowledge of another. All cases of recollection involve (at least) three terms: the subject who remembers, the object that reminds him of what he remembers, and the object he remembers. Secondly, the knowledge of what is remembered must be distinct from the knowledge of the reminding object. This a puzzling condition, and Gosling takes it to mean that "it must be possible to know or be acquainted with what we are reminded by, without knowing or being acquainted with what we are reminded of, and vice versa: I may be reminded of Simmias by his portrait, but not by Simmias himself."[32] But I am not sure that this is right because, for one thing, such a consideration does not play a prominent role in Plato's argument; for another, as we shall see, this aspect of recollection, as stated, is covered by Plato's fourth condition.

My own view is that Plato is stating a different condition here: If A reminds me of B, then my coming to know A is not (not: need not) on that occasion sufficient for my coming to know B. For suppose that I am looking at Simmias, who is wearing a brown tunic; can we say that (my looking at) Simmias reminded me of his tunic? No, for looking at Simmias, I am also looking at his tunic. On the other hand, I can be reminded of the tunic if my looking at Simmias when he is not wearing it brings it to my mind. Similarly, my seeing Simmias running may remind me that the bell that has been annoying me for the last five minutes signals the beginning of a lecture on ethics; even though the two events are simultaneous, one may remind me of the other if my coming to know the first does not by itself imply my coming to know the second. Notice also that on Gosling's condition, my seeing Simmias wearing his tunic could actually qualify as a reminder of the tunic, since knowing Simmias is in fact independent of knowing his tunic, and it is possible to know one without knowing the other.[33]

The third condition, given at *Phaedo* 73e1–3, is rather loose, and not quite necessary:

> This, then, is recollection: especially if it happens to someone in connection with things he has long since forgotten because of the passage of time and of not thinking about them.

Coming to know the equal itself is such a star instance of recollection. Here, too, I must disagree with Gosling, who interprets this passage as stating a necessary condition: "I am not said to be reminded of someone or something except in some respect in which I had at least temporarily forgotten them."[34] This is indeed true, but, as the text shows, not what Plato is saying at this point. He only wants to point out that given that the other conditions are met, and that knowledge of one thing brought to mind another, which was not there at the time (i.e., which was temporarily forgotten), we are especially justified in calling this recollection if the thing remembered has been forgotten for a long time.

The fourth condition is the most crucial one for our purposes. At 74a1–

2, Socrates, having explained the general conditions of recollection, distinguishes between being reminded of *B* by *A* through some association *A* and *B* possess for the subject (as when a portrait of Simmias [73d9], or Simmias himself [73e5–6], reminds us of Cebes) and being reminded of *B* by *A* through some similarity between them (as when Simmias' portrait reminds us of Simmias himself: 73e9–10). In "remembering through similars," Socrates now adds (74a5–7),

> isn't it also necessary that one realize whether or not what reminds him lacks something in respect of being similar to that which is remembered?

When I first read this passage, I was bewildered; eventually I came to disbelieve what I thought it said. Why should Plato make this a necessary condition for recollection, and why did he think that it was obvious, as Simmias' immediate assent at 74a8 indicates? Is it really necessary for me to realize that Simmias' portrait, which reminds me of Simmias, does not match the color of his hair? Must I, in one breath, realize that I am looking at Simmias' portrait and that the portrait is inaccurate? Finally, why *can't* the portrait be accurate?[35]

I can see only one possible way of saying that the portrait must be inaccurate: one could argue that the color of Simmias' hair depends on the lighting in which it is seen, and that the illumination is constantly changing; therefore, the portrait cannot capture the right color over time. This may be thought plausible; but, by this argument, we would have to conclude that one never even sees the real color of Simmias' hair. For the color at any moment is different from what it has been or will be at all other moments; thus we should have to conclude that even our sight gives us an imperfect approximation to the color of Simmias' hair. But surely this is not what Plato had in mind. And even if he did, we should note that this still would not give him (or us) good reason to say that portraits must be inaccurate. For nothing prevents the portrait from attributing to Simmias exactly the right color of hair (or any other characteristic) at a given moment, from a given perspective, or in given conditions. The portrait's "imperfection" does not consist in its deficiency in resembling Simmias in a given respect, but in its incapacity to capture some characteristic of Simmias in all its dimensions. This point can be made by saying that a portrait cannot possibly capture all the characteristics of its model. And this does not preclude the portrait from matching its model exactly in some characteristics (namely, these in which it resembles it). And the fact that the portrait does not duplicate all the features of its model must be clear to the spectator if he is to be aware that he is looking not at the model itself, but at a different thing, its portrait or copy, which resembles the model in certain relevant respects!

My suggestion, then, is that Plato is not maintaining the implausible idea that the approximation view attributes to him, namely, that if two things are similar to each other, and one is a copy of the other, the copy can never reproduce exactly that very characteristic that makes it a copy in the first place. Rather, Plato believes that if one thing is a copy of another then it must lack some characteristic of its model, and that one must realize this if one is to realize that he is confronted with a copy in the first place. In this way, Plato's notion of "copy" is different from our notion of "duplicate," and he distinguishes the two in his statement of this condition.[36] If our two similar objects share every characteristic, then we shall no longer be confronted by a copy, portrait, or image (εἰκών) and its original. Particularly, in the case of recollection, we shall not even be aware of being confronted by two distinct objects at all. But then the second condition on recollection will not have been met, and no remembering will occur: we will be seeing (hearing, etc.) what we take to be the very object that we were supposed to remember.

It is important to keep in mind in this context a passage in the *Cratylus* (432a–d), where Socrates shows Cratylus that pictures (and likenesses in general, including *onomata*: names or words) cannot reproduce every property of their original. If a god, Socrates says, made a likeness of Cratylus, matching not only his color and shape, as painters do, but also made everything inside just as it is (ἀλλὰ καὶ τὰ ἐντὸς πάντα τοιαῦτα ποιήσειεν οἷάπερ τὰ σά, 432b5–6), then what we would have would not be Cratylus and his image, but, simply "two Cratylusses."

The implication is clear that painters can, and do, match exactly the "color and shape" of their subject, but that they cannot match all its properties. If they did, they would no longer be constructing a likeness, but a duplicate. Socrates completes his point by asking Cratylus if he is not aware "how far likenesses *fall short* of being such as the things are of which they are likenesses" (ἢ οὐκ αἰσθάνῃ ὅσου ἐνδέουσιν αἱ εἰκόνες τὰ αὐτὰ ἔχειν ἐκείνοις ὧν εἰκόνες εἰσίν, 432d1–3). The vocabulary is that of the *Phaedo:* likenesses fall short of their model—not because they cannot *exactly* reproduce *any* of its properties, but because they cannot *at all* reproduce *some* property (or properties) of their model.[37]

It is a difficult question for the approximation view how, since according to its account copies cannot match exactly any of their models' properties, we come to realize that an object is a copy of a different one in the first place. (Notice that this is the same criticism, in relation to copies and originals, that we raised at the very beginning of this section in relation to particulars and Forms.) This view appears more plausible if we think of portraits and their subjects only. For a portrait, one might say, may not match any property exactly, but it may match a number of properties approximately, and, on balance, it resembles its subject more than it resembles any other object. Even if we grant this, which is very doubtful,[38] we must still remember that portraits are only of incidental concern to Plato:

his main interest is to show that sensible objects are likenesses of the Forms in which they participate. But sensible objects resemble each Form only in one respect: the only characteristic common to the equal itself and to equal particulars is that they, too, are in their way equal. And if their equality is only approximate, if, that is, it is really inequality, how can we connect them with the equal itself in the first place?[39] Since the alternative that might have applied to portraits is no longer available to us, we should conclude that we would never realize that equal, just, or large particulars "desire" to be like their respective Form, which we do realize, Plato says, at the very moment when we begin to employ our senses.

These, then, are Plato's conditions on recollection:

If a person, P, is reminded of B by becoming aware of A, then,

1. A and B are distinct;
2. Becoming aware of A was not on that occasion sufficient for becoming aware of B;
3. In particular, we are said to recollect B especially if we have long forgotten it.

Further, if A and B are similar, then,

4. P must realize that A is only similar to, and not identical with, B, in that it does not duplicate every property of A; in Plato's words, A must fall short of being such as B is.

Plato shows, by the example of the equal itself, that our knowledge of the Forms satisfies these conditions. First he shows that the equal itself is distinct from all sensible equal objects, which are responsible for our becoming aware of it (*Phd.* 74a9–c10). He then states that given that equal things are similar to the equal itself, they fall short of being just like it (74c11–d8). He goes on to argue that we realize their inferiority through our senses, which we exercise from the moment we are born and that thus our knowledge of the Forms is prior to and independent of our knowledge of equal particulars, for otherwise the comparison could not have been made (74d9–75d6). Finally, he argues in a way strongly reminiscent of *Meno* 98a2–4 and *Laches* 190c6 that, since people cannot "give an account" (διδόναι λόγον, 76b4–9) of the Forms, their knowledge must have been lost. Our knowledge of the Forms is thus forgotten, acquired before birth and before our senses began to function (75d7–76c10). Therefore, he concludes, our soul must have existed before our birth (76c11–77a5).

IV

The approximation view fails to make Plato's theory of recollection coherent. Let us now try to show, by exploiting the suggestion made in our discussion of Plato's fourth condition, how Socrates' distinction between sensible equal objects and the equal itself supports his claim that the former are inferior to the latter.[40]

Since Socrates' peculiar claim that sensible equals are inferior to the equal itself (74d4–8) is not given explicit justification, it is reasonable to expect that it has received some support in what has just preceded it. And since what has preceded it is the distinction between these two classes of objects, our task is to read that argument in a way which will provide the support the imperfection claim needs.

What is the characteristic that allows Socrates to make the distinction? The problem is that his claim that

> sticks and stones, sometimes, still being the same, appear equal to one, unequal to another (74b8–9)

is too vague and incomplete to be understood as it stands. One alternative, older and more widely accepted than the second, has been to take the indefinite pronouns "one" and "another" as masculine and to render this passage as follows:

> Two stones or two logs equal in length sometimes seem equal to one man, but not to another, though they haven't changed.[41]

A number of considerations against this view, some less persuasive than others, have been given by N. R. Murphy and K. W. Mills.[42] Among them we might single out the claim that on Hackforth's interpretation Plato's second premiss appears to be irrelevant. For that premiss, stated at *Phaedo* 74c1–2, is:

> But now, what about the equals themselves? Have they ever appeared to you to be unequal, or equality to be inequality?[43]

But what Plato should have asserted is not that the Form of equality can never appear to be unequal (or inequality) to Simmias, but that this could never happen to anyone. Antisthenes, for example, would not have been bothered by this claim, since equality never appeared to him to be anything at all. Also, Murphy argued, on this approach the first premiss is "pointless, since we could infer only that one of the two [men] had made a mistake."[44] Now these points have been widely discussed and, on balance, Hackforth's view and Murphy's suggestion to take the pronouns as neuter and read Plato as saying "that sticks and stones without themselves changing have contrasted predicates in different relations, but the equals themselves . . . have not"[45] have proven equally inconclusive.

I propose to bypass most of the debate and offer a different consideration that might strengthen Murphy's approach. According to Hackforth, we have a pair of objects, equal to each other in length, which, perhaps because of perspective, seem equal to some people and unequal to others.

These objects, in other words, are supposed to remain in the same relation to each other while people disagree about their equality. And as long as we concentrate on this particular example, Hackforth's interpretation seems, if not confirmed, at least plausible. But surely Plato is not interested only in the predicate "is equal (to . . .)" but also in all those predicates for which he will postulate Forms, including "is larger (than . . .)," "is smaller (than . . .)," "is good," "is just," and "is beautiful."

Let us now take one of these predicates and ask how the argument would distinguish, for example, just particulars from the just itself. According to Hackforth, Plato would claim that the same just act would appear just to some people and unjust to others. But now that perspective cannot provide the easy answer, the question why Plato would believe this becomes crucial. Plato did actually believe that people disagree about what is just, pious, brave, or beautiful. But his belief did not concern acts like returning a knife to its maniacal owner: this, he thought, was patently unjust (*Rep.* 331c–d); he did not doubt that humans are beautiful compared to apes (*Hippias Major* 289a); he did not question Socrates' bravery at Delion (*La.* 181b) or at Potidaea (*Smp.* 219e5–221c1). What he did doubt was that returning what one owes is always, in all contexts, just; whether a human being is beautiful no matter what that person is being compared to; whether retreating or advancing is always brave. In a specific context, Plato would not hesitate to call an action just or brave, a person beautiful or virtuous. What he did hesitate to believe was that the grounds usually given for such claims would always, in all circumstances, support the same conclusion, as he thought good grounds should.

But if this is so, then Hackforth's interpretation of our argument cannot account for its generalization, which should capture all those predicates for which Plato postulates Forms. Although a log may from a certain angle appear unequal to another log of equal dimensions, a just act will not appear unjust unless the context in which it was considered has changed:[46] returning a knife to its rightful owner is not just if its owner happens to be a homicidal maniac.

My claim is that Hackforth and those who agree with him have been misled by an accidental feature of the particular example that Plato used in his argument. They thus took it that Plato claims that things can appear both *F* and not *F* in the same context to different observers. But although Plato could have said this about pairs of equal things, he could not have said it about the other predicates for which he designed his argument. What he could have said, and what I think he did say, is that no earthly equal, beautiful, large, good, pious, or just object can appear equal, beautiful, large, good, pious, or just in every relation. If any did, it would be in itself equal, or beautiful, and so on. But all earthly things depended for their beauty, and their equality, on the presence of other things and on a comparison with them, and this distinguished them from the Forms that were essentially what these earthly things were only accidentally.

If we accept the idea that what distinguishes sensible particulars from Forms is the fact that particulars possess their properties only in an incomplete manner, only in relation to other particulars, while the Forms possess them completely, in themselves, not only does the general argument become coherent, but also the imperfection claim receives the support it needs. Just as Simmias' portrait matches Simmias' hair color exactly at a given moment, so equal particulars resemble equality exactly, in relation to specific objects to which they are equal. And just as Simmias' portrait cannot match Simmias perfectly (either in all his properties, or in respect of hair color over time), so equal particulars cannot match equality in all respects. For they are equal only to some things and not to others, and without any change in themselves (but only in their relations) they can be truly considered as both equal and unequal—while equality is always equal, and depends on nothing other than itself for this. And just as Simmias' portrait "falls short" of being just like Simmias, so equal particulars "fall short" of being just like the equal itself. But their imperfection does not consist in their being approximately what the Forms are exactly; it consists in their being accidentally what the Forms are essentially.

It is in this way that Socrates, in distinguishing equal particulars from the equal itself, also shows that sensible objects are inferior to the Forms. And here we have one of the reasons why the Forms that Plato postulates all correspond to incomplete predicates. His problem was that sensible objects *still being the same,* would appear to be both equal and unequal, both beautiful and ugly, and so on. He postulated the Forms in order to show that despite their compresence these properties did correspond to distinct entities, and that the terms associated with them did have distinct, and univocal, meanings. But for this problem to even arise, the *same* sensible particulars would have to be qualified by contrary properties. And for these particulars to remain the same, there would have to be some properties that those particulars possessed in themselves, independently of their relations to other objects, properties that would allow their reidentification over time. These properties all corresponded to complete terms, they did not confuse the soul by appearing together with their opposites, they did not require the postulation of Forms, and the way in which they applied to sensible particulars actually provided Plato with the model on which he conceived of the relation between the Forms and the properties for which these Forms stood.

Plato, then, did think that the Forms have perfect instances in the sensible world (these are the "characters" of the *Phaedo*), and that they are contained in the particulars that participate in them. What is imperfect is the way in which those perfect instances are possessed by sensible objects, an imperfection that allows us to say of everything that we consider as just or beautiful or equal that is also unjust, ugly, or unequal. Contrary to the idea underlying the approximation view, I think that Plato was writing not so much with Pythagoras but with Parmenides in mind. His question, as the absence of mathematical discussion in the early dialogues indicates, was not of a sort that would have taxed mathematicians. It was the question how we can even understand each other when we say that sensible objects are equal, beautiful, good, or large, since these words seemed to refer to exactly the same things to which their contraries also referred; and the question how things can both be and not be what we say they are. To these Eleatic challenges, the theory of Forms replied that none of these objects is equal, beautiful, good, or large, but that there is a whole class of different, intelligible, objects—objects that always and only are, and never are not, which we know not by the senses but by recollection, and which, by being the meanings of our words and by being instantiated by sensible objects, allow us to understand each other and to know when we are speaking truly of the changing sensible world.[47]

NOTES

1. A comprehensive survey will be found in Gregory Vlastos, "Degrees of Reality in Plato," in R. Bambrough, ed., *New Essays on Plato and Aristotle* (London and New York, 1965), 1–19.

2. A. E. Taylor, *Plato* (London, 1922), 41; ch. II, *passim*. See also *Platonism and Its Influence* (Boston, 1924), ch. II, *passim*.

3. A. E. Taylor, *Plato: The Man and His Work*, 6th ed. (Cleveland, 1966), 187.

4. Ibid., 188.

5. John Burnet, *Plato's Euthyphro, Apology of Socrates, and Crito* (Oxford, 1924), n. ad loc., 37.

6. John Burnet, *The Phaedo of Plato*, Oxford, 1911, n. ad loc., 55, italics in the text. See also Burnet's *Platonism* (Berkeley, 1928), 41–43.

7. W. D. Ross, *Plato's Theory of Ideas* (Oxford, 1951), 25.

8. Ibid., 23.

9. Paul Shorey, *What Plato Said* (Chicago, 1933), 172–73.

10. Hugh Tredennick, *The Last Days of Socrates* (Baltimore, 1959), 14.

11. Apart from the texts quoted above, see Burnet's comment on *Phd.* 75c11, op. cit., 58, and on *Eu.* 5d3, op. cit., 31. For a more recent statement of this view, see J. E. Raven, *Plato's Thought in the Making* (Cambridge, 1965), 69–70, 96.

The paradigm involved here is so strong that Burnet felt justified in writing this (*Platonism*, 41–42): "[The geometrician is] certainly not [speaking] of any triangle that we can perceive by the senses (for all these are only approximately triangles), not even of any we can imagine. He is speaking of what is 'just a triangle' (αὐτὸ τρίγωνον) and nothing more. It is neither equilateral, isosceles, or scalene. And so it is with all other geometrical terms. It is clear from the way in which the subject is introduced in the *Phaedo* (65d4) that this was the original sense of the doctrine of 'forms.'"

But a glance at *Phd.* 65d–e shows that no geometrical terms or Forms are involved in that passage! Socrates directly introduces the Forms as intelligible entities by the example of *the just itself* at 65d4, and goes on to mention the beautiful itself, the good itself, largeness, health, and strength. The only vaguely "mathematical" Form is largeness, μέγεθος; and there are no obvious parallels between the properties of being large (or tall) and being a triangle.

12. That is, Plato generalized to *at least* these contexts. Some believe that he also generalized to all contexts; cf. Ross, op. cit., 24.

For the sake of fairness we must mention that Ross does not subscribe to the historical thesis about the genesis of the theory of Forms (op. cit., 13–16). But his treatment of imperfection belongs to the same category as that of the other writers quoted above.

13. See J. Gosling, "Similarity in *Phaedo* 73b *seq.*," *Phronesis* 10 (1965): 151–61. This article has been extremely helpful to me, and I draw heavily from it in what follows.

14. C. M. Gillespie, "The Use of *eidos* and *idea* in Hippocrates," *Classical Quarterly* 6 (1912): 179–203, esp. 202: "Prof. Taylor's contention that Plato found the words already in current use with the specific technical sense of 'simple beings,' 'monads,' 'things-in-themselves,' and merely applied them to a new kind of hyperphysical monad [is unfounded]. . . . My examination seems to indicate that at the time of Socrates the words *eidos* and *idea* show two trends of meaning in the general vocabulary of science. The first is mainly physical, but without mathematical associations: . . . the *form* of a bodily object. . . . The second is semi-logical, classificatory; used especially in such contexts as 'there are forms, kinds' of anything, whether a substance like the 'moist' or a disease or whatnot."

15. See the passage quoted from Tredennick above.

16. See the first quote from Taylor above.

17. I. M. Crombie, *An Examination of Plato's Doctrines*, vol. 2 (London and New York, 1963), 279.

18. "Predication and Forms of Opposites in the *Phaedo*," *Review of Metaphysics* 26 (1973): 461–91.

19. See, for example, *Laches* 190e5–6, *Hi.Ma.* 289a1–6, *Rep.* 331c–d.

20. See Wilfrid Sellars, "Vlastos and 'The Third Man,'" *Philosophical Perspectives* (Springfield, 1967), esp. 25–31.

21. I leave the range of predicates for which this explanation is appropriate open, much like Socrates does at, among other places, *Phaedo* 100b–c.

22. See R. E. Allen, "Participation and Predication in Plato's Middle Dialogues," in G. Vlastos, ed., *Plato I: Metaphysics and Epistemology* (Garden City, N.Y., 1971), 178: "A crooked line is not an imperfect instantiation of straight linearity; on the contrary, it is a full and complete instantiation of the *kind* of crooked line that it is, and the kind is repeatable, though the line itself is not . . . to say that something is deficient with respect to one character is merely an awkward way of saying that it quite fully has another."

23. For a detailed discussion see K. W. Mills, "Plato's *Phaedo* 74b7–c6," *Phro-*

nesis 2 (1957): 128–48; 3 (1958): 40–58. A number of references are given in this article. I will give some additional ones below, but see also R. S. Bluck, "Plato's Form of Equal," *Phronesis* 4 (1959): 5–11; Richard Haynes, "The Form equality, as a set of equals," *Phronesis* 9 (1964): 17–26; and J. M. Rist, "Equals and Intermediaries in Plato," ibid., 27–37.

24. Peter Geach has argued that the Form of equality actually consists of two perfectly equal objects in "The Third Man Again," in R. E. Allen, ed., *Studies in Plato's Metaphysics* (London and New York, 1965), 265–77.

25. W. D. Ross, op. cit., 22; R. Hackforth, *Plato's Phaedo* (Indianapolis, 1965), 69 n. 2; R. S. Bluck, op. cit., and *Plato's Phaedo* (London, 1955), 67 n. 2.

26. Burnet, *The Phaedo of Plato,* n. *ad* 74c1, 56; R. Loriaux, *Le Phédon de Platon, Commentaire et traduction,* vol. I (Namur, 1969), 143–46.

27. This is also the opinion of G.E.L. Owen, "The Platonism of Aristotle," in P. F. Strawson, ed., *Studies in the Philosophy of Thought and Action* (London, 1968), 147–74. My conversations with Professor Owen on this subject have been extremely valuable.

28. Or, according to the variant manuscript readings (cdd. TW) τότε . . . τότε, "sometimes equal, sometimes unequal." This reading, however, does not introduce any new considerations, as we shall see.

29. Ross, op. cit., 23.

30. It is instructive to compare, at this point, Plato's discussion of perspective at *Republic* 597–98. The physical bed does not change, whatever the angle from which we look at it; it only appears different. Painting represents not the bed as it is, but as it appears (598a–b). Variations due to perspective have no implications as to the *ontological* character of physical objects, and are therefore unlikely to account for the ontological distinction that Plato is trying to draw in the *Phaedo*.

31. Gosling, op. cit.

32. Ibid., 154.

33. See also ibid., 159.

34. Ibid., 154–55. A similar point is made by Aristotle in *De Memoria et Reminiscentia,* 451a31 *ff.* See Richard Sorabji, *Aristotle on Memory* (Providence, 1972), 53.

35. It is important to notice that Plato envisages as real possibilities both that the object may and that it may not lack anything in respect of being similar to what it reminds us of. Plato's point is, I think, very sensible. Not all similar objects are related as copy to original: two mass-produced earthen jars, for example, are not. He is saving a place in his scheme for such objects in this statement.

36. Cf. n. 35.

37. My debt to Gosling is obvious; he is the first to have pointed out the relevance of the *Cratylus* passage to the *Phaedo;* see pp. 157–59 of his article.

38. I don't really agree even with this claim: how one can tell that an object is a picture of another is a much more complicated affair. But this approach may seem to some to have "initial credibility."

39. Socrates' inclusion of the "larger" and the "smaller" in his list of Forms at *Phaedo* 75c9 makes this point crucial. If sensible objects were all only approximately large, then they should all be small, and they would all strive to be like the "smaller."

40. The interpretation of 74a9–12 is not our concern. Whether we take it to mean "we say that something, namely, the equal itself, is equal," or "we say that something equal exists, namely, the equal itself," the rest of the argument remains, for our purposes, unaffected.

41. This is Hackforth's translation, op. cit., 69; Bluck, *Plato's Phaedo*, 67, translates as follows: "[D]o not stones that are equal, or pieces of wood, very often seem—the self-same objects—to one man, equal, to another, unequal?" Cf. Burnet, *The Phaedo of Plato*, n. *ad* 74b8, 74; R. D. Archer-Hind, *The Phaedo of Plato* (London, 1883), n. *ad* 72e–76d, 77.

42. N. R. Murphy, *The Interpretation of Plato's Republic* (Oxford, 1951), 111, n.; K. W. Mills, op. cit. Loriaux also accepts this view, without argument, in *L'Être et la Forme selon Platon* (Paris, 1955), 18–19; he does not argue for it in *Le Phédon de Platon*, 149–53.

43. Hackforth, op. cit., 69; cf. Bluck, op. cit., 67.

44. Murphy, op. cit., 111, n.; Mills, op. cit., 131–33, argues that both interpretations are subject to this shortcoming. But this is not true if the "appears" is taken to mean, as it is taken below, "appears and in fact is."

45. Murphy, op. cit., 111, n.; I have deleted the Greek in Murphy's sentence.

46. Unless, that is, it is considered as an action-type to be found in many tokens.

47. I am very grateful to John Cooper, who read a draft of this paper and saved me from some, though not all, of my errors. (Those that remain, he could do nothing about.) An older debt, acknowledged belatedly here, is due to Michael Friedman.

Eight

CONFUSING UNIVERSALS AND PARTICULARS IN PLATO'S EARLY DIALOGUES

THAT SOCRATES did not always find it easy to make himself understood by his interlocutors in Plato's early dialogues, and that this difficulty was caused by his radically new approach to philosophy, is standard doctrine and, for what it is worth, true. Along with this standard doctrine, however, comes the following explanation of his difficulty; and this explanation, it can be argued, is not true.

It is said that when Socrates is made to ask questions like "What is the pious and what the impious?" (*Euthyphro* 5d7), "What is courage?" (*Laches* 190d8, e5), or "What is the beautiful?" (*Hippias Major* 287d3), he is asking for the definition of a universal. For the "average" Greek of his time, however, this is a radically new question about a radically new sort of object, and Socrates' interlocutors do not understand it. They usually answer it as if it were a different, if related, question: they tend to provide concrete instances of the universal in question rather than a definition, however inadequate, of the universal itself. Socrates always tries, but does not always succeed, to make himself clear: Meno, for example, is supposed never to get the point.

This approach is indeed common. We can find it, for example, in John Burnet:

> In several of Plato's dialogues Socrates is made to criticize the confusion of the universal . . . with some particular of which it is predicated.[1]

R. E. Allen states this view as follows:

> As universals, Forms play a regulative role in dialectic; they are the antecedents of *esti* in questions of *ti esti,* "What is it?" and they therefore specify the nature of that question, and so restrict the range of answers that can be sensibly given to it. . . . Because holiness and temperance and beauty are universals, answers to the question of what they are cannot merely provide examples of them.[2]

I. M. Crombie also accepts this approach, and tries to explain why Socrates' interlocutors missed Socrates' point:

> [O]ne can ask what the beautiful is (meaning "What is beauty?") or what man, or the man, is (meaning "What is the essential nature of mankind?").

When this idiom is used no distinction is drawn between the property (beauty) and the class of things which have the property (the beautiful in the sense of that which is beautiful). It is thus natural for the man in the street, when asked what the beautiful is, to think first of the class and to reply by citing some of its prominent members or sets of these. . . . One has to labour, as Socrates labours with Hippias, to show the man in the street what is wanted. . . . Socrates explains that he wants no instance, but "that the presence of which to anything makes that thing beautiful."[3]

So "What is the beautiful?" is supposed to be ambiguous in Greek. Socrates' interlocutors tend to take it as "What is beautiful? Point out a beautiful thing," while Socrates himself always takes it as "What is beauty? What is it that enables us to point out things as beautiful?" The innovation of Socrates and Plato is held to have been their insistence on this ambiguity and their belief that the former question cannot be answered unless the latter is answered first.

It is beyond question that something about what Socrates was asking was not clear to his interlocutors, but this view does not account for it. This well-established interpretation does not fit the text of Plato's dialogues, and it commits us to a very peculiar view of the philosophical setting for Plato's work.

I

In discussing the *Euthyphro,* P. T. Geach employs the approach that I want to criticize.[4] Socrates, in this dialogue (*Eu.* 5d7), asks Euthyphro to tell him "what is the pious and what the impious," and when Euthyphro answers (5d8 ff.), Socrates

> adopts a line of argument that we find paralleled in many dialogues. If Euthyphro really knows that his own action is pious, then he must be able to say what is pious; he must not give examples of pious actions. (370–71)

Socrates is dissatisfied with Euthyphro's answer, Geach continues, because he makes two assumptions:

> (A) that if you know you are correctly predicating a given term 'T' you must "know what it is to be T," in the sense of being able to give a general criterion of a thing's being T; (B) that it is no use to try and arrive at the meaning of 'T' by citing examples of things that are T. (371)

Geach calls the way of thinking involved in making these assumptions "the Socratic fallacy, for its *locus classicus* is the Socratic dialogues" (371). He certainly is not alone in reading Plato in this manner; but the question should be reopened: does Socrates commit this "Socratic" fallacy? I am not disputing whether making these two related assumptions constitutes a fallacy—my question is more simpleminded. Is it really clear that Euthyphro and others like him respond to the Socratic question by citing concrete instances of universals instead of universals themselves, and does Socrates ever complain that they do?

My answer to both these questions is categorically negative. My argument for this will consist in a careful reading of the relevant Platonic texts without assuming in advance that these texts exhibit instances of the confusion between universal and particular, definition, or criterion, and concrete example.

This is what Euthyphro actually says in response to Socrates' question:

> I say then that the pious is what I am now doing: prosecuting anyone who is in the wrong in questions of murder or of sacrilegious theft or fails to do the right thing in any situation of this sort, whether he is [your] father or mother, or anyone else for that matter; and not prosecuting is impious. (*Eu.* 5d8–e2)[5]

The temptation to suppose that Euthyphro has offered a concrete example of a pious action rather than a statement of what constitutes piety may spring from concentrating exclusively on his opening words: "the pious is what I am now doing." But this is not all that he says; it is, in fact, the smallest part. The main burden of his statement falls on what follows this phrase, and that is very general and abstract indeed; its force is that to prosecute anyone who has wronged the religious order is (the) pious, or, for that matter, piety, and that its opposite is (the) impious.

Of course, this is not an adequate definition of piety, as Socrates will presently show. Naive as Euthyphro may be, however, he simply does *not* say that his prosecution of his father, a particular action, is pious (or, even worse, piety). He says that every prosecution of a religious wrong is pious, and that since his action is such a prosecution, it, too, is pious.

We might then ask why Euthyphro brings his own action into his response at all, if his point is the very general one that I think we should attribute to him, and not the particular point that he is usually supposed to be making.

To answer this we must recall that Socrates has been pressing Euthyphro to say how he knows that prosecuting his own father, which Euthyphro is about to do, and about which he is obviously sensitive, touchy, and, in a slightly perverse way, proud (cf. 4b7–32, 6a3–5), is in fact pious. Now prosecuting one's own father is not an everyday affair, and Plato relies on this to set up the dialectical situation of the dialogue.[6] It is a strange, uncommon, and disputable action that Euthyphro is engaged in, and Socrates, or anyone else, need not accept the assumptions that constitute the "Socratic" fallacy in order to question Euthyphro on what he takes piety to be. If someone claimed that stealing from the poor is just, it would be a good idea, and not a logical error, to ask him what he means by justice, and even to suppose that he has some explicit view on the subject. This is what Socrates has done (and it is all that he has done), and Euthyphro mentions his action in his reply in order to respond to that challenge. Avenging religious wrongs, he says, is pious, and his action is pious because it is an avenging of a religious wrong.[7] There is thus no evidence so far that Euthyphro misunderstands Socrates' question in the way that is usually supposed. He says that to be pious is to do so-and-so in such-and-such circumstances, and this, inadequate as it may be, is not pointing to a particular; it is, if we want to keep to this vocabulary, specifying a universal.

It is a bad answer, however, and in Socrates' refutation (6d) some have seen an accusation that Euthyphro provided a concrete example rather than a definition of piety. This interpretation has been so widely accepted that it has even entered a number of translations of this passage; this, for example, is Lane Cooper's version:

> For, my friend, you were not explicit enough before when I put the question. What is holiness? You merely said that what you are now doing is a holy deed—namely, prosecuting your father on a charge of murder.[8]

In this way, Socrates is represented to take Euthyphro to have offered "My prosecution of my father" as his answer to the question "What is piety?" But we have seen that this is not what Euthyphro said. Why then does Socrates, if I am right, have this reaction?

Well, *does* Socrates have this reaction? Here is the last part of his statement in Greek:

ἀλλά μοι εἶπες ὅτι τοῦτο τυγχάνει ὅσιον ὂν ὃ σὺ νῦν ποιεῖς, φόνου ἐπεξ-ιὼν τῷ πατρί.

These translations assume that the crucial last phrase is epexegetic, that it specifies what Euthyphro is now doing, namely, prosecuting his father. But Socrates has not used the infinitive (*epexienai*) of the Greek verb for "to prosecute," but its present participle, which must be translated not as "prosecuting" but as "in prosecuting," thus:

> You said that what you are now doing, in prosecuting your father, is pious.

And this is a very different statement. Socrates is not saying that Euthyphro only said that his particular action is pious; on the contrary, he acknowledges the Euthyphro has offered an explanation of that action's being pious. His point is this: You said that what you are now doing in prosecuting your father, *namely, avenging a religious wrong,* is pious. Rather than giving us evidence that Socrates' interlocutors confused universal and particular, this passage, read correctly, shows that this problem is absent from the *Euthyphro;* and, by being so often misread, it provides us with an instance of a universally accepted interpretation imposing an unnatural reading on a particular text.[9]

What is it then that Socrates dislikes about Euthyphro's answer? To answer this we must notice that Socrates' objection is not wholly contained in the statement that we have just been discussing. In fact, he concedes that Euthyphro may have been correct in what he said (*isōs*, 6d6). Euthyphro, we should notice, has actually given an argument:

Prosecuting my own father is pious
> because (1) prosecuting one's father in such circumstances
> > is avenging a religious wrong,
> and (2) avenging a religious wrong is (the) pious.

Socrates accepts this as far as it goes. But he thinks that it does not go far enough: "Still, Euthyphro, you do say that many other things are pious," he goes on to say (*Eu.* 6d6–7). What are these many other pious things, these "many other piouses," as he puts it? I suggest that, consonant with my interpretation, they are other explanations of why particular actions are pious, and not these particular actions themselves. That is, Socrates remarks and Euthyphro agrees (6d8), as well he might, that avenging religious wrongs is not the only explanation why actions are pious. There are many other nonoverlapping explanations; for example, sacrificing before a journey. Euthyphro thus admits in this exchange that he is prepared on occasion to give a different principle, instead of *(2)* above, in similar arguments. And *this* is what Socrates objects to, as he in fact goes on to say at 6d9–e1: it is the unity, and not the universality, of the pious that Euthyphro has failed to capture. Since sacrificing before a journey is also (what it is to be, or the) pious, and since it is different from avenging religious wrongs, Euthyphro has not yet said what the pious is, especially since he has explicitly admitted (5c8–d6) that the pious is one and the same in all that is pious, that there is a single explanation of all piety. Given this admission, to which Socrates refers at 6d9–e1, Euthyphro's answer, in characteristic elenctic fashion, is shown to be inconsistent with it. He does not, to repeat, confuse universals with their instances: he offers too narrow a definition of what to be pious is. In this way he either excludes obviously pious things (all sacrifices before journeys, for example); or else he admits, contrary to his earlier claim, that there is, after all, nothing common to all those things that we consider pious. The "many other piouses," *pace* Burnet,[10] are not particular pious things, but distinct explanations of what makes everything that is pious, pious.

I will return to a number of questions raised in this discussion later in this essay. What I hope to have shown so far is that the "Socratic" fallacy is not committed by Socrates in the *Euthyphro*: that Euthyphro does not confuse universals with particulars, that Socrates does not take him to have done so, and that he does not object to Euthyphro's first definition on the illegitimate grounds that Geach and the standard approach attribute to him. Furthermore, a quick look at the *Charmides,* the *Laches,* and the *Meno* will show that this sort of confusion is not to be found in these early definitional dialogues any more than it is to be found in the *Euthyphro.*

II

Gerasimos Santas has stated that the *Charmides* does not exhibit the confusion between universals and their instances.[11] He writes that

> all the definitions [of temperance in this dialogue] have the generality required of a Socratic definition. Unlike most typical Socratic dialogues where a definition is sought, Charmides and Critias do not begin by giving the wrong *kind* of definition . . . somehow they seem to know the sort of thing that Socrates is after, which is rather surprising in the case of Charmides at least since he has just met Socrates for the first time. (110)

Santas contrasts the *Charmides,* in this respect, with the *Euthyphro,* the *Laches,* and the *Meno.* And I agree that some of the definitions in these dialogues lack a required generality; but I do not agree that this is the same as to confuse universals with particulars. Having shown this for the *Euthyphro,* I will now try to show it for the other two works. In that way, I hope to show that there is nothing surprising in Charmides' response to Socrates.[12]

At *Laches* 190d3–4, we find Socrates asking: "Let us then first try to say what courage is," and Laches responding as follows:

> Know well that if someone were willing to fight the enemy, remaining at his post, and did not retreat, he would be courageous. (190e5–6)

It should be obvious that Laches says nothing even remotely close to the idea that, say, Aeschylus or his performance at Marathon is courageous (or, even worse, courage). Courage, he says, is to fight the enemy and not to retreat. His definition, of course, is not general enough; but where is the confusion between what is courageous and what it is to be courageous?

In this context, the word "example" is peculiarly ambiguous. We can say that Charmides is an example of beauty, that Aeschylus is an example of courage, and that Nicias is an example of piety. We can also say that the examples in question are Charmides' beauty, Aeschylus' courage, and Nicias' piety. Or we can finally say that the examples are physical beauty, fighting steadfastly, and sacrificing before a journey.

Now if I asked you what beauty is, and you answered by citing Charmides, his beauty, or even physical beauty, we could say that you have not yet answered my question correctly. But it is not clear that you would have made the same error in all these cases. In the last case, you would have given a partial or incomplete answer. You would not have yet said what makes everything beautiful beautiful, because there is, or so it seems, more than beauty that meets the eye. I might even react by saying that you have merely given me an example of what beauty is, that you have merely specified one of a number of ways of being beautiful, while what I want to know is that which makes all these ways of being the same thing, that is, beautiful. It is only a specification of this (if there is such a thing, as Socrates always assumes) that will answer my question.

If, on the other hand, you pointed at Charmides, I should have to say much more than this. I might still say that you have merely given me an example of beauty, but I would not go on to speak of ways of being beautiful. I would have to start all over again, because in that case you would have totally missed my point; you would have really answered a different question. You would not simply have given me an inadequate answer, but no answer at all.[13]

The point is that saying that Euthyphro and Laches answer the Socratic question by giving examples, being ambiguous, does not by itself imply that they confuse universals with their concrete instances. The two errors are not the same. Further, since Socrates complains (*La.* 191c7 ff.) that Laches' answer is not general enough, we have there an indication that Laches' error is the weaker of the two. The stronger error, confusing universals with their instances, does not actually constitute a failure in respect of generality: no matter how complete we make our list of courageous individuals, we will never begin to supply the sort of answer that Socrates wants. We will never give any, let alone a single, explanation of what makes all these things courageous.

With this in mind, we need to spend very little time on the *Meno*. Again, Meno does not answer Socrates' question, "In the name of the gods, Meno, what do you claim virtue to be?" (*M.* 71d5), by mentioning a particular or even a set of particulars. He replies (71e1–72b5) by citing different *kinds* of virtue, different *ways* of being virtuous, not particular virtuous things. And the point he is never convinced of is not the distinction between virtuous men on the one hand and what it is to be a virtuous man on the other, but the idea that there is something in common between being a virtuous man, being a virtuous woman, being a virtuous child, and the many other ways there are of being virtuous (72a1). He thinks that virtue is, at least in this respect, different from health, size, and strength (72e2–73a5); that, in the case of virtue, there is no single, all-embracing explanation.

Why then is it so often thought that Meno cannot distinguish universals from particulars? Apart from the influence of an already accepted interpretation, one could cite Socrates' famous analogy with the bees as a possible, though not very good, reason (*M.* 72a6–c5). Socrates there likens the many virtues that Meno mentions to a swarm of bees, and insists that as the bees do not differ insofar as they are bees, so the many virtues cannot differ in respect of being virtues. And because bees are particular objects, it may have been thought that what Meno offered were also particular objects. But, of course, this is an analogy, and this inference is illegitimate. The virtues are likened to the bees in respect of being "many and of every sort" (72b2–5), not in respect of being particulars. Socrates' point can be made, in keeping with Meno's words, in terms of kinds of virtue: Meno claims that there are many kinds of virtue; but all these are kinds of the same thing—virtue; what then is this one thing of which they are all kinds? To this, of course, Meno responds that there is no such thing in the case of virtue.

Finally, that the many virtues are not particulars becomes more clear at 74a7–10. Meno has tried to say that virtue, "if you want a single thing in every case, is to be able to rule people" (73c9–d1). Socrates now complains that again they have, in their search for the one virtue, found many. And these many virtues are courage, temperance, wisdom, magnificence, and many others (74a4–6), which are not likely to be considered as particulars by anyone. They are different ways of being virtuous, just as in the *Euthyphro* all we found were different ways of being pious, and in the *Laches,* different ways of being courageous.

III

We have left the *Hippias Major,* another early definitional dialogue, until last, for this work seems to offer a perfectly clear-cut case of the universal/particular confusion, and has often been used as a reason for reading that confusion into other dialogues as well. But our conclusions so far may have shaken our absolute confidence in the usual interpretation of the first steps of the Socratic elenchus, and we may be prepared at least to question the import and significance of Hippias' misunderstanding of Socrates.

The passage that concerns us begins at *Hippias Major* 287c1. Hippias readily concedes to Socrates (287c1–d2) a number of points. Just people, he agrees, are just by justice, wise people are wise by wisdom, good things are good by the good, and beautiful things are beautiful by the beautiful. The construction, common in Plato's work (see *Eu.* 6d10–11, *Phd.* 100–105, *Prm.* 132a1–b2), is the instrumental dative; and there seems to be no significant distinction between abstract nouns ("justice," *dikaiosunē*) and neuter adjectives preceded by the definite article ("the beautiful," *to kalon*). Hippias also agrees that justice, wisdom, the good, and the beautiful "are something" (*esti ti*). And now Socrates asks Hippias to say what the beautiful, which is something, is (*Hi.Ma.* 287d2–3).

All of a sudden, Hippias is at a loss. Is the question, he asks, what is beautiful (*ti esti kalon*, 287d4–5)? No, Socrates answers, the question is what is the beautiful (*hoti esti to kalon*, 287d6). Hippias cannot see a difference between these two (287d7–9), and Socrates repeats his question (287d11–e1). Finally, Hippias claims to get the point:

> I understand, my friend, and I will say in reply . . . what the beautiful is, and I will never be refuted. For, know well, Socrates, that, if the truth be told, a beautiful maiden is beautiful (*parthenos kalē kalon*, 287e2–4).[14]

Obviously, Hippias is still far from being clear; but what is he unclear about? On the usual approach, we would have to say that he understands what it is to specify beautiful things, but that he does not understand what it is to specify what beauty is. He does not understand that, when preceded by the definite article, the adjective "beautiful" does not function as a common descriptive predicate true of particular objects (a function with which he is perfectly at home), but, if you will, as a referring expression denoting the universal, the property of, beauty. He thinks that "beautiful" is, in all its applications, a general term true of particulars; hence his confused reply, "a beautiful maiden is beautiful."

Let us suppose for the moment that this is in fact his reply. Is the belief that we just attributed to him sufficient to explain his confused statement? I think that it is not: Hippias must be more confused than that, because of what he earlier conceded, without argument, to Socrates: that beautiful things are beautiful *by the* beautiful, and that *the* beautiful is something. Although he claims to understand these ideas, and thus the function of "the beautiful," perfectly, he cannot understand the difference between asking what is that by which things are beautiful and asking what some beautiful object happens to be.

We must then attribute to Hippias a compound confusion. Not only does he not understand Socrates' question, and thus that "the beautiful" is true of something other than concrete particulars alone; if only that were the case, he should not have accepted the claim that the beautiful is what makes such objects beautiful and that it can be defined or at least spoken about.[15] He also, inconsistently, accepts these claims.

We are then to take it that Socrates' educated interlocutors were all some sort of naive nominalists. They could deal with sentences of the sort "*a* is *F*" but did not even understand sentences of the sort "*a* is the *F*." Socrates is supposed to have met with difficulty precisely in making them understand this latter sort. Concentrating just on our text for the moment, we should ask how we can reconcile this supposed nominalism with Hippias' willingness to consider the beautiful as that on account of which beautiful things are beautiful.

Our text shows that Hippias is willing to accept this idea, but unwilling, or unable, to understand the difference between the question "What is the beautiful?" and the question "What is beautiful?" We cannot deny this, but we can, and do now, ask what his unwillingness shows. Does it show, as is commonly supposed, that he reduces the former question to the latter, to a question about particulars? Or could it perhaps show that he actually does the opposite, that he reduces, that is, the latter to the former? His misunderstanding alone does not settle the issue. To decide, we must examine his answer, "*parthenos kalē kalon.*" What does he, and Socrates, take the import of this statement to be?

If we take it as "A beautiful maiden is beautiful," as "*a* is *F,*" then we must attribute to Hippias the compound, and as far as I can tell, inexplicable confusion that we have been discussing. For, in that case, what could he have possibly meant by his admission that the beautiful makes things beautiful? In view of this, we should try to interpret his reply in a manner that will both make his earlier admission understandable and explain why he cannot distinguish between "What is the beautiful?" and "What is beautiful?" What then if we take his reply not with the force of "A beautiful maiden is beautiful," but with the force of "Being a beautiful maiden is (what it is to be) beautiful," "To be a beautiful maiden is (to be) beautiful"?

Linguistically speaking, this reading is not impossible. Plato may be writing as Sophocles wrote in the famous ode of the *Antigone* (332–33):

$$\pi o\lambda\lambda\grave{\alpha} \ \tau\grave{\alpha} \ \delta\epsilon\iota\nu\grave{\alpha} \ \kappa o\grave{\upsilon}\delta\grave{\epsilon}\nu \ \mathring{\alpha}\nu\text{-}$$
$$\vartheta\rho\acute{\omega}\pi o\upsilon \ \delta\epsilon\iota\nu\acute{o}\tau\epsilon\rho o\nu \ \pi\acute{\epsilon}\lambda\epsilon\iota,$$

which can very naturally be translated as

> Many things are marvelous and nothing
> is more marvelous than being human,

and which significantly goes on to speak of *anthrōpos,* man, as *touto,* "that," not *houtos,* "he," and to attribute causal efficacy to it. Similar constructions occur in Euripides' *Helen* (560–61):

$$\vartheta\epsilon\grave{o}\varsigma \ \gamma\grave{\alpha}\rho \ \kappa\alpha\grave{\iota} \ \tau\grave{o} \ \gamma\iota\gamma\nu\acute{\omega}\sigma\kappa\epsilon\iota\nu \ \phi\acute{\iota}\lambda o\upsilon\varsigma,$$

> To know one's friends is also (to be) a god,

and *Hippolytus* (627–28):

$$\tau o\acute{\upsilon}\tau\omega \ \delta\grave{\epsilon} \ \delta\tilde{\eta}\lambda o\nu \ \acute{\omega}\varsigma \ \gamma\upsilon\nu\grave{\eta} \ \kappa\alpha\kappa\grave{o}\nu \ \mu\acute{\epsilon}\gamma\alpha,$$

> And from this it is clear that woman is a great evil.

My idea is that the structure of Hippias' statement is of this sort, that "beautiful maiden" does not denote any particular beautiful maiden, but being a beautiful maiden; that "beautiful" is not a bona fide general term, but that it has a peculiar, strong sense,[16] close to what we would mean by the expression "is to be beautiful."

The advantages of this interpretation are considerable. First, we don't have to attribute to Hippias the gross inconsistency that the alternative approach requires. On our present suggestion, Hippias admits that the beautiful is that by which beautiful things are beautiful and proceeds to say that being a beautiful maiden is what explains why (some) beautiful things are beautiful. Second, we can see why he does not notice a difference between the two questions. He takes the primary import of statements of the form "a is F" to be that of "a is the F." Third, we can account for his answer not being satisfactory, and, more importantly, for the argument that Socrates uses against it; to this we shall turn presently. Finally, we can explain the peculiar force of this and other statements about the F that we find in Plato's writings: Hippias' statement does imply that every beautiful maiden is beautiful, and that is why Socrates appeals to particular beautiful maidens in his refutation; but it also concerns another "thing," what it is to be a beautiful maiden, which is why Socrates also appeals to the *genos* (race, species, kind) of beautiful maidens, and which Hippias identifies with what it is to be beautiful. Hippias, in other words, answers that to be a beautiful maiden and to be beautiful are one and the same thing.

Socrates now asks if saying that being a beautiful maiden is being beautiful is sufficient to specify that by which everything that is beautiful is beautiful (*Hi.Ma.* 288a6–11), and it is this point that Hippias misunderstands, as his reply indicates: would anyone dare say that to be a beautiful maiden is not (to be) beautiful, that it is (to be) ugly (288b1–3)?

Hippias thus makes the same sort of answer that we earlier saw Euthyphro make. He does not mention a particular beautiful thing, but a way of being beautiful; and, like Euthyphro, he considers this a statement of what to be beautiful is. When Socrates claims that being a beautiful mare is also (to be) beautiful (288b8–c3), Hippias misses the point that we want a single explanation of all beauty, and sticks to what he considers a sufficient condition for being beautiful.[17] Socrates now gets him to admit that being a beautiful pot is also (a way of being) beautiful (288c9–e7). Hippias, after some argument, accepts this with a qualification:

> Being well-wrought, this (sort of) utensil, too, is beautiful, but it will not do to judge that all this (i.e., being a beautiful pot) is beautiful in comparison to maiden, mare, and "all the other beautifuls." (*Hi.Ma.* 288e6–9; cf. *Eu.* 6d6–7 on the "many other piouses")

Socrates pounces on this. As Heraclitus said, he remarks, the most beautiful ape will be ugly when compared to the *genos* (family, species) of human beings; similarly, it seems, Hippias wants to say that the most beautiful pot will be ugly when compared to the *genos* of maidens. But once we allow comparisons, we may compare the family of maidens to the family of gods, and conclude that, in that context, the most beautiful maiden is, after all, ugly. And the claim is generalized to cover not only being beautiful but also being wise and, in a characteristic ellipsis, "all such things" (*Hi.Ma.* 289a8–b7).

What follows from this is that Hippias has not yet said what the beautiful, what it is to be beautiful, is. He has only specified "what happens to be, on his own admission, no more beautiful than ugly" (289c1–3). Socrates' complaint has nothing to do with particulars being confused with universals; it is simply that being a beautiful maiden does not by itself explain the beauty of anything. Being a beautiful maiden (or horse, or lyre) is compatible with being ugly. In this way, he refutes the cornerstone of Hippias' claim, that "no one will dare say that being a beautiful maiden is not beautiful" (288b1–3). And he also exhibits the characteristic pattern of argument that we have seen him employ in the *Euthyphro* and in the *Laches,* and which can also be found in the *Charmides* and in the first book of the *Republic.*[18]

So, by taking *parthenos kalē kalon* as "Being a beautiful maiden is being beautiful," we can account for Hippias' acceptance of the reality of the beautiful and also for his doubting that to ask what that is, is different from asking what is beautiful: it is this latter question that he reduces to the former, and not the other way around. We can also account for Socrates' argument against Hippias' definition, and for the distributive force of that statement, which allows both of them to move from beautiful maidens individually to beautiful maidens in general. And we can finally place this exchange within a broad class of arguments that Socrates has with his interlocutors in giving them to understand what is peculiar about his definitional questions: what is at issue is never the abstractness, but the uniqueness, of the pious, of courage, of justice, of virtue, or of the beautiful.

IV

We have now seen that Plato's writing fails to support the idea that Socrates' interlocutors were confused in that they mentioned particulars in answering requests for definitions of universals. To believe that this was their confusion is to commit ourselves to the following being the case. Socrates' contemporaries, we would have to say, knew well how to employ general terms, true of individual objects; in fact, this was the only way in which they used general terms. They also knew that singular terms designated, or named, those individual objects. Socrates, however, raised, for the first time, the following question:

> Let us consider a significant subject-predicate sentence such as: "Socrates is pious." Concerning the subject-term, "Socrates," we know that there is something which it signifies, or designates, or is a name of, viz. the Athenian philosopher Socrates. Now it seems reasonable to raise the question: Does also the predicate-term, the adjective "pious," designate something? Is there an entity of which that term is the name?[19]

Suppose, for a moment, that this is a "reasonable" question; is there a reasonable answer to it? My own reaction would be to say that I do not know, or even that, of course, there isn't. But it is notorious that Socrates' interlocutors (even Meno) are quite willing to answer affirmatively.[20] Their willingness in this respect has prompted the view, stated among others by Theodore de Laguna,[21] that

> the first proposition to be noted, as forming part of the general theory of Ideas, is that universals . . . exist. . . . On this score Socrates never meets with any opposition. He does sometimes meet with a certain difficulty in understanding, as when Hippias assures him that the beautiful as such is a beautiful girl. (447)

On this view, the existence of universals is taken for granted in the Socratic dialogues. The difficulty arises because Socrates' interlocutors, having granted this, go on to mistake the question "What is this universal?" for the request "Point out a particular of a certain sort."

This view has some peculiar implications. To hold it, we must believe both that Socrates' contemporaries were naive nominalists, so that we can explain why they always take the question "What is the F, or F-ness?" to be concerned only with F particulars; and, also, that they were naive realists, so that we can explain why they find nothing problematic in the idea that there is an entity, the F or F-ness, that the predicate F names. Further, we must believe that Socrates, faced with an antecedently understood use of adjectives as general terms and with a domain of particular objects to account for that use, insisted that such terms also have a different, referential use and introduced a new domain of objects in order to account for it.

Now perhaps all this is not impossible. But we have seen that this is not quite what happens in Plato's early dialogues. Furthermore, we can give a different model, which is more plausible in itself and accounts for what Plato wrote. Here, I can only sketch this model, without much background support; I can only offer my earlier reading of the dialogues as internal evidence in its favor.

Suppose that we make a shift, and not consider that the copula in Greek is most commonly used as it is used in English, "sc. to indicate that the individual named by the subject-term is a member of the class of those possessing the attribute expressed by the predicate-term."[22] Suppose that we say instead that often in Greek sentences, as in *parthenos kalē kalon esti,* or *phonou epexienai tōi patri hosion esti,* the use of the copula commits the speaker to saying that to be a beautiful maiden is to be beautiful (in other words, that it is *the* beautiful) or that to prosecute one's father for murder is to be pious (in other words, that it is *the* pious). That is, what if the logical form of a number of Greek sentences of the grammatical form "*a* is *F*" were taken to be "*a* is the *F*" or "To be *a* is to be *F*"?

This would commit us to a different general model. Socrates need no longer be thought to introduce a new, naming use of predicate-terms that his contemporaries both understand (in agreeing that the *F* is something) and cannot use (in saying that the *F* is a particular *F* thing). We can say instead that Socrates is simply showing his contemporaries that given this naming use of predicate-terms, to which they all agree, neither Charmides, nor his beauty, nor being a beautiful youth, nor even physical beauty in general, can be beautiful; that is, what it is to be beautiful. He is not introducing both a different use of predicate-terms and a different domain of objects to account for it. He is simply insisting that given an agreed-upon use of such expressions, the things that are commonly offered as what those expressions "name" (*onomazei,* the catchall semantical term that Plato almost exclusively uses; cf. *Crat.* 385c7–d6, *M.* 74d3–74a9, *Phd.* 102a10–103e5) cannot be what those expressions really name.

On this approach, everybody agrees that the beautiful is what "beautiful" names, as is in fact the case in the dialogues; but, when asked what that thing is, no one can offer a proper answer, as is again the case in the dialogues. According to my suggestion, the agreement is built into the situation with which Socrates was confronted and with which he confronted his contemporaries; his point, proceeding as it does from antecedently accepted premises, is characteristically elenctic. On the alternative approach, Socrates would first have to convince his interlocutors that "beautiful" named the beautiful. But, as the dialogues show, they considered that idea a commonplace, and he never had to try. And if they did consider it a commonplace, it becomes very difficult to understand why they mistook his question to be about particular objects, of which "beautiful" is true, but which it does not name.

Now one could say that Plato's goal was to show how confused his contemporaries were. This is true, and my view does depend on the idea that Socrates' interlocutors were confused: this is why Socrates used the elenchus on them. But the confusion is not the same in both cases. The intense confusion that the usual view is committed to is often made more palatable by speaking of them as average people, men in the street, as Crombie would have it. But Socrates' interlocutors were not, except in a literal sense, men in the street: they were people of exceptional promise (like Charmides and Lysis), of some distinction and sophistication (Laches, Meno, and Euthyphro), or even of considerable authority (like Protagoras and Hippias). None of them was the common person about whom, but never to whom, Socrates is made to speak in Plato's dialogues. Socrates' interlocutors could have been confused. But could they have been so confused that they misunderstood completely the distinction between universals and particulars while they were supposed to be in the very process of drawing it?

NOTES

1. John Burnet, *Plato's Euthyphro, Apology of Socrates, and Crito* (Oxford, 1924), 32.

2. R. E. Allen, *Plato's "Euthyphro," and the Earlier Theory of Forms* (London, 1970), 70.

3. I. M. Crombie, *Plato: The Midwife's Apprentice* (London, 1964), 44.

4. P. T. Geach, "Plato's *Euthyphro:* An Analysis and Commentary," *The Monist* 50 (1966): 369–82.

5. The translations, unless otherwise noted, are mine.

6. See, for example, Socrates' undisguised shock at 4a5–b6, and Euthyphro's response at 4b ff.

7. Perhaps one might be tempted to find the "Socratic" fallacy in what Socrates says at 6e3–6: "So teach me what this characteristic [*idea*] is, so that by looking at it and by using it as a standard, I can consider pious anything that you or anyone else does, and which is like it, and not consider pious whatever is not like it." This statement implies that a definition of piety will settle all questions of what is and is not pious; it may even imply that only such a definition will settle them. But it does not imply that we cannot decide whether *anything* is or is not pious unless we first have the definition. And it is this latter idea that constitutes the "Socratic" fallacy, not the reasonable point that we cannot settle *all* cases of piety and impiety without a definition.

8. In Edith Hamilton and Huntington Cairns, eds., *Plato: Collected Dialogues* (New York, 1963), 174. Compare R. E. Allen, op. cit., 27: "You said that the thing you are now doing is holy, prosecuting your father for murder," and Hugh Tredennick, *Plato: The Last Days of Socrates* (Baltimore, 1954), 24–25: "You said that what you are doing now—prosecuting your father for manslaughter—was a pious action."

9. M. Croiset, *Platon: Oeuvres Complètes* (Paris, 1953), vol. 1, 190, translates this as follows: "Tu t'es contenté de me dire que, en accusant ton père d'homicide, il se trouve que tu as fait un acte pieux." He takes, that is, the participial construction correctly; ironically, however, and probably because of his philosophical interpretation of the dialogue, he inserts the gratuitous "un acte" in the translation.

It should be noticed in this connection that H. W. Smyth, *Greek Grammar* (Cambridge, Mass., 1920), does not mention such a possible use in his discussion of the participle (454–79), while he does mention it in his discussion of the infinitive (442). The only epexegetic uses of the participle listed in J. D. Denniston, *Greek Prose Style* (Oxford, 1960), 83, involve the repetition of the main verb, and have a sense quite different from what must be attributed to this construction in the *Euthyphro*.

It is also very important to recall that when, at *Euthyphro* 6d8–10, Plato uses "prosecuting anyone etc." as an epexegesis of "what I am now doing," he employs the infinitive and not the participial construction.

10. Burnet, op. cit., 36: "one or two particulars of which *to hosion* [the pious] can be predicated."

11. Gerasimos Santas, "Socrates at Work on Virtue and Knowledge in Plato's *Charmides*," in E. N. Lee, A.P.D. Mourelatos, and R. M. Rorty, eds., *Exegesis and Argument: Studies in Greek Philosophy Presented to Gregory Vlastos* (Assen, 1973), 105–32.

12. I am not certain that Santas identifies these two failures here; he does not discuss this issue. In his "Socrates at Work on Virtue and Knowledge in Plato's *Laches*," in Gregory Vlastos, ed., *The Philosophy of Socrates* (Garden City, N.Y., 1971), 177–208, Santas says that Laches' first definition of courage is not general enough (185, 188), but he also says that Laches gives examples, instead of a definition, of courage (187). This is, as I shall argue presently, at least a misleading way of speaking.

13. I cannot discuss here the intermediate case, saying that Charmides' beauty is (what it is to be) beautiful, which presents a crucial ambiguity of its own, combining as it does both a reference to a particular (Charmides) and a reference to a universal (beauty). The problems connected with "entities" of this sort are apparent, among other places, in *Phaedo* 100–105, and in the opening chapters of Aristotle's *Categories*.

14. Doubtless in order to cushion a linguistic shock, Jowett translates this by "a beautiful maiden is a beauty," in Hamilton and Cairns, op. cit., 1540.

15. On the connection between "being something" and definability in Plato, see G.E.L. Owen, "Plato on Not-being," in Gregory Vlastos, ed., *Plato I: Metaphysics and Epistemology* (Garden City, N.Y., 1971), 223–67, esp. 247.

16. I have partially discussed this sense of Greek predicates in my "Predication and Forms of Opposites in the *Phaedo*," *Review of Metaphysics* 26 (1973): 461–91, and in this book's essay "Plato on the Imperfection of the Sensible World." I am grateful to Susan Glimcher for discussing the linguistic point with me.

17. In the *Phaedo*, Socrates holds that the *F* itself can never be not-*F* and that it is the single explanation of why all *F* things are *F*. He considers these two ideas as jointly necessary and sufficient conditions for an adequate definition of the *F* itself. See *Phd.* 100e8–101b2, and Nehamas, "Predication and Forms of Opposites in the *Phaedo*," 465 ff.

18. On the *Charmides*, see 159b1–160d3, and Santas, "Socrates at Work on Virtue and Knowledge in the *Charmides*," 116–17. On the *Republic*, see the argument at 331c–d.

19. Anders Wedberg, "The Theory of Ideas," in Vlastos, *Plato I*, 28–52. I have changed the specimen predicate in this quotation, taken from page 28, from "human" to "pious" in order to make it one of the predicates with which Plato was concerned in his early dialogues.

20. *Euthyphro* 5c8–d6 and *Hippias Major* 287c1–d2 constitute *explicit* admissions of the reality of "universals." So does *Protagoras* 330c1–2, d2–5, which may be surprising when we think of Protagoras' extreme "subjectivism."

21. Theodore de Laguna, "Notes on the Theory of Ideas," *Philosophical Review* 43 (1934): 443–70.

22. Gregory Vlastos, "A Note on 'Pauline Predications' in Plato," *Phronesis* 14 (1974): 95–101, 95.

Nine

SELF-PREDICATION AND PLATO'S THEORY
OF FORMS

—τὸ τί ἦν εἶναι ἑκάστῳ τῶν ἄλλων τὰ εἴδη
παρέχονται.

They furnish the Forms as what it is for each of the
others to be.
Aristotle, *Metaphysics* A7.988b4–5

CONSIDER this famous passage of the *Phaedo*:

[I]f anything is beautiful other than the beautiful itself, it is beautiful for no
other reason but because it participates in that beautiful; and I mean this for
everything. Do you agree with this sort of explanation [*aitia*]?[1]

In its context, this statement suggests that Plato accepts the following
three ideas:

1. Beauty (which is here merely an example) is beautiful.
2. Whether anything else is beautiful is an open question.
3. If anything else can be actually considered beautiful, this must be explained
   in terms of its participation in Beauty, which is itself beautiful in a way which
   does not seem to require such an explanation.[2]

These are strange ideas, for what strikes us as requiring explanation is not
so much why ordinary things are beautiful, or large, or just, but rather why
Plato is at all tempted to say that they are not. Plato's view seems to be
that, strictly speaking, only Beauty is beautiful, and that it takes philosophy
to show that anything else is. To understand why Plato holds this view we
must understand his general view of predication, that is, how he construes
the attribution of characteristics to things, how he interprets sentences of
the form "*a* is *F*." I think that there is something unusual in his interpretation; otherwise, he should not have been willing to consider as obviously
true only those sentences in which the subject-term purports to refer to
the very Form of *F*-ness.

By "self-predication" I shall understand simply the idea that Beauty is
beautiful—in general terms, that the *F* itself is *F*—independently of any
particular analysis we might give to it.[3] So construed, self-predication is

clearly part and parcel of the theory of Forms; but it is also clear that it is acceptable in Plato's writings independently both of the theory and of specific knowledge of what the relevant Form is. Thus Protagoras agrees that Justice is just and Piety, pious (*Prt.* 330c3–e2); Hippias, that Beauty "will never appear ugly to anyone anywhere" (*Hippias Major* 291d1–3); and Euthyphro, that the *eidos* of Piety is pious (*Euthyphro* 6e3–6),[4] long before each one of them is shown not to know what Justice, Beauty, or Piety is, and without any commitment on their part to the existence of the separate Forms. And when Plato does introduce the Forms, self-predication is still acceptable prior to the successful discovery of what any particular Form is.[5]

Self-predication thus preceeds the theory of Forms. In addition, the idea appears in Plato's early dialogues for a reason: it plays an important role in Socratic definition.

When Laches, for example, tries to define being brave as standing one's ground and not retreating, Socrates rejects his effort by arguing that on occasion one may actually be brave in retreating (*La.* 190e4–191b3, cf. 192b10–193c5). To Cephalus' idea that Justice is returning what one owes, Socrates counters that on occasion one may, in returning what is owed, be unjust (*Republic* 331c1–d3), and to Polemarchus' refinement of this proposal he objects that what it implies, namely, harming one's enemies, is actually never just (*Rep.* 335e5, cf. 334d12–e2). Finally, when Hippias claims that Beauty is being a beautiful maiden, Socrates' response is that being a beautiful maiden is compatible with being ugly and hence "no more beautiful than ugly" (*Hi.Ma.* 289c5).

What is important for our purpose is Plato's willingness, which is obvious in the last two instances above, to move from the fact that something is compatible both with the possession and with the nonpossession of a given characteristic *F* to its being both *F* and not *F* itself. For example, Socrates' attitude seems to be that if people can be brave on some occasion without standing their ground, then standing their ground is on no occasion what accounts for the bravery of those who are brave.[6] These two points are explicitly connected by Plato himself at *Phaedo* 101a5–b1, where he argues that the explanation of something's being *F* can never be appealed to in order to account for something's being not-*F*, and that this explanation must itself be *F*.[7]

We may express this point by saying that standing their ground is never what makes people (or their actions) brave.[8] Alternatively, we could say that standing one's ground is not itself brave and thus cannot provide a good answer to Socrates' question—a question aiming at knowledge of what being brave is. Anything that can under any conditions be characterized as not-*F* fails to be itself *F*, that is, it fails to be the *F* itself—and Socrates does reject proposed candidates precisely on the ground that they are not-*F* as well as *F*.[9] It is this point that Plato makes, in the context of the theory of Forms, at *Republic* 479c3–5.[10]

With the one exception of Hippias (who is characterized as slow rather than reluctant; *Hi.Ma.* 287c–291a), Socrates does not find it difficult to convince his interlocutors that the *F* is *F*. This is something usually conceded at the very beginning of his discussions. What *is* difficult is to find out what *that,* the *F* itself, is. Many candidates are disqualified because they are no more *F* than not-*F*, and this seems to be incompatible with the fact that the *F* itself is *F*. Our question is why this should be so, why "the *F* itself is *F*" should be incompatible with being in any way not-*F*, why it should imply being *F* in every way.

This approach toward self-predication suggests that at least sometimes Socratic definition should follow a particular pattern. The search should begin with an agreement (explicit or tacit) that the *F* itself is *F*; a plausible candidate should then be selected, and its name substituted for the subject-term in the self-predication. One should then try to determine whether the resulting sentence is true. This pattern can actually be found—for example, in the second elenchus of Euthyphro (*Eu.* 6e ff.). Socrates there expresses the view that Piety is pious by means of his paradigmatic vocabulary at 6e3–6.[11] Euthyphro agrees, and goes on to offer what is just a substitution instance of the self-predication:

> What is pleasing to the gods is pious, and what is not pleasing [to them] is impious. (*Eu.* 6e10–7a1)

Socrates then argues that since the gods disagree among themselves, the very same things will be both pleasing and not pleasing to them (8a4–5), and that therefore, on Euthyphro's account,

> the same things would be both pious and impious. (8a6–7)

But his question, he continues, was what is itself pious,

> not what happens, the very self-same thing, to be both pious and impious. (8a11–12)

The conclusion is that since what is pleasing to the gods is both pious and impious, it cannot be the pious itself.

This pattern is also discernible at *Republic* 331d4–335e5, as well as in the *Hippias Major,* where Socrates complains that Hippias' answer would have been a good one had his question "originally been what is both beautiful and ugly" (*Hi.Ma.* 288c9–d5). That we can find it, is, I hope, some evidence that we are not completely on the wrong track. In addition, its existence explains a peculiar feature of such elenchi. For to Socrates' question, "What is the *F*?," the answer often given is not "*a* is the *F*," but "*a* is *F*" (cf. also *Eu.* 9e1–3, *Rep.* 331e3–4). We can now see that such answers, rather than betraying confusion on the part of Socrates' interlocutors, or even on Plato's own, are perfectly legitimate, since they are just instances of the self-predication that governs the elenchus.[12]

A self-predication, then, is not a *discovery* we make about a particular Form after we have found out what it is, but rather a truth known antecedently, which can even supply a condition of adequacy on the Form's definition: whatever the F itself turns out to be, it must be F in a suitable sense; and this sense in turn involves always and in every case being F. We must now try to capture the sense in which the F itself is F, accounting at the same time for the fact that Plato did not feel that he had to argue for this strange idea, but that he did feel that every other sentence of the form "a is F" created a philosophical problem.

My suggestion is that we should accept the following analysis of self-predication:

The F itself is $F =_{df}$. The F itself, whatever it turns out
to be, is what it is to be F.

The suggestion actually is that Plato tends to interpret every sentence of the form "a is F" as "a is what it is to be F," and that his difficulties with ordinary predication stem exactly from this interpretation. But we will come to this later. For the moment, we should note how such an analysis of "Justice is just" helps to show how both

Returning what one owes is (what it is to be) just

and

Doing one's own is (what it is to be) just

are proper answers to Socrates' question "What is Justice?" since both are instances of the self-predication, though only the second, according to Plato, is true.

So construed, self-predications describe the Forms,[13] but what they describe is the Forms' very nature.[14] They are thus not just ordinary predications, yet they are not pure tautologies either. They are not, on any occasion, absurd: nothing is logically or metaphysically wrong with Justice, doing one's own, being what it is to be just, with Motion being what it is to move, or with Plurality being what it is to be plural.

Now if Plato understands all predication on this model, we can explain why nothing other than the Form can be strictly speaking F. For neither Socrates (a "particular") nor returning what one owes (a "universal") is just, since neither is what it is to be just.[15] If Plato thinks that a characteristic can only be attributed to a thing if it constitutes that thing's very nature, nothing but Justice (which simply is that nature) can be just. For, to paraphrase the *Phaedo* (102b8–c4), when we say that Socrates is just we do not say in words what is in fact the case: for Socrates is not just in virtue of being Socrates, in virtue, that is, of his nature, but only in virtue of the justice that he happens to possess.[16] And since being just is not the nature of anything other than Justice, nothing that we know about these things in themselves (that is, nothing we know about their nature) will help us determine whether they can ever be considered just. We can only determine this if we can establish an appropriate relationship (participation) between such things and something else, distinct or separate from them (*chōris, chōriston*).

To learn what Justice is, is therefore to learn something very important about those things that make a claim to being considered (but that are not) just: anything can be considered, or said to be, just that can be seen as a doer or as a doing of one's own; it must participate in, or be a case of, doing one's own.[17] In coming to know what Justice is, we come to know the one thing to look for in every case—though discerning it may be so difficult in practice (since nothing is in itself, or purely, a doer or a doing of one's own) that some may despair of its existence:

> Each [Form] is in itself one; but by appearing everywhere in combination with actions, bodies, and with the others, it appears to be many. (*Rep.* 476a5–7)

On this interpretation of self-predication we need no longer suppose, as has in the past seemed necessary, that the predicate "just" has a different sense when it applies to Justice than it has when it applies to its participants.[18] The predicate has only one sense, and so, unfortunately for sensibles, does the "is" that connects subject and predicate; this is why *only* Justice is just, why, in general terms, the Forms are said to be, in contrast to sensibles, "purely" or "really."[19] The imperfection of the Form's participants does not consist in *what* they are, but rather in *how* they can be said to be just.[20]

This interpretation may also help to show that Plato's conviction that each Form is in every case one and the same,[21] that it is always and without change *F*,[22] that it is simply and alike *F*,[23] and that it is *F* in every possible respect[24] depends not on metaphysical prejudice but on compelling reasons.

Suppose, for example, that we define Justice as *X*, having characteristics *ABC*. Having *ABC* is therefore just, that is, what it is to be just. Now suppose that something else, *Y*, distinct from *X* and consisting in having characteristics *DEF*, makes an equal claim to being the just itself. Having *DEF* must therefore also be just, in the same way. Given our interpretation of "is" we can now argue validly to the following disjunctive conclusion: either *ABC* and *DEF* do not make an equal claim to be the just itself, and only one of them is, or if their claims are in fact equal, neither is successful, and something distinct from both of them is really just. For, by hypothesis, *ABC* and *DEF* are distinct, and *ABC* is just. Hence, *DEF* cannot be just. For, if it were, then since *ABC* is not *DEF*, *ABC* would not be what *DEF* is, that is, just. Thus, *ABC*, which has been defined as the just itself would turn out not to be just. The same argument could also be made for *DEF*. Given this understanding of "is," and its accompanying principle that the *F* itself is *F* (which is, I shall suggest, a special case of Parmenides' notorious principle, "Never shall this be proved, that what is not is")[25] anything that does not make an *exclusive* claim to being *F* is immediately disqualified. If two things make an equal claim, neither of them is *F*, hence neither of them is the *F*, and there must be something else, distinct from both of them, which is really *F*, and to which the previous two are somehow related:

> [A] further one would appear whose *eidos* (aspect, form) they, in turn, would both have and that, not these two, would then be what [*F*] is.[26]

It is important to notice that we can construct parallel arguments for the other, equally Parmenidean, characteristics that Plato attributes to the Forms. For example, if *X* is what it is to be just, then *X* must be always and without change just. For if *X* were at any time characterizable as not just, this would violate the Parmenidean principle that "what is must be and cannot not be,"[27] and it would show that *X* is identifiable independently of its being just.[28] But then it follows that *X* cannot be what it is to be just: nothing is identifiable independently of its nature, and a thing's nature is precisely that respect in which a thing never changes.[29] Such arguments all depend on the assumption that what is *F* cannot in any way appear to be not-*F*. And this assumption can make claims to self-evidence (rather than seeming to depend on prejudice or confusion) if we see the "is" of predication in Plato as specifying the very restrictive concept "is what it is to be." In this way, by construing self-predication as a more fully spelled-out version of Parmenides' principle of being, we are enabled to give both theses more plausibility and more of a historical context.

It is widely agreed that the later Presocratics were concerned to show, against Parmenides, that the sensible world has a measure of reality because of the existence of objects (atoms, the elements, or the *homoiomerē*) that meet Parmenides, conditions on being, and that underlie appearance and constitute the reality of which the sensible world is the appearance:[30]

> The Parmenidean logic had rudely checked the course of Greek thought . . . it determined the subsequent course of Presocratic philosophy which was in the main a series of attempts to save the world of nature without transgressing the rules of the new logic.[31]

It is also agreed that in the *Sophist* Plato tries directly to refute the Parmenidean principle that unless something is *F* in every way it is not *F* in any way. Yet

> few students of ancient philosophy would expect to find in the earlier dialogues . . . arguments or passages recalling the verses of Parmenides.[32]

If the argument of the preceding pages is correct, however, then it may be plausible to suppose not only that Plato's vocabulary echoes Parmenides', but that he, along with his contemporaries, worked within a Parmenidean framework for a large part of his life—until he turned to overthrow that framework in his later works. His generalization of Socrates' moral concerns into the theory of Forms represents, ironically, one of the last Presocratic systems—broader and more magnificent, to be sure, than Atomism or Empedocles' system of cycles, but still their competitor: a first among equals.

Thus the Forms, and only the Forms, are *F* in a way that seems to satisfy Parmenides' conditions on being, and thus they constitute reality. If this is so, however, what are we to say of the many other things that we want to, that we even have to, consider beautiful, or large, or just? My suggestion has been that Plato follows Parmenides to the extent of thinking that there is, strictly speaking, only one way of having a characteristic, namely, being that characteristic itself. This is precisely what the interpretation of "*a* is *F*" as "*a* is what it is to be *F*" implies; and, of course, it also follows from the interpretation that only the *F*, and nothing else, is *F*. Plato, that is, follows Parmenides in not distinguishing clearly between having a property and being a property, between being *F* and "receiving" *F*, to use Aristotle's expression from *Physics* A3. Aristotle, in fact, denies that the conclusion that only the *F* is *F* follows from this interpretation of "a is *F*": the argument, he says, is inconclusive (*asumperantos*), for "the being of [*F*] will be different from that which has received it."[33] Not having made this distinction, Parmenides seems to have argued that what constitutes reality is not things but rather the nature of such things; he also seems to have concluded that everything other than this nature, everything other than what-is, is in no way, that everything other than being is "deceptive appearance" (B8.52.60, cf. B1.30).

Plato, it seems to me, was unwilling to follow Parmenides in denying all reality to sensible objects. Though he does not think that, for example, Charmides, or being a beautiful youth, is beautiful (since such claims, by means of the arguments that we rehearsed above, can be shown to entail contradictions of the form "The *F* is not *F*"), he tries to preserve a measure of these things' claim to being considered beautiful by showing that they bear an appropriate relationship to Beauty, to what is itself beautiful. Thus he offers as a second-best alternative to—and *not* as an analysis of—

such things' being beautiful the idea that, rather than *being* beautiful, they *participate* in, or that they resemble, or that they in some way possess, the one thing that alone really is beautiful.[34]

Before we go on to examine this aspect of the theory of Forms, and its semantical implications, we should stop to consider a serious objection to this general interpretation of self-predication. This objection contends that given this interpretation, Plato's argument that the Forms are distinct (*hetera*) from their participants at *Phaedo* 74a9–c6 is a failure.[35] In that argument, Plato tries to show that the equal itself is distinct from all sensible equals on account of the fact that though equal things are unequal, the equal itself is never unequal.[36] Let us now use "the F" as a term referring to the Form, and "this F" as a term referring to any participant in that Form. Plato's point can now be put as follows: though it is always and without exception true that the F is F, it is not always and without exception true (in fact, he seems to believe, it is never true) that this F is F.

The objection now is that if we interpret

    1. The F is F

as

    2. The F is what it is to be F,

Plato's argument fails, in that it can be shown that this F is in fact F. For it is quite true that

    3. The F is not what it is to be not-F,

and it is equally true that

    4. This F is not what it is to be not-F,

since no unequal thing, for example, is what it is to be unequal, that is, inequality. But, given our interpretation of "is," (4) is equivalent to

    5. This F is not not-F,

which is, in turn, equivalent to

    6. This F is F,

and, therefore, sensibles, no less than the Forms themselves, turn out to be F, which contradicts our approach to self-predication.

I would reply to this objection that what Plato is trying to point out is that F-things can be considered no more F than not-F, and that this characteristic is what distinguishes them from the Forms. That is, Plato believes that though "This F is not not-F" has a claim to being true, so does the claim

    7. This F is not F,

and the problem with sensible objects is that neither claim is better supported than the other. And precisely because both (6) and (7) are equally true, Plato concludes that neither of them is true, and that sensibles cannot be said "either to be or not to be, either both or neither" (*Rep.* 479c3–5). Plato concludes that sensibles are never *F* on account of the fact that there is as good reason for saying that they are *F* as there is for saying that they are not-*F*. The objection is correct in pointing out that given our interpretation of "is," it follows from Plato's argument that we can say that *F*-things are *F*. It overlooks the fact, however, that, given that same interpretation, it is equally true to say that *F*-things are not *F*, and that it is the contradiction generated by these statements (given, again, this interpretation of "is") that forces Plato to separate Forms from sensibles, and to limit the application of "being" to the Forms.

However, though Plato is unwilling to speak of sensibles as being (either *F* or not-*F*), he is not willing to stop talking altogether of their having characteristics. And it is this unwillingness on his part that prompts him to introduce the relation of participation, a relation that is, to repeat, an alternative to, and not an analysis of, *being F*. It is, then, for this reason that Plato feels that he must explain why ordinary things are beautiful, large, or equal: why, as he puts it, they are "named after" the Forms (*epōnumian ischein*, *Phd.* 102b2). Just as, on the ontological level, only the beautiful itself is beautiful, so, on the semantical, the word "beautiful" is strictly speaking only the name (*onoma*) of the beautiful itself and of nothing else. The word, we may say, is only "derivatively" the name of beautiful things.[37]

It is important to notice, however, that in this context a "name" (*onoma*) cannot be construed either as an arbitrary identifying tag, conventionally (or even causally) associated with an object, or as a term denoting its referent through any set of characteristics which that object happens to possess.[38] Rather, Plato seems to think that "beautiful" names only the beautiful because he thinks of an *onoma* as revealing the nature of what it names, and that it is only if this very strong semantical relation obtains that a word can pick out an item in reality. An *onoma*, therefore, is only in a strictly literal sense a *proper* name for Plato. This attitude toward language seems to me to be presupposed by the many commonplace puns on proper names in Greek literature,[39] as well as by the following statement attributed to Pericles by Thucydides:

> and it has been called by the name "democracy" because it has been set up not for the few but for many . . .[40]

This suggests that the characteristic on account of which democracy is given its name (*onoma*) is not a chance property of the system, but something that determines it in an essential manner. More specifically, this attitude is presupposed by Plato's willingness to speak of names as something that things in the world do or do not *deserve* (*axiousthai, Phd.* 103e3).

On this view, the predicate "just" is the name (*onoma*) only of what it is to be just, and not of anything that merely happens to be just. The catchall semantical term *onoma* involves this very strong relationship between word and thing, and for this reason, I disagree with an assumption that governs much recent discussion of predication and self-predication in Plato. This is the assumption that an *onoma* is either a proper name (and thus has a conventionally grounded relation to its referent) or a predicate construed along the lines of class membership.[41] If we accept this assumption, then when Plato says that "beautiful" is a name of the beautiful, we are faced with a dilemma; either "beautiful" is a proper name of the beautiful and the self-predication reduces to the tautology "The beautiful is the beautiful"; or, to avoid this result, "beautiful" is a bona fide predicate of the beautiful, and Beauty turns out to be, with serious consequences for the theory of Forms, a member of the class of beautiful things.[42] Yet, I think that Plato's discussion of the way in which sensibles are named after the Forms, at *Phaedo* 102–4, shows that instead of assuming that an *onoma* can ever specify an accidental property of a thing, he introduces the notion "being named after" precisely in order to capture this linguistic operation. By contrast, he retains *onoma* and *onomazein* (naming) for cases where a word expresses the nature or essence of its referent.[43]

Semantic vocabulary does not play a major role in Plato's early dialogues. As far as we can tell, Socrates, concerned with the question of the nature of virtue, did not stop to consider what we are to say about the rejected candidates for the *F* itself—things which, though not *F* strictly speaking, are still in a way *F*. In the *Meno*, however, we meet with semantic terminology. Socrates there argues that though both being round and being straight "are called by some one name" (*heni prosagoreueis onomati*), that is, the name "shape," there must be something else

> which occupies the round no less than the straight . . . that which you name "shape" indeed . . . (74d7–e1)

He then goes on to ask:

> What on earth, then, is that of which this word, "shape," is the name? (74e11)

His argument seems to be that since neither being round nor being straight is what it is to be a shape, neither is what the name "shape" names. And we cannot possibly construe "names" as "is true of" (the relation expressed by class membership) in this context, since this is precisely the sense in which both the round and the straight are "called by some one name" and this sense is being contrasted with naming. The correct sense of "names" here must be that of specifying the very nature of what being a shape is.

We should notice two points. First, that once this semantical relation is openly employed, the question, what to say about all the things that we call "*F*" but which are not really (are not actually named) *F* comes to the fore, inconspicuous as it may have previously been. And with its emergence (which occurs in the *Meno,* a dialogue independently acknowledged to signalize the beginning of Plato's middle period) is associated the introduction of the theory of Forms. For the theory aims to answer exactly this question, by appealing to participation on the ontological level, and to "being named after" on the semantical level.[44]

The second point to notice is that on this construal of *onoma,* it follows that if something has any name, it can only have one name. For if a name specifies what a thing is, no two distinct names can apply to the same thing, since nothing can have two natures.[45] Conversely, no name can name more than one thing, for these two, by hypothesis, distinct things would then have to have the same nature, and thus be one. Interestingly, the arguments for this position would parallel, on a semantical level, the arguments we rehearsed above in relation to the ontological status of the Forms, and which derive from Eleatic assumptions. The basic semantical principle that governs naming, and that we might call the One-Name Assumption is this:

> If *w* is the name of *a*, then *w* is the only name *a* has, and *a* is the only object named by *w*.

The One-Name Assumption can be located in the presentation of the theory of Forms in the *Parmenides,* when Socrates contrasts Forms and sensibles by characterizing the latter as *talla ha dē polla kaloumen* (129a3). The expression can be translated as "the others, which we call 'many'"; "many," however, can function either as a referring expression, as a term by which sensibles are collectively denoted, or as a placeholder for the predicate, in which case the phrase should be taken as "the others, which we call many things" or "the others, which we call by many names." On the latter reading, which I prefer, the Forms' participants are things that can be denoted by more than one name (the possibility being grounded in their participation in many Forms, after each of which they are named); by contrast, the Forms are things that can be called only by one name.[46]

This last idea, the One-Name Assumption, is, of course, too restrictive; the Forms, too, must be capable of bearing more than one name. This is why the attack on Parmenides in the *Sophist* contains as its integral part the theory of the blending of Forms. For this latter theory asserts that the Forms, too, participate in one another, and its purpose, significantly, is to show in what manner we call in each case the very same thing by means of many names. (*Sph.* 251a5–6)

This dual attack on Parmenides, semantical no less than ontological, supports the idea that the One-Name Assumption goes hand in hand with the ontological principle that we discussed above, and that both spring from an Eleatic approach to language and reality.

The overall consequence of this discussion is that Plato turns out to be both more naive and more sophisticated than we sometimes suppose. He is not concerned with the more contemporary problem of universals, but then neither does he make elementary errors about it. He is concerned with articulating the very concept of predication; this is, if I am right, one of the central purposes of the theory of Forms. He does not begin with an antecedently existing understanding of predication; there was no theory about how a single thing can have many characteristics, or how a single thing can be denoted by more than one word. Certainly, Plato did not start out believing that to say that something is large is to say that a general term, true of objects in general, is true of some given individual, and end up with a strange notion of being, according to which each general term must also function as the proper name of an abstract entity, which is more real than the objects with which he began.[47]

Rather, Plato begins with a peculiar notion of being, stemming from Parmenides and, as far as we can tell, broadly accepted in his time. According to this conception, nothing is that is not what it is to be something, and each word can pick out at most one thing in the world, the very nature of what the word names. Beginning with this, Plato concludes with a very sophisticated justification of predication, an operation with which this notion of being is, strictly speaking, incompatible. He assumes that "being" has only one sense, and that nothing is that does not meet in every way a set of very stringent conditions. Yet we do say that many other things also are: the theory of Forms aims to show that though this is not strictly speaking correct, neither is it just delusion.

The main weakness of the theory is its very commitment to Parmenides' principle, according to which nothing is F is any way that is not F in every way. It is not until he writes the *Parmenides* and the *Sophist* that Plato questions this assumption and concludes that everything that is in some way F will also not be F in some other way, that "being" does not have only one sense, and that even being itself, without contradiction, is not. During Plato's middle period, the F itself (which is in every way F) competes with the many F things for the appelation "F," and is the only thing that deserves it: it is another thing, distinct from them, whose claim to being F is the only one acceptable.

The *Parmenides* rightly emphasizes this separation between Forms and their participants in its first part, and the principles that underlie it in its second. It is not a little to Plato's credit that he realized that the explanatory value of the postulation of the Forms ultimately depends on denying that principle, and that he was willing and able to overhaul the very framework on which his theory originally depended. In his "parricide" of Parmenides (*Sph.* 241d3), Plato conceived predication; and without the theory of Forms, which made him Parmenides' intellectual offspring, his parricide could never have occurred.

NOTES

1. *Phaedo* 100c4–8; and cf. *Parmenides* 128e6–129b1, *Symposium* 211b1–5.

2. See my "Predication and Forms of Opposites in the *Phaedo*," *Review of Metaphysics* 26 (1973): 461–91, esp. 464, and Norio Fujisawa, "῎Εχειν, Μετέχειν, and Idioms of 'Paradigmatism' in Plato's Theory of Forms," *Phronesis* 20 (1975): 30–49, esp. 35–36.

3. The term was originally introduced, along with a particular analysis, in Gregory Vlastos's important paper, "The 'Third Man' Argument in the *Parmenides*," in R. E. Allen, ed., *Studies in Plato's Metaphysics* (London and New York, 1965), 231–63. The term shall also be used to refer to sentences in which self-predication occurs.

4. It may be possible to find self-predication at *Euthyphro* 5d1–5 as well, though the sense of the text there is not so clear. On a number of possible translations, such, for example, as R. E. Allen's, the passage does not contain a self-predication: "Or is not the holy, itself by itself, the same in every action? And the unholy, in turn, the opposite of all the holy—is it not like itself, and does not everything which is to be unholy have a certain single character with respect to unholiness?" (*Plato's "Euthyphro" and the Earlier Theory of Forms* [London, 1970], 26). But it is also possible to construe *pan* at 5d4 adverbially and with what precedes it in the text and translate: "Is not whatever turns out to be unholy (i.e., the unholy itself) like to itself and having wholly one character with respect to unholiness?" Cf. Parmenides, DK B8.22: *epei pan estin homoion,* which has given rise to a similar dispute. G.E.L. Owen ("Eleatic Questions," *Classical Quarterly* 10 [1960]: 84–102, esp. 92–93), followed by Michael C. Stokes (*One and Many in Presocratic Philosophy* [Washington, D.C., and Cambridge, Mass., 1971], 134–35) takes *homoion* adverbially, while A.P.D. Mourelatos (*The Route of Parmenides* [New Haven, 1970], 111 n. 30) takes it adjectivally. This debate can be resolved if we follow Owen and take *homoion,* as well as *pan,* adverbially, yet not as modifying *estin* (which is why Mourelatos rejects this reading) but, instead, an implicit predicate "*F*": *pan estin homoion* becomes "it is all alike *F,*" echoed, if that is true, closely by the *Euthyphro.*

5. For example, *Symposium* 210e–212a, which is deeply committed to self-predication, does not in fact ever say what Beauty is; the *Phaedo,* despite its essential reliance on self-predication both in its introduction and in its employment of the theory (74a–75d, 100b–105e), does not contain even a specimen definition of a Form; the self-predication of *auta ta homoia* is accepted at *Parmenides* 129b1–2

without any statement of what this thing is (and cf. on the use of *teras, Phd.* 101b1), and so is the self-predication of the one and the many at *Prm.* 129b6–7.

6. Socrates' approach is well described by Gerasimos Santas, "Socrates at Work on Virtue and Knowledge in Plato's *Charmides*," in E. N. Lee, A.P.D. Mourelatos, R. M. Rorty, eds., *Exegesis and Argument: Studies in Greek Philosophy Presented to Gregory Vlastos* (Assen, 1973), 105–32. Socrates, Santas writes, "has not been trying to show that the characteristic Charmides hit upon, quietness of behavior, is contrary to the characteristic of temperance, but rather that it is irrelevant to it; some cases of quietness may be cases of temperance—possibly even all—depending on some further characteristic of the performance" (117).

7. See "Predication and Forms of Opposites in the *Phaedo*," 465–66 (n. 2 above) and, for discussion of different views of this passage, David Gallop, *Plato's "Phaedo"* (Oxford, 1975), 184–86. It is significant that Aristotle adopts in a general way the second part of this condition. Cf., for example, *Metaphysics* a, 993b24–27: "A thing has a quality in a higher degree than other things if in virtue of it the similar quality belongs to the other things as well (e.g. fire is the hottest of things; for it is the cause of the heat of all other things)" (Ross translation).

8. This relation is expressed variously in Plato's texts: cf. *Euthyphro* 6d11 (*hōi*), *Protagoras* 332c1–2 (*hupo* + genitive), *Hippias Major* 288a10 (*di'ho*), *Charmides* 160d7 (*poiein*).

9. Cf. *Hi.Ma.* 289c4–5, c9–d1; *Eu.* 8a7–8.

10. The many explanations offered by the "lovers of sights," Socrates says, "play a double game, and we cannot securely think that any one of them is or is not, either both or neither."

11. If the view supported in n. 4 above is correct, the self-predication has been already accepted by Socrates and Euthyphro at 5d1–5.

12. I have tried to support such a claim in the essay "Confusing Universals and Particulars in Plato's Early Dialogues" in this book.

13. For a list of conditions that successful interpretations of self-predications must satisfy, see Sandra Peterson (subsequently, "Peterson"), "A Reasonable Self-Predication Premise for the Third Man Argument," *Philosophical Review* 82 (1973): 451–70, esp. 461.

This particular condition is satisfied by Vlastos's original view of self-predication in "The 'Third Man' Argument in the *Parmenides*," a view on which "*F*-ness is *F*" is taken as a bona fide predication, asserting that *F*-ness is an *F* thing, along with its participants—albeit superlatively so. This interpretation faces a number of difficulties:

(a) It depends on a questionable assumption about the ways in which words are connected with things for Plato; see below, pp. 184–88.

(b) It has the consequence that no single predicate applies both to the Form and to its participants: "If the Form, Largeness, is superlatively large, while large mountains, oaks, etc., are only deficiently large, it must follow that the single word *large* stands for two distinct predicates ["large$_1$" and "large" respectively]. Now since Largeness is, by hypothesis, the Form of the predicate "large," it cannot be the Form of the different predicate "large$_1$." There must then be two Forms, Largeness and Largeness$_1$" ("The 'Third Man' Argument in the *Parmenides*," 253–54).

But if this is so, then it is not clear that to say that Largeness is large (i.e., large$_1$) is illegitimately to assimilate it to individuals that are large (252). In addition, it remains obscure why the Forms' possession of their properties can explain their participants' possession of their own, distinct properties.

(c) The theory of Forms is burdened by a number of paradoxes, discussed by Vlastos in "The Unity of Virtues in the *Protagoras*" and "An Ambiguity in the *Sophist*," both in *Platonic Studies* (Princeton, 1974), 221–69, 270–322, and in "A Note on 'Pauline Predications' in Plato," *Phronesis* 19 (1974): 95–101. Vlastos resolves such paradoxes (e.g., that Motion is a thing that moves, though all Forms, according to the theory, are at rest) by arguing that where they result, the self-predication must be interpreted as a distributive statement (a "Pauline" predication), true only of the Form's participants and not of the Form itself.

This view still must face the objections raised against taking self-predications as ordinary predications in the cases where paradoxes are not involved. In addition, it *reduces* talk of the Forms to talk about their participants and thus runs the risk of eliminating ontological commitment to Forms. Vlastos's replies to this objection ("An Ambiguity in the *Sophist*," 274 n. 13, 320–22; "A Note on 'Pauline Predications' in Plato," 100–101) do not seem to me sufficient, for the only way we can try to secure reference to Forms in Pauline predications is by introducing quantifiers purporting to range over them but which actually do not pick out any free variables in the sentences that follow them. "The relation of B to A is such that necessarily everything that is B is also A" is not committed to the existence of anything over and above the values of "everything"; cf. W. V. Quine, "On What There Is," in W. V. Quine, *From a Logical Point of View* (New York, 1968), 1–21, esp. 12–14, and Wilfrid Sellars, "Abstract Entities," in *Philosophical Perspectives* (Springfield, Ill., 1967), 229–69.

(d) To return to Vlastos's original view, we should note that it makes it difficult to account for the asymmetry that Plato finds to exist between, say, "Beauty is beautiful" and "Charmides is beautiful"—an asymmetry indicated by the fact that the latter, and only the latter, needs to be explained according to Plato. On this view, the asymmetry can only be located in the very sense of "beautiful," as we saw in *(b)* above. But then we are faced with a dilemma: either both Beauty and Charmides are beautiful in the same sense—and Charmides is as perfectly (superlatively) beautiful as Beauty, or Beauty is as imperfectly (deficiently) beautiful as Charmides—or they are beautiful in different senses, and it is not clear why Charmides is beautiful by participating in Beauty, which is beautiful in another sense of the predicate. We shall see below that the asymmetry in question, which allows Plato to deny that Charmides is in fact beautiful, must be located not in the sense of the predicate "beautiful," but by postulating a single, restrictive sense of "is" in which Beauty is, and Charmides is not, beautiful—the predicate itself having the very same sense in both applications.

14. R. E. Allen, "Participation and Predication in Plato's Middle Dialogues," in Allen, *Studies in Plato's Metaphysics*, 43–60, has insisted on this aspect of self-predication. The main problem with this view is that Allen, assuming that a term true of an object for Plato must be either its proper name or its accidental predi-

cate, and holding against Vlastos that it cannot be the latter, concludes that "Beauty is beautiful" just means "Beauty is Beauty." But:

(a) It is doubtful that "Beauty," "the beautiful itself," and "beautiful" are ever synonymous, as Allen has to claim; cf. Vlastos, "The Unity of Virtues in the *Protagoras*," 263 n. 111.

(b) The view cannot account for Socrates' argument at *Prt.* 330b7–332a3; cf. Peterson, "A Reasonable Self-Predication Premise for the Third Man Argument," 460 n. 16.

(c) The view considers the Forms as standards, but construes standards in a disputable manner. To read "Beauty is beautiful" as a tautology on the grounds that this is the proper logical form of "The standard meter is a meter long" while its denial is self-contradictory is dubious. Cf. Colin Strang, "Plato and the Third Man," in Gregory Vlastos, ed., *Plato I: Metaphysics and Epistemology* (Garden City, N.Y., 1971), 184–200, esp. 187–91, and, for a systematic attack on this view, Saul Kripke, "Naming and Necessity," in Donald Davidson and Gilbert Harman, eds., *Semantics of Natural Language* (Dordrecht, 1972), 253–355. And cf. D. Halliday and R. Resnick, *Physics* (New York, 1964), 3: "Accurate measurements taken after the standard [meter] was originally determined show that it differs slightly (about 0.023%) from its intended value."

15. I have argued that the distinction between universals and particulars is not relevant to Socrates' definitional concerns in "Confusing Universals and Particulars in Plato's Early Dialogues," op. cit.

16. An interesting discussion of self-predication and of the questions raised by this passage can be found in Charlotte Stough, "Forms and Explanations in the *Phaedo*," *Phronesis* 21 (1976):1–30. Our views are similar, especially in our agreement that Plato's concept of *being* is one that antedates the concepts of identity and predication; cf. Stough, 12 with n. 16.

17. Capturing the close relationship between the Form's being *F* and its participants' being *F* is the goal both of Vlastos's distributive approach and of Peterson's interpretation of "*F*-ness is *F*" as "*F*-ness makes whatever participates in it *F*" (though this is a simplified version of Peterson's elaborate view; cf. Peterson, 461–62, for a fuller statement). The problem is that the former approach *reduces* the self-predication to a statement about the Form's participants (see n. 13 *(c)* above), and thus cannot account for the explanatory function that the Form has. The latter view, by contrast, reduces the self-predication to an assertion of the explanatory connection, and does not attribute to the *F*-ness anything over and above the second-order property "makes whatever participates in it *F*." In this way, the fact that Justice is what makes its participants just is taken to be the whole content of the statement that Justice is just, instead of appealing to this latter as the ground for the ability of Justice to provide that explanation. It is interesting, in this connection, to appeal to a distinction recently drawn by Hilary Putnam, "On Properties," in *Mathematics, Matter, and Method* (London, 1975), 305–22, esp. 316–17, between "causal" and "canonical" descriptions of properties. "Justice makes its participants just" is then a *causal* description of Justice, and though it is connected to, it is not identical with, say, "Doing one's own is just," or "Justice is doing one's

own," which is the Form's canonical description, and which accounts for the Form's causal or explanatory role.

18. This is an essential feature of Vlastos's view in "The 'Third Man' Argument in the *Parmenides*" (op. cit.), of Allen's identity interpretation, and of Peterson's approach. Vlastos's "Pauline" interpretation avoids this feature, by denying the application of the predicate to the Form altogether when the relevant difficulties arise.

19. *eilikrinōs, pantelōs, ontōs: Phd.* 74d4–7, 102a10–103a2; *Rep.* 479a5–d5, 523e3–524a10. For fuller discussion and references, see Gregory Vlastos, "Degrees of Reality in Plato," *Platonic Studies* (op. cit.), 58–75, and my essay "Plato on the Imperfection of the Sensible World" in this book.

20. The asymmetry between Forms and their participants, if asymmetry it is, would "belong to the 'being' rather than to the '*F*' in 'being *F*'," as Wilfrid Sellars writes in "Vlastos and the 'Third Man,'" *Philosophical Perspectives*, 28.

21. *hen, tauton: Eu.* 5d1, 6d9–e1; *La.* 191d10–11; *M.* 72c6–d1, 74a7–10, 75a6–9; *Rep.* 476a4–7, 479a3–5, 597c1–d2; *Prm.* 131a8–c10, 132a1–b1.

22. *aei, aei on, hōsautōs aei echei, aei kata tauta echei: Phd.* 78d1–2, 79e3–5; *Smp.* 211a1; *Crat.* 439d4–5, e1–5; *Rep.* 479a2–3, 484b4; *Tim.* 48e6, 51a1.

23. *monoeides: Phd.* 78d5; *Smp.* 211b1.

24. This generic idea is expressed in a number of ways, e.g., at *Symposium* 211a2–5: Beauty is not beautiful *(a)* only in some respect and not in another (*tēi men . . . tēi de*), *(b)* only at some time and not at another (*tote men . . . tote d' ou*), which is connected with its being unchangingly beautiful (cf. n. 22 above), *(c)* in relation to some things and not to others (*pros men . . . pros de;* also *tōi men . . . tōi de, Phd.* 74b7–c3, and cf. *Hi.Ma.* 289a1–b7), *(d)* here but not there, for some but not for others (*entha men . . . entha d'ou, tini men . . . tini d'ou*).

25. DK B7.1: *ou gar mēpote touto damēi, einai mē eonta.* Plato does not explicitly deny this principle until his writing of the *Sophist: Sph.* 237a3–b3, 241d1–7, 258c6–e3; for an extended discussion of Plato's Eleatic concerns in that dialogue, see G.E.L. Owen, "Plato on Not-Being," in Vlastos, *Plato I,* 229–67, to whom a serious debt is hereby acknowledged.

26. *Republic* 597c7–9, replacing Plato's term "bed" with a variable. In this way, perhaps, we can supply Plato with an argument for his conclusion that there can only be one Form for each relevant predicate, and thus provide an answer to Strang's question: ". . . the first two Beds, simply *qua* a plurality, require a further Bed above them. But why are we obliged to deny that the first two Beds are Forms?" (Strang, 192–93). The reason is that if two things are equally *F,* neither of them is strictly *F,* and thus neither can be the Form. In the same way, we may also provide a justification for Plato's pervasive "One-Over-Many" Assumption (cf. Strang, "Plato and the Third Man," 186–87).

27. Parmenides DK B2.3: . . . *estin te kai . . . ouk esti mē einai.*

28. I use "identifiable" here in the sense of Malcolm Schofield, "Plato On Unity and Sameness," *Classical Quarterly* 24 (1974): 33–45, esp. 39.

29. Cf. Mourelatos, *The Route of Parmenides,* 107: "What a thing *gets* to be (or *comes* to be) is not what the thing really is, i.e. in its essence or nature."

30. A recent discussion of this idea can be found in David J. Furley, "Anaxagoras in Response to Parmenides," in Roger A. Shiner and John King-Farlow, eds., *New Essays on Plato and the Presocratics* (Guelph, 1976), 61–86.

31. Harold Cherniss, "The Characteristics and Effects of Presocratic Philosophy," in David J. Furley and R. E. Allen, eds., *Studies in Presocratic Philosophy*, vol. I (London, 1970), 1–28, 22.

32. Friedrich Solmsen, "Parmenides and the Description of Perfect Beauty in Plato's *Symposium*," *American Journal of Philology* 92 (1971): 62–70, 62.

33. *Physics* A3.186a28–29. Aristotle's criticism of Parmenides in this chapter, and some of the similarities between Parmenides' view and the theory of Forms and between this criticism and Plato's own attack on Eleaticism at *Sophist* 244b–245d, are discussed by W. Charlton, *Aristotle's "Physics"* I, II (Oxford, 1970), 59–62.

34. Cf. *Phaedo* 100d4–6, 102b8–c4, and, on the construal of the latter passage, Stough, "Forms and Explanations in the *Phaedo*," op. cit., 17 n. 24.

35. This objection was made to me by M. F. Burnyeat.

36. I have discussed the structure of this argument in "Plato on the Imperfection of the Sensible World."

37. The term, but not its analysis, is taken from Allen, "Participation and Predication in Plato's Middle Dialogues," op. cit., 45–47.

38. Different attempts to attribute to Plato contemporary theories of reference, and the difficulties they encounter, are discussed by J.M.E. Moravcsik, "Recollecting the Theory of Forms," in W. H. Werkmeister, ed., *Facets of Plato's Philosophy* (Assen, 1976), 1–20. An interesting discussion of Plato's approach to reference can be found in Gail Fine, "Plato on Naming," *Philosophical Quarterly* 27 (1977): 289–301. Fine and I agree that "for '*n*' to name *x*, it must reveal the *tupos* or outline of the essence of *x*; that is, it must correctly describe *x*'s essence," (298), though Fine goes on to compare Plato's view with John R. Searle's theory of proper names ("Proper Names," in P. F. Strawson, ed., *Philosophical Logic* [Oxford, 1967], 89–96). However, Searle does not require the cluster of descriptions associated with a name to concern the essence of that referent, and his view is therefore not parallel to Plato's.

39. Among the most notable of these is the pun of *Prometheus Bound*, lines 85–86: *pseudōnumōs se daimones Promēthea kalousin:* "the gods call you 'Prometheus' pseudonymously." See also *Odyssey* 1.62, 5.340, 19.407–9 for puns connected with the etymology of "Odysseus." Needless to say, one should also think of the *Cratylus*, and cf. J. V. Luce, "Plato on Truth and Falsity in Names," *Classical Quarterly* 19 (1969): 222–32, esp. 225–26.

40. Thucydides II.37.1.

41. This assumption, generally implicit, has recently been stated by Vlastos, "The Unity of Virtues in the *Protagoras*," 238 with n. 46; cf. 225 n. 8. The interpretation of predication as expressing class membership is given by Vlastos, "A Note on 'Pauline Predications' in Plato," op. cit., p. 98. Plato usually employs the copula, Vlastos writes, as "it is most commonly used in Greek (as in English) subject-predicate sentences, sc. to indicate that the individual named by the subject-term is a member of the class of those possessing the attribute expressed by

the predicate-term." But though Plato may well *employ* the copula in some such manner, it does not follow that he would analyze its employment in the way that Vlastos accepts. Though Plato uses the copula (it is difficult, in fact, to imagine how he might not have), he may not have arrived at a correct theory of how the use is to be construed. And his philosophical problems stem not from his *employment* of predication, but of his *analysis* of what it is to say of something that it is beautiful, just, or large.

42. Cf. notes 13 and 14 above. Allen's identity view, we can see, accepts the first horn of this dilemma, while Vlastos's original view chooses the second. Vlastos's distributive interpretation preserves the assumption by construing "beautiful" as a bona fide predicate of beautiful things, rather than as a term true of the Form.

43. Vlastos finds Plato making the distinction between proper names and descriptive predicates at *Phaedo* 104a5–7 ("The Unity of Virtues in the *Protagoras*," 238). Plato writes: "Don't you think that [Three] may always be called both by its own name and by the name of the odd, though [the odd] is not identical with Three?" Vlastos glosses this as follows: "Here 'names' is evidently used in the two different senses I have specified. In '"Three" names Three' to 'name' is to refer. In '"odd" names Three' to name is to describe" (239). We should remark:

(a) Plato does not write that three *may* be called by its own name, but rather that it *must* be called by its own name (*prosagoreutea*), which brings us closer to the idea of things deserving, or having a claim to, their own name, and away from the conventional associations of "reference."

(b) Plato has been distinguishing between Forms and their participants by saying that while the tall itself is (and is named) tall, Simmias, who *is not* tall, is named after it (*epōnumian echei*), because he participates in it (102c10–d2; cf. Aristotle, *Metaphysics* A6.987b7–10). "Being named after" seems to be Plato's term for Vlastos's "qualifying predicate." When Plato comes to discuss three and odd, he does not seem to draw a distinction between names on the one hand and predicates on the other (since "odd" is not an accidental predicate of three). Rather, he seems to be distinguishing two ways of naming within the strong sense of "name," which we have been discussing: Three is not only (what it is to be) three, but is also (essentially) odd.

44. Cr. Stough, "Forms and Explanation in the *Phaedo*," op. cit., 21, with n. 30.

45. If this is true, it may have some interesting implications for Socrates' theory of the unity of virtue. For if virtue is truly one thing for Socrates (so, Terry Penner, "The Unity of Virtue," *Philosophical Review* 82 [1973]: 35–68), then its names ("justice," "virtue," "temperance," etc.) must also be one name. Though Socrates does not discuss this, I think we could justify this claim by arguing that all these names, insofar as they have the same *logos*, that is, knowledge of good and bad, are in fact the same name. The same name can, on this account, be embodied in different words, i.e., sounds. Cf. *Cratylus* 389–90, and Charles Kahn, "Language and Ontology in the *Cratylus*," in *Exegesis and Argument*, 152–76. I have discussed this point with Alan Code, Marc Cohen, and Michael Wedin; they remain unconvinced.

46. One part of this assumption is exhibited at *Parmenides* 147d1–e6, where it

is said that no matter how many times a name is said (that is, to however many things in however many occasions it is applied), what it names is "that . . . of which it is the name" (d4), and that we "always apply it to that nature (*phusis*) of which it is the name" (e5–6). I think we can find this denied at *Philebus* 18b–d, where Theuth is said to apply the name "element" to each and every sound of the human voice: *heni te hekastōi kai sumpasi stoicheion epōnomase*. Linguistically, at least, this echoes *Parmenides* 147e1–2: *ouk ep' allōi oude allo ti onomazeis ē ekeino houper ēn onoma*.

47. This common approach to Plato can be found very clearly in Anders Wedberg, "The Theory of Ideas," in Vlastos, *Plato I,* 28–52, esp. 28–29.

Ten

PARTICIPATION AND PREDICATION IN PLATO'S LATER THOUGHT

I

ONE of the central characteristics of Plato's later metaphysics is his view that Forms can participate in other Forms. At least part of what the *Sophist* demonstrates is that though not every Form participates in every other (252d2–11), every Form participates in some Forms (252d12–253a2), and there are some Forms in which all Forms participate (253c1–2, 256a7–8). This essay considers some of the reasons for this development, and some of the issues raised by it.

For it *is* a development in Plato's thought that the Forms are capable of participating in one another, a new feature that distinguishes his later views from the metaphysics of the *Phaedo* or the *Republic*. It is, of course, true that in the *Republic* (476a6–7) Plato mentions the "mutual combination" of Forms, of which there are at least verbal echoes in similar expressions in the *Sophist*.[1] But verbal echoes are all these are: in the *Republic*, this combination refers to the fact that pairs of opposite Forms (e.g., the beautiful and the ugly, the just and the unjust) are manifested by the same sensibles and cannot be easily seen for what they really are; in the *Sophist*, however, the Forms combine in the different sense that some of them are characterized by the very features constituted by others.[2]

One might suppose that the fact that Plato never in his middle dialogues mentioned that Forms participate in other Forms does not establish that he did not believe that they could. And, naturally, by itself it does not. But our hypothesis is given some necessary support from other considerations.

One such consideration is provided by the role participation plays in Plato's middle dialogues. In the *Phaedo* (74a ff.), Plato argues that no sensible equal object is identical with the Form of equality, the equal itself. This argument is very complicated and its interpretation is highly controversial.[3] But Plato's conclusion clearly depends on his view that every equal object other than the Form is also unequal, whereas this could never be the case with the equal itself. Furthermore, this feature makes equal objects, as Plato puts it, "inferior" (φαυλότερον, ἐνδεέστερον) to the Form. Plato generalizes these points at 75c–d and again at 78c ff.,[4] where he contrasts "being," which is always in the same state, with "the many beautiful, . . . equal and all other" such objects that are in constant change.[5]

This contrast is drawn more systematically in the *Republic*. Here (476ff.), Plato distinguishes between what totally (παντελῶς) or purely (εἰλικρινῶς) is on the one hand and what in no way (μηδαμῇ) is on the other. He argues that "the many beautiful" objects are no more beautiful than ugly, that "the many just" objects are no more just than unjust, and so on. He concludes that all such things "are ambiguous, and one cannot securely think that any one of them either is or is not either both or neither" (479c3–5). He finally claims that they are located between being (479c7) or pure being (479d5) and not-being.

It is crucial to notice that the intermediate realm to which Plato assigns sensible things is not simply the conjunction of the two extremes. Plato does not think that an object really is beautiful and also really is not. The suggestion is, on the contrary, that the two extremes exclude each other. The intermediate object belongs neither here nor there. A sensible object is neither (really) beautiful, since it is also ugly, nor is it (really) ugly, since it is also beautiful. It makes as much, or as little, of a claim to be the one as it does to be the other. It literally does not rest at either end; it is in this sense that the sensible world "rolls about between" the two extremes (*Rep.* 479d4–5), and it is this that makes it imperfect. It is in this sense that it only appears to be, but is not, beautiful, large, or just.

Now it might be argued that this passage does not, as I claim, support the view that what participates in the *F* is imperfectly *F*, that participation and being are, on Plato's middle-period view, incompatible. The argument would be that what intermediate things are not is *pure* being and *total* not-being. And though these two extremes do indeed exclude each other, their mutual exclusion does not show that a participant in the *F* (though it naturally cannot be *purely F*) cannot *be F*. But this argument is not convincing. It depends crucially on the view that Plato envisages a distinction between pure being on the one hand and (simple?) being on the other. Yet such is clearly not the case. Plato introduces the two extremes by means of the expressions "pure being" and "total not-being" at *Republic* 477a and argues that the former is coordinate with knowledge (ἐπιστήμη) while the latter is coordinate with ignorance (ἄγνοια). He then distinguishes knowledge from belief (δόξα) at 477a–478a and goes on to claim, dropping the qualification without any sign of discomfort and without any apology, that knowledge is, to be sure (γέ που), coordinate with being. He makes the same point at 478b3–4 when he argues that since knowledge is of what is (τὸ ὄν), the object of belief must be other than what is—again, without qualification. Thus, as he concludes, belief is neither of what is nor of what is not (478c6); what remains, distinct not only from pure being and not-being but from being and not-being as well, is the sensible world, consisting of the Forms' participants. Plato, therefore, does not distinguish between what purely is and what is—insofar as participants are not pure beings, they also are not-beings.[6]

But the very imperfection of these objects should give us pause. For if they are imperfectly beautiful, large, or just, they are beautiful, large, or just *in a way*. If they were not, the question of their imperfection would not arise. What is it, then, that accounts for our being able to call them "beautiful," "large," or "just"? What provides the way in which they are what we claim them to be? Plato's answer to these urgent questions is provided by the relation of participation, which obtains between these many things that seem to be, but are not, beautiful, large, or just, and the one thing in each case that really is beautiful, large, or just—that is, the corresponding Form. By contrast to these things, the Form is purely, totally, and really (εἰλικρινῶς, παντελῶς, ὄντως); it is always the same, and it is never qualified by its opposite. As Socrates puts it in the *Phaedo,* in Plato's most extensive discussion of participation, "largeness itself will never condescend to be both large and small at the same time" (102d6–7). We should notice, incidentally, that though sensible objects are beautiful, large, or just *in a way,* their participation in the corresponding Forms is not similarly qualified: participation is not itself a relation that obtains in a way or to a degree. Plato explicates being *F* in a way by appealing to participating, *tout court,* in the *F*. The only passage suggesting a different view comes from the *Lysis*. Here, at 217e1–3, Socrates asks if an object will always be such as what is present to it (παρεῖναι) or if the manner of this presence is relevant to the possession of the corresponding quality, and accepts the second alternative. He introduces this general point (which he then applies to good and evil, wisdom and foolishness) by means of the example of hair, which appears white if dyed but is white through age. The example, however, concerns the tangible presence of a quality, and the dialogue is a very early work, from which the separated Forms of Plato's middle period are totally absent. For these reasons, the weight of the evidence, culled from Plato's explicit discussions of participation, primarily in the *Phaedo* and the *Parmenides,* is overwhelmingly in favor of the view that though it explicates the relative possession of a quality, the relation itself is not one that can be similarly qualified.

This interpretation of participation suggests that the relation is not simply introduced to account for cases where an object is qualified by a characteristic, *F*, without being identical to it. Rather, it is introduced to account for the possibility that something which is not really *F* (in that it is, in the sense discussed above, also not-*F*) can still be said to be *F* with some claim to truth, or at least to plausibility. It provides an explanation of why things that are not really beautiful seem to be so and can be spoken of, even if only in a derivative sense, as "beautiful." The capacity to participate seems to go along with an incapacity to be—and it is to that extent unlikely that the Forms (pure, total, and real beings) should have the capacity or the need to participate in anything.

The same point is suggested by the manner in which Socrates introduces the theory of Forms in the *Parmenides* (128e5–130a2). He appeals to it, of course, in order to mark the distinction between the Forms of likeness and unlikeness on the one hand and their participants on the other.[7] The Forms' participants are all sensibles (ὁρώμενα, 130a1), though not necessarily particulars. But the fact that they are sensible supports the view that no Forms are among them.

It seems clear that Socrates introduces the theory in order to vindicate some sort of antieleatic monism. Though it is not clear what sort of monism Zeno and Parmenides are supposed to hold, we can still say that Socrates appeals to the Forms as the proper domain of the expression "the things that are" (τὰ ὄντα). His point is that if we are clear about which are the things that are, then the contradictions that Zeno has been raising for pluralism are not genuine, since they apply not to what is itself but only to what participates in what is—not, for example, to similarity and to dissimilarity, but only to things that participate in them, and that they are not therefore genuine contradictions.

Notice Socrates' statement of 129b1–3:

εἰ μὲν γὰρ αὐτὰ τὰ ὅμοιά τις ἀπέφαινεν ἀνόμοια γιγνόμενα ἢ τὰ ἀνόμοια ὅμοια, τέρας ἂν οἶμαι ἦν.

For if someone showed that the similars themselves turned out to be dissimilar(s), or the dissimilars, similar(s), that would, I think, be monstrous.

This is reminiscent of Zeno's antipluralist conclusion at 127e1–3:

εἰ πολλά ἐστι τὰ ὄντα . . . ἄρα δεῖ αὐτὰ ὅμοιά τε εἶναι καὶ ἀνόμοια, τοῦτο δὲ δὴ ἀδύνατον.

If beings are many . . . they must on that account be both similar and dissimilar; and this is quite impossible.

Socrates agrees with Zeno up to a point: he accepts the view that things that are cannot be qualified by their own contraries. But then he limits drastically the range of things that can be said to be with respect to similarity and dissimilarity: he limits that range to similarity and dissimilarity themselves. Other things, he insists, can be so qualified—but then these *are* not, they only participate in being, similar or dissimilar.

In this distinction, Socrates concedes (in fact, he insists) that similarity itself is one and not many. In that sense he is, like the Eleatics, a sort of monist: there is one thing that is similar, one that is dissimilar, and so on. Until we can be certain whether the Eleatics held that there is only one thing in the world (a thesis we might call "numerical" or "harsh" monism) or that there is only one of each kind of thing ("kind" monism), we cannot be certain about the extent of Socrates' disagreement with them. They all agree at least on the thesis that sensibles are not—Socrates never denies this. But he insists that the many things that are not similar can still be called "similar" insofar as they participate in similarity: on this point the disagreement is clear.[8]

Socrates thus *gives* being to Zeno and Parmenides; he agrees with their conditional. But he argues that when we call something other than the *F* itself *F,* we are not saying that it *is F,* which, he concedes, would generate Zeno's contradictions; we are only saying that it participates in being *F.* This is a major concession on his part, for it is to accept the thesis that what is *F* cannot in any way be not-*F.* Generalized, this becomes the principle

(P) What is cannot not be,

which is the heart of Parmenides' "Truth." Socrates, however, claims that accepting (P) does not imply that nothing else can properly be called *F.* For in doing so, *pace* Zeno and Parmenides, we are not saying that it is, but only that it participates in *being F.*

It is clear that this reply to Eleaticism cannot be accepted unless at least two conditions are met. First, we must be told clearly what participation is and how it can accomplish its end. Secondly, it must be shown that the theory preserves the inviolability of those things which, according to it, are. Does the theory, in other words, satisfy condition (P), as it seems intended to do?

Socrates' challenge to Zeno is to argue first that no Form can be qualified by its own opposite: similarity cannot be dissimilar nor dissimilarity, similar (129b1–3); the one cannot be many nor the many, one (129b6–c1). Now if it could be shown that the one itself is many, or that the large itself is not large, this would be sufficient to show that Socrates' theory is inconsistent, since it fails to satisfy condition (P). But could it also be that a weaker argument might accomplish this purpose? What if one, for example, could show that

The large itself is one and many?

I draw this distinction because though Socrates begins his exposition with the claim that no Form can be qualified by its own opposite, he then seems to generalize his view. For he seems to claim (129d6–e4) that he would be astonished if it were shown that the Forms could in general "mix and separate" among themselves. What is not clear is whether he denies that pairs of opposite Forms can combine (but then why should he deny that they separate?) or that Forms in general cannot, that there are no participation relations among them (in which case the separation would refer to the fact that some Forms do not participate in some others). The verbal expression of Socrates' view does not settle the issue.[9] But it is important to notice what Parmenides, in his criticism of Socrates' theory, undertakes to show. Though he does suggest that the small itself turns out, on Socrates' view, to be large (131d7–e1), he does not argue explicitly that, say, the one itself turns out to be many, which would have corresponded to Socrates' original narrow challenge. Rather, he argues that every Form, assumed to be one in the theory, turns out to be many, whether its participants possess all or part of it (131a3–e7). He takes this to be a serious challenge to the theory, and this in turn suggests that Socrates had indeed asserted the broader thesis we mentioned above.

Socrates had introduced participation in Forms in order to avoid Zenonian contradictions, and in order to explain how a single subject can be qualified by two opposite predicates. As far as I can see, he doubts that the Forms are subject to the same predicament (ἀπορία, 129e6), and this suggests that he believes that being and participation exclude each other. Part at least of what Parmenides tries to show in his criticism is that Socrates must conclude that the Forms, too, are subject to participation. Now Socrates' theory is interesting insofar as it holds that statements like "a is F and not F" concern not things that are, but only things that participate in being. If such statements concern things that are, then indeed they are contradictions and cannot be maintained. But if they concern only their participants, then they can be rephrased as "a participates in the F and also in the not-F" and have no vicious consequences. If Parmenides, however, shows that such statements are in fact true of things that are as well, then he may be showing that the Forms have no more claim to being than do their participants. But then what is the point of the theory?

Thus the intention of the middle theory of Forms seems to be to keep participation and being apart. This is supported by the "separation" of Forms from their participants, a frequent target of Aristotle's criticism of the theory (e.g., *Metaphysics* A6.987b ff.; M4.1078b ff.) and a feature of the theory on which the *Parmenides* insists again and again (*Prm.* 128e7–129a1, 129d7–8, 130b2–5, c1–2, c6–d2). This is particularly obvious at 130b2–3, where Parmenides asks Socrates if it was his own idea to distinguish "separately (χωρίς) on the one hand some Forms themselves and on the other separately (χωρίς) again the things that participate in them." It is true, of course, that the context suggests that the participants here are sensible objects. It might, accordingly, be thought that separation depends only on the fact that the Forms are all intelligible and not sensible. But it is very unlikely that Socrates' theory envisages an intelligible class of participants in Forms (i.e., other Forms). His original response to Zeno's view

involves a general distinction between the one Form and its many participants without raising issues of intelligibility or sensibility (128e5–129a6).
He then maintains (129a6–c2), again without relying on any such distinction, that Zeno's difficulties apply only to participants, and hence are not
real difficulties. He continues with specific examples drawn from the sensible world (129c2–e4). And he recapitulates by issuing his challenge, this
time explicitly in terms of sensibles (129e4–130a2). In short, it is Socrates
who thinks that all participants in Forms are sensible objects. His separation of the Forms from them, not the Forms' intelligibility, is the point at
issue.

In general, separation implies at least that no Form is among its own
participants (cf. *Phaedo* 74a–75d, *Republic* 476c–d). And since it is closely
associated with the view that the Forms are in a perfect way what their
participants are only imperfectly (what, that is, they both are and are not),
separation also suggests that the middle theory of Forms draws an exclusive distinction between perfection, being, and the Forms on the one
hand, and imperfection, participation, and the many sensibles on the
other. This is also suggested by the fact that though Plato, in his middle
period, often considers the relation of copy to original as a possible model
for participation (e.g., *Phd.* 73c–75d, *Prm.* 132c–133a), he never seems
to consider that any Form (not even the Good itself) is a model of which
the others are copies.[10]

On the whole, then, it seems that in Plato's middle dialogues participation is a relation that obtains between sensibles and Forms, and which
allows sensibles, though they do not strictly deserve it, to be called by the
names that properly apply only to Forms. By contrast, it is clear that in the
Sophist participation also obtains between one Form and another.

Now that this categorical barrier has, for some reason, been crossed, we
may want to ask whether participation can obtain between a Form and
itself. Can a Form be among its own participants? The question is not
without interest.

II

In the *Sophist*, the Eleatic Stranger undertakes to demonstrate the "powers
of combination" (254c5) of five important Forms.[11] He first wants to be
sure, however, that the Forms he has chosen are indeed five, and he gives a
number of proofs to the effect that Motion, Rest, Being, Same, and Different are all distinct from one another. At the end of the last of these proofs
he says:

> We must then say that the nature of the Different is fifth among the Forms
> which we chose. . . .[12] And we shall say that it goes through all of them; for

each one is different from the rest[13] not on account of its own nature, but on account of participating in the Form of the Different. (255d9–e6)

Now this statement suggests that in "going through" all the Forms, the Different goes through itself as well. As since to be "gone through" by a Form seems to be identical with participating in it, the statement suggests that the Different participates in itself. But this idea, that a Form can participate in itself, is (and has been felt to be) peculiar. Gregory Vlastos, for example, translates the relevant part of the Stranger's statement as follows:

And we shall say it . . . goes through them all (i.e., through Rest, Motion, Being, Identity).[14]

Grammatically, however, it is not at all obvious that "all" here should be construed to refer only to those Forms that are distinct from the Different.[15] The text, as it stands, says that every Form is different from all the others not because of its nature, not because of the particular Form that it is, but because it participates in the Different. This grammatically more plausible reading seems to imply that the Different is itself different from the other Forms not because of what it is, but because of what it participates in. Since, however, what the Different is and what, in this case, it is supposed to participate in are the same (namely, itself), it is not easy to see what distinction Plato has in mind here. For this reason, the passage is often translated so as to avoid this implication. But, as we have seen, this translation is weak on purely linguistic grounds; and it becomes weaker when we notice that Plato implies that the Same, too, participates in itself in writing, at 256a7–8, that Motion "is the same because everything participates in the Same." If we want, therefore, to avoid the idea that Forms can participate in themselves, we must try to do so on interpretive and philosophical grounds.[16]

On such grounds, however, the view that the Different does not differ from the other Forms by its own nature has at least one advantage over its alternative. The claim that "the Different *is* different in virtue of its own nature (that is, different from the other Forms)"[17] is faced with a difficult question. What is, in this case, the function of the arguments that precede this passage and in which Plato tries to *demonstrate* that the Different is distinct from the other Forms? If the very nature of the Different guaranteed its distinctness from every Form, then simply naming it "the Different" would ensure that it was so distinct. At most, we would need an existence proof to the effect that there is such a thing as the Different, and the rest would follow. We would not need what we get—a series of complicated arguments of dubious soundness distinguishing the Different from the other Forms by showing that not drawing the distinction has unwelcome consequences.

It is then probable that Plato wrote deliberately that the Different is different from the other Forms not because it is, but because it participates in, itself. Now what is the import of the contrast between being and participating, between these two ways of being different?

For we have to agree, I think, that here we do have two ways of being different. Nothing is different from anything else because of its own nature, but only because it participates in the Different, which is itself different from everything else for the same reason. But everything, every Form at least, is *something* because of its own nature. What is it then that the Different is on account of its own nature? What is the nature of the Different?

The answer to this question is, quite simply: different—whatever, that is, Plato assumed the Different to be as we went through the demonstrations of its distinctness from the other Forms. Simple as this answer is to state, however, its import and significance are difficult to understand. This is partly due to the fact that it involves two deceptively similar but deeply divergent statements about the Form. First, the statement that the Different is different. Secondly, the statement that the Different is different from other things.

The first statement does not assert that the Different is different from anything else; it only tells us, not very informatively, what its nature is. And though the nature of Difference is what accounts for things being different from one another, it is not part of that nature itself to be different from any other object. The statement,

The Different is different,

is therefore a self-predication, and should be interpreted as having the form:

The Different is what it is to be different.[18]

Such an interpretation removes all air of paradox from this and other sentences of this sort in Plato. Consider, for example, a sentence that has been thought to cause serious problems for the theory of Forms:

Plurality is plural.

How could Plato have accepted anything like this? How could he even protest that it could not be false (*Prm.* 129c–d) since he believes quite explicitly that each Form is one? How could Plurality be plural; Largeness, large (larger than what?); and Equality, equal (equal to what?)?[19] And, indeed, if we assume that these are normal subject-predicate statements, in which a general term is asserted to be true of their subject, such paradoxes are unavoidable. But if we construe our sentence as

Plurality is what it is to be plural,

the paradox disappears, since the implication that plurality is many things also disappears. Nothing prevents what it is to be plural from being one. In fact, on this approach, every self-predication is not only nonparadoxical, but true.[20]

In contrast to the self-predication, the second statement says,

The Different is different from everything else.

The truth of this statement is not grounded in the nature of the Different any more than the difference of Motion from everything else is grounded in the nature of Motion. Rather, it is grounded in the fact that the Different, like everything else, partakes of the Different and is distinguished from other things in virtue of possessing characteristics that it does not share with them. The Different is, in short, a thing different from every other thing.

Generalizing this claim, we might say that

The F participates in the F

is an explanation of the fact, if it is a fact, that

The F is an F-thing,

an explanation of the fact that a particular Form happens to be characterized by the very feature that it constitutes. By contrast, the self-predication only tells us what feature it is that the Form constitutes. And whether that feature characterizes itself is an open question, the answer to which is quite independent of the truth of the self-predication. That Beauty is what it is to be beautiful does not in itself imply that Beauty is a beautiful thing any more than the fact that having the same measurements is that what it is to be equal implies that having the same measurements is an equal thing. As a matter of fact, Beauty is for Plato a beautiful thing. But the truth of this is grounded in the truth of the relevant self-participation, not in the truth of the self-predication itself.

If this is true, it would seem that Plato has come to the view that to have a characteristic is to participate in the Form that constitutes that characteristic. He has also come to the view that there are no exceptions to this principle, even when the subject in question is the Form itself. We shall see that this view differs radically from his position in the middle dialogues, where he was willing to attribute features only to Forms and simply on the ground that the relevant self-predications were true, as they all of course were.

For the moment, consider this passage from the *Parmenides:*

For thus Being would most certainly be. . . . Being would participate in Being in respect of being a thing that is, and in Not-being in respect of not being a thing that is not, if it is to be perfectly. (162a6–b1)

This passage, which also makes the parallel case for Not-being, raises many difficult questions: for our purposes, we need to notice that Plato writes that Being must participate in itself if it is to be a thing that is, and if it is to be perfectly (μάλιστα, τελέως). Just as the nature of the Different did not guarantee that the Different was different from other things, so the nature of Being does not guarantee that it is a thing that is. What is very significant about this passage is its insistence that Being must participate in itself if it is to be perfectly; we shall return to this issue later. Our present aim is to notice that the mutual exclusiveness of participation and perfection that was central to the middle theory of Forms seems to have received a serious blow in this passage. And the apparently natural question, "But what else would be if Being itself were not?" may be as misleading as the rhetorical statement that Socrates had once made in the *Protagoras:* "Hardly anything would be pious if Piety itself were not pious" (*Prt.* 330d8–e1).

III

At this point, it would not be unreasonable to object that the *Parmenides* is poor ground in which to look for evidence about Plato's views on participation. For only a few pages before the statement we have been discussing, Plato, in the course of giving an argument that apparently depends on the principle that if anything participates in a Form then it is not identical with it, seems to claim that no Form can participate in itself. Cornford translates this passage (*Prm.* 158a3–6) as follows:

> As having unity, [each part of a certain whole] will plainly be other than unity; otherwise it would not have unity, but simply be unity itself; whereas nothing but unity itself can be unity.[21]

Harold Cherniss has taken this passage to show that Plato was quite aware of the distinction between predication and identity, between having unity and being unity. He has also found Plato to be arguing here that nothing that has a certain feature can itself be that feature, and has tried to block some of the force of the "Third Man" argument in this manner.[22]

But if Plato held this view, he would also have to hold that the one itself cannot have unity, that it cannot be one thing. This unfortunate implication was noticed by Vlastos, who tried to avoid it by translating our passage as follows: as participating in the one, each part of the whole in question

> must clearly be other than the One; otherwise it would not participate in the One, but would *be* the One itself . . . whereas it is impossible for anything, except the One itself, to be the One.[23]

Vlastos agrees with Cherniss that Plato distinguishes here between identity and predication. But he argues that Plato does not believe that one excludes the other:

> All that is said here is that if *anything participates in the One,* it (the participant) cannot be identical with the One. It is not said that *if anything has unity,* it cannot be identical with the One.[24]

Vlastos distinguishes between participating in Unity on the one hand and having unity on the other, and claims that the former is a species of the latter. To participate in Unity, he argues, constitutes only one way of having unity; the One itself has unity without participating in itself. Though he does not agree with Cherniss that being a feature excludes having that feature, he does think that being a feature excludes participating in it. On this construal as well, therefore, the passage forbids the participation of a Form in itself.

A similar position has been taken by Frank Lewis:

> Plato's counterfactual. . . . "If a thing were not other than one, then it would not participate in the one," would be inexplicable dogma if it were not supported by a general principle prohibiting the participation by a Form in itself.[25]

There is therefore a consensus on the part of those who discuss this passage that Plato does not believe that a Form can be among its own participants.

Let us now notice that Vlastos and Cornford translate these occurrences of the term "one" (ἕν) in Plato's Greek as "the One" and "unity" respectively, that is, as a proper name of the Form.[26] Yet Plato has actually written the following:

> And clearly [each part] would participate in the One (τοῦ ἑνός) being other than one (ἕν); for otherwise it would not participate, but would be itself one (ἕν); whereas now it is impossible to be one (ἑνί) except in the case of the One itself (αὐτῷ τῷ ἑνί).

In short, despite a number of specific differences among its commentators, this passage is generally taken to show that Plato accepts the principle that if anything participates in the One then it cannot be the One.[27] I will now question the grounds for this basic agreement.

Plato marks a distinction between being one and being the One. He writes that if something participates in the One, then it is other than one. And, having noticed the distinction between the proper name "the One" and the predicate "is one," we must decide how to construe the predicate. We cannot take it simply as "is one thing" or "has unity," for in that case the passage will imply that, since everything other than the One is other than one, only the One itself will have unity and be one thing. But this contradicts Plato's basic point in this argument, which is to show how things distinct from the One (τἆλλα τοῦ ἑνός, 157b8) can—in fact, must—have unity. To account for this, and to preserve Plato's linguistic distinction between "the One" and "is one," I would like to suggest the following. Let us suppose that the sentence

This is other than one

is closer in form to

This is other than red

than it is to

This is other than John.

I am not claiming that ἕτερον ("other") does not express the nonidentity of individuals in Plato; if examples are needed, *Parmenides* 139c2–3 makes this quite clear:

ταὐτὸν μὲν ἄρα ἑτέρῳ ἢ ἕτερον ἑαυτοῦ οὐκ ἔσται.

It will not be the same as something else or different from itself.

But I do claim that Plato puts ἕτερον and ταὐτόν ("the same") to another use as well. We can locate this use, for example, at *Republic* 435a7–8:

Ἆρ οὖν . . . ὅ γε ταὐτὸν ἄν τις προσείποι μεῖζόν τε καὶ ἔλαττον, ἀνόμοιον τυγχάνει ὂν ταύτῃ ᾗ ταὐτὸν προσαγορεύεται, ἢ ὅμοιον;

Will it then be the case . . . that what one calls the same, whether bigger or smaller, will be similar or dissimilar in respect of what it is said to be the same?

The text goes on to substitute the predicate "just" for the expression "the same"; it thus shows that this latter term can function like a second-order predicate. If it is being used in this way, the statement

a is the same as *b*

is to be construed as

a is the same as *b* in respect *F*,

and all that follows from it, as Plato is quite aware, is that *a* and *b* are similar to each other.[28] Another such case can be found at *Sophist* 224b1–2:

οὐκοῦν καὶ τὸν μαθήματα συνωνούμενον πόλιν τε ἐκ πόλεως νομίσματος ἀμείβοντα ταὐτὸν προσερεῖς ὄνομα;

So then you will call by the same name him who buys up learning and exchanges it for money from city to city?[29]

A passage that uses ἕτερον in this manner is *Sophist* 252b9–10:

οἱ μηδὲν ἐῶντες κοινωνίᾳ παθήματος ἑτέρου ἕτερον προσαγορεύειν.

Those who allow nothing to be called different in virtue of sharing in a different characteristic (or: in the characteristic of something different),

which shows that ἕτερον can be used in cases where there is no question of individuals being involved. We are told that something is (called) different if two distinct terms ("names," ὀνόματα) can apply to it.[30] Plato, significantly, goes on to show in this argument that this manner of being different or "many" does not imply that the same subject becomes a different subject or that one individual becomes many individuals. This, of course, was what the notorious (but mysterious) late-learners and the other philosophers discussed in this part of the *Sophist* had considered as the implication of applying many different terms to one subject. Plato is concerned to show that such fears are groundless.

This use of "same" and "other" has an important consequence: it allows Plato to show why these fears are unjustified. The discussion of the late-learners (*Sph.* 251c8–d3) aims to show that to say

Man is good

in addition to saying

Man is man

is in fact to say that

Man is other than man.

But to say this last is not to *deny* that Man is man (or that a man is a man). It is simply to say that Man has some other features as well, in addition to being man. And this is not incompatible with (ἐναντίον) being man. Thus, in general terms,

a is other than *F*,

which can even be given as the analysis of

a is not *F*,

does not by itself atribute to *a* the *lack* of the feature that the *F* constitutes, but only the *possession* of some feature distinct from the feature constituted by the *F*. Such a statement is therefore compatible with the truth of

a is *F*.

This, notice, remains the case even if the subject of the statement is the *F* itself. For in saying that

The beautiful itself is other than beautiful

or even that

The beautiful itself is not beautiful

we need not be saying that the nature of Beauty is not what it is, but only that Beauty possesses some other characteristic as well. It is this analysis that finally enables Plato to deny the doctrine of Parmenides, to reject principle (P), and to assert that even Being itself is not (*Sph.* 237a, 241d, 258d).

We can now at last return to our passage in the *Parmenides*. Plato has written that things other than the One must still be in a way one: they must participate in the One. He has also written that whatever participates in the One must be other than one. We have taken this to mean that whatever participates in the One is other than what it is to be one. Plato supports this claim by arguing that if something were not other than one, it would not participate in the One but would simply be itself (i.e., what it is to be) one. If something that is one, that is, were not *something* other than what it is to be one, it would not participate in the One, but simply be what it is to be one. But only the One, Plato claims, can be what it is to be one. Notice now that the converse does not hold. That is, from the fact that the One is what it is to be one, it does not follow that it cannot be something else as well, and hence that it cannot participate in itself. The argument, though it does not require that the One participate in itself, does not preclude that possibility. For being what it is to be one is not incompatible with being something else as well. And, in fact, whatever participates in the One must have some characteristic other than its being one; it must, at the very least, possess a feature that will allow us to answer the question (which can always be asked): One what? For example, it may have to be one *whole* or one *part*, for

> it is necessary both for the whole and for the part to participate in the One; for the former will be one whole, of which the parts are parts, while whatever is part of a whole is in each case one part of that whole. (*Prm.* 158a6–b1; cf. 144e7–145a3)

Thus, in order to participate in the One, a subject must have some characteristic in respect of which it is unitary. If all that we could in principle say of the One itself were that it is one, then it is not clear that we can say that it is something that is one, that it is one thing. This is the general idea that I was earlier trying to suggest by distinguishing between simply being different on the one hand and being a different thing on the other.

I think that we can finally conclude that Plato's present argument in the *Parmenides* does not obviously prevent the One from participating in itself. The One can be other than one, though the argument does not require it. As a matter of fact the One will, for independent reasons, have to be much that is other than one if we are to say anything truly of it. But this argument does not require that what participates in a Form must be itself distinct from that Form; it only requires that it must be something that is in turn itself distinct from that Form. This condition, we have seen, can be met even by the very Form in question, which is thus enabled, if it turns out to be necessary (as in the case of the Different and the One, but not, for example, in the case of Motion), to participate in itself. Self-participation, according to the view I am putting forward, is optional; more importantly, it does not follow from self-predication as we have construed it, and which is obligatory in the case of every Form.[31]

It might be objected to this interpretation of Plato's argument that it is incompatible with the passage 158b1–2:

οὐκοῦν ἕτερα ὄντα τοῦ ἑνὸς μεθέξει τὰ μετέχοντα αὐτοῦ;

Then what participates in the One will participate in it being different from it?

The problem is that it seems as if Plato here ignores the distinction between "other than one" and "other than the One" on which our interpretation depends, and claims that if anything participates in the One it must be distinct from it. This a serious objection, but I think it can be met in the following way. The reason why Plato feels free to conclude his argument as he does is that his discussion in this section of the *Parmenides* concerns the question whether in fact everything that is distinct from the One (τἆλλα τοῦ ἑνός) can or cannot participate in it (156b6 ff.). The passage we have been considering is part of the proof that they can—that, indeed, they must. In giving this proof Plato appeals to some general conditions for the participation of any object in the One (or, for that matter, in any Form). These conditions allow Forms to participate in themselves; in particular, they allow the One to participate in itself. But this is not Plato's interest in this passage; he does not, as I have said, even assert it. Having appealed to those general conditions in giving his proof, he now returns to his special subject and restricts his attention to it—to everything, that is, that is other than the One.

IV

We have already remarked that the idea that Forms can participate in other Forms represents a new development in Plato's thought. This development, in turn, constitutes a serious advance in Plato's view of the nature of predication, the attribution of properties to subjects. And this advance is most evident, I think, in his acknowledgment that Forms can even on occasion participate in themselves.

In the dialogues in his middle period, Plato often writes that a Form's participants bear the feature that that Form constitutes in a way inferior to (ἐνδεέστερον, φαυλότερον) the way in which the Form is characterized by it, and which he describes as pure, total, real, or perfect (εἰλικρινῶς, παντελῶς, ὄντως, τελέως).[32] Plato's view is particularly plain in the *Symposium*, where the lover's ascent from lesser to greater beauties terminates with the Form of Beauty itself, the only thing that is really beautiful, beautiful by nature, divinely and without qualification in any respect, "pure, untainted and unmixed" (εἰλικρινές, καθαρόν, ἄμεικτον; *Smp.* 211e1).

The linguistic evidence is familiar, though its interpretation is still a matter of dispute. Given my view of self-predication, I think that by making such comparisons Plato does not mean that along with its participants, the Form, too, possesses the feature that it constitutes, that properties attach not only to their proper subjects but to themselves as well—and in a better way at that. In his middle dialogues Plato seems to me to believe, say, that the *only* beautiful thing is the Form of Beauty. He believes this because he thinks that the only way of being beautiful is to be what it is to be beautiful, and that to be what it is to be beautiful is to be beautiful in every way. He thinks that to be beautiful at all is to be naturally beautiful, and that to be naturally beautiful is to be the very nature of beauty itself.

A natural question arises at this point. Self-predications, on the interpretation I have suggested, are harmlessly true. Yet here we have Plato holding a view about beauty that is anything but that. Is this consistent with my interpretation? I think that it is. The difficulty with which Plato is faced, the counterintuitive view we have seen him hold, is not due to the logical form of the self-predications themselves. Such sentences state what the nature of, say, beauty is. The difficulty comes when Plato maintains that the conditions that something must satisfy in order to be the nature of beauty (among which are at least uniqueness, unchangeability, and eternity) must also be satisfied by anything that is to be considered, strictly speaking, beautiful. But these conditions are, of course, different in the two cases. When Plato in his middle dialogues denies that participants in beauty are truly beautiful, he has in mind that no such object can possibly satisfy these conditions. The imperfection of such objects consists in the fact that they are characterized by beauty only in certain contexts, or only at some times. One could say that *while* and *to the extent that* beauty applies to them they are really beautiful, and in a way that is correct. But what concerns Plato is that beauty applies to them in these qualified ways, for some time and to some extent: this is what renders them imperfect, not really beautiful. In the criticisms of the theory of Forms in the *Parmenides* Plato came to see that this identification was illegitimate. He eventually saw his way to keeping self-predication without also accepting those consequences that, he had thought, prevented things other than Forms from being truly characterized by features that did not constitute their nature.

Plato's middle view thus involves a comparison between Forms and their participants to the inevitable detriment of the latter. And Plato introduces the relation of participation precisely in order to account for the fact that sensible objects seem to be beautiful despite the fact that they are, strictly speaking, not. His point is not that Beauty, as well as beautiful things, is beautiful, but that things that are not beautiful still *seem* that way.[33]

This identification of what is naturally beautiful with the very nature of beauty seems to me to have been seriously weakened by the time when Plato, in the *Theaetetus*, attacks those who

> in the case of what is just and unjust, pious and impious, insist on claiming that none of them is such as to have its own being by nature. (172b2–5)

Plato is discussing here the relativism of Protagoras and some others "who will not go as far as Protagoras."[34] He offers as his alternative to relativism a carefully stated thesis to the effect that Justice and Piety have a nature that is independent of what different people take them to be—and not the more radical thesis that Justice or Piety is more truly just or pious than anything the relativists would propose in any particular case. Of course, Plato need not have asserted the stronger view at this point: the weaker view he accepts is a sufficient alternative to the relativist thesis. But his avoiding it is not insignificant, since in a context not unrelated to this he had once attacked the "lovers of sights" who offered different accounts of the features of sensible things (*Rep.* 475d ff.) precisely on the ground that the Forms, which *he* offered as accounts, were more real than their participants (which was all that *they* had to offer).[35]

The view that sensibles necessarily bear their characteristics in a way inferior to that in which Forms do is also undermined in the *Philebus*, where we find the very same vocabulary that Plato in his middle dialogues used in order to describe the perfection of the Forms extended so as to apply to what in the context seem to be sensible objects. At 52d ff. Socrates engages to show that purity, not intensity, is the mark of true pleasure (52d6–8). In order to convince Protarchus of this view, Socrates argues that truth or genuineness (ἀλήθεια) in general consists in purity and not in magnitude. His example is *the white* (τὸ λευκόν, 53a1; this may be either the color white, or white things in general). Socrates here claims that the truest (ἀληθέστατον, 53a9) and most beautiful (κάλλιστον, 53b1) white is that which has the greatest purity (καθαρότης, 53a5; μάλιστ᾽ εἰλικρινές, 53a8), that white "in which there is no portion of any other color" (53a7). He finally concludes (53b4–6):

> We shall therefore be quite correct in saying that a small but pure white is whiter and more beautiful and more true than a large mixed white.[36]

Much about this argument is unclear, but it does suggest that sensible things may contend for perfection. Plato appears to be willing to extend his use of this distinctive family of terms, previously reserved for the Forms, to the sensible world as well. Purity and truth are no longer necessarily characteristics only of Forms:

> Every pleasure, whether small in comparison to large, or little in comparison to much, so long as it is pure of pain, is more pleasant, more true and more beautiful. (53b10–c2)

As Aristotle was to put it, "that which lasts long is not whiter than that which perishes in a day."[37]

Plato's usage is actually not quite consistent on this point, as *Philebus* 59c2–6 shows. In this passage, Plato uses the vocabulary of purity in a way that suggests that he may not, after all, be willing to apply it to anything other than intelligible objects. But it seems to me that there begins to emerge in his thinking a distinction between, say, what it is to be large on the one hand and the largest thing on the other. This distinction, which is suggested by his willingness to consider some sensibles as perfect instances of what we say they are, also drives a wedge between the two notions of participation and imperfection, which had been up to now closely connected in his thought.[38]

We have remarked that, in the middle dialogues, *to be* and *to participate* were mutually exclusive. Only the Form of Beauty, and nothing else, is beautiful. In addition, the Form is not qualified by contrary predicates, as we have seen Socrates insist in the opening pages of the *Parmenides*. But if this is so, it does not participate in any Forms, and it does not possess imperfectly the characteristics that they constitute and that they, and only they, possess perfectly. Since Beauty is the only truly beautiful thing, it cannot participate in itself either, since participation functions just in order to account for the fact that some things that are not beautiful still appear to be so. Yet in the *Sophist* we find Forms participating in other Forms and even, in some cases, in themselves as well.

Now Plato, I think, from his earliest to his last dialogues, always accepts the idea of self-predication.[39] He never gives up his view that Beauty is beautiful, that is, what it is to be beautiful, that Largeness is large or that Difference is different. What he does give up is his belief that to be what it is to be beautiful, large, or different is the perfect (in fact, the only) way of being beautiful, large, or different. He comes to see, if my account is right, that from the fact that something is the nature of beauty, it does not follow that it is naturally beautiful or the most beautiful thing. And it is just for this reason that he introduces the notion of self-participation: in order to account for those cases in which, as is the case with the Different, the One, and perhaps also with the Beautiful, the very nature of a characteristic happens to be an instance of it.

To realize this is also to realize that to participate in Beauty, in what it is to be beautiful, to be beautiful in the qualified way that every beautiful thing is beautiful, is not at all a second-best way of being beautiful. This, of course, had been the core around which the middle theory of Forms had been constructed. But Plato comes to realize that nothing is beautiful in an unqualified way or that to be what beauty is is not to be beautiful in every way and hence not the perfect way of being beautiful. To be what it is to be beautiful is not, just on that account, to be supremely or even reasonably beautiful—just as to be what it is to be different is not, just on that account, to be a thing different from any other.

Now if participation and imperfection are separated, if to participate in a Form is not to have in an inferior way the corresponding characteristic, nothing prevents Forms from participating in one another and thus from receiving one another's "name." This is the starting point of the positive discussion of the *Sophist*. The dialogue's central problem is stated in a number of ways,[40] but it can ultimately be expressed by either of the following questions: What are the real counterparts of the linguistic forms "Being" and "Not-being" (τὸ ὄν and τὸ μὴ ὄν)? How can Being be said not to be and Not-being to be? These questions may not appear obviously related, but Plato shows, in the course of his argument, that they are closely connected. Suppose that Not-being were totally incapable of being in any way, just as according to the middle theory of Forms Beauty was totally incapable of not being beautiful in any way. Then, apart from the paradox that Not-being would *be* what it is not to be, we would have to face the following problem. If it could not be anything, it would have no characteristics at all, and it would therefore be impossible to find anything of which "Not-being" was the name. Whatever we picked out as a candidate would have to have some characteristic in virtue of which it was picked out in the first place, and it would therefore *be* something. The referent of "Not-being" must therefore be some "things," it must accordingly have some (= many) names, and it must participate in many Forms, including Being itself. Similarly, if Being could not be in any way, the expression "Being" would not name anything, for we must be able to say of Being more than just that it is what it is to be (for example, that it is a whole, *Sph.* 244d15 ff.). But if Being is some "things," then it is other than being (in the sense we have discussed) and hence not being; in addition, being anything is not being something else. Hence Being must not be some "things" if it is to be anything at all, it must participate in many Forms, including Not-being itself, after which it comes to be named.

This reading of the *Sophist* is not original with me, and I have not begun to be adequate to it.[41] But I want to introduce a previously unnoticed consideration in its favor. This is the fact that it allows us to see clearly why Plato, having shown that Being and Not-being are equally baffling (250d8–e4) and having expressed the hope that both can be understood together (250e5–251a3), begins his solution with the apparently unrelated plan to explain

in what way we call the very same thing in each case by many names.[42]

It also allows us to explain why Plato ends his demonstration of the reality of Not-being as well as his solution to the problem of false statement by referring back explicitly to this very problem (259b–d, 263d1–4).[43]

Plato's reason for beginning and ending his discussion in this manner is that the problems that he is trying to solve are generated by the assumption, central to the middle theory of Forms, that the mark of reality is to be named only by one name.[44] Beauty, for example, is named only by the term "beautiful": it is the only thing that is beautiful, and beautiful is all that it is. Its participants, on the other hand, are both many in the sense that more than one of them has an equal claim to that name, and in the sense that each is not only beautiful but other things as well, by the names of all of which it (and everything else that shares in the relevant characteristics) is, however imperfectly, called. Socrates' exclusive distinction between being and participating in the opening of the *Parmenides* was intended to show that a conservative pluralism, with being applying only to Forms and participating only to sensibles, was a plausible alternative within the basic limits set by Eleatic monism. But Parmenides, in attacking the theory and in the negative hypotheses of that dialogue, and the Eleatic Stranger, at *Sophist* 237c–250e, demonstrate that to be named only by one name is ultimately not to be named by any name and thus not to be anything at all. Now clearly Plato did not refrain from speaking about the Forms in his middle dialogues. He attributed all sorts of features to them, and the description of dialectic in the middle books of the *Republic* presupposes that the Forms must be related to each other in complicated ways. The difficulty is that, given his exclusive distinction between being and participation, the theory provided no mechanism for explaining how it was that Forms could possess the many properties they had to possess if they were to be real objects and if they were to function as Plato had intended them to function. An account had to be given of how Forms could have many names without thereby becoming many things. A theoretical way had to be found to allow real things to have more than one feature.

This is the problem of the *Sophist,* which finally answers the question, "To what are we to apply this name, 'Not-being'?"[45] by saying, "To everything" (258d5–e3). Everything that is, including Being itself, is not; everything that is not, including Not-being itself, is. It is crucial for Plato's account of how this is possible that he have an explanation of how everything can be called by many names without thereby becoming many different objects. This explanation, in turn, depends on the account of "other than," which we have discussed. To be other than *F*, to be not-*F*, implies by itself only being *something* other than *F*; this something need not be the contrary of *F*, or even a feature incompatible with it.

Plato's explanation involves the notion of participating in whatever is primarily named by each name, which is the nature of the feature in question. That there is such a thing in every case is not something about which Plato ever changed his mind: this is what the idea of self-predication as I have construed it comes to; and we find it asserted, for example, at *Sophist* 258b7–c4. What he did change his mind about was the question whether something could be such a thing and also have many names. In his middle period he did not think it possible. But the problems his theory generated led him to an analysis of otherness and negation that enabled him to assert that what Beauty, or Largeness, or Otherness, is can be many things without ceasing to be itself.

What these "things" are is, of course, properties. Having many properties is not being many subjects. Beauty is many things in virtue of participating in them, in virtue of bearing to them that relation that Plato had earlier introduced in order to account for the claim of some things that are not beautiful to be called "beautiful" nonetheless. But Plato came to see that the phrase "are not" is illegitimate in this context. To be a beautiful thing, more beautiful than some, less beautiful than others, beautiful for some people, not beautiful for others, beautiful during one part of its existence, not beautiful during another—all this, he realized, does not logically detract from the beauty of the thing in question. And though the nature of Beauty is not itself qualified in any such way (it is not itself beautiful from one point of view, not beautiful from another, etc.), this is not because it is a more perfectly beautiful being, but because it is not a beautiful thing at all just on that account. It is simply that which beautiful things have in common and on account of which they are beautiful.

In arriving at this realization and in extending the ability to have many names—that is, to bear predicates—to Forms as well as to their participants, Plato finally left behind the tradition from which he had emerged. This tradition, he realized, was common to thinkers ranging from the sophists to the sage he most venerated and who was, astonishingly, discovered in the many-headed sophist's hiding place—a place that, even more astonishingly, he had himself supplied. In the *Sophist* Plato liberated himself from that tradition and showed that to have a characteristic is not an imperfect way of being that characteristic. In this, I think, he offered us the first solid understanding of the metaphysics of predication in Western philosophy.[46]

NOTES

1. *Sophist* 251d9: ἐπικοινωνεῖν ἀλλήλοις; 253a8, e1: κοινωνεῖν.

2. Cf. G.E.L. Owen, "A Proof in the *Peri Ideōn*," in R. E. Allen, ed., *Studies in Plato's Metaphysics* (London, 1965), 305 with n. 5; and also my "Predication and Forms of Opposites in the *Phaedo*," *Review of Metaphysics* 26 (1973): 461 with n. 2. One should at this point also mention *Phaedrus* 254b, where Plato speaks of "the nature of beauty . . . standing on a pure pedestal along with (μετά) temperance," which may suggest that the two Forms qualify each other. Plato's highly metaphorical language does admit that interpretation. But though parts of Socrates' "Great Speech" in this dialogue point backward to the metaphysics of the *Republic*, his subsequent discussion of the method of division (265c ff.) points forward to the *Sophist* and the *Politicus*. The *Phaedrus* thus appears to belong to Plato's later period, even if only to its beginnings. Cf. Leonard Brandwood, *A Word Index to Plato* (Leeds, 1976), xvi–xviii, for a stylometrically justified placing of the *Phaedrus* in that later group.

3. I have discussed this argument in the essay "Plato on the Imperfection of the Sensible World," where some of the claims made here are defended in some detail. See also n. 18 below.

4. That the subject remains the same is indicated by the extremely close parallelism between the language of 75d2–3 and that of 78d1–2.

5. That such change need not refer to successive temporal stages but to the contemporaneous "compresence of opposites" is argued for in "Plato on the Imperfection of the Sensible World" and in T. H. Irwin, "Plato's Heracleitianism," *Philosophical Quarterly* 27 (1977): 1–13.

6. The same point can be made in connection with *Timaeus* 27d ff., assigning, after G.E.L. Owen ("The Place of the 'Timaeus' in Plato's Dialogues," in Allen, *Studies in Plato's Metaphysics*, 318–38), an early date to that work. Plato here distinguishes exclusively between what always is and never becomes on the one hand and what always becomes and never is on the other. He envisages no further distinction between what always is and what is. As Owen remarks, the *Timaeus* advocates "that the expression ἔστι [is] be reserved for pronouncements about ἀίδιος οὐσία [being which ever is]" (322). Since this is a recommendation or, as we might say, a technical usage, it will not do to point to texts where Plato uses the idiom "is *F*" of sensible objects as constituting in themselves evidence against my view. Thus, for example, Socrates says, at *Phaedo* 102e1–5, that in contrast to tallness that will not tolerate to become short and thus other than it is, "I, still being who I am, am, the same person, short." Plato does not refrain from using the copula in talking of sensible objects; he objects to a particular philosophical interpretation of that usage. In this passage, he has already said that "that Simmias is taller than Socrates is not in fact as we say in words" (102b8–10). This whole discussion of the *Phaedo* is aimed at showing how things that *are not F* still deserve

that appellation (ἐπωνυμία). For detailed discussion, see my "Predication and Forms of Opposites in the *Phaedo*," *Review of Metaphysics* 26 (1973): 461–91.

7. See *Parmenides* 129a2–3. Similarly, in connection with the one and the many at 129c4, d3.

8. At *Parmenides* 129d4, Socrates says that the many things "become" similar. This naturally prompts the question whether this does not suggest that they really are similar once they have undergone the relevant becoming. In one sense they are similar: Socrates even goes on to say that "they *are by partaking* in both [Forms] similar and dissimilar" (129a8). But it is precisely the fact that they are *both* that prevents them from being, strictly speaking, either. "Really being *F*" is a highly restrictive notion, and excludes being not-*F* in any way; cf. n. 30 below.

9. Cf. *Parmenides* 129e5–130a2.

10. This suggestion was made to me by Daniel Devereux. Against the view that "paradigmatism" can still be found in the late *Politicus* (285d–286b), cf. G.E.L. Owen, "Plato on the Undepictable," in E. N. Lee, A.P.D. Mourelatos, and R.M. Rorty, eds., *Exegesis and Argument* (Assen, 1973), 349–61.

11. That these are not *the* most important Forms is argued by F. M. Cornford, *Plato's Theory of Knowledge* (Indianapolis, 1957), 273 with n. 2. On Plato's use of μέγα and μέγιστον to mean *important*, cf. *Sophist* 218c7–d2, *Politicus* 285e–286a.

12. Strictly, "Fifthly we must say that the nature of the Different is among the Forms which we chose." For the construction, ἐν οἷς προαιρούμεθα, see Lewis Campbell, *The Sophistes and Politicus of Plato* (Oxford, 1867), note *ad loc.*

13. ἄλλων here could be taken to depend on ἕκαστον and not on ἕτερον. We could then translate, "each of the others is different." This should be more congenial to those who think that only Forms other than the Different are different in virtue of participating in it. So far as I know, however, this alternative (which is grammatically less plausible because of the greater proximity of ἄλλων to ἕτερον) has not been adopted.

14. Gregory Vlastos, "Self-Predication in Plato's Later Dialogues," in *Platonic Studies* (Princeton, 1973), 340 with n. 13. A similar view of this passage is accepted, without argument, by Frank Lewis, "Plato on 'Not,'" *California Studies in Classical Antiquity* 9 (1976): 92.

15. The antecedent of πάντων αὐτῶν at 254e3 is τὰ εἴδη ἃ προαιρούμεθα (cf. n. 11), of which the Different is the fifth, at 254d9–e1; that is, all five important Forms.

16. Daniel Devereux has objected that "all" (πάντα) can be given the sense of "all the rest" because at 256d11–12 the Stranger claims that Not-being necessarily is in relation to all the Forms, but then proceeds to give "a *separate* account of how Being is not" (his italics). Devereux infers from this that 256d11 ff. must have referred to "all the rest, apart from Being." But this does not follow. As Russell Dancy also pointed out, we can simply take it that, having made a general and unqualified claim about all the Forms, the Stranger proceeds to draw explicitly its most startling consequence. This consequence is not only startling; it constitutes the thesis which the Stranger is trying to establish in this stretch of his argument, and it is therefore doubly worthy of explicit discussion.

17. Vlastos, "Self-Predication in Plato's Later Dialogues," 340, n. 13.

18. A detailed presentation and defense of this view can be found in this book in "Self-Predication and Plato's Theory of Forms." This essay offers a number of considerations in support of my view that the Forms' participants are only imperfectly what we say they are. Following the practice of that essay, I use the term "self-predication" for sentences of the form "The *F* is *F*" independently of any particular analysis they receive. A self-participation, by contrast, is a sentence of the form "The *F* is an *F*-thing" (see below). For example, according to this usage, Gregory Vlastos in "The 'Third Man' Argument in the *Parmenides*," *Philosophical Review* 63 (1954): 319–49, analyzes self-predications as self-participations. I regret this divergence from more common practice, but it is important for my view; cf. below n. 39.

19. Such difficulties are discussed by Gregory Vlastos in "The Unity of Virtues in the *Protagoras*," and "An Ambiguity in the *Sophist*," in *Platonic Studies*, 221–69 and 270–322; also in "A Note on 'Pauline Predications' in Plato," *Phronesis* 19 (1974): 95–101.

20. Gregory Vlastos, in "On a Proposed Redefinition of 'Self-Predication' in Plato," *Phronesis* 26 (1981): 76–79, argues that this interpretation makes self-predications true because, ultimately, it collapses them into straightforward identity-sentences. As such they are equivalent to assertions of such trivial facts as "Plurality = Plurality" or "Justice = Justice." The issue is far too complex to take up in detail here. A Form, like an Aristotelian primary substance, is identical with its nature or essence: it *is* that nature or essence. But from the fact that the subject of a sentence is identical with its predicate (as is the case in essential predication) it does not follow that the sentence is an assertion of that identity. "Doing one's own is what it is to be just," though it may imply an identity is not equivalent to it. According to Plato,

The Good = The last Form the philosophers come to know

is true, while

The Good is what it is to be the last Form the philosophers come to know

is false. It could be objected that these sentences do not concern the essence of the Good. But this is not a problem. For the point is that the "is" of identity (if such a *sense* of the verb exists at all) relates a subject to any property that attaches solely to it, while the expression "is what it is to be," as also in Aristotle, relates a subject only to those characteristics that constitute its nature. Self-predications may imply identity-sentences, but are not equivalent to them. Cf. below, n. 41.

21. F. M. Cornford, *Plato and Parmenides* (Indianapolis, n.d.), 207.

22. Harold Cherniss, "The Relation of the *Timaeus* to Plato's Later Dialogues," in Allen, *Studies in Plato's Metaphysics*, 370–72.

23. Vlastos, "Self-Predication in Plato's Later Dialogues," 335–36.

24. Ibid., 337.

25. Frank Lewis, "Did Plato Discover the *Estin* of Identity?" *California Studies in Classical Antiquity* 8 (1975): 121.

26. Cf. Lewis, "Did Plato Discover the *Estin* of Identity?," 121–22.

27. Cornford, it should be remarked, does not discuss this issue explicitly.

28. Cf. *Parmenides* 139e8: . . . τὸ ταὐτόν που πεπονθὸς ὅμοιον, and Aristotle, *Metaphysics* Δ9.1018a15–17.

29. This passage shows that when used in this way, "same" and "different" range over terms ("names") and not over the individuals whose predicates are in question. Sometimes, the term "name" is dropped, and the grammatical forms we are discussing are the result.

30. Cf. *Sophist* 251a5–c6, *Philebus* 14b7–e4. We should notice that *Theaetetus* 159a6–8 seems to combine the use of both terms. Plato's usage seems to me to foreshadow Aristotle's more careful distinction between being the same or different in number, in species, in genus, or in some less important way; cf. *Met.* I3.1054a32–b14. For a use of ἕτερον as a second-order predicate, cf. *Met.* Z15.1040a12–14.

31. G.E.L. Owen ("Notes on Ryle's Plato," in Oscar P. Wood and George Pitcher, eds., *Ryle: A Collection of Critical Essays* [Garden City, N.Y., 1970], 359–60) offers an interpretation of this passage with which mine partially overlaps. He finds that Plato here raises the hope that he may be revising his earlier restrictive view that "being not-x excludes being x in any way whatever" (355). The hope is raised, according to Owen, by the fact that "things other than the One are carefully said to be 'not *the* One' before the phrase is replaced in 158c by 'not one'" (359). This replacement, Owen feels, shows that Plato still thinks that what is not one can neither be identical with the One nor participate in it (cf. Owen's premisses [15] and [16], 355–56). I agree that 157b–158c raises these hopes, but I do not think that they are as vain as Owen holds. I find Plato to be farther along the way of liberalizing his view that something either is *F* in every way or not at all. As we have seen, the expression "is not one" is introduced earlier than Owen thinks, at 158a, and in such a way that denying that something is one implies only that it has a characteristic additional to unity, not that it lacks unity altogether. Hence the view that what is other than the One is not one does not imply that it is in no way one. I agree with Owen, however, that an illegitimate move is made in 158c. He takes it to be the inference from the fact that what is not the One, and hence not one, to the conclusion that it is an unlimited plurality (as opposed to its Being nothing at all [cf. Owen's premiss (10), 353]). I think that though this conclusion is in fact unacceptable, it is not deduced from the premiss Owen mentions (which would involve Plato in an unacceptable view of predication) but from the premiss that what is not the One *does not participate in the One* when it is in the process of coming to be one.

32. Cf. *Phaedo* 74d4–7, 102a10–103a2; *Republic* 477a2–7, 479a5–d5, 523e2–524a10, 597a5. And see Gregory Vlastos, "Degrees of Reality in Plato," in *Platonic Studies*, 58–75, and this book's essay "Plato on the Imperfection of the Sensible World."

33. Cf. the essay "Self-Predication and Plato's Theory of Forms."

34. Cf. John McDowell, *Plato's "Theaetetus"* (Oxford, 1973), 172–73, and Cornford, *Plato's Theory of Knowledge*, 81–83.

35. Cf. *Rep.* 585d7–9.

36. σμικρὸν ἄρα καθαρὸν λευκὸν μεμειγμένου πολλοῦ λευκοῦ λευκότερον ἅμα καὶ κάλλιον καὶ ἀληθέστερον ἐὰν φῶμεν γίγνεσθαι, παντάπασιν ἐροῦμεν ὀρθῶς.

37. *Nicomachean Ethics* I.6.1096b4–5; Ross's translation.

38. The view I support here owes a large debt to Julius Stenzel's pioneering work, *Plato's Method of Dialectic,* trans. D. J. Allan (New York, 1973). On the question of perfection, for example, Stenzel believes that already in the *Parmenides* "Plato begins intentionally to neglect the contrast between higher and lower value, which he had previously so often stressed, and which gave colour to the separation of the Ideas" (56). Stenzel emphasizes the receding importance of the ontological separation of Forms from their participants when he writes that "[t]he 'participating' things and the 'form' in which they participate stand on one plane; each 'participant' *is* that 'in which it participates', and *vice versa*" (59). He insists that every Form is, in Plato's later dialogues, both one and many (e.g., 58–59, 93–95). Where I disagree with Stenzel is in his (admittedly qualified) view that the Forms in the later dialogues become more and more like concepts (e.g., 86, 90). Further, I think that his account of how even the "indivisible Form" (τὸ ἄτομον εἶδος) is still many does not go far enough: he claims that this is so because "the concept of its essence, its λόγος, is a combination of all the higher concepts" (94). This is true. But where Plato makes his real advance is in articulating a theory of predication that allows for this possibility in the first place. Stenzel at best hints at that theory, but does not detail it.

39. This has been denied, for example, by Colin Strang, "Plato and the Third Man," in Gregory Vlastos, ed., *Plato I: Metaphysics and Epistemology* (Garden City, N.Y., 1971), 187–88, following G.E.L. Owen, "The Place of the *Timaeus* in Plato's Dialogues," in Allen, *Studies in Plato's Metaphysics,* 314 n. 4. Strang and Owen, however, construe self-predication as (unrestricted) self-participation. My own view is that Plato never accepted this latter position, but that in his late dialogues he did introduce a restricted self-participation thesis in addition to unrestricted self-predication, about which he never had any doubts. Cf. n. 18 above.

40. Cf. *Sophist* 236d9–237a1, a3–4; 237b10–c4; 241b1–3, d5–7; 246a1–2; 250d7–e2; 258d5; 263d1–2.

41. The original impetus for this general interpretation of the *Sophist* was given by G.E.L. Owen, "Plato on Not-Being," in Vlastos, *Plato I,* 223–67, and by Michael Frede, *Prädikation und Existenzaussage* (Göttingen, 1967). Frede's distinction between two uses of "is," one in which the subject is said to be in relation to something that is not distinct from it, and one in which a subject is said to be in relation to something that is distinct from it (12–29), is seriously connected with the theses I advance above. Self-predication, as I construe it, is a special case of Frede's first use of the verb "to be." Identity, we should notice is, according to Frede, also a special case of this sort of predication (71–72), and should not be identified with self-predication (cf. 31–33).

42. *Sph.* 251a5–6. Cornford comments: "The transition here necessarily seems a little abrupt" (*Plato's Theory of Knowledge,* 253).

43. For the connection between calling one thing many, and calling the same thing different, cf. 251b1–3, b8–9; 252b9–10; 259d2–4.

44. Cf. the essay "Self-Predication and Plato's Theory of Forms."

45. *Sph.* 237c1–2; for the parallel with Being, cf. 250e1–2.

46. I am grateful to John Cooper, Daniel Devereux, Michael Frede, Patricia Kenig Curd, Avrum Stroll, and Robert Turnbull for discussing with me the issues this essay addresses.

Eleven

EPISTĒMĒ AND *LOGOS* IN PLATO'S LATER THOUGHT

IN RETURNING to the form of his early elenctic dialogues in the *Theaetetus*, Plato once again brings into prominence Socrates' old definitional question as well as the apparent impossibility of ever answering it in a satisfactory manner. The essay that follows raises some problems about the general features of that question in the hope of coming to a better understanding of its specific object in this dialogue: the nature of knowledge, of *epistēmē*.[1]

Socrates begins the main discussion of the *Theaetetus* by telling his young interlocutor, in a very traditional manner, that he wants "to know what exactly knowledge itself is."[2] The construction *what knowledge is* and others similar to it are emphasized on a number of occasions at the opening stages of the investigation. When Socrates, for example, appeals to the definition of clay in order to explain why Theaetetus' first attempt to define knowledge fails, he asks him to suppose that "someone had asked concerning clay . . . what exactly it is." Further on, he speaks of "someone who does not know what something is" as well as of "someone who is asked what knowledge is." As a final instance, we can cite his exhortation to Theaetetus to try hard "to grasp the account of what knowledge is."[3]

Plato, however, had never been consistent in the terms he used in order to specify Socrates' concern. In the *Euthyphro*, for example, though Socrates wants the seer to "teach him exactly what the form [of the pious] is," he later on suggests ironically that surely Euthyphro knows "both the pious and the impious."[4] Similarly, in the *Theaetetus*, Socrates often abandons the construction *what x is* as the object of verbs of questioning, answering, knowing, and explaining, and substitutes instead the simpler construction *x*, the accusative of the noun in question. So, for example, he claims that "if someone does not know knowledge, he does not understand the knowledge of shoes either" and that "whoever ignores knowledge does not understand shoemaking or any other craft."[5] At another point he objects that Theaetetus' answer is only "the knowledge of something," while later on he discusses how difficult it is "to discover knowledge."[6]

Plato's grammatical inconsistency has recently been taken to indicate a deeper philosophical problem. Assuming that when the construction is *what x is,* the verb "to know" of which it is the object "needs to be taken in the sense in which we know that something is the case (French *savoir*)," while when the construction is the simple accusative "it would be natural to take 'know' in the sense in which we talk about knowing objects (French *connaître*)," John McDowell states the problem as follows. Plato's idiom, he argues,

> would . . . naturally incline him to understand knowing, say, what knowledge is as a matter of acquaintance with an object, designated indifferently by the phrase "what knowledge is" or the word "knowledge." . . . More generally, Plato's idiom would be an obstacle in the way of his achieving clarity about the distinction between knowing objects and knowing that something is the case.[7]

Now it is actually not clear that the distinction between *connaître* and *savoir* can be usefully applied to Plato's account of *epistēmē*.[8] More to our purposes, it is not at all clear that the distinction itself can be justified. As Gail Fine put it in discussing this issue, "*connaître*-knowledge essentially involves knowledge of truths" and cannot therefore "be invoked as an alternative to propositional knowledge."[9] Fine disputes McDowell's claim that Plato confuses the knowledge of propositions with the knowledge of objects. She argues that Plato was quite aware of the fact that all knowledge of objects involves knowledge of propositions. Her own position is that, with a minor qualification, the notion of propositional knowledge, knowledge that something is the case, captures fully what Socrates wants to know when he asks what *epistēmē*, virtue, beauty, or (for that matter) clay, is.[10]

This, however, is the first question I want to raise in what follows. How satisfactory an account of Plato's view of *epistēmē* can we give by relying on the notion of propositional knowledge? The *Theaetetus* is the perfect text of which to ask this question, since its own question is "What is knowledge?" and thus allows us to approach our problem from two directions. Since to be able to answer Socrates' question is to know what the thing to be defined is, we can look at the *sort* of answer that Socrates finds satisfactory. And since his present question concerns knowledge itself, we can look at the *specific* answers the dialogue has to offer.

It is clear that in one sense the knowledge Socrates is after will in fact be propositional. "If we know something, we can say what it is," Plato claims in the *Laches* (190 c6), combining our two constructions, and dismaying those of his commentators who find such a condition much too strong.[11] But this, I think, is only part of the story.

First, we should recall Socrates' notorious complaint in the *Euthyphro* that to say that the pious is what is loved by the gods is not to indicate the being (*ousia*) of piety but only some less intrinsic feature of it (*pathos*).[12]

Secondly, it can be argued that Socrates actually knows a number of truths about the objects of his search before he begins to try to define them. For example, in the *Theaetetus* itself, a guiding principle of the search is that *epistēmē* cannot involve error and falsehood.[13] Yet this sort of knowledge is not considered to constitute even a partial answer to his question.[14]

A third factor suggesting that the notion of propositional knowledge does not exhaust Plato's interest in *epistēmē* is his very lack of concern as to whether what Socrates wants to discover is, say, knowledge or what knowledge is. It may be true, though it is far from clear, that "a sentence of the form 'a knows x' can always be transformed into a sentence of the form 'a knows what x is'; and the latter, in turn, is readily transformed into 'a knows that x is F,"[15] but the converse chain of implication certainly does not hold. If it did, then (to connect our present consideration with the previous two) Socrates would know what the pious is given his knowledge that it is loved by the gods. Yet despite this apparent asymmetry, Plato actually finds no difficulty in transforming sentences of the form "a knows what x is" into "a knows x" and conversely. His indifference suggests that what we have been calling propositional knowledge, knowledge to the effect that x is F for any quality F, is only necessary and not sufficient for knowledge of what x is. We could make this same point by saying that the chain of implications is convertible only when certain values of F are involved, namely, properties that constitute the nature or essence of x. For to know what x is and thus to know x itself is just to know its essential properties.

What all this is leading to is the far from novel view that Socrates is actually concerned only with the knowledge of essences, however that notion is to be construed. He cares neither about direct acquaintance with objects nor about knowledge of any proposition that happens to be true.[16] But before we put this old point to some original use, let us stop to notice a novel consideration in its favor. This is that our essentialist construal of Socrates' concern provides us with an adequate and satisfying interpretation of his notorious argument in the *Theaetetus* that any attempt to define *epistēmē* by listing its branches is bound to fail.[17]

Theaetetus' first answer to Socrates' question is that *epistēmē* is geometry, shoemaking, carpentry, and the other sciences and crafts (*Tht.* 146c–e). Socrates refutes this first by drawing an analogy. Had he been concerned with clay, he says, it would have been ridiculous to list different sorts of clay, since someone who does not know in general what clay is cannot be expected to know in particular what potters' clay is. And since, say, carpentry is knowledge of how to make things in wood, Socrates cannot be expected to know what it is since he does not know what knowledge in general is.

The argument has proved difficult to understand. For example,

McDowell claims that it depends on the implausible principle that in order to understand a phrase of the form "knowledge of *x*" or an expression equivalent to it but not containing the word "knowledge" in it (e.g., "carpentry") one must already "in some sense know what knowledge is" (114). But Burnyeat has shown that Socrates is not discussing linguistic expressions; he is after what Burnyeat calls "philosophical" knowledge. And though the argument does not depend, according to Burnyeat, on McDowell's implausible principle, it is nonetheless fallacious.[18] For Plato, Burnyeat argues, rejects Theaetetus' answer on the basis of the following argument:

> Socrates does not know what knowledge of making things in wood is.
> Carpentry is knowledge of making things in wood.
> Therefore, Socrates does not know what carpentry is.

Burnyeat thinks that this argument is fallacious because it depends on substituting "carpentry" for "knowledge of making things in wood" in the opaque context created by the verb "to know." But, he claims, Socrates' ignorance of carpentry does not follow from his ignorance of knowledge of making things in wood any more than his ignorance of Alcibiades follows from his ignorance of the defiler of the Herms.

Fine gives this argument a more sympathetic treatment. She is "inclined to think" that it is valid because, according to her, it depends on the Platonic principle that knowledge must be based on knowledge: to know something is to know the elements of its definition.[19] But though Plato may accept some such principle, his present argument is much more direct and does not need to be fortified with extra premisses. We can make a much simpler response to Burnyeat's charge.

The response is the following. Admittedly, the verb "to know" does often generate an opaque context. But the construction *what x is,* which specifies the property that constitutes the essence of *x,* that is, the very nature of *x,* neutralizes that opacity. Suppose, for example, that I do not know what H_2O is. Then, given that H_2O is water, I do not know what water is. And I remain ignorant of this even if I can use the term "water" as fluently as anyone else in the world. Conversely, if I know what H_2O is, given again that it is water, I also know what water is, even if, as it may happen, I cannot use the term "water" properly. Even if I do not know what "water" means, I may still know what water is.

This suggestion has two interesting consequences for the interpretation of Plato, though I can do no more than mention them here. First, since essences are known transparently, it is possible for someone to know what something is without being in a position to describe oneself as having that knowledge. For example, though I may know that water is H_2O, I may not know that this is an essential feature of water or that the substance before me is in fact water. In both cases, there is the temptation to say that by becoming aware of these facts I recover knowledge that I already possessed without knowing that I did. This temptation, I think, is ultimately connected with some of Plato's reasons for holding that knowledge is recollection. The second consequence is related to the fact that, according to such an essentialist construal of knowledge, in order to know what water is one must know what H_2O is and what in turn that is and so on until one can finally be said to know everything that water is. Since, always according to such a view, accidental features are not part of what things ("really") are and since knowledge involves all the essential features of its objects, we might say that to know something at all is to know it fully and completely, to know it perfectly. These qualifications, in turn, capture both the linguistic flavor and the conceptual force of Plato's attitude toward *epistēmē*.

Returning to our present argument, we can now see that, no matter how fluent his Greek, if Socrates does not know what knowledge of making things in wood is then he does not know what carpentry is. Knowledge of what things are is independent of being familiar with any particular expression that stands for them.[20] If there are essences, then to know a thing's essence is to know the thing itself: to know what x is is to know x. This, rather than a confusion between "propositional" and "direct" knowledge, is what lies behind the grammatical indifference that Plato exhibits and that started us on this discussion. To know the thing itself, moreover, is to know it under some privileged description permitting the inference that one (transparently) knows what that thing is even if one does not know that some other description applies to it. Socrates' refutation of Theaetetus' first answer is thus valid and straightforward.

Though, as we have said, the view that Socrates wants to know the essence of things is not new, its implications, as our preceding discussion may have suggested, have not always been clearly articulated. I now want to turn to one of this view's serious implications for the analysis of Plato's account of *epistēmē*. In its full force, this implication has so far, to the best of my knowledge, escaped the notice of previous discussions of this question.[21] This is that if Socrates wants to determine the essence of the objects of his search, and if only correct definitions give *epistēmē* or knowledge of these objects, then it follows that not every true belief can be transformed into *epistēmē*. If it is appropriate to talk of "transforming" beliefs into knowledge at all, then at best only a subset of all true beliefs can be turned into knowledge, even if they satisfy some further conditions as well. These are beliefs that concern the essences, or features that follow from the essences, of the things they are about. Beliefs about accidental features of things, as we shall see, are excluded. A further crucial consequence of the interpretation we are discussing is that the very idea of "adding" some further condition to true belief in order to turn it into knowledge is misguided.

These points become important when we turn to the third part of the *Theaetetus* (201c–210d) in which Plato, having previously failed to define *epistēmē* either as perception or as true belief, attempts to define it as true belief in addition to or accompanied with (*meta*) *logos*. He examines three ways of construing *logos*" (as sentence, as enumeration of elements, and as a statement of the way in which an object differs from everything else) before he concludes that this last effort, too, is at least apparently unsuccessful. The expression "true belief plus a *logos*," being the main object of investigation, occupies the center of his attention.[22]

The prevalence of this expression in the third part of the *Theaetetus* and Plato's ubiquitous insistence that *logos* and *epistēmē* are closely connected[23] have led a number of philosophers to find in the dialogues the first statement of what is now widely accepted as the general form of the definition of knowledge. That *epistēmē* is said to be true belief plus *logos* has been taken as a version of the view that knowledge of a proposition p involves, first, the belief that p, secondly, the truth of that belief, and, thirdly, an adequate justification for holding that belief. Accordingly, Plato's failure to define *epistēmē* in these terms and the negative ending of the *Theaetetus* are accounted for by the inherent difficulty of this still unsolved problem.

Among philosophers concerned primarily with the theory of knowledge we find, for example, A. M. Quinton writing that "the argument for including justification as well as truth and belief in the definition of knowledge goes back to Plato's *Theaetetus*."[24] D. M. Armstrong locates the "first recorded occurrence" of this analysis of the concept of knowledge in the *Meno*.[25] Finally, Roderick Chisholm claims that "Plato himself suggests" that the problem of defining knowledge must be approached by assuming,

> first, that if one man knows and another has true opinion but does not know, then the first man has everything that the second man has and something else as well. Then, having made this assumption, we ask: what is that which, when added to true belief, yields knowledge?[26]

Such an approach to knowledge depends essentially on the view that any true proposition that is believed can be known if it is believed with justification. Though, according to some of the varieties of this general scheme, some propositions may be more basic than others, all true propositions that are believed justifiably are known. Further, the justification that is necessary to transform a belief into knowledge is thought to be added to the belief in question. That is, each belief is identifiable quite independently of its justification.

When we turn to philosophers concerned primarily with the explication of Plato we find, for example, Glenn Morrow writing: "By what procedure . . . can a true belief be transformed into a necessarily true belief? This . . .

is the important question still unanswered at the end of the *Theaetetus* and the object of Plato's concern."[27] Paul Friedländer, to cite just one more instance, claims that "knowledge differs from true opinion or belief by virtue of the fact that an account, *logos,* is added to the latter. This is not far from Plato's own view."[28]

Needless to say, this position has often been denied. Harold Cherniss, speaking for a number of scholars, has put the point forcefully: "If true opinion and knowledge are not identical, the former cannot be an essential element of the latter. The common assumption of a relationship between 'right opinion' and knowledge is due to the external similarity of their results, but the rightness of any particular opinion is simply accidental as Plato succinctly shows."[29] But the matter is not so simple. The passage to which Cherniss refers, Plato's discussion of the jury at *Tht.* 201a–c, does not in any way show that opinions can be right only accidentally. On the contrary, Plato allows that the judges can be justly persuaded (with a pun on *dikaiōs*) and still lack knowledge. So, too, in the *Meno,* the problem with correct opinion is not that it is correct only accidentally, or even that it is only momentary; the problem is that it does not remain in the soul "for a long time" (*polun . . . chronon,* 98a1), which is a different difficulty altogether. If anything, it might be argued, both dialogues may be taken to be suggesting just what Cherniss denies: that knowledge and belief may overlap. For Plato seems to be saying that the eyewitness can know what the judges can only have opinions about, and that the traveler knows the road to Larissa at which others can only guess.[30]

More recently, Nicholas White has described the analogy between Plato's concerns and contemporary epistemology as "misleading" on the grounds that Plato "has in view, in the first instance, a notion of knowledge which figures, not in statements of the form '*s* knows that *p,*' but in statements of the form '*s* knows *x*' where 'x' does not stand for a sentence or proposition."[31] But though, as we have seen, Plato is in fact interested in statements of the latter sort, we have also seen that their equivalence to statements of the form "*s* knows what *x* is" directly reintroduces propositions into the analysis of *epistēmē.* We cannot therefore sever the connection between Plato's concerns and contemporary interests so easily.

Two important recent discussions of the third and final part of the *Theaetetus* exhibit a qualified, even ambiguous attitude toward ascribing to Plato an interest parallel to the contemporary epistemological approach. The first is that of Gail Fine, who attributes to Plato what she calls an "interrelation" model of knowledge. This is the view that nothing can be known in itself, but only as an element occupying a particular place within a structured field, knowledge of which is involved in knowing all its elements.[32] To know an object, therefore, is to know the field to which it belongs. Fine claims that, by making this model explicit, Plato comes to hold "a modified version of the thesis that knowledge is true belief with an account," a position she finds Plato to hold in the *Meno,* the *Phaedo,* and the *Republic.* But the modification is not serious: it is "only that knowledge involves true beliefs with several accounts, explaining the interrelations among the elements in a discipline" (369). The idea that any true belief can be turned into knowledge is clearly involved in Fine's ultimate definition of knowledge according to Plato as "correct belief about *x* with the ability to produce accounts properly relating *x* to other suitably interrelated objects in the same field" (394).

The idea that Plato accepts such an interrelation model of knowledge seems to me correct, though I doubt that we can find that model in the *Theaetetus* itself. I will return to these issues below. For the moment I am concerned with the view that such a model allows us to establish a relatively close connection between Plato's account of *epistēmē* and the contemporary analysis of propositional knowledge.

We must first remark that, as Fine shows, the *logos* that Plato considers to be essentially involved with *epistēmē* is not sentence or statement in general, but an account or definition of the thing known (373–74, 387 ff.). Plato immediately dismisses the construal of *logos* as statement on the grounds that if that were so, everyone who is not mute or congenially deaf would be assured of having *epistēmē* in virtue of expressing true beliefs (*Tht.* 206d1–e3). Furthermore, the *Sophist,* in a part that explicitly construes *logos* as sentence (261d–264b), makes true and false belief, not *epistēmē,* coordinate with true and false *logos.*

But if the *logos* in question is an account or definition of what is known, it is not clear how its addition to a true belief about something can turn that true belief into knowledge. As Burnyeat has put it in "Paradoxes in Plato's Distinction between Knowledge and True Belief," the second of the discussions I mentioned above, it is not clear what this emphasis on *logos* as definition has to do with "the epistemological question, 'why, on what grounds do you believe that p?' Neither here [*Tht.* 201c–21d] nor anywhere else in the dialogue does Plato so much as mention the now familiar analysis of knowledge in terms of justified true belief" (180). Burnyeat's own view is that Plato is not here concerned with our concept of knowledge, but with our concept of understanding instead.[33] This is also a view I accept; I return to it below as well. What I want to emphasize at this point is that although Burnyeat is eager to distinguish between Plato's account of *epistēmē* and the answer to the epistemological question above, he is still willing to accept what I will call the "additive" model of *epistēmē.* According to this model, *epistēmē* is reached when a second, independent factor is combined with true belief.

In his discussion of the example of the wagon at *Tht.* 207a–c and in his effort to show that what is at issue here is not knowledge but understanding, Burnyeat writes that no extra increment of certainty, no further assurance that it is in truth a wagon (and not e.g. a cardboard mock-up), is achieved by being able to enumerate all the constituent parts of a wagon. What is added to correct belief is an understanding of what a wagon is. ("Paradoxes in Plato's Distinction," 188)

In parallel manner, in "Aristotle on Understanding Knowledge," he claims that Plato believes "roughly, that what you need to add to true belief to yield *epistēmē* is something that will secure understanding" (135).

This brings us to the second question I want to raise in this essay. Is it reasonable to suppose, and to attribute to Plato the supposition, that if I hold a true belief about something I can transform that true belief into *epistēmē* by adding to it a *logos* of the thing in question that connects it with other objects in its field and yields understanding of it?

Fine and Burnyeat seem to consider this a reasonable supposition, and thus accept the additive model of knowledge we mentioned above. In this, I think, they betray a deeper commitment to the essential appropriateness of the epistemological question. According to Fine, to know *x* is to have a correct belief about it plus an account connecting it to the other elements in its field. Let us apply this to one of Plato's own examples, grammar (*Tht.* 206a, *Sph.* 253a, *Phil.* 17a–b, 18b–d). Given the above characterization and assuming that I am a grammarian who knows how the letters of the alphabet are interrelated, it follows that I can have *epistēmē* of the fact that (as I believe correctly) this particular token of *a* is in italics. A similar point is true in connection with Burnyeat's view. For it implies that if I believe correctly that some particular wagon belongs to Laius and if I am an accomplished wagonbuilder, then I have *epistēmē* of the fact that this is Laius' wagon.

Put in this manner, the additive model is very difficult to accept. Why should knowledge of grammar make me better able than you to know that this *a* is in italics? Why should my understanding of what a wagon is enable me to know better than you do that this wagon belongs to Laius? Such considerations are irrelevant to the transformation of these true beliefs into *epistēmē*. To know that this *a* is in italics (if such a thing is, for Plato, a matter of knowledge), I must be able to see it, to identify it correctly, and to recognize italic font. To know that the wagon belongs to Laius, I must know its history. Nothing less, and nothing more, will do.[34] What is, without doubt, a correct emphasis on the function and importance of definition in Plato's view of *epistēmē* is forcing us to move away from the idea that its addition to a true belief can turn that belief into knowledge.

Apart from being in itself counterintuitive, the additive model conflicts with much of what Plato says about *epistēmē* in his later dialogues. He does often place *epistēmē* against fields of objects and thinks of possessing it as having the ability to articulate the modes of combination of the elements of these fields. "Not everyone," we read at *Sph.* 253a8–12, "knows which letters can combine with which"; one needs the grammatical art (*technē*) to be able to do this. Similarly, only the musically educated possess the art of knowing which notes mix with which (*Sph.* 253b1–4). This, Plato continues, is true of all the arts, and also of dialectic, which proceeds through knowledge (*epistēmē*) to demonstrate which Forms do and which do not combine with others (*Sph.* 253b8–c3). In the *Philebus*, too, to have musical and grammatical knowledge is to be capable of dealing with all the interrelations of notes and letters respectively: "No one can come to learn each [letter] itself by itself apart from all the rest"; the inventor of grammar, "considering that their connection (*desmos*) is one and makes them all in a way one, announced that there was one art concerning them, and called it 'grammar'" (17c–d2).

The crucial consequence of Plato's comments seems to me to be that the domain of every *epistēmē* and *technē* is in each case *exhausted* by the interrelations among its objects and the rules of their combination. Nothing that Plato says here suggests that he envisages that acquiring *epistēmē* about some domain will turn every true belief one has about its members into an item of *epistēmē*.

So our negative answer to the question whether we should attribute the additive model of knowledge to Plato has, in turn, generated a new question: if it is not the case that all true beliefs are candidates for knowledge, which are those that are? To begin answering this question, it will be helpful to recall the problem with which we began our present discussion. That problem was that the *logos* of a thing is quite irrelevant to a large number of true beliefs about it—to the belief, for example, that this *a* is in italics or that that wagon belongs to Laius. The thing's *logos* is therefore also irrelevant to those characteristics that the beliefs in question concern. The first step toward our answer is thus to determine which set of beliefs about a thing, and which set of its characteristics, is suitably related to its *logos*. The second, as we shall see, is to give a clear characterization of this suitable relation.

The first step is easier to take than the second. What properly belongs to "dialectical knowledge" (*dialektikē epistēmē*), Plato writes in the *Sophist* (253d1–3), "is to divide according to kinds and not to think that the same Form is a different one or that a different Form is the same." This characterization of dialectic is notoriously cryptic, but it will help to see it as parallel to Plato's statement in the *Theaetetus* (207d–208a) that one cannot know something (*epistēmona einai*) if one thinks that "the same thing sometimes belongs to the same thing and sometimes to a different one or that now one thing and now another belongs to the same." This is not itself patently obvious, but Plato goes on to give an example of the second error: it would be to think that the first letter in the Greek for "Theaetetus" is theta while that in "Theodorus" is tau (both words begin with a theta in Greek). And though he does not tell us what the first error consists in, we may easily surmise that it would be, for example, to think that the Greek words for "Theaetetus" and "Timon" both begin with a theta.[35]

Such characteristics of letters concern their interrelations with other letters, with those objects along with which they form the domain studied by grammar. This suggests that in general the characteristics for which we are searching are those characteristics of things that constitute their interrelations with the other things of their domain. The same point is also suggested by the method of division, which is followed in the two dialogues that form the *Theaetetus*'s dramatic sequel, the *Sophist* and the *Politicus*. For the aim of these dialogues, along with the never-composed *Philosopher*,[36] is in very traditional vocabulary "no mean task": it is to focus on the three kinds—sophist, statesman, philosopher—and "to define clearly in connection with each one what exactly it is."[37] Needless to say, the method of division itself, by means of which this traditional Socratic goal is to be pursued, is anything but traditional—we shall have more to say about this below. What is important for our current purposes is to notice that this method is directed precisely at the articulation of the connections between sophistry, statesmanship, philosophy, and the other arts and sciences. To define the sophist is to locate the sophistic art (once we have, partly through the middle sections of the *Sophist*, determined that it is an art) within the structured family of the arts and crafts in general. The Socratic question, which, as we have seen, explicitly governs the dialectic of these late Platonic dialogues, concerns the essence of its objects. The correct answer to that question constitutes *epistēmē* of what is thereby defined. It follows, therefore, that the beliefs that are candidates for knowledge are those that concern a thing's essence. In addition, we have seen, such beliefs concern the interrelations of each thing with others belonging along with it to the same structured domain.[38]

At least one welcome consequence of this idea is that it explains why the *logos* of a thing is relevant to its *epistēmē*. For the characteristics we have been discussing are all relevant to the *logos*, the definition, of the thing in question. The *logos* is a summary statement of the path within a network of objects that one will have to follow in order to locate a particular member of that network.[39] But each object along that path itself occupies a unique position within that network, and is defined by its interrelations to all other things and their positions. Thus a thing's *logos*, apparently short as it may be, is implicitly a very rich statement since it ultimately involves familiarity with the whole domain to which that particular object belongs. Those characteristics are therefore objects of *epistēmē* that concern a thing's interrelations within its field, since such characteristics are explicitly or implicitly connected with the *logos* of the thing in question. Accordingly, it is true beliefs about these characteristics that, when suitably related to a thing's *logos,* are candidates for *epistēmē.*

And this brings us to the second part of our question: What is the suitable relation for which we are looking? We have seen that the most explicit *logos* will not, by being added to a belief about a thing's accidental properties, turn that belief into *epistēmē.* This is at least part of what the negative ending of the *Theaetetus* suggests.[40] In this respect, Plato's view is a direct forerunner, perhaps even a competing contemporary, of Aristotle's explicit position that what is accidental is not knowable.[41]

Will, then, the addition of *logos* to true beliefs about essential properties help matters? Suppose that you correctly believe that the letter sigma cannot under any circumstances be preceded by the letter gamma, while it can be both preceded and followed by the letter alpha. Suppose, further, that in many respects your grammatical knowledge is still incomplete; perhaps you are even ignorant of some of the rules governing the use of sigma: not being an Athenian, you do not know that double sigma is interchangeable with double tau. And now suppose that you become an expert grammarian, and that you thereby acquire the full *logos* of sigma. Can you add it to your belief in order to turn it into knowledge? How can you, since this belief is part of the *logos* of sigma in the first place? What turns it into *epistēmē* cannot be the addition of an independent *logos,* but its incorporation, along with similar beliefs, into a *logos* of sigma.

The additive model of knowledge thus faces a dilemma. Either a *logos* can be added to a true belief, but this cannot generate *epistēmē* since the belief in question can only be accidental; or (the content of) a true belief can become (the content of) *epistēmē,* but not by the addition of a *logos* of which, since it is an essential belief, it is actually already a part.[42]

A great virtue of the approach I am suggesting we take is that it allows us, in no uncertain terms, to take Plato fully and literally at his word when at the end of the *Theaetetus* he writes:

> It would seem . . . that knowledge is neither perception, nor true belief, nor an account added to true belief.[43]

Now Plato, to be sure, does not argue along the lines I suggested in the previous paragraph. He argues that if *logos* is simply a statement, then its addition to true belief turns every expressed true belief into *epistēmē,* which is impossible (206d1–e3); that if *logos* is the simple enumeration of the elements constituting a thing, then its addition to a true belief is not sufficient to turn it into *epistēmē* (206e3–208c3); and, finally, that if *logos* is the ability to distinguish a thing from everything else, then its simple addition will either be presupposed by all true belief or the addition of its knowledge will make our definition circular (208c4–210a9). I think that

these arguments are sound even if *logos* is construed according to the interrelation model of *epistēmē*. And though I cannot offer a detailed justification of this claim here, I hope that this can be excused since Plato ultimately depends for his conclusion on the considerations we have raised in
the preceding part of our discussion. If this is so, then, Plato is quite correct to end the dialogue negatively and to close with the claim that *epistēmē* cannot consist in the addition of *logos* to true belief.

What has prevented everyone so far from taking this negative conclusion at face value is Plato's rhetorical question at *Theaetetus* 202d6–7:

> For what *epistēmē* could there be apart from both *logos* and true belief?

It is clear that Plato takes this question seriously, and that he accepts the
view that *epistēmē* involves both true belief and *logos*. But at this point, the
commitment to the additive model of knowledge, which is motivated by
the influence of the epistemological question even on those who deny its
immediate relevance to Plato, leads in a misleading and dangerous direction. For it forces the assumption that if such a connection exists it must
consist in the addition of *logos* to true belief in order to yield *epistēmē*. In
fact, it forces the assumption that this is exactly the connection that Plato
envisages in others of his dialogues and that therefore he cannot be giving
it up in the *Theaetetus*.[44]

Now it is undeniable that the connection between *epistēmē* and *logos* is
ever-present in Plato. In the *Phaedo,* for example, which is almost always
cited in this connection, Plato writes of people in whom "*epistēmē* and
correct *logos* are present"; he later claims that "if someone knows, then he
is capable of giving a *logos* of what he knows"; again, he mentions the
"being itself of which we give an account as to what it is."[45] In the *Republic* he describes the dialectician (dialectic being, of course, the supreme
epistēmē) as one "who is capable of grasping the account of each thing."[46]
In the *Symposium* he asks: "Don't you know . . . that to have true belief
and not to be able to give a *logos* is neither to have *epistēmē*—how could
something without *logos* be *epistēmē*?—nor ignorance?"[47]

Yet *not once* in any of these contexts does the expression "true belief plus
(*meta*) *logos*," which is rampant in the *Theaetetus,* appear. Even in the
Meno, which is appealed to more than any other dialogue in this context,
true beliefs are only said not to "be worth much until one binds them
down with an account of the explanation . . . *epistēmē* differs from true
belief by this bond."[48] Surely nothing but an antecedent commitment to
the additive model would convince one without further argument that the
connection Plato envisages between belief and *logos* is that of addition.

The expression *meta logou* ("along with an account") occurs, in connection with knowledge and outside the *Theaetetus,* only in two instances in
the *Timaeus.* In the first, Plato is contrasting the world of the Forms with

the world of becoming and describes it as "comprehensible with thought along with an account."[49] It is clear, however, that there can be no question in this context of adding this account to belief, since what it is said to accompany is "thought" (*noēsis*) from which belief (*doxa*), which relates only to the world of becoming, is being sharply distinguished. Furthermore, the preposition *meta*, which depends on "comprehensible" at least as directly as it depends on "thought," carries more its sense of accompaniment rather than the sense of addition that is primary in the *Theaetetus*. In the second instance, Plato is contrasting true belief with intelligence, and describes the latter as being "always along with true account."[50] And again, it is clear, the question of adding *logos* to belief does not arise. Interestingly enough, Plato simply does not use the expression *meta logou* in connection with knowledge with anything like the frequency exclusive attention to the *Theaetetus* would suggest; in fact, as we have just seen, he hardly uses it at all. When he does use it, he generally is concerned with the idea of action under reason's guidance, and with self-control.[51]

If, then, the connection between *logos* and true belief is not one of addition, and if Plato seriously thinks that both of them are elements of *epistēmē*, what can their connection be? When does a true belief become knowledge? Our answer to this question is bound to be speculative since Plato has nothing explicit to say on this subject after the *Theaetetus*. We have seen that those true beliefs are candidates for knowledge that concern the essence of the things they are about. We have also seen that, having become knowledge, such beliefs are parts of the *logos* of the thing in question. We might therefore suggest that those beliefs can qualify as *epistēmē* concerning something that is expressed in or through that thing's *logos*.

This suggestion seems immediately open to the objection that it limits the range of *epistēmē* intolerably, since it apparently implies that very few beliefs about each object will ever count as knowledge of it. What about, the objection continues, all those beliefs that, though not contained or expressed in the *logos* of something, are still intimately connected with it? What about, that is, the rich structure of the knowledge of things that, as Aristotle shows in the *Posterior Analytics*, we can have about things given their definitions, the principles of the science that concerns them, and the syllogistic rules?[52]

It is at this point, I think, that the interrelation model of *epistēmē* comes to our assistance. For on this model, as we have seen, the *logos* of each thing is intimately connected with the *logos* of everything else in its domain. And what counts as *epistēmē* is the large set of beliefs that is expressed through the totality of statements about the interrelations of the members of that domain. This is why, in my opinion, Plato, though willing to use the singular *logos* in writing that we must "seek and present what [the sophist] is through a *logos*," is equally willing to use the term's plural and write that "it is always necessary in connection with everything to come to an agreement through *logoi* about the thing itself rather than about its name only without *logos*."[53] And though the expression *dia logōn* can simply mean "conversing," it can also take on the narrower meaning we have attributed to it here. It certainly has that narrower meaning in Plato's statement that if the dialectician is to "demonstrate correctly which kinds combine with which and which do not admit one another [he] must proceed with a certain knowledge through *logoi*" (*Sph.* 253b9–c1). Plato, in any case, is willing to use the expression in a suggestively ambiguous manner. So, in the *Politicus,* Socrates says that while he and the younger Socrates have their name in common, it is much more important to see whether they are akin to one another through *logoi:* through conversation, we get to know others better; through definition, we get to know what is akin to what and so, strictly speaking, what each thing is.[54]

Though it seems that, at least in Plato's later thought, not every true belief is in principle a candidate for knowledge, it also seems clear that he does not believe that the domains of *epistēmē* and belief are completely separate.[55] On the contrary, Plato appears willing to allow that there can be *epistēmē* of anything that belongs to the structured fields that we have been discussing. The letters and musical notes that are his main examples in the *Theaetetus,* the *Sophist,* and the *Philebus* are sensible objects about which we can have beliefs and about which, when our beliefs are structured appropriately, we can also have *epistēmē*. At the very least, Plato seems to believe that we can have *epistēmē* of the types to which such objects belong.

Plato makes this point in general terms at *Philebus* 61d10–e4, where he freely envisages *epistemai* of changing things, differing from *epistēmai* of unchanging things only in being "less true," and elaborates his view at 62a2–d6. Even *Phil.* 58e–59c, which some find incompatible with this position, does not challenge it.[56] The passage does not deny that there is knowledge of changing, sensible objects but only that there is "intelligence or knowledge possessing the greatest truth" about them (59b7–8). This, it should be clear, is not to say that we can have no knowledge of the sensible world; it is only to say, as Plato does say, that the further a domain is amenable to mathematical and hence systematic treatment, the clearer and truer its *epistēmē* will be. The metaphysical basis of Plato's view seems to be the idea that the more changeable some objects are, the more unstable their interrelations are going to be. And since knowledge, for Plato, concerns only what is unchanging and stable, there will be that much less to have *epistēmē* of in connection with them. And along with this degrees-of-truth theory of *epistēmē* Plato tends, in his later period, to emphasize more and more the systematic understanding of fields rather than the knowledge of particular facts.[57]

Perhaps, then, we have now answered the question why the *Theaetetus* ends negatively: none of its candidates is satisfactory; adding *logos* to true belief does not yield knowledge. But in so doing, we have raised a new question, to which I now turn in closing. If Plato does have an alternative view of *epistēmē*, that is, true belief expressed in accounts, why does he not produce it in the *Theaetetus*? Why, moreover, does he not in any of the dialogues following the *Theaetetus* present the answer we have attributed to him?

Like all questions that concern an absence, this one, too, can only receive a speculative (though, I hope, not idly speculative) answer. In the *Theaetetus*, the first answer Socrates receives to his question consists of a list of different sorts of *epistēmai* in no particular order and with no explanation of why they are given as they are. Having offered the argument we discussed at the beginning of this paper, Socrates presents a second reason for rejecting this answer. Though one could reply to his question simply and shortly, he says, Theaetetus' answer forces one to "traverse an interminable road."[58] The word *aperantos*, "interminable," is closely connected etymologically and semantically with the word *apeiros*, "unlimited," "indefinite," or "infinite."[59] Theaetetus understands this connection since, in explaining his method for defining the notion of power, he appeals to the fact that this goal could not be reached by enumeration given the fact that the powers are *apeiroi* (*Tht.* 147d7). Socrates then asks him to do the same with *epistēmai*: as he encompassed all powers, many as they are, in one form, he must now express all *epistēmai* in one account (*Tht.* 148d5–7). And, following their discussion about Socrates' midwifery, Theaetetus makes his first effort: *epistēmē*, he says, is perception (*Tht.* 151e1–3).

What is remarkable about this procedure is its similarity to the method of Plato's early dialogues, which receives its most explicit discussion at *Meno* 71d–77b. Here, too, we have things of many sorts—virtues, bees, and shapes. Each of them differs from the others in many respects, and some are even opposite to one another (*enantia*, 74d7). Nevertheless, Socrates wants to know that respect in which the members of each kind of thing do not differ (72c2–3), that form which they all have and which makes them all what they are (72c7–8), that which is in all of them the same (75a4–5).

But turn now to the opening pages of the *Philebus*, and the impression is overwhelming that Socrates and his interlocutors have exchanged roles. For it is now Protarchus who claims that pleasures cannot differ from each other insofar as they are pleasures (*Phil.* 13c5; cf. 12d8–e2), as Socrates had earlier claimed about bees and virtues. And it is now Socrates who insists that pleasures do indeed differ from one another just as colors and shapes do; for though shape is "all one in kind," its parts can be very different from, even "most opposite" (*enantiōtata*) to, one another (12c–13b). Now it is not Socrates' willingness to distinguish parts within a unity that is important: he had already done this in the *Meno*. What is remarkable in its stark contrast to his earlier practice is his insistence that both pleasures and *epistēmai* must be investigated not only in their unity but also, in fact primarily, in their difference and multiplicity: he no longer seems to want the short unitary answer that he had so passionately sought earlier.[60]

In the ensuing obscure discussion of the one and the many (*Phil.* 14c ff.), Socrates uses the examples of grammar and music. He is illustrating his view that in trying to establish what something is we must look for the determinate number of sorts of things that belong to it—not for its basic absolute unity or for its ultimate unlimited multiplicity (16c–17a). We must, he says, construct something like a table of the precise interrelations of these sorts. Voice, for example, is both one and unlimited (17b3–4). But since this is true of everything,

> we are not yet wise in virtue of either of them, on account, that is, of knowing either its unlimitedness or its unity; what makes each one of us grammatical is knowing how many things it is and of what sorts. (17b6–9)

Socrates makes a similar point about music (17c11–e6) and recapitulates at 18a6 ff. It is crucial, he says, to grasp the specific number of the sorts of voices (i.e., phonetic sounds) there are and of the connections that govern them and make them one; we must rush neither from the one to the unlimited, nor from the unlimited to the one. What makes these all one, he rather startlingly concludes (18c–d), is not the single Form he had previously been looking for but their manner of combination (*desmos*), which, in the nature of the case, must itself consist of a large number of interrelations. He finally returns to pleasure and knowledge at 18e3–4. Though they are each one he says, "our argument requires us" to explain how each is both one and many, and how many precisely each one is before it appears in its unlimitedness (18e8–19a2).

What emerges from this is that Socrates' definitional question remains strikingly unchanged throughout Plato's life from his earliest dialogues to, for example, the *Sophist* (218c5–7). But, equally strikingly, the sort of answer that Plato considers proper to that question alters drastically between his writing of the *Theaetetus* and of the *Philebus*. And my speculation is that though Plato may well have reached a unitary answer to the question "What is knowledge?" by the end of the *Theaetetus,* he refrains from giving it because he has also reached the view that any such unitary answer is bound to be misleading, or at least uninformative.[61]

We must not, the *Philebus* tells us, rush "straight at the one" (18b1). Yet the unitary answer we have been discussing does just that. What we need instead is a clear and exhaustive determination of how many *epistēmai* there are, to what sorts they belong, how they are related to one another, and how they combine in terms of generality, clarity, and truth to form the hierarchical structure discussed at *Philebus* 55d–59c. The answer to Socrates' question, whether it is about knowledge or anything else, can never— if it is to give knowledge—consist either of a haphazard list or simply of an all-encompassing formula.

The answer can only be given by means of the long and complicated divisions through which the *Sophist* and the *Politicus* attempt to define their subject matter. Both dialogues try to define a species of art (*technē*) or science (*epistēmē*), that of the sophist and that of the statesman (cf. *Pol.* 258b2–7). In both dialogues the art in question is defined by being located within a determinate network of other arts and sciences. And the process by means of which the definition is reached provides, at the same time, both an explanation of the aporetic ending of the *Theaetetus* and an illustration of the obscure opening of the *Philebus*.

Plato, therefore, does try to answer the question of *Theaetetus*. But his answer is not cryptically contained within the dialogue itself, either negatively (as Cornford argued) or positively (as Fine suggested). His answer is given in the two dialogues that follow the *Theaetetus*. Or, rather, part of this answer only is given in those dialogues. For the project of definition has now been shown to involve the mastery of the whole field to which the object of definition belongs, and hence a science of the field in question. Despite the immense importance of the *Sophist* for Plato's metaphysics, the dialogue, along with the *Politicus,* is only a small part of the grandiose project of defining *epistēmē,* the outlines of which we glimpse rather darkly at *Philebus* 55d–62d.

By seeing knowledge as the object of knowledge in Plato's late dialogues, we are now able to see how the dramatic sequels to the *Theaetetus* are also its doctrinal complements. And by making knowledge the object of knowledge, Plato himself was able to exhibit, in one stroke, both the correct method and the content of dialectic, which he took, after all, as the very essence of knowledge itself.[62]

NOTES

1. I retain, with qualifications to follow, the usual translation for *epistēmē*.
2. *Theaetetus* 146e9–10: γνῶναι ἐπιστήμην αὐτὸ ὅτι ποτ' ἐστίν.
3. *Tht.* 147a1–3: εἴ τις . . . ἔροιτο . . . περὶ πηλοῦ ὅτι ποτ' ἐστίν . . . ; 147b2: ὃ μὴ οἶδεν τί ἐστιν; 147b10–11: . . . τῷ ἐρωτηθέντι ἐπιστήμη τί ἐστιν; 148d1–2: . . . προθυμήθητι . . . [περὶ] ἐπιστήμης λαβεῖν λόγον τί ποτε τυγχάνει ὄν.

4. *Euthyphro* 6e3–4: . . . δίδαξον τὴν ἰδέαν τίς ποτέ ἐστιν with 15d4–5: . . . εἰ μὴ ᾔδησθα . . . τό τε ὅσιον καὶ τὸ ἀνόσιον. Cp. 6d1–2 with 6d10–11 and 15e1. Cf. also *Laches* 190b7–9 and 190c6, *Menexenus* 79d6–e3, *Parmenides* 134b6–12, *Cratylus* 439c–440b.

5. *Tht.* 147b4–5: Οὐδ᾽ ἄρα ἐπιστήμην ὑποδημάτων συνίησιν ὁ ἐπιστήμην μὴ εἰδώς; 147b7–8: Σκυτικὴν ἄρα οὐ συνίησιν ὃς ἂν ἐπιστήμην ἀγνοῇ, οὐδέ τινα ἄλλην τέχνην.

6. *Tht.* 147b11–c1: . . . τινός . . . ἐπιστήμην ἀποκρίνεται; 148c6–7: . . . ἐπιστήμην . . . ἐξευρεῖν.

7. John McDowell, *Plato: "Theaetetus"* (Oxford, 1973), 119–20. McDowell detects this problem in various parts of the dialogue; see his references on p. 120.

8. M. F. Burnyeat, "The Simple and the Complex in the *Theaetetus*," unpublished manuscript (1970), 19–20.

9. Gail J. Fine, "Knowledge and *Logos* in the *Theaetetus*," *Philosophical Review* 88 (1979): 379.

10. Fine, "Knowledge and *Logos*," 367. For the qualification, see ibid.

11. For example, P. T. Geach, "Plato's *Euthyphro*: An Analysis and Commentary," *Monist* 50 (1966): 369–82. But see "Confusing Universals and Particulars in Plato's Early Dialogues." For a defense of Socrates along different lines, see T. H. Irwin, *Plato's Moral Theory* (Oxford, 1977), 294. I discuss Irwin's view briefly in n. 14 below.

12. *Euthyphro* 11a. Similar points are made at *Menexenus* 71b, *Gorgias* 448e.

13. *Tht.* 152c6: ἀψευδές. For the correct construal of Socrates' argument, see F. C. White, "Ὡς ἐπιστήμη οὖσα: A Passage of Some Elegance in the *Theaetetus*," *Phronesis* 17 (1972): 219–26.

14. It can be, and has been, objected to me that Socrates need not or that he cannot have knowledge of anything if he does not already know its definition. Accordingly, he must, at best, have true beliefs about it. This view has recently been defended by Irwin, op. cit., 294, and *Plato: "Gorgias"* (Oxford, 1979), 113. But it seems to me that the need to draw this distinction on Socrates' behalf springs from the antecedent conviction that *epistēmē* just is propositional knowledge. For if it is, and Socrates claims that he cannot have *epistēmē* of anything concerning some object unles he has *epistēmē* regarding its definition, then the only thing left for him to have is belief (the mental state that, when suitably justified, constitutes knowledge of fact). But if, as I am trying to suggest in this essay, we are not to see the *epistēmē/doxa* distinction as strictly parallel to the distinction between knowledge and belief, then this expedient is unnecessary. As I will argue, the notion of propositional knowledge is much broader than the notion of *epistēmē*. Socrates, therefore, can deny that he has *epistēmē* of something without denying that he knows, as a matter of fact, that it is so. My solution to Geach's criticism, op. cit., depends on the view that what Socrates denies having *epistēmē* of (the teachability of virtue, the piety of prosecuting one's father, etc) concerns highly controversial issues involving the essence of the objects in question.

15. Fine "Knowledge and *Logos*," 367. Whether "*a* knows *x*" can be transformed into "*a* knows what *x* is" depends on many factors. If *knows* means *is*

acquainted with, for example, and "what *x* is" specifies *x*'s essence, the inference clearly fails.

16. Cf. Richard Robinson, *Plato's earlier Dialectic,* 2d ed. (Oxford, 1953), 49–53.

17. *Tht.* 147a–b. The answer makes its givers ridiculous (γελοῖοι) for two reasons. First (πρῶτον, 147a7) because of the issue we are discussing. Secondly (ἔπειτα, 147c3) because it fails to encompass all *epistemai* and all clay within a short, single formulation. This second point is not sufficiently noticed. We shall return to it toward the end of our discussion.

18. M. F. Burnyeat, "Examples in Epistemology: Socrates, Theaetetus, and G. E. Moore," *Philosophy* 52 (1977): 388–90.

19. Fine, "Knowledge and *Logos,*" 393 n. 29. The principle (KBK) is originally introduced on p. 367.

20. It might be objected here that Plato's claim that one does not understand (συνίησιν) the name of something if one does not know what it is (*Tht.* 147b2) suggests that Plato rejects the view I advocate here. But this would be a mistake. As Burnyeat argues ("Examples in Epistemology," 387–88), the "understanding involved here is not identical with but presupposes linguistic familiarity with the terms in question." What Burnyeat does not see is that his view also allows him to construe the second version of this argument that he attributes to Plato as valid (390).

21. One should except the statement by Fine referred to in n. 9 above. But Fine does not pursue the point and, I think, ultimately offers a construal of Plato's view of *epistēmē* that is incompatible with it. Burnyeat, too, makes a similar suggestion in "Paradoxes in Plato's Distinction between Knowledge and True Belief," *Proceedings of the Aristotelian Society, Supplementary Volume* 54 (1980), 180, but follows it in a different direction.

22. Cf. *Theaetetus* 201d1–2; 202c7–8; 296c3–5; 208b8–9, e3–5; 210b1.

23. E.g., among many places, *Men.* 97e–98a; *Phd.* 73a, 76b, 78d; *Rep.* 534a–b; *Tim.* 28a, 51e; *Smp.* 202a; *Sph.* 253b.

24. A. M. Quinton, *The Nature of Things* (London, 1973), 122.

25. D. M. Armstrong, *Belief, Truth, and Knowledge* (Cambridge, 1973), 137.

26. Roderick M. Chisholm, *Theory of Knowledge* (Englewood Cliffs, N.J., 1966), 5.

27. Glenn R. Morrow, "Plato and the Mathematicians: An Interpretation of Socrates' Dream in the *Theaetetus* (201e–206c)," *Philosophical Review* 79 (1970): 313.

28. Paul Friedländer, *Plato: The Dialogues (Third Period),* trans. Hans Meyerhoff (Princeton, 1976), 184.

29. Harold Cherniss, "The Philosophical Economy of the Theory of Ideas," in R. E. Allen, ed., *Studies in Plato's Metaphysics* (London, 1965), 6.

30. Both passages, I must admit, are troublesome for the view advanced in this paper: neither seems to connect *epistēmē* with the knowledge of essence. But both passages are surrounded with difficulty in any case. For example, it is not clear how traveling the road to Larissa can provide one with the *aitias logismos* ("account of the explanation") that Plato considers necessary for *epistēmē* at *Meno* 98a3–4. The

eyewitness passage, on the other hand, does not fit well with Plato's overall emphasis on the connection between *epistēmē* and understanding in the *Theaetetus* (for difficulties in integrating this with Plato's overall strategy, see Burnyeat, "Paradoxes in Plato's Distinction," 186–88). But it can also be suggested that, despite what Socrates says, the eyewitness cannot be said to have *epistēmē* since all perceptual awareness is liable to the many errors discussed at *Tht.* 192a–194c. For this point, see E. S. Haring, "The *Theaetetus* Ends Well," *Review of Metaphysics* 35 (1982): 512 with n. 9. Haring also finds a positive message in the dialogue's negative ending, and her discussion is worth consulting.

31. Nicholas P. White, *Plato on Knowledge and Reality* (Indianapolis, 1976), 176–77.

32. Fine, "Knowledge and *Logos* in the *Theaetetus.*" The interrelation model of knowledge was actually first located in the dialogue by May Yoh, "On the Third Attempted Definition of Knowledge, *Theaetetus* 201c–210d," *Dialogue* 14 (1975): 430: ". . . in Plato's view, to name [elements] involves an act of discrimination, and to discriminate is to set them in proper relation to each other. They are thus not isolated from others and will no longer be alogon (*sic*); for there will be some *logos* of their inter-relation." Yoh, however, proceeds to connect this promising model, quite gratuitously, with the theory of Forms.

33. "Paradoxes in Plato's Distinction," 186–88. Cf. also Burnyeat's "Aristotle on Understanding Knowledge," in E. Berti, ed., *Aristotle on Science: "The Posterior Analytics"* (Padua and New York, 1980), 97–139, esp. 133–36. See also J.M.E. Moravcsik, "Understanding and Knowledge in Plato's Philosophy," in *Neue Hefte für Philosophie* 15/16 (1978): 53–69. An extensive recent discussion can be found in Jon Moline, *Plato's Theory of Understanding* (Madison, 1982).

34. Gail Fine has objected to me that on her view more than knowledge of wagons (for example) is necessary for the knowledge that this wagon belongs to Laius: "I believe this wagon is Laius' when, e.g., I see him sitting in it; I know it's his when I add to this belief others about, e.g., how he came to be there, or ask him if it's his wagon, and so on." This may in general be correct, but I cannot see how it is applicable to Plato's concern with *epistēmē*, even on the additive model, if we accept the view that what must be added to true belief is *logos* and that *logos* is definition. For the beliefs cited here do not seem to be related to the *logos* of the object in question. They do not connect the wagon to other objects in an appropriate field. In addition, if we assume that the fact that "this wagon is Laius'" is a matter of knowledge, it is not clear that a definition of what a wagon is is necessary for knowledge of that fact.

35. See Fine, "Knowledge and *Logos*," 387–88; White, 178 with n. 53; McDowell, 253–54. All three discussions correct previous readings of this passage, e.g., those of F. M. Cornford, *Plato's Theory of Knowledge* (Indianapolis, 1957), 157–58, and Morrow, "Plato and the Mathematicians," 309–10. But, perhaps because of Plato's emphasis, they all seem to be aware only of the second and not also of the first of the errors that Plato discusses here.

36. The attempt of Jacob Klein to show that the *Philosopher* was never to be written, but that what the philosopher is is implicit in the practice of the dialectic

art in these three dialogues, does not seem to me convincing. See his *Plato's Trilogy* (Chicago, 1977).

37. *Sophist* 217b2–3: καθ' ἕκαστον μὴν διορίσασθαι σαφῶς τί ποτ' ἔστιν, οὐ σμικρὸν οὐδὲ ῥάδιον ἔργον. Cf. *Sophist* 218c6–7: . . . τί ποτ' ἔστιν, ὁ σοφιστής, and cp. *Politicus* 258b3, πολιτικὸν διαζητεῖν with *Theaetetus* 148c6–7, ἐπιστήμην . . . ἐξευρεῖν.

38. These domains, I think, consist of types of which sensible objects are tokens. Such a view is suggested by J.M.E. Moravcsik, "Forms, Nature and the Good in the *Philebus*," *Phronesis* 24 (1979): 88 ff.

39. See, for example, the final "weaving together of the name" of the sophist at *Sophist* 268c5–d5. For recent discussion of the method of division, see J.M.E. Moravcsik, "The Anatomy of Plato's Divisions," in E. N. Lee, A.P.D. Mourelatos, and R. M. Rorty, eds., *Exegesis and Argument* (Assen, 1973), 324–48; also, J. L. Ackrill, "In Defence of Platonic Division," in Oscar P. Wood and George Pitcher, eds., *Ryle: A Collection of Critical Essays* (Garden City, N.Y., 1970), 373–92, though Ackrill, in my opinion, places too much emphasis on the idea that Platonic division is an operation upon concepts and not upon natural objects and their kinds. An excellent earlier treatment is to be found in Julius Stenzel, *Plato's Method of Dialectic*, trans. D. J. Allan (New York, 1973).

40. On this issue, I disagree with Fine, who thinks that the dialogue's negative ending simply suggests that only several *logoi,* and not a single one, can turn a true belief into *epistēmē* and that this is all that Plato means it to suggest ("Knowledge and *Logos*," 394–97). I don't see how the addition of many *logoi* can help to turn a belief about a thing's accidental properties into *epistēmē* where a single one will fail (cf. McDowell, 257). Now Fine argues (392 n. 28) that what may be needed is not the addition of any *logos* distinguishing a thing from others but that of a *logos* specifying a thing's essence. It is, however, still unclear how an essential *logos* (which is what I have been concerned with all along) can transform an accidental belief into *epistēmē*. Even if Plato, like Aristotle, believes that features that follow from a thing's essence but are not part of it are objects of *epistēmē*, this is still a far cry from his thinking that any true belief about an object can become *epistēmē* if it is accompanied by its *logos*. I therefore do not accept Fine's view that Plato's final argument against defining *epistēmē* as true belief accompanied by *logos* "fails for reasons Plato himself already provided" and that Plato does not take this failure seriously (394). Plato, I think, is quite serious about the dialogue's failure. And this failure contains, as we shall see, an important additional lesson.

41. Aristotle, *Posterior Analytics* A6.75a18–27, A30; *Metaphysics* E2.1026b2–24, 1027a19–28, esp. 27–28: ἐπιστήμη οὐκ ἔστι αὐτοῦ. For an account motivating Aristotle's denial that we can have *epistēmē* of "perceptible physical objects and their contingent (accidental) properties," see Burnyeat, "Aristotle on Understanding Knowledge," 114–15. See also Jonathan Barnes, *Aristotle's "Posterior Analytics"* (Oxford, 1975), 124–28.

42. There do remain beliefs about features of things that, though not parts of their essence, in some way follow from it. But, as I will suggest, the *logos* of a thing, though apparently short, involves a large number of its features because it is a

summary specification of the relations between that thing and all the other members of its domain along with their features, which consist in further such relations.

43. *Tht.* 210a9–b2. McDowell, 257, begins to suggest the point I am insisting on, but pursues it in a very different direction: "The argument of [209d4–210a9] might well prompt the following thought: true judgement concerning a thing, and knowledge as to what it is, are not related in such a way that an addition to the first can convert it into the second. "This," he infers, "suggests that true judgement concerning a thing already implies knowledge as to what it is." The inference is resistible, however. The point may suggest that those true judgments constitute knowledge as to what a thing is that are expressed (not in addition to, but) through *logoi*. Notice, in this connection, that even Cornford, *Plato's Theory of Knowledge,* 162–63, does not take Plato at his word. The problem, as he sees it, is that Plato has deliberately not appealed to the proper sense of *logos,* which concerns the Forms.

44. Cf. Fine, "Knowledge and *Logos,*" 369; Yoh, 420–21; McDowell, 229; Julia Annas, "Knowledge and Language: The *Theaetetus* and the *Cratylus,*" in Malcolm Schofield and Martha Craven Nussbaum, eds., *Language and Logos: Studies in Ancient Greek Philosophy Presented to G.E.L. Owen* (Cambridge, 1982), 137 with n. 1.

45. *Phaedo* 73a9–10: . . . ἐπιστήμη ἐνοῦσα καὶ ὀρθὸς λόγος; 76b5: ἀνὴρ ἐπιστάμενος περὶ ὧν ἐπίσταται ἔχοι ἂν δοῦναι λόγον; 78d1: αὐτὴ ἡ οὐσία ἧς λόγον δίδομεν τοῦ εἶναι.

46. *Republic* 534b3–4: Ἦ καὶ διαλεκτικὸν καλεῖς τὸν λόγον ἑκάστου λαμβάνοντα τῆς οὐσίας; Cf. b4–6, b8–d1.

47. *Symposium* 202a5–7: Τὸ ὀρθὰ δοξάζειν καὶ ἄνευ τοῦ ἔχειν λόγον δοῦναι οὐκ οἶσθ᾽ . . . ὅτι οὔτε ἐπίστασθαί ἐστιν—ἄλογον γὰρ πρᾶγμα πῶς ἂν εἴη ἐπιστήμη—οὔτε ἀμαθία;

48. *Meno* 98a3–8: . . . οὐ πολλοῦ ἄξιαί εἰσιν, ἕως ἄν τις αὐτὰς δήσῃ αἰτίας λογισμῷ . . . καὶ διαφέρει δεσμῷ ἐπιστήμη ὀρθῆς δόξης. For some discussion, see R. S. Bluck, *Plato's "Meno"* (London, 1961), 412–13.

49. *Timaeus* 28a1–2: . . . νοήσει μετὰ λόγου περιληπτόν.

50. *Timaeus* 51e3: . . . ἀεὶ μετ᾽ ἀληθοῦς λόγου.

51. E.g., *Protagoras* 324b1–2; *Republic* 517b4–7; *Phaedrus* 256a5–6; *Laws* 647d4–6, 772a1–3. *Sophist* 265c7–9 mentions *logos* and *epistēmē* together, but it is not telling. Cf. Aristotle, *Posterior Analytics* B19.100b10: . . . ἐπιστήμη δ᾽ ἅπασα μετὰ λόγου ἐστί, which cannot support the additive model, and *Nicomachean Ethics* VI.6.1140b33.

52. Myles Burnyeat kindly discussed this point with me.

53. *Sophist* 281b7–c1: . . . λόγῳ . . . ; c4–5: . . . διὰ λόγων.

54. *Politicus* 257d2–258a3: . . . διὰ λόγων . . . ; on the contrast between name and thing, see, for example, *Pol.* 262d4–6 and *Sph.* 218c1–3.

55. Such a view is held, for example, by Cherniss, "The Philosophical Economy of the Theory of Ideas," and, of course, by Cornford, *Plato's Theory of Knowledge.* For an argument against finding this view in the *Republic,* see Gail Fine, "Knowledge and Belief in *Republic* V," *Archiv für Geschichte der Philosophie* 60 (1978): 121–39, with full references. Though I am not always in agreement with Fine's

reconstruction of Plato's argument, I am in substantial agreement with her conclusions.

56. Fine, "Knowledge and Belief," 122 n. 3, considers this passage inimical to her position. But see I. M. Crombie, *An Examination of Plato's Doctrines*, vol. I (London, 1962), 57.

57. Burnyeat discusses such a view in detail, and makes some necessary qualifications, in "Paradoxes in Plato's Distinction," 180–88. He points out that this construal explains Plato's insistence that to have *epistēmē* one must become master of a proof or explanation oneself, his finding teaching as problematic as he does, and his emphasis on definition as part of *epistēmē* (186–87). Burnyeat also seems to draw a distinction, however, between teaching morals and mathematics on the one hand, where "teaching does not produce knowledge" (i.e., understanding), and practical skills on the other, where "there is an honest job for teaching to do" (187). I am inclined to think that, whether or not Plato was aware of it, the problem is the same in all cases. Though one can indeed be taught to be a shoemaker, it is not clear that one can be taught to be a *good* shoemaker—this is where the difficulty is. Similarly, one can be taught some mathematics—most people are; but how does one teach a student to be a good mathematician, "really to understand" mathematics? The question of morals is naturally the most complicated by far. Whereas in shoemaking, mathematics, and the other crafts we can distinguish between a shoemaker, say, and a good shoemaker, the distinction collapses in regard to virtue. The only thing that is to be taught here is how to be *good,* pure and simple: there is nothing else to teach.

Following C.A.J. Coady, "Testimony and Observation," *American Philosophical Quarterly* 50 (1975): 149–55, esp. 154, and B.A.O. Williams, "Knowledge and Reasons," in G. H. von Wright, ed., *Problems in the Theory of Knowledge* (The Hague, 1972), 1–11, Burnyeat makes a number of interesting comments about the transmissibility of knowledge as opposed to the intransmissibility of understanding. A suggestive parallel asymmetry holds between description and interpretation (activities that, to some extent, are coordinate with knowledge and understanding). If I describe an object *x* to you, and I am in an appropriate position for doing so, you can go on to describe *x* yourself; but you cannot do the same with an interpretation of *x* unless, in some way, you go through the interpretation yourself (notice that nothing prevents you from describing my interpretation without engaging in it yourself, and that the objects of description and interpretation need not be distinct). This seems to me a much more promising manner of distinguishing between these two activities than the effort to find differences between their truth-claims and truth-conditions. For the latter approach, see Robert J. Matthews, "Describing and Interpreting a Work of Art," *Journal of Aesthetics and Art Criticism* 36 (1977): 5–14.

58. *Theaetetus* 147c2–6. Socrates is here referring to the example of clay, but the context shows that his point is intended to apply to knowledge as well.

59. Cf. for example, *Crito* 119a4: ἀπέραντος . . . ἀριθμὸς ἀνθρώπων.

60. *Phil.* 13e–14a, esp. 14a8–9: πολλαί . . . καὶ διάφοροι. T. H. Irwin has remarked that Socrates' practice in the *Philebus* may not after all be so different from his practice in the early *Charmides*, where he carefully distinguishes different

kinds of knowledge from each other. But the main difference consists in Plato's view in the *Philebus* that the answer to the question about knowledge must be *simply* a vast map specifying the position of each kind of knowledge within it. The very distinctions among the kinds of knowledge, suitably articulated, constitute those very kinds, and the total articulation constitutes knowledge itself.

61. At this point, I must qualify my agreement with Fine on the question of Plato's acceptance of the interrelation model of *epistēmē* in the *Theaetetus*. This model is clearly involved in the examples of the *Sophist* and the *Philebus*, in the practice of the *Sophist* and the *Politicus* (that is, in the method of division), and in the theory of the *Philebus*. But I am not certain that it is spelled out in the *Theaetetus*, though Plato is clearly working his way toward it. The only strong evidence Fine presents for her view is the passage 206a–b ("Knowledge and *Logos*," 385). Now Plato does claim that to know a musical note is to know to what strings it belongs (*Sph.* 206b1–2), which supports the interrelation model. But he does not say this of letters: on the contrary, he speaks of coming to learn "each itself by itself" (206a6–7), which is precisely what he considers impossible at *Phil.* 18c7–8. At best, then, the evidence is equivocal, and we should take a cautious attitude toward this issue. G.E.L. Owen, "Notes on Ryle's Plato," in Wood and Pitcher, *Ryle*, 365, unequivocally rejects the view Fine supports.

62. I am deeply indebted to M. F. Burnyeat, Gail Fine, and J.M.E. Moravcsik for their detailed comments on this essay. Hugo Bedau, Daniel Dennett, Charles Kahn, David Sachs, and Jerome Schneewind also gave me a number of useful suggestions.

PART III

Plato: Questions of Beauty and the Arts

Twelve

PLATO ON IMITATION AND POETRY
IN *REPUBLIC* X

PLATO'S ATTITUDE toward the poets is bald and uncompromising: He wants no part of them. And though he takes no pleasure in his attitude, for he takes pleasure in poetry, he takes the attitude seriously. His argument in Book X of the *Republic* is neither exaggerated nor ironical. He does not rely on two different senses of "imitation" in order to exclude only that part of poetry that it might be thought reasonable to despise. He does not exploit a subtle distinction in order to retain serious poetry once he has succeeded in eliminating poetry that merely entertains. His proscription allows of no exceptions.

But though his view is more stern than it has sometimes been comfortable to suppose, its scope is also narrower. Book X of the *Republic* contains an outrageous attack on poetry and—this is part of my argument in what follows—on poetry only. Plato does not "banish the artists." In fact—this is another part of my argument—he does not even banish the painters.

That Plato banishes only poetry, though painting is in his eyes equally *mimesis* (imitation), suggests that being imitative is not by itself a sufficient reason for exclusion from the city. What distinguishes painting from poetry in this respect is a pressing question, especially when we realize (as I hope we shall) that Plato's argument against poetry depends on a series of analogies with painting. These are close enough to have convinced many of Plato's readers, though not Plato himself, that painting and all "fine" art, not only poetry, is to be outlawed. But by turning our attention to the differences between painting and poetry that account for the asymmetry in Plato's treatment of these two practices, we may find that though the action he advocates is, as usual, quite drastic, his motivation, as is also usual, is not half as perverse as we have been fearing.

I

Plato states his position on poetry in the preamble to *Republic* X (595a1–c5). This is that "in no way are we admitting [in our city] as much of it as is imitative" (595a5). His reason for holding this position, which he also states in the preamble, is that tragedy and all such imitations are hazardous to the reason (*dianoia*) of their listeners—of those at least who do not possess as an antidote the knowledge of what these things really are. (595b5–7)[1]

We must notice that the subject here is only poetry and that the reason why it is not admitted to the city is that it harms the soul of its listeners. This suggests that Plato is not going on to offer two arguments against poetry—first, that it is imitative (595c7–602b11), and second, that it is bad for the soul (602c1–606d8).[2] Rather, the general discussion of imitation and the demonstration that poetry is one of its species are only parts of the single argument against poetry that we find announced at the very beginning of the book. In addition, noticing this point is helpful in distinguishing Plato's view of poetry from his view of painting, for if being imitative were a reason for banishment, painting, being the paradigm of imitation, should surely be banished. Yet the opening of the book says only that poetry is to be banished. The reason for this, we shall see, is the difference in the seriousness of their bad effects.

Before we turn to this question, however, we must discuss a serious difficulty that the preamble raises for the interpretation of Plato's view of poetry. For though the present claim is that no imitative poetry (*hosē mimētikē*) is admissible in the city (595a5), the discussion of poetry in Books II and III concluded by admitting "the unmixed imitator of good character" (*ton tou epieikous mimētēn akraton,* 397d4–5). Furthermore, Book X itself finally allows "so much of poetry as consists of hymns to the gods and praises of virtuous people" (*hoson monon hymnous theois kai enkōmia tois agathois poiēseōs,* 607a3–4). If such poetry is imitative, Book X contradicts not only Book III but itself as well. If it is not, how much poetry is thereby allowed after all in the city?[3]

Plato has been forcefully defended against the charge of inconsistency by J. Tate, who, in a series of papers that are still very influential, argued that Plato uses "imitation" in two senses. The imitation he banishes at 595a5 is imitation of a bad sort, while the imitation he admits at 397a4–5 is of a good sort, and the contradiction disappears.[4]

Plato's earlier discussion of imitation in Books II and III concerns the elementary education of the young Guardians. In his city, as in Athens (cf. 376e2–3), children begin their education through poetry. Having discussed the subjects appropriate for them, Plato goes on (392c6 ff.) to discuss style (*lexis*), and distinguishes pure narration (the dithyramb), pure imitation or impersonation (tragedy),[5] and their combination (epic). He then raises the question whether the Guardians should be educated by the use of imitation,[6] and claims that the answer depends on whether they are to be imitative themselves (394e1–2). It is precisely at this point that Tate locates the two senses of "imitation"; for, he claims, "the answer is both 'no' and 'yes.' "[7]

Yet all that Socrates says here is that the young Guardians will be allowed to imitate only characters like those into which they should grow (394c4–5). To imitate other sorts as well would be an instance of *polupragmosunē* (doing more than one thing; cf. 395b–c) and might make them like the characters they would in that case imitate. But nothing here, it seems to me, implies that "imitation" has two senses; all that is implied is that one and the same activity can have different sorts of objects.[8]

Plato now combines the above formal specification of imitation[9] with the range of its possible subject matter. A good person would recite mostly by narration, but would occasionally imitate *(a)* good people doing good things, *(b)* less often, good people in bad situations, and *(c)* only with difficulty and "only for fun" (*paidias charin*) bad people doing good things (395c5–c10). An unworthy person would imitate anything and would use little narration (397a1–b2). A third style, finally, would consist in a mixture of these two (397c9–10). Adeimantus now approves only the first of these three modes, that of "the unmixed imitator of good character" (397d4–5), a sort (I suppose) of a purified Homer.

Tate, however, describes what Adeimantus approves as the

> *nonimitative* style, which nevertheless contains such kinds of imitation as the virtuous poet will not disdain to practice. Plato could scarcely have made it clearer than the style that is nonimitative in the first sense is yet imitative in the second sense, the sense in which the Guardians are imitative.[10]

On Tate's view, therefore, Plato at 595a5 only excludes imitation in the bad sense of 397a1–b2, and nothing else: "The poetry that is admitted is imitative in one sense and nonimitative in another sense."[11]

Plato's attack on poetry is therefore significantly disarmed—if, indeed, it still is an attack at all. But it is clear that *Republic* 394–97 does not generate two senses of "imitation." Plato simply allows the young Guardians to listen to, and to tell, tales that, if they involve imitation, imitate good characters or good actions, and forbids them to do much else. The different styles all imitate, in the same sense, different objects. The conflict between Books III and X cannot be resolved in this manner.

In specifying what sorts of poetry are acceptable in Books II and III of the *Republic*, Plato has consistently enraged generations of readers. We should comment (and we can do no more than that on this occasion) on whether this rage has been justified: Very briefly, my own view is that it has not. Plato's attitude toward what young children should recite, read, and learn from (for *this* is his subject at this point) is quite reasonable. We find it unthinkable that he should imagine that great poetry like Homer's could be harmful. But in thinking of it as "great poetry" we are begging the question, for we place it within a complex cultural context, within a long tradition, and within a world ("Homer's world, not ours," in Auden's words) that we know to be long dead. We do not look at the Homeric poems as a primer, from which one learned to read, to speak, to think, and to value. The relevant comparison is not between ourselves and fourth-century Athenians in respect to our reactions to Homer. (And, in any case, how many *children* today read Homer? And of those who do, in watered-down versions of the *Tales-from-Homer* type, how many read of Odysseus and Calypso, or Demodocus' lay of Ares and Aphrodite?)[12] The proper comparison would involve contemporary children, mass education, and mass entertainment. Instead of learning from Homer, children today learn from primers that are often, for example, sexist; we find nothing wrong or narrow-minded in protesting against them. They are entertained by, and learn what friendship and companionship are, from "The Smurfs" and "Power Rangers"—ubiquitous and intrusive purveyors of bad taste, deformed paradigms, and questionable values.[13] And though we may not want to legislate such things out of existence, we do not, or would like not to, let children watch them. On the reverse side of this coin, the positive effort that goes into making children's literature appropriate to them, correctly or incorrectly, is a Platonic legacy.

In short, we quite agree with Plato that censorship for children is appropriate. We quite agree with him that art has great power, and that we must channel it correctly. We do not agree on whether censorship should be practiced on Homer (but this, I have argued, depends on a wrong comparison) and on whether it should be legislated by the state. But on the last issue we cannot any longer charge Plato with being a philistine; we can only charge him with being illiberal. And this is neither new, nor surprising, nor (as many have feared about his views on Homer) inconsistent with his own poetic powers.

We still have to face the conflict between Books III and X: The former seems to allow imitative poetry, the latter to forbid it. This conflict, I am afraid, cannot be ultimately eliminated; but it is not as stark and glaring as it has often seemed to be. In discussing this last issue, we shall gain some understanding of why Plato seems to return to the question of poetry in Book X, something that has made this last part of the *Republic* seem suspiciously like an afterthought.[14] I shall suggest that Plato does not clearly *return* to the banishment of poetry in Book X, but that he raises the question in a systematic form for the first time. Books VIII and IX of the *Republic* consist mainly of a discussion of threats against the unity of the soul and of the city. Book X belongs primarily with them, and shows that poetry is one of these threats and that the city is proof against it.

Now Book X seems to begin with a reference to the earlier discussion in

Book III, but this reference is not absolutely clear. Socrates does say that he is now convinced (*ennoō*, 595a2) that the city has been well organized (*ōkizomen*, 595a2); his reason for thinking this is that he recalls (*enthumētheis*, 595a3) that poetry is not being admitted to it (595a5). But I am not certain that we have to take his recollection to refer to the discussion in Book III, which concerned primarily the control and not the exclusion of poetry. We might instead take it to refer to his realizing that nowhere after Book III (to which I shall presently turn) is there any provision made for poetry in the organization of the city: This omission, we should realize, would have been glaring to an Athenian audience, in whose life poetry (tragic, epic, and lyric) played a crucial part. Finally, his comment, "It appears even clearer now that it is not to be admitted" (*ou paradektea nun kai enargesteron . . . phainetai*, 595a5–6), need not be taken to imply that an earlier attempt to banish poetry has already been made, but only that such an attempt, had it been made before the soul had been divided, would have been much more difficult to justify.

The actual discussion of poetry in Books II and III concerned the elementary education of the young Guardians, and Plato, I think, was quite willing to allow imitative poetry to play a crucial role in that enterprise. He considers the use of poetry proper in education (cf. 376e2–4, where Plato expresses a remarkably positive attitude toward traditional education), since he thinks that imitation can become "habit and nature" (395d1–3);[15] if, therefore, a child's objects of imitation are also examples for imitation, he thinks that they will be beneficial. His claims about poetry (and the other arts, which he does not here contrast with poetry) at 401a–402a show that he is thinking of the very beginning of the Guardians' education.[16] He believes that by proper imitation, a child not yet capable of understanding (*prin logon dunatos einai labein*, 402a2)[17] can develop a preference for beauty and goodness and will embrace understanding in friendship when it does finally arrive (402a3–4). On this question, Plato anticipates Aristotle, who also thinks that imitation is natural and that human beings "learn at first by imitation,"[18] though Plato differs from Aristotle in thinking that imitation in poetry becomes harmful once understanding has set in—that is, once the soul has developed all its separate parts.[19]

Though children can learn from imitation, the adult inhabitants of the city are not to be exposed to it.[20] This is Plato's primary concern, the main target of his argument in Book X, and what his refusal to admit poetry in the city comes to; when he writes here that imitative poetry is not being admitted, we need not look for another sense in which imitation is (or has already been) admitted. The discussion in Books II and III lays the foundations for the omission of any reference to poetry as a component in the city's life in the bulk of the *Republic,* and Book X explains why that omission has been made.[21]

Precisely because the foundations for the exclusion of poetry are laid in Books II and III, however, Plato, by the time of his writing of Book X, has come to see his attitude toward poetry as a single policy. This, at least, is what is suggested by his statement at 607b1–3:

> Let this, then, be said in our defense in recalling that it was reasonable to send poetry away on that occasion since it has such a nature.

For this does refer back to 398a–b, where the poet who imitates everything is not allowed to enter the city. Because of the reference, we cannot totally avoid the conflict between Books II and III on the one hand and Book X on the other, which we have been discussing. But if we realize that there is more to the proscription of poetry than the single passage 398a–b, and that the major burden of that proscription is carried by Plato's silence as to the role of poetry in his city's life, then the conflict loses a great part of its immediacy and seriousness.

Book X, therefore, can now be seen as a part of the long discussion of the perversions of the soul and of the city that begins with Book VIII: Poetry creates a "bad constitution" (*kakēn politeian*, 605b7–8) in the soul just as, for example, an excess or defect of wealth can destroy the "constitution within" the wise man (*tēn en hautōi politeian*, 591e1). Though not perfectly consistent with Books II and III, Book X is not simply an incomprehensible return to a subject that these two books seem to have exhausted; for a crucial part of its function is to justify the omission of poetry from the life of the city's adult inhabitants—a subject not accounted for in Books II and III. Thus Book X of the *Republic* is neither a "digression"[22] nor a "coda,"[23] neither an "appendix"[24] nor a "retrospect."[25] It is, rather, a step of a carefully constructed description of the ways in which the soul can be less than perfect and thus lose the rewards of the life of justice—to a final accounting of which Plato significantly turns in the last part of Book X.

II

We must now look at the actual argument that Plato offers in Book X of the *Republic* for the banishment of poetry—that it brings disarray into the soul. The first part of this argument consists of a discussion of imitation, and the conclusion of that discussion is that imitation is worthless as a source of knowledge and that

> the imitator knows nothing of any account about what he imitates and imitation is merely play (*paidia*) and not anything serious (*spoudē*). (602b7–8)

But that something is play is not enough to exclude it from the city. This inhuman attitude would be in conflict with Plato's view at 424e5–426a6 that *paidia* should be forbidden only if it is lawless (*paranomos*) and thus destroys good character (which is, essentially, Plato's argument against poetry as well). Plato clearly does not dislike *paidia* for itself,[26] but only if it usurps the place of what must be taken seriously.[27] The demonstration that imitation is merely play does not provide a reason for banishing poetry, but is only one of the steps leading to that final conclusion.

At 597c7 Socrates asks, in his traditional manner, for a definition of imitation;[28] in reaching it, he appeals to the theory of Forms. A number of factors make the appeal strange: First, the theory is not mentioned in the preamble to the book, in contrast to the divided soul, which is;[29] second, the version of the theory that is introduced is enormously peculiar;[30] third, little of what Socrates says about the Forms is actually relevant to his definition of imitation. It is important for him to show that imitation is at two removes from reality. But showing this does not clearly require the dubious one-over-many argument of 596a ff., or Forms of artifacts, or God as the creator of such Forms. In addition, the theory here attributes to the craftsman a knowledge that, being of Forms, has been so far considered as the distinguishing (and very hard to acquire) characteristic of the philosopher. But since these questions are not central to my purpose, I shall not pursue them any farther.[31]

The question that we must ask is why Plato reaches his definition of imitation through a discussion of painting (596d–597a), which he describes as a way of making "things that appear but that are not truly real" (596e4). Since his primary concern is with poetry, why does he not depend directly on its features in order to define imitation?

This is by no means the only occasion where Plato employs this strategy. He introduces painting for the second time in distinguishing the three sorts of objects that there are: natural objects (Forms), physical objects, and painted objects. The painter cannot be said to be a maker of either of the first two, but is only an imitator of what God and the craftsman make.[32] The definition thus reached is this:

> Do you call the imitator [a maker] of the product at two removes from reality?[33] (597e3–4)

Only now is this general definition applied to the tragic poets and all other imitators (597e6–8), who are also said to make things at two removes from "the king" and the truth.[34]

Plato introduces the painter for a third time at 597e10 ff. and, by means of distinguishing between the way physical objects really are and the way they appear, claims that painting concerns an appearance (*phantasma*) and not truth—a result that he then generalizes to all imitation (598b6–8).[35] Again, he argues that the painter's products are deceitful, and that therefore this is true of all imitation.[36] After a detailed discussion of poetry on the basis of these conclusions, the painter is used to introduce the additional argument for the imitator's ignorance (601b9–602b8). Finally, the appeal of imitation to the lower parts of the soul is also introduced by means of painting, and only then is it generalized to poetry (602c ff.).

But why does Plato depend so crucially on painting? We tend quite automatically to take painting as our model for the representational arts, and this procedure has raised few questions.[37] But the little we know about the earl history of *mimeisthai* ("to imitate") and its cognates suggests that these terms were originally connected with speech and poetry rather than with painting, with hearing rather than with seeing. In view of this, Plato's practice of depending on painting for his views of imitation and poetry needs to be explained.

In an important though idiosyncratic work, Hermann Koller has argued that *mimesis* was originally connected with music and dancing and that its sense was therefore that of "representation" and even "expression" rather than of "imitation."[38] He finds this last sense, which he claims is specific to painting, invented in *Republic* X.[39] Some of Koller's conclusions have been criticized by Gerald Else,[40] but one serious aspect of the problem seems to me not to have been completely resolved.

In disagreeing with Koller, Else tries to find in the earliest occurrences of these terms the connotation of counterfeiting and its attendant distinction between appearing and being, which he considers crucial to the sense "imitation." But this effort, it seems to me, fails. Consider, for example, the *Delian Hymn to Apollo*, where (163) it is said that the Delian maidens

know how to *imitate* the voice and dance of all people
pantōn d' anthrōpōn phōnas kai krembaliastun mimeisth' isasin

Koller, because of the presence of dancing, thinks that the sense of "imitation" is totally inappropriate here.[41] Else, by contrast, finds it unavoidable.[42] But when we think of the continuation, "anyone would think that he himself was speaking, so well is their song put together," it seems to me that though the connection with music proves little, we need not suppose that the maidens "impress and flatter their guests by imitating their native accents and dances" either.[43] Rather, the maidens are said actually to speak different dialects and to know how to perform dances from different areas: They *act like* other people, and no deception is involved.

The case is quite similar with Aeschylus, *Choephoroi* 564:

amphō de phōnēn ēsomen parnēsida glōssēs autēn Phōkidos mimoumenō.

Else's translation, "We will put forward a Parnassian accent, imitating [mimicking] the sound of the Phocian dialect," seems to me gratuitous.[44] Orestes may much more plausibly be taken to be telling Pylades, who was Phocian to begin with, that they must, quite simply, speak Phocian to each other.

The sense of *acting like* someone else is, we should notice, exactly what is needed in interpreting Theognis 370:

mōmeuntai de moi polloi . . . mimeisthai d' oudeis tōn asōtōn dunatai.

To account for this case, Else needs to postulate a second sense of the verb, "an extension of the meaning from physical mimicry to moral imitation."[45] But on my suggestion the line can be smoothly translated thus:

Many make fun of me . . . but none of the unwise can act like me.[46]

It does not, therefore, seem clear that *mimesis* was from its very beginning connected with *mimicking*. It is clear that the term and its cognates were more often used in connection with speaking and acting rather than with painting, and it is also clear that even in the latter half of the fifth century they did not go hand in hand with the Platonic notions of the counterfeit, the merely apparent, the deceitful, and the fake.[47] A number of cases in Herodotus illustrate very well the sense *acting like,* which we have found above.[48] Thucydides' claim that Pausanias' behavior "appeared more like a *mimesis* of tyranny than like a generalship" and thus cost him his life could not be explained by appealing to the sense *counterfeiting;* on the contrary, the necessary sense seems to be that of *emulating.*[49] Even Democritus, who did in fact rely on the distinction between seeming and being in many aspects of his thinking, does not seem to me to appeal to it, as Else claims he does,[50] in DK B39:

One must either be or imitate a good human being

agathon ē einai chreōn ē mimeisthai.

It is not plausible to take this as advice to pretend to be good. Rather, we should take it as advice to the effect that, if one cannot be good, one should do the next best thing—act like someone who is.[51]

By the end of the fifth century, however, the contrast between imitation and reality may be found in the dramatic poets—see, for example, Aristophanes *Frogs* 108–9 and Euripides *Ion* 1429.[52] It seems to me plausible that this connection might have been already established in painting, especially if we consider Xenophon, *Memorabilia* III.x.1–8, as an accurate report. In that passage, the "illusionist" painter Parrhasius eagerly agrees with Socrates that painting is a "likeness of the visible" (*eikasia tōn horōmenōn,* x.1) and insists that all that he can imitate (*apomimeisthai, mimēton*) is the look, and not the character, of people. Parrhasius is finally persuaded, however, that character can also be imitated—but only insofar as it "appears through (*diaphainei*) the face and bearing" of the subject. A similar connection between painting and appearance is made in Socrates' ensuing conversation with the sculptor Cleiton. Even though Xenophon's evidence is hardly contemporary (Parrhasius seems to have been born before 460 B.C.[53] and this conversation may have occurred around 420–410), the report does give some evidence that a connection between painting and the way things look may have been in existence by the end of the fifth century B.C.

We are now in a position to explain why Plato relies so heavily on painting in his discussion of imitation in *Republic* X.[54] "Imitation," as it was traditionally applied to poetry, speaking, and dancing, meant primarily *acting like* someone else. It did not carry with it the connotation of imitating only the appearance as opposed to the reality of the object imitated, or the connected notion of deceiving and counterfeiting. In fact, the crucial role that poetry played in education seems to have depended precisely on a conflation between appearance and reality.[55] Plato, however, wants to argue in *Republic* X that the poets, even when their imitations are successful, can do no more than imitate the look, not the nature, of things. To make this controversial point, to argue that poetry really is not just imitation in the sense of *likeness* but imitation of *appearance,* Plato appeals to painting, which can easily be said to be an imitation of the look of its subjects, considers it as representative of all imitation, and applies its characteristics to poetry as well.

It has long been claimed both by opponents and by defenders of Plato's views on art that artists need not imitate only sensible objects (which they do, according to Plato, by reproducing their appearance) but also that they can somehow directly imitate the Forms. This idea, whose later origin (notably in Plotinus)[56] has been noticed by M. H. Abrams and Monroe Beardsley,[57] has been connected in various ways with Plato. Some claim merely that it is compatible with his view of art as imitation,[58] while others argue more strongly that Plato actually believed that art imitates the Forms.[59]

Both versions of this approach to Plato are wrong, textually and philosophically. The main texts on which this approach is based are either neutral on this question or they contradict this very claim they are used to support. For example, Tate appeals to *Republic* 402b–c in order to show that "the truly *mousikos* (musical) perceives the ideas and their images."[60] Now, it is true that this passage mentions forms (*eidē*) of virtues. But these forms are not the Forms of Plato's theory, which have not yet been introduced at this point of the *Republic*. The presence of the word *eidos* is clearly not sufficient to establish the presence of the theory, especially since these forms are present in sensible objects (*enonta*) and not separate from them, as the theory requires them to be. The passage only claims that we must learn to recognize the many varieties of virtues and vices in the world and in our images of them. The implication, in Adam's words, is that the poet "copies from the life" and not from the intelligible world.[61]

Republic 500e–501b, a passage often used in this connection, likens the construction of the perfect city to the work of a painter using "a divine paradigm" (501e3). Tate considers this a description of the "genuine kind of imitation."[62] But this misses the point of Plato's simile, which is not that there is such a painter, but that this is what the philosopher is. Nor is *Republic* 472d helpful in locating a painter who imitates the Forms,[63] for though the passage shows that Plato did not think that artists are confined to reproducing the appearance only of actually existing things, this does not imply that in painting someone more beautiful than any existing person, the painter would be imitating the Form.[64]

We close this discussion with two texts outside the *Republic*. First, Plato's *Laws* 817b–c, which claims that the inhabitants of Plato's city are the true tragedians, for they live the best life—the truest tragedy. Far from supporting the claim that true poetry imitates the Forms,[65] this passage makes the same point as *Republic* 500e–501b: The best kind of poetry is not poetry at all, but a good life; hence, unless by virtue of a pun, there is no good poetry.[66] Second, Plato's *Phaedrus* 248d–e, a much misread passage in which the "musical" (*mousikos*) is among the best kinds of life that a soul can choose, in contrast to the life of the imitator, which is sixth down on Plato's list. Taking "musical" to refer to some sort of artist, commentators have seen Plato here distinguishing between a true artist and a mere imitator.[67] But the *Phaedrus* has been discussing the soul and the proper relations between its parts. The best lives are lived by the most harmonious souls. And for such souls we find the term *mousikōtatos* ("most musical," *Republic* 411e–412a; cf. *mousikos,* 591d1). This is the person who uses musical education and physical education for their true purpose, the harmonious agreement of reason and spirit that produces control over appetite. This, and not "the arranger of strings," is the true musician—the liberal, civilized character whom Plato considers responsible for one of the best sorts of life a human being can have.[68] The "musical," in this as well as in other contexts, is not the artist but the gentleman who patronizes the artists and knows what to take from them.[69]

Turning to the philosophical basis of the idea that art can imitate the Forms, we should begin by recalling the persistent commonplace that in *Republic* X Plato accuses art of being an imitation of an imitation. But in fact Plato never says this, either in his book or in any other part of his work. Further, not once in *Republic* X is *mimesis* used to refer to the relationship between sensible objects and Forms.[70]

Plato does say, once, that the craftsman makes things "looking toward" (*pros . . . blepōn,* 596b7) the Form, but this is not sufficient to establish that the relationship between the product and the Form is one of imitation[71]—that is, nothing in the text implies that the relationship between a work of art and its subject is the same as that between a physical object and its Form or Forms.[72] And this is one of the main philosophical reasons why the painter and the poet cannot imitate the Forms: for this would just be to produce physical objects—beds or good people. To "imitate" the Forms is a request that it is logically impossible for the artist to satisfy,[73] for in virtue of satisfying it, the artist would cease to be an artist.

In his remarks on this subject, Collingwood wrote that the artist "makes not a bed or a battle or a hero or a villain, but an object *sui generis,* to be judged not by the standards by which such things are judged, but by a standard peculiar to itself."[74] Collingwood, indeed, tried to show that Plato thought of art as an activity distinct from all others: not knowledge, not perception, but imagination—with its own laws, principles, and values, and even with its own way to truth. Though not unlike Collingwood's own philosophy, this is exactly the reverse of Plato's view of art, for there is little that is more striking in Plato's attitude than his absolute refusal to accord to the activity and to the products of *mimesis* an independent status of their own.

This refusal is presupposed, for example, by his crucial statement at *Republic* 394e8–9 that

> the same person is not capable of imitating many things well as he can one,

a statement that is an application of the principle that each person can be good only at one practice. Here the conditions for what constitutes a distinct activity are not supplied by the activity itself, not by the rules it follows, but only by its object: if the object is different, the imitation is different too.[75] Playing the hero, Plato seems to think, is an activity distinct from playing the villain (395b3–6); it is his commitment to such a position that underlies his unwillingness to allow the poet who can imitate anything and everything (398a–b) into his city. And despite his one later reference to *mimesis* as an object of knowledge, it is remarkable how little Plato thinks of it as an art along with the many other arts that he discusses in the *Republic* (cf. 601a4–6).

When one turns from the practice of *mimesis* to its objects, the picture remains the same. The objects of imitations are hardly entities in their own right. Even to speak of "an appearance of a bed" is slightly misleading in this context, for appearances can be thought to have their own ontological status. But Plato seems to block this approach by insisting the the painter produces *a bed;* and though it is a bed "in a way" (*tropōi ge tini,* 596e10), this seems to qualify more the degree than the manner in which the imitator's product is a bed.[76] Thus Plato speaks of a painter making not a picture of a cobbler, but "a cobbler who seems to be" (600e7–601a7). Imitation, he says, can "fashion *everything,* because it touches everything in small part—and that is an image" (598b6–8).

Plato's metaphysical view is manifested in a linguistic vacillation on his part. At 598b4–5 he characterizes painting as an "*imitation* of appearance" and not of reality (*phantasmatos mimēsis*), while at 599a2–3 he claims that poets "*produce* appearances" (*phantasmata poiousin*). Similarly, he characterizes poets as "*imitators* of images" at 600e5 (*mimētas ei-dōlōn*), while he describes Homer as a "*maker* of an image" at 599d3 (*eidolou dēmiourgos*). To think of an artist as an imitator of appearance is to think of the appearance as the *object* of imitation, as something existing in the world before the artist begins to work, as what the artist copies or represents. The appearance in this case is a part of the physical object that is the artist's model. To think of an artist as a maker of an appearance, by contrast, is to think of the appearance as the *product* of imitation, as something that comes into being as a result of the artist's work, as the result of the artist's representation. That Plato does not seem to mark this distinction has some important implications, since it suggests that he is thinking of the object of imitation and of the product of imitation as being the same object—if not in number, at least in type. It almost seems as if he believes that the painter lifts the surface off the subject and transplants it onto the painting: this idea is also suggested, we should notice, by his use of the word *ephaptesthai* at 598b7–8, which we quoted above: Imitation, he claims, *touches* a small part of everything—the image. This image is both the surface of the subject and the product of the painter; the difference between the painted bed and the real bed is that, though they have identical appearances, the latter is in three dimensions while the former is only an image with no depth.

On such a view the limiting case of imitation is the creation of a duplicate of the model. This metaphysical version of the story of Pygmalion is not only consistent with Plato's attitude, but also actually occurs in the famous passage (432a–c) of the *Cratylus,* for Socrates argues there that if one took an image (*eikōn*) of Cratylus and proceeded to add to the color and shape already belonging to it (the appearance) everything else that belongs to Cratylus, then the final product will be a second Cratylus. Thus the painted Cratylus is conceived as an incomplete Cratylus, as the very appearance, which is only part of the real Cratylus, and which can be turned into the latter simply by the addition of details that it lacks.

Thus the imitator of an *F* thing produces a seeming *F* thing, an object whose identity is constituted by the thing that it seems to be, not by any properties that it might have in its own right. And that its objects lack such properties is a central reason why *mimēsis* is in Plato's eyes not an art; for it would have to be such properties, and only such properties, that could provide criteria for when the practice was and was not pursued well and an account of what the practice consists in.[77] As it is, if we try to base such criteria on the objects imitated rather than on their imitations, then the result simply is that a painting of, say, a bed is better the more what it produces looks like a real bed, and the more the practice itself looks like carpentry. My suspicion is that this is precisely what Plato thinks, and that it is the reason why he does not accord imitation an independent status of its own.[78]

Plato's view in the *Republic* is, I think, inconsistent with his statement in the *Sophist* that "an image, though not really being [what it is an image of], really is [an image]" (240b12–13). But to come to that conclusion Plato had to revise substantially a number of views he held when he wrote the *Republic,* and we cannot discuss these issues on this occasion. Our present concern is with what we might call the utter transparency of imitation, its almost total lack of substantiality both as practice and as product. It is precisely this transparency that, in Plato's eyes, justifies one of his most extreme views, that

> if one could make both things, both what is imitated and the image, do you think that anyone would abandon himself to the making of images and consider that as his most precious possession in life?[79] [599a6–b1; cf. 599b3–7]

As the products of *mimesis* are images of real things, so the practice of *mimesis* is the image of a real practice. The point of the first part of the argument against poetry in Book X of the *Republic* is to demonstrate the total heteronomy of *mimesis*. Being thus heteronomous, the imitation of the waging of war, the governing of cities, and the improvement of character can proceed without even true opinion (*pistis*) about such issues, much less knowledge (*epistēmē*) about them.[80]

III

Everything that has been said so far, however, makes *mimesis* "some sort of game and nothing serious" (*paidian tina kai ou spoudēn,* 602b8), and though this is indeed a lowly status, it does not justify its banishment. It is only after this part of his argument has been completed, at 602c1 ff., that Plato goes on to show, by means of the divided soul, why poetry (which now more clearly becomes the subject of his discussion) is to be excluded from the city.

Plato's argument for this conclusion is immensely complicated, and not always very clear.[81] Its first stage depends, as we have said, on yet another analogy (the last) between painting and poetry. Plato writes that painting "exploits a weakness in our nature" (*hēmōn tōi pathēmati tēs phuseōs epithemenē*—namely, our susceptibility to error and illusion (602c7–d5). By contrast, measuring, counting, and weighing help us in "being ruled" not by what appears to be the case but by the results of calculation (602d6–9). Calculation is attributed to the *logistikon en tēi psychēi* (602e1–2), the calculating part of the soul, which was distinguished from spirit and appetite at 436 ff. Sometimes, it seems, though the calculating part has performed its measurements, contrary results still appear to it (*tanantia phainetai,* 602e4–6).[82] Yet "we have agreed that it is impossible for the same thing to have contrary opinions about the same matters" (602e8–9). As Murphy points out,[83] this is not, strictly speaking, accurate, since it is not clear that the principle stated and discussed at 436a–437d can cover contrary opinions. Still, how the division is accomplished is less important to our purposes than its results.

For what is it that this logically imperfect principle divides? And into what does it divide it? I find the obvious answer, that the soul is divided into reason and appetite once again, difficult to accept. For one thing, this would involve the attribution of thinking to appetite.[84] And though this is not a serious difficulty, the suggestion raises the more difficult question of what the appetite has to do with perceptual error and illusion. Why should our *desire* tell us that the immersed stick is bent?

Most importantly, however, the idea that the soul is here divided into reason and appetite would entail that the principle on which the division depends has been wrongly applied. At 439a–b, for example, the principle was used to show that if the soul has two opposed tendencies, then the soul itself has two parts, not that there is another object, distinct from the soul, that is the subject of one of the opposing tendencies. The principle claims that if an object O has two opposed tendencies T^1 and T^2, then O consists of two parts, O^1 and O^2, each one of which bears one of the two tendencies; not that O bears one tendency and a distinct object, P, the other. Since in our present passage the calculating part of the soul is said to have two opposing beliefs (602e4–6), it must be the calculating part itself that is further divided. Our principle does not allow us to introduce a distinct object, appetite, and attribute to it one of the two conflicting beliefs.

If this is so, we can take Plato to be distinguishing between two aspects of reasoning, both belonging to the rational part of the soul: the uncritical acceptance of the senses' reports on the one hand, and reflective judgments about them on the other. This may seem more plausible if we look at Plato's anatomy of the soul as an attempt to characterize different and partially independent sources of human motivation.[85] His original division of the soul in Book IV distinguished, very roughly, among rational, emotional, and appetitive motives. His present argument is making a finer distinction within our rational motives. In fact, Plato seems to be appropriating Socrates' account of the only two possible sources of motivation in the *Protagoras* (356c–357a). Socrates had argued there that human action was motivated either by "the power of appearance" (*hē tou phainomenou dunamis*) or by "the measuring art" (*hē metritikē technē),* and that if the latter were present, it would always dominate. In this passage, Plato seems to be arguing that these are by no means the only sources of motivation, since they are species of rational motivation only, and that Socrates' model in the *Protagoras* was overly simple. More importantly, he also seems to be arguing that the measuring art is not always victorious over the power of appearance. Sometimes we act on what our senses tell us, sometimes on what we know to be the case despite what they tell us, and sometimes on what they tell us despite our knowledge that it is not the case.

The only consideration that might make us think again before considering that what is opposed to measurement is a part of the rational part of the soul is the contempt with which Plato seems to speak of it at 603a7–b4, especially his use of the derogatory term *phaulon* ("base") at 603a7 and b4. However, in an extremely similar context in the *Philebus* we read the following:

> . . . if one were to set apart from each art arithmetic and measuring and weighing, might we say that the remaining part of each would be base (*phaulon*)?
> It would indeed be base (*phaulon*). (55e1–4)

The part that is left of each art is that part that depends on experience and trial and error. The fact that Plato is willing to consider such lower-level cognitive activities as "base" shows that he may well be using that term in our present passage to describe a lowly aspect of the soul's rational element.[86]

Having made this distinction, Plato goes on to discuss poetry in detail (603b6 ff.). And it is clear that in what follows his argument against poetry depends on his view that it appeals to and strengthens the irrational elements in the soul. For example, it is difficult to interpret differently his discussion of giving in to grief and tears at 603e–604a (cf. 606a) and his putting together reason and custom (*logos kai nomos*), enjoining one to be controlled on the one hand, and the passion itself (*auto to pathos*) pulling one toward grieving on the other at 604a–b. This is surprising because the discussion of painting seemed to have little if anything to do with the irrational elements of the soul. Still, I think that this incongruity is only apparent and that neither Plato nor my account is incoherent.

The difference is that in his discussion of painting Plato has been concerned only with the effect of painting, whatever its subject matter, on its spectator. His claim has been that at least sometimes painting induces us to think of a painted object as real, and even to persist in thinking so despite our knowledge that it is not (602d1–4; cf. 598c1–4). But the first part of his discussion of poetry (602b6–605a7) is concerned not with the effect of poetry on its audience, but with the subject matter of the poem itself. This is shown by the fact that the discussion opens with a careful statement of what poems are about at 603c4–8; poems, Plato writes, represent people acting willingly or unwillingly, thinking themselves to profit or to be harmed by their actions, and in all such situations (*en toutois dē pasin*) either grieving or rejoicing. And in all such situations (*en hapasi toutois*) no agent is in harmony with himself: Everyone is torn by conflict (603c10–d7). This conflict, we have seen, concerns reason and what is irrational in the soul; but it is, as the passage makes clear, part of the subject matter of poetry. Plato claims that poetry represents such conflict because it must in most cases depict behavior springing from irrational motives (604e1–6); the poets, if they are to be successful among the many, must depict the "irascible and variable" character (605a2–6). Poetry, therefore, tends to appeal to the irrational aspect of the soul much more than painting, since the domination of reason is what gives most poets their object of imitation. Moreover, in this passage Plato seems to oppose reason both to spirit (*thumos*) and to appetite (*epithumētikon*). It has been claimed that this is evidence that he was never serious about the existence of spirit or emotion as a part of the soul in the first place.[87] But emotion is in fact a source of motivation, and Plato thought so for good reasons.[88] The explanation of why he opposes reason to spirit and appetite together, it seems to me, is simply that he does not need to distinguish these two for his present purposes. He wants to claim that poetry is likely to depict conflicts between reason on the one hand and some lower part of the soul on the other. Sometimes, that lower part is appetite (for example, *aphrodisia, epithumētika*, 601d1–2); sometimes it is spirit (for example, *achthos, lupē*, 603e7–8; *thumos*, 606d1). And this is why he describes what the poets depict by using the terms "irascible and variable" (605a5), which have been associated, respectively, with spirit and appetite in his earlier discussion.[89]

Now, finally, poetry is banished (605a–c). And Plato's reason for this is that he thinks that poetry is much more dangerous to the soul than painting. Poetry's threat is in two parts. Both practices are imitative, and thus both imitate (or produce) deceptive appearances, appearances that we tend to take as reality even in the knowledge that they are not so. This claim, which was made for painting at 602c1–603b5, is made explicitly for poetry at 605b8–c4. To this extent painting and poetry are analogous.

But the appearance that poetry presents as reality is not only much more compelling (because of the greater complexity of poetry, especially dramatic poetry, as an art form), but also, in Plato's eyes, irrational and bestial as well. Even if poetry depicted virtuous characters, it would do no more than create a way in which someone who *seemed* virtuous, but who might in no way *be* virtuous, would act. To consider that as what constitutes virtue (to take that appearance as reality, an attitude common enough to be natural) would have been repellent enough to him:

> *Prosōpon*, the Greek word for mask, also means face, aspect, person, and stage figure (*persona*); we should allow mask and face to draw semantically close

> together, and then we should enrich the face far beyond our own conception,
> until it is able to embrace (as it did for the Greeks from the time of Homer)
> *the look of a man together with the truth about* him.[90]

This attitude toward the mask, or the appearance in general, is exactly what horrifies Plato, for it occurred not only in what he took to be the best of cases, those where an apparently good character is presented as really good, but much more dangerously, it also occurred in the more common cases where what Plato would consider vicious characters were presented by the poets as good. This is worse than simply to confuse the metaphysics of one's audience—though, to be sure, the theater always does this.[91] It is to pervert one's audience in such a way that they would no longer be able (as Plato thought the Athenians were not) to tell the good from the bad, or to act on the good even if they knew what it was.

Plato's argument against poetry thus involves, first, the opposition of reason to the irrational parts of the soul, which is involved in the subject matter of poetry and in what aspects of the personality it influences (cf. 606d1–7); second, it involves the opposition between two aspects of reasoning, which is involved in explaining why one can be tempted to act even on what one knows not to be correct. It is this opposition that accounts for our tendency to take as models for imitation what are merely products of imitation.

Painting, whatever it depicts, is trivial compared to poetry (cf. 598b8–c4); painting is truly a *paidia* and no more. But poetry can be of harm even to the best among us: This is the gravest (*megiston*) objection against it (605c6–8, c10; 606b5–8). The best people must be those who can, at least in principle, distinguish between representation and reality, those who know the distance between the theater and life and that one is not to behave in the world as characters are made to behave in poetry (605d–e). But even such people, Plato insists, finally succumb: They, too, take pleasure (*chairomen*, 605d3) and praise the poet who can make them act in the theater as they would be ashamed to act in life,[92] and who finally succeeds in making them act that way in life as well.

Despite the pleasure he obviously took in poetry himself,[93] Plato was willing to banish it because he saw it only as an imitation of an education, and of a bad education at that. What he allows of poetry at 607a4, "hymns to the gods and praises of noble people," seems to me negligible and tailor-made for special occasions.[94] The question he does not seem to have asked (or perhaps he did, and his theory of the soul gave him the wrong answer)[95] was why even the best people do take pleasure in poetry, why they rejoice in characters distressed, sorrowful, and suffering, why they enjoy being involved in awful, horrible disasters—why, that is, the phenomenon called "distance" today occurs. Had he asked that question, he might have noticed two things. First, that what is at fault for our taking representation for reality may not be the deceitful nature of representation itself, but our own wrong views about it—for example, the assumption that to represent the world is to duplicate its surface, which implies that a representation is a sort of partial object, that an appearance is an incomplete reality. To question this assumption is to take the first step toward granting representation a status of its own. And in taking this step, he might also have noticed that the pleasure of the best people is not at the sorrow represented but at the representation of the sorrow. He might have seen what he did not, that poetry and representation, imitation in general, can be done badly or that it can be done well, that it is, in a word, art.[96]

NOTES

1. Cf. 598d4–5, 605c5–8, 606b5–7. The term *akouontes* (listeners) given Plato's contrast between *akoē* (hearing) and *opsis* (sight), which pertains to painting (603b6–7), suggests that Plato is avoiding (not forgetting) to mention the painter on this occasion.

2. Cf. James Adam, *The Republic of Plato* (Cambridge, 1921), vol. II, 408, n. on 603b–605c: "Poetry, is . . . the counterpart of Painting; its products are low in point of truth, and it feeds our lower nature. We exclude the Poet from our city on both grounds." This view of the structure of Plato's argument is shared, with greater or lesser clarity, by Alistair Cameron, *Plato's Affair with Tragedy* (Cincinnati, 1978), 47; E. F. Carritt, *The Theory of Beauty* (London, n.d.), 39; R. C. Cross and A. D. Woozley, *Plato's Republic: A Philosophical Commentary* (New York, 1966), 275; William Chase Greene, "Plato's View of Poetry," *Harvard Studies in Classical Philology* 29 (1918): 1–75, esp. 52–53; G.M.A. Grube, *Plato's Thought* (New York, 1964), 189–92; Eva Keuls, "Plato on Painting," *American Journal of Philology* 95 (1974): 100–127, esp. 100; Leonard Moss, "Plato and the *Poetics*," *Philological Quarterly* 50 (1971): 533–42; esp. 536–37; Richard Lewis Nettleship, *Lectures on the Republic of Plato* (New York, 1968), 341–43; Eva Schaper, *Prelude to Aesthetics* (London, 1968), 44–47; Paul Shorey, *The Republic of Plato* (London, 1935), vol. II, lxii; Shorey, *What Plato Said*, abr. ed. (Chicago, 1965), 201. I. M. Crombie, *An Examination of Plato's Doctrines* (London, 1962), vol. I, 145, notices that the imitativeness of poetry does not by itself constitute an argument against it in Plato's eyes, but does not develop the point.

3. For example, Paul Friedländer, *Plato: An Introduction* (Princeton, 1969), vol. I, 122–23, claims that all of Plato's dialogues (which he considers poetry) are thus allowed back into the city. Cf. Morriss Henry Partee, "Plato's Banishment of Poetry," *Journal of Aesthetics and Art Criticism* 29 (1970): 209–22, esp. 219. R. G. Collingwood, *The Principles of Art* (Oxford, 1938), 48, argues that Plato does not want to exclude Pindar or lyric poetry in general.

4. J. Tate, "'Imitation' in Plato's *Republic*," *Classical Quarterly* 22 (1928): 16–23; "Plato and 'Imitation,'" *Classical Quarterly* 26 (1932): 161–69; "Plato, Art, and Mr. Maritain," *New Scholasticism* 12 (1938): 107–42. Tate's resolution of the

conflict is accepted by, among others, Cross and Woozley, *Plato's* Republic, 279; W. J. Verdenius, *Mimesis: Plato's Doctrine of Artistic Imitation and Its Meaning to Us* (Leiden, 1949), 21–24; Whitney J. Oates, *Plato's View of Art* (New York, 1972), 36. A variant of Tate's view is held by all those who think that according to Plato good art imitates the Forms; on this position see note 60 below. Grube, *Plato's Thought*, 186 n. 3, notes his disagreement with Tate, but does not attempt to resolve the difficulty. Shorey, *The Republic of Plato*, vol. II, 419 n. *c*, makes use of a similar distinction.

5. Cf. Grube, *Plato's Thought*, 185–86. Plato here characterizes imitation as "making oneself like another either in voice or in bearing" (393c5–6).

6. Some find at 394a7–9 an anticipation of the argument of Book X: cf. Shorey, *The Republic of Plato*, vol. I, 232. Adam, *The Republic of Plato*, vol. I, 147, n. on 394d, and vol. II, 384, n. on 595a, doubts that such a connection is made here. For reasons that will appear below, I accept Adam's view.

7. Tate, " 'Imitation' in Plato's *Republic*," 17.

8. Tate seems to me actually to concede this point when he writes that the two "sorts" of imitation are "formally" the same though "really" very different (" 'Imitation' in Plato's *Republic*," 17–18). The only real difference is in the objects imitated, and this is not sufficient to generate two different kinds of imitation.

9. Plato's distinctions between different forms of recitation, also found in Aristotle's *Poetics*, 1448a20–22, are repeated without significant alteration by René Wellek and Austin Warren, *Theory of Literature* (New York, 1942), 215–16.

10. Tate, " 'Imitation' in Plato's *Republic*," 18; my italics.

11. Tate, "Plato on 'Imitation,' " 161.

12. On difficulties with sexually explicit passages in Homer, cf. W. E. Gladstone, *Studies on Homer and the Hoemric Age* (Oxford, 1858), vol. II, 238–64.

13. "Art delights in unsavoury trivia and in the endless proliferation of senseless images (television)," in Iris Murdoch, *The Fire and the Sun: Why Plato Banished the Artists* (Oxford, 1977), 65.

14. See Gerald F. Else, *The Structure and Date of Book 10 of Plato's Republic* (Heidelberg, 1972), followed by Laszlo Versenyi, "Plato and Poetry: The Academicians' Dilemma," in John H. D'Arms and John W. Eadie, *Ancient and Modern: Essays in Honor of Gerald Else* (Ann Arbor, 1977), 119–38.

15. The *porrō* ("for long") of 395d1 should not be taken to imply that Plato thinks that the Guardians will engage in imitation for many years. This passage is actually concerned with the dangers of imitating bad models, and the word qualifies the situation of someone who is a good person to begin with: Even such a person, if allowed to imitate bad models for a long time, may become bad. With 395c7–d1, *hina mē ek tēs mimēseōs tou einai apolausōsin*, cp. *Prt.* 326a3–4, *hina ho pais zēlōn mimētai kai oregētai toioutos genesthai*.

16. Cf. *Republic* 376e–377b, which puts training in poetry and music before training in physical education. This is the earliest education given to children. The same point is made at *Prt.* 325a–326b, which describes learning the alphabet, poetry, and the playing of the cithara as the first education outside the home; only later is physical education introduced as an activity to be pursued by children (326b ff.). Cf. also *Laws* 654a6–7, *thōmen paideian eirai prōtēn dia Mousōn te kai*

Apollōnos ("Shall we consider that the earliest education is that which proceeds through the Muses and Apollo?"). Isocrates, *Antidosis* 266–68, characterizes the education of young children (*hēn hoi paides en tois didaskaleiois poiountai*) as education concerning letters and music; *Antidosis* 183 places practice in gymnastics along with training in philosophy, and this considerably later in life.

17. According to one tradition in Stoicism, probably deriving from Zeno, reason comes into human beings at the age of fourteen; according to another, reported by Aëtius, and probably due to Chrysippus, the age at which reason is developed is the *prōtē hebdomas*—that is, the seventh year of life. Cf. Hans von Arnim, *Stoicorum Veterum Fragmenta* (Leipzig, 1905–24), vol. I, 40–41.

18. *Poetics* 1448b5–9. Moss, "Plato and the *Poetics*," 540, thinks that, in contrast to Aristotle, Plato considers imitation to be an "acquired taste." But both our present passage and 607e, to which he also refers, support the contrary conclusion. Cf. *Rep.* 595a–b; Plato's statement that poetry harms its listeners' *reason* and that the discussion of its banishment had to wait for the division of the soul suggests that adult and underage audiences may react differently to poetry.

19. It is characteristic of Plato to consider a necessary step in an upward progression as something to be discarded and even despised once it has performed its function. This is clear, for example, in the ascent of *erōs* in the *Symposium:* The beauty of a single body does not only cease to be an object of love once the lover has been enabled, partly by its means, to perceive the beauty of all bodies; it actually becomes an object of contempt (*kataphronēsanta*). Plato expresses a similar attitude in connection with an epistemic ascent at *Rep.* 516a–b.

20. Plato does not seem to envisage the composition of new poems once a sufficient repertory has been established; cf. 424b3–c6, where he fears that new poems may introduce surreptitiously unacceptable new modes of composition and recitation.

21. The only other mention of poetry in such a context outside Book X is at 586b, where tragedians are excluded from the city, quite incidentally, "because they praise tyranny."

22. Nettleship, *Lectures on the Republic of Plato,* 340.

23. Crombie, *An Examination of Plato's Doctrines,* vol. I, 143.

24. Shorey, *The Republic of Plato,* vol. II, lxi.

25. Adam, *The Republic of Plato,* vol. II, 384, n. on 595a–597e.

26. At *Laws* 685a6–b1, Plato characterizes the whole enterprise of that work as a *paidia* of old men; and at 803c2–8 he describes people as playthings (*paignia*) of the gods, and living as play (*paizonta . . . paidias . . . diabiōnai*). *Timaeus* 52d2 describes physical science as *paidia.*

27. See the discussion of how philosophy must not be pursued as a game at *Rep.* 539c5–d1; and cp. *Sph.* 237b10–c4.

28. *mimēsin holōs echois an moi eipein hoti pot' estin;* this question and the ensuing discussion with Glaucon on the difficulty of the problem suggest that little of theoretical importance for imitation was established in Books II and III.

29. This may give some support to the claim that poetry is not banished *because* it is imitative.

30. The large literature on this subject is well known. A good discussion can be

found in Harold Cherniss, "On Plato's *Republic* X 597B," *American Journal of Philology* 53 (1932): 233–42.

31. *paidias charin,* I make the following tentative comments.

a. A neglected paper by J. A. Smith ("General Relative Clauses in Greek," *Classical Review* 31 [1917]: 69–71) challenges, on grammatical grounds, the usual translation of 596a6–7: "We are in the habit of postulating one single Form for each plurality of many things to which we give a common name." Smith argues that this translation presupposes that the relative clause, *hois tauton onoma epipheromen* ("to which we give a common name"), is general, specifying the pluralities to which Forms correspond. But, partly on the authority of William Goodwin, *Syntax of the Mood and Tenses of the Greek Verb* (Boston, 1900), secs. 532, 534, Smith doubts that the clause is general. If it were, he argues, it would have been more correct of Plato to use not *hos* with indicative, as he does here (and, I add, in another nongeneral clause at 479a1–3), but either *hos* with subjunctive and *an* (cf. 479b10) or indicative with *hosos* or *hostis* (cf. 426d4–6). If that is so, the "manys" (*polla*) to which Forms correspond are not defined by the relative clause, but are thought to be known antecedently. Their having a common name is therefore a characteristic that they may share with other groups that are not "manys" in the proper way and to which no Forms correspond. Smith also suggests, however, that *tauton* should not be translated as "common" (which is the customary translation of *koinon*) but as "the same" and as referring back to the Form (71). He thus takes *tauton onoma* ("same name") to carry the implications of, say, *homōnumon* ("homonym," "named after") at *Phd.* 78e2. His version of 596a6–7 would then be something like this: "We are in the habit of postulating one single Form for each group of 'manys'—to which, in that case, we give the same name as that which the Form has." This suggestion, which is not implausible, needs further textual support, especially from a study of Plato's usage of relative clauses—a project much more complicated and systematic than the three instances I produced above, and well beyond the scope of this paper. I thank John J. Keaney for discussing this question with me.

b. 596a10, *thōmen dē kai nun hoti boulei tōn pollōn* (Adam's text) is translated, for example, by Shorey, as "let us take any multiplicity you choose." This translation construes the genitive *tōn pollōn* as a partitive, and suggests that we are selecting some from among a previously agreed-upon set of "manys." This is a natural reading, but it should not prevent us from seeing that it is possible also to take *tōn pollōn* as a genitive of the whole, as in *Laws* 801c5–6: *thōmen dē kai touton tōn peri mousan nomōn kai tupōn hena:* this means: "Shall we set this *as* one among the laws and forms concerning music?" It involves not a selection from, but an addition to, a set. We might then translate 596a10 as follows: "Let us now set whatever you want as among the manys" (that is, among those groups to which Forms correspond). Thus, and consonant with the previous point (*a*), the generation of Forms of artifacts would be an extension, and not an application, of the usual methods of the Academy. John Cooper has objected that the phrase *hoti boulei* tells against this reading. For, he asks, "Are we *really* being asked to extend the theory to *any* direction one wants? No. Rather, only in a *particular* direction." This is true, but I don't think that it dislodges my proposal; for Socrates, who makes this suggestion, immediately goes on to introduce beds and tables, thus securing the direction he wants the argument to take. Glaucon is never allowed to express his own preference.

c. The Forms of bed and of table may have been chosen by Plato precisely so that, because of their lowliness (*atimotēs kai phaulotēs,* cf. *Prm.* 130c6–7), the imitator can be put down. These are the very implements that separate the "city of pigs" from the most primitive human city at 372d–e, and are clearly connected with food and with sex—the lowest desires in Plato's scheme. Cf. Charles Griswold, "The Ideas and the Criticism of Poetry in Plato's *Republic* Book X," *Journal of the History of Philosophy* 19 (1981): 135–50.

d. That God is the creator of these Forms may appear less incredible (and less in contradiction to *Tim.* 28a–29a, according to which God uses the Forms as patterns) if we recall that these are Forms of artifacts and not of natural objects and kinds, which are what the demiurge of the world uses as his standards. In addition, Socrates' claim that there is a bed "in nature," *hēn phaimen an, hōs egōimai, theon ergasasthai,* involves the potential optative, and could be taken as the rather ironical statement, "We could say, I suppose, that God makes it." Finally, that nothing in Plato's definition of imitation actually depends on God's creating the Forms makes the contradiction (though still not really resolved) less pressing.

32. The painter is said here to imitate both the physical object and the Form (597e1–2). But the point that matters is that the painter produces something distinct from, and consequent upon, the other two. Plato immediately goes on to say that the painter imitates not the Forms but the works of craftsmen (598a1–3).

33. I have supplied an implicit *dēmiourgon* despite Adam's claim (*The Republic of Plato,* vol. II, 392, n. on 597e) that it is unnecessary. The word has already been applied to the painter at 596e6. In the immediately preceding exchange it was claimed that the painter does not make a *bed* (597d11–12), but that he is only an imitator of it (597e1–2). But, as 596e6 has suggested and as the sequel will confirm (cf. 599a1–2, d3), the imitator is a maker of a sort. And the question is, If imitation is making, what is it that it makes?

34. On the difficulties of identifying this king, cf. Adam, *The Republic of Plato,* vol. II, 464–65.

35. Plato speaks indifferently of the imitator both as imitating (598b3–4, 600e5) and as making (599a2–3, d3) appearances or images.

36. It is sometimes claimed that in using the term "phantasm" (*phantasma*) to describe the objects of painting, Plato is thinking of art that is specifically deceptive and not of art that is true to its model. For example, J. P. Maguire, "The Differentiation of Art in Plato's Aesthetics," *Harvard Studies in Classical Philology* 68 (1964): 389–410, appeals to *Sph.* 235d–236b, where "eikastic" art, which accurately reproduces its model, is distinguished from "phantastic" art, which does not (392–93). He writes that "it is the . . . 'phantastic' school which seems to be referred to in *Republic* X and identified with art simply" (393). But the *Sophist* (whose doctrine of images is in many ways different from that of the *Republic*) takes these two as species of a genus, imitation (*mimētikē,* 235d1). An *eikōn* is a species of image (*eidōlon*), which is distinguished by its accuracy; a "phantasm," which is inaccurate, is another. But in its three occurrences in connection with art

in the *Republic,* at 401b–c, *eikōn* is equivalent to "image" (*eidōlon, mimēma*), as also is "phantasm" in Book X (see the texts referred to in n. 35). More importantly, Plato's discussion of the deceptiveness of art in Book X, does not in any way depend on the possible inaccuracy of the representation. He is concerned with the fact that a representation, accurate or inaccurate, may be mistaken for the reality it represents.

37. Plato's procedure is noted by Keuls, "Plato on Painting," but her interests take her in another direction (110).

38. Hermann Koller, *Die Mimesis in der Antike* (Berne, 1954).

39. Koller, 63.

40. Gerald F. Else, "Imitation in the Fifth Century," *Classical Philology* 53 (1958): 73–90.

41. Koller, 37.

42. Else, 76.

43. Else, 76.

44. Else, 77.

45. Else, 77; he lists this as a distinct sense of the term on page 79.

46. We cannot possibly examine all the texts involved in this dispute here. Else seems correct in this view of Aeschylus Frag. 57 Nauck[2], as against Koller (74–75), but his reconstruction of a hypothetical context that allows him to find in this "earliest appearance" of *mimos* "an implication that Koller finds nowhere before Plato" (the implication of deception) is much too speculative (75–76). His view of Pindar *Pythian* 12.21, though possible, does not exclude the sense "reproduce" as opposed to "imitate" for *mimēsait';* so also with his interpretation of Pindar Frag. 94b Snell, 1.15 (77). He interprets Aeschylus Frag. 364 Nauck[2], *liburnikēs mimēma manduēs chitōn,* as "a shirt that *copies or simulates the appearance* of a Liburnian cloak" (78; my italics). But this imports philosophical presuppositions that the text does not obviously require: "Copied from" or "made like" are not, I think, inappropriate translations. Else's claim that Aeschylus Frag. 190 Mette shows that *mimēma* had from its earliest occurrences the connotation of "replica" (78) is correct, though "replica" and "image" (where the latter is taken specifically as "appearance") need not be, as Else supposes, equivalent.

47. Cf. Richard McKeon, "Literary Criticism and the Concept of Imitation in Antiquity," *Modern Philology* 34 (1936–37): 1–35. For Plato, McKeon writes, "the word 'imitation' indicates the lesser term of the proportion of being to appearance: If God is, the universe is an imitation; if all things are, shadows and reflection are imitations; if the products of man's handicrafts are, his representations of them are imitations" (9).

48. For example, iv.16: Aryandes wanted to equal (*parisoumenos*) Darius, so he imitated him (*emimeeto*) in circulating silver coins in emulation of the king's golden Darians; for this presumption, Aryandes was executed. Similarly, v.66–68, where Cleisthenes is said to have emulated (*emimeeto*) his grandfather. We must also note Herodotus' use of *mimesis* to refer to a portrait (iii.57: *mimēsis pugmaiou andros*).

49. I.95.3. The same is true of VII.63.3. Neither passage, especially the second, carries the suggestion of "aping" that Else claims for them. Cf. Euripides, *Hippo-*

lytus 114, where the old servant claims that he must not imitate (*mimēteon* = act like) the young Hippolytus in not praying to Aphrodite.

50. Else, "Imitation in the Fifth Century," 83.

51. The notion of the next best thing also appears in Democritus B38: *kalon men ton adikeonta kōluein. ei de mē, mē xunadikeein* ("It is noble to stop whoever is acting unjustly; but if not, not to cooperate in the injustice"). Cf. Eric Havelock, *Preface to Plato* (Cambridge, Mass., 1963), 58.

52. It is not clear, however, that Euripides, *Helen* 74–75, is a good instance of the sense "anything imitated, a counterfeit, copy" under which it is listed in LSJ s.v. *mimēma:* Teucer yells at the real Helen, not realizing who she is, "May the gods spit at you because you are so much (*hoson mimēm' echeis*) like Helen." For other references, cf. Else, "Imitation in the Fifth Century," 79–82.

53. Cf. R. G. Steven, "Plato and the Art of his Time," *Classical Quarterly* 27 (1933): 149–55, esp. 150.

54. Plato has already mentioned painting in connection with a contrast between appearance and reality at 583b and 586b–c. For a discussion of Plato's overall attitude toward painting in the *Republic,* cf. Nancy Demand, "Plato and the Painters," *Phoenix* 29 (1975): 1–20. Demand finds his treatment of painting in Book X harsher than, and inconsistent with, his treatment in earlier books and explains this discrepancy by the hypothesis that *Republic* X was composed considerably later than the first nine books of the work. We have seen that this is also the view of Else, *The Structure and Date of Book 10 of Plato's Republic.*

55. For an extreme but provocative statement of this view, cf. Havelock, *Preface to Plato.*

56. Plotinus, *Enneads* V.viii.1. John Dillon has pointed out to me that Plotinus may have been influenced by Cicero, *Orator* ii.8–10.

57. M. H. Abrams, *The Mirror and the Lamp: Romantic Theory and the Critical Tradition* (New York, 1953), 42–44; Monroe C. Beardsley, *Aesthetics: Problems in the Philosophy of Criticism* (New York, 1958), 394.

58. For example, David Daiches, *Critical Approaches to Literature* (Englewood Cliffs, N.J., 1956): "Why it did not occur to Plato that the painter, by painting the *ideal* object, could suggest the ideal form and thus make direct contact with reality . . . is not easy to see," 20. Cf. also Grube, *Plato's Thought,* 202.

59. The literature on this question is enormous.

Some scholars think that good art imitates Forms and is still recognizably art. Such is the view of Tate, "'Imitation' in Plato's *Republic*," 21–22, and "Plato and 'Imitation,'" 164–65; Leon Golden, "Plato's Concept of Mimesis," *British Journal of Aesthetics* 15 (1975): 118–31; Victor Goldschmidt, "Le problème de la tragédie d'après Platon," *Questions Platoniciennes* (Paris, 1970), 103–40; Henri Joly, *Le renversement Platonicien* (Paris, 1974); Iris Murdoch, *The Fire and the Sun;* Carritt, *The Theory of Beauty,* esp. 31–32; Greene, "Plato's View of Poetry," 34–35; Maguire, "The Differentiation of Art in Plato's Aesthetics," 394; R. C. Lodge, *Plato's Theory of Art* (London, 1953), 182.

Some of these join other scholars in believing that Plato's objections to art are only objections to the art of his time on the grounds that it is too realistic and illusionistic. Cf. Cherniss, "On Plato's *Republic* X 597B," 241; Greene, "Plato's

View of Poetry," 54; Nettleship, *Lectures on the Republic of Plato*, 353; Friedländer, *Plato*, vol. I, 119; Tate, "Plato and 'Imitation,'" 164–65. The idea that Plato attacks not art in general but only the art of his time (with or without reference to the theory of Forms) has been much discussed by historians of Greek painting. The classic work by Pierre-Maxim Schuhl, *Platon et l'art de son temps (Arts Plastiques)*, 2d ed. (Paris, 1952), established the picture of Plato as a forceful participant in a "lutte entre les anciens et les modernes"; cf. Steven, "Plato and the Art of his Time." Different views have recently been expressed by Keuls, "Plato on Painting," who connects what she considers Plato's gradually increasing distaste for the plastic arts with the rise of the scientific pretensions of the Sicyonian school, and by Demand, "Plato and the Painters." My own view is that this debate has assumed proportions greater than those it deserves since Plato, at least in *Republic* X, does not banish the painters and since, as Demand herself shows, his earlier references to painting in the *Republic* are not as pejorative as it is often thought.

Other scholars, again, believe that true art is really philosophy—for example, Oates, *Plato's View of Art*, 40: David Gallop, "Image and Reality in Plato's Republic," *Archiv für Geschichte der Philosophie* 47 (1965): 113–31. Those scholars who think that Plato's dialogues constitute true poetry also seem to me to accept such a view—for example, Friedländer, *Plato*, vol. I, 118–22: Partee, "Plato's Banishment of Poetry," 219. The objection to this view is mainly that it establishes what it seeks to avoid—that there is no *poetry*, or *art*, that imitates Forms.

60. "'Imitation' in Plato's *Republic*," 18; cf. 21. So also Shorey, *The Republic of Plato*, vol. I, 260 n. *a*. On *Rep.* 401c, see also Verdenius, *Mimesis*, 14.

61. Adam, *The Republic of Plato*, vol. I, 168, n. on 402c. Contrast further the plurals *ta tēs sōphrosunēs eidē* (the forms of temperance, etc.) with the emphasis on the uniqueness of each *eidos* at, for example, 476a ff.

62. Tate, "'Imitation' in Plato's *Republic*," 21. But contrast Shorey, *The Republic of Plato*, vol. I, 504 n. *a*.

63. So Gallop, "Image and Reality in Plato's *Republic*," 116, and Adam, *The Republic of Plato*, vol. I, 328, n. on 472d. Contrast again Shorey, ibid.

64. Tate, "Plato, Art, and Mr. Maritain," 111, claims that 599d and 607a show "that genuine art is once removed (not twice) from the ideal world." But 599d simply says that if Homer had been only once removed from reality, then he would have known what makes people truly virtuous, and would have functioned as a legislator. The reference to 607a is even less convincing.

65. So Tate, "Plato and 'Imitation,'" 167.

66. Cf. Epicurius, *ap.* Diogenes Laertius X.xxvi.121: "Only the wise man will have the right view of music and poetry: And he will live, not write, poems" (*monon te ton sophon orthōs an peri te mousikēs kai poiētikēs dialexesthai. poiēmata te energein, ouk an poiēsai*).

67. For example, Tate, "'Imitation' in Plato's *Republic*," 22.

68. Cf. Charles M. Young, "A Note on *Republic* 335c9–10 and 335c12," *Philosophical Review* 83 (1974): 97–106, esp. 104–5.

69. I am indebted to Paul Woodruff for discussing this issue with me.

70. The term is used at *Timaeus* 48e2, but it is a notorious fact that Plato never settled exactly what that relationship was.

71. No mention is made of imitation at *Cratylus* 388a–389a, the only other passage where Plato describes the making of artifacts in terms of looking at the Forms.

72. Often this is not noticed, but the point is made by J.-P. Vernant, "Image dans la théorie Platonicienne de Mimêsis," *Journal de Psychologie* 2 (1975): 133–60; "L'Idée de lit ne peut être imitée de cette façon [that in which the sensible bed is imitated by the artist]. Son rapport avec le lit du menuisier n' est pas homologue à la semblance de ce dernier avec l'image du peintre" (158).

73. Cf. Vernant, 139–41; and Collingwood, "Plato's Philosophy of Art," *Mind* 34 (1925): 154–72, esp. 158.

74. Collingwood, "Plato's Philosophy of Art," 159. A more extreme view is that of Walter Pater, *Plato and Platonism* (New York, 1894), who, on the basis of *Republic* 341d, found that Plato anticipates the doctrine of art for art's sake (241).

75. With Socrates' comment here that people don't seem to be able to compose both tragedies and comedies, compare his position in the *Symposium* that comedy and tragedy actually should be written by the same author (223d). It is interesting to recall in this connection the many parts that each actor in a Greek drama would have to play.

76. On the background of Plato's attitude, cf. Gregory Vlastos, "Degrees of Reality in Plato," in Renford Bambrough, ed., *New Essays on Plato and Aristotle* (London, 1965), 1–19.

77. Cf. Terence Irwin, *Plato's Moral Theory* (New York, 1977), 73–75.

78. To avoid a possible misunderstanding, I should say that nothing said above implies that two different paintings of Socrates, since both are of Socrates, are identical to each other. The two paintings can be quite distinct frescoes, or canvases, or what have you—but they are identical as *paintings,* according to this view, since their content is the same. In addition, their quality, on this view, can vary in accordance to the degree of their likeness to their model.

79. To Plato's statement compare, ironically, the following: "Art is not the most precious manifestation of life. Art has not the celestial and universal value that people like to attribute to it. Life is far more interesting." This is the view of Tristan Tzara, "Lecture on Dada," in Robert Motherwell, *The Dada Painters and Poets* (New York, 1951), 248.

80. A similar point is made in the additional argument at 601b9–602b5, where *mimesis* is called craft or art (*technē*). Still, it is no more an art than the bed the painter makes is a bed (with "three arts," *treis technas,* at 601d1, cp. "three beds," *trittai klinai,* at 597b5). This argument involves the claim that at least in some cases knowledge and belief have the same object (for example, cf. 601e5–6), and this seems to contradict the epistemology developed in Book V. But see Gail Fine, "Knowledge and Belief in *Republic* V," *Archiv für Geschichte der Philosophie* 60 (1978): 121–39.

81. Some of its complications are noticed by N. R. Murphy, *The Interpretation of Plato's Republic* (Oxford, 1951), 239–43.

82. Cf. Terry Penner, "Thought and Desire in Plato," in Gregory Vlastos, ed., *Plato II: Ethics, Politics, and Philosophy of Art and Religion* (Garden City, N.Y., 1971), 100.

83. Murphy, *The Interpretation of Plato's Republic,* 241.

84. Adam, who accepts this traditional view himself, notes this as a difficulty, *The Republic of Plato,* vol. II, 406, n. on 602c ff. Penner, "Thought and Desire in Plato," is not disturbed by this fact, since it is part of his view that the appetitive part of the soul does engage in (rudimentary) thought (100–101).

85. Cf. John M. Cooper, "Plato's Theory of Human Motivation," *History of Philosophy Quarterly* 1 (1984): 3–21, and Gary Watson, "Free Agency," *Journal of Philosophy* 72 (1975): 205–20.

86. Cf. John M. Cooper, "The Theory of Good in Plato's *Philebus,*" *Journal of Philosophy* 74 (1977): 713–30.

87. Penner, "Thought and Desire in Plato," 113.

88. Cooper, "Plato's Theory of Human Motivation."

89. "Irascible" (*aganaktētikon*) is connected with spirit and emotion via "rage" (*orgē*) and "raging" (*orgizesthai*) at 440a5, d2: "variable" (*poikilon*) is connected with appetite via *poikilou* at 588c7 and *polueidia* at 580d11.

90. John Jones, *On Aristotle and Greek Tragedy* (New York, 1962), 44; my italics.

91. From a very different point of view, Marshall Cohen tries to show that art does not always involve distance and that it *does* have a direct effect on its audience ("Aesthetic Essence," in George Dickie and R. J. Sclafani, *Aesthetics: A Critical Anthology* [New York, 1977]). He writes (487–88) that "the muzzles of the battleship *Potemkin,* pointed at the audience, are positively menacing." *Positively,* perhaps; but *really?*

92. On the strong reaction of Greek audiences to poetic recitation, cf. *Odyssey* viii.521 ff.; Xenophon, *Symposium* iii.11, *Ion* 535c–e. On naturalism in Greek acting style, cf. Peter Walcot, *Greek Drama in Its Theatrical and Social Context* (Cardiff, 1976), ch. 5.

93. *Republic* 607e–608b uses the violent language of *Phaedrus* 255b–256b to describe the lover of poetry and his fight against giving in to it.

94. Cf. *Laws* 801e1–4, which makes essentially the same point. Considering the *Laws'* use of "prayers" (*euchai*) and Socrates' own description of his prayer to Pan at the end of the *Phaedrus* as an *euchē* (279b6–c7), it does not seem to me that such a view as Collingwood's, *The Principles of Art,* 48, is correct. On "praise" (*enkōmion*), see *Smp.* 177a–b, and the speeches that make up the bulk of that dialogue.

95. Cf. Thomas Gould, "Plato's Hostility to Poetry," *Arion* 3 (1964): 70–91. Since Plato's hostility is, if my argument is correct, very specific, Gould's diagnosis, which appeals to what he considers Plato's all-embracing systematic dualism, can be challenged. Still, Gould stresses correctly that Plato was unwilling to make any serious exception to his banishment of poetry. Cf. also Murphy, *The Interpretation of Plato's Republic,* 224; and, of course, Havelock, *Preface to Plato, passim.*

96. I am grateful to J.M.E. Moravcsik and Phillip Temko, who organized a conference on Plato's philosophy of art and beauty, for which this essay was originally prepared. John Cooper made extensive comments on that version, and James Bogen, Charles Young, and Cass Weller were kind enough to discuss these issues with me.

Thirteen

PLATO AND THE MASS MEDIA

BOOK X OF THE *Republic* contains a scathing attack on poetry that is still, by turns, both incomprehensible and disturbing.[1] Plato's banishment of the poets from his model city has always been a cause of interpretative difficulties and philosophical embarrassments, even for some of his greatest admirers. But I am now beginning to believe that the difficulties are not real and that the embarrassments are only apparent, and my purpose in what follows is to offer an outline—I cannot do more than that on this occasion—of my reasons for thinking so. I am convinced that close attention to the philosophical assumptions that underlie Plato's criticisms reveals that his attack on poetry is better understood as a specific social and historical gesture than as an attack on poetry, and especially on art, as such. But placed within their original context, Plato's criticisms, perhaps paradoxically, become immediately relevant to a serious contemporary debate.

I

The interpretative difficulties of Book X are relatively easy to dispose of. The first is that this book seems to return to a subject that Plato, as we know, had already discussed extensively in Books II and III. But the fact is that the subject of Book X is different. The earlier books concern the function of poetry in the education of the young Guardians, in which it plays an absolutely central, if rigidly censored and controlled, role. Book X, however, concerns the almost total exclusion of poetry, with the exception of a few "hymns to the gods and praises of noble people" (607a4), from the life of the adult citizens—an exclusion that must have been absolutely shocking to Plato's Athenian audience, accustomed as it was to a large variety of dramatic festivals and poetic contests throughout each year.[2] Moreover, Book X addresses this new subject by new means, on the basis, namely, of the metaphysics, epistemology, and psychology developed in Books IV–IX and unavailable to Plato (595a5–b1) on the earlier occasion.

The second difficulty, which has bothered many commentators, concerns a conflict between Plato's first discussion of poetry and his return to it in Book X. The latter notoriously begins with the statement that all mimetic poetry has already been excluded from the city, while Book III has actually encouraged the young to engage in the imitation of good characters (397d4–7). I once tried to eliminate this conflict, without ultimate success, on the basis of the distinction drawn in the previous paragraph.[3] But the conflict can in fact be eliminated on the basis of another distinction. This is the contrast between being an imitator (*mimētēs*) on the one hand and being imitative (often expressed by the term *mimētikos*) on the other.

Plato clearly allows the young Guardians to be imitators of good characters. But actually he allows them to imitate bad characters, if it is necessary and if they do so not seriously (*spoudēi*) and only in play (*paidias charin*)—that is, in order to satirize and ridicule them (396c5–e8). Plato forbids not imitation, which he considers essential to education, but imitativeness, the desire and ability to imitate anything independently of its moral quality and without the proper attitude of praise or blame toward it (395a2–5, 397a1–b2, 398a1–b4). When Socrates says in Book X that "all mimetic poetry" (*poiēseōs hosē mimētikē*) has been excluded from the city, he does not refer to all imitation but only, as his own word shows, to poetry that involves and encourages imitativeness: the conflict disappears.[4]

The elimination of these interpretive difficulties may help to show that Book X is an integral part of the *Republic*.[5] But this only adds to the philosophical embarrassments it creates. Why, after all, does a work of moral and political philosophy end with a discussion of aesthetics? The obvious answer is that Plato simply does not distinguish aesthetics from ethics. His argument against poetry depends on ontological principles regarding the status of its objects and on epistemological views about the poets' understanding of their subject matter, but his concern with poetry is ethical through and through. It is expressed in just such terms both at the very beginning of the argument, when Socrates claims that tragedy and all imitative poetry constitute "a harm to the mind of their audience" (595b5–6), and at its very end, when he concludes that if we allow poetry in the city "pleasure and pain will rule as monarchs . . . instead of the law and that rational principle which is always and by all thought to be the best" (607a5–8).[6]

It is just this obvious answer, however, that causes the greatest philosophical embarrassment by far because it suggests that Plato is utterly blind to the real value of art, that he is unable to see that there is much more than an ethical dimension to art, and that even in its ethical dimension art is by no means as harmful as he is convinced it is.

It is against this embarrassment that I want to defend Plato, though I do not want to have to decide whether he was right or wrong in his denunciation of Homer and Aeschylus. I believe, and hope to convince you as well, that the issue is much too complicated for this sort of easy judgment. But I do think that Plato's view deserves to be reexamined and that it is directly relevant to many contemporary concerns. Plato's attitude toward epic and tragic poetry is in fact embodied in our current thinking about the arts, though not specifically in our thinking about epic and tragedy. Though his views often appear incomprehensible, or reprehensible, or both, we often duplicate them, though without being aware of them as his. If this is right, then either Book X of the *Republic* is more reasonable and more nearly correct than we are ever tempted to suppose or we must ourselves reevaluate our own assumptions and attitudes regarding the arts.

First, a preliminary point. Plato is not in any way concerned with art as such. This is not only because, if Paul Kristeller is correct, the very concept of the fine arts did not emerge in Europe until the eighteenth century.[7] The main reason is quite specific: Plato does not even include painting in his denunciation. His argument does in fact depend on a series of analogies between painting and poetry, and he introduces all the major ideas through which he will eventually banish the poets by means of these analogies. This has led a number of scholars to conclude, and to feel they should explain why, Plato banished the artists from his model city. But a careful reading shows that neither painting nor sculpture is outlawed by Plato.[8] This suggests, as we shall see in more detail below, that no general account of Plato's attitude toward the arts is required. It also implies that we must determine which specific feature of imitative poetry makes it so dangerous that, in contrast to the other arts, it cannot be tolerated in Plato's city.

This feature, on which Plato's argument against poetry crucially depends, is that poetry (in telling contrast to painting and, particularly, to sculpture) is as a medium inherently suited to the representation, or imitation, of vulgar subjects and shameful behavior:[9]

> The irritable part of the soul gives many opportunities for all sorts of imitations, while the wise and quiet character which always remains the same is neither easy to imitate nor easy to understand when imitated, especially for a festival crowd, people of all sorts gathered in the theaters. (604e1–5)

Plato makes his "greatest" objection to poetry on the basis of this idea. Not only average people but good people as well, even "the best among us," are vulnerable to its harmful influence (605c6–10). Socrates speaks for these select individuals when he says that, confronted with the excessive and unseemly lamentation that is the staple of tragic and epic poetry, "we enjoy it, surrender ourselves, share [the heroes'] feelings, and earnestly praise as a good poet whoever affects us most in this way" (605d3–5; cf. *Philebus* 48a, *Ion* 535a, *Laws* 800d). And yet, at least in the case of the best among us if not also among the rest of the people as well, this sort of behavior is exactly what we try to avoid when we meet with misfortunes of our own: in life, Plato claims, we praise the control and not the indulgence of our feelings of sorrow. How is it then that we admire in poetry just the kind of person we would be ashamed to resemble in life (605d7–e6)?

Socrates tries to account for this absurdity by means of the psychological terms provided by the tripartition of the soul in Book IV of the *Republic*. The lowest, appetitive, part of the soul, which is only concerned with immediate gratification and not with the good of the whole agent, delights in shameful behavior as it delights in anything that is not measured. Now poetry depicts the sufferings of others, not our own. The rational part of the soul, accordingly, is in this case indulgent toward the appetite, and allows it free expression. The whole agent, therefore, in the belief that such indulgence is harmless, enjoys the pleasure with which poetry provides the appetite (606a3–b5).

What we fail to realize is that enjoying the expression of sorrow in the case of others is directly transferred to the sorrows of our own. Cultivating our feelings of pity in spectacles disposes us to express them in similar ways in our own case and to enjoy (or at least to find no shame in) doing so: thus it ultimately leads us to make a spectacle of ourselves (606a3–b8). Plato now generalizes his conclusion from sorrow in particular to all the passions:

> So too with sex, anger, and all the desires, pleasures, and pains which we say follow us in every activity. Poetic imitation fosters these in us. It nurtures and waters them when they ought to wither; it places them in command in our soul when they ought to obey in order that we might become better and happier . . . instead of worse and more miserable. (606d1–7)

In short, Plato accuses poetry of perverting its audience. Poetry is essentially suited to the representation of inferior characters and vulgar subjects: these are easy to imitate and what the crowd, which is already perverted to begin with, wants to see and enjoys. But the trouble is that all of us have an analogue to the crowd within our own soul (cf. 580d2–581a1). This is the appetitive part (the counterpart to the third and largest class, the money lovers, in Plato's analogy between city and soul), to the desires and pleasures of which we are all more or less sensitive. And since—this is a most crucial assumption to which we shall have to return—our reactions to poetry are transferred directly to, and in fact often determine, our reactions to life, poetry is likely to make us behave in ways of which we should be, and often are, ashamed. Poetry "introduces a bad government in the soul of each individual citizen" (605b7–8). But this is to destroy the soul and to destroy the city. It is precisely the opposite of everything the *Republic* is designed to accomplish. This is why poetry is intolerable.

We must now turn to Plato's deeply controversial assumption that our reactions to life follow on the lines of our reactions to poetry: the whole issue of the sense of Plato's charges against poetry and of their contemporary importance depends just on this idea. On its face, of course, this assumption can be easily dismissed. Enjoying (if that is the proper word)

Euripides' *Medea* is not likely to dispose us to admire mothers who murder their children for revenge nor to want to do so ourselves nor even to tend to adopt as our own Medea's ways of lamenting her fate.[10] But this quick reaction misses precisely what is deep and important in Plato's attitude.

To begin to see what that is, we should note that Plato's assumption does not seem so unreasonable in connection with children. Almost everyone today would find something plausible in Plato's prohibition that children imitate bad models "lest from enjoying the imitation they come to enjoy the reality" and something accurate in his suspicion that "imitations, if they last from youth for some time, become part of one's nature and settle into habits of gesture, voice, and thought" (395c7–d3). On this issue, Aristotle, who disagrees on so many issues regarding poetry with Plato, is in complete agreement: "We should also banish pictures and speeches from the stage which are indecent . . . the legislator should not allow youth to be spectators of iambi or of comedy" (*Politics* VII.1336b14–21).[11] But, also like Plato, Aristotle does not confine his view to children only: "As we know from our own experience . . . the habit of feeling pleasure or pain at mere representations (*ta homoia*) is not far removed from the same feelings about realities" (*Pol.* VIII.1340a21–25).

To a great extent, in fact, Aristotle's vindication of tragedy against Plato involves the argument that poetry is actually morally beneficial. And the reason for this is that *katharsis* both excites and purifies emotions that, in Stephen Halliwell's words, "although potent, are properly and justifiably evoked by a portrayal of events which, if encountered in reality, would call for the same emotional response."[12] The assumption that there is some direct connection between our reactions to poetry and our reactions to life is common to both philosophers. The main difference is that Aristotle argues, against Plato, that this parallel tends to benefit rather than to harm the conduct of our life.

The Platonic argument seems plausible in the case of children because many of us think (though this view is itself debatable) that, unclear about the difference between them, children often treat representations simply as parts of and not also as symbols for reality. They do not always seem able, for example, to distinguish a fictional danger from a real one. But Plato, as we have seen, believed that the case is similar with adults. Their reactions to poetry, too, determine their reactions to life because, to put the point bluntly, they are exactly the same kind of reactions. And the reason for this is that, as he believed, the representations of poetry are, at least superficially, exactly the same kind of objects as the real things they represent. The expression of sorrow in the theater is superficially identical with— exactly the same in appearance as—the expression of sorrow in life. Though actors do not, or need not, feel the sorrow they express on the stage, this underlying difference is necessarily imperceptible and allows the surface behavior of actors and real grievers to be exactly the same.

"Paradoxically," Jonas Barish has written, "Plato makes much of the ontological difference between an actual thing and its mimetic copy (or the dream of it) yet allows little psychological difference."[13] On the account I have just given, however, Plato's view is not at all paradoxical. It is precisely because the difference between imitations and their objects *is* ontological, a difference that cannot be perceived, that our reactions to both, which are based on our perception, are so similar. Plato's view is that the pleasure we feel at the representation of an expression of sorrow in poetry is pleasure at that expression itself, and for that reason likely to dispose us to enjoy such behavior in life. He does not consider the possibility that the pleasure may be directed not at the expression of sorrow but at its representation, and that this representation is an independent object, having features in its own right and subject to specific principles that determine its quality.[14]

What I mean by this is that for Plato representation is *transparent*. It derives all its relevant features, the features that make it the particular representation it is, solely from the object it represents, and which we can see directly through its representation (we shall have to return to this "directly"). The imitation of an expression of sorrow is simply sorrow expressed, identical in appearance to the real expression of sorrow, though not actually felt.

All imitations are treated in Book X of the *Republic* simply as apparent objects, as appearances of their subjects, and not as objects with a status of their own (597e7–601b8). God, carpenter, and painter all produce a bed (596b5), though the painter's bed is only "apparent" (598b4). The painter does not primarily produce a painting, a physical object with a symbolic dimension; the portrait of a cobbler is simply "a cobbler who seems to be" (600e7–601a7). The clear implication is that the poets produce apparent crafts and apparent virtues in their imitations of what people say and do; they duplicate the appearance of people engaged in the practice of a craft or of virtuous activity (600e3–601b1). Even more frequently, of course, they duplicate the appearance of vicious activity—this is the seductive, and appropriate, subject matter of poetry. Imitators, for Plato, lack a craft of their own (and are, in this respect at least, like sophists and rhetoricians). They therefore do not know the nature of what they imitate, and simply transcribe the appearance of various things and actions by means of colors and words.[15]

This metaphysical view is reflected in Plato's ambivalent language.[16] Painters, he writes, are both *imitators* and *makers* of appearances (598b3–4, 599a2–3); Homer is a *producer* of images, though poets in general are *imitators* of images (599d3, 600e5). In the latter case, the image is the object of imitation, something that exists before imitation begins. In the former, it is the product of imitation, and comes into being only as imitation proceeds. This ambivalence suggests that for Plato the object and the product of imitation are identical in kind, that is, totally similar; it is almost as if the imitator lifts the surface of the imitated object and transfers in into another medium. What is different in each case is the depth—physical in the case of painting and psychological in the case of poetry—which imitation necessarily leaves untouched. If it were in some way possible to add to the imitation this missing dimension, we could produce a duplicate of its subject or, if no antecedent subject exists, a new real thing. The real object is the limiting case of the representation: this is exactly Plato's argument at *Cratylus* 432a–c; it is the metaphysical version of the myth of Pygmalion.

II

The metaphysics of Pygmalion is still in the center of our thinking about the arts. To see that this is so, and why, we must change subjects abruptly and recall Newton Minow's famous address to the National Association of Broadcasters in 1961. Though Minow admitted that some television was of high quality, he insisted that if his audience were to watch, from beginning to end, a full day's programming,

> I can assure you that you will observe a vast wasteland. You will see a procession of game shows, violence, audience participation shows, formula comedies about totally unbelievable families, blood and thunder, mayhem, violence, sadism, murder, western badmen, western goodmen, private eyes, gangsters, more violence, and cartoons.[17]

This general view of the vulgarity of television has been given a less extreme expression, and a rationale, by George Gerbner and Larry Gross:

> Unlike the real world, where personalities are complex, motives unclear, and outcomes ambiguous, television presents a world of clarity and simplicity. . . . In order to complete a story entertainingly in only an hour or even half an hour conflicts on TV are usually personal and solved by action. Since violence is dramatic and relatively simple to produce, much of the action tends to be violent.[18]

An extraordinary, almost hysterical version of such a view, but nevertheless a version that is uncannily close to Plato's attitude that the lowest part of the soul is the subject-matter of poetry, is given by Jerry Mander. Television, he writes, is inherently suited for

> expressing hate, fear, jealousy, winning, wanting, and violence . . . hysteria or ebullience of the kind of one-dimensional joyfulness usually associated with

some objective victory—the facial expressions and bodily movements of anti-social behavior.[19]

Mander also duplicates, in connection with television, Plato's view that poetry directly influences our life for the worse: "We slowly evolve into the images we carry, we become what we see."[20] This, of course, is the guiding premise of the almost universal debate concerning the portrayal of sex, violence, and other disapproved or antisocial behavior on television on the grounds that it tends to encourage television's audience to engage in such behavior in life.[21] And a very sophisticated version of this Platonic point, making use of the distinction between form and content, has been accepted by Wayne Booth:

> The effects of the medium in shaping the primary experience of the viewer, and thus the quality of the self during the viewing, are radically resistant to any elevation of quality in the program content: as viewer, I become *how* I view, more than *what* I view. . . . Unless we change their characteristic forms, the new media will surely corrupt whatever global village they create; you cannot build a world community out of misshapen souls.[22]

We have seen that Plato's reason for thinking that our reactions to life duplicate our reactions to poetry is that imitations are superficially identical with the objects of which they are imitations. Exactly this explanation is also given by Rudolph Arnheim, who wrote that television "is a mere instrument of transmission, which does not offer any new means for the artistic interpretation of reality."[23] Television, that is, presents us the world just as it is or, rather, it simply duplicates its appearance. Imitations are substitutes for reality. In Mander's words,

> people were believing that an *image* of nature was equal . . . to the experience of nature . . . that images of historical events or news events were equal to the events . . . the confusion of . . . information with a wider, direct mode of experience was advancing rapidly.[24]

Plato's argument against poetry is repeated in summary form, and without an awareness of its provenance, in connection with television by Neil Postman: "Television," he writes, "offers viewers a variety of subject-matter, requires minimal skills to comprehend it, and is largely aimed at emotional gratification."[25] The inevitable result, strictly parallel to "the bad government in the soul," which Plato would go to all lengths to avert, is, according to Postman, an equally dangerous "spiritual devastation."[26]

Parallels between Plato's view and contemporary attitudes such as that expressed in the statement that "daily consumption of 'Three's Company' is not likely to produce a citizenry concerned about, much less committed to, Madisonian self-government," are to be found wherever you look.[27]

Simply put, the greatest part of contemporary criticisms of television depends on a moral disapproval that is identical to Plato's attack on epic and tragic poetry in the fourth century B.C. In this respect, at least, we are most of us Platonists. We must therefore reexamine both our grounds for disapproving of Plato's attack on poetry and our reasons for disapproving of television.

It is true that television is also the target of another criticism, a purer aesthetic criticism concerned with the artistic quality of television works. This is not a criticism that Socrates, who confesses to "a love and respect for Homer since childhood" (595b9–10) and who describes his love of poetry in explicit sexual terms (607e4–608b2), would ever have made. We will discuss this criticism in the last section of this essay.

III

My effort to establish a parallel between Plato's deep, complex, and suspicious hostility toward Homer and Aeschylus, on the one hand, and the obviously well-deserved contempt with which many today regard much of television programming, on the other hand, may well appear simply ridiculous. Though classical Greek poetry still determines many of the criteria that underlie the literary canon of our culture, most of television hardly qualifies as entertainment. Yet my position does not amount to a trivialization of Plato's views. On the contrary, I believe, we are bound to miss (and have already missed) the real urgency of Plato's approach if we persist in taking it as an attack against art as such. Plato was neither insensitive to art nor inconsistent in his desire to produce, as he did, artworks of his own in his dialogues; he neither discerned a deep characteristic of art that pits it essentially against philosophy nor did he envisage a higher form of art that he would have allowed in his city.[28] Plato's argument with poetry concerns a practice that is today paradigmatically a fine art, but it is not an argument directed at it as such a fine art. At this point, the history of art becomes essential for an understanding of its philosophy. Though Plato's attack against poetry in the *Republic* may be the originating text of the philosophy of art, his argument, without being any less profound or disturbing, dismisses poetry as what it was in his time: and poetry then was popular entertainment.

The audience of Attic drama, as far as we now know, was "a 'popular' audience in the sense that it was a body fully representative of the great mass of the Athenian people"[29] and included a great number of foreign visitors as well.[30] During the Greater Dionysia in classical times no fewer than 17,000 people,[31] perhaps more,[32] were packed into the god's theater. Pericles, according to Plutarch, established the *theōrikon*, a subsidy to cover the price of admission and something more, which ended up being distributed to rich and poor alike, and made of the theater a free entertainment.[33]

The plays were not produced in front of a well-behaved audience. The dense crowd was given to whistling (*syringx*), and the theater resounded with its "uneducated noise" (*amousoi boai plēthous, Lg.* 700c3). Plato expresses profound distaste for the tumult with which audiences, in the theater and elsewhere, voiced their approval or dissatisfaction (*Rep.* 492c). Their preferences were definitely pronounced if not often sophisticated. Since four plays were produced within a single day, the audience arrived at the theater with large quantities of food. Some of it they consumed themselves—hardly a silent activity in its own right, unlikely to produce the quasi-religious attention required of a fine-art audience today and more reminiscent of other sorts of mass entertainments. Some of their food was used to pelt those actors whom they did not like,[34] and whom they often literally shouted off the stage.[35] In particular, and though this may be difficult to imagine today, the drama was considered a realistic representation of the world: we are told, for example, that a number of women were frightened into having miscarriages or into giving premature birth by the entrance of the Furies in Aeschylus' *Eumenides.*[36]

The realistic interpretation of Attic drama is crucial for our purposes. Simon Goldhill, expressing the recent suspiciousness toward certain naive understandings of realism, has written that Electra's entrance as a peasant in the play Euripides named after her "is upsetting not because it represents reality but because it represents reality in a way which transgresses the conventions of dramatic representations, indeed the representations of reality constructed elsewhere in the play." In fact, he continues, "Euripides constantly forces awareness of theatre as theatre."[37] This, along with the general contemporary claim that all art necessarily contains hints pointing toward its artificial nature and undermining whatever naturalistic pretensions it makes, may well be true. But it does not alter the fact that it is of the essence of popular entertainment that these hints are not, while the entertainment still remains popular, consciously perceived. Popular entertainment, in theory and practice, is generally taken to be inherently realistic.

To be inherently realistic is to seem to represent reality without artifice, without mediation and convention. Realistic art is, just in the sense in which Plato thought of imitation, transparent. This transparency, I believe, is not real. It is only the result of our often not being aware of the mediated and conventional nature of the representations to which we are most commonly exposed. As Barish writes in regard to the theater, "it has an unsettling way of being received by its audiences, at least for the moment and with whatever necessary mental reserves, as reality pure and simple."[38] Whether or not we are aware of it, however, mediation and convention are absolutely essential to all representation. But since, in such cases, they cannot be attributed to the representation itself, which, transparent as it is, cannot be seen as an object with its own status and in its own right, they are instead attributed to the represented subject matter: the slow-moving speech and action patterns of soap operas, for example, are considered (and criticized) as representations of a slow-moving world.

Attributed to subject matter, mediation and convention appear, almost by necessity, as distortions. And accordingly (from the fifth century B.C. through Renaissance and Puritan England as well as Jansenist France in connection with the theater, through the eighteenth- and nineteenth-century attacks on the novel, to contemporary denunciations of the cinema and of television) the reality the popular media are supposed to represent has always been considered, while the media in question are still popular, as a distorted, perverted, and dismal reality. And it has regularly involved campaigns to abolish or reform the popular arts or efforts on the part of the few to distance themselves from those arts as far as possible. And insofar as the audience of these media has been supposed, and has often supposed itself, to react directly to that reality, the audience's undisputed enjoyment of the popular arts has been interpreted as the enjoyment of this distorted, perverted, and dismal reality. It has therefore also been believed that this enjoyment both reflects and contributes to a distorted, perverted, and dismal life—a vast wasteland accurately reflected in the medium that mirrors it.

This is the essence of Plato's attack against poetry and, I believe, the essential idea behind a number of attacks against television today. Nothing in Plato's time answered to our concept of the fine arts, especially to the idea that the arts are a province of a small and enlightened part of the population (which may or may not be interested in attracting the rest of the people to them), and Plato holds no views about them. His quarrel with poetry is not disturbing because anyone seriously believes that Plato could have been right about Homer's pernicious influence. Plato's view is disturbing because we are still agreed with him that representation is transparent—at least in the case of those media that, like television, have not yet acquired the status of art and whose own nature, as opposed to what they depict, has not yet become in serious terms a subject in its own right.[39] And because of this view, we may indeed react to life, or think that we do, as we react to its representations: what is often necessary for a similarity between our reactions to life and our reactions to art is not so much the fact that the two are actually similar but only the view that they are. Many do in fact enjoy things on television that, as Plato wrote in regard to poetry, some at least would be ashamed, even horrified, to enjoy in life.

The problem here is with the single word "things," which applies both to the contents of television shows and to the situations those represent. What this suggests is that what is presented on television is a duplicate of what occurs in the world. No interpretation seems to be needed in order to reveal and to understand the complex relations that actually obtain between them.

By contrast, no one believes that the fine arts produce such duplications. Though we are perfectly willing to learn about life from literature and painting (a willingness that, in my opinion, requires close scrutiny in its own right), no one would ever project directly the content of a work of fine art onto the world. The fine arts, we believe, bear an indirect, interpretative relationship to the world, and further interpretation on the part of audience and critics is necessary in order to understand it. It is precisely for this sort of interpretation that the popular arts do not seem to call.

IV

Yet the case of the *Republic* suggests that the line between the popular and the fine arts is much less settled than is often supposed. If my approach has been right so far, Plato's quarrel with poetry is to a great extent, as much of the disdain against television today is, a quarrel with a popular form of entertainment. Greek drama, indeed, apart from the fact that it was addressed to a very broad audience, exhibits a number of features commonly associated with popular literature. One among them is the sheer volume of output required from any popular genre. "Throughout the fifth century B.C. and probably, apart from a few exceptional years, through the earlier part of the fourth century also," Pickard-Cambridge writes, "three tragic poets entered the contest for the prize in tragedy and each presented four plays."[40] If we add to these the plays produced by the comic poets, the plays produced at all the festivals other than the City Dionysia (with which Pickard-Cambridge is exclusively concerned), and the plays of the poets who were not chosen for the contest, we can see that the actual number of dramas must have been immense. The three great tragedians alone account for roughly three hundred works. And this is at least a partial explanation of the fact that so many plays were different treatments of the same stories. This practice is imposed on popular authors by the demands of their craft and is in itself a serious source of satisfaction for their audience.[41]

The most important feature of popular art, however, is the transparency to which we have already referred. The idea is complex, and it is very difficult to say in general terms which of a popular work's features are projected directly onto reality since, obviously, not all are. A television audience knows very well that actors shot during a show are not really dead, but other aspects of the behavior of such fictional characters are actually considered as immediate transcriptions of reality. On a very simple level, for example, it is difficult to explain otherwise the fact that the heroines of *Cagney and Lacey* invariably buckle their seat belts when they enter their car, whether to chase a murderer or to go to lunch. And many aspects of their relationship are considered as perfectly accurate transcriptions of reality. Popular art is commonly perceived as literally incorporating parts of reality within it; hence the generally accepted, and mistaken, view that it requires little or no interpretation.

Arthur Danto has recently drawn attention to art that aims to incorporate reality directly within it, and has named it the "art of disturbation." This is not art that represents, as art has always represented, disturbing reality. It is art that aims to disturb precisely by eradicating the distance between it and reality, by placing reality squarely within it.[42] Disturbational art aims to frustrate and unsettle its audience's aesthetic, distanced, and contemplative expectations: "Reality," Danto writes, "must in some way . . . be an actual component of disturbatory art and usually reality of a kind itself disturbing. . . . And these as components in the art, not simply collateral with its production and appreciation."[43] "Happenings" or Chris Burden's viciously self-endangering projects fall within this category. And so did, until relatively recently, obscenity in the cinema and the theater.

The purpose of disturbational art, according to Danto, is atavistic. It aims to reintroduce reality back into art, as was once supposedly the norm: "Once we perceive statues as merely designating what they resemble . . . rather than containing the reality through containing the form, a certain power is lost to art."[44] But contemporary disturbational art, which Danto considers "pathetic and futile," utterly fails to recapture this lost "magic."[45]

This failure is not an accident. The disturbational art with which Danto is concerned consists mainly of paintings, sculptures, and "happenings" that are essentially addressed to a sophisticated audience through the conventions of the fine arts: you dress to go see it. But part of what makes the fine arts fine is precisely the distance they have managed, over time, to insert between representation and reality; this distance can no longer be eliminated. Danto finds that disturbational art still poses some sort of vague threat: "Perhaps it is for this reason that the spontaneous response to disturbational art is to disarm it by cooptation, incorporating it instantaneously into the cool institutions of the artworld where it will be rendered harmless and distant from forms of life it meant to explode."[46] My own explanation is that the cool institutions of the artworld are just where the art of disturbation, which is necessarily a fine art, has always belonged.

Disturbational art aims to restore "to art some of the magic purified out when art became *art*."[47] This, I believe, is not a reasonable goal: once a genre has become fine, it seldom if ever loses its status; too much is invested in it. And yet, I want to suggest, "the magic purified out when art became *art*" is all around us, and just for that reason almost totally invisible. The distinction between representation and reality is constantly and interestingly blurred by television—literally an art that has not yet become *art*—and that truly disturbs its audience: consider, as one instance among innumerably many, the intense debate over the influence on Soviet-American relations of the absurd miniseries *Amerika* in the spring of 1987.[48]

As a medium, television is still highly transparent. Though, as I have admitted, I do not yet have a general account of which of its features are projected directly onto the world, television clearly convinces us on many occasions that what we see *in* it is precisely what we see *through* it. This is precisely why it presents such a challenge to our moral sensibility. The "magic" of television may be neither admirable nor even respectable. But it is, I am arguing, structurally identical to the magic Plato saw and denounced in Greek poetry, which also, of course, was not *art*.

Plato's attack on poetry is duplicated today even by those who think of him as their great enemy and the greatest opponent of art ever to have written. It is to be found not only in the various denunciations of television, many of which are reasonable and well supported, but even more importantly in the total neglect of television on the part of our philosophy of art. Aesthetics defends the arts that can no longer do harm and against which Plato's strictures hardly make sense. His views are thus made incomprehensible and are not allowed to address their real target. Danto writes that every acknowledged literary work is "about the 'I' that reads the text . . . in such a way that each work becomes a metaphor for each reader."[49] The key word here is "metaphor": we do not literally emulate our literary heroes, in the unfortunate manner of Don Quixote; we understand them through interpretation and transformation, finding their relevance to life, if anywhere, on a more abstract level. But such literal emulation was just what Plato was afraid of in the case of tragic poetry, and what so many today are afraid of in regard to television: "We become what we see." Plato's attack on "art" is still very much alive.

V

A reasonable reaction to these speculations is that whatever the similarities between Plato's attack on poetry and contemporary attitudes toward television, the difference between the media themselves is immense. Not only did Greek poetry have its Homer and its Aeschylus, but Plato was acutely, even painfully aware of its beauty. Toward such beauty, Socrates says, "we shall behave like lovers who see their passion is disastrous and violently force themselves away from the object of their love" (607e4–6). But television, almost everyone seems to agree, has no aesthetic value: it is not only harmful but ugly; why bother?

This issue is extremely complicated, and I can only touch on it lightly here. The common view that television is aesthetically worthless seems to me profoundly flawed. This is not because I think that television is aesthetically valuable, but because this sort of statement is the wrong sort of statement to make. Television is a vast medium that includes a great variety of genres, some of which have no connection of any kind with the arts. A similar statement would be something like "Writing is good (or bad)," which wears its absurdity on its face. Even a more specific view to the effect, say, that "Literature is valuable" seems obviously untenable once we consider the huge numbers of absolutely horrible literary works most of which are, mercifully, totally forgotten.

We must therefore gradually develop principles and criteria suited for the criticism of television. We need to articulate classes and categories to help us organize its various species and genres—the kind of project with which, for example, the serious study of poetry first began. We need principles that will be more than mechanical applications of the principles developed already for other arts and that, naturally, television always miserably fails to satisfy.[50] We need, for example, especially in connection with broadcast television, to face the fact that the unit of aesthetic significance is not the individual episode—though individual episodes are all we ever see—but the serial as a whole.[51] The fact that the serial somehow inheres in its episodes raises radically new aesthetic questions as well as venerably old metaphysical ones. As Aristotle remarked when, after dismissing Parmenides and Melissus as physical thinkers of any significance, he nevertheless proceeded to discuss their views in detail, "there is philosophy in the investigation" (*Physics* A2.185a20).

We finally need, as Stanley Cavell has correctly pointed out, to think seriously about the fact—and is *is* a fact—that "television has conquered." Two questions need to be asked: "First how it has happened; and second how we [intellectuals] have apparently remained uninterested in accounting for its conquering."[52] The first question can only be answered through the development of television criticism. The second also requires such criticism, but also an explanation of why the criticism has been so slow in developing. Cavell attributes this to the fear of

> the fact that a commodity has conquered, an appliance that is a monitor, and yet what it monitors . . . are so often settings of the shut-in, a reference line of normality or banality so insistent as to suggest that *what* is shut out, that suspicion whose entry we would at all costs guard against, must be as monstrous as, let me say, the death of the normal, of the familiar as such.[53]

But, I think, there is another aspect to this fear, another—connected— reason for it. It is a reason provided directly not by what television shuts out but precisely by what it lets in, by what it shows and by the conditions under which we look at it.

Broadcast television, which until recently was practically identical with the medium itself, works primarily through the serial. Each episode, precisely because it instantiates the serial of which it is a member, is essentially repetitive, however novel a story line it may exploit on a particular occasion. The set is always the same. The character's personalities are usually the same.[54] Their habits, their facial and verbal expressions, their peculiarities are the same. The surroundings in which conversations occur are the same. The groupings in which those conversations occur are the same. Membership in the serial is established through this sameness, which is therefore essential to the genre. And the serial is repetitive in another dimension as well: it is broadcast at exactly the same time each week. Watching a particular show—and to come to appreciate a show at all requires watching a number of episodes: the features they share as members of a species cannot be otherwise noticed and interpreted as such—imposes a rigorous routine on the viewer. Unless one owns a recording machine, one must arrange one's life, one must establish a routine, in order to accommodate the show. And what one sees then, with or without a recording machine, is nothing other than the representation of routine itself.

Routinization, however, is either something we want to avoid or something we want to forget. Television brings it, as it were, home to us. It imposes a routine on its viewers, it portrays routine for them, and it suggests that their own life mirrors what it portrays. Television will be resisted as long as routine remains, in the absence of criticism and interpretation, its most salient feature. Interpretation is necessary in order to determine whether there are other features there to be noticed and, perhaps, appreciated. In the meantime, of course, the critics may themselves be trapped in routine: this danger is endemic to the enterprise. But nothing, in principle, deprives the depiction of routine of aesthetic value just as nothing, in principle, prevents the depiction of foolishness, cruelty, murder, incest, ignorance, arrogance, suicide, and self-mutilation from constituting, as it has on at least one occasion, an unparalleled work of art.

Notes

1. Poetry is also discussed in Books II and III (376e–403c) of the *Republic*. Plato's negative attitude, of course, is not confined to this work. The *Ion,* one of his early works, is devoted to the issue whether rhapsodes, and poets, possess a *technē,* or rational craft, and to the proof that they do not. The heavy censorship of poetry is brought up on a number of occasions in the *Laws,* his last work, e.g., at 659b–662a, 700a–701b, 802a–c, 829a–e. The case of the *Phaedrus* is more complicated and ambiguous, for the following reason. Though it is true that Socrates, in his

"Great Speech," praises poetry as a "divine madness" and puts it in the same group as medicine, prophecy, and—of all things—philosophy (243e–245c), this statement is made within a rhetorical context. And Socrates, in his later discussion of rhetoric claims that an orator must always make use of what his *audience,* in this case Phaedrus, is likely to find persuasive, not necessarily and strictly speaking the truth (271c–272b). Cf. John M. Cooper, "Plato, Isocrates, and Cicero on the Independence of Oratory from Philosophy," in John J. Cleary, ed., *Proceedings of the Boston Area Colloquium in Ancient Philosophy,* vol. I (Washington, D.C., 1986), 77–96, esp. 80–81.

2. Four major festivals were held in Athens and its vicinity: the Anthesteria, the Lenaia, the Rural Dionysia, and the Great or City Dionysia. Each involved a variety of dramatic and poetic performances. The major study of these festivals is Arthur Pickard-Cambridge's *The Dramatic Festivals of Athens,* 2d ed. (Oxford, 1968). Ion's recitations of Homer may have occurred as part of such festivals, but they may have also taken place independently; we know (530a2–3) that he had participated in a festival at Epidaurus.

3. "Plato on Imitation and Poetry in *Republic* X," in this book.

In what follows, I will rely on the analysis of Plato's argument in Book X offered in this article, to which I will refer as "Plato on Imitation."

The most forceful earlier effort to resolve the conflict in Plato's favor had been that of J. Tate, who, in a series of articles, tried to distinguish between a good and a bad sense of "imitation" and to limit Plato's exclusion to the latter; cf. "Plato on Imitation," 48–49 and notes, for references to Tate's work and for criticism of his position.

4. This resolution of the conflict follows the view of G.R.F. Ferrari's "Plato and Poetry," in *The Cambridge History of Literary Criticism,* vol. 1: *Classical Criticism,* ed. George A. Kennedy (Cambridge, 1989), 92–148.

5. This has been most forcefully denied by Gerald F. Else, *The Structure and Date of Book 10 of Plato's "Republic"* (Heidelberg, 1972: *Abhandlungen der Heidelberger Akademie der Wissenschaften, phil.-hist. Kl., Jg. 1972, Abh. 3*) as well as in his posthumously published *Plato and Aristotle on Poetry* (Chapel Hill and London, 1986). A number of commentators on the *Republic* have found it difficult to see how Book X fits with the work's overall argument; cf. "Plato on Imitation," 54 and notes, for references. Most recently, Julia Annas has described the book as an "excrescence" in her *Introduction to Plato's "Republic"* (Oxford, 1981), 335.

6. I have generally, though not always, relied on the translation of the *Republic* by George Grube (Indianapolis, 1974).

7. Paul O. Kristeller, "The Modern System of the Arts," *Journal of the History of Ideas* XII (1951): 496–527, XIII (1952): 17–46.

8. A detailed defense of this claim can be found in "Plato on Imitation," 54–64.

9. Plato has many reservations in connection with painting and sculpture. He argues in this book, for example, that painting produces only imitations of things, that it can fool simple people, and that it confuses the mind. In the *Sophist,* he attacks at least one species of sculpture because it essentially misrepresents the proportions of its original (235c8–236a7). This is only a sample, but a fair sample

of the sorts of objections he raises against these two art forms. He does not attack them on moral grounds. It is interesting in this connection to note that Aristotle claims that painting does represent people "who are worse than we are" (*Poetics* 2.1448a5–6). But Aristotle did not consider this an objection either to painting or, of course, to poetry.

10. There is a crucial problem here concerning the way in which the action depicted in an artwork is described. Are we to be moved by Medea's murder of her children or by the impossible situation in which this stranger, a woman in a man's country, is placed? These are questions of interpretation, which I shall have to avoid here.

11. I have used Jonathan Barnes's revision of the Oxford Translation in *The Complete Works of Aristotle* (Princeton, 1984).

12. Stephen Halliwell, *Aristotle's "Poetics"* (London, 1986), 200. Halliwell's book is extremely valuable in its demonstration of the common ethical and psychological ground between Plato and Aristotle on poetry.

13. Jonas Barish, *The Anti-Theatrical Prejudice* (Berkeley, 1981), 29. Barish makes a similar point in connection with Tertullian's view, which is even more extreme than Plato's: "In the world of Tertullian's polemic," he writes, "the difference between art and life has no status. . . . For Tertullian [to witness a spectacle] is to approve it in the most literal sense: to perceive it as raw fact and to rejoice in it as fact. 'The calling to mind of a criminal act or a shameful thing . . . is no better than the thing itself'" (45). Tertullian, of course, is also interested in showing that a sin in intention is as damning as a sin in act, but his conflation of representation with reality, as Barish shows, is rampant.

14. On this point, I disagree with Ferrari, "Plato and Poetry." Ferrari is admirably clear on the fact that Plato is concerned not so much with feelings themselves, but with their expression, in poetry. On the basis of this he argues that Plato's suspiciousness of poetry is justified. But Ferrari, like Plato, identifies the representation of (the expression of) sorrow with that expression itself. This identification, I am arguing, is illegitimate.

15. It might be asked at this point why someone who did have knowledge of a craft could not produce a more profound imitation of it. This is a very vexed question. The short answer, which is defended at length in "Plato on Imitation," is that to produce something in the full knowledge of what it is is simply not any longer to produce an imitation, but a further instance of it.

16. A more extensive treatment of this point can be found in "Plato on Imitation."

17. Quoted in Eric Barnouw, *Tube of Plenty: The Making of American Television,* rev. ed. (Oxford, 1982), 300.

18. George Gerbner and Larry Gross, "The Scary World of TV's Heavy Viewer," *Psychology Today* (April 1976): 44. It should be remarked in this context (and this is a subject I propose to discuss in detail elsewhere) that the short length of many television programs is not necessarily a shortcoming. It is a convention of the genre and, as such, it can be exploited in very interesting ways, much as, say, the fact that the classical tragedians, on the average, had to compose four plays for presentation within a single day, between sunrise and sunset. The question is raised

by David Thornburn in "Television Melodrama," in Richard P. Adler, ed., *Understanding Television: Essays on Television as a Social and Cultural Form* (New York, 1981), 73–90.

19. Jerry Mander, *Four Arguments for the Elimination of Television* (New York, 1978), 279–80.

20. Mander, 219. A similar view is expressed by Michael Novak, "Television Shapes the Soul," also reprinted in Adler, *Understanding Television,* 19–34.

21. A fascinating alternative view is proposed in Gerbner and Gross, "The Scary World of TV's Heavy Viewer." Their research suggests that the more television one watches the more one tends to be afraid of the violent world that is so often depicted there: the heavy viewer is likely to withdraw from this world rather than to engage in the behavior depicted on television.

22. Wayne C. Booth, "The Company We Keep: Self-Making in Imaginative Art," *Daedalus* 111 (1982): 56–57.

23. Rudolph Arnheim, "A Forecast of Television," in Adler, *Understanding Television,* 7.

24. Mander, *Four Arguments,* 26.

25. Neil Postman, *Amusing Ourselves to Death: Public Discourse in the Age of Show Business* (New York, 1985), 86.

26. Postman, *Amusing Ourselves to Death,* 155. Postman's attack on television, duplicated, among other places, in Booth's "The Company We Keep," in Martin Esslin's otherwise sympathetic *The Age of Television* (New York, 1981), and in Douglass Cater's "Television and Thinking People," in Adler, *Understanding Television,* 11–18, demands serious and extensive attention. The basic idea on which this sort of attack depends is a contrast between the medium of print, which is assumed to be complex, articulate, and highly suited to the communication of complicated information on the one hand and the visual media, especially television, on the other: television is supposed to be incapable of answering serious questions, of examining complicated issues in depth, and of truly involving the rational capacities of its audience—this is said to be due both to some technical features inherent in the television image and to the immense time constraints to which television is always subject. The irony here is very deep. Almost every argument this approach uses to demonstrate the inferiority of television to writing repeats, without most of those authors' knowledge, the arguments Plato used in the *Phaedrus* to demonstrate the inferiority of *writing* to speech and, in the *Gorgias* and the *Theaetetus,* the inferiority of rhetoric to dialectic. The fact that Plato's arguments for the superiority of speech over writing can be so easily used to show the superiority of writing over another form of communication is a subject with far-ranging implications that I propose to discuss in detail on another occasion.

27. Ronald K. L. Collins, "TV Subverts the First Amendment," *New York Times,* September 19, 1987.

28. References to such interpretations of Plato can be found in "Plato on Imitation," nn. 4, 60, 75, 96, and in the passages to which those notes are appended.

29. Peter Walcot, *Greek Drama in Its Theatrical and Social Context* (Cardiff, 1976), 1.

30. Arthur Pickard-Cambridge, *The Theatre of Dionysus in Athens* (Oxford, 1946), 140–41.

31. Ibid., 144.

32. If, that is, we are to believe Plato's statement that Agathon faced an audience of over thirty thousand at the Lenaia on the day preceding the dramatic date of the *Symposium* (175e).

33. Pickard-Cambridge, *The Dramatic Festivals of Athens,* 266–68.

34. Demosthenes, *De Corona* 262. The passage refers directly to the Rural Dionysia, but there is no reason to suppose that the situation in the City Dionysia was significantly different.

35. Pollux, iv.122; Demosthenes, *De Corona* 265.

36. *Vita Aeschyli;* Pollux, iv.110. Whether the story is or is not true is not important; what matters is that stories of this sort circulated and were found believable.

37. Simon Goldhill, *Reading Greek Tragedy* (Oxford, 1985), 252–53.

38. Barish, *The Anti-Theatrical Prejudice,* 79.

39. In some cases where television is examined as a medium, the standards applied to it are implicitly drawn from other media and art forms and, not surprisingly, yield the conclusion that (by those unacknowledged standards) it is an utter failure as a serious art. This is particularly obvious in the case of Postman, *Amusing Ourselves to Death.*

40. Pickard-Cambridge, *The Dramatic Festivals of Athens,* 79.

41. This is well discussed in John G. Cawelti, *Adventure, Mystery, and Romance: Formula Stories as Art and Popular Culture* (Chicago, 1976). See also Janice A. Radway, *Reading the Romance: Women, Patriarchy, and Popular Literature* (Chapel Hill, 1984), esp. 5–6, 29, 34. It should be pointed out, though, that, on the basis of Euripides, *Hippolytus* 451–56, and Aristotle, *Poetics* 9.1451b25, Pickard-Cambridge doubts that the Athenian audience was familiar with the myths explored in drama. He considers "even without the context . . . an easy and obvious joke" the comic poet Antiphanes' complaint (Frag. 191K) that the tragic poets, whose stories were known to their audience, had an advantage over the writers of comedy (275–76 and notes). I do not find the joke either easy or obvious. On Aristotle's statement, cf. D. W. Lucas, *Aristotle: "Poetics"* (Oxford, 1968), n. *ad loc.*

42. Arthur C. Danto, "Art and Disturbation," in *The Philosophical Disenfranchisement of Art* (New York, 1986), 117–33. Some of the ideas of the following paragraphs are also presented in my review of Danto's book, *The Journal of Philosophy* LXXXV (1988): 214–19.

43. Danto, "Art and Disturbation," 121.

44. Ibid., 128.

45. Ibid., 133.

46. Ibid., 119.

47. Ibid., 131.

48. The show's director at one point denied that his hostile portrayal of United Nations troops and Soviet characters was significant, since this was after all a work of fiction, but insisted that his strongly sympathetic and always more complex

portrayal of his American characters was intended to show how Americans really are, and should be the main focus of his audience's attention.

49. Danto, "Philosophy as/and/of Literature," in *The Philosophical Disenfranchisement of Art,* 155.

50. Cf. Thornburn, "Television Melodrama," in Adler, *Understanding Television.*

51. Stanley Cavell, "The Fact of Television," *Daedalus* 111 (1982): 77–99.

52. Ibid., 75.

53. Ibid., 95.

54. This statement needs to be qualified in light of shows like *Hill Street Blues, St. Elsewhere,* or *L.A. Law,* which allow for some character development. Such development, however, is both slow and conservative.

PART IV

Plato: Individual Works

Fourteen

THE *SYMPOSIUM*

THE *SYMPOSIUM* is one of Plato's best known and most influential works. Its importance and its popularity derive from a number of factors that are as exhilarating in themselves as they are difficult to put together into a unified whole. The dialogue presents at least four different aspects to its readers, and it is read for at least four different reasons. First of all the *Symposium* contains a series of speeches on the subject of love (*erōs*), and this is the main reason most readers are attracted to it. Second, it contains one of the most explicit and vivid descriptions of a Platonic "Form," the Form of Beauty, which, according to Socrates' speech, is the final object of all love (209e–212a); the dialogue accordingly provides crucial information on the nature of those objects that Plato considered the ultimate constituents of reality. Third, the *Symposium* provides an extraordinary portrait of Socrates, through his own words, through the comments of the other participants in the feast that is the dialogue's subject, and through the long speech of Alcibiades (215a–222b). Finally, on a more formal level, the *Symposium* is one of the most artfully dramatic works of philosophy ever composed. Plato's success in presenting abstract philosophical ideas of an otherworldly sort through a lighthearted, often comic piece of writing is in itself an object of admiration and study.

The *Symposium* is an account of a banquet given by the young poet Agathon to celebrate his first victory (with his first play, no less) at the dramatic contest held in conjunction with the Lenaian Festival in Athens in 416 B.C. Socrates, who would have been over fifty at that time, is by far the oldest member of the company. The account of the banquet is given by a certain Apollodorus, sometime between 406 and 400 B.C., as we can gather from his statement that, at the time he is asked to relate what occurred at the feast, Agathon has been absent from Athens "for many years" (172c). As for the actual dialogue, two allusions to historical events (182b, 193a) show that Plato must have written it after 385 B.C.,[1] while the fact that Phaedrus speaks only hypothetically of a regiment composed of lovers (178e–179b) implies that it was completed before 378 B.C., when the city of Thebes established just such a regiment, the famous "Sacred Band."

We have no positive evidence that the dinner Plato describes actually ever took place. On the other hand, nothing excludes the possibility, even though the historical Aristophanes, who is on very good terms with everyone here, had already attacked Socrates in his play *The Clouds* and would soon turn against Agathon in his *Thesmophoriazousai*. Nevertheless, Plato goes out of his way to suggest that Apollodorus, the dialogue's narrator, is only repeating an account he has heard from someone else (173b). Since Plato uses such an indirect approach in the *Parmenides,* a dialogue relating a conversation that could not have taken place, we may speculate that at least the details of the occasion the *Symposium* describes, if not the occasion itself, are Plato's own invention.

This speculation is made more plausible when we consider the fact that the crucial part of Socrates' speech on *erōs* is supposed to be an account of the views of Diotima, a priestess from Mantineia, of whom we know nothing other than what Socrates tells us here. In addition, Diotima in her speech makes an allusion to the view Aristophanes has just presented at the banquet (204d–e, 212c). This, too, suggests that even if Diotima actually existed, what she is represented as saying to Socrates cannot have been composed, as Socrates claims, long before the party during which he relates it. Furthermore, Plato's having Socrates admit that he cannot understand Diotima (206b) and having Diotima warn him that he may not be capable of being initiated into "the final and highest mystery" of love (210a) may well be Plato's way of indicating that the views involved toward the end of Socrates' speech are not Socrates' but Plato's own.[2]

"Dinner party" or even "feast" is not a perfect translation of the Greek word *symposion,* which literally means "drinking together." Though food was always served on such occasions, it was consumed quickly at the start of the evening so that the participants could get to the real purpose of the affair. This was heavy drinking, usually under the direction of an elected "leader" (*symposiarchos*), who had the authority to propose endless toasts, usually drunk in order from left to right, and to establish how much each guest would have to consume. Entertainment, both musical and sexual, was commonly supplied by flute-girls (*aulētrides*), and the evenings would often end with the guests dropping off to an exhausted sleep on the couches on which they had been eating and drinking throughout the evening.

The guests at Agathon's dinner, however, are suffering the aftereffects of the previous night's drinking, and they decide early on to drink lightly and to send the flute-girl away (176a–e). Instead, they decide to have a conversation on—or, rather, a series of speeches in praise of—*erōs* (176e–177e). Such speeches, too, are given in order from left to right, making Socrates, who comes to the dinner late and shares Agathon's couch, the last to take the floor.

The general Greek word for "love" is *philia,* which applies indifferently to the feelings of friends, family members, and lovers. *Erōs* refers to particularly intense attachment and desire in general. Most commonly, however, it is applied to passionate love and desire, usually sexual, and to the god who personified that state. Since Greek lacked our convention of capitalizing the initials of proper names, it is only possible to tell what the word refers to in each case from the context, and our translation constantly shifts between "he" (to refer to the god) and "it" (to refer to the state). *Erōs* and *philia* can coexist; this becomes obvious in Phaedrus' discussion of the example of Alcestis, who alone was willing to die in her husband's place: "Because of her love (*erōs*), she went so far beyond his parents in family feeling (*philia*) that she made them look like outsiders" (179c).

But despite the case of Alcestis, which is also mentioned (though with a vastly different interpretation) by Diotima (208d), the love discussed and praised in the *Symposium* is primarily homosexual. It is true that Eryximachus in his speech generalizes the phenomenon to apply to almost everything in the world and that Aristophanes places homosexual and heterosexual love on exactly the same footing. But Pausanias and Agathon are totally unconcerned with heterosexuality; Phaedrus mentions it almost as an afterthought; and Socrates places it, along with the desire to procreate, outside the "ladder of love" that leads from the love of one particular beautiful boy to the love of Beauty itself.

Plato's emphasis on homosexual love is not always easy for his twentieth-century audience to understand. It is, actually, a remarkable fact that the *Symposium,* the first explicit discussion of love in Western literature and philosophy, begins as a discussion of homosexual love and soon leaves behind all love of individuals: the real objects of love, as the concluding parts of Socrates' speech (208c–212a) urge, are fame, beautiful bodies in general, beautiful souls, the beauty in laws, practices, and the sciences, and finally Beauty itself, in all its purity and generality.

In fact, these two features of the *Symposium*—that the love addressed is primarily homosexual and that it soon becomes very abstract and general indeed—are interconnected. Greek homosexual relations often had a crucial educational and ethical dimension, which Plato took over and developed in the abstract direction dictated by his theoretical philosophical views.

In ancient Athens, it was both accepted and expected that older men would fall in love with and seek sexual gratification from younger (that is, adolescent) boys. Such relationships generally existed side by side with conventional marriage on the part of the older man, the "lover" (*erastēs*), and with the expectation of it on the part of the boy, the "beloved" (*erōmenos*). The affairs were asymmetrical in a number of ways. For one thing, the boy was supposed to be won only with difficulty and to resist the passionate and often extravagant advances of the lover. Second, once won, the beloved was expected not to enjoy the sexual act; on the contrary, enjoyment was a sign of a depraved nature. As Xenophon wrote in his own

Symposium (viii.21), "The boy does not share in the man's pleasure in intercourse, as a woman does; cold sober, he looks upon the other drunk with sexual desire."[3] Finally, the relationship, at least ideally, involved the lover in the role of ethical and intellectual teacher and the boy in the role of his student. The latter had everything to learn from and nothing to teach the former; in fact, a proper homosexual relationship was often a crucial part of the socialization of the sons of good families into adult civic life. Once the boy reached adulthood, he ceased being a beloved and became a friend: the affair was over. Long-lasting relationships between adults, like that between Agathon and Pausanias (cf. 193b–c), were the exception rather than the rule. Actually, Athenian attitudes toward homosexual affairs were not entirely consistent. Young boys were protected by their families from the advances of older men, who were nevertheless urged to pursue them and were admired for their conquests. Despite the ethical benefits of such relationships, giving in to a lover, especially too quickly, was often considered a disgrace.

The praises of *erōs* in the *Symposium* can be roughly divided into two groups. The first three speeches, by Phaedrus, Pausanias, and Eryximachus, naturally fall into one category, and the second three, by Aristophanes, Agathon, and Socrates, into another.

The first group of speeches is rather conventional in its praise of *erōs* for its effects, though all three speakers seem to be trying to come to terms with the double standard implicit in the attitudes of Athens toward pederasty and to defend *erōs* against charges that must have been commonplace at the time.

None of these speeches, however, is purely conventional. Phaedrus' passionate emphasis on virtue and self-sacrifice, for example, goes beyond common practice. His style is simple, but carefully balanced and concise. His enthusiasm, however, carries him to say extravagant things: that love is the best guide to virtue (a view also shared by Socrates, but on the basis of a radically different conception of *erōs*) and that virtue is most valuable when connected with love. The virtue that interests him is the courage that leads to self-sacrifice, and in developing that theme he twists the legend of Orpheus to suit his purposes (179d). Love has no dark side in Phaedrus' eyes, and his praise of its effects its indiscriminate.

Pausanias is unwilling to share Phaedrus' unlimited enthusiasm. He continues to praise *erōs*'s effects but distinguishes between a vulgar and a noble kind of love. The former, he argues, is aimed indifferently at women as well as at boys: its purpose is purely sexual gratification. The latter, which is exclusively homosexual, is concerned with the welfare of the beloved's soul. There is something self-serving and self-righteous in Pausanias' rather prim attitude. And it is not at all impossible that Aristophanes, who developed the hiccups while Pausanias is talking (185c–e), may have exploited his problem to make fun of Pausanias. In any case, it is worth bearing in mind that Aristophanes is hiccupping during at least part of Pausanias' high-minded oration.

Pausanias' distinction between noble and vulgar love is taken over by Eryximachus, who stretches the meaning of "love" into "attraction" or even "harmony." This, in turn, enables him to credit love, without defining it any further, with beneficial effects not only in medicine (which, he never tires of reminding us, is his own field) but also in music, meteorology, and divination. Eryximachus' style, like his manner throughout the *Symposium,* is extremely pedantic. Plato is clearly satirizing his self-importance and his extraordinarily good opinion of the significance of medicine. In general, it is remarkable how many of the speeches in this work contain elements of parody: even Socrates' habit of engaging in dialectic through the method of question and answer does not escape unscathed (194a–e, 199b ff.).

Aristophanes' magnificent speech, with which the second group of speeches begins, is in sharp contrast to Eryximachus' vague abstractions, bringing the discussion back to the subject of the feelings of individual people for one another. Aristophanes tells a myth according to which human beings were originally of three sexes—male, female, and male-female—and had twice as many limbs and organs as we have today. For a number of reasons, the gods decided to split them in half, and accordingly each one of us today is searching for a half of the same original nature with whom to spend the rest of our life. Love is the desire to find our other original half, and our sexual preference is determined by the sex of the original double being from which each of us is descended. Aristophanes' story thus interprets both homosexual and heterosexual love as absolutely natural, but it makes another crucial contribution to the speeches' progression.

Aristophanes' speech is stunning in its originality. Although it contains parody in its use of myth, it is on the whole a highly serious work, and its view of love has no parallel in earlier Greek literature. It actually anticipates more romantic modern versions of love, particularly the idea that love draws together two unique individuals to join as one person. For all its comic elements, a sad note sounds frequently in the speech: the goal of loving, the forging of one person out of two, is not to be achieved. What we have instead is the temporary satisfaction of sexual relationships, and these are at best a promise of a more permanent happiness and a closer union.

By giving an explanation, however fanciful, of the desire people have to spend large parts of their life in the company of someone else, Aristophanes shifts attention from the benefits of love to its nature—something the first group of speeches either neglected or underemphasized. And this is precisely the strategy Agathon adopts in his own encomium: "You must explain what qualities in the subject of your speech enable him to give the benefits for which we praise him," he says at the very beginning of his contribution (195a). He then proceeds, in a masterful parody of oratory, to praise *erōs* as the youngest, the most beautiful, and the most virtuous of the gods and to account for Love's benefits by relating them directly to his youth, beauty, and virtue.

This is, delightfully, the most comic of these six speeches. And though Agathon is a tragedian, Socrates will later contend that a good tragic poet should also be able to write in comic vein (223d). No doubt Plato means us to notice that neither his tragic nor his comic poet—Aristophanes— follows exclusively his own special muse. Here, the young speaker, quite drunk already in his own honor, is unmistakably playing for laughs. He indulges in an unrestrained parody of Gorgianic style and sophistic argument, enlivened with salacious double entendres, and punctuated with digs at the age and ugliness of his couch partner, Socrates. Still, as he himself insists, though much of the speech is mock-serious, parts of it are meant in earnest.

Socrates has nothing but praise for Agathon's method of speaking first of the features of *erōs* and only then of its benefits, which fits well with his own dialectical practice (cf. *Meno* 71b). But he accepts none of the conclusions Agathon has reached through that method. In characteristic manner, which does however seem a little out of place on such an occasion, he questions Agathon in the manner in which he usually questions his interlocutors in Plato's more explicitly dialectical works (199c–201c). He gets Agathon to agree that *erōs* is the desire for beauty (a first attempt at a definition of its nature). He then claims that, since no one desires what one already has or is, *erōs* cannot be beautiful. For that matter, in view of the fact that all good things are beautiful, *erōs* cannot be good or virtuous either (199c–201c).

Having silenced Agathon, Socrates now tactfully tells him that he himself had made the mistake of thinking that *erōs* was beautiful and good at one point in life. He was corrected by Diotima, a priestess from the city of Mantineia, who was his teacher in all matters of love, and he now goes on to relate his conversation with her. The upshot of this conversation is that *erōs* turns out to be neither beautiful nor ugly but something "in between"; and the same is true for his goodness, his divinity, and his wisdom: "he is in love with what is beautiful, and wisdom is extremely beautiful. It follows that Love *must* be a lover of wisdom (*philosophos*/philosopher), and, as such, is in between being wise and being ignorant" (204b).

The reason Agathon and the younger Socrates were tempted to attribute all good qualities to *erōs* turns out to be that they conceived of it on the model of the beloved, who is the object of desire and is thus young, beautiful, and good and not—as would have been correct—on the model of the lover, who lacks these features but is still close enough to them to recognize and appreciate them (204c). We must keep this idea in mind, for it will become important when we turn to the *Symposium's* portrait of Socrates. But the point is also important in the immediate context, because it shows that Plato has already begun to mold the conventional conception of love to suit his own philosophical needs. We have seen that the lover was traditionally expected to be his beloved's teacher: wisdom, that is, was the lover's contribution to a relationship in which the beloved supplied only physical beauty. But by counting wisdom among beautiful things, Socrates has turned the lover from a purveyor into a pursuer of wisdom. This, in a way, is one of the most crucial ideas presented in the *Symposium,* and it governs all that follows in Socrates' speech: philosophy, the pursuit of wisdom, is motivated by love; it is, in fact, love's highest expression.

Diotima defines *erōs* in general as the desire for the continual possession of good things (206a). But since this is equivalent to defining it as the desire for happiness (204e), she tries to offer a more specific account that will apply to love and sexual desire in particular. She goes on to say that love specifically is the desire to reproduce and to "give birth in beauty" (206b, e). "All of us," she claims, "are pregnant . . . both in body and in soul, and as soon as we come to a certain age, we naturally desire to give birth" (206c).[4] This desire to reproduce, which is also a desire for immortality (206e–207a), may involve physical offspring, glory, or good deeds in general—anything that springs from the individual but stays behind after the individual's death.

For Plato, and so for Socrates and Diotima in the *Symposium,* the most lasting offspring are virtuous acts. These are produced by a lover who is attracted by a noble soul within a boy's beautiful body (lovers who are only pregnant "in their body" are attracted to women, according to Diotima) and who, together with his beloved, leaves behind him "more beautiful and more immortal" children (209c). Such, for example, are "the children" of the great poets and the great lawmakers of Greece (209d).

Socrates' speech could well have ended at this point. To be sure, there are serious differences between it and the speeches that preceded it. It begins, for example, with a dialectical bout, which is, to say the least, unusual in the context of a formal encomium. Socrates' attribution of the views he presents to Diotima and his recounting of his imaginary conversation with her are unprecedented in the history of rhetoric. The idea that *erōs* is "a philosopher" and the definition of love is the desire to give "birth in beauty" are clear innovations on Plato's part, and the tone of the speech, despite some light touches here and there, is much more serious than that of any of the others, rising to a remarkable crescendo at 208c–209e. Despite all these differences, however, Socrates' speech has, up to this point, been quite continuous with all the others. Socrates has concentrated on the love of individuals for one another and, despite his various disagreements with the earlier speakers, has attributed to this love the same general sort of benefits that Phaedrus and Pausanias had introduced into the discussion. His speech is more complex than any other, but it has not so far added anything truly novel to the picture of *erōs*.

It is just here, however, at the point where Plato's readers, familiar with the conventions of formal speeches of praise (*encōmia*), would have been ready for Socrates to stop, that something remarkable occurs. Instead of winding his speech down, Socrates reports that Diotima told him that everything she had said about love up to this point, far from exhausting the topic (as it would have been perfectly natural to suppose), constituted only the means and stepping-stones for something else, "the final and highest mystery" of love. And she tells him that, though she will try to explain that mystery to him, he may well be unable to understand it (210a).

Now we are on completely new ground. Diotima describes a kind of "ascent" of love (210a–210d). A lover first falls in love with a single beautiful body, which inspires him to give birth to beautiful ideas. But the lover, as we know, loves beauty, and the beauty in all beautiful bodies is the same: the lover, therefore, will realize that his reasons for loving a single individual are also reasons for his becoming a lover of all beautiful bodies, and he values his earlier love less than before. The lover now sees that the beauty of the soul is nobler than the beauty of bodies, and he turns to the creation of "such ideas as will make young men better." In looking for such "ideas" or "discourses" (*logoi*), the lover will come to realize that the "activities and laws" that such ideas express are themselves beautiful in their own right, and he will devote himself to them instead. But these activities and laws, in turn, manifest and depend upon knowledge, and the lover now becomes attached to nothing less than "the great sea of beauty, and, gazing upon this, he gives birth to many gloriously beautiful ideas and theories, in unstinting love of wisdom (*philosophia*)."

These are radically new ideas. Plato begins with the ordinary concept of love as a bond uniting two people. He then exploits the view that homosexual affairs had an educational dimension, connects it with his own idea that love is a desire for wisdom, and combines it with what for him is a fundamental assumption, namely, that if we love or desire something for some reason, X, then that reason, X, is the primary object of our love or desire.[5] So at each step of the ascent, the lover "rises" to a love of whatever it is that explains the beauty of, and hence his love for, the object on the step below. Love, then, which by now has almost become another word for philosophy, has left the bonds between individual people far behind: nothing of that sort could have been expected from the first part of Socrates' speech.[6]

But even the love of knowledge, Diotima continues, is not the final stage of this ascent. Emphasizing the novelty and the controversial nature of what we are about to be told (210e), she now reveals "the reason for all [these] earlier labors." If a lover has gone about things correctly, he will at some point "all of a sudden" (*exaiphnēs:* we will return to this) see "the reason for all his earlier labors." This reason, for the sake of which everything else has been undertaken, is Beauty itself, that which makes everything else beautiful and the ultimate object of all *erōs,* according to Plato's highly revisionary and bold view.

This "Form" of Beauty is pure, unchanging, beautiful in every way, not to be seen with the eyes of the body, and separate from all the things that derive their beauty from it. It exists independently of all beautiful things, and nothing that happens to them can ever affect it. About the relationship between Beauty and the many beautiful things for whose beauty it is responsible and which it explains, we learn nothing in the *Symposium* (or, for that matter, in the dialogues where the theory of Forms is given more systematic exposition: cf. *Phaedo* 100d). What we do learn is that, despite its many forms and various objects, all love—whether we know it or not—is directed at the very nature of Beauty. And so *erōs,* which we first approached as the desire to possess sexually the body of another person, turns out to be a desire for immortality, for wisdom, and for the contemplation of an object that is not in any way bodily or physical. Furthermore, only when a lover devotes himself to the pursuit of Beauty as a whole "will it become possible for him to give birth not to images of virtue . . . but to true virtue" (212a). Sexual desire, properly channeled, leads not simply to gratification but to the good life.

The end of Socrates' speech is radically different from anything that has preceded it: the whole atmosphere of Agathon's feast seems to have changed. But Plato does not allow this serious, almost hieratic mood to last for long. One of the greatest dramatic features of the *Symposium* is the way in which seriousness alternates with lightheartedness, instruction with banter, self-revelation with irony. And one of the work's most artful reversals occurs at the end of Socrates' speech, with the drunken entrance of Alcibiades, who does his best to turn the sober feast into a drinking contest (212c ff.).

The noise Alcibiades and his party make at Agathon's door is heard "all of a sudden" (*exaiphnēs*): Plato seems to be marking explicitly a reversal in the atmosphere that Diotima had created by her own reversal of the mood that had prevailed earlier when she introduced the Form of Beauty, which also, as we saw, comes "all of a sudden" into view (210e).[7] But even if

Alcibiades' boisterous entrance seems hardly compatible with Diotima's revelation (in fact, it seems to be quite the opposite), his contribution to the dialogue is as central as hers, and what he has to reveal is quite as important.

We have already seen that Diotima has argued that *erōs* should be conceived not on the model of the beloved but on that of the lover: he is neither beautiful nor totally ugly, but beauty's pursuer; he is neither wise nor foolish, but wisdom's admirer (*philosophos*); he is neither god nor mortal, but a "spirit" (*daimōn, daimonion,* 202d–203a). Now, throughout the *Symposium,* Socrates has been said to love beautiful young men and boys; he is the perfect philosopher; and he is even referred to as *daimonios* by Alcibiades (219c). This suggests that the model on which *erōs* is to be conceived is not so much the lover in general but Socrates in particular; after all, he has already admitted that "the only thing I say I understand is the art of love" (177d). At the same time, the identification of Socrates with the lover and with love itself suggests that Socrates is not the proper object of love: his role, like that of the lover and love itself, is that of the pursuer, not of the pursued.

And yet the matter is more complicated. As Alcibiades makes his way to Agathon's couch in order to crown Agathon with a wreath he has brought for that purpose, he fails to see that Socrates is also lying there. It is only after he is ready to lie down that Alcibiades finally becomes aware of Socrates, turns to him, and says, "You always do this to me—all of a sudden (*exaiphnēs*) you'll turn up out of nowhere where I least expect you!" (213c). Thus, after Socrates has been implicitly identified with love and the lover and while both he and Alcibiades seem to be in agreement over the fact that Socrates is the lover and Alcibiades his beloved, Alcibiades' language connects Socrates with Diotima's description of the ultimate object of love, the very Form of Beauty. This is a crucial point, but not much is made of it here. Plato seems to be placing what we will later be able to see as a subtle hint as to how we are to understand Socrates in this work. We shall return to it below.

Alcibiades is asked to make his own contribution to the praise of *erōs,* but he refuses because he claims that Socrates is too jealous for him to dare to praise anyone else in his presence. A great deal of good-natured banter about who is jealous of whom follows, and Eryximachus finally suggests that Alcibiades should speak in praise of Socrates, which he proceeds to do (215a ff.).

Given the subtle connections already established between Socrates and *erōs,* this is less of a change of subject than we might suppose. And in fact Alcibiades' witty encomium of Socrates develops a number of themes from Diotima's speech (which confirms that both speeches are Plato's creations). Socrates, he says, is like the statues of Silenus—far from beautiful on the outside but full of lovely little figures of the gods inside (215a–b). This shows Socrates to be neither perfectly beautiful nor totally ugly, and it also offers a concrete image of Diotima's metaphor of the lover's being pregnant "both in body and in soul." That he is a philosopher is, of course, the most obvious fact about him (218a–b), and Alcibiades returns again and again to the fact that Socrates is full of the best and most virtuous ideas and arguments (215b–216c, 221d–222a). And that he is almost superhuman is intimated not only by his incredible stamina and courage (219e–221c) but also by the comparison with Silenus, who was the semidivine companion of Dionysus and, as we have mentioned already, by Alcibiades' application to him of the word *daimonios*.

All these hints connecting Socrates with *erōs*, however, seem to be shaken by the conclusion of Alcibiades' speech. Alcibiades here mentions Socrates' "deception" (222a–b). What this deception is has been foreshadowed both by the use of "all of a sudden" at 213c and by another unobtrusive remark at 217c, where Alcibiades, describing his unsuccessful attempts to seduce Socrates, says that he invited him to dinner "as if *I* were his lover and he my young prey!" In his conclusion, Alcibiades comes out and accuses Socrates explicitly, and only half in jest, of a conscious and devious practice: "He has deceived us all: he presents himself as your lover, and, before you know it, you're in love with him yourself!"

We have now come full circle. Agathon's speech conceived and praised love as the beloved; Diotima identified love with the lover and, implicitly, with Socrates; Alcibiades, still thinking of Socrates as love, now reveals him to be, in reality, the beloved. But the circle has made a tremendous difference. Plato gives us in Socrates a union of lover and beloved, beguiler and beguiled. But the personification of *erōs*'s two aspects in Socrates inevitably leads further. Unlike Agathon's unthinking love for love, which makes *erōs* an end in itself, to love Socrates, as Alcibiades knows and makes clear to the company, is to love what Socrates, as *erōs*, loves: the possession of beauty, wisdom, and goodness. To love Socrates is to be a philosopher. And, as we know from many of Plato's other Socratic dialogues, this is exactly what Socrates wanted of those he approached in his direct yet ironic manner.

This very serious point is made through the broad comedy that characterizes the whole episode of Alcibiades. But, of course, the point could not be made without the very serious speech of Diotima, which sets the stage for Alcibiades' antics. And Diotima's speech, in turn, depends crucially on a refutation of the views presented with the utmost elegance in Agathon's lovely trifle. The serious and the comic exist side by side in this dialogue, and each is equally crucial for the philosophical ideas the work communicates. That serious philosophy can be done at the same time that entertaining, even comic, events and conversations are depicted is not only true but may actually be the message with which the *Symposium* itself ends. Early into the morning hours, after everyone else has left or drifted off to sleep, Socrates is trying to prove to Agathon, the tragic poet, and to Aristophanes, who wrote comedies, that "the skillful tragic dramatist should also be a comic poet" (223d).

Whether this interpretation of the dialogue's end is or is not correct, the *Symposium* is a philosophical masterpiece because it is such a successful literary work. It presents a revisionary, otherworldly conception of love and a metaphysical vision to support that conception. But it is only by showing Socrates to be as much at home in everyday life as he is in the search for wisdom, as capable of being a good man here and now as he is devoted to the pursuit of a Beauty that does not exist in this world, as sturdy a drinker as he is an astute dialectician, that Plato has succeeded in convincing generations of readers that his idea of love is not simply a wild philosophical fantasy but rather an ideal according to which life can almost be lived. The various aspects of the dialogue do fit together after all. The *Symposium* is to be read and savored for all these reasons: for its philosophical views—the theory of love, the description of the Form of Beauty; for its literary elements—the brightness of the occasion it depicts, the portrayal of the various speakers, the characterization of Socrates; and for the product of the interaction between these two—the demonstration that living according to that theory has produced, whatever our misgivings, a hero of our culture.

Notes

1. It is remotely possible that, at 193a, Aristophanes may be referring to an earlier division of the Mantineian Alliance on the part of the Spartans in 418 B.C. (cf. Thucydides V.81). But the word Aristophanes uses here is not strictly appropriate to that action, and, in any case, the allusion at 182b (to the subjection of Ionia, on the coast of Asia Minor, to the Persian Empire, which occurred in 386 B.C.) is sufficient to fix the date of the dialogue.

2. A number of the views Socrates expresses in the first part of his dialogue with Diotima are views compatible with other views expressed in Plato's Socratic dialogues. But the idea that love is the desire for "birth in (the presence of) beauty" (206c ff.) and everything that follows, including, of course, the revelation of the Form of Beauty as the ultimate object of *erōs* (209e–212a), is Plato's; cf. Vlastos, "The Individual as Object of Love in Plato," in his *Platonic Studies* (Princeton, 1981), 3–42.

3. Quoted in K. J. Dover, *Greek Homosexuality,* (Cambridge, Mass., 1978), 52. This study is indispensable for an understanding of Greek, especially Athenian, attitudes.

4. On this strange reversal, which makes the pregnancy the cause and not the

outcome of intercourse, see M. F. Burnyeat, "Socratic Midwifery, Plantonic Inspiration," *Bulletin of the Institute of Classical Studies* 24 (1977): 7–16.

5. See John A. Brentlinger, "The Nature of Love," in *The "Symposium" of Plato,* trans. Suzy Q. Groden, ed. John A. Brentlinger (Amherst, 1970), 113–29.

6. Whether love for individuals *as* individuals is completely abandoned or merely receives lesser emphasis is a complex and disputed question. See Gregory Vlastos, "The Individual as Object of Love in Plato," 32–34, for the former view, and T. H. Irwin, *Plato's Moral Theory* (Oxford, 1977), 168 and n. 59, for the latter.

7. The same word is used at 223b to mark the sudden entrance of an even drunker group, which brings about the disintegration of the party after the end of Alcibiades' speech.

Fifteen

THE *REPUBLIC*

HOMER'S WORLD still exists. Its seas, its islands, its rivers, plains and mountains are there for all to see. Many do indeed see them as they visit the ruins of buildings through which the ancient Greeks celebrated their power and commemorated their past. But these ruins are more than landscape. They are also a vivid metaphor for the fact that what is geographically continuous is socially, psychologically, institutionally, and spiritually sundered from us—for the fact that this is really, in W. H. Auden's words, "Homer's world, not ours."

If our world and Homer's are no longer the same, that is largely because of Plato, and perhaps most of all because of Plato's most famous book, the *Republic*. This work was its author's main weapon in his fight to forge a new world, to replace the quarrelsome magnificence of Achilles and Odysseus with the rational grandeur of Socrates, and its success can be measured by comparing our present attitudes to the protagonists of the *Odyssey* and the *Iliad* on the one hand and to the dominant figure of the *Republic* on the other. We still admire Homer's heroes, but we can no longer try to emulate them. And though we may not always admire Socrates, the question of emulation does not arise in his regard: he has become part of what we are; to the extent we do not admire him, we are at war with ourselves.

This is not to say that the doctrines explicitly asserted in the *Republic* are widely accepted. On the contrary, Plato's paternalistic political authoritarianism, his radical metaphysical distinction between a sensible and an intelligible world, only the latter of which can be known, his conviction that the moral life can guarantee happiness, his exclusion of what we now consider literature from his ideal state, his conviction that philosophers should be given ultimate political power, his proposal for the common possession of spouses and children among the elite of his city—these are all views that, if they can be contemplated at all, are nothing short of wildly controversial. And yet, the foundations of most of the ideas we do contemplate and consider commonplace today are found in the *Republic*.

The *Republic* has most often been read as a work of utopian political philosophy, and it has provoked the most diverse interpretations and the most violent disagreements. Here is an example, drawn practically at random. Immanuel Kant, the great German philosopher, took the central idea of the work to be "a constitution founded on the greatest possible human freedom, according to laws which enable the freedom of each individual to exist by the side of the freedom of others," and characterized it as, "to say the least, a necessary idea, on which not only the first plan of the constitution of a state, but all its laws must be based."[1] Sir Karl Popper, by contrast, who finds the doctrine of the *Republic* "barbaric," writes that "Plato is not even interested in those problems which men usually call the problems of justice, that is to say, in the impartial weighing of the contesting claims of individuals. Nor is he interested in adjusting the individual's claims to those of the state."[2]

But the *Republic* is not just a work of political philosophy. In much broader terms, it delimits the range of questions and the sort of methods relevant not only to philosophers and classicists, not only to historians of thought and culture, but also to educators, to political, social, and even natural scientists (whose mathematical approach to their endeavors dates from the scientific revolution's rediscovery of Platonism), to artists and critics, to the governing and the governed, the powerful and the powerless. It does not simply underlie some of our more abstruse theories. It is part of the fabric of our common sense.

The *Republic* raises its questions in a relentlessly interconnected manner. Plato realizes that the nature of the good human life cannot be determined independently of the place of human beings within society; that the nature of society depends on the education of its citizens; that proper education requires a view of knowledge and of the nature of the world that can be known; that theories of knowledge presuppose psychological accounts of the individuals that are to be educated; that psychology dictates particular attitudes toward the arts. Moral theory, metaphysics, epistemology, theory of education, political and social philosophy, philosophy of science, psychology, and aesthetics are all established here, for the first time, as aspects of a single enterprise. None of these subjects is more central to the *Republic* than any other. The work's real topic is the enterprise they constitute as a whole. That enterprise is philosophy.

The *Republic* is therefore not only a work of philosophy. It is in fact the first work of philosophy ever written. Nothing composed before it, including Plato's own earlier works, is comparable to it in magnitude, ambition, or scope. The *Republic* inaugurates philosophy as a practice and discipline and establishes what we still consider its nature. It constructs a new image of the individual; from now on, reason becomes essential in defining what counts as human and in solving both private and public problems. The emphasis on rationality, on the existence of objective truth, and on the unbreakable connection between the search for truth and the attainment of happiness are the features that separate Plato's world from Homer's. For the first time, wisdom replaces glory as the true aim of human life.

Plato was perfectly aware of the magnitude of the task he had set himself. Though Socrates, who is the main speaker of this dialogue, constantly expresses his uncertainty about the specific views he proposes, the work as a whole exudes an air of absolute confidence in the substance of its project. But this confidence is not advertised. It is not asserted in the work but emerges through it. The *Republic* praises the most abstract, rigorous, and theoretical modes of thought at the expense of the practical, the rhetorical, and the literary. Nevertheless, it is itself a literary work of the first order, and it is as a literary work that it succeeds in establishing the priority of abstract reason. It works by indirection. As we dispute, for example, Plato's idea that the philosophers should govern our city, we grant him his view that reason should rule our life. The *Republic* argues for, but also seduces us into, rationality.

Like all seductions, this one too proceeds by small, inconspicuous steps: each one individually leaves us more or less where we already were; all together lead us to a place we could never have imagined before. Plato introduces his shocking blueprint for a radically new conception of the ideal life and the ideal state by means of an offhand remark by an old gentleman, Cephalus, who says early on in Book I that he is not afraid to die because his wealth has allowed him to live without lying and without owing any debts "of sacrifice to God and of money to man" (331). Socrates interprets this remark, somewhat arbitrarily, as a definition of justice, and sets the wheels of his dialectical machine in motion. But even the spirited exchange of Book I of the *Republic*, in which various definitions of justice, successively more revisionary, are proposed and tested, is a tiny step compared to the increasingly revolutionary ideas presented in the other nine books.

The question with which the *Republic* begins, then, is "What is justice?" This soon becomes "Why be just at all?" "Why be good if all the advantages go to those who are not?" This second question, put to Socrates at the beginning of Book II, is urgent because it appeals to one of the most persistent images in our culture: on the one hand, the unconscionable cad who lives a rich, privileged, honored, and envied life, never caught and brought to account; on the other, the just and moral individual who passes through life unnoticed—at best unrewarded, perhaps ridiculed, at worst deeply and irreparably wronged. Since this seems more the rule than the exception, what reason can there be for being moral? Goodness appears to have little to do with the greatness of Odysseus, with the success of the rulers of the ancient world, or, indeed, with the fame of many of our own contemporaries.

The *Republic* is a prolonged effort to eradicate this image. It attempts, instead, to paint a picture in which the life of justice is the best and happiest human life. Painting this picture is a long and complex process. It requires a representation of the structure of the human soul, of the nature of the social organization in which such a soul can survive and thrive, of the manner in which such a soul and state can come about, and of the nature of the world that makes their existence possible and right.

Before we turn, however briefly, to the elements of which Plato's picture consists, it is necessary to take a few steps back. To understand the picture, we must first see the background against which Plato constructs it.

This background consists, first, of a debate raging through ancient Athens from the middle of the fifth century B.C. well until 375 B.C., when the *Republic* was probably composed. The debate concerned what the Greeks called *aretē:* What is *aretē,* and how do people acquire it? In particular, can *aretē* be taught?

Aretē is usually translated as "virtue." But this is not right. *Aretē* is much broader than the narrower, strictly moral English word and also applies to animals as well as to inanimate objects. In the *Republic,* for example, Socrates speaks of the *aretē* of eyes and of knives (352–353). Anything that has a function has a corresponding *aretē* which it exhibits when it performs that function well. Homer speaks of the *aretē* of horses, Herodotus praises the *aretē* of Indian cotton, and Thucydides the *aretē* of fertile soil. Far from being confined to morality, *aretē* refers to whatever it is that makes something a good instance of its kind.

As applied to human beings, *aretē* could be understood as "success." Our question, then, would become, "What is success, and can it be taught?" The ancient question thus acquires an immediate contemporary resonance. We are faced today with an obsession with (an ill-defined concept of) success, with a vast industry devoted to imparting its secrets through books or self-help manuals, with itinerant "experts" holding "seminars" from city to city. Many believe that what such "experts" teach is not "real" success, and that what really should count as success cannot be taught at all. In all this, our situation is remarkably similar to the debates swirling within and around classical Athens over the notion of *aretē* and the ability of the sophists, its professional teachers who toured the various Greek cities, to impart it to those who were willing to pay their considerable fees.

In more general terms, which would apply even to the inanimate objects we mentioned above, we might try to understand *aretē* as the quality that makes something outstanding in its group, as the feature that accounts for its justified notability. This idea involves three sets of elements: the inner structure and quality of things, their reputation, and the audience that can appreciate them. This is as it should be. *Aretē* (like "success") always had a public aspect; it is related to the Homeric word *kleos,* which is essentially tied to fame, and preserves this connotation even in postclassical Athens: when the orator Hypereides, for example, wrote that those who die for their country "leave *aretē* behind them," he was thinking of it in such public terms.

But what is it to have a justified reputation in the world? Each of this formula's three elements may create a problem. If we identify *aretē* with justification, with the inner reasons why someone deserves a good reputation, people who possess *aretē* may well seem to others to lack it. If we emphasize reputation instead, cads who appear to have *aretē* but lack its substance will receive its rewards. And, finally, who is to judge who possesses the right combination of features?

Prompted by the personality and fate of Socrates, who had died in 399 B.C., Plato makes an unprecedented effort to solve these difficulties together. This is the second component of the context within which we must locate the picture drawn in the *Republic*.

A fruitful way of reading this work is to see it in part as an attempt to rehabilitate Socrates in the eyes of the world. As Plato saw him, Socrates was utterly convinced that *aretē* was not reputation but goodness, not public fame but an inner disposition of the soul that he made it his life's work to acquire. He was, as Plato described him in the closing words of the *Phaedo,* "the best, the wisest and the most just of all the men we have known." But Socrates was not only unrecognized as a good man; on the contrary, he was executed as a common criminal, charged with impiety and with undermining the faith of the young in the city's traditional values. For Plato, Socrates' case represented the greatest possible discrepancy between the inner aspect of *aretē*—the reasons for which one should have a good reputation—and the reputation one actually did have. Instead of being rewarded for what he was, Socrates was condemned on its account by a city incapable of appreciating him.

But the *Republic* is more than simply a rehabilitation of Socrates. Much more radically and ambitiously, it aims to establish a world in which what happened to Socrates can never happen again, a new world in which goodness and reputation can never again drift apart. It also aims to construct a society in which the appearance of a person like Socrates will not be a lucky exception, as Plato thought he had been in Athens, but the product of long-term social planning. Plato designs a city in which every generation will possess and honor the equivalents of Socrates—the people he calls philosophers.

That is why Plato pays so much attention in this work to the third element in our account of *aretē,* to the people who are to judge goodness; and why a discussion of the moral question of how life is to be lived so quickly turns into an examination of political and social problems. Turning away from the Athenian democracy that had executed Socrates, Plato tries to imagine a city with the right sort of people, able to discern goodness and willing to honor it appropriately. He describes the inner disposition that makes people good, the structure of a state in which good people will possess the most exalted position, and the populace that will understand that one justifies the other. The *Republic,* whose unity has been so often disputed, emerges as a remarkably coherent work once we read it within the context provided by the debate over *aretē* and by Socrates' fate.

Book I, as we have said, ends inconclusively. The sophist Thrasymachus has argued that far from being a case of *aretē,* justice is a feature exhibited by the weak and the foolish: much better to live unjustly, usurping power, grabbing whatever one wants, and satisfying one's desires whatever they may be. Socrates tries to refute Thrasymachus' claims, but his argument is not persuasive. At the beginning of Book II, therefore, Glaucon and Adeimantus, who profess to agree with Socrates that the life of justice is much better than the life of injustice, ask him to offer a complete and convincing defense of justice "in itself." Plato, then, undertakes to prove the radical thesis that it is better to live a just life even if, as it happens, one acquires a reputation for injustice and is punished for it (the case of the historical Socrates) than to live unjustly with all the rewards that life confers if one is lucky enough to escape detection. Justice, even totally undetected, brings happiness in its train; injustice, even completely unexposed, makes for a miserable life.

Plato believes that, independently of any political considerations, the just and the moral life guarantee happiness, and therefore people in their right mind will always choose them over any other alternative. But he also realizes how difficult it is to become virtuous within a degenerate state. Socrates, he had already intimated in his *Meno,* may have represented no more than a divine accident; and even in the *Republic* he has him argue that, in imperfect cities, the best natures are most prone to the greatest corruption and that it is only his own "divine sign," a mysterious voice that came to him from time to time, that allowed him to retain his integrity (496). The moral issue, therefore, is necessarily implicated in politics.

It is for this reason that the argument to prove that justice secures happiness begins, in the middle of Book II, by constructing a perfect state and explaining what makes that city just. Plato's conceit for taking this route is that since both cities and individuals are just, it will be easier to find out what justice is if we look for it in the greater of the two: Justice in the city is exactly like justice in the soul "writ large." The metaphor is brilliant and far from merely decorative.

Cities are necessary because people are not self-sufficient. Production is most efficient when individuals work only at what they can do best. Socrates designs his perfect city on the principle that people must engage only in the one activity for which they are naturally suited: "The work is better and is done more easily when each man works at the one craft for which nature fits him" (370). This crucial principle, suitably transformed, will eventually become the definition of justice.

The city contains three classes of people: artisans, who will satisfy its practical needs; "auxiliaries" who will be its professional military contingent; and guardians or rulers, who will make decisions concerning overall governance. Everyone in the city—men and women, as Plato insists—is exposed to the same educational system. The better one does, the higher one rises in the city's hierarchy, from artisan to auxiliary to guardian.

Plato's proposals for elementary education in Books II and III of the *Republic* have been rabidly denounced because of his ruthless censorship of the great poets, of Homer and Aeschylus, whose works are to provide the city's primers. Yet Plato's approach is perfectly justified. Blinded by the fact that children today are educated through books or television programs composed specifically for them, we see their specially designed, socially acceptable features as products of sensitive creation rather than violent excision. We overlook the fact that even if our means sometimes differ, our practice and goals are exactly the same as his.

It is true that our values are not always the same as Plato's, and we have less trust in the state. But, as surely as he did, we also censor children's educational material—and we do it on similar grounds: we too agree that the practice of "imitation" or representation, "if it is begun in youth and persisted in, leaves its impress upon character and nature, on body and voice and mind" (395). Bad models produce bad people. We even produce bowdlerized versions of the same Greek myths and poems he despises to sit beside our abbreviations of the Bible and Shakespeare. Despite our uncomprehending contempt for Plato's suspiciousness of "art," our elementary education is thoroughly Platonist.

Similar considerations apply to Plato's notorious proscription of poetry and dramatic festivals from the life of the adult citizens of his state. To us, this seems like an almost incomprehensible attack on "art" by one of the greatest artists in the world. But, whatever one reads on the subject, Plato never "banished the artists"—painting and sculpture remain within his city. His target was poetry, which he denounced as what it primarily was in his time, a popular entertainment. Poetry, he claimed, inevitably confuses its audience's ability to discriminate between reality and imitation, between authentic and fake; it is essentially suited for depicting vulgar and repulsive subjects: good characters do not make for good dramatic material; finally, it predisposes its audience, even "the best among us," by enjoying in imagination what it abhors in reality, to live in profoundly harmful ways. Scratch beneath the surface of all the attacks on the popular arts through the ages, from William Prynne's attack on the theater and on Shakespeare, to the Jansenists' abhorrence of the dramatic representation of religious events, to the despisers of novels whom Jane Austen satirized in *Northanger Abbey,* to the disdain for photography in the late nineteenth and early twentieth centuries, to the contemporary contempt for cinema and television, and you will find one or another version of Plato's arguments against poetry. Here, too, our common sense is the relic of Plato's idiosyncratic imagination—his ideas are our facts.

The structure of the perfect city (to return to the main argument) is established by the beginning of Book IV. Plato now tries to locate the virtues, particularly justice, within it. The city will be wise because its guardians or rulers administer its affairs. It is courageous because the auxiliaries discriminate correctly between what is and what is not to be feared. It is temperate, it exhibits "self-mastery," because the three classes are agreed on who is to rule and who is to obey within it. And, finally, the city is just because each class "attends to what belongs to it, each doing its own work" (434). Justice often refers to being satisfied with one's possessions, to not desiring what others have. No class in the city wants more than what naturally belongs to it, none attempts to usurp the prerogatives of the others. This is for Plato the definition of social justice.

But social justice is not Plato's ultimate goal. What he wants to show is that the just individual leads the happiest life. To make this point, he now draws an extraordinarily novel and influential analogy (influential enough to seem commonplace today) between the state and the individual "soul." Just as the state is composed of three classes, so, he argues in Book IV, the soul consists of three parts. One is the set of desires for basic needs like food, drink and sex; this "appetitive" element aims at its immediate satisfaction. It is often hindered in its pursuits by another part, which aims at the long-term satisfaction of the whole person or soul. Plato identifies this "calculating" element, which desires knowledge and can weigh the short- and long-term benefits of various courses of action, with reason. Finally, he establishes the existence of a third, "spirited" element, intermediate between the other two, motivated by ambition and focused on honor, and generally allied to reason. For the first time, the human individual is described in terms of a complex, structured hierarchy.

Appetitive desires can be generally satisfied with goods that can be bought. The appetitive element of the soul corresponds to the class of artisans in the city, the group which Plato often calls the "money-loving" class. Reason, which oversees the proper functioning of the whole person, is the analogue of the guardians who watch over the city as a whole. And the spirited element, a precursor of our own notion of the emotions, corresponds to the auxiliaries, who, aiming at honor, are trained to aid the guardians in their governing of the city.

On the basis of this analogy, Plato now argues that the virtues of the soul are parallel to the virtues of the city. An individual is just, he claims, "if the parts within him are doing severally their own work" (441). Reason, the seat of wisdom, should therefore rule the soul with the aid of the spirited element, in which courage resides, and both will keep the desiring element in check, hindering its blind pursuit of satisfaction, preventing it from acquiring mastery over the soul, and thus ensuring a life of temperance and self-control.

Plato's concept of justice as "psychic harmony," as the internal agreement of the parts of the soul about what each one of them should do, is not obviously equivalent to the common notion of justice: the latter involves respecting one's obligations, not stealing, cheating, or lying, and avoiding what is generally considered to be immoral behavior. Perhaps, it has been argued, psychic harmony can indeed ensure happiness; but Plato has to show that it is justice that accomplishes this end, and these two are far from the same. The objection is serious, but it can be answered.

Plato believes that people whose internal structure is in proper order, who care for their overall good and are neither extremely ambitious nor overwhelmingly acquisitive, will have no reason and no motive to behave, in the intuitive sense of the term, unjustly. Why should they, if under reason's rule they desire only what is good for them and what they can secure by means of their natural abilities? Furthermore, Plato believes that people will act justly in the intuitive sense only if they possess the psychic harmony he values so highly. If they lack psychic harmony, unbalanced desires will push them inevitably toward immoral behavior.

In the end, Plato defines justice as the healthy state of the soul. "People," Glaucon says, "think that when the constitution of the body is ruined life is not worth living, not with all the foods and drinks and wealth and dominion in the world; and are we to believe that, when the constitution of the very principle of our life is in confusion and ruin, life is then worth living, though a man do whatever he please?" (445).

In a serious sense, then, Plato has changed the subject. Aretē, exemplified by justice, has now become an internal affair. Real success consists not in ordinary accomplishments, not even in just behavior as commonly understood, but in an inner arrangement that places the desires of reason in charge of the whole personality. The preponderance of the lower, appetitive desires is now defined as a true disease of the soul. Plato believes that these desires, unless kept in constant check, cannot possibly be satisfied: they can only be indulged, and the more they are indulged, the stronger they become. The stronger they become, the less satisfaction we can derive from a life devoted to their pursuit. Injustice, as the lack of psychic harmony, is misery. Self-control, measure, and rationality ensure that one is an outstanding human being. And being outstanding is the most important element in being a happy person, a person who has the right desires and the ability to satisfy them.

How convincing is this view? Plato has claimed that a just person is a truly healthy person, and that no one would choose a diseased life over a healthy one. Diseases of the soul produce pains and displeasures more acute that diseases of the body. But something is missing from this argument—a robust and detailed representation of the healthy person and of the pleasures attending the psychically healthy life. The bulk of the central books of the *Republic* is devoted to constructing such an exemplar, and once again this means introducing politics into the picture.

Plato claims that his admittedly impractical reforms—in particular, the guardians' lack of personal possessions, their sharing of their spouses, male and female, and their ignorance of who their biological children are (449–473)—cannot possibly become reality unless an even more impractical reform is made. This is his famous proposal that "philosophers bear kingly rule in cities, or those who are now called kings and princes become genuine and adequate philosophers" (473).

However utopian Plato's ideal of the philosopher-kings still seems, we cannot begin to imagine how shocking the proposal must have appeared to its original audience. "Philosophy" has by now become a common word, even though its exact sense is still in dispute. This was not true in Plato's time. The *Republic* was a radically innovative effort to establish the term's legitimacy: it argues that the word corresponds to a genuine practice, which Plato introduces here for the first time. He describes a drastically new activity that leads to a previously unimagined way of life. He wages war against all the other institutions and activities—religion, poetry, traditional social wisdom, the new democratic politics, rhetoric, sophistry, and even the newly developed mathematical sciences—which claimed to provide people with good modes of living.

Plato elbows his way through these institutions, opens up a new space, establishes philosophy within it, and claims that philosophy leads to human perfection. The life of reason is both the life of justice as he has defined it so far and the happiest human life possible. The philosophical passion for knowledge and truth, which disdains every lower desire, emerges only after a long education through which self-control is acquired; it cannot be distinguished from the ability to rule oneself; and the ability to rule oneself is the best qualification for the responsibility of ruling the city. The pursuit of knowledge makes one the best possible human being; the best possible human being, who also is the ruler in the right state, occupies the most exalted position within it. Philosophy and psychic harmony are one. They ensure the health of the soul and the happiness of the person. In the perfect state they are accompanied by the duty to rule. The perfect person is the perfect citizen. Socrates' successors can never share his fate.

Plato finds philosophy as difficult to explain as he considers it, once explained, demanding to practice. Books V to VII outline its nature and the education that can lead a few capable people to its practice. They consist of a combination of complex arguments and striking images.

Philosophy for Plato consists essentially in the belief that the world possesses an intelligible nature distinct from the sensible appearances with which we are generally acquainted. The intelligible is more real and more valuable than the sensible, and it is the object of any knowledge we can ever have. Philosophers, especially from their training in mathematics, understand that the objects of knowledge are only illustrated, but never understood, through their sensible representations. As a result of their education, they eventually become aware of the existence of the Forms, of the single intelligible essences that underlie and give substance to the multiple, changing sensible phenomena that surround us. Any doubts about the existence of an intelligible world or of a set of objective, absolute truths regarding it are incompatible with philosophy: they are at the other side of the line that separates philosophy from sophistry. Even today, when those suspicious of the notion that truth is objective claim to be philosophers, they strike a false note: the key is still given by the *Republic*.

The features of philosophy as Plato understands it are difficult to explain to others. In one of his most famous images, he compares our life to that of prisoners in a cave, able to see only shadows of objects projected on its back wall. He writes that as most of us are incapable of realizing that we are only seeing shadows, we are even less able to imagine that there is a whole world of real objects outside the cave altogether. No wonder that philosophers, when they try to explain what they have seen there, become the subjects of ridicule (514–518).

It takes fifty years for philosophers finally to understand the greatest of the Forms, the Form of the Good. This mysterious object, which Plato says is to Forms what the sun is to sensible objects (508), represents the perfection of the intelligible structure of the world, and the fact that all within it is arranged for the best. Full understanding of the Good results in a fully good person, a person whose reason, by means of its understanding, has acquired complete control over the soul's baser needs and desires. Only the philosophers therefore are perfectly just, and thus perfectly happy. Knowledge, goodness, and happiness are one, though they can only be achieved by a very few people. The rest are to allow themselves to be ruled by these few in order to come as close as possible to the good life (590).

The philosophers are capable of seeing the world in its total perfection and also the place within it of each one of us, depending on our character and ability. They are therefore capable of telling the rest of the people in the city what life is best for them, and how they can attain the maximum psychic harmony of which they are capable. Plato's identification of knowledge with goodness represents a rationalism of the most extreme sort. Is it also as authoritarian as it is often taken to be? This question is more complex.

The fundamental assumption on which Plato's system depends is an image of living a life as practicing a craft, as a process that proceeds by definitive rules and whose product depends on how well its rules are applied. To put the point bluntly, just as we willingly take the advice of shoemakers on the most appropriate shoes, so, he believes, we should be willing to take the advice of the philosophers on what life is best for us. The image of life as a craft is, to say the least, profoundly questionable. But it is not clear that any other general image of what life is like is obviously better than Plato's. Today we believe in the value of freedom, even if it results in the gravest of errors. He was unwilling to sacrifice happiness, even if it meant renouncing autonomy. The issue is still open, and the *Republic* continues to invite us to consider it.

Plato's text also raises a host of other problems. It may be true that in the individual case, devotion to contemplation is not easily distinguished from justice conceived as psychic harmony: a life of contemplation involves the harmony of one's various desires. But in the case of the city as a whole, the analogy fails. For it is no longer clear that the philosophers' contemplation of the Forms is compatible with their role as rulers. Why should the philosophers, whose best activity and happiest life consist in the contemplation of the Forms, return to the public life required of the rulers of the city? If contemplation and justice as psychic harmony are one, would we not commit an injustice if we took them away from the one activity for which they are best suited? Is Plato conceding this point when he writes that we must "compel" them to become guardians (521), that this is not something they will do willingly?

But the *Republic* would not be the work it is if it were not full of problems of this sort. On one level, it clearly leaves its readers with many more questions than answers. On another, deeper level, however, it is a book that, for better or worse, we cannot do without. It is here that the idea originates that social accomplishments do not secure happiness or even real success, unless they are moral accomplishments recognized by a society of the right sort. And it is here that the power of reason to create such a society, on the basis of an understanding of the real nature of the world, is announced for the first time and established once and for all.

It is in the *Republic* that, along with Nietzsche, we should seek in order to "comprehend what idiosyncracy begot that Socratic equation of reason, virtue, and happiness." For Nietzsche, this was the "most bizarre of all equations." Perhaps it is, and perhaps it is not. In any case, this equation describes much of the structure of our lives. And it is worth recalling that it does not represent a fact of nature but was first presented by Plato, through argument and metaphor, through demonstration and image, in the *Republic*. Whatever one's misgivings about it (and one can have many), it can no longer simply be dismissed. It is part of us. Because of the *Republic*, Plato—to use again, in closing, Auden's words—"is no more a man to us / but a whole / climate of opinion." Climates of opinion can change: they can be improved or they can be discarded. In either case, they must first be understood. There is no better place to start understanding our own than this work in which Plato's admiration of Socrates blossomed into an image of a world in which, unlike ancient Athens, Socrates has been forever safe.

NOTES

1. Immanuel Kant, *Critique of Pure Reason,* trans. F. Max Müller (Garden City, N.Y., 1966), A316/B373.

2. K. R. Popper, *The Open Society and Its Enemies,* vol. 1: *The Spell of Plato* (New York, 1962), 106.

Sixteen

THE *PHAEDRUS*

GENERAL REMARKS

ODYSSEUS HAD NEVER WANTED to take part in the Greek expedition against Troy that is the subject of Homer's *Iliad:* strange and dangerous things often happen away from home. He pretended to be mad, but the great trickster was himself tricked by Palamedes into admitting his sanity and joining the departing armies.[1] Odysseus, however, may have been right not to want to leave Ithaca. None of the Greek heroes met with so many troubles and strange adventures, and none was absent as long as Odysseus, who spent twenty years abroad before finally returning home.

In the *Phaedrus,* Plato strikes an unusual variation on the theme of leaving home—of abandoning, even for a short while, the surroundings to which one is accustomed. We know from another of his dialogues, the *Crito,* that Socrates never left Athens for any reason except military service; he even refused to attend festivals that were held in the countryside, and he had no desire to know what life in other cities was like (*Crito* 52d). Phaedrus himself remarks here that Socrates is totally out of place (*atopōtatos*) in the country: "Not only do you never travel abroad," he says; "as far as I can tell, you never even set foot beyond the city walls" (230d).

But Socrates *has* set foot beyond the city walls on this occasion. The *Phaedrus* is the only Platonic dialogue in which Socrates leaves the city in order to engage in philosophical conversation.[2] And even though he only takes a short walk in the country, what happens to him is in a way stranger than any of Odysseus' adventures. Odysseus, after all, survived the dangers and monsters he faced by staying the same, by acting as he always had before: with craftiness, wiliness, courage, and prudence. But Socrates seems to become almost a different person once he leaves Athens. Odysseus met external enemies: strange gods, weird monsters, unknown peoples. Socrates, who claims that, not "knowing himself," he wonders whether he is "a beast more complicated and savage than Typho, or . . . a tamer, simpler animal with a share in a divine and gentle nature,"[3] discovers by the banks of the river Ilisus parts of himself he had never known before. The "monsters" he meets, though not malevolent, come from within.

Why, then, does he leave? Because Phaedrus, cast here in a role a bit like that of Palamedes, tricks him into abandoning his usual urban haunts.[4]

More accurately, Phaedrus lures him outside the city with the promise that he will read to him a speech on love (*erōs*) that Lysias, the great orator of the final years of the fifth century B.C., had just composed. Socrates, who confesses that he is "sick with passion for hearing speeches" and calls himself "a lover of speeches" (228b–c), tells Phaedrus that he would follow him to the ends of the earth in order to hear what Lysias has to say on the topic (227d). And so the two friends look for a place in the country where they can listen to the speech in comfort and quiet.

Odysseus pretended to be mad in order to stay home and survived abroad by the powers of his reason. Socrates, who is the embodiment of reason in Athens, seems to lose his composure, if not his mind, the moment he leaves the city. His uncharacteristically lyrical praise of the spot where they have chosen to sit stuns Phaedrus. Socrates replies that the promise of hearing the speech has worked magic on him; like a donkey marching endlessly in fruitless pursuit of feed dangled in front of its nose, he will follow Phaedrus wherever he goes as long as he is carrying Lysias' speech (229b–230e).[5]

The very idea that the prospect of listening to a speech would have such an effect on Socrates is surprising; it should alert us to the exceptional nature of the situation portrayed in this dialogue. Socrates, as Plato pictures him, has never been "a lover of speeches." On the contrary, he has consistently expressed his aversion to long discourses. Throughout the dialogues, he insists that he can only discuss matters by means of the short question-and-answer method we know as the elenchus: he can neither make nor indeed understand long speeches (see, e.g., *Protagoras* 334c–335c, *Gorgias* 449b–c, 461d–462a). In the *Phaedrus,* however, he not only listens avidly to Lysias' speech; he also criticizes it and even produces two long speeches of his own, one of which, the second or "Great Speech" (243e–257b), is one of the most famous rhetorical accomplishments of classical Greece.

What has happened to change Socrates so radically? His own explanation is that he has come to be possessed by the gods and spirits that inhabit the enchanted place where he and Phaedrus have found themselves: the speeches he makes, he insists again and again, are not his own creations but theirs (235c–d, 238d, 241e–242a, 262c–d). Of course Socrates in the *Phaedrus* and in these other works is Plato's own creation. And the question we need to ask is not primarily why Socrates is behaving so strangely in this case, but rather why Plato has taken his very urban and rational Socrates and made him willing to leave Athens, vulnerable to possession by the nymphs (*numpholēptos,* 238d) and by the gods (*enthousiazōn,* 241e) and capable of composing such magnificent orations. For, in the process, Plato has himself produced one of the strangest dialogues he ever wrote. The whole of the *Phaedrus,* no less than Socrates or the magical place where its action takes place, is an unending source of enchantment, of unexpected situations, of puzzlement and speculation.

Though the *Phaedrus* is one of Plato's greatest and most widely read dialogues, its structure constitutes a perennial subject of debate. Since later antiquity, its central subject has commonly been taken to be the way in which love leads to philosophy—the subject of Socrates' second speech. After all, Plato had already addressed that very idea in the *Symposium*, another work consisting almost entirely of speeches; and the *Phaedrus*, with its three speeches on love, is commonly taken as its companion piece. Our interest in the *Phaedrus* often centers on the question of how the metaphysics, epistemology, and psychology of the *Republic*, which was written after the *Symposium* and in all probability before the *Phaedrus*, affect the view of *erōs* presented in the latter work.[6] And the magnificence of Socrates' Great Speech, which is a panegyric on love and quite overwhelms the rest of the work, makes it difficult to believe that anything other than *erōs* could be Plato's central topic. But if the speeches contain Plato's main topic, why does the long discussion of rhetoric that follows them never address their substance? If love is the main theme of the *Phaedrus*, why is it forgotten in the dialogue's second half?

In order to be able to address the question of the structure of the *Phaedrus* as a whole, we must first make some remarks about the nature of its parts.

The *Phaedrus* is an account of a conversation between Socrates and Phaedrus. It is impossible to pinpoint the "dramatic date" of the work, that is, the time when the conversation is supposed to have taken place. In fact, there does not seem to have been a time when this meeting between Phaedrus and Socrates could have occurred. Because of his alleged involvement in the notorious mutilation of the statues of the god Hermes, Phaedrus was exiled from Athens from 415, when the crime was committed, until 403 B.C. The conversation cannot have occurred between 403 and 399 B.C., when Socrates was executed, since there is a strong indication that Sophocles and Euripides, who both died in 406 B.C., are still alive when the action of the dialogue takes place (268c). It is also unlikely to have occurred any earlier than 415, before Phaedrus' exile, because Lysias, whose company Phaedrus has just left as the dialogue opens, lived abroad in the city of Thurii in Italy for a number of years and returned to Athens only in 412, after Phaedrus had already left.

We can be a little more positive about the *Phaedrus'* date of composition: that is, the time when Plato actually wrote the dialogue. It seems to be later than the *Republic*, close to the *Parmenides*, and earlier than the *Sophist*.[7] Although, like most efforts to date Plato's works, this view partly depends on speculation, we can say with some confidence that the *Phaedrus* was written between 375 and 365 B.C., at the time when Plato was entering the third phase of his philosophical development, following his early, Socratic period and his middle phase, which is associated with the flourishing of the theory of Forms as most people know it today.

The *Phaedrus* is a dialogue in the most literal sense. Unlike a number of others of Plato's works, it is a conversation between two and only two people.[8] Phaedrus, who is a mature man when this conversation is supposed to have taken place,[9] is portrayed as a great admirer of Lysias in particular and of rhetoric in general. Though a friend of Socrates, he seems to have little appreciation or understanding of Socrates' approach to life and thought. He loves rhetoric, but he seems to think of it as a contest aiming to produce a more novel or comprehensive speech than one's opponent that ends only when one of the contestants is forced to give up (see 243d, 257c). His attitude toward philosophy is not unlike his approach to rhetoric. Though he thinks that life would be unbearable without the pleasures of philosophical conversation (258e), it is not clear that he understands the profound effect that philosophical ideas can have on one's life. Socrates' Great Speech may in fact be intended to convince him, as far as a man of his character can be convinced on that issue, that philosophy is life's most serious activity.

Socrates describes Phaedrus as a "begetter" of speeches (261a). His description is justified by Phaedrus' eagerness to memorize Lysias' speech, by his insistence that Socrates compete with Lysias with speeches of his own, and by the fact that the idea of praising *erōs* in the *Symposium,* where Phaedrus is characterized as "the father of the subject," was originally his own. But Phaedrus' seriousness does not match his enthusiasm. Socrates makes a great effort to get Phaedrus to realize that rhetoric must be pursued with a regard for the truth of what one is talking about. And since truth is what we get to know through philosophy, Socrates argues that philosophy is a necessary element in the rhetorician's art. In addition, Socrates wants him to understand that rhetoric and philosophy, whether in oral or written form, are not simply means of urbane entertainment but efforts to establish views according to which life can be led. Whether Phaedrus learns either lesson in the course of his conversation with Socrates remains an open question at the end of the dialogue.

PART ONE: INTRODUCTION AND SPEECHES (227A–257B)

The *Phaedrus* falls naturally into two parts. The first (227a–257b) consists of an introductory conversation and three speeches on *erōs*.

The kind of love addressed by the three speeches is almost exclusively love between men—a central feature in the life of the ancient Greeks in general and the Athenians in particular.[10] Today, such relationships are often called "homosexual," but the term should be used with care. "Homosexuality" usually denotes an exclusive sexual preference for members of one's own sex and, often, a particular style of life that revolves around it. In ancient Athens, however, though there were men who lived exclusively with other men, as we learn, for example, in regard to Pausanias and Agathon in the *Symposium* (193b–c),[11] most paederastic relationships were different from what we now consider homosexual affairs.

It was a common though by no means a universally approved practice in ancient Athens for older men to fall in love with young, usually adolescent, boys. Such a difference in age, which may or may not form part of homosexual relationships, was essential to paederasty. In addition, paederasty did not in general interfere with marriage or other relationships with women. The older man (*erastēs*) would most often already be married, while the younger one (*erōmenos*) would be expected to marry when he reached the appropriate age.

In paederastic affairs, the boy was expected not to give in easily to his admirer, who was in turn expected to engage in passionate and extravagant gestures of love and devotion. Even if the boy was finally won over, it was not expected that the sexual encounter would bring him great pleasure— at least it was expected that he would not show signs of being pleased too readily. What was expected was that the *erastēs* would act as an ethical and intellectual teacher of his *erōmenos*. What the two participants thus took from their relationship was, at least in theory, radically different: the older man received pleasure; the younger, education and edification. Paederasty was in many cases an instrument of socialization and teaching.

In his speech (230d–234c), Lysias focuses on this aspect of paederastic relationships and turns it around to his own paradoxical purposes. The speaker urges a young boy to accept him as a lover precisely because the older man is not in love with him, and argues that in general someone who does not love a boy will be better for him, as a friend and teacher, than someone who does. The central idea of the speech is that love makes men passionate while it lasts, but, once it is gone, makes them at best indifferent to, at worst enemies of, their earlier loves. By contrast, a man who enters into a sexual relationship with a boy without love does so "with no thought of immediate pleasure; [he] will plan instead for the benefits that are to come, since [he] is master of [himself] and [has] not been overwhelmed by love" (233b–c). Nonlovers, the speaker argues, are much more likely to become and remain friends (*philoi*). The whole speech depends on an exaggerated interpretation of the utilitarian aspects of paederasty: the basic premise is that if education and long-lasting friendship are the goals of such relationships, nonlovers are much more likely to secure them for boys than are lovers. The speaker paradoxically appears to renounce *erōs* (which involves passionate sexual desire) as a ploy to gain sexual favors.

Lysias' speech, which turns all accepted ideas about paederasty on their head, is what is known as an "epideictic" speech. Epideictic speeches were exhibition works. They were intended to show what a speech writer was capable of doing even with an unpromising subject. They often functioned as advertisements for their authors' talents. The more unusual the position supported, and the better argued it was, the better the advertisement. Phaedrus clearly thinks of Lysias' speech as an immense accomplishment, and is eager to have Socrates agree with his view.

Socrates, though, will have none of it. He claims that the speech is both crudely constructed and repetitive. The fact that he is willing to criticize the speech at all, instead of pleading, as usual, ignorance of rhetoric, is already surprising enough. But this is only the first of many surprising events in this work. The next is about to occur.

Socrates has already indicated that he finds himself in an unusually inspired state (234d). He now claims that he has heard much better speeches on the same topic. He is not sure whether they are the work of Sappho or Anacreon (the great early love poets of ancient Greece) or of some other author. But he is sure of the following: "My breast is full," he tells Phaedrus, "and I feel I can make a different speech, even better than Lysias'. Now I am well aware that none of these ideas can have come from me—I know my own ignorance. The only other possibility, I think, is that I was filled, like an empty jar, by the words of other people streaming in through my ears" (235c–d). Though he does not completely deny his ignorance, Socrates claims, for once in all of Plato's work, to be able to deliver a speech.[12]

So an inspired Socrates, though unwilling to accept full responsibility for what he is about to say, proceeds to make his own speech on Lysias' subject (237b–241d). He begins with a definition of love as an irrational impulse that overpowers our desire to do what is right and attracts us inescapably to beauty. On the basis of this definition and a stark contrast between reason, which desires the good, and irrational impulse, which seeks pleasure and gratification, he argues that the lover is bound to be harmful to the boys he pursues. *Erōs* is a kind of madness, and all madness—especially the madness of love—must be avoided at all costs: it will destroy the soul as well as the body of the boy; it will consume his property, provoke his disgust, and ultimately leave him without a friend and protector. Socrates' speech is a direct counterpart to Lysias'; all that Socrates leaves out is the complementary argument that the nonlover is beneficial. His speech, that is, stops short before the explicit attempt at seduction.

In this way, Socrates produces a counterepideictic speech and makes an implicit claim to have beaten the orator at his own game. This, naturally, is a very peculiar situation, since Lysias is one of the great orators of the time, while Socrates officially disavows any knowledge of rhetoric. We must therefore keep in mind the question of what it is that Plato is trying to suggest by having Socrates outdo Lysias even though Socrates claims to have no knowledge of rhetoric as such knowledge was understood at the time.

But Socrates' victory is hollow. Deeply dissatisfied with his performance, he claims that his "divine sign" (see *Apology* 31c–d) has let him know that he should not leave the place where he and Phaedrus have found themselves before he makes amends for a very grave error on his part. What is that error? It is the very speech he has just given—even though he had earlier claimed that the speech was not his own but something he had heard from others, perhaps even the product of divine inspiration. Socrates, that is, acknowledges that he is far from completely free of responsibility for what is wrong with his speech. And what is wrong with the speech is that it attacks *erōs* because, being a kind of madness, it is worse than and cannot be preferred to any rational state of mind. Socrates' first speech, therefore, is an argument to the effect that *erōs* is an evil to be avoided—an argument that represents a conventional (if playful) stance in early Greek love poetry.

Socrates, however, is now faced with the feeling that his first speech was blasphemous, since *erōs* is a god or at least something divine (242e) and cannot therefore be bad in any of the ways his speech had asserted.[13] In an exchange full of religious and mythological allusions, he recants his earlier speech and claims that he cannot absolve himself unless he makes another speech, this time in praise of *erōs* (241d–243e).

Socrates' second speech is for many of Plato's readers the centerpiece of the *Phaedrus*.[14] The speech is a magnificent, imaginative construction; it leaves the two that precede it so far behind that it is sometimes difficult even to remember that they actually form part of the dialogue. The first two speeches recount the disadvantages of *erōs* when it comes to capturing the affections of a boy. The Great Speech is a hymn to the indispensability of *erōs* for human life as a whole. The other speeches consist of playful arguments seeking love while denying it; they are firmly located within the world of everyday life. The third speech constructs, by means of argument and myth, a grandiose and apparently serious picture of the human soul and its fate, both when it is embodied and when, free of the body, it travels across the heavens in the company of the Olympian gods. *Erōs*, as Socrates had argued in his earlier speech, still turns out to be a kind of madness, but madness is no longer assumed to be necessarily bad. On the contrary, Socrates now credits it with some of the greatest gifts with which human life is blessed. *Erōs* emerges as the moving force behind the best possible human life. And as we might well expect when Plato addresses the question of the best human life, that life turns out to be the life of the philosophers. As in the *Symposium, erōs* leads to philosophy. But in contrast to the *Symposium,* where its irrational aspects receive little if any notice, in the *Phaedrus erōs* is primarily a madness—a madness, moreover, that enables us to live in a truly rational manner. The paradoxical conclusions of the earlier speeches are swept aside by the far greater paradox presented in this praise of love: Losing one's mind is a prerequisite for truly finding it and for living according to the values reason dictates. But the speech, as we shall eventually see, is not without its own playful side; Socrates, in fact, describes it by that term himself at 268c.

Socrates begins his speech with the claim that madness, which he had classified as an evil in his first speech, is much more complex than he had allowed there. Many benefits, he argues, come to us through madness; he mentions the importance of the madness of prophets and seers, the madness that sometimes presages absolution from family curses, and the madness of poets (244a–245b). He then leaves this topic and turns to a proof of the immortality of the human soul; the soul, he argues, is a self-moving thing and the principle of motion for everything else. But the principle of motion must be ever-moving: if it ever stopped, everything else would also come to a stop; and if the soul were to start moving again, it would have to do so by means of some further principle—which would show that it was not a principle after all. And since life and motion go hand in hand, the soul, ever-moving as it is, is also ever-living (245b–246a).

At this point, Socrates abandons the logical style he has used in his proof of the soul's immortality and produces what he explicitly describes as a simile (cf. *eoiketō,* 246a) for its structure. He likens the soul to a winged two-horse chariot driven by a charioteer. The teams that correspond to the souls of the gods (or perhaps to the gods themselves) are in perfect internal harmony.[15] But in all other cases the charioteer has an uneasy relationship with his horses. One of them is docile and obedient, while the other is wild and (so to speak) has a mind of its own. The winged soul lives by itself, independently of body. But when souls lose their wings, they fall downward from heaven and enter bodies, to which they impart motion and life: such complexes of body and soul constitute what we call mortal animals (246a–d).

The chariots of the gods, each followed by the souls that are the god's natural companions, travel around heaven and regularly see from its outer rim a "place beyond" that it is impossible to describe accurately: "What is in this place is without color and without shape and without solidity, a being that really is what it is, the subject of all true knowledge, visible only to intelligence, the soul's steersman" (247c). Reason, which is what the charioteer stands for in Plato's simile, is nourished by this otherwise invisible being, which includes true justice, true self-control, true knowledge, and all the other objects that in his middle dialogues Plato had called the Forms and that constitute the world's real and ultimate structure.

But while the gods circle the outer rim of the heavens without trouble, the crowds of the lesser souls that follow them are fighting with one another for a glimpse of the place beyond heaven's rim and of the beings that would nourish them. Their view is therefore partial. Some, indeed, succeed in seeing enough to remain aloft. Many, undernourished as they are, have their wings broken as they jostle one another in their effort to rise above heaven. Without wings, they fall earthward, enter human bodies, and lead different lives, in accordance with how much contact they had with the Forms while they were still disembodied. Those who had the best view become philosophers, lovers of beauty, cultivated people, or devotees of erotic love. Those who saw the least become tyrants—rulers of cities who, according to the eighth and ninth books of the *Republic,* are the most contemptible human beings because they are slaves to desires that are in fact impossible to satisfy.

There thus begins a cycle of reincarnation that lasts for ten thousand years—it takes that long, Socrates says, for the soul to grow its wings again. The only exception is provided by those souls that choose the life of a philosopher or of the right sort of lover of boys who combines *erōs* with philosophy: these souls can return to the heavens after three reincarnations and within three thousand years. The others keep choosing new lives every thousand years, sometimes going from human to beast, sometimes the other way around. The most important factor in this cycle is how much the disembodied soul had seen of the Forms while it was traveling around heaven. The more one has seen, the more truly human one is. For to be truly human is to think abstractly, and abstract thought is nothing but "the recollection of the things a soul saw when it was traveling with gods, when it disregarded the things we now call real and lifted up its head to what is truly real instead" (249b). Such recollection, which Plato had discussed in the *Meno* and in the *Phaedo,* is precisely the activity of philosophers. Philosophers have little regard for merely human affairs; they live, so to speak, in another world; everyone else therefore thinks that they are mad instead of realizing that they are the most sane and perfect of human beings (246d–249d).

The reference to the apparent madness of philosophers brings Socrates back to his original account of the benefits of madness in general. He now introduces a fourth kind of madness—the kind "which someone shows when he sees the beauty we have down here and is reminded of true beauty," the Form of Beauty in the place beyond heaven. This is the madness of love (249d). Recollection, he says, is very hard: our souls have seen little of the Forms, whose images on the earth are very indistinct. But there is one glorious exception—Beauty. Beauty "was radiant" when our souls traveled the heavens; and, unlike the other Forms, its earthly images enter our soul through vision, the sharpest of our senses, and are therefore much stronger than those of the rest. What counts as an image of Beauty? Socrates' answer is clear: In the best case, it is a beautiful boy who is no longer an object of value simply in himself but is also a reminder of the true Beauty that nourishes our soul and provides, eventually, a way out of the circle of reincarnation.

Those people who retain enough of their memory of Beauty are so taken with the boy's beauty that they are ready to worship him as a god. Their souls' wings begin to grow again. Plato uses a protracted metaphor, describing sexual excitement and the general agitation that overtakes a man in love in terms of the soul's feathers growing, swelling, and piercing their covering. The man literally loses his mind. He is willing to do anything for the boy he loves, to give up everything, to follow him wherever he goes, and to sleep at his doorstep—even if it is merely to catch a fleeting glimpse of him.

Erōs, then, is losing one's mind to Beauty. It is superficially directed at the boy, but the ultimate driving force behind it is the recollection of and the desire to possess again the Beauty that the soul saw during its disembodied travels. Moreover, Beauty itself is a proxy for the rest of the Forms, which it helps us recollect, however imperfectly, and which it makes us desire all the more. The earthly images of Beauty, the beautiful boys who were treated in such a cavalier fashion in the previous two speeches, now turn out to be our closest link to immortality and to a life that, by devoting itself to the recollection of the Forms, is our best road back to that blessed state: the stakes have been radically raised (249d–253c).

But *erōs* is not easy. Falling in love with a boy does not by itself guarantee that one will become a philosopher. The complexity of the soul, which is represented in Plato's simile by the charioteer and his two horses and recalls in many details the tripartition of the soul in the fourth book of the *Republic* (and its further elaboration in books eight and nine), explains why people react so differently to sexual and erotic desire. The charioteer (reason) and the obedient horse (the "spirited" element of the *Republic*, whose goal is honor) work together; but the second horse, which represents the appetitive part, works against them. While the first two hold themselves back from treating the boy improperly, the wild horse keeps pulling the whole soul forward and close to the boy so that it can accomplish its own goal—sexual pleasure.

Socrates describes the conflict in the soul in detailed and moving terms. In the process, Plato offers a highly revisionary account of paederasty. According to this account, sexual gratification is the goal neither of the boy nor, much more surprisingly, of the *erastēs*. Plato admits that most often, of course, the lover gives in to the wild horse and uses the boy only for his pleasure. But in a few cases, after a long and painful struggle, the wild horse is subdued. The lover now respects the boy and approaches him only in the proper manner, as a good friend. The boy gradually begins to be attracted by the older man and his obvious good will; and as they spend more and more time together, he in turn begins to fall in love with the man. But his love, Socrates points out, is not really love for the man himself, who, after all, does not even have to be beautiful. Rather, it is (though the boy does not know this) love for his own image reflected back at him through his lover's eyes: he too, then begins to fall in love with the image of Beauty he himself constitutes and therefore, indirectly, with Beauty itself.

Even companionship of the best sort, however, brings the two lovers in close physical contact, and the wild horse once again asserts its need and desire. Socrates describes two outcomes. The lovers may overpower their appetite completely and spend their time together chastely devoted to philosophy—that is, to the effort to recollect and understand the nature of true Beauty, Justice, Virtue, and the other Forms. If this is how they live, he claims, they will die happy and have to face only two more reincarnations of the same sort before their souls are liberated from their bonds to mortal body and return to heaven. But some lovers may be weaker than the previous pair. They may give in to their sexual urges and consummate their love affair in a way that, for Plato, is far from ideal. But it need not be too far: provided that sex is not the main goal of their relationship and that they treat each other properly in a serious and long-lasting friendship, there is a good chance that, upon their death, they will begin a longer but ultimately successful voyage back to the disembodied state that, Socrates argues here, constitutes human perfection (253c–256e).

The central idea of Lysias' speech was that lovers cannot be trusted to secure for boys the long-term advantages that were supposed to make paederastic affairs worthwhile. Socrates' first speech described the lover as a madman, distasteful and embarrassing in the short term, changeable and unreliable thereafter. In both cases the idea was that love itself interferes with paederasty, if the point of paederasty, as was widely assumed, was to socialize the boy into the life of a well-to-do Athenian citizen who was serious about his obligations toward his family, his friends, and his city.

Socrates' second speech looks far beyond such issues. Though love is still a madness, it is not the madness brought about when base desire overcomes reason (cf. 238b–c); rather, it is the result of the recollection of Beauty and of the other Forms that, however much we desire them, we cannot ever fully possess while we are still embodied. Love is a madness produced by an unsatisfiable rational desire to understand the ultimate truth about the world, prompted in the first instance by the desire to possess true Beauty. It is a madness sparked by a vision of truth and leading to its clearer apprehension; it is the madness of philosophy. *Erōs* is indispensable to paederasty because it provides the only entry into its real purpose: helping oneself and one's beloved to recall what the soul had seen in its travels around the heavens. And since that is the world of the Forms, which is the true object of knowledge, a good paederastic relationship is, for Plato, equivalent to the life of philosophy itself. The rewards of paederasty have nothing to do, as in the previous speeches, either with sexual pleasure or with worldly advantages; instead, they bring about a final liberation from "this thing we are carrying around now, which we call a body, locked in it like an oyster in its shell" (250c) and a return to the blissful existence of a well-balanced soul in its disembodied state.[16] Love moves the soul to the stars (cf. *Timaeus* 41e–42d).

It was important to give this brief outline of the views Plato has Socrates express in this speech, flat and inadequate as such an outline is bound to be, because so many of these views seem to correspond, as we have already said, to ideas Plato had presented in a number of dialogues earlier than the *Phaedrus*. Thus, the idea that *erōs* is really a mechanism of philosophy had already been presented in the *Symposium*. The theory that knowledge, particularly the knowledge of Forms, is recollection formed part of the *Meno* and the *Phaedo*. The theory of the divided soul, which was absent from the *Symposium*, became crucial in the *Republic*. The theory of Forms, introduced through an account of love and Beauty in the *Symposium*, was integral to the *Phaedo* and the *Republic*.[17] And the notion that the Form of Beauty is the most beautiful object in the world, the idea of "paradigmatism" according to which each Form is the perfect exemplar of the property for which it stands, is central to the metaphysics and epistemology of all these middle works. But in the *Phaedrus* these ideas are embedded in a highly rhetorical speech that Socrates will, in fact, later attempt to disown. A reading of the entire dialogue, therefore, must ask what attitude Plato is taking here toward the theories he had presented in these earlier works. This question is connected to the more general issue of the structure and unity of the *Phaedrus* as a whole.

PART TWO: DISCUSSION OF RHETORIC AND WRITING (257B–279C)

The second part of the *Phaedrus* treats in dialogue form issues concerning the principles of rhetorical composition supposedly raised by the speeches of the first. But the discussion addresses rhetoric in purely formal terms. Socrates and Phaedrus consider the proper composition of speeches, the knowledge that the good orator must possess, the relationship between rhetoric and philosophy, and the advantages and disadvantages of writing speeches in particular and of writing in general. *Erōs,* which was the subject

of all three speeches and which assumed nothing less than cosmic importance in Socrates' Great Speech, is forgotten. How can we account for this
strange fact?

That the second part of the *Phaedrus* is silent on *erōs* is strange, however,
only if we assume that love is the *Phaedrus'* central topic. We have already
said that this assumption has been often made, even by Plato's ancient
readers, who gave the *Phaedrus* such subtitles as "Of the Beautiful" and
"Of Love and of the Mind." But as Friedrich Schleiermacher observed as
early as 1836, "the superadded titles of this dialogue . . . have been understood almost universally in indicating the true subject of it, have been
translated and used in quotations, though love and beauty appear only in
one part of the work, and could not, therefore, to an unprejudiced person,
obtain as the true and proper subject of it."[18] And Schleiermacher goes on
to argue, quite correctly, that not only is it impossible that the particular
question of whether boys should favor men who do not love them over
those who do could

> have been in Plato's mind the main-subject matter . . . but not even love in
> general. For in either case this beautiful work, worked up as it evidently is
> with the greatest pains, would appear deformed in a most revolting manner,
> utterly contravening the maxim that it must be fashioned like a living crea-
> ture, having a body proportioned to the mind, with parts also in due propor-
> tion [cf. 264c]. For the whole of the second half would then be nothing but
> an appendage strangely tacked on, and not even tolerably well fitted. (Schle-
> iermacher 49)

Schleiermacher himself believes that the true subject matter of the *Phaedrus* is philosophy itself and that the dialogue (which he believed to be the
first Plato ever composed)[19] is a blueprint for the philosophical edifice
Plato already had in mind to construct. This is difficult to accept. What
seems more reasonable, as we shall see in more detail below, is to suppose
that the main subject of the dialogue is rhetoric—its nature, the proper
way of pursuing it, if any, and its relation to philosophy. On such a reading,
the three speeches that form its first part turn out to be examples Plato
puts forward in order to support the conclusions he reaches in the second.
Taking the speeches as examples of rhetorical structure explains why *erōs*
does not appear in the subsequent discussion. Plato is more interested in
what the speeches show about the practice of rhetoric than in what they
reveal about the nature of love. But it also allows us to explain (as we
must) why, among so many other possible subjects, Plato chose to compose his sample speeches on the topic of *erōs*. Neither their form nor their
subject will appear random any longer.

Collectively, the speeches represent situations that were relatively common in the competitive atmosphere within which rhetoric grew in classical

Athens.[20] If we take the first two, the speech of Lysias and Socrates' first effort, as a pair, we see that they both argue for a similar conclusion: Lovers are harmful. The two speeches represent a contest as to who, Lysias or Socrates/Plato, can compose a better speech on the very same topic. If, on the other hand, we group Socrates' two speeches together, we can see them as an instance of the commonplace fact that trained orators were able (and proud of their ability) to speak impressively on both sides of every issue. Does this then mean that Socrates must believe that the two speeches are equally convincing? Not if we accept his own suggestion (262d, 265c–266a) that the two are really a single long oration, in which a bad kind of love is distinguished from a good kind. In that case, the speeches would only appear to give equal support to contradictory views; in reality they would be compatible with each other and both would contain a measure of truth, the first no less than the second.[21] Combining the speeches, and attributing to *erōs* a complexity beyond the farthest reaches of Lysias' imagination, thus gives Socrates an overall victory against his opponent.

But even if the speeches are formally connected with one another in these ways, the question of their subject still remains unanswered. If they are intended only as examples for the subsequent discussion of rhetoric, we need to ask why Plato chose *erōs* as his exemplary theme. Is his choice of love completely random? How could it be, given that it is a subject to which he had already attributed such crucial importance in the *Symposium* and which, in the *Phaedrus*, enables him to introduce so many of his views on other philosophical issues? But if it is not random, if Plato introduced it for some particular reason, what is his attitude toward the status of *erōs* and of those other issues? Why does Socrates not discuss them at all? Why does he take a dismissive tone toward his speech (cf. 262a–c, 265b–d)?

We must now examine, again in very rough and general terms, the points regarding rhetoric that Plato makes in the second part of the dialogue.

Amazed at the beauty of Socrates' second speech, Phaedrus confesses that he is not sure Lysias could compose a better one. And he also adds that Lysias might be unwilling to continue the competition because he had recently been attacked on the grounds that speechwriting is a shameful occupation and not worthy of a gentleman's attention (257c). Socrates responds that writing speeches is not itself shameful; shame only attaches to composing speeches, orally or in written form, badly. So the question becomes when speeches are composed well and when not; and this is equivalent to asking when rhetoric is and when it is not correctly practiced. Instead of returning to Athens, the two friends decide to stay in the country and continue their discussion, on a philosophical level now, through the early afternoon. Socrates, in addition, points out the cicadas singing overhead. Consonant with the respect for myth and traditional theology that his visit to the countryside has produced in him, he describes the cicadas as the Muses' messengers. They are watching them, he says, and will report to the Muses whether the two friends have spent their time lazily drifting off in the summer heat or have been engaged in the sort of philosophical discussion that is a tribute to the cicadas' patron goddesses (258b–259e).[22]

Socrates begins the discussion by asking whether rhetoricians should always know the truth about their topics. Phaedrus offers the commonplace response that this is not at all necessary. Orators, he continues, need to know only what their *audience* considers to be just or good or noble, not what is really so (if anything is): it is by manipulating their audience's preconceived views, not by appealing to the actual truth, that rhetoricians succeed in convincing them of their own—the rhetoricians'—position (cf. *Gorgias* 452d). Conviction in this rhetorical context is connected to manipulation; what an audience already believes, whether or not it is true, allows them to be manipulated much more effectively than the actual truth, which they may well not believe at all.

Socrates responds by arguing at length that rhetoric can be pursued systematically, as a "craft" or "art" (*technē*),[23] only if orators do actually know the truth about their subject. First he claims that orators who are ignorant of what is truly good or just may cause great harm to their audience. Second, he argues that only those who know precisely the truth about a subject can lead their audience, step by indiscernible step, away from their own beliefs and toward the conclusion they want by presenting arguments that diverge from the truth as little as possible. Only they know how least to diverge from the truth so as to be believable. In addition, their knowledge allows them to be aware when their opponents are in turn trying to mislead them and to resist them successfully: "If you are to deceive someone else and to avoid deception yourself, you must know precisely the respects in which things are similar and dissimilar to one another" (262a). Since knowledge of the truth is necessary for the ability to treat rhetoric systematically, and since Plato believes that the search for truth is philosophy, the main (and surprising) implication of Socrates' controversial argument is that finally only philosophers can be adequate rhetoricians (259e–262c).

Phaedrus and Socrates now turn to Lysias' speech in order to determine whether it has been composed systematically, as a result of *technē*, or haphazardly. It turns out that the speech proceeds by piling argument upon argument without concern for structure or for the relations among its various parts.[24] In particular, Socrates criticizes Lysias for beginning his speech without a definition of *erōs* that would allow the audience to have a clear idea of their topic (262d–264e).

Having established that speeches must be carefully constructed, Socrates now examines his own two efforts. Though he begins by treating them as independent works, he ends up thinking of them as one long speech divided into two parts. Their common element is that they both depend on a definition of *erōs* as madness, which they divide into two kinds—a bad one attacked in the first speech, and a good one praised in the second. Everything else in his speeches, Socrates now shockingly says, "was really a game." The only things that mattered were two: first, that the speeches collected all the phenomena that fall under *erōs* together and offered a general definition of that notion; second, that they divided madness, the genus to which *erōs* belongs, into its various kinds and finally located *erōs* itself within it, so as distinguish its bad aspect from its good, to criticize the former and celebrate the latter (265a–266b).

Such "collections and divisions," of which Socrates claims to be a lover (*erastēs*), turn out to be, in fact, the methods of dialectic, or philosophy.[25] So, the single serious idea that Socrates' two rhetorical speeches are supposed to illustrate is the practice of the method of philosophy. *Erōs* has disappeared altogether.[26] Philosophy, Socrates implies again, is necessary for the correct pursuit of rhetoric. But Phaedrus replies, quite correctly, that even though they may have succeeded in defining philosophy, rhetoric, which is after all their main topic, still eludes them (266c–d). For one thing, he claims, Socrates has left totally out of the picture all the many tropes and modes of argument that various teachers of rhetoric have identified in their handbooks. Socrates, who turns out to have detailed knowledge of the technical aspects of rhetoric, responds that these can be of no help to a rhetorician who does not know how to put them together and how to utilize them in accordance with some general principles in order to construct acceptable speeches. Rhetoric requires much more than acquaintance with formal tricks (266d–269c).

What exactly, then, does rhetoric require in addition to its technical features? Socrates replies that as in the case of every *technē*, rhetoric must proceed through an understanding of the objects it involves. Rhetoric is a directing of the soul toward certain views and conclusions by means of speeches (261a, cf. 271c). Rhetoricians, therefore, must know the nature of the soul and its various kinds; they must also know the various kinds of speeches there are and how different souls are affected by them; and they must be able to detect the sort of soul they address in each particular case and therefore the kind of speech that is most appropriate to it. Only on the basis of such general understanding will the formal mechanisms classified by the various teachers of rhetoric find their place and fulfill their function (269d–272c).

We shall see that this grandiose conception of rhetoric, which actually places it so close to philosophy itself that the two may appear identical,[27] is important for answering our earlier question concerning the silence of the second part of the *Phaedrus* regarding *erōs*. For the moment, however, let us follow Socrates as he takes up a challenge to the conception of rhetoric he has just articulated. He imagines that one could object that the abstract study he has been recommending is quite useless to the practicing orator. According to this argument, which we have already encountered in the dialogue, the rhetorician only needs knowledge of what is plausible—that is, what the audience will consider plausible in each particular case: the knowledge that rhetoric requires is practical and concrete; it concerns what people believe to be true, not the truth itself. Truth has nothing to do with persuasion—only verisimilitude does. Socrates' response is that no one can know what is plausible without knowing what is true. After all, he claims, what is plausible is identical with what is likely to be the case; likeness to the truth is what makes something likely; and knowledge of the truth is therefore necessary in order to know what is likely and, for that reason, plausible (272c–274a).[28]

Rhetoric correctly conceived, therefore, requires knowledge of the truth about the subject of one's discourse. It also requires knowledge of the nature of the soul. It involves the ability to discern the kind of soul one is faced with in each particular case. And it also requires the ability to tell the truth in such a way that our audience, even if it is of limited ability, will be drawn toward it. The ornamentation that is an essential element of rhetoric is not directed at entertaining or manipulating an audience: its purpose is to bring that audience as close to the truth as it can get.

Having argued that rhetoric can be systematically practiced only by those who know the kinds of truths he has enumerated, Socrates turns to the question of when writing is and when it is not proper (274b–278e). This passage has received great attention in recent years, partly because of Jacques Derrida's influential interpretation of it as an attack on writing that necessarily undermines itself.[29] Derrida believes that Plato aims to argue that writing is in all cases inferior to oral communication. For Derrida, this is a general tendency of Western philosophy, which, he argues, has tended to consider speech a more direct, more comprehensible, and less ambiguous mode of communication than writing. Speech is presumed to be clear, a direct expression of thought; and speakers can always explain their meaning if it is misunderstood. Derrida, in a detailed reading of the passage to which we cannot do justice here, argues that Plato's attack fails in a peculiar way because, even as he tries to distinguish speech from writing, Plato needs to describe the former in terms of concepts and metaphors drawn from the latter. So, for example, Plato claims that speech, "the living, breathing discourse of the man who knows, of which the written one can be fairly called an image," is actually "*written down* . . . in the soul of the listener" (276a). But if speech has to be characterized in terms of writing, Derrida argues, speech itself must be characterized with the imperfections that attach to writing. What follows, he claims, is that there is no mode of communication that is free from misinterpretation, ambiguity, and appropriation by another person independently of its author's intentions. All the problems Plato identifies for writing apply to speech as well.

The interpretation of this passage is too complicated to discuss in any detail here, though it is well worth careful consideration in the course of reading the dialogue. Two alternative interpretations that deserve to be briefly mentioned are the following. One is that Plato is not here attacking all writing, but only a certain attitude toward it, an attitude that induces us to take for granted anything written, to refuse to question it, to consider it true, simply on the grounds that it has been written. But the same is true of oral discourse. Speech should no more be taken for granted than writing. Phaedrus may perhaps be willing to accept uncritically others' views, rhetorically or philosophically expressed, in speech or in writing. But in fact both speech and writing need to be questioned, put to the test, and made material for reflection. Socrates' strictures apply equally to speech and to writing so long as these are accepted as authoritative without first being examined in regard to their truth.[30]

A second, preferable, way of reading this passage is to claim that Plato's discussion is not essentially connected to the difference between speech and writing. Though of course the discussion of the *Phaedrus* applies directly to speech and writing, it is a special case of a much more general debate, repeated over and over again, concerning the trustworthiness of a new and not yet understood mode of communication in comparison to that of an accepted medium. We generally tend to connect the older medium to rationality and to successful communication exclusively; we tend to describe the new one as less rational and much less likely to succeed in communicating ideas. What is often true in such discussions is that we make an unfair comparison: we judge the new medium according to its ability to communicate the type of ideas for which the older one had been designed, and it is no surprise that it fails in that regard. Moreover, we tend to identify the ideas suited to the old medium and the manner in which that medium communicates them with what is rational. Accordingly, even if the new medium is sometimes judged to be successful in communicating its own ideas by its own methods, we are tempted to consider these ideas at best as inferior to the former, at worst as irrational and harmful. For example, it is true, as Plato claims, that writing cannot answer questions in the way a speaker can in the course of a discussion. This is, from one point of view, a disadvantage of writing over speech. But speech cannot possibly communicate ideas that are as complex or textured as the ideas that can be expressed through a medium as permanent and as capable of review as writing. Each medium has its own advantages and disadvantages, and it is much more difficult than we often think to make a direct comparison between them. Nevertheless, we do. The general strategy for such comparisons is presented in the *Phaedrus* for the first time in Western thought; speech and writing are simply the media of communication that were at issue at the time. But we can find that strategy manifested again and again in the most different situations, with the same considerations applied to the most diverse examples. Its most recent instance is the negative comparison of the visual media, especially television, to writing. What is particularly ironic is that almost every argument Plato gave in the *Phaedrus* in favor of speech and against writing is now given in favor of writing and against television. This suggests that what matters in each specific case is not the pair of media being compared, but the fact that, having already accepted one medium as an effective and rational method of communication, we are bound to consider the other ineffective and unreasonable. We thus put the other medium at an inherent disadvantage from the very beginning, and we are prevented from taking its own claims seriously.[31]

At the end of their discussion of writing, Socrates tells Phaedrus that authors who write with a knowledge of the truth, able to defend their own works and aware that their writings are not themselves of great worth, should be considered philosophers. Those, on the other hand, whose main goal is to produce written texts without concern for the truth or for the shortcomings of their products should be considered rhetoricians or speech writers. Even in its written form, rhetoric can be part of the activity of philosophy, provided that it is properly practiced (278c–e).

We now, finally, can turn directly to the complex question we could not answer without first having formed a general idea of the contents of the *Phaedrus:* Is this work unified? Do its two parts constitute elements in a single, coherent structure?

First, we must agree on what counts as unity in this context. Even this question is disputed. Malcolm Heath, for example, has made a strong case for thinking that the unity of the dialogue lies in its formal aspects, in the fact that though its two parts have radically different subjects, the work still satisfies Aristotle's criteria for having a unified plot.[32] Nevertheless, it would be more satisfying to show that the *Phaedrus* does after all address a single subject throughout and that its unity is not merely formal.

If the subject of the *Phaedrus* were *erōs*, it would be impossible, as we have seen, to find such a thematic unity in the work: *erōs* is simply not discussed in the dialogue's second part. But, as we have also seen, there is a subject that is central to every part of the work—rhetoric. We have already said that we need not read the *Phaedrus* as a treatise on *erōs* with an irrelevant, long discussion of rhetoric tagged on. We can read it instead as a sustained discussion of rhetoric in which Plato constructs three speeches on the topic of love as examples of what rhetoricians are capable of doing and as objects of criticism or praise.

Such a view immediately explains the formal relations we noted above among the three speeches of the *Phaedrus*. In a discussion of rhetoric, it makes sense to portray the competitive situations in which rhetoricians found themselves in the course of practicing their profession. But our approach generates two new questions. The first is why Plato chooses *erōs* as the subject of his exemplary speeches. If *erōs* were itself the dialogue's central subject (or even, as Heath argues, one of two subjects addressed in the work), this question would not have to be raised. But our reading implies that Plato could have composed the dialogue's speeches on any topic that could be addressed by rhetoric; why, among such a large range, did he decide on *erōs*? The second question concerns the status of the speeches, especially the status of the Great Speech. This, in turn, can be broken down into two further problems. First, the Great Speech, like the rest of the *Phaedrus,* is in fact a written discourse and therefore subject to Plato's objections against writing. Even though, within the dialogue's fiction, it is spoken by Socrates, and not written in the way that Lysias' speech has been written down, it is (along with the whole dialogue) a piece of writing so far as Plato's readers are concerned. What, then, does Plato think of the speech's contents? What, indeed, does he think of the whole of the *Phaedrus*? Second, even within the fiction of the dialogue, in which Socrates delivers it orally, the speech is a work of rhetoric, and must fall short of the accuracy that philosophy (and only philosophy) possesses in Plato's eyes. The speech is long and of great beauty, and it presents views that have been central to Plato's philosophy. But can Plato believe its contents in view of its inferior status?

Let us first consider Plato's choice of *erōs* as the subject of the speeches of the *Phaedrus*. Plato had already addressed *erōs* rhetorically in the *Symposium,* and he may well have thought it an appropriate subject for this discussion of rhetoric—all the more so if he has changed some of his views on *erōs* in the meantime. And it seems clear that, on some issues at least, Plato has in fact changed his mind. The *Phaedrus,* for example, depends crucially on the notion of the divided soul, which Plato first introduced in the *Republic* and which accounts for the difficulty that lovers have in controlling their sexual appetites even after they have begun to realize that love is primarily directed not toward sex but toward philosophy. By contrast, the *Symposium* does not appeal to such a divided soul. An undivided soul, all of it always desiring what it considers best, is subject to no such conflicts. It cannot possibly be tempted by desires for the body once it has determined that the soul is more beautiful and therefore worthier of love. And according to the *Symposium,* lovers desire the higher objects of love as soon as they become aware of their existence: leaving their earlier loves behind, those who can see far enough progress toward true love, which is love of the Form of Beauty (*Symposium* 210a–211b2).[33]

Plato may have had a second reason for considering *erōs* an appropriate subject. Precisely because he believes that it is a force that moves the soul to the Forms and to philosophy, he can use it in order to introduce various philosophical views that might otherwise not easily have found a place within the dialogue. *Erōs* provides an entry into the heart of Plato's philosophy.

Finally, we might consider the following possibility. The best way to persuade people to devote themselves to philosophy is by showing them what philosophy is and what benefits they can derive from it. But most of us lack the knowledge, or the kind of soul, that can respond directly to the dry and technical collections and divisions of which Socrates, for one, is a lover. For those without the right soul, love for another human being, which is a phenomenon many come to know at some time or other during their lifetime, may be as close as they will get to the philosophical life—*erōs* knows how to awaken souls and give them wings, raising them from the deathlike condition that is what Plato believes life on earth is. *Erōs* is the only force that will "direct the soul" of most of us, and especially the soul of Phaedrus as he is portrayed in this dialogue. And that is another reason why it is a perfect subject for the speeches through a discussion of which Plato tries to distinguish rhetoric from philosophy.[34]

But this now brings us to the second question we asked above: Can Plato be serious about the views he expresses in Socrates' Great Speech? Socrates himself characterizes his speech as "playful"—though, to be accurate, he also says that it is "appropriate and respectful" (265b–c). But without such a rhetorical exhortation (and, in many cases, even with it), the mere experience of *erōs* would surely not prove enough to move those who have it toward philosophy: its rewards are most often pursued in other directions. Does Plato, though, believe the content of his rhetorical effort, when in the second part of his dialogue he takes such pains to separate rhetoric from philosophy? If even true rhetoricians cannot speak the plain truth but must embellish it to make it attractive and convincing to their audience on each particular occasion, how much of the Great Speech is true and how much of it is, so to speak, an inflection of the truth produced for Phaedrus' benefit?

At 277b–c, Socrates claims that true rhetoricians will have to understand the method of collection and division that they will apply both to their topics and to the souls of their listeners. This enables them to give the speech that is appropriate on each occasion, "a complex and elaborate speech to a complex and elaborate soul and a simple speech to a simple one." The knowledge Socrates attributes to the true rhetorician here (cf. 271c–272c) is at least in part the knowledge he had earlier attributed to the dialectician or philosopher (265c–266c). In other words, whatever exactly the relationship is between "true rhetoric" and philosophy, a true rhetorician will know how best to bring an audience as close to the truth as it is possible for them to come in view of their abilities.

Phaedrus is not a philosopher's ideal listener; his soul is not "simple" but "complex and elaborate." The "mythical" speech in praise of *erōs*, therefore, must have been designed especially for him and for his interests. It is thus an example of true rhetoric, spoken by someone who knows the truth but has tailored his presentation to his listener's character. Socrates' speech does not therefore present the unadorned truth about philosophy or the theory of Forms. It is an artful construction that inflects the truth in order to appeal to Phaedrus' specific needs and abilities. This is an important reason, incidentally, why we should not assume without further argument that Plato is prepared to defend the views expressed in the speech in just the form he presents them here: they need not be, and almost certainly are not, the truth just as Plato sees it.

This point has been appreciated by many readers of the *Phaedrus*.[35] But a question that has not been given enough attention is this: Let us suppose that the Great Speech does inflect the truth; which part of it is the truth and which the inflection? Is there a distinct part that Plato himself believes more or less literally and another that he composes for Phaedrus' sake? The most obvious answer, and the answer given or presupposed in most discussions of the *Phaedrus*, is that Plato believes in the theory of Forms, in the doctrine of the divided soul, in the theory of recollection, in the transmigration of the soul—in all the theories, that is, that the speech contains. Accordingly, the inflection consists in his vivid mythological imagery, especially the story of the soul as a winged chariot traveling in the company of the gods and of its fate.

But this view runs into a serious problem: We have good reason to think that by the time he wrote the *Phaedrus*, Plato no longer accepted the theory of Forms as it is presented in the Great Speech. The method of collection and division, which is described as the method of philosophy in the dialogue's second part, goes hand in hand with the theory of Forms as we find it in Plato's later dialogues, particularly the *Sophist* and the *Philebus*.[36] But that theory is obviously not the same as the theory of Forms we find in Plato's middle works, especially the *Phaedo* and the *Republic*. This middle theory was subjected to serious criticisms in the *Parmenides*, and its paradigmatism was particularly put to the test. Paradigmatism consists in the idea that each Form is the perfect exemplar of the feature for which it stands: Beauty, for instance, is the most beautiful object in the world; Largeness, the largest. This idea, of course, is at the heart of Socrates' Great Speech. If Beauty were not itself beautiful, there would be no reason for the soul to recollect it upon seeing a beautiful boy. And if the

Form were not supremely beautiful—much more beautiful than the boy—there would be no reason to be drawn toward it instead of remaining solely in love with the boy.

Another feature of the middle theory of Forms is that it is not at all clear that it allows the Forms to be related to one another. Each Form is complete in itself, its nature independent of everything else (see *Symposium* 211a–b); Plato often describes our coming to know the Forms, as he does in the *Phaedrus*, by metaphors drawn from sight. Such metaphors reinforce the notion that each Form is an independent object that can be seen in its entirety by itself. But the theory of Forms of the Great Speech is incompatible with the theory that the second part of the dialogue implies. The method of collection and division depends on the idea that the Forms are closely connected with one another and that to know a Form is to know its connections: to divide a Form (itself an impossible task according to the middle theory attacked in the *Parmenides*, which asserts that each Form is indivisible) is to determine the Forms to which it is related as a genus is related to its species. According to the late dialogues, the Forms constitute a great network of essentially interrelated objects. And this is not at all the picture of the Great Speech. The Forms of the middle theory are, as the *Parmenides* insists, "separate" both from each other and from their many instances. There is no way to account for the relation, if any, between the Forms and their instances (*Parmenides* 130b–134e). But when the *Philebus* discusses collection and division it leaves us with an impression at least that the connections between the world of Forms and the world of sensible objects are much more intimate. Division of a Form, for example, may end precisely when we reach the countless objects that fall under it.[37]

The theory of Forms is not the only obstacle to claiming that Plato accepts the views of the Great Speech in their literal form. The fact is that most of these views do not appear in Plato's later work. For example, after his dramatic presentation of the theory of recollection—which had been so crucial to the *Meno* and the *Phaedo*—in the Great Speech of the *Phaedrus*, Plato simply never appeals to it again: not, for example, in the *Theaetetus*, which is explicitly devoted to establishing the nature of knowledge. Further, though the doctrine of the tripartite soul does reappear in the *Timaeus*, it does so in significantly different form. While all three parts of the soul are immortal in the Great Speech, only reason defies death in the *Timaeus*.[38]

What, then, if we were to turn our usual picture of the Great Speech around? What if we were to think that the truth Plato accepts does not consist of the philosophical theories the speech contains? What if Plato simply wants to communicate instead the idea that philosophy is the most important part of life? In that case, the theories of the speech, which Socrates presents so colorfully, will turn out to be the means by which he tries to move Phaedrus to realize that philosophy is superior to a life that finds its greatest pleasures in rhetoric. It is not clear that Socrates is perfectly successful in his effort, but at least Phaedrus is willing to continue their conversation into the afternoon instead of returning to the city, in order to persuade Lysias to compose a hymn to *erōs* that will outdo Socrates' own (257c). If only for a short while, Phaedrus actually *engages* in philosophy with Socrates.

The countryside, for which Socrates has left Athens, has turned him, surprisingly, into an accomplished rhetorician. Much more surprisingly, however, it has provided him with an opportunity to cast doubt on views that, within the fiction of Plato's dialogues, he had developed within the city walls. This Odysseus returns home from abroad a different man indeed.

If we suppose that Plato makes Socrates present picturesque views of Forms and souls to delight Phaedrus and to direct his soul toward philosophy, we can draw a further conclusion. Since Plato treats these theories no longer as ends in themselves but as means, we can now read Socrates' Great Speech as Plato's farewell to the theory of Forms it describes. What the speech shows is that the middle theory of Forms is as good as a good story—good enough to lead some people to philosophy, and perhaps even good enough to have led Plato himself to it. But once you do get there— really there—you realize that philosophy consists in the austere practice of collection and division, defining the kinds of things there are and distinguishing each from everything else. The theory of Forms as we came to know it in Plato's middle works has had its use; and it may still have an important role to play in firing the imagination. In fact, it has played just that role during a great part of the history of Western philosophy: generations of readers, reading the speech as Phaedrus is supposed to have listened to it, have turned to philosophy because of the beauty of the vision of Plato's middle theory of Forms; not many have ended up believing it.

It might seem strange that Plato would produce such a beautiful piece of prose in order to part company with his own views. But the beauty of the speech makes the parting all that more moving. The *Phaedrus* is not simply discarding a rusted tool that has outlived its usefulness. It is leaving behind a set of views that had led to the most valuable form human life can take; without such views such a life could not have been articulated in the first place. Socrates' Great Speech exudes gratitude for what first made that life possible. It is a farewell to a dying friend; but its beauty has secured that friend an undying afterlife. And since Plato first introduced the Forms, in the *Symposium*, through a speech on *erōs* (210e–212b), nothing would have been more appropriate than to have taken leave of them through a speech on the same topic.[39] *Erōs* is literally the beginning and the end of the theory of Forms of Plato's middle dialogues, and the *Phaedrus* is Plato's valedictory address to it.

The *Phaedrus* is thus a companion piece to the *Parmenides*. Both dialogues, in extremely different ways, leave the middle theory of Forms behind. Both emphasize that the activity of philosophy is more important than the specific views one holds. This is, according to our reading, the main thrust of Socrates' Great Speech. Similarly, Parmenides claims that even if the theory of Forms as Socrates had presented it is indefensible, some version of it is necessary if dialectic is to be at all possible (135b–c). Philosophy in general—not the literal content of any particular philosophical theory—constitutes in both cases the primary concern.

If Plato does not literally believe the philosophical theories of the Great Speech, does this mean that the speech cannot help us determine his views? Is there no point in reading it for information on Plato's substantive doctrines? There is. Even if Plato no longer accepts the theory of Forms in the version contained in the Great Speech, this does not imply that he was not earlier himself devoted to what is here primarily an artifice to move Phaedrus to philosophy. There is no reason to believe that the theory of Forms in the *Phaedrus* is not, at least to some extent, an accurate rendition of what he himself considered his earlier views to have been. The Great Speech can give us important information about the philosophy of the *Symposium,* the *Phaedo,* and the *Republic.*

But the *Phaedrus* is a written work, and we have seen that Plato has warned his readers not to put much trust in writing. What, then, should our own attitude toward the dialogue be? What should we believe of what we read here? Plato himself writes that written texts cannot be taken very seriously; writings that are recited without giving their audience the opportunity to question them and learn from them produce only conviction and not knowledge (277e). Perhaps, then, the *Phaedrus* itself, like all of Plato's texts and like all the rhetorical works to which he assimilates writing, should not be taken too seriously? Perhaps the whole dialogue, like the speeches in it, is itself a "game"?

But what does it mean to avoid taking the *Phaedrus* seriously? It does not mean that we are to consider it simply a long joke. It means that, like rhetoric, the dialogue also cannot produce knowledge but only conviction.[40] But, unlike rhetoric, it can still be questioned, because, like so many others of Plato's works, it leaves its own questions unanswered. To question the *Phaedrus,* therefore, is to continue asking its questions. Asking its questions, questioning the answers we give them, and even disputing the interpretation of Socrates' Great Speech given here, are, of course, doing philosophy. And so, not to take the *Phaedrus* seriously in the proper sense is to take philosophy itself seriously. But to take philosophy seriously, perhaps paradoxically but also appropriately for a work that delights in paradoxes and twists of its own, is to take the *Phaedrus* as well very seriously after all.

NOTES

1. To prove that he was mad, Odysseus took to plowing a rocky piece of land where nothing could grow. Palamedes, however, placed Odysseus' infant son, Telemachus, on the plow's path. Odysseus then swerved in order not to kill the child, and his madness was shown to have been a ruse. This story is not mentioned in either the *Iliad* or the *Odyssey*, but it can be found in Hyginus' *Fabulae* or *Genealogiae* 277.1.

2. It should be noted that the *Republic* describes a conversation that takes place in the Piraeus, Athens' port. But the two localities were adjacent, connected by the famous "Long Walls" that were destroyed when Athens lost the Peloponnesian War in 404 B.C. In a literal sense, going to Piraeus (which Socrates may well have done more than once) was not going beyond the city walls.

3. See 230a.

4. Palamedes appears, in a different context, in the *Phaedrus*; see 261b.

5. This simile is only one aspect of the *Phaedrus* that anticipates some of the strange happenings in Shakespeare's *Midsummer Night's Dream:* Socrates is not the only literary character to have been enchanted by the woods surrounding ancient Athens. In Shakespeare's play, Bottom is given a donkey's head by Puck; and Titania, the queen of fairies, is made to fall in love with him. Four lovers— Lysander, Demetrius, Helena, and Hermia—also find their affections strangely changed once they have left Athens for the countryside.

6. An interesting argument to the effect that Plato does not have, in any strict sense, a theory of *erōs* is offered by G.R.F. Ferrari, "Platonic Love," in Richard Kraut, ed., *The Cambridge Companion to Plato* (Cambridge, 1992), 248–76. It should also be said that there is no firm external evidence that the *Phaedrus* was in fact written after the *Republic*. However, the most coherent account of Plato's philosophical development depends on the relative dating of the works assumed here, and defended below.

7. Socrates' second speech seems to allude to many of the ideas Plato expressed in the *Meno*, the *Phaedo*, and the *Republic*. They include the view that knowledge is recollection, the idea of the transmigration of the soul, and the assumption that the Forms are perfect exemplars of the qualities for which they stand: thus, for example, the Form of Beauty is the most beautiful thing in existence. The brief discussion of collection and division (265c–266c) as the correct method of pursuing philosophical issues anticipates its detailed application in the *Sophist*. If we assume that the *Parmenides*, in which the theory of Forms of the *Republic* comes under criticism, was written between the *Republic* and the *Sophist*, in which a new method of dialectic is followed, then it is reasonable to suppose that the *Phaedrus* was written not long before or after that work.

8. Other dialogues that fall in this category include the *Euthyphro*, the *Crito*, the *Ion*, the *Hippias Major*, the *Hippias Minor*, and the *Menexenus*.

9. At 236b, Socrates refers to Lysias as Phaedrus' *paidika,* that is, as the boy with whom Phaedrus, in the position of an older man, is in love. The point may be a joke, but it strongly suggests that Phaedrus cannot be younger than Lysias. Similarly, at 275b, Socrates says that Phaedrus is Lysias' *erastēs,* thus reinforcing the same point. At 242a–b he claims that Phaedrus has himself produced or caused others to produce more speeches than any of his contemporaries, with the exception of Simmias of Thebes; this too suggests that he cannot be a very young man at the time of this discussion. There is no evidence in the dialogue to suggest that Phaedrus is himself a young boy trying to decide what sort of life—and lover—he should choose or that the work revolves centrally around that issue (as argued by Martha C. Nussbaum, *The Fragility of Goodness: Luck and Ethics in Greek Tragedy and Philosophy* [Cambridge, 1986], ch. 7). Though Socrates does occasionally address Phaedrus as *pai* (roughly, "child") and *neania* (roughly, "youth," "young man"), this is not telling. Such terms of intimacy were as common then as they are now. Consider, for example, that Socrates refers to Agathon, who is thirty years old, as a *meirakion* (roughly, "adolescent boy") at *Symposium* 223a.

10. For a general discussion of the subject, see K. J. Dover, *Greek Homosexuality* (Cambridge, Mass., 1978), and Michel Foucault, *The Uses of Pleasure* (New York, 1985).

11. Aristophanes actually parodied Agathon's effeminate ways in his *Thesmophoriazousai.*

12. Socrates, of course, also delivers a speech on *erōs* in the *Symposium.* But there he explicitly attributes the speech to Diotima, and even delivers it as if it were coming directly from her. There is no explicit acknowledgment within the fictional world of the *Symposium,* as there is in the *Phaedrus,* that the speech is really his own (though Plato gives a number of hints to that effect to his readers).

13. Some commentators, e.g., Rowe, (C. J. Rowe, *Plato: Phaedrus, with Translation and Commentary* [Warminster, 1986]), find serious differences between the view of *erōs* expressed here and the discussion in the *Symposium* (201e–203b), where *erōs* is said to be not a god but a spirit, and neither good nor bad, but "in between" the two. But we should not exaggerate these differences. Plato's present statement that *erōs* is "a god or something divine" is compatible with *erōs* being a "spirit" (*daimōn*); and his view that he therefore "can't be bad in any way" is compatible with his not being good—which are just the positions he had taken in the *Symposium.*

14. On this tendency (which he traces back to Marcilio Ficino), see C. J. Rowe, "The Argument and Structure of Plato's *Phaedrus,*" *Proceedings of the Cambridge Philosophical Society* 32 (1986): 106–25.

15. Whether Plato's simile envisages that the gods have souls or that they simply are souls is not absolutely clear. Many points in Socrates' second speech are obscure in this way. Consider, for example, the rather obscure description of "the place beyond heaven" a little further on (246c–247d), or the issue of the extent of the soul's wings: do they belong to the horses only (246a) or to the whole complex (251b–c)? The speech leaves many such questions open, and we should not be too insistent in pressing it for answers.

16. Plato, we must remember, had already described philosophy in the *Phaedo*

(64b–65d) as the mode of life closest to the life that the soul leads after death, free from body and sense.

17. On the relative dating of the *Symposium* and the *Phaedo,* see n. 39 below.

18. Friedrich Schleiermacher, *Introductions to the Dialogues of Plato* (New York, 1973), 48.

19. Schleiermacher places the *Phaedrus* first partly because he reads it as Plato's announcement of the nature and superiority of philosophy over other practices—a programmatic statement of his views in general. He also locates in it an "excessive, and almost boisterous and triumphant exultation," "an ostentation of power and superiority"; and he finds that its "spirit is youthful throughout" (59–62). His view of the dialogue's position in the sequence of Plato's dialogues is not entertained seriously by scholars today.

20. Note, for example, that when Phaedrus realizes that Socrates' second speech is intended as a praise of love, he promises that he will force Lysias to respond with a speech on that very subject (243d–e).

21. Socrates actually makes this point himself at 265e–266a.

22. G.R.F. Ferrari (*Listening to the Cicadas: A Study of Plato's "Phaedrus"* [Cambridge, 1987]) builds his ambitious overall interpretation of the *Phaedrus* on a reading of this episode. His study is worth consulting on all the issues raised by this complex work.

23. The Greek word *technē,* often translated as "art," is actually quite different from that English word. It connotes, in contrast to our "art," a systematic body of knowledge that can be taught and that follows rather well formulated rules. I have kept, however, to the traditional rendering in this discussion. An alternative translation might be "craft"; "science," which some translators prefer, is too strict a notion and corresponds more accurately to the Greek *epistēmē.*

24. In contrast to Lysias', Socrates' own first speech proceeds in a very organized manner. After the definition of love, the speaker constructs the following sequence. He lists the bad effects of a lover on, first, the boy's mind; second, on his body; and third, on his possessions, family, and friends—that is, in descending order of importance. He then describes how unpleasant an older man's company is bound to be while he is still in love with the boy and goes on to anticipate the obnoxious behavior of such a man once the love affair is over. The conclusion lists these five points precisely in the reverse order from that in which they were presented, ending with what the speaker clearly considers most important, the harm lovers do to the souls of their beloved. According to the principle of composition enunciated at 264c, Socrates' speech is clearly superior to Lysias'. One might argue, however, that the latter is not at all haphazard, but that it is constructed in such a way that it will appear to be so and therefore informal and unstudied—as different from the usual supplications of other men toward boys as the speaker's unusual desires are from theirs.

25. Collection and division are the backbone of Plato's dialectical method in his late works. It is plausible to claim that they are presented here for the first time. They are practiced in detail in the *Sophist* and the *Statesman*. The *Philebus* discusses them in more general terms (14c–20c).

26. *Erōs* is mentioned in the discussion of collection and division, but only as the example on which the method was practiced. Nothing substantive is said about it.

27. The exact relationship between "true" rhetoric and philosophy is very difficult to determine. The question is discussed well, if not conclusively, in the debate between C. J. Rowe, "The Argument and Structure of Plato's *Phaedrus*," and Malcolm Heath, "The Unity of Plato's *Phaedrus*," *Oxford Studies in Ancient Philosophy* 7 (1987): 150–73.

28. This argument, its weaknesses, and its immense influence on the rhetorical tradition are discussed by John J. Cooper, "Plato, Isocrates and Cicero on the Independence of Oratory from Philosophy," in John J. Cleary, ed., *Proceedings of the Boston Area Colloquium in Ancient Philosophy* 1 (1985): 77–96.

29. Jacques Derrida, "Plato's Pharmacy," in his *Dissemination* (Chicago, 1981), 61–171.

30. This, greatly simplified, is the view of Ferrari, *Listening to the Cicadas,* 214–22.

31. An egregious case of this type of argument can be found in Neil Postman's *Amusing Ourselves to Death* (New York, 1985). Postman simply applies Plato's argument regarding speech and writing to writing and television without any idea as to its origins. In this way he fails to appreciate, and to guard against, the irony of praising writing over the visual media for exactly the reasons Plato prefers speech to writing. See also the essay "Plato and the Mass Media" in this book.

32. See Malcolm Heath, "The Unity of Plato's *Phaedrus*," who argues that the unity of the dialogue does not depend on a thematic connection between its two parts. He attributes to the work a "formal unity," a notion that he derives from Aristotle's discussion of the unity of drama in the *Poetics*. The unity of the *Phaedrus*, like the unity of a number of Greek plays, according to Heath, consists not in its addressing a single subject, but in the unity of its plot, which he construes as the fact that "the sequence of events that it narrates unfolds in accordance with necessity and probability; given these people in this situation, that is indeed what they would do and say" (161).

33. Dorothea Frede, in "Out of the Cave: What Socrates Learned from Diotima," *Nomodeiktes* 27 (1993): 387–412, argues that the fact that the divided soul is not mentioned in the *Symposium* does not show that this dialogue was written before the *Republic*. Plato, she claims, only uses the divided soul when he needs it, and so we can draw no conclusions from his silence regarding it in the *Symposium* (403 n. 15). But note that, as we have just argued, the theory of the divided soul makes a big difference to how *erōs* is presented in the *Symposium* and in the *Phaedrus*. Plato, in other words, should have used the theory of the divided soul if it was available to him when he was composing the former dialogue. Other differences between the two works can also be detected, though they are not quite so many nor are they so obviously connected with general conclusions about Plato's life and philosophical development as Martha Nussbaum, for example, claims in *The Fragility of Goodness*, ch. 7.

34. The connection between *erōs* and persuasion (*peithō*) is an old one in Greek thought: desire is compelling, like a powerful speech. It is even reported that Sap-

pho had written that Persuasion was the daughter of Aphrodite. See D. A. Campbell, *Greek Lyric* (Cambridge, 1991); and Sappho, Fragments 90 and 200.

35. See again the essays by Rowe and Heath referred to above.

36. In his discussion of the similarities between rhetoric and medicine, Socrates at one point (270c–d) says that in order to understand the nature of anything we must know what capacity that object has of acting on and being acted upon by what other things in the world. The idea here is identical to the "criterion" or "definition" (*horos*) of what it is to be that Plato attributes to the Eleatic Stranger in the *Sophist* (247d–e). The view that such "dynamic" relations constitute the nature of real objects contrasts seriously with the notion that the Forms cannot be affected by other things, which seems presupposed in the middle dialogues and is criticized at length in the *Parmenides*.

37. See Dorothea Frede, *Plato: "Philebus"* (Indianapolis, 1993), xx–xxx, for a good discussion of this very complex problem.

38. All three parts of the soul are immortal, as far as we can tell, in the *Republic* as well. There is no indication here, as there is in the *Timaeus* (41d–42d, 69d–72d), that the two lower parts are mortal and accrue to the soul simply because it is incarnated.

39. This argument presupposes that the *Symposium* was written before the *Phaedo*. The issue is murky, and there is no external evidence to decide it. On internal grounds, it seems plausible to date the *Symposium* first: it envisages an undivided agent, very much as the earlier *Protagoras* does, and in contrast to the divided agent (composed of body and soul, each a source of motivation in its own right) of the *Phaedo* and the divided soul of the *Republic;* in addition, the *Symposium's* portrait of Socrates is much more consonant with that of Plato's early dialogues than with the otherworldly picture so starkly painted in the *Phaedo*.

40. Cf. Rowe, "The Argument and Structure of Plato's *Phaedrus*," 120.

INDEX OF PASSAGES CITED

GENERAL INDEX

Grote, George, 27 and 50n1, 100, 110, 111
Grube, G., 295n6
Guthrie, W. K. C., 23n6, 58n61, 85, 87–88, 94, 126

Hackforth, R., 152–53
Halliwell, S., 283, 296n12
Heath, M., 347, 348, 357n27, n32
hen, to. See One, the
heterosexuality, in the *Symposium,* 305–6
Homer: Plato's attitude toward, 287; reception of, 253–54; world of, 316
homosexuality: and education, 333; in the *Phaedrus,* 332–33; in the *Symposium,* 305–6. See also *erōs*

identity: and naming, 209; and predication, 207–11. *See also* being; "is"; One
ignorance, Socratic: concerning *aretē,* 6, 7, 13, 31–32, 33–34, 37, 43–44, 47, 54–55n37, 66, 69, 76–77, 90–91, 116; concerning rhetoric, 334. *See also* irony, Socratic
imitation: and appearance, 263, 268; distinguished from knowledge, 256–57, 258, 284; and education, 280; effects of, xxix–xxx, 322; of the Forms, xxxii–xxxiii, 257, 260, 261–62; and narration, 253; and poetry, xxxiv, 251–78; objects of, 253, 262–64, 268; and painting, 257–60; semantics of, 273–74n36; of sensibles, 260; transparency of, 264, 284–85, 286, 288–89, 290–91; types of, 252–53, 257–60; and understanding, 255. See also *mimēsis;* poetry
imperfection, of particulars: and context, 142–43, 146–47, 152–54; and measurement, 140–41; and participation, 215; and perspective, 142–43, 152–53
individualism, of Socrates, xxx, 50
intellectualism, of Socrates, 27–58, 45–46, 59–82
interlocutors, of Socrates, 73–74, 121n19, 172–73
irony: complex, 70–72, 101; definitions of, 71–72, 81n36, 103; as educational tool, 70–72, 101; Platonic, 72–73; simple, 101; Socratic, 47, 70–72, 100–101, 102–3. *See also* ignorance, Socratic

Irwin, T. H., 13–14, 25n41, 29, 30, 32, 39, 40, 41, 52n17, 53n29, n30, n31, 55n37, 90, 111, 117, 218n5, 242n11, n14, 247n60
"is", definitions of, xxxiii, 133, 172–73, 180–81, 190n13, 193–94n41, 212, 218–19n6, 220n20
Isenberg, A., xxxviin11
Isocrates: educational system of, 109–10; as philosopher, 120; on philosophy, 109; on Plato and Socrates, 108

Joachim, H. H., 137n32
Jones, J., 267–68 and 278n90
Jowett, Benjamin, xxxi, 5
justice: and *aretē,* 321, 324–25; and the good life, 318–19; as a virtue, 35–36

Kahn, C., 105n19, 106n31, 122n26, 248n62
Kalligas, P., 26n51, 107n36
Kant, Immanuel, xx–xxi, 316–17
Keaney, J. J., 272n31
Kerferd, G., xxxi, 111–12, 113–14, 115
Keuls, E., 274n37, 276n59
Kierkegaard, S., 71, 83, 84, 94, 96, 97, 99, 102, 106n28
Kirk, G. S., 130
Klein, J., 3, 24n16, 244–45n36
Knightenhelser, K., 121n10
knowledge: and accidents, 235; and acquaintance, 6, 29–30; additive, 231–33, 235–38, 244n34; and *aretē,* 45, 48–49, 60; and being, 197; and belief, 6, 7, 13–15, 16–19, 21–22, 30, 34, 36, 67, 228, 231, 232, 233–39; and definition, 232; definitions of, 224–29; by description, 6; dialectical, 233; distinguished from imitation, 256–57, 258, 284; distinguished from understanding, 20–22; and the elenchus, 67; essentialist, 228; of ethics, 69–70; and the good life, 27–28, 37–39, 40, 315; and inquiry, 9; interrelational, 230–31, 234–35, 237–39; and *logos,* 229, 231, 232, 233–39; multiplicity of, 240–41; nature of, 224–48; objects of, 9, 14, 20–21, 238–39; permanence of, 20; philosophical, 67; possessed by Socrates, 101–2; propositional, 225–26, 228, 230, 242n14; and recollection, 49–50, 147–51; and rhetoric,

B 395